G. FATTORUSSO
EX LIBRIS
FLORENTIA
SEMPER
CLARIORA
SEQUOR
UTILE
DULCI
M. A. FALORSI
MERVEILLES DE L'ITALIE
WONDERS OF ITALY

ITALY

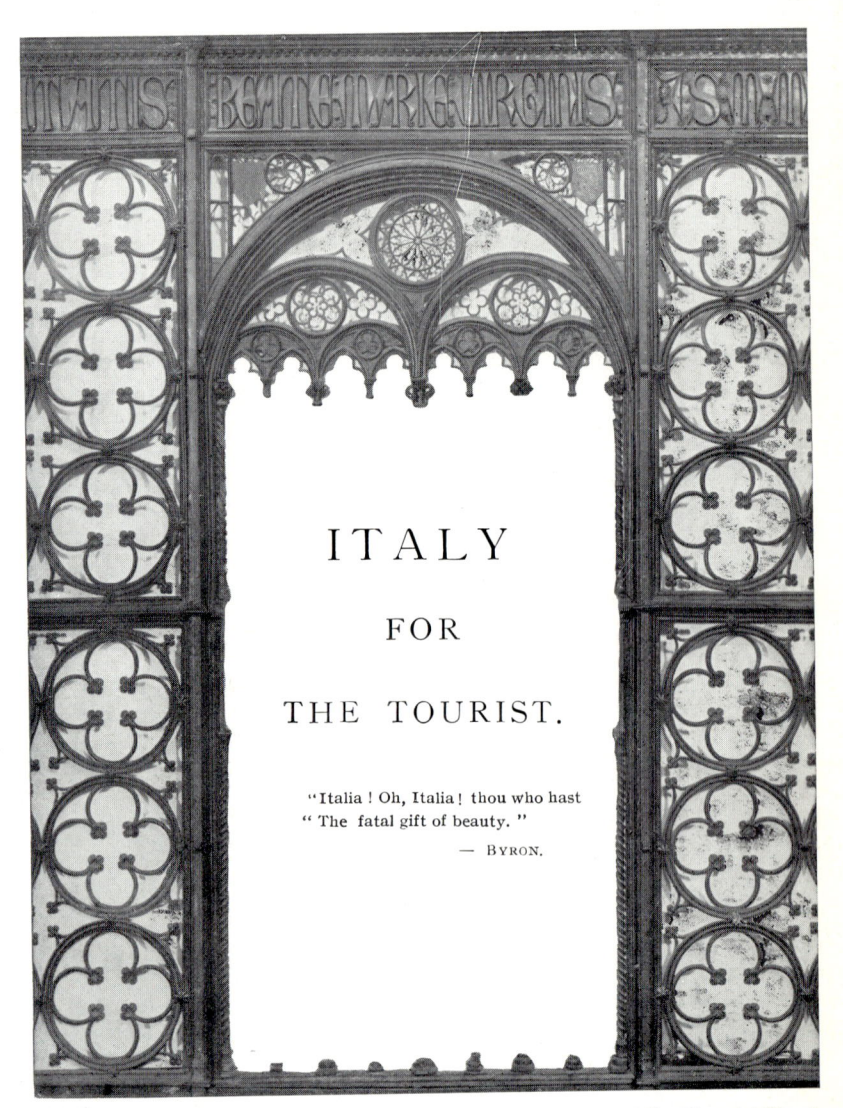

FOR

THE TOURIST.

"Italia! Oh, Italia! thou who hast
"The fatal gift of beauty."
— BYRON.

FLORENCE, CHURCH OF SANTA CROCE, Fifteenth century bronze gate of the Rinuccini Chapel.

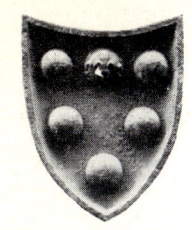

THE MEDICI ART SERIES.
Edited by G. & M.-L. FATTORUSSO.
di P. BRUSCOLI.

WONDERS OF ITALY

Non nobis sed omnibus.

« Oh Land of Beauty, garlanded with pine
« And luscious grape-vines, 'neath whose vaulted skies
« Of blue eternal, marble mansions rise,
« And roseate flowers from every lattice shine,
« Still have the Nations striven of yore
« For thy fair fields, lovely as Eden's plains;
« Thy temples; and thy cities by the main
« Throned hoar and gray upon the rocky shore.
« Who hath seen thee, — oh never in his breast
« The heart grows wholly old! some youthful zest
« Of life still lingers: some bright memory!
« And when the nightingales in Autumn chill
« Fly forth, a yearning stirs his spirit still
« To fly with them toward sunny Italy! »

DANTE EXPOUNDING HIS POEM.
(Detail from the picture on p. 210).

ADORATION OF THE MAGI, 1423, BY GENTILE DA FABRIANO (1360-1440).

Florence, UFFIZI GALLERY.

G. FATTORUSSO

WONDERS OF
ITALY

THE MONUMENTS OF ANTIQUITY, THE CHURCHES, THE PALACES,
THE TREASURES OF ART

HISTORY BIOGRAPHY RELIGION LITERATURE FOLKLORE

A HANDBOOK FOR STUDENTS AND TRAVELLERS

WITH

NUMEROUS CHRONOLOGICAL AND GENEALOGICAL TABLES
OF FORMER SOVEREIGN HOUSES AND ILLUSTRIOUS PERSONALITIES

700 PAGES 3275 ILLUSTRATIONS FROM PHOTOGRAPHS
AND TWENTY-FOUR FULL PAGE PLATES IN COLOUR

SIXTEENTH EDITION REVISED, 1974

THE MEDICI ART SERIES

FLORENCE: EDITRICE GIUSEPPE FATTORUSSO

DI P. BRUSCOLI

Printed in Italy.

The illustration on the frontispiece is a reproduction of a medallion of children, by A. della Robbia, *that adorns the façade of the Foundling Hospital, Florence.*

COPYRIGHT BY R. M. L. FATTORUSSO, 1956.
ALL RIGHTS RESERVED.

First published 1925.
Second edition 1926.
Third edition, January, 1927.
Fourth edition, January, 1928.
Fifth edition revised, June, 1928.
Sixth edition enlarged and revised, 1930.
Seventh edition entirely revised and enlarged, 1937.
Eighth edition entirely revised, 1948.
Ninth edition entirely revised and enlarged, 1949.
Tenth edition newly revised and enlarged, 1950.
Eleventh edition, 1952, 1953, 1956.
Twelfth edition entirely revised, 1959.
Thirteenth edition revised, 1962.
Fourteenth edition revised, 1966.
Fifteenth edition entirely revised, 1971.
Sixteenth edtioin revised, 1974

PRINTED IN FLORENCE - ITALY.

TURIN. THE CASTELLO MEDIEVALE ON THE RIVER PO.

PREFATORY NOTE

VICTORY. *By* CONSANI.
(*Pitti Gallery, Florence*).

THE object of this book is to facilitate the traveller's itinerary in Italy, by indicating at a glance the most notable places and works of art in the cities through which he travels; to recall familiar places and things to those who have seen them or suggest them to others to whom fate denies the opportunity of visiting this incomparable country; finally to serve as a repertory for purposes of reference to the general student of Art.

The very general approbation bestowed by the public upon the preceding editions of *Wonders of Italy*, has encouraged me to redouble my efforts in this edition — which has been considerably enlarged and revised throughout—in order to secure a still higher character than it before enjoyed, and I have the gratification of presenting a volume embracing all the most important monuments with accurate descriptions, besides spirited views mirroring this Land of Beauty.

My authorities in compiling the historical notes and ascriptions are given in a list of the books I have consulted. For the chief attraction of the book—the illustrations— I would again express my indebtedness to Messrs. Fratelli Alinari and Giacomo Brogi of Florence and to Signor D. Anderson of Rome for their courteous permission to reproduce their photographs. I take this opportunity to express my thanks to Messrs. Stianti Brothers and to the " Impronta Press ", who have taken a special care in the printing of the book.

G. F.

MARBLE ORNAMENT ON THE TOMB OF GALEAZZO VISCONTI. *Certosa di Pavia.*

CONTENTS

Sonnet . . . . *Page*	1
Prefatory Note	5
INTRODUCTORY	9

PIEDMONT:

AOSTA, SUSA.	12
TURIN	15

LIGURIA:

GENOA	26
SANTA MARGHERITA	41
RAPALLO	41
BORDIGHERA	43
SAN REMO	43

LOMBARDY:

MILAN	48
MONZA	63
COMO	64
LAKE COMO, GARDA	65
LAKE MAGGIORE	68
PAVIA	69
BERGAMO	74
BRESCIA	76
CREMONA, CREMA	77
MANTUA	78

VENETIA:

VENICE	81
PADUA	155
VERONA	159
VICENZA	167
TRENTO	168
TRIESTE	169

EMILIA-THE MARCHES:

BOLOGNA . . . . *Page*	172
PARMA	177*
PIACENZA, MODENA	177
FERRARA	178
RAVENNA	181
RIMINI, FORLÌ	188
ANCONA, LORETO	189
URBINO	190

TUSCANY:

FLORENCE	191
PISA	313
LUCCA	325
PISTOIA	326
PRATO	328
SIENA	329
SAN GIMIGNANO	352
VOLTERRA	355
AREZZO	356

UMBRIA:

PERUGIA	358
ASSISI	365
ORVIETO	377
CITTÀ DI CASTELLO, SPOLETO . .	389
GUBBIO, NARNI, TERNI	390

LATIUM:

ROME	392
TIVOLI, FRASCATI	512
CIVITA CASTELLANA, TUSCANIA . .	514
SUBIACO, VITERBO	515
FOSSANOVA, ANAGNI, OSTIA . . .	516

CAMPANIA:

NAPLES . . . . *Page*	519
POMPEII	541
SORRENTO	548
CAPRI	550
AMALFI	552
POSITANO	554
ATRANI	555
RAVELLO	556
SALERNO	557
PÆSTUM	558
POZZUOLI, ISCHIA	559
MONTECASSINO	560
CAPUA	iv[i]
BENEVENTO	iv[i]

ABRUZZI-APULIA:

AQUILA, SULMONA . . . . . . *Page*	562
TROJA, TRANI	563
BRINDISI, ALTAMURA	564
BARI, LECCE, BITONTO	565

SARDINIA:

CAGLIARI, SASSARI	566B
UTA, SACCARGIA	566D

SICILY:

PALERMO	569
TAORMINA	579
SYRACUSE	580
MESSINA, CEFALÙ	582
AGRIGENTO (Girgenti)	583

GENEALOGICAL TABLES OF VARIOUS SOVEREIGN HOUSES FORMERLY RULING IN ITALY.

THE HOUSE OF SAVOY KINGS OF ITALY . . . . *Page*	16*
THE VISCONTI, Seigneurs and Dukes of Milan	73
THE SFORZA, Dukes of Milan	73*
THE GONZAGA, Marquis of Mantua	80
THE ESTENSI (HOUSE OF ESTE), Marquis of Ferrara	178*
THE MONTEFELTRO, Seigneurs and Dukes of Urbino	190*
THE DELLA ROVERE, Dukes of Urbino	190A
THE MEDICI (Elder Branch), Seigneurs of Florence	287A
THE MEDICI (Junior Branch) GRAND-DUKES of Florence	287B
SOVEREIGNS OF THE KINGDOM OF NAPLES AND OF SICILY	518
INDEX AND APPENDIX	585

ANGEL PLAYING. *Detail from the painting by* GIOV. BELLINI (p. 134).

WORKS CONSULTED
NOT INCLUDING ENCYCLOPÆDIAS.

ADDISON (J. DE W.) *The Art of the Pitti Palace.*
ALIGHIERI (DANTE) *Divina Commedia.*
BERENSON (B.) *Painters of the Renaissance.*
BURCKHARDT (J.) *Civilization of the Renaissance.*
CAFFIN (C. H.) *How to Study Pictures.*
CAROTTI (G.) *Storia dell'Arte.* Milano.
CARTWRIGHT (JULIA) *The Painters of Florence.*
CLEMENT (C. E.) *Legendary and Mythological Art.*
COTTERILL (H. B.) *Medieval Italy.*
CROWE & CAVALCASELLE. *History of Painting.*
CRUTTWELL (M.) *The Florentine Churches.*
DENNIE (JOHN) *Rome. The Pagan City.* London.
DENNISTOUN (J.) *Memoirs of the Dukes of Urbino.*
DOUGLAS LANGTON. *History of Siena.*
EASTLAKE (Sir CHARLES) *Handbook of Painting.*
GARDNER (E. G.) *The Story of Florence.*
GARNETT (R. A.) *History of Italian Literature.*
HALLAM (H.) *Europe during the Middle Ages.*
HEADLAM (C.) *Venetia and Northern Italy.*
HEYL CHARLES (C.) *The Art of the Uffizi Palace.*
HEYWOOD (W.) *A Pictorial Chronicle of Siena.*
HORNER (The Misses) *Walks in Florence.*
HUTTON (E.) *Venice and Venetia.*
HYETT (F. A.) *A History of Florence.*
JAMESON (Mrs.) *Sacred and Legendary Art.*
LANCIANI (R.) *Pagan and Christian Rome.*
LINDSAY (Lord) *History of Christian Art.*
LUCAS (E. V.) *A Wanderer in Florence.* London
MACHIAVELLI. *History of Florence.*
MATHER (Jr. F. J.) *A History of Italian Painting.*
MAU (AUGUSTUS) *Pompeii its Life and Art.*
MAUCLAIR (C.) *Florence.* London.

NORWAY (A. H.) *Naples Past and Present.* London.
NOYES (ELLA) *The Story of Ferrara.*
PASSAVANT (J. D.) *Raphaël d'Urbin.* Paris.
PERKINS (CHARLES C.) *Tuscan Sculptors.*
PERKINS (F. MASON) *Giotto.* London.
RADCLIFFE (A. G.) *Schools and Masters of Painting.*
REINACH (S.) *Apollo.* London.
REYMOND (MARCEL) *La Sculpture Florentine.*
RICCI (CORRADO) *Art in Northern Italy.*
RICHTER & TAYLOR. *Golden Age of Christian Art.*
RIO (A. F.) *The Poetry of Christian Art.*
ROBINSON (J. C.) *Italian Sculpture.*
ROSCOE (W.) *Life of Lorenzo the Magnificent.*
RUSKIN (JOHN) *Mornings in Florence.*
SCOTT LEADER. *The Renaissance of Art in Italy.*
SISMONDI (J. C. L.) *The Italian Republics.*
SLADEN (DOUGLAS) *How to See Italy by Rail.*
STALEY (E.) *The Guilds of Florence.*
SYMONDS (J. A.) *The Renaissance in Italy.*
SYMONDS (J. A.) *Sketches in Italy.*
TAINE (H.) *Naples, Rome, Florence and Venice.*
VASARI (GIORGIO) *Le Vite de' Pittori, Architetti.*
VAUGHAN (H. M.) *The Naples Riviera.*
VENTURI (A.) *Storia dell'Arte Italiana.*
VILLARI (P.) *Life and Times of Savonarola.*
VILLARI (P.) *Mediaeval Italy.*
WATERS (W. G.) *Italian Sculptors.*
WEY (FRANCIS) *Rome.*
WILLIAMS EGERTON (R.) *Hill Towns of Italy.*
WÖLFFLIN (H.) *The Art of the Italian Renaissance.*
YOUNG (Colonel G. F.) *The Medici.* London.
YRIARTE (CHARLES) *Florence.* Paris.

BÆDEKER'S, MUIRHEAD'S, MURRAY'S, HARE'S, GRANT ALLEN'S, *Guide Books.*

ANGEL plucking the strings of a lute.
Detail from a painting by CARPACCIO (p. 141).

THE ROMAN IMPERIAL EAGLE. *Ancient sculpture from Trajan's Forum. (Church of Santi Apostoli, Rome).*

ITALY
HISTORICAL SKETCH

JULIUS CÆSAR.
Marble statue placed in the "Via dei Fori Imperiali".

THE beginning of the Romans, who preceded the Italians, is hidden in mystery and legend. The Latins are said to have descended originally from the mountain glens of Umbria. Be that as it may, between 753 B. C., the legendary date of the founding of the city of Rome by Romolus and A. D. 476, when the empire of the last of the Augusti passed under the rule of the Byzantine emperors, the Roman nation had risen to supreme power and had sunk again into decay.

Odoacer (476), who established the first kingdom of Italy and placed it under the suzerainty of the Byzantine emperors, heads a long list of foreign rulers —Greeks, Franks, Germans, Spaniards and Austrians— who successively governed the peninsula from distant capitals. The Byzantine rule gave way before the invasion of the Lombards, who remained in possession of Northern Italy until the middle of the 8th century. The rule of the Frankish emperors, of whom Charlemagne was the first and greatest, then began and continued for nearly two centuries (774-962). Finally King Berengarius was deposed by Otho I. of Germany and Italy passed (961) under new masters. The German emperors labored to destroy the prestige

— 8A —

of the Papacy. This controversy, waged with varying success for three centuries, culminated in the bloody civil strife between the papal and imperial factions—the Guelphs and the Ghibellines. But in time the influence of the stronger princes restored order, and the peninsula was divided among five principal powers—the Duchy of Milan, the republics of Florence and Venice, the Holy See and the Kingdom of the Two Sicilies.

For more than two centuries and a half Italy was a pawn in Europe's game of war. Between 1796 and 1815 appeared the ephemeral readjustments of territorial lines, jurisdictions and sovereignties incident to the Napoleonic régime. Under this régime had been developed a sentiment of nationality that rebelled at the despotism practiced by princes returning in bitterness of spirit from their exile.

In 1848 the spirit of revolution was epidemic in Europe. The Young Italy party, with Giuseppe Mazzini at its head, then arose seeking the establishment of a republic. In 1849, however, with the fall of the last republic at Rome, Italy's hope of liberation seemed finally crushed. But King Victor Emmanuel II. of Savoy who had for his foremost minister the statesman Cavour, was determined on accomplishing that which he had set out to do. At the cost of sacrificing Nice and Savoy, the King secured an offensive alliance with France against Austria, and in 1861 Victor Emmanuel II. was crowned King of Italy at Turin. But by a convention with France, Italy was bound to hold Papal Rome inviolable. In 1866 Venice was acquired by Italian activity in alliance with Prussia in the war of that power with Austria. As for Rome, Victor Emmanuel, released from his obligations by the downfall of the French Empire in 1870, entered the city and removed his capital thither from Florence.

The King to whom United Italy owed its existence died and was succeeded by his son Humbert, in 1878, who ruled until 1900 and was succeeded by his only son Victor Emmanuel III.

DOME OF ST. PETER'S. *View taken from the Pincian Hill.*

FLORENCE. UFFIZI GALLERY.

THE MADONNA DELLE ARPIE
with St. Francis and St. John the Evangelist. By ANDREA DEL SARTO, A. D. 1517.

This Madonna, called of the *harpies* from the figures at the corners of the pedestal, is the masterpiece of Andrea del Sarto, the greatest colourist of the Florentine school. The Madonna, with her eyes cast down, stands statuesquely; she holds a book resting on her thigh, on which the Infant Christ steps, while with childish grace and playfulness he climbs her neck. The companion figures, St. Francis and St. John the Evangelist, stand on either side; two little angels support the Virgin, whose face is a highly idealized portrait of the painters' wife, while the Evangelist on the right, is believed to be a portrait of the master himself.

In this picture the full type of the Renaissance was assained. The composition is well balanced, the extremities of the figures admirably drawn, the pictorial richness unsurpassed: nothing can exceed the harmonious fusion of tones in which the outlines of the work are almost obliterated.

RIVIERA DI LEVANTE.   PORTOFINO.

VIEW OF PORTOFINO ON THE ITALIAN RIVIERA.

    This Italian Riviera is full of a delightful scenery. Smiling villages, each with its note of individual charm, are scattered all along the wondrous coast. The Riviera is subdivided by the gulf whose central point is the fair city of Genoa; hence the names that distinguish the coasts that lie East and West of Genoa: *Riviera di Levante* and *Riviera di Ponente*. The view of Portofino given above is so full of loveliness that it must be counted among the most superb in Europe.

ISOLA BELLA LAKE MAGGIORE. Lombardy.

ITALY
THE LAND OF WONDERS

> " Fair Italy,
> " Thou art the garden of the world, the home
> " Of all Art yields, and Nature can decree;
> " Even in thy desert, wat is like to thee?
> " Thy very weeds are beautiful, thy waste
> " More rich than other clime's fertility;
> " Thi wreck a glory, and thi ruin graced
> " With an immaculate charm which cannot be defaced."
> — BYRON.

A COUNTRY so beautiful and so interesting as Italy needs no introduction to the traveller. Its historic associations of a glorious past, its noble monuments and priceless treasures of Art are in themselves allurements enough. But there is besides, the charm of natural beauties, of lofty mountains and luxuriant valleys, of picturesque shores and lovely lakes, of an ideal climate and blue skies, while to all who reverence the human spirit in its highest manifestations that must needs be holy ground, where, at every turn, you come upon traces of the most illustrious men that ever lived. During several centuries its people produced much that is great and even imperishable in Art and Science; its intellectual leaders gave a powerful impulse to creation, in both of these by revivifying classical antiquity; the number of petty potentates who held their courts in its various subdivisions created a hundred centres of interest, and the secret of Italy's charm consists partly in the consciousness that its cities are connected with the earliest developments of European civilization, that there was scarcely any great epoch in the history of mankind but found here its theatre and its heroes.

The traveller from the north feels himself suddenly transported into a new world as soon as he passes the barrier of the Alps. This enchanted land is in truth a land of wonders; every city and almost every little town is important either historically or picturesquely. There is entertainment to suit all tastes and desires; there is food for all minds, joy for every soul. Within the circle of a few hundred miles, are to be seen cities, each of which might be regarded as the capital of a distant kingdom. Those who delight in Art can find enough to do for a lifetime. The traveller of archeological bent, fond of old ruins, can study the ruins of monuments reared by the greatest and most ancient nations of the earth. Whoever is in quest of health has at his disposal all kinds of summer and winter resorts, all kinds of mineral springs besides the charm of pleasant surroundings. Little wonder, therefore, if Italy has been called the Land of Wonders.

THE NINE MUSES. Detail of the Triumph of Apollo (p. 179).

VIEW OF MONTE CERVINO.

Italy was the soul of the world and all were wooing her; she was the focus of all ancient culture, and this focus each nation desired to possess as its own. As far back as historic records reach, Italy has always been the Paradise of the earth; it almost seems as though Nature herself were anxious to protect this shrine of her beauties, for on three sides she has protected her by the sea and on the north has built a gigantic wall formed by the great chains of the Alps.

PIEDMONT

TURIN
AOSTA SUSA THE ALPS

AOSTA. Honorary Arch of Augustus. *Erected 23* B. C.

— 11 —

2. - *WONDERS OF ITALY.* Photo ALINARI, ANDERSON, BROGI.

PIEDMONT.

The Alps, the highest and vastest chain of mountains in Europe, form a natural barrier between Italy and the rest of the Continent. The Romans first obtained some knowledge of them by Hannibal's passage (216 B.C.) across them. Since then this formidable barrier has been stormed by innumerable invaders and the traces of the various incursions remain in the colossal construction of the numerous roads or passes so frequented now by travellers and motorists. One of the oldest of these passes is that of the Great St. Bernard, on the summit of which is the world-famous Hospice (8000 feet), 'the most elevated habitation in Europe.' This Hospice or Convent was founded in the 11th cent. by St. Bernard of Menthon. The monks here pass their lives in the perilous offices of rendering assistance to travellers in distress. Every evening one of them, accompanied by a trusty servant and attended by large strong dogs, descends a part of the mountain in search of benighted travellers who are wandering in the snow, or buried under the avalanches. The dogs are trained to this sort of service and perform their duty admirably; they will scent a man at a great distance, and, notwithstanding the thick fogs or the deepest snow, always know how to find their way. By the watchfulness and active exertions of these pious ecclesiastics the lives of many individuals who would fall victims to the rigour of the climate, are saved every year.

VIEW OF MONTE ROSA. (15.200 ft.).

GENERAL VIEW OF AOSTA. *In the distance are the Alps.*
Aosta was the birthplace of St. Anselm († 1109), archbishop of Canterbury from 1903.

OZEGNA. THE CASTLE. 15 cent.

IVREA. CASTELLO DELLE QUATTRO TORRI.

PIEDMONT.

VIEW OF MONTE BIANCO (15.782 ft.).

PIEDMONT, the district " at the foot of the mountains ", a territorial division of North Italy, enclosed on all sides except towards the Lombard plain by the semicircle of the Alps and the Apennines, embraces the provinces of Turin, Novara Cuneo, Alessandria and Vercelli. There are numerous summer resorts in the Alpine valleys. The history of Piedmont is closely interwoven with that of its dynasty, the *House of Savoy*, which first became conspicuous about the year 1000, and whose territorial possessions were constituted a county of the empire in the 12th century. *Humbert I.* ' Biancamano ' († 1056), is generally regarded as the founder of the dynasty; *Amadeus VI.*, extended the power of his House; *Amadeus VIII.*, raised to the ducal dignity by the Emperor Sigismund added Piedmont to his possessions. Beginning with Emanuel Philibert (1580 and during the 17th and 18th centuries Piedmont was the only Italian state that took an active part in Europian fighting; in the 19th century Piedmont became the stronghold of the *Risorgimento* (indipendence movement) and the strongest instrument in the unification of Italy.

CASTLE OF FENIS (AOSTA). *Gothic style (14th century)*

SUSA. Triumphal Arch. *Erected* 7 B. C.

Photo ALINARI.

PIEDMONT.

NOVARA. CHURCH OF SAN GAUDENZIO. By TIBALDI. Height of the dome 397 ft.

AGLIÈ. THE CHATEAU. Erected in 1775. Now a residence of the Duke of Genoa.

PINEROLO. THE CATHEDRAL. 11th cent. Romanesque-Gothic style.

ASTI. THE CATHEDRAL. Erected in 1348. Gothic style. The birthplace of Vittorio Alfieri († 1803), tragic poet.

Only a few miles from Pinerolo is the territory inhabited by the Waldenses, a Protestant community founded by Peter Waldo about 1170 in the south of France, and who were driven by cruel persecutions to take refuge in the Piedmontese valleys. It was during the persecution of 1655 that elicited a protest from Cromwell in England and that Milton wrote his famous sonnet, "On the Late Massacre in Piedmont."

SALUZZO. THE CATHEDRAL. 16th cent.

SALUZZO. PALAZZO CAVASSA. 15th cent.

Photo ALINARI.

GENERAL VIEW OF THE CITY FROM THE CAPUCHIN MONASTERY.

TURIN

TURIN, the ancient *Augusta Taurinorum* of the Romans, reached its first period of importance in the fifteenth century, when it came into the possession of the House of Savoy, who has made Italy free and united. To day Turin is the chief city of Piedmont, as brilliant and beautiful as any city of modern times,—broad streets, stately palaces, churches, public monuments, and gardens are conspicuous everywhere. The streets are ornamented with arcades, and remarkably regular (as in the time of the Romans); the most important all converge to the Piazza Castello, a huge square space near which stand the chief public buildings, while in the centre of the square itself is the Palazzo Madama (p. 17), a strange imposing edifice, having on one side a late-Renaissance façade, whilst on the other are octangular towers and heavy doorways which belong to the Middle Ages.

Turin possesses a fine Picture Gallery, a most interesting Museum of Egyptian Antiquities, and an Armoury, which is considered the best in Europe.

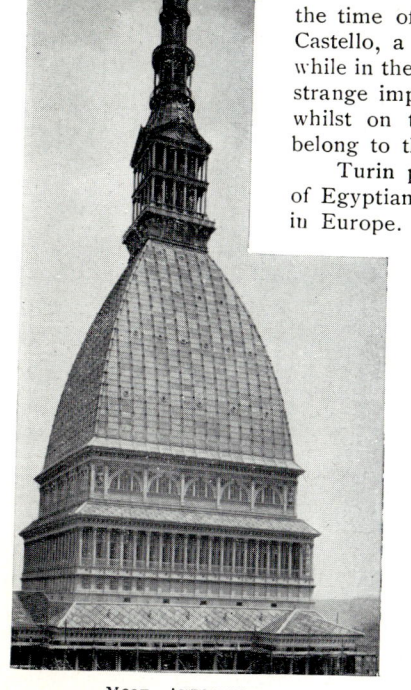

MOLE ANTONELLIANA.
The Tower, 540 ft. high, has been damaged in 1953.

CHURCH OF SUPERGA. *Erected in 1720.*
Charles Albert and other Savoy princes are buried in the crypt.

Photo ALINARI, BROGI.

TURIN — THE CITY.

Monument to Amedeus VI. † 1383. The "Conte Verde." By PALAGI.

Monument to Victor Emmanuel II. † 1878. By PIETRO COSTA.

Monument to Camillo Cavour. † 1861. Designed by DUPRÈ. (1873).

Palazzo Carignano. *Erected by* GUARINI (1680). *King Victor Emmanuel II, was born in this palace.*

Court of the Palazzo Paesana.

The Porta Palatina. *A Roman gateway restored in 1910.*

Royal Castle of Moncalieri.

Photo ALINARI, BROGI.

"HISTORICAL SUPPLEMENT".

GENEALOGICAL TABLE OF THE HOUSE OF SAVOY

The Kings of Italy.

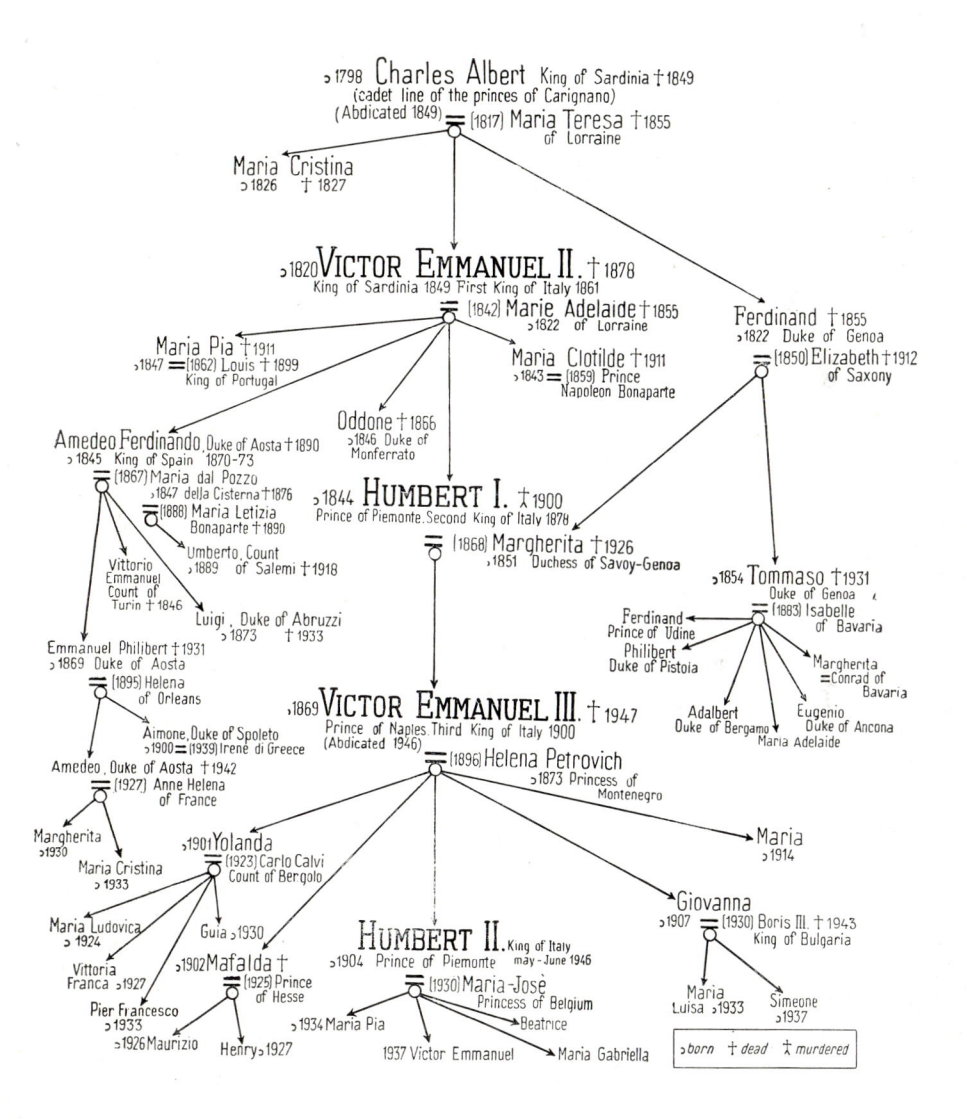

∽1798 **Charles Albert** King of Sardinia †1849
(cadet line of the princes of Carignano)
(Abdicated 1849) ═ (1817) **Maria Teresa** †1855
of Lorraine

Maria Cristina
∽1826 †1827

∽1820 **Victor Emmanuel II.** †1878
King of Sardinia 1849 First King of Italy 1861
═ (1842) **Marie Adelaide** †1855
∽1822 of Lorraine

Ferdinand †1855
∽1822 Duke of Genoa
═ (1850) **Elizabeth** †1912
of Saxony

Maria Pia †1911
∽1847 ═(1862) Louis †1899
King of Portugal

Maria Clotilde †1911
∽1843 ═(1859) Prince
Napoleon Bonaparte

Oddone †1866
∽1846 Duke of
Monferrato

Amedeo Ferdinando, Duke of Aosta †1890
∽1845 King of Spain 1870-73
═(1867) Maria dal Pozzo
∽1847 della Cisterna †1876
═(1888) Maria Letizia
Bonaparte †1890

∽1844 **Humbert I.** †1900
Prince of Piemonte. Second King of Italy 1878
═ (1868) **Margherita** †1926
∽1851 Duchess of Savoy-Genoa

∽1854 **Tommaso** †1931
Duke of Genoa
═ (1883) **Isabelle**
of Bavaria

Vittorio Emmanuel
Count of Turin †1846

Umberto, Count
∽1889 of Salemi †1918

Luigi, Duke of Abruzzi
∽1873 †1933

Ferdinand
Prince of Udine
Philibert
Duke of Pistoia

Margherita
═Conrad of Bavaria

Emmanuel Philibert †1931
∽1869 Duke of Aosta
═(1895) Helena
of Orleans

Adalbert
Duke of Bergamo

Eugenio
Duke of Ancona
Maria Adelaide

Aimone, Duke of Spoleto
∽1900 ═(1939) Irene di Greece

∽1869 **Victor Emmanuel III.** †1947
Prince of Naples. Third King of Italy 1900
(Abdicated 1946)
═ (1896) **Helena Petrovich**
∽1873 Princess of Montenegro

Amedeo, Duke of Aosta †1942
═(1927) Anne Helena
of France

Margherita
∽1930

Maria
∽1914

Maria Cristina
∽1933

∽1901 **Yolanda**
═(1923) Carlo Calvi
Count of Bergolo

Maria Ludovica
∽1924

Guia ∽1930

Giovanna
∽1907 ═(1930) Boris III. †1943
King of Bulgaria

Vittoria Franca ∽1927

∽1902 **Mafalda** ‡
═(1925) Prince
of Hesse

Humbert II. King of Italy
may-June 1946
∽1904 Prince of Piemonte
═(1930) **Maria-José**
Princess of Belgium

Maria Luisa ∽1933

Simeone
∽1937

Pier Francesco
∽1933

∽1926 Maurizio

Henry ∽1927

∽1934 Maria Pia

Beatrice

1937 Victor Emmanuel

Maria Gabriella

∽born †dead ‡murdered

A dynasty which ruled over the territory of Savoy and Piedmont for nine centuries and, until 1945, over the Kingdom
[continued on following page].

— 16* —

G. FATTORUSSO, Editor.

"HISTORICAL SUPPLEMENT".

CAMPAIGN SUIT OF DUKE E. PHILIBERT    CAMPAIGN SUIT OF A PRINCE OF SAVOY.
Royal Armoury or *Armeria Reale*, Turin.

The *Armoury*, is one of the most important collections of armour in Europe. Besides old battle-axes and other 16th century weapons, it contains Piedmontese ensigns of the War of Independence, arms and souvenirs of Victor Emmanuel II., Humbert I. and Charles Albert, a sword of Napoleon I. and a lock of his hair. In the Great Hall are beautiful suits of armour of the Martinengo family, a gigantic suit of armour worn at the Battle of Pavia (1525) by an equerry of King Francis I. of France. But the finest of all, however, are the suits of Duke Emmanuel Philibert † 1580, and Prince Eugene of Savoy.

HOUSE OF SAVOY *(continued from preceding page)*

of Italy. The founder of the house was Umberto Biancamano (Humbert the White-handed), † 1056, a feudal lord, who, in 1003 was count of Nyon on the Lake of Geneva, and in 1024 of the Val d'Aosta. In 1034 he obtained the county of Savoy as a reward for helping King Conrad II. the Salic to make good his claim on Burgundy. His descendants were created (1101) imperial counts of Savoy by Emperor Henry IV. † 1106. The following are the component parts which by successful wars, conquests and marriages were united under the authority of the dynasty : Piedmont, the *Principality of Carignano* the *Marquisate of Ivrea*, the *Counties of Nice* (1388), of *Asti*, ceded by Charles V. in 1531, the *Marquisate of Saluzzo* (1588), the *Duchy of Monferrato* (1630) ; several dismemberments of the *Duchy of Milan*, namely the *Provinces of Alessandria, Tortona* and *Novara* (1736), lastly the *Genoese territories*. By the Treaty of Utrecht (1713) the island of *Sicily* was ceded to Savoy and the title of king bestowed upon the duke. In 1720 Victor Amadeus II. was forced to cede Sicily to Austria in exchange for *Sardinia*, which with Savoy and Piedmont, etc. constituted the KINGDOM OF SARDINIA till its dissolution in 1860, when Savoy was ceded to France and the remaining portion merged in the new ITALIAN KINGDOM under Victor Emmanuel II. Henceforth, the destinies of Italy were bound up with the advance of the house of Savoy (Casa Sabauda), with its growth in wealth, military resources and political self-consciousness, and with its ultimate acceptance of the task, accomplished (1918) of freeing Italy from foreign tyranny and forming a single nation out of many component elements.

TURIN — THE CITY.

Monument to Prince Ferdinand of Savoy. By A. Balzico. (1877).

Monument to Duke E. Philibert. † 1580. *Bronze by* Carlo Marochetti, 1838.

E. Philibert of Savoy, the hero of St. Quentin (1557), spent 25 years in the service of the emperor Charles V., as governor-general of the Low Countries.

Monument to Charles Albert. † 1849. *Bronze by* Marochetti.

Palazzo Madama. Designed by Juvara. *Western façade, eighteenth century.*
Originally erected by William II. of Montferrat on the Roman east gate of the town, remains of which were incorporated in the palace.

Palazzo Madama. *Eastern façade dating from the 13th and 15th cent.*

Grand Staircase of the Palazzo Madama Designed by Juvara.

Castello del Valentino. (In the style of a French chateau). *Begun in 1650 for the wife of Vittorio Amedeo I.*

— 17 —

Photo Alinari, Brogi.

3. - WONDERS OF ITALY.

TURIN — THE CHURCHES.

THE CATHEDRAL (*San Giovanni Battista*).
Designed by BACCIO PINTELLI. A. D. 1498.

DOME OF THE CAPPELLA DEL SANTISSIMO SUDARIO. (*Cathedral*).

INTERIOR OF THE CATHEDRAL.
Renaissance style.

CAPPELLA DEL SS. SUDARIO. (Holy Shroud).
By GUARINI 1694. (*Cathedral*).

TOMB OF GIOVANNA D'ORLÈ.
(*Cathedral*).

The churches in Turin are distinguished by richness of ornament and good architecture.

The Cathedral or church of *San Giovanni Battista*, situated immediately behind the Royal palace, was designed by *Baccio Pintelli* and erected by the architect *Meo del Caprina*. It is built in the form of a Latin cross and contains numerous works of art in painting. Behind the high altar is the celebrated Cappella del Santissimo Sudario or Holy Shroud, with walls entirely lined with black marble, contrasting singularly with the white marble monuments, while the light from the curiously shaped dome above enhances the effect. The monuments were erected in 1842 by King Charles Albert to the memory of four of his ancestors: Emmanuel Philibert († 1580), Prince Thomas († 1656), Charles Emmanuel II. († 1675), Amadeus VIII. († 1451). In an urn over the altar is preserved a portion of the shroud in which the body of our Saviour is said to have been wrapped by Joseph of Arimathea after the descent from the cross. This precious relic was brought from Jerusalem to Chambery in the year 1452 and after many vicissitudes brought to Turin by Emmanuel Philibert in 1578.

CHURCH OF THE SANTI MARTIRI. *16th cent.*

Photo ALINARI, BROGI.

TURIN — PICTURE GALLERY.

"LA CONSOLATA." *Erected by* GUARINI 1679-1714.

THE TWO QUEENS. *By* VELA. (*La Consolata*).

La Consolata, which derives its name from a miraculous picture of the Virgin, the object of much veneration, is formed by the union of two churches opening into each other; the most ancient dating from the 10th cent. The adjoining campanile is a relic of an ancient convent founded by the monks of Novalesa. In a chapel to the left of the entrance are two kneeling statues in marble of Maria Teresa, Queen of Charles Albert, and Maria Adelaïde, Queen of Victor Emmanuel II. (both of whom died in 1855).

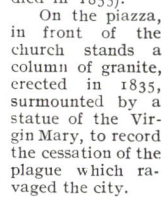

On the piazza, in front of the church stands a column of granite, erected in 1835, surmounted by a statue of the Virgin Mary, to record the cessation of the plague which ravaged the city.

San Filippo, is the largest church in Turin, its dome fell in just as it was nearing completion and was restored by JUVARA.

SANTA CRISTINA. *By* FIL. JUVARA.

SAN DOMENICO. *Gothic style. Founded in 1354, repeatedly restored.*

CHURCH OF SAN FILIPPO. *By* GUARINI *and* JUVARA.

CHURCH OF SAN LORENZO. *By* GUARINI.

Photo ALINARI, BROGI.

TOBIAS AND THE THREE ANGELS.
By BOTTICELLI.

Tobias and the Archangel.
By PIERO POLLAIUOLO.

THE QUEEN OF SHEBA BEFORE SOLOMON.
By PAOLO VERONESE.

Tobias had been sent on a mission by his father Tobit who was afflicted with blindness. Tobias was accompanied by a stranger, who, it transpired, was the Archangel Raphael disguised. While on the way they came to the River Tigris, and as the young Tobias went down to wash himself, a fish leaped out of the river and would have devoured him. But the angel directed him to drag the fish to shore, take out its heart, liver and gall and put them up safely; explaining that these parts of the fish are of virtue in exorcising devils and in healing blindness. In the course of his mission Tobias was married to Sarah, whose seven previous husbands had died in the bridal-chamber, slain by the jealousy of the demon. By Raphael's directions Tobias was enabled to exorcise the demon, and with his wife and the angel returned home. And when his blind father came to greet him, he rubbed the gall on his eyes and Tobit's eyesight was miraculously restored.

In Botticelli's picture, the Archangel Raphael leads the youthful Tobias; to the left is St. Michael, the Angel of Judgment sword in hand; to the right Gabriel, the Angel of Redemption holding the lily. Tobias with his fish represents the Christian, the believer, guided through his life-pilgrimage by the angelic guardian and minister of divine mercy.

MADONNA DELLA TENDA.
By RAPHAEL.

ENTOMBMENT. *By* F. FRANCIA. A. D. 1515.

ST. PETER and Donor.
By G. FERRARI.

TURIN — PICTURE GALLERY.

MARGUERITE OF VALOIS. *By* F. CLOUET.

THE CHILDREN OF CHARLES I. *By* VAN DYCK (1635).

The fine portrait of the children of Charles I of England, painted by Van Dyck in a range of colours fast and dull, is rather cold, but the vigour of the touch and the powerful character of these famous and childish faces give us on the whole a melancholy and piercing charm. On the left is Charles, Prince of Wales and the future Charles II, with a long red satin dress, laying his right hand on the head of a spaniel. In the center is Princess Maria (later the wife of William of Nassau) stands with a naive coquetry in her white satin frock; on the right, James, Duke of Jork shows an apple to her brothers.

ANTOON VAN DYCK (1599-1641), was the most distinguished of Ruben's pupils. He spent five years in Italy devoting himself to the study of the great masters. On his return to Antwerp he at once became the great courtpainter of his time. Afterwards he went to England and was patronized by King Charles I. and during nearly eight years worked at the portraits of the English aristocracy. He died in London and is buried at St. Paul's.

THE PASSION OF OUR LORD. *By* HANS MEMLING. (15th century).

— 21 —

Photo ALINARI, ANDERSON, BROGI.

TURIN — ROYAL PALACE.

THE ROYAL PALACE. *Erected in 1646-58.* The bronze statues in front, Castor and Pollux, are by *Sangiorgio*.

THE GRAND STAIRCASE. Showing the statue of Charles Albert.

THE GREAT HALL or "Sala degli Svizzeri."

THE LIBRARY.

THE ROYAL ARMOURY.

CAMPAIGN SUIT OF PRINCE EUGÈNE.

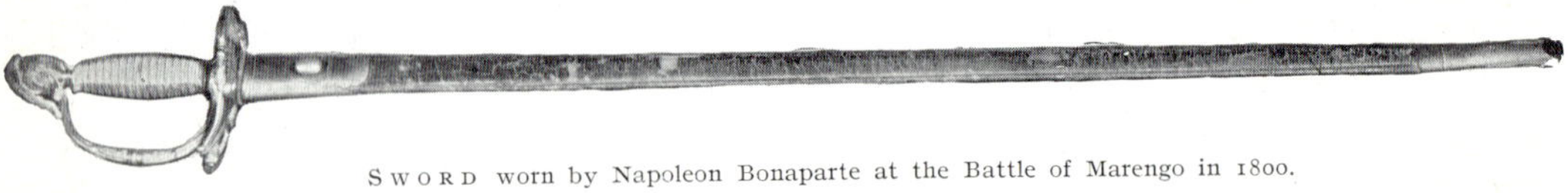

SWORD worn by Napoleon Bonaparte at the Battle of Marengo in 1800.

Inaugurated by King Carlo Alberto in 1833, the Royal Armoury contains one of the finest collections of arms in the world, and many splendid horses, covered with the skins of the real animals which belonged to celebrated personages.

— 22 —

Photo ALINARI, BROGI, FOTOCELERE.

LEONARDO DA VINCI. *Drawing in the Royal Library.*

CASTLE OF STUPINIGI. *By F. Juvara. (18th century).*
A summer residence of the King.

VEZZOLANO. THE ABBEY.
Erected in the 12th cent.

VERCELLI. CHURCH OF S. ANDREA.
Erected in the 13th cent.

LAKE OF ORTA. Isola San Giulio.
This, though one of the smallest of the Italian Lakes, is nevertheless as lovely as the others and better known lakes.

Photo ALINARI, BROGI, FOTOCELERE.

LIGURIA

THE "RIVIERA"

RIVIERA DI LEVANTE. VIEW OF PORTOFINO.

GENOA
SAN REMO BORDIGHERA ALASSIO
SANTA MARGHERITA RAPALLO

WONDERS OF ITALY.

VIEW OF THE CITY AND THE HARBOUR.

GENOA

GENOA, the queenly city of the Tyrrhenian Sea, the birthplace of Columbus, the leading commercial centre of Italy, lies at the foot of the Apennines. Her peculiar situation on the slope of steep hills surrounding a bay gives rise to an inevitable picturesqueness and a never ending series of views. The ancient greatness of the city, her wealth and splendour are indicated by the magnificent churches and Renaissance palaces, famous for their beauty and their vast collections of works of art.

The greatest architect of the Genoese palaces was *Galeazzo Alessi* (1512-72), a pupil of Michelangelo, born at Perugia. His style is imposing and uniform and he displayed great ingenuity in making the best of unfavourable sites. As for painting, there are many works by Rubens and Van Dyck, who resided for many years in Genoa; the latter left many portraits of members of the Genoese nobility. The native painters are of little importance; they are *Luca Cambiaso* (1527-85), *Giovanni Battista Paggi* (1554-1627) and *Benedetto Castiglione* (1616-70).

MONUMENT TO COLUMBUS († 1506).

Christopher Columbus, born in Genoa, went to sea at 14. On Oct. 12 1492, after two months of great peril he first touched land at the Bahamas. The statue of the Discoverer at the top rests on an anchor, while a figure typifying America kneels at his feet. The sitting figures below symbolize Religion, Wisdom, Fortitude and Geography. The reliefs between them represent scenes from the life of the great Navigator.

The Great Lighthouse.

The lantern is 520 ft. above the sea; the powerful reflectors show a light visible for nearly 30 miles.

— 27 —

Photo ALINARI, BROGI.

4. - WONDERS OF ITALY.

GENOA — THE CATHEDRAL.

CATHEDRAL OF SAN LORENZO. Fourteenth century.

Statue of the so-called « Arrotino », scissor-grinder.

The Cathedral of San Lorenzo was founded in A. D. 985; re-erected in the eleventh century in the Romanesque style, and again in 1307 in the Gothic style. In the sixteenth century it was provided with a Renaissance dome by the architect *Galeazzo Alessi*, the friend of Michelangelo and the architect to whom Genoa owes its architectural splendor. The lower part of the façade is an imitation of French Gothic churches, while the alternate courses of black and white marble show Pisan influences. The solemn interior, striped with black and white marble, contains many works of art in sculpture and painting. In the left aisle is the famous chapel of San Giovanni Battista, built *Dom.* by *Gaggini* in 1496 and richly decorated with statues by *Guglielmo della Porta, Matteo Civitali, Sansovino* and other artists. In consequence of the crime of Herodias' daughter, women are forbidden to enter the chapel except on one day of the year. The Treasury of the cathedral contains many valuable objects of ancient art among which is the *Sacro Catino* (the Holy Grail?), an ancient Oriental glass vessel taken by Genoese crusaders at Caesarea in 1101, which is said to have been used by Our Saviour at the Last Supper (See p. 39).

THE GOTHIC PORTALS OF THE FAÇADE. 13th cent.
Over the central door is a relief of the martyrdom of St. Laurence.

INTERIOR OF THE CATHEDRAL

Photo ALINARI, BROGI.

GENOA — THE CATHEDRAL. Chapel of St. John the Baptist.

STATUE OF ST. JOHN, by SANSOVINO. CHAPEL OF ST. JOHN THE BAPTIST.
(In consequence of the crime of Herodias' daughter, women are forbidden to enter this chapel).

SARCOPHAGUS of the 13th cent. containing the ashes of the Baptist.

Photo ALINARI, BROGI.

GENOA — THE CHURCHES.

CHURCH OF SAN MATTEO.
Gothic style, 13th cent.

CHURCH OF SANTO STEFANO.
Romanesque-Gothic.

CHURCH OF SAN DONATO.
Romanesque style, 12th cent.

SAN MATTEO. Above the altar Andrea Doria's sword presented to him by Pope Paul III.

ST. IGNATIUS OF LOYOLA. *By* RUBENS.

THE ASSUMPTION. *By* G. RENI.

(*Paintings in the Church of Sant'Ambrogio*).

TOMB OF ANDREA DORIA. *By* MONTORSOLI.
(*Crypt of the church of San Matteo*).

PORTAL OF THE INNER FAÇADE.
(*Church of S. Maria di Castello*).

Photo ALINARI, BROGI.

GENOA — THE CHURCHES.

Church of Santa Maria in Carignano.
Designed by Galeazzo Alessi, 1552.

Church of the Santissima Annunziata.
Erected by G. della Porta. 1587. The Portico is by Barabino.

Church of San Siro.
(Seventeenth century).

Madonna. By Niccolò Barabino.
(Church of the Immacolata).

The Santissima Annunziata.
(Sixteenth century).

Church of the Immacolata Concezione.

Church of Santa Maria delle Vigne.

Photo Alinari, Brogi, Fotocelere.

GENOA — THE PALACES. Palazzo Doria del Principe.

CEILING OF THE LOGGIA. STUCCO AND PAINTED ORNAMENTS, *designed by* PERIN DEL VAGA.

JUPITER OVERTHROWING THE TITANS. *By* PERIN DEL VAGA.

THE LOGGIA WITH PORTRAITS OF THE DORIAS.

THE GREAT HALL. (*First floor*).

CHIMNEY - PIECE. *By* SILVIO COSINI.

The Palazzo Doria del « Principe » so called from the title granted by Charles V. to Andrea Doria, ranks as one of the most important. The palace was presented in 1522 to Andrea Doria who had it remodelled by *Montorsoli* in 1529 and adorned with frescoes and grotesques by *Perin del Vaga*.

Andrea Doria (1468-1560), was at first the admiral of the French fleet, but disgusted at the breach of faith shown by Francis I. he decided to transfer his allegiance from France to Spain and became the admiral of the Emperor Charles V., and having obtained a promise that Genoa should be an independent Republic, drove the French out of the city and established a new constitution (1528) in which all party interests were made subordinate to the real welfare of the State. The famous Golden Book « Il Libro d'Oro » was opened and on its pages were recorded the names of those who should rule; the Grand Council of Four Hundred (the Parliament) was set up and the old quarrels were forgotten and there was peace for twenty years, when mutual distrust and personal ambition triumphed once more and led to the famous (unsuccessful) conspiracy of Giovanni Fieschi (1547), who fell into the harbour as he was crossing a plank to step into a galley and was drowned by the weight of his armour.

Photo ALINARI, BROGI.

GENOA — THE PALACES. *Palazzo Reale.*

HALL OF VAN DYCK. *A private theatre adjoins the apartment.*

THE SAMIAN SIBYL. By GUERCINO.

THE BALL ROOM.

HALL OF THE MIRRORS.

STATE APARTMENTS.

The *Palazzo Reale* erected about 1650 for the Durazzo family by the Lombard architects FALCONE and CANTONE was purchased by the House of Savoy in 1817. The richly decorated interior contains numerous works of art by VAN DYCK and many other Italian Masters

THE PORTAL.

THE ROYAL PALACE. VIEW OF THE COURTYARD.

Photo ALINARI, BROGI.

GENOA — THE PALACES. Palazzo Rosso.

THE LITTLE GALLERY.    SALA DELL' ALCOVA.

The rooms are named after the ceiling fresco paintings which were executed by CARLONE, D. PARODI, PIOLA and DE FERRARI.

ANTONIO BRIGNOLE.    PAOLA ADORNO BRIGNOLE.   PORTRAIT OF A LADY.
Portrait details by VAN DYCK.   *By* PARIS BORDONE.

The *Palazzo Rosso* (so named from its red colour), formerly the property of the Brignole Sale family, was presented together with the renowned picture gallery contained in it to the city of Genoa in 1874 by the Duchess of Galliera († 1889).

ADORATION OF THE MAGI. *By* BONIFAZIO VERONESE.    CLEOPATRA. *By* GUERCINO.

The Renaissance palaces of the Genoese aristocracy are of the greatest importance to the student of Art.

Photo ALINARI, BROGI.

GENOA — THE PALACES. *Palazzo Rosso.*

CEILING OF THE SALA DELL'AUTUNNO. (Autumn).

SALA DELLA GIOVENTÙ. (Test of Youth).

PORTRAIT OF A PATRICIAN.
By PARIS BORDONE.

PORTRAIT OF F. FILETTO.
By GIOVANNI BELLINI (?).

THE BOTANIST.
By MORETTO DA BRESCIA.

ST. SEBASTIAN.
By GUIDO RENI.

ST. FRANCIS OF ASSISI.
By B. STROZZI („ Il Cappuccino ").

PHILIP II. OF SPAIN.
By VAN DYCK.

Many of the Genoese palaces, which surpass in number those of other cities of Italy, were erected by the architect *Galeazzo Alessi* († 1572), a pupil of Michelangelo.

Photo ALINARI, BROGI.

5. - *WONDERS OF ITALY.*

GENOA — THE PALACES.

MADONNA. *By* GERARD DAVID.
CHRIST AND THE TRIBUTE MONEY. *By* A. VAN DYCK. 
S. CECILIA. *By* BERN. STROZZI. 

Paintings in the Palazzo Bianco.

The *Palazzo Bianco* contains a great many works of art. Formerly the property of the Brignole Sale family, the palace (like the *Palazzo Rosso*) with its collections was bequeated to the city of Genoa in 1889 by the Duchess of Galliera.

JENNER vaccinating his son. *By* MONTEVERDE.
ALLEGORY OF LOVE. *By* RUBENS. 
S. FRANCIS. *By* MURILLO. 

Paintings in the Palazzo Bianco.

The Atrium and Staircase.   PALAZZO DELL' UNIVERSITÀ.   The Court.

This is the finest court and staircase at Genoa. The palace was begun as a Jesuit college by BARTOLOMMEO BIANCO in 1623 and created a University in 1812.

— 36 —

Photo ALINARI, BROGI.

GENOA — THE PALACES.

PARADISE. By B. STROZZI.  PIETÀ. By BERNARDO STROZZI. S. AUGUSTINE. By B. STROZZI.
Paintings in the Accademia Ligustica.

The Sala Rossa.   PALAZZO MUNICIPALE, FORMERLY DORIA TURSI.   The Council Room.

The *Palazzo Municipale* or Town Hall possesses a magnificent court and staircase. In the council chamber are mosaic portraits of Columbus and Marco Polo. In the other rooms are the violins of Paganini and Sivori, three letters of Columbus (only the copies are shown), Italian and Flemish tapestries.

PALAZZO MUNICIPALE (Doria Tursi). *Erected by* LURAGO. 1564.

HALL WITH THE MONUMENT TO TOLLOT. *Palazzo Municipale* (Doria Tursi).

— 37 —

Photo ALINARI, BROGI.

GENOA — THE PALACES.

PIAZZA XX SETTEMBRE.   PALAZZO DUCALE.

The *Palazzo Ducale* originally built in the 13th century was the residence of the doges. The old building, remodelled in the 16th century, was modernized by SIMONE CANTONI after a fire in 1777.

PORTAL of the Palazzo Negroni.
By PARODI *and* ANSALDO.

VESTIBULE of the Palazzo Balbi.
By G. PETONDI. 1780.

PORTAL of the Palazzo Durazzo.
By ALESSI *and* PARODI.

PORTAL *by* GIOVANNI DA BISSONE (Palazzo Doria).

In medieval times, when Genoese streets were narrow, the decoration of palaces was restricted to the marble doorways.

GENOA — THE CITY.

PIAZZA AND CHURCH OF SAN PIETRO IN BANCHI.

The Piazza Banchi and the Old Exchange are in the heart of the old city. From here runs the Via degli Orefici where the delicate silver filigree work for which Genoa is famous may be seen spread out in profusion.

TABERNACLE. By DOMENICO PIOLA.
(*Via degli Orefici*).

The *Torre degli Embriaci* illustrated here is the only relic left of the 12th century castle of Guglielmo Embriaco, the Genoese captain who distinguished himself in the first Crusade.

The Crusades have a special connecting link with Genoa, since it was from here that Godfrey de Bouillon, going to Jerusalem, set sail in the *Pomella* as a private pilgrim in 1095. Having been insulted at the very door of the Holy Sepulchre, Godfrey burning for vengeance against the Turks returned to Europe. He found Pope Urban II. who had already been worked upon by Peter the Hermit, holding a council of 310 bishops at Clermont for the purpose of organizing an expedition to drive the infidels from Jerusalem. Godfrey's report at once settled the question and the Pope gave Peter the Hermit the fatal commission that was to lead uncounted thousands to death. The first Crusade, under the leadership of Godfrey, was proclaimed and ecclesiastics were sent in all directions to preach the Holy War. Two of these, the bishops of Arles and Gratz came to Genoa and preached to the inhabitants with such success that an army of enthusiasts sailed from here in 1097. Landing at Syria, the Genoese displayed great valour in helping capture the town of Antioch; on their return home, however, they stopped at Myra in Licia and carried off from a Greek monastery the ashes of St. John the Baptist, which are now preserved in San Lorenzo (p. 29). In the following year the Genoese sent a larger force to the Holy Land under the command of Guglielmo Embriaco. He landed at Joppa and marching on Jerusalem found the Crusaders led by Godfrey de Bouillon still unsuccessful. Embriaco and his men set to work and rendered the allied forces such efficient help that the garrison was overpowered and the Holy City captured (1099). But Embriaco's main title to fame rests on the capture of the town of Caesarea (1101), which he achieved with unassisted Genoese forces after a most obstinate resistance. The booty that fell to the Genoese was very considerable and they returned home laden with spoil, bringing along the famous Catino (p. 28) which Guglielmo Embriaco offered to the church of San Lorenzo

TORRE DEGLI EMBRIACI.

PIAZZA CORVETTO
and the bronze equestrian statue of Victor Emmanuel II.

CORSO ITALIA
and the new Lido of Genoa.

Photo ALINARI, BROGI.

GENOA — *THE CAMPOSANTO.*

GENERAL VIEW OF THE CAMPOSANTO *or Cemetery of Staglieno. Laid out in 1850.*

TOMB OF MAZZINI († 1872).
Italian Patriot and Revolutionist.

VIEW OF ONE OF THE GALLERIES.
Cemetery of Staglieno.

The Camposanto at Genoa, occupying a vast area on the northern site of the city, is regarded as one of the finest in existence. It abounds in monuments whose rivalry in decorations has brought about a wonderful display of statuary

Photo ALINARI, BROGI.

LIGURIA — *RIVIERA DI LEVANTE.*

VIEW OF PORTOVENERE (*near La Spezia*)

THE ITALIAN RIVIERA. The district or strip of coast we now speak of as « The Riviera », was part of ancient Liguria; and Liguria it remains to-day, the name being retained and constantly used as regards the Italian portion at least. It is only since 1860 that Mentone, Nice, etc., have belonged to France. Since then, the French section of the Riviera is known as « La Côte d'Azur ».

The Italian Riviera, by far the largest portion, is a country quite as charming as the other and perhaps better known Riviera, « La Côte d'Azur ». There is the same beautiful Mediterranean — deep, blue crested with white caps or opalescent in the evening glow; there are the same headlands grown with pine and cedars, the same fertile valleys with even quainter villages; there are the same delightful walks under olive trees and along the craggy cliffs.

The Italian Riviera is full of delightful scenery and possesses a charm distinctly and individually its own. It is subdivided by the gulf whose central point is the fair city of Genoa; hence the names that distinguish the wondrous coasts that lie East and West of Genoa: « *Riviera di Levant* » and « *Riviera di Ponente* ».

VIEW OF RAPALLO, S. MARGHERITA AND PUNTA PORTOFINO FROM MONTALLEGRO.

RAPALLO, eighteen miles from Genoa, is one of the most protected spots on the coast much frequented as a winter resort and for sea-bathing. The vegetation here is quite tropical, camellias and oleander bloom everywhere in the open air. The houses are chiefly on arcades; near the sea is a picturesque watch-tower, similar to those seen on the Riviera of Amalfi (p. 555). It was erected after the town had been raided by Dragut Rais, that terrible corsair, the scourge and terror of Italy and Spain, who, in 1549 landing here at night surprised and sacked the town, carrying off a great number of men and women into captivity and leaving the usual marks of Turkish atrocities.

Photo ALINARI, BROGI.

LIGURIA — RIVIERA DI LEVANTE.

VIEW OF SANTA MARGHERITA.

SANTA MARGHERITA, is situated on a beautiful and sheltered bay of the Gulf of Rapallo. The beauty of the region, and particularly the charm of the coast line, has rendered it a favorite winter resort. Three miles from Santa Margherita is the delightful fishing village of *Portofino*; and beyond is the famous old *Abbey of San Fruttuoso* illustrated on page 46.

VIEW OF RAPALLO.

Photo ALINARI, BROGI.

LIGURIA — *RIVIERA DI LEVANTE.*

VIEW OF PORTOFINO.

PORTOFINO. It was from this little harbour that Richard *Coeur de Lion* embarked for Palestine in 1190. On the hill-side is the old Benedictine convent of San Gerolamo della Cervaia, founded in 1361; within its walls many distinguished personages, obliged from stress of weather to land at Portofino, were hospitably received. Thus in 1377 Pope Gregory XI. with a great fleet, on his way from Avignon to Rome, put into the shelter of the harbour and spent the night in the convent. Pope Urban VI. was here in 1385, the Emperor Maximilian in 1490, Adrian VI. in 1522, and John of Austria after his victory over the Turkish fleet at Lepanto. Here too Francis I. of France, detained by contrary winds on his way to Madrid as the prisoner of Charles V. was confined for a night.

SAN FRUTTUOSO is a picturesque little village, not far from Portofino, situated inside a narrow bay. The abbey, founded before the 10th century, has a church in the primitive gothic style and a small cloister where are the tombs of a Doria family (from 1275 to 1305) and a romanesque sarcophagus.

NERVI, at about eight miles from Genoa, for the beauty of its landscape and its mild climate, is an attractive and favourite winter resort.

ABBEY OF SAN FRUTTUOSO.

VIEW OF NERVI.

Photo ALINARI, BROGI.

6. - *WONDERS OF ITALY.*

LIGURIA — *RIVIERA DI PONENTE.*

GENERAL VIEW OF SAN REMO.

SAN REMO is the best known of the resorts on the Italian Riviera. Its climate is renowned for its mildness and evenness, and vegetation attains here a higher point of lavish fertility. It owes the shelter it enjoys from harsh winds to the rocky promontories which shut in its deeply curved bay to the east and west. The nucleus of the original town lies far back inland, but the newer edifices, the palatial hotels and the villas built for the accommodation of visitors in winter are far nearer the sea-front.

VENTIMIGLIA, the frontier town between Italy and France, occupies the site of the Roman *Albium Intemelium*. From here an attractive walk or drive leads to the *Giardini Hanbury*, one of the finest botanical gardens in Europe. They were founded in 1867 by the late Sir Thomas Hanbury, who, after spending a number of years as a merchant in China, bought the 15th century house that stood on the promontory of Mortola, and planted the terraces with a wonderful collection of rare trees and plants from Africa, Australia, America and the Far East. Running through the gardens one can see a stretch of the *Via Aurelia*, the old narrow road built by the Romans before the Christian era, and which they used to reach their port of harbour a few miles to the west, named *Portus Herculis Monaeci* (the modern Monaco). There Romans landed and embarked on their way to and from Liguria. In those days the coast and surrounding district was a bare rock, until the Middle Ages, when the Genoese commenced to build a castle with towers and formidable walls, to resist the incursions of the Saracens; and the protection which this fortress gave soon created a population on the promontory.

In the middle ages Monaco became a centre of strife in the struggles of the Guelphs and Ghibellines. The Grimaldis, who represented the Guelphs, succeeded in capturing the stronghold and were finally left masters of the district. A member of their family having expelled the Sacacens from Monaco in the 10th century, received from the emperor Otho I., the lordship of that city; its territory in course of time became the Principality of Monaco (and Montecarlo).

PANORAMIC VIEW OF BORDIGHERA.

BORDIGHERA is a chosen place of residence. Since Doctor Antonio's adventure the town has undergone a considerable change. Its gardens are most beautiful, palm-trees flourishing in the greatest profusion. Several attractive excursions can be made from here, such as Dolceacqua with its ruined medieval castle, the home of a thousand fantastic legends.

Photo ALINARI, BROGI.

LIGURIA — RIVIERA DI PONENTE.

SAN REMO. The Promenade.

This magnificent promenade is adorned with beautiful palms; many of them are as much as eighty feet high, and the palm branches used in the solemnities of Palm Sunday at Rome are all sent from here.

These splendid trees recall the interesting story of the momentous occasion when San Remo received the privilege from Pope Sixtus V. in 1586, at the time of the raising of the great granite obelisk which stands in front of St. Peter's at Rome. The Pope made the occasion one of great solemnity, by threatening death to anyone who should speak during the operation. All went at first, the immense mass was slowly rising upon its base when suddenly it ceased to move. In the construction of his apparatus, the architect had omitted to allow for the tension of the ropes produced by the enormous weight; at the critical moment, when there seemed scarcely any hope of the huge stone being successfully raised into its place, the sailor Bresca of San Remo at the peril of his life broke the breathless silence by shouting « Acqua alle funi ! » (water on the ropes), thus solving the difficulty. In return for this service Sixtus V. granted to the Bresca family the privilege of providing the yearly supply of palm-branches for St. Peter's on Palm Sunday.

VIEW OF DOLCEACQUA.

The ruinous stronghold of the Dorias rises above like enchanted castle in a fairy tale.

ALASSIO AND ITS BEACH.

ALASSIO is perhaps the prettiest place along the wonderful Riviera. Its beach soft as a velvet carpet is one of the finest in Italy.

Photo ALINARI, BROGI.

Portrait of LEONARDO DA VINCI. *Biblioteca Ambrosiana.*

MILAN. THE CASTELLO SFORZESCO. The old residence of the Dukes of Milan.
Erected in the 15th century by the Sforza, on the foundations of the 14th century Viscontean castle.

LOMBARDY

MILAN
THE LAKES PAVIA BERGAMO
BRESCIA CREMONA MANTUA

* CASTLE OF SIRMIONE. Lake of Garda.

CORONATION OF OTHO III. *Marble relief by* MATTEO DA CAMPIONE *in the cathedral of Monza.*

CHRONOLOGY OF MILANESE HISTORY.

B. C.

408. — Milan is founded by the Gauls.
222. — Milan (Mediolanum) is conquered by the Romans.

A. D.

305-402. — Milan becomes the residence of the Western Emperors. During this period the city equals Rome in extent and importance.
312. — Constantine the Great issues the toleration edict at Milan preparatory to the establishment of Christianity as the State religion.
375. — Saint Ambrose becomes Bishop of Milan.
388. — Theodosius, emperor, resides at Milan.
402. — The Emperor Honorius transfers his residence at Ravenna.
402. — Alaric, King of the Goths, invades northern Italy.
452. — Attila, *Flagellum Dei*, invades Italy and sacks Milan.
538. — Milan is again sacked and razed to the ground by the Franks and Burgundians. 300.000 of the inhabitants of all ages are massacred; the women sold as slaves.
568-774. — Milan under the domination of the Lombards who choose Pavia as the capital of their new kingdom called *Lombardy*.
756. — The Frankish King Pepin marches into Italy and attacks the Lombards.
774. — Charlemagne enters Milan and founds the so-called Kingdom of Italy.
774-1045. — After the fall of the Lombard kingdom the Archbishops of Milan become the real rulers of the city.
1035-45. — Archbishop Aribert in power. This ambitious and warlike prelate assumes the right to dispose of the crown of Italy. He invents the *Carroccio*, which was afterwards adopted by the principal cities of northern Italy.
1157. — Milan is strong and prosperous.
1162. — With the exception of a few churches Milan is totally destroyed by the Emperor Frederic Barbarossa.
1167. — Formation of the League of Lombardy, and defensive alliance against the Emperor. Milan is rebuilt by the allied cities.
1176. — Battle of Legnano. The Milanese and their allies defeat Frederick Barbarossa who loses all hope of re-establishing the empire of Charlemagne.
1221. — Milan becomes a republic. A *Podestà* is elected.
1237. — In a battle against Frederick II. Milan suffers a terrible defeat.
1250. — Strife between nobles and people (Guelfs and Ghibellines). Struggle for predominance between the Houses of the *Della Torre* and of the *Visconti*.
1252. — The Dominican Pietro da Verona, Inquisitor of Milan, is murdered.
1277-1447. — The *Visconti* Lords of Milan.
1310. — Matteo Visconti is appointed Imperial Vicar by Henry VII. of Luxembourg.

1386. — Gian Galeazzo Visconti begins the Duomo. He founds the Certosa di Pavia (1396).
1395. — The Visconti are created Dukes of Milan (p. 73)
1447. — Death of Filippo Maria, the last of the Visconti.
1447-50. — Milan becomes a republic, the " Golden Republic of Sant'Ambrogio. "
1450-1535. — The *Sforzas* reign at Milan.
1450. — Francesco Sforza becomes Duke of Milan.
1479. — Lodovico " il Moro " rules Milan. His splendid patronage of arts and letters made of Milan the richest centre of the æsthetic culture of the Renaissance.
1491. — Beatrice d'Este marries Lodovico. A period of great brilliance and prosperity follows in the history of Milan.
1494. — Charles VIII. of France invades Italy as the ally of Lodovico.
1500. — Louis XII. of France invades the Milanese. Lodovico is captured and carried off to France. He is imprisoned in the castle of Loches where he died of grief in 1508. Milan ruled by French governors.
1512. — Battle of Ravenna, the French are expelled from Milan. Maximilian, eldest son of Lodovico, is restored to the throne and made duke, by Pope Julius II. and Emperor Charles V.
1515. — Battle of Marignano (Melegnano). Milan falls into the hands of Francis I. of France. Maximilian is forced to abdicate and retires to France where he dies in 1530. Milan once more under a French governor : the Constable Bourbon.
1522. — The French suffer a terrible defeat by the forces of Charles V. and those of Leo X. and lose Milan. Francesco, second son of Lodovico, is made duke of Milan.
1524. — Francis I. at the head of a large army again enters Milan and drives the duke into flight.
1525. — Great battle of Pavia. Francis I. is taken prisoner, the French are expelled from Milan by the Emperor Charles V. Duke Francesco returns and continues to reign as vassal of the Emperor. He dies in 1535 and with him the House of Sforza becomes extinct. The duchy of Milan becomes a mere province of Charles V.'s vast empire : the " Holy Roman Empire. "
1535-1713. — Milan under Spanish rule.
1713. — Milan with the rest of Lombardy passes into the hands of Austria.
1785. — Alessandro Manzoni is born at Milan.
1797. — Milan becomes the capital of the " Cisalpine Republic. "
1799. — Milan is retaken by the Austrians, and regained by the French the following year.
1805. — Napoleon I. is crowned in the Duomo with the Iron Crown (p. 64).
1848. — Bloody insurrection against the Austrians who are compelled to evacuate the city for several months.
1859. — Milan is united with the new Kingdom of Italy.

GENERAL VIEW OF MILAN FROM PORTA TICINESE.   *In the centre the campanile of Sant'Eustorgio (p. 55).*

MILAN

MONUMENT TO LEONARDO († 1519).
By MAGNI. *Erected in 1872.*

Not far from Leonardo's monument and in the same piazza is the *Teatro della Scala*, designed by PIERMARINI and opened in 1779. It is the largest opera house in Italy, so called from its having been erected upon the site of the church of Santa Maria della Scala, founded by the wife of Barnabò Visconti, of the Della Scala family, Lords of Verona. The building externally unimpressive, but famous in operatic art, and capable of containing 3000 spectators, has always been admired for the excellence and magnificence of its internal arrangements. The theatre was damaged by the war in 1943 and faithfully rebuilt.

MILAN is the principal financial center of Italy and one of the richest manufacturing and commercial cities in the country. It has had a very long and important history and played a most prominent part in the making of Modern Italy. In the first centuries of the Christian era Milan was a vast, populous and magnificent city (when it became the seat of the Western Emperors), second in importance only to Rome. Nothing remains, however, of her temples, her peristyles, her theatres, her double walls. From the 5th to the 12th century the city was subjected to all the evils attending upon the greatest scourges of humanity, — war, famine, and plague. It was besieged forty-eight times, and stormed twenty-eight times, and so injured by warfare that only a few churches of the early-Christian and Romanesque period have survived. In the 11th century the city was ruled by the Archbishops, one of whom, Aribert, devised the famous *Carroccio*. In the 14th century the *Visconti* (p. 73) became lords of Milan, and thenceforth the city steadily increased in wealth and power. In the middle of the 15th century the *Sforza* succeeded as Dukes of Milan, and under their rule and liberal patronage of Arts Milan became the capital of one of the richest states in Italy. During the reign of Lodovico Sforza (Il "Moro"), the city burst forth into the splendours of a New Athens: scholars, poets, artists, architects, musicians, engineers, flocked to his magnificent court. It was at this period that the great Leonardo da Vinci came to Milan, and by order of Lodovico painted the celebrated "Last Supper."

Photo ALINARI, ANDERSON, BROGI.

MILAN — THE CATHEDRAL (Duomo).

THE CATHEDRAL. *Founded in 1386, by* Gian Galeazzo Visconti, Lord of Milan.

PIAZZA DEL DUOMO. On the left is the *Galleria Vittorio Emanuele*, on the right the *Royal Palace*.

Photo ALINARI, ANDERSON, BROGI, FOTOCELERE.

MILAN.

THE STAINED GLASS-WINDOWS OF THE CATHEDRAL (*detail*), *by* ANTONIO DA PANDINO (*15th cent.*).

MILAN — THE CATHEDRAL (Duomo).

VIEW OF THE APSE AND CHOIR WINDOWS.

MARBLE WORK ON THE ROOF.

The Cathedral of Milan is one of the wonders of the world. The first architects were probably *Marco da Campione* and *Simone da Orsenigo*, but a host of architects-sculptors were associated with the work: *Heinrich von Gmünd, Hans von Freiburg, Jean Mignot, Filippo degli Organi* of Modena, *Giovanni Solari* and his son *Guiniforte Solari, Francesco di Giorgio* of Siena, *Giovanni Antonio Amadeo, Giovanni Dolcebuono, Cristoforo Solari, Tibaldi, Ricchini* and others. The central spire surmounted by a statue of the Virgin rises 354 feet from the ground; the octagonal dome, designed by *Amadeo*, marks the transition from the Gothic to the Renaissance style.

The Facade, begun early in the sixteenth century, was completed by order of Napoleon I. in 1805-1809.

BRONZE DOOR OF THE MAIN PORTAL.
BY LODOVICO POGLIAGHI (1906).

MADONNA AND CHILD and Angels.
(Detail from the bronze door).

Photo ALINARI, ANDERSON, BROGI, FOTOCELERE.

MILAN — THE CATHEDRAL (Duomo).

A capital of the gigantic pilars in the interior of the church.

VIEW OF THE GRAND NAVE.
The whole church, even the roof is of marble.

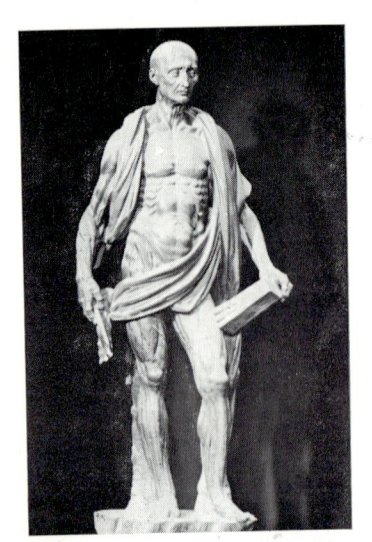

ST. BARTHOLOMEW carrying his skin.
By MARCO AGRATE.

The absence of ornaments in the interior adds to the impressiveness of its grandeur. The prodigious height of the pillars, the solemnity of the vast space, leave in the memory an impression of wondrous beauty.

In the middle of the church is a huge seven-armed bronze Candelabrum of most elaborate workmanship. Its base is adorned with fantastic figures of sirens, winged dragons, and other animals, including symbolical figures of Fortune, Architecture, Music and Old Testament scenes. In the right transept is a statue by *Marco Agrate* representing St. Bartholomew flayed, and carrying his own skin, with the inscription, — " Non me Praxitel sed Marcus finxit Agrates." In the crypt is the tomb of S. Carlo Borromeo. The coffin that contains his remains is richly adorned with silver, gold, and jewels.

THE GREAT BRONZE CANDELABRUM.
Executed in the thirteenth century (?).

— 52 —

Photo ALINARI, ANDERSON, BROGI.

MILAN — THE CATHEDRAL (Duomo).

The Cathedral of Milan is one of the largest and most sumptuous churches in the world; an example of the richest possible and most florid style of Gothic architecture that can be imagined. In fret-work, in carving and in statues, it surpasses all the churches in Christendom. The whole of it, even the roof is of marble, and taking into account both the large and small statues, it is said to contain over two thousand.

This marvellous edifice was commenced in 1386 by the splendour-loving Gian Galeazzo Visconti, and dedicated by him to *Mariae Nascenti* — to the Birth of Motherhood — as the inscription on the façade announces. Its earliest architects though Italian in name had certainly been schooled in Northern Gothic, for the huge structure shows scarcely a trace of the essential characteristics of genuine Italian Gothic. The building operations lasted for centuries, owing to the dissensions between the innumerable Italian architects and the German and French masterbuilders who were frequently associated in the work, and the church was not consecrated till the year 1577.

The Interior is most impressive. A wondrous and almost inexplicable sensation of awe and reverence overpowers those who enter the solemn, consecrated aisles! This mystic influence is not only due to the vastness of the space and the beauty of the proportions; to the forest of clustered pillars which support

VIEW OF THE TRANSEPT showing the magnificent bronze pulpits.

the roof; to the dim, religious light which streams in through the great stained glass windows: it is to the consciouness that millions of people have knelt and prayed here for centuries....

The original plan of the church was simpler than its development in subsequent times; it was intended to have only one altar, according to the Ambrosian rite, but the length of time spent in its construction, the frequent interruptions to its progress, the love of hange which animated the different architects, occasioned a departure from strict adherence to that design. The plan of the Duomo is in the form of a Latin cross, with double aisles separated by fifty-two gigantic pillars, and a transept also flanked with aisles. The whole temple is 490 feet long, 298 feet broad, and 268 feet high in the interior; it covers an area of 14.000 square yards and holds about 40.000 people.

VIEW OF THE CHOIR AND THE AMBULATORY.

Photo ALINARI, ANDERSON, BROGI.

MILAN — SANT'AMBROGIO.

General View. BASILICA DI SANT'AMBROGIO. *The Façade and the Atrium.*

The *Basilica of Sant'Ambrogio* was founded in A. D. 386 by St. Ambrose, bishop of Milan, who, according to tradition, baptized St. Augustine here. Of the early church, very little remains. The present edifice, representing the most remarkable example of Romanesque architecture, probably dates from the 12th cent.; but it preserves the features and atmosphere of the ancient basilica. Beneath the arcades of the very fine atrium, similar in form to the older one which it replaced, are tombstones, antique inscriptions and frescoes. The façade consists of a *Nartex* surmounted by a gallery of five open arches graduated in height corresponding with the lines of the gables. The campanile on the left is a fine Lombard tower of 1128; that one on the right dates from the 9th century. Outside this church the Lombard kings and the German emperors took their oath before they went inside to be crowned.

The imposing interior, entirely re-decorated, contains a great number of works of art among which the High Altar casing or *paliotto* that was presented by Archbishop Angilbertus about 835. This marvellous masterpiece of medieval art, the work of the goldsmith Wolvinius, is made of gold and silver plates enriched with uncut jewels and enamel of the most exquisite colours. The silver reliefs on the front represent scenes from the Life of Our Saviour; those on the sides angels, archangels, and Milanese saints. On the back, in a series of twelve square panels, are depicted the principal incidents of the life of St. Ambrose, while in the four medallions in the center are the archangels Michael and Gabriel, below them the Archbishop Angilbertus presenting a model of the altar to St. Ambrose, who crowns the donor, and St. Ambrose placing a crown on the head of Wolvinius, the goldsmith. The central part consists of two folding doors which give access to the shrine in which is deposited the body of the Great Archbishop Ambrose.

Canopy over the high-altar. *12th cent.*

PALIOTTO. Side view with busts of saints and angels.    DETAIL OF THE PULPIT. (*11th cent., romanesque art*).

— 54 —

THE JOURNEY AND THE ADORATION OF THE MAGI.
Marble altarpiece executed in 1347 (*Cappella dei Magi*).

The relief given above is in the Cappella dei Magi, where is also preserved a huge stone sarcophagus in which the "bones of the Magi" were kept until they were carried off to Cologne by Rinaldus, Archbishop of that city, when Milan was taken by Frederick Barbarossa.

Among other works of art the church, the interior of which with its three aisles is a typical fully-developed Lombard basilica, contains a triptych by Borgognone and the tomb of Uberto III Visconti, with the stupendous sarcophagus by Giovanni di Balduccio on which is carved the Coronation of the Virgin.

The basilica of S. Eustorgio founded in the 4th cent. to receive the relics of the Magi presented to Archbishop Eustorgius of Milan by the Emperor Constantine, was rebuilt in the 13th cent. and made over to the Dominicans. It was here that the tribunal against heresy was first set up, and from the open-air stone pulpit which overlooks the Piazza, St. Peter Martyr (Fra Pietro da Verona), Inquisitor General, fulminated his denunciations against heretics. But his strenuous efforts, his cruelties to stamp out heresy by the medieval plan of persecution, led to his death. On 28th April 1252 he was stabbed in a forest as he was journeying between Milan and Como; his martyred body was brought to this church and enclosed in a marble sarcophagus, until enough funds were collected from the pious for the erection of a nobler shrine.

Balduccio's magnificent monument was begun in 1336 and completed three years later. The sarcophagus is supported by eight exquisite allegorical figures of (front) Justice, Temperance, Fortitude and Prudence; and (rear) Charity hugging two children, Faith with the Chalice and the Cross, Hope with a cornucopia of fresh flowers, and Obedience bearing the yoke and the Gospels. The legend of the Saint is represented in a series of eight reliefs around the sarcophagus. The story begins at the back with the preaching of the Saint in the Piazza, and is continued through his martyrdom, funeral ceremony, canonization by Innocent IV. in 1253, and his appearance in succour to mariners in a storm. These panels are separated by statuettes of SS. Peter, Paul, Eustorgius, Thomas Aquinas, and the Doctors of the Church. Upon the lid of the sarcophagus are represented in relief the martyred saints John and Paul, and the donators — Cardinal Orsini, and the King and Queen of Cyprus. In the tabernacle is the Madonna and Child enthroned attended by SS. Dominic and Peter Martyr; the figures of Christ and two angels on top complete this elaborate shrine "which has few equals in unity of design, earnestness of feeling, and a judicious use of the symbolism of Christian art."

TOMB OF ST. PETER MARTYR.
By BALDUCCIO DA PISA. A. D. 1339 (*Cappella Portinari*).

Photo ALINARI, ANDERSON, BROGI.

Santa Maria delle Grazie, a church of brick and terracotta with a very beautiful exterior, was erected from 1465 to 1490 by Guiniforti Solari. In 1492, by order of Lodovico il Moro, the church was partly rebuilt by Bramante to whom are due also the striking tribune and the cupola, a marvellously fine work with its mingling of red brick and marble in the rows of windows beneath an open arcade. In the church there are some fine frescoes by Gaudenzio Ferrari; these frescoes, full of exuberant imagination, are among the best works of this artist. In the apse are fine stalls of carved and inlaid wood.

Adjoining it, is the convent leading from the cloister to the former refectory on the walls of which Leonardo da Vinci painted his celebrated " Last Supper."

CHURCH OF SANTA MARIA DELLE GRAZIE (*15th cent*).

The small but picturesque *Church of St. Satiro* was founded by order of the Archbishop Ansperto, in 9th century, and rebuilt in 1478 by Bramante who added the sacristy, now a baptistery. In the interior Bramante, with a clever perspective device, gave the perfect illusion of a semi-circular apse. The Cappella della Pietà, that is the ancient baptistery, has a graceful decoration and a Deposition in terracotta by Agostino De Fondutis. The campanile is in the 9th century Lombard style.

CHURCH OF ST. SATIRO, *by* BRAMANTE. (*15th century*).

CAMPANILE OF S. GOTTARDO.

Photo ALINARI, ANDERSON, BROGI.

MILAN — SANTA MARIA DELLE GRAZIE.

THE "CENACOLO" OR LAST SUPPER. By LEONARDO DA VINCI. A. D. 1495-98

Painted by order of Lodovico Sforza in the Refectory of the Monastery of Santa Maria delle Grazie.

This celebrated composition, the great masterpiece of the artist, combines all the best characteristics of the master's style. Leonardo has chosen to represent the dramatic moment when our Lord announces his approaching betrayal. The words, "One of you shall betray me," have been pronounced, and the whole company is thunder-struck. A storm of passionate feeling bursts forth; each disciple starts forward to express his grief and horror, and repel any implied accusation. In the midst of the tumult Christ sits motionless. He bows His head in silence, and His silence is more eloquent than words, — it seems to corroborate the accusation, "It cannot be otherwise, one of you shall betray me!"

To understand the wonderful skill with which the scene has been arranged one should first examine the delicate equilibrium of the design; the manner in wich the groups are contrasted, the relation they bear to each other, the expressions of the faces. Then pass on to consider the marvellous head of the Saviour, in whose features the painter has been able to combine dignity, solemnity, and majesty, with resignation and love.

In the composition of the scene Leonardo departs from the traditional arrangement by placing Judas among the rest of the disciples, instead of alone, opposite to them. The twelve Apostles are distributed in four groups of three on the right and left of the Saviour. *On the right hand* of Christ is St. John, who leans backwards in sorrow; Peter reaches impetuously forward to inquire who is the traitor; Judas, whose face is seen in profile, starts back terror-stricken, in his confusion he upsets the salt; St. Andrew, an elderly grey-bearded head, lifts both hands in astonishment; St. James Minor, resembling the Saviour in his mild features, reaches his hand on the shoulder of St. Peter; Bartholomew, on the extreme end of the table, has risen from his seat and leans forward as if to catch the words of Christ. *On the left* of the Lord is St. James Major who, with extended arms shrinks back in horror; St. Thomas is seen behind, the forefinger of his right hand raised, threatening, directed to Judas; St. Philip, young and with a beautiful head, with his hands on his breast protests his love and innocence. St. Matthew turns eagerly to his companions and with both his hands points to our Saviour; St. Thaddeus speaks to Simon and expresses consternation; Simon, the oldest of the twelve, is thoughtful and distressed.

Although now a total wreck, this monumental masterpiece is still perhaps the most impressive picture in the world, and well calculated to convey an idea of Leonardo's powers of invention. The design and the preparations for the execution had been carefully elaborated by the master, and the picture itself was completed within three years. A contemporary author writes that Leonardo was indefatigable in the execution of this work; he would mount the scaffold at day-break and continue there till night, forgetting to eat or drink. At other times he would stand for hours with arms in front of it and meditate upon the work, or paint but a stroke or two as the result of days of thought, or of the sudden inspiration of the moment. Fifty years after it was finished the picture began to deteriorate; the seeds for its rapid decay were sown by Leonardo himself, who, in order to be able to work with deliberation was tempted to paint 'a tempera' upon the dry wall, instead of fresco. Thus, the pigments not having been absorbed into the surface they gradually crumbled away. The hand of the 18th cent. restorers and the vandalism of the French soldiers (1796) who used the Refectory as a stable, have almost completed the ruin of this stupendous masterpiece of the Renaissance — the epitome of Leonardo's labours. But even in its decay it testifies to the almost superhuman depth and creative power of the Master.

LEONARDO DA VINCI born in 1452, died at Amboise in 1519. Of noble physical type, he was endowed with a combination of intellectual qualities such as probably no other man possessed. His manners were most polished, he conquered by the magnetism of his incalculable personality. Wherever he went he attracted crowds of enthusiastic disciples. In his mind science and art seemed married to one another. His unresting spirit in its thirst after knowledge left no departement of natured unexplored. He appears to have had an extensive knowledge of architecture, engineering civil and military, and mechanics generally, botany, anatomy, mathematics and astronomy; besides being a painter, he was likewise sculptor, poet, musician and philosopher.

Photo ALINARI, ANDERSON, BROGI.

The Nuptials of the Virgin. «Lo Sposalizio». *Painted by* Raphael. a. d. 1504.

This delightful altarpiece painted for the church of S. Francesco in Città di Castello (Umbria), is reminiscent of the Sposalizio of Perugino in the Museum at Caen. In both paintings a small polygonal building, representing the Temple at Jerusalem, rises in the background. The arrangement of the figures is simple and beautiful: Mary and Joseph stand opposite each other, the High Priest in the centre solemnly joins their hands; Joseph is in the act of placing the ring on the Virgin's finger. The latter is attended by a group of graceful virgins, while on Joseph's side are the disappointed suitors breaking their rods, — only the one held by Joseph has blossomed into a lily, the sign, according to the legend, that he was the chosen one.

Photo Alinari, Anderson, Brogi.

MILAN — THE BRERA GALLERY.

MADONNA OF THE "ROSE-BOAER." *By* BERNARDINO LUINI.

MARTYRDOM of ST. SEBASTIAN. *By* VINCENZO FOPPA (1427-92).

MADONNA with ST. CLARA. *By* BORGOGNONE.

The *Burial of St. Catherine* is one of Luini's most charming creations. The tranquil, refined character of the head of the saint and the expression of death, are exceedingly fine. St. Catherine, a virgin of Alexandria (ca. 307), in consequence of her refusing to submit to the licentious Emperor Maxentius, was condemned to be torn to pieces on a wheel set with spikes and knives. The wheel having broken, she was decapitated; her body was then taken up by angels and deposited on Mount Sinai. There it rested in a marble sarcophagus, and there a monastery was built over it in the 8th century. St. Catherine was a female endowed with intellect, eloquence and chastity.

THE BURIAL OF ST. CATHERINE OF ALEXANDRIA. *by* BERNANDINO LUINI.

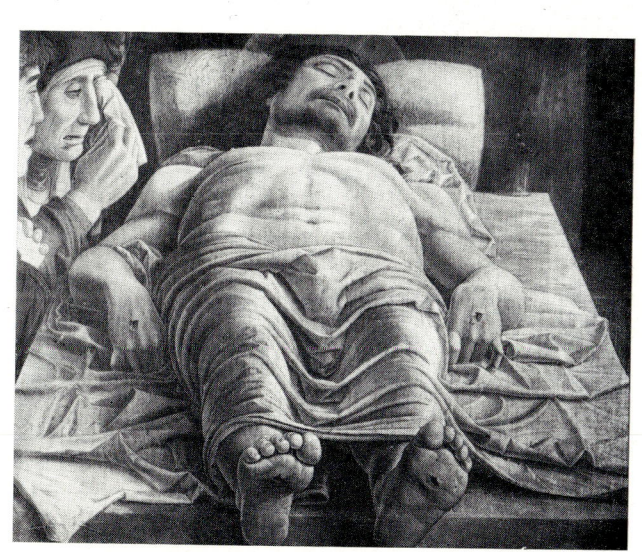

THE DEAD CHRIST, *by* MANTEGNA.

HEAD OF CHRIST. *Drawing by* LEONARDO.

8. - *WONDERS OF ITALY.*

Photo ALINARI, ANDERSON, BROGI.

PREACHING OF ST. MARK AT ALEXANDRIA. *Oil painting by* GENTILE BELLINI. A.D. 1507.

BELLINI'S *Preaching of St. Mark at Alexandria*, left unfinished when Gentile died, was completed by his brother Giovanni. This large composition is extremely interesting for the numerous figures in oriental costumes, whilst the architectural background bears evidence of the master's visit to Constantinople, which was marked by the following uncommon incident.

In the year 1479 the Sultan Mahomet II. having requested the Republic of Venice to send him the best painter, Gentile was unanimously selected by the authorities. In the Turkish capital the artist was treated with great consideration, and made portraits of the Sultan, and of many other notable personages. His sojourn, however, was hastily cut short. It is related that one day he showed the Sultan a picture of Herodias's daughter with the head of John the Baptist in a charger. The Sultan objected that the appearance of the severed neck was anatomically incorrect, and when he saw that Gentile did not understand his mistake, he summoned a slave and had him instantly decapitated in the presence of the horrified artist, that he might see for himself what was the true action of the muscles under such circumstances. Gentile was immediately convinced, and took the first opportunity to escape from the scene of such experiments.

MADONNA AND CHILD.
By CARLO CRIVELLI *(ca. 1468-93).*

MADONNA AND ANGELS.
By ANDREA MANTEGNA.

FINDING OF THE BODY OF ST. MARK by the Venetians.
(See *p. 102*). *By* TINTORETTO A.D. 1548

PIETÀ. *By* GIOVANNI BELLINI. *An early work.*

Photo ALINARI, ANDERSON, BROGI.

MILAN — THE BIBLIOTECA AMBROSIANA. MUSEO POLDI-PEZZOLI.

HOLY FAMILY. By LUINI.
(*Biblioteca Ambrosiana*).

LUCREZIA CRIVELLI (?). By BELTRAFFIO.
(*Biblioteca Ambrosiana*).

MADONNA and Saints. By BORGOGNONE.
(*Biblioteca Ambrosiana*).

The *Biblioteca Ambrosiana*, founded by Cardinal Federigo Borromeo at the beginning of the 17th century, contains the Library and a most interesting Picture Gallery. In the hall of the Picture Gallery dedicated to Leonardo is exposed, together with the works attributed to the great Master and his pupils, also the celebrated *Codice Atlantico*, consisting in 402 sheets with drawings and writings of Leonardo.

The *Museo Poldi-Pezzoli* consists in valuable collections of paintings, ancient bronzes, sculptures, enamels, cameos and tapestries, which the nobleman G. C. Poldi-Pezzoli bequeathed to the city of Milan. The *Portrait of a Lady* by Antonio del Pollaiolo, showed in this museum and formerly attributed to Piero della Francesca, is a most lovely picture. The outline of the face is perfect, the eye and the hair are exquisitely painted; it is a simple convincing likeness. The picture represents the wife of Joannes de Bardi.

PORTRAIT. By LEONARDO.
(*Biblioteca Ambrosiana*).

BEATRICE D'ESTE. By LEONARDO.
(*Biblioteca Ambrosiana*).

BETROTHAL OF ST. CATHERINE. By LUINI.
MADONNA. By BOTTICELLI. 
PORTRAIT. By A. DEL POLLAIOLO. 
Paintings in the *Museo Poldi-Pezzoli*.

Photo ALINARI, ANDERSON, BROGI.

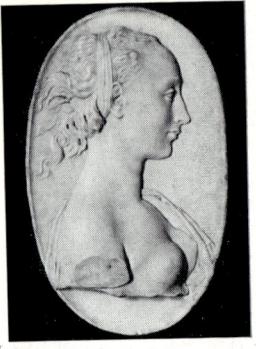

MILAN — *MUSEO ARCHEOLOGICO*.

Marble relief attrib. to DONATELLO. 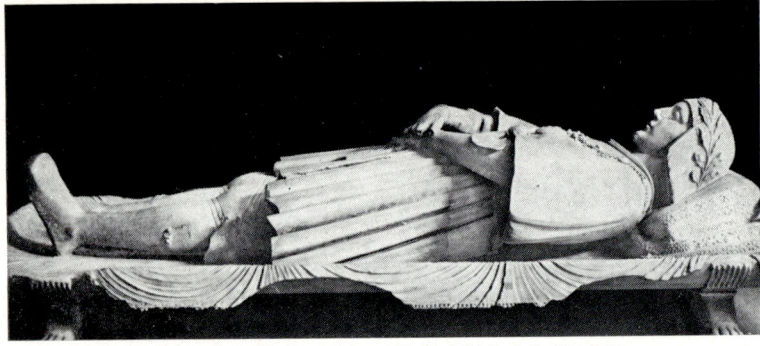   EFFIGY OF GASTON DE FOIX. *Part of the tomb by* BAMBAIA.

Gaston de Foix, nephew of Louis XII and Governor of Milan, routed the Spanish and Papal troops at the battle of Ravenna (1512) but was slain in the moment of victory when pursuing the fugitives. The tomb was ordered in 1515 by Francis I and left incomplete at the expulsion of the French in 1522.

The *Museo Archeologico*, located in the Castello Sforzesco, possesses an interesting collection of antique, medieval and modern sculptures.

The equestral statue of Bernabò Visconti, Duke of Milan, was executed during Bernabò's lifetime. Bernabò († 1385), celebrated for his cold-blooded cruelty, was an enemy of Urban V and having incurred that pope's displeasure, the pontiff sent two envoys — Benedictine abbots — to expostulate with the duke; directing that if he did not yield to the papal commands, he should be excommunicated. Having failed in their negotiation, the ambassadors solemnly delivered into Bernabò's hands the bull of excommunication. He received it without comment placing it in his pocket. The envoys then took leave, and he, as if to pay them honour, escorted them with a large retinue ouside the city gate. On the party arriving at a bridge, the duke stopped, and abruptly asked the envoys if they preferred to eat or drink. The two prelates, surprised at this address and glancing down at the turgid river, answered that eating seemed preferable; whereupon the duke drawing from his pocket the papal document enjoined them to eat it; and both, to escape with their lives, were obliged to swallow not only the parchment bull but the seals and all; after which they were allowed to return to the Pope.

PIETÀ RONDANINI. *By* MICHELANGELO.    MONUMENT TO BERNABÒ VISCONTI. *By* BONINO DA CAMPIONE (1370).

Photo ALINARI, ANDERSON, BROGI.

MILAN — THE CITY.

The entrance to the Galleria Vittorio Emanuele
(built in 1865-67, by G. Mengoni) as seen from the duomo.

Loggia degli Osii. Erected in 1316.
From the balcony (centre) sentences were pronounced upon criminals.

Court of the Palazzo Marino.
Built by Galeazzo Alessi in 1558.

Ospedale Maggiore. Length of façade 935 ft. Founded
by Duke Francesco Sforza and his wife Bianca Maria in 1456.

Colonnade of San Lorenzo.
These Corinthian columns are a relic of a porticus of Roman times.

Photo Alinari, Anderson, Brogi.

MONZA. THE CATHEDRAL. *Lombard-Gothic style.*
Erected in the 14th cent. by MATTEO DA CAMPIONE († 1396),
on the site of a church founded in 595 by Queen Theodolinda.

MONZA. PALAZZO COMUNALE
or Town Hall. *Erected in the 13th cent.*
(Called also *Palazzo Arengario*).

The greatest possession of the cathedral of Monza is the celebrated Iron Crown of the Lombards. It consists of a wide band of gold adorned with precious stones, while the rim of iron inside is said to have been made from a nail of the True Cross brought by the Empress Helena from Palestine. With this the Lombard kings and the German emperors, — Frederick Barbarossa, Henry VII. of Luxembourg, etc. — were crowned.

THE IRON CROWN (*Corona Ferrea*).

It was used by Charles V., who crowned himself with it at Bologna in 1530, and by Napoleon I., in 1805 who placed it on his won head with the words, « Dieu me l'a donnée, gare à qui la touche ».
The Treasury of the cathedral contains many objects of historical interest, and the gifts made by Theodolinda to the church she founded.

INTERIOR OF THE CATHEDRAL.
Restored in the 17th cent.

Banquet of Herod. Salome presenting St. John's head to her mother. *By* MASOLINO DA PANICALE. (*Castiglione*).

THE MARRIAGE OF THE VIRGIN. *By* B. LUINI.
(*In the Santuario della Beata Vergine, Saronno*).

Photo ALINARI, ANDERSON.

COMO — THE CATHEDRAL.

THE CATHEDRAL (*begun in 1396*) AND THE BROLETTO (*1215*).

Como, the ancient *Comun*, lies at the south-western end of the Lake Como and is enclosed by an amphitheatre of mountains; it is a charming little Lombard town, rich in scenic beauty and warlike reminiscences. Among the most famous natives of Como are the Elder and the Younger Pliny, Pope Innocent XI, Paulus Jovius, the historian, and Alessandro Volta, the physicist.

The *Cathedral*, or Duomo, built entirely of marble is one of the finest cathedrals of Northern Italy, and declared by Simonds to be " perhaps the most perfect building for illustrating the fusion of Gothic and Renaissance styles." Begun in 1396, the present edifice dates mainly from the middle of the 15th century. The Gothic façade was erected in 1487 and terminated with early Renaissance decorations and sculptures by the brothers *Tommaso* and *Jacopo Rodari*. The octagonal dome is by *F. Juvara*. The main portal is exceedingly rich in ornamentation, full of figures of saints and heroes, framed in carved stone-work. The seated figures of the two Plinys in the niches or tabernacles on either side of the principal entrance, date from 1498. The southern portal, built in Bramante's style, is a marvel of rich carving. The northern door is known as the " Porta della Rana ", from the carved frog once at the foot of the jamb. The interior of the church, that is remarkable for its noble proportion, contains works by Bernardino Luini, Gaudenzio Ferrari and T. Rodari.

To the left of the Duomo is the *Broletto*, built in alternate patterns of black and white stones, in 1215.

MEETING OF ST. ELIZABETH WITH THE VIRGIN, *by* RODARI.
Relief in the lunette of the PORTA DELLA RANA.

PLINY THE YOUNGER, *by* AMUZIO DA LURAGO (?).
Statue in the niche at the side of the main doorway.

Photo ALINARI, BROGI.

THE ITALIAN LAKES — *LAKE COMO.*

VIEW OF COMO AND LAKE.

CERNOBBIO. *View of the façade of* Villa d'Este.

The Lake of Como, is perhaps the most beautiful of the Italian Lakes, it was the chosen resort of intellectual and social life existing within the boundaries of the Roman world. Here the beauties of Lake Maggiore are reproduced in small but perhaps yet more effective scale; here Nature has freely lavished her choicest gifts and the traveller finds a delightful series of pictures by the alternations of pretty townlets with solitary landscape, villas combining classic elegance with rustic peace, with always the mountains and Alpine scenery in the distance.

Cernobbio is one of the most attractive and pleasant places on lake Como. The Villa d'Este was built in 1568 by Card. Tolomeo Gallio. In 1816-20 it was the home of the unfortunate Queen Caroline of England.

VIEW OF BELLAGIO FROM CADENABBIA.

Photo ALINARI, BROGI.

LOMBARDY. THE ITALIAN LAKES.

LAKE OF GARDA. The west side of the Gardesana.

THE LAKE OF GARDA, the *Lacus Benacus* of the Romans, celebrated in Latin, Italian and German lore, is the largest of all the Italian lakes; three great provinces meet on its shores: the Trentino, Venetia and Lombardy. The country around is uncommonly picturesque and varied, fringed with almost tropical vegetation, delightful resorts (Gardone Riviera, Riva, Salò, Sirmione, Arco, etc.), country houses and elegant villas are to be seen everywhere.

LAKE OF LUGANO. View of Melide with the Monte Arbostora.

The Lake of Lugano lies partly in Italy and partly within the Swiss Canton of Ticino; the charm of the landscape is due to this blending of different elements that complete each other.

— 67 —

THE ITALIAN LAKES — *LAKE MAGGIORE.*

LAKE MAGGIORE. VIEW OF THE BORROMEAN ISLANDS FROM STRESA.

LAKE MAGGIORE is about forty miles long; its Northern shores touch the rugged mountains of Switzerland. The banks are thickly inhabited with an almost uninterrupted succession of little towns, summer resorts, villas and hotels, so that one may walk from one village to another almost without knowing it.

STRESA is the most popular place on Lake Maggiore. From here the traveller sees one of the most enchanting spectacles in the world, for on the broad sheet of water, sparkling in the sunlight, he sees the three beautiful Borromean Islands, so named from the illustrious family of Borromeo. Two of these, Isola Madre and the Isola dei Pescatori are inhabited only by fishermen and their families, but the third, the famous Isola Bella, with its princely chateau and its fairy-like garden which rises in a series of terraces from the waters, is the most idyllic spot imaginable. There are innumerable interesting excursion (to Monte Mottarono the " Rigi of Northern Italy " 4892 ft.) which may be made to points in the vicinity, all easy of access, each with its own peculiar attractions. Stresa was the home of the philosopher Antonio Rosmini, † 1855.

ISOLA BELLA. THE GARDENS.

SANCTUARY OF ST. CATHERINE.

The gardens of Isola Bella were laid out in the 17th century, and are stocked with beautiful exotic trees and plants, — cedars, magnolias, laurels, camellias, oleanders, azaleas, rhododendrons, etc.

— 68 —

Photo ALINARI, BROGI.

PAVIA — THE CHURCHES.

VIEW OF THE CITY AND THE TICINO RIVER. *The Bridge dates from* 1353.

PAVIA was the capital of the Lombard Kings until the conquest of Charlemagne. It became later the faithful ally of the German emperors several of whom being crowned in the Basilica of San Michele. In the 14th cent. it was handed over to the Visconti of Milan, and was a very prosperous town. Here in 1525 was fought the Battle of Pavia, in which Francis I. King of France was defeated and taken prisoner by the army of Charles V. It was on this occasion that the king wrote to his mother " Madame tout est perdu, hors l'honneur " (All is lost save honour). Of the numerous towers and churches it once possessed only a few survive to-day. Pavia is the birthplace of Lanfranco († 1089) archbishop of Canterbury in the reigns of William the Conqueror and William Refus; Boethius was imprisoned here and during his confinement he wrote the famous *De Consolatione Philosophiae*, the " Consolations of Philosophy," a book translated by King Alfred and by Chaucer. He was put to death and his remains were interred in the old church of San Pietro in Ciel d'Oro. Petrarch frequently resided at Pavia as the guest of Galeazzo II. Visconti.

SAN PIETRO IN CIEL D'ORO. (11th cent.).

San Pietro in Ciel d'Oro, an old monastic church, rebuilt about 1100 in the Romanesque style, and mentioned by Dante (Par. X. 128), is famous for the *Arca di Sant' Agostino* it contains, which was probably executed by *Matteo* and *Bonino da Campione*. This most sumptuous marble monument is enriched with 95 statuettes of saints, prophets and Virtues; 50 bas-reliefs representing incidents in the life of St. Augustine of Hippo; and numerous architectural accessories which form an *ensemble* of the most imposing character. On the sarcophagus is the recumbent effigy of the Saint, whose relics were brought to Pavia in 723. The Lombard king Liutprand († 744) is also buried here.

It was in the church of San Michele, originally built by the Lombard kings that Charlemagne (771), Berengar (888), and his successors Berengar II. (950), Adalbert and Arduin, Margraves of Ivrea (1002), were crowned " Kings of Italy. " Henry II. (1004), Frederick Barbarossa (1115) and other German emperors received the Lombard crown in Monza.

BASILICA DI SAN MICHELE. (14th cent.).

LEFT SIDE OF THE ARCA DI SANT'AGOSTINO 14th cent. (*San Pietro in Ciel d'Oro*).

— 69 —

Photo ALINARI, BROGI.

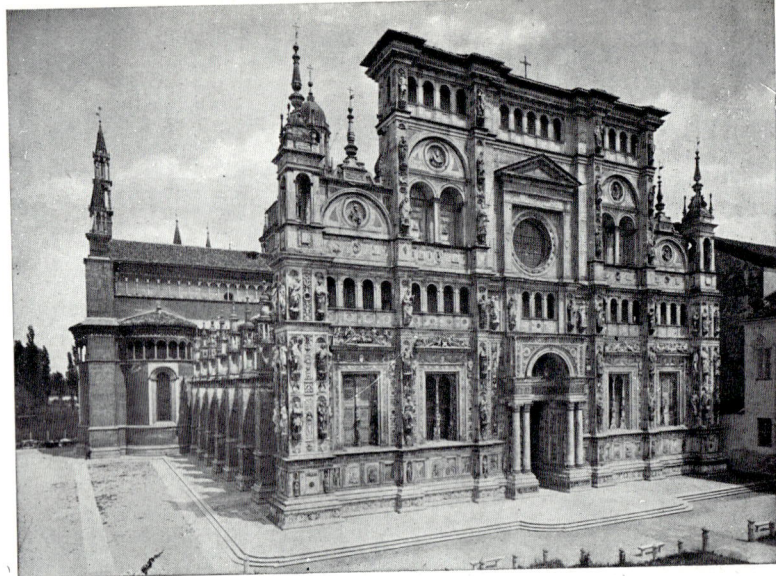

PAVIA — THE CERTOSA.

The *Certosa di Pavia* or Carthusian monastery was begun in 1396 by Gian Galeazzo Visconti, Lord of Milan, in fulfilment of a vow made by his wife.

The central portion of the church with its high nave and Gothic pillars is reminiscent of the Duomo of Milan; the apse shows signs of the transition period from Gothic to Renaissance, the façade which belongs to the latter part of the 15th century is completely Renaissance.

This celebrated Façade was commenced in the year 1473, from designs prepared by the painter *Borgognone*. In greater part it is the work of the two brothers MANTEGAZZA and AMADEO. Every portion of it is covered with white marble sculptures. Medallions imitating Roman coins, with portraits of emperors and other mythological figures form the base; statues of saints and martyrs fill the niches of the pilasters; arabesques form the frame-work of the windows; Biblical stories and scenes from the lives of the saints and the "unsaintly" founder (Galeazzo Visconti) fill every available space.

With its wealth of ornamental work about its front, its interior, and its cloisters, the Certosa forms a perfect museum of sculpture, — an epitome of Lombard Art. Generations of artists, and each succeeding Duke, from Galeazzo Visconti to the last of the Sforzas, contributed his share towards this mighty monument which is considered "the richest and most wonderful in the world."

FAÇADE OF THE CHURCH. *Begun* A. D. 1473.

Sculptural work on the façade.  — Window on the façade.  — Bas-reliefs on a window.

The monastic buildings were completed early in the 15th century; the cloisters continued after 1450. The richness of the terracotta-decoration over the arcades of the cloisters is such as scarcely another edifice in Italy can boast of.

Plinth of the façade with medallions imitating Roman coins.

Photo ALINARI, BROGI.

PAVIA — THE CERTOSA.

VIEW OF THE LITTLE CLOISTERS.

INTERIOR OF THE CHURCH.

The ground plan of the church is in the form of a Latin cross. The beautiful and imposing interior is mainly Gothic—a style that dominated Lombardy for about two hundred years—while the transepts and the choir show signs of the transition period from Gothic to Renaissance.

Besides the Visconti and Sforza monuments — given on page 72 — the church contains an array of artistic works: rich bronze screens divide the nave from the transepts; paintings, tombs, and monuments are set against the walls; while the greatest profusion of an infinite variety of precious marbles is found inlaid in mosaic on the numerous altar-fronts.

MAIN PORTAL OF THE CHURCH.

Relief with THE LAYING OF THE FIRST STONE OF THE CERTOSA.

The marble reliefs by the main portal of the church were executed by BENEDETTO BRIOSCO and represent: on the right, "The Foundation of the Carthusian Order in 1804" and "The Laying of the First stone of the Certosa in 1396"; on the left, "The Consecration of the Church in 1497" and "Translation to the Certosa of the body of the founder Galeazzo Visconti in 1474".

Photo ALINARI, ANDERSON, BROGI.

PAVIA — THE CERTOSA. Sepulchral monuments in the Church.

The VISCONTI became lords of Milan in 1310. Matteo, the founder, was appointed Imperial Vicar by Henry VII. of Luxemburg. When he died (1322), he was succeeded by his son Galeazzo who died in prison (1328), and his grandson Azzo who consolidated his power by the murder of his uncle Marco. Azzo died in 1339 and was followed by Giovanni, Archbishop of Milan. On the death of the latter (1349), the lordship passed into the hands of his three nephews— Matteo, Galeazzo, and Bernabò. Matteo was killed (1355) by his brothers, who then ruled the territories between them. Galeazzo died in 1378 and was succeeded in his portion of the domain by his son Gian Galeazzo who shared the dominion with his uncle Bernabò, whose daughter he married. Gian Galeazzo was the veritable Viscontean " viper, " and his career forms a very important chapter in Italian history. Crafty, hypocritical, and ambitious, he determined to supplant his uncle and father-in-law, and to re-unite the whole principality beneath his own sway. For seven years he shut himself in the Library of Pavia and pretended to be absorbed in religious observances. One day in 1385 he announced his intention of proceeding on a pilgrimage to Our Lady of Varese and expressed his desire to greet his uncle on his way there. He passed near Milan, and his uncle with a couple of followers came forth to meet him. Gian Galeazzo embraced him tenderly, and then gave an order in German to his bodyguards who seized Bernabò. Gian Galeazzo marched immediately to Milan and in a General Council was proclaimed sole lord of Milan. Bernabò was imprisoned and died of poison soon after. Considering however, what the people could give the people might take away, Galeazzo afterwards stipulated to pay the Emperor Wenceslaus 20.000 gold sequins for the title of hereditary Duke of Milan. Once established on the throne, Gian Galeazzo set out to conquer the neighbouring states, which one after the other fell into his grasp by the most despicable arts: fraud, violence, plots of diabolical cunning.... He was no soldier himself, but he took into his service all the chief *condottieri* of the day paying them high prices. Yet, with all his occupations of war and statesmanship, he found time to encourage literature, and stimulate every form of Art which might glorify his state. The Duomo of Milan, the Certosa of Pavia owed their foundation to his sense of splendour. In the midst of his great schemes, when master of the greater part of Lombardy, the Romagna and Tuscany, while he only awaited the surrender of Florence to put on the royal mantle and diadem already prepared for the ceremony of his coronation as King of Italy, he died of the plague in 1402. His two sons, Giovanni Maria and Filippo Maria, who were mere boys, succeeded to the dominions under the regency of their mother, but the Duchess Catherine proved incompetent and the vast tyranny of Gian Galeazzo fell to pieces rapidly.

TOMB OF GIAN GALEAZZO VISCONTI († 1402).
By CRISTOFORO ROMANO. A. D. 1497.

The SFORZA'S rule of Milan began in 1450, with Francesco Sforza, the great *condottiere* and son-in-law of the last Visconti. Francesco ruled in right of his wife as Duke, and on his death (1466), was succeeded by his eldest son Galeazzo Maria who was murdered (1476) because of his abominable crimes. After the death of Duke Galeazzo his widow Bona of Savoy governed for a time on behalf of her infant son Gian Galeazzo. In 1480, however, her late husband's brother Lodovico (il " Moro "), managed to banish her, installed the boy-Duke in the Castello Sforzesco where he was practically a prisoner and proceeded to govern in his name. Henceforth Gian Galeazzo, feeble in body and mind, became a mere ornamental figurehead, and when in 1490 he came of age his uncle Lodovico refused to surrender the rule to him, and at the same time strengthned his hold on the throne by giving influential posts to his adherents and gradually introducing his own effigy on coins. At this time Milan was one of the richest States, not only of Italy, but of the world. Lodovico had carefully developed her resources while gathering round him men of genius of every kind—Leonardo da Vinci, Bramante, etc.—and the city had been transformed into a new Athens. In 1489, the beautiful Isabella of Aragon came to Milan as a bride of the young Duke Gian Galeazzo, and two years later the marriage between Lodovico and the accomplished Beatrice d'Este took place; the wedding festivities which followed on these occasions were of great magnificence. Yet, amid all these splendours Lodovico's situation was exceedingly awkward. The friction and rivalry between Isabella and Beatrice had at last become so intolerable that Gian Galeazzo with his wife withdrew to the Castle of Pavia. Isabella indited a piteous letter to her grandfather, King Ferrante of Naples imploring him to right her husband. Ferrante determined to resort to force to overthrow the usurpers, and Lodovico having resolved to make himself Duke and finding himself threatened by the allied forces of Naples and Florence invited Charles VIII. of France to attack Naples to urge the old Angevin claim. His aim was to stir up trouble which would prevent the other Italian states from interfering with him. Charles was easily persuaded to this and his invasion of Italy (1494) formed a turning point, not only in the history of Milan, but of Italy, as it opened the gates of Italy to foreign despotism. Four years later Louis XII. (Duke of Orleans) succeeding to the throne of France, in right of his grandmother Valentina Visconti, set himself to claim the dukedom of Milan. In order to press his claim he entered Italy at the head of a large army, attacked Milan (1500), and captured Lodovico who was carried off to France to end his career in a dungeon at Loches.

MONUMENT OF LODOVICO IL MORO († 1508) AND BEATRICE D'ESTE († 1497).
By CRISTOFORO SOLARI. A.D. 1499. (*Detail*)

Photo ALINARI, BROGI.

— 72 —

"HISTORICAL SUPPLEMENT"

GENEALOGICAL TABLE OF THE HOUSE OF VISCONTI
Seigneurs and Dukes of Milan.

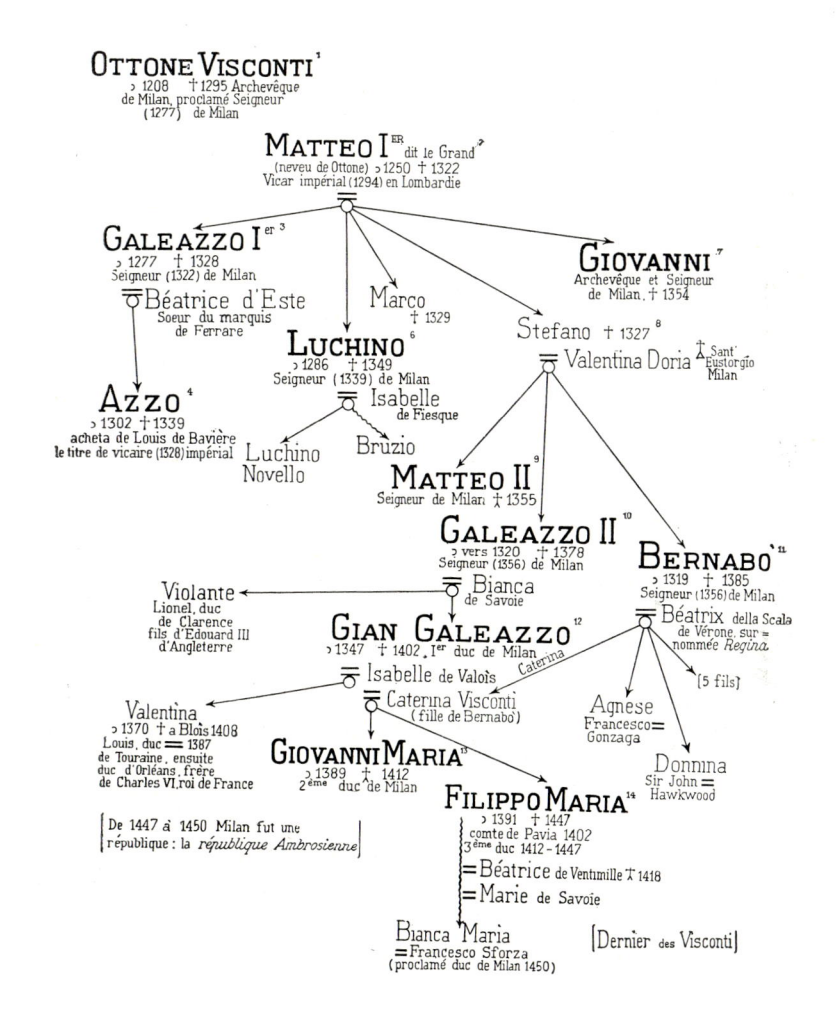

OTTONE VISCONTI[1]
> 1208 † 1295 Archevêque de Milan, proclamé Seigneur (1277) de Milan

MATTEO Ier dit le Grand[2]
(neveu de Ottone) > 1250 † 1322
Vicar impérial (1294) en Lombardie

GALEAZZO I[er][3]
> 1277 † 1328
Seigneur (1322) de Milan
= Béatrice d'Este, Soeur du marquis de Ferrare

Marco † 1329

GIOVANNI[7]
Archevêque et Seigneur de Milan, † 1354

Stefano † 1327 [8] — Sant' Eustorgio Milan
= Valentina Doria

AZZO[4]
> 1302 † 1339
acheta de Louis de Bavière le titre de vicaire (1328) impérial

LUCHINO[6]
> 1286 † 1349
Seigneur (1339) de Milan
= Isabelle de Fiesque

Luchino Novello

Bruzio

MATTEO II[9]
Seigneur de Milan † 1355

GALEAZZO II[10]
> vers 1320 † 1378
Seigneur (1356) de Milan
= Bianca de Savoie

BERNABO[11]
> 1319 † 1385
Seigneur (1356) de Milan
= Béatrix della Scala de Vérone, sur= nommée Regina
[5 fils]

Violante
Lionel, duc de Clarence fils d'Edouard III d'Angleterre

GIAN GALEAZZO[12]
> 1347 † 1402, Ier duc de Milan
= Isabelle de Valois
= Caterina Visconti (fille de Bernabô)

Caterina

Agnese
Francesco = Gonzaga

Donnina
Sir John = Hawkwood

Valentina
> 1370 † a Blois 1408
Louis, duc = 1387 de Touraine, ensuite duc d'Orléans, frère de Charles VI, roi de France

GIOVANNI MARIA[13]
> 1389 † 1412
2ème duc de Milan

FILIPPO MARIA[14]
> 1391 † 1447
comte de Pavia 1402
3ème duc 1412-1447
= Béatrice de Ventimille † 1418
= Marie de Savoie

[De 1447 à 1450 Milan fut une république : la *république Ambrosienne*]

Bianca Maria
= Francesco Sforza
(proclamé duc de Milan 1450)

[Dernier des Visconti]

VISCONTI, the name of a celebrated Italian family which long ruled Milan. In the 11th century they possessed estates on Lakes Como and Maggiore. A certain Ottone, who distinguished himself in the First Crusade, is known to have been viscount of Milan in 1078. The real basis of the family's dominion was laid, however, by another Ottone (d. 1295), a canon of Desio, appointed archbishop of Milan by Pope Urban IV., in 1262. The Della Torre family, who then controlled the city, opposed the appointment and not until his victory at Desio in 1277 was Ottone able to take possession of his see. He imprisoned Napoleon Della Torre and five other members of his family.

His nephew, Matteo, born 1250, succeeded him as political leader of Milan, and in 1310 the emperor Henry VII. made him imperial vicar of Lombardy. An able general, who by successful wars gained possession of a great part of Northern Italy. Matteo relied for his conquests more on diplomacy and bribery, and was esteemed as a model of the prudent Italian despot. He died in 1322.

GENEALOGICAL TABLE OF THE HOUSE OF SFORZA
Dukes of Milan.

Muzio Attendolo SFORZA
⁕1369 †1424 D'abord cultivateur, puis *condottiere*. Fondateur de la Famille.

- **Bosio** comte de Santa Fiora
- **Francesco Alessandro** Régent, puis duc de Milan ⁕1401 †1466
  = (1441) Bianca Maria Visconti †1468
  - Tristano
    Beatrice = d'Este (ainée)
    - Drusiana = Giacomo Piccinino
  - Filippo
    Ottaviano †1477
    - Ippolita †1484
      = Alfonso †1495 d'Aragon, duc de Calabre, puis roi de Naples
  - Ascanio †1505
  - Sforza Maria duc de Bari †1479
  - Elisabetta Maria = Guillaume VI marquis de Montferrat
  - **Galeazzo Maria** duc de Milan ⁕1444 †1476
    = Bonne de Savoie †1504
    - Caterina (la Dame de Forli) ⁕1463 †à Florence 1509 = Jerôme Riario Seigneur de Forli = Jean de Medicis
      - Jean des Bandes Noires
    - Ermes
    - Carlo
      Ippolita = Alessandro Bentivoglio
    - **Gian Galeazzo** duc de Milan Banni par Ludovic ⁕1469 †1494
      = Isabelle d'Aragon †1524
      - Francesco conte de Pavie ⁕1490 emmené en France par Louis XII, mourut abbé de Marmoutiers, en 1511
      - Bonne †1557 = Sigismond roi de Pologne
      - Ippolita †1501
      - **Massimiano** duc de Milan dès 1512 ⁕1491, defait à Marignan en 1515 par François Ier alla finir ses jours en France †à Paris en 1530
    - Anna †1497 = Alfonso duc de Ferrare
    - Bianca Maria †1510 Maximilien Ier empereur
  - **Ludovico Maria** dit *le More* ⁕1451, duc de Milan 1480-1499 prisonnier (1500) de Louis XII mourut à Loches en 1508
    = Béatrice d'Este †1497
    - Bianca = Galeazzo di San Severino
    - Cesare
    - Gian Paolo †1535
    - **Francesco Maria** dernier duc de Milan 1521 ⁕1492 †1535
      = (1534) Christine de Danemark il n'eut pas d'enfants Ses Etats passerent à l'emper. Charles-Quint
- **Alessandro** Seigneur de Pesaro ⁕1409 †1473
  - Ginevra = Bentivoglio de Bologna
  - Costanza Varana de Camerino
  - Costanzo †1483 = Camilla Marzana de Sessa
  - Battista = Federigo duc d'Urbin
  - ...vanni †1516 ...3) Lucrezia Borgia = Ginevra Tiepolo ...anzo

SFORZA, the name of a famous Italian family. They were descended from a peasant condottiere Giacomo or Giacomuzzo (abbreviated into Muzio) Attendolo, born in 1369, who gained command of a band of adventurers by whom he had been kidnapped. He took the name of Sforza in the field, became constable of Naples under Joanna II., fought against the Spaniards, served Pope Martin V., by whom he was created a Roman count, and was drowned in the river Pescara, near Aquila. His natural son Francesco (1401-1466) served the Visconti and married in 1441 Bianca, the only daughter of Filippo Maria Visconti, duke of Milan and received as dowry among other cities the promise of succession to the duchy of Milan. The short-lived Ambrosian republic, which was established by the Milanese on the death of Visconti (1447), was overthrown by Francesco, who forced his way into power, made his triumphal entry as duke of Milan on March 1450.

MADONNA ENTHRONED AND TEN SAINTS.
By LORENZO LOTTO. (*Church of S. Bartolommeo*).

PALAZZO DELLA RAGIONE. *Gothic style.*

BERGAMO, the ancient Roman *Bergomum*, was the birthplace of Gaetano Donizetti and of the famous commander of the Venetian republic Bartolommeo Colleoni, who is buried in the beautiful *Cappella Colleoni* given on the next page. As we look at the monument of this brave, clever and virtuous Condottiere it is interesting to recall the curious military system and mode of warfare which prevailed in Italy from the close of the 13th until the 16th century.

The innumerable feuds and petty wars of which Italy was the scene in medieval times had been mainly waged by troops of cavaliers and nobles. But after the decline of the Imperial authority—when the nobles were either expatriated or reduced to impotence—the Papacy and the republics got the upper hand and Italy was divided into different states and despotisms, which used to be constantly at war with one another. Priests and merchants were alike unwilling to engage in war and endure the hardships of the field; therefore, they took mercenary troops into their pay to do their fighting for them. The emperors, when they periodically descended into Italy for the purpose of asserting their rights or replenishing their exchequers, were usually accompanied by armies, a part of which they sometimes left behind. These discharged soldiers formed themselves into independent companies — *compagnie di ventura* — under their own leaders who obtained the title of *condottiere*, and who were ready to sell the services of their companies to the highest bidder. At first foreign mercenaries were employed by some of the great Italian captains and by the communes; then we find that the captains or *condottieri* were themselves foreign (the Duke of Guarnieri, Fra Moriale, Sir John Hawkwood...). Later on again the chief *condottieri*

PORTRAIT. By LORENZO LOTTO.   CESARE BORGIA. By GIORGIONE.   PORTRAIT. By BECCARUZZI.
Painting in the Accademia Carrara.

were Italians (Alberico da Barbiano, Braccio da Montone, Carmagnola, Francesco Sforza, Niccolò Piccinino, Colleoni, Federigo d'Urbino, Giovanni delle Bande Nere, father of Cosimo I. de' Medici, etc.). As a rule these hired troops did not belong to the country for which they were fighting, hence they had no feeling of patriotism or loyalty. They sometimes fought first on one side and then on the other, irrespective of country or the justness of the cause; they really fought mainly for money, lands and power, and occasionally it was possible for a *condottiere* to obtain the lordship of a city or a district out of some province which he had been summoned to aid or to subdue. Francesco Sforza even rose to be Duke of Milan. These armies often behaved much more like freebooters and marauders than like soldiers, and the *condottieri* sometimes were required to give their wives and children as hostages, and notwithstanding this, neither felt nor inspired confidence. They lived in an age of broken faith, no wonder then if they often were full of contempt for all sacred things and displayed all the duplicities, cruelties, and tortuous policies to which the most accomplished villain of the time could have aspired. Still, it is pleasant to notice that many of the captains were very fine men, and that, like Bartolommeo Colleoni, they were brave and sincere, considerate and generous to their soldiers, compassionate and merciful to their enemies.

Photo ALINARI, ANDERSON.

BERGAMO. — *CAPPELLA COLLEONI*.

Monument to Bartolommeo Colleoni († 1475),
with reliefs from the life of Christ.
Designed by G. A. Amadeo.

Cappella Colleoni. *Erected by* Amadeo *in 1470-76*.

The *Cappella Colleoni*, adjoining the church of S. Maria Maggiore, is one of the gems of early Renaissance art. The building was designed by *Amadeo* for the famous general Bartolommeo Colleoni, who desired to erect within it a splendid monument to himself.

The façade is lavishly covered with marble and richly ornamented with fine sculptures of Christian and Pagan subjects. The interior decorated by *Tiepolo* contains the sepulchral monuments of Colleoni and of his beloved daughter Medea. The tomb of the founder is surmounted by a gilded equestrian statue of the general, made by an unknown sculptor of Nuremberg. It stands upon a sarcophagus supported by short columns resting on a base elevated upon four columns.

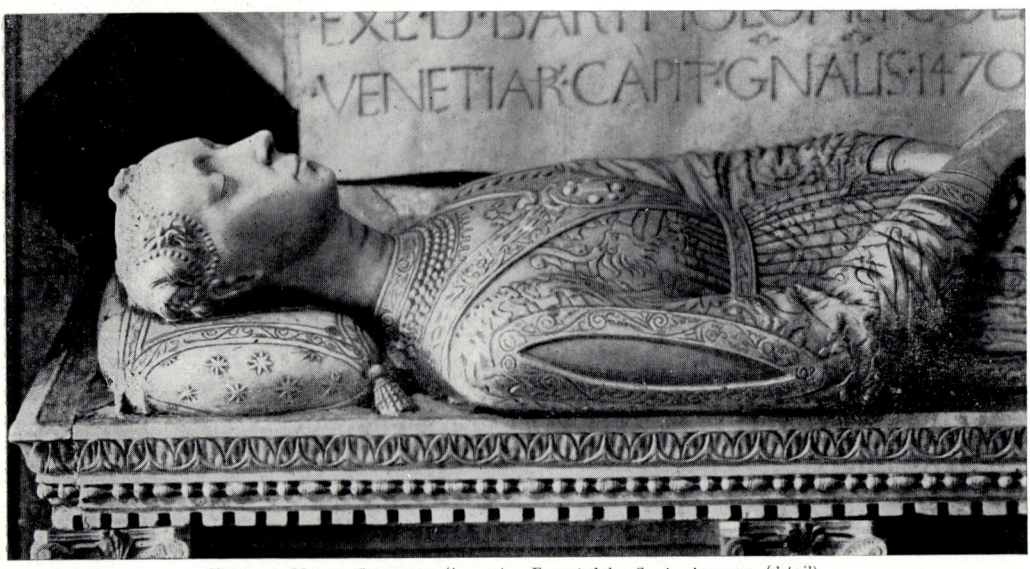

Tomb of Medea Colleoni († 1470). *Executed by* G. A. Amadeo (*detail*).

Brought hither from the church of Baselia, this is one of the most charming works of its kind in Italy. The recumbent effigy of Medea, "a masterpiece of grace and virginal purity," is clad in a brocade robe, with a string of pearls round her long slender neck. Her eyes are serenely closed, and her arms peacefully folded upon her bosom.

Photo Alinari, Brogi.

BRESCIA.

The Duomo Nuovo (*left*) and the Rotonda (*right*) or Duomo Vecchio.

Church of S. Maria dei Miracoli *Early-Renaissance period.*

Brescia has a very remote origin, and already in Roman times was a flourishing town. In the Middle Ages, thanks to its manufactory of weapons it became one of the wealthiest cities of Lombardy. The city possesses an excellent Museum of Roman Antiquities (*Museo Civico dell'Età Romana*) situated in the picturesque remains of temple erected by Vespasiano (73 A. C.); a Christian Medieval Museum (*Museo Civico dell'Età Cristiana*) containing numerous works of art such as reliquaries, enamels, majolica-ware, etc.; a Picture Gallery (*Pinacoteca Tosio Martinengo*) to which a visit is essential for a proper appreciation of the Brescian painting; two Cathedral, the Duomo Nuovo begun in 1604 by G. B. Lantana and the Duomo Vecchio that is a circular building of the 12th century, besides many edifices of the early-Renaissance period. Brescia is especially noteworthy in the history of painting as the birthplace of " Il Moretto " (Alessandro Buonvicino, 1498-1555), who combined some of the best qualities of the Venetian school and distinguished himself for his sober colouring, a " silver tone " which has a peculiar charm. Another minor master, Romanino (1485-1566), who successfully imitated Titian and Giorgione, was also a native of Brescia.

The *Municipio*, usually called the *Loggia*, was begun in 1492 by T. Fromentone in the early-Renaissance style and completed in 1574 by J. Sansovino who built the upper part. On the groundfloor is a deep colonnade in front of which are some pilars.

The Loggia, *designed by* Fromentone.

Coronation of the Virgin, *by* Moretto.
(*Church of SS. Nazaro e Celso*).

The Saviour, *by* Raffaello.
(*Paintings in the Tosio*

Madonna and Saints, *by* Moretto.
Martinengo Gallery).

— 76 —

Photo Alinari, Brogi.

BRESCIA. CREMA. CREMONA.

THE BROLETTO (12th cent.).    STATUE OF VICTORY.    MONTE DI PIETÀ (15th cent.).

The *Statue of Victory* in the Museum of Roman Antiquities is a bronze figure; Victory is about to write on a shield and under her left foot is a helmet. This statue is a precious specimen of ancient plastic art, excavated in 1826. The *Monte di Pietà* is a plain Renaissance building, begun in 1484; the handsome loggia was erected by P. M. Bagnadore in 1597. The *Broletto* is a massive building, begun in 1187 but not entirely completed until the 16th century; it was the town-hall.

Near Brescia the Chevalier de Bayard *sans peur et sans reproche* (the fearless and faultless knight), was wounded in a fierce batle (1512) against the Venetians.

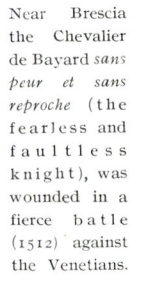

MARY MAGDALENE BEFORE CHRIST.
By ROMANINO. (Church of S. Giovanni, Brescia).

CHRIST AND THE WOMAN TAKEN IN ADULTERY.
By TITIAN. (Church of Sant' Afra, Brescia).

CREMONA, the home of Amati, Stradivari and Guarneri, the manufacturers of the famous Violins, has one of the finest towers in Italy, the "Torrazzo," 360 ft. in height. The imposing Cathedral, consecrated, in 1190 is built in the Lombard-Romanesque style.

Cremona is a city of great antiquity. It was conquered by the Romans in 218 B. C. and became a flourishing town. In the 5th century it was destroyed by the Huns, but was rebuilt in the 6th by the Lombard King Agilulf. Early in the 14th century it was sacked by Henry VII. of Luxembourg and subsequently came into the possession of the Visconti and the Dukes of Milan.

CREMA. THE CATHEDRAL. 13th cent.   CREMONA. THE CATHEDRAL. 12th cent.

Photo ALINARI.

MANTUA.

MANTUA. THE REGGIA OR DUCAL PALACE. *The Castello di S. Giorgio (14th cent.).*

MANTUA was the home of Virgil, who celebrated the place in his *Georgics*. The city played an important part in the storms of the Middle Ages, when the Gonzagas obtained its mastery; it then attained importance and prosperity.

The Gonzagas were genuine lovers of art and literature and made of their court a brilliant center of civilization. Francesco Gonzaga I. (1407-44) was created Marquis of Mantua by the Emperor Sigismund. He invited the humanist Vittorino da Feltre, to educate his sons, and through him made his court a renowned centre of culture, a " sanctuary of manners, deeds, and words." He was followed by Lodovico (1444-78), a lover of the arts and letters, who established the first printing offices in Mantua, where the first book printed was the *Decameron* of Boccaccio. It was at this time that the painter Mantegna entered the service of the Gonzagas, and decorated the Marquis' nuptial chamber. The next prince, Gian-Francesco II. (1484-1519), made his court, the resort of poets: Ariosto, author of *Orlando Furioso*, Bembo, Poliziano who composed in 3 days his famous drama, *Orfeo*. Gian-Francesco's wife, was the gentle Isabella d'Este, the greatest connoisseur in art of her time. With judicious taste she collected valuable books from Aldo's press, gems and rare brocades, musical instruments of rare workmanship, and commissioned painters to paint for her pictures the theme of which had been sketched out by her own poetic invention. With these and other works of art she adorned her little apartment called *Il Paradiso* consisting of four little *Camerini* interesting for their decoration and splendid coffered ceilings, on one of which the motto of the princess, " nec spe nec metu ", is often repeated.

LODOVICO GONZAGA MEETING HIS SON CARDINAL FRANCESCO.  THE FAMILY OF LODOVICO GONZAGA. *Camera degli Sposi. Frescoes by* MANTEGNA.

Photo ALINARI, BROGI.

MANTUA — *PALAZZO DEL TÈ.*

PALAZZO DEL TÈ. *The Court. Designed by* G. ROMANO.

VENUS AND MARS. *Fresco by* G. ROMANO.

The *Palazzo del Tè*, a summer residence of the Gonzagas, was erected by GIULIO ROMANO (1525) for Federigo, son of Gian Francesco and Isabella d'Este. The rooms of this 'most noble pleasure-house,' are full of sensational, and occasionally indelicate, mythological and allegorical frescoes, designed by Giulio Romano and carried out with the assistance of his pupils. In one room is represented the notorious «Overthrow of the Giants»,—colossal figures depicted in all possible attitudes, crushed between

BANQUET FOR THE MARRIAGE OF CUPID AND PSYCHE. *Frescoes by* GIULIO ROMANO.

enormous masses of rock and falling buildings. In another chamber, the most important, is represented the *Story of Psyche*, as told by Apuleius in his «Golden Ass». The incidents in the fable are here illustrated with every variety of fantastic invention and insolence of freedom; and these compositions are important not only for a study of the life and manners of the people who inhabited or frequented this room, but for the influence the pictures exercised on later art.

Detail of wall fresco by MANTEGNA.
(*Camera degli Sposi, Castello di Corte, Mantua*).

Photo ALINARI, ANDERSON

"HISTORICAL SUPPLEMENT"

GENEALOGICAL TABLE OF THE HOUSE OF GONZAGA
Marquis of Mantua

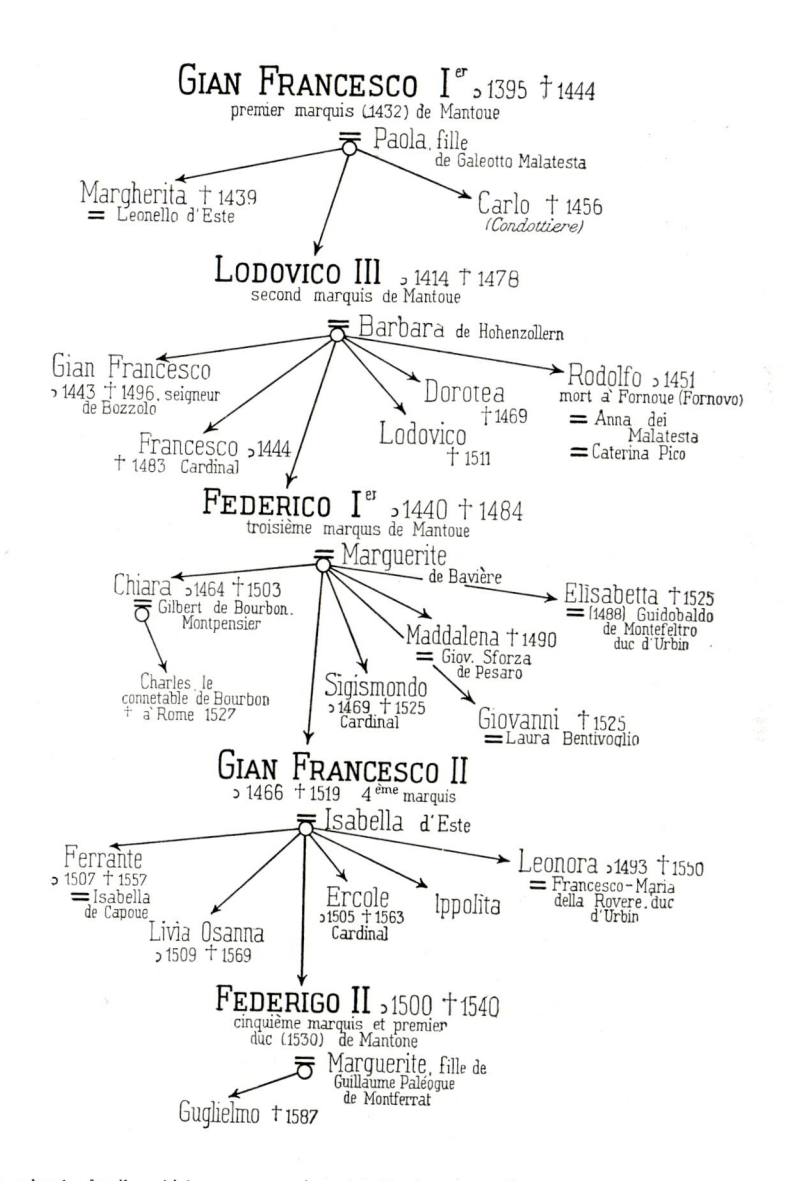

Gian Francesco Ier ⚭ 1395 †1444
premier marquis (1432) de Mantoue
= Paola, fille de Galeotto Malatesta

- Margherita †1439 = Leonello d'Este
- Carlo †1456 (Condottiere)
- **Lodovico III** ⚭ 1414 †1478 second marquis de Mantoue
  = Barbara de Hohenzollern
  - Gian Francesco ⚭ 1443 †1496, seigneur de Bozzolo
    - Francesco ⚭ 1444 †1483 Cardinal
  - Dorotea †1469
  - Lodovico †1511
  - Rodolfo ⚭ 1451 mort à Fornoue (Fornovo)
    = Anna dei Malatesta
    = Caterina Pico
  - **Federico I**er ⚭ 1440 †1484 troisième marquis de Mantoue
    = Marguerite de Bavière
    - Chiara ⚭ 1464 †1503 = Gilbert de Bourbon, Montpensier
      - Charles, le connetable de Bourbon † a' Rome 1527
    - Maddalena †1490 = Giov. Sforza de Pesaro
    - Sigismondo ⚭ 1469 †1525 Cardinal
    - Giovanni †1525 = Laura Bentivoglio
    - Elisabetta †1525 = (1488) Guidobaldo de Montefeltro duc d'Urbin
    - **Gian Francesco II** ⚭ 1466 †1519 4ème marquis
      = Isabella d'Este
      - Ferrante ⚭ 1507 †1557 = Isabella de Capoue
        - Livia Osanna ⚭ 1509 †1569
      - Ercole ⚭ 1505 †1563 Cardinal
      - Ippolita
      - Leonora ⚭ 1493 †1550 = Francesco-Maria della Rovere, duc d'Urbin
      - **Federigo II** ⚭ 1500 †1540 cinquième marquis et premier duc (1530) de Mantone
        = Marguerite, fille de Guillaume Paléogue de Montferrat
        - Guglielmo †1587

An Italian princely family which gave sovereigns to Mantua from the year 1328 to 1708. (See following page).

— 80 —

HOUSE OF GONZAGA.

In 1329, the emperor Louis of Bavaria sold the office of imperial vicar to Luigi of Gonzaga (d. 1360), who during the fierce Hohenstaufen struggles in Northern Italy supplanted the tyrant Bonacolsi and became "Capitano del Popolo" in Mantua. His successors were his son Guido (d. 1360) and his grandson Luigi II. (d. 1382), and Gian Francesco (d. 1407), who fought successfully against Milan and Venice. Then, Gian Francesco I. (d. 1444) received for his military services to the emperor Sigismund the title of marquess of Mantua. His grandson, Federigo I. (d. 1484), served under various foreign sovereigns, including Bona of Savoy and Lorenzo the Magnificent. Subsequently, Federigo's son Gian Francesco (d. 1519) commanded the allied Italian forces against Charles VIII. of France at the battle of Fornovo, and with the help of his wife, the famous Isabella d'Este, he promoted the fine arts and letters. He was succeeded by his son Federigo II. (d. 1540), captain-general of the papal forces. After the peace of Cambrai (1529) his ally and protector, the emperor Charles V., raised his title to that of Duke of Mantua in 1530. His son Guglielmo subdued a revolt in Monferrato and was presented with that territory by the emperor Maximilian II. His grandson Vincenzo II. (d. 1627) appointed as his successor Charles, the son of Henriette, the heiress of the French family of Nevers-Rethel, his great grandson Ferdinand Charles, acquired Guastalla by marriage in 1678, but lost it soon afterwards, finally in 1708 Austria annexed the duchy.

Ceiling painting by MANTEGNA.
(*Camera degli Sposi, Castello di Corte, Mantua*).

VENETIA

VENICE. THE GRAND CANAL. VIEW OF THE RIALTO BRIDGE.

VENICE
PADUA   VICENZA   VERONA
TRENTO   TRIESTE   AQUILEIA

WONDERS OF ITALY.

VIEW OF VENICE AS SEEN FROM THE ISLAND OF SAN GIORGIO MAGGIORE.

VENICE

"There is a glorious city in the sea!
"The sea is in the broad, the narrow streets,
"Ebbing and flowing; and the salt sea weed
"Clings to the marble of her palaces."

— ROGERS.

THE LION OF ST. MARK.
A work of the 15th century.

VENICE, the "Queen of the Adriatic," is one of the most famous and singular towns in the world. Beautiful and majestic mellowed by years of splendour, her aspect is like a dream, and her history like a romance. Her noble and magnificent palaces, her churches, campanili and cupolas seem to raise vision-like as from the stroke of the enchanter's wand from the bosom of the waters.

Old chronicles ascribe the origin of Venice to the exiled inhabitants of the neighbouring Roman lands who, driven in terror from their homes by the Gothic barbarians, sought refuge on the islets in the lagoon, and built their homes on the island of Rivo Alto. The little community at first confined to this small spot of land was increased by a constant migration of fugitives and gradually the other islands were covered with houses and peopled. Isolated and secure in their island fastenesses, the inhabitants enjoyed a considerable degree of comfort and tranquillity and grew rich and powerful at a time when the rest of Western Europe was sinking lower and lower in barbarism.

Founded in the fifth century as a place of refuge during the invasions of Italy by the Huns, Venice took shape as an independent State about the end of the seventh century, to assume later the form of a republic; the Doge or chief magistrate ranking as one of the sovereign powers of Europe.

— 81 —

VENICE — *VIEWS OF THE CITY.*

VIEW OF THE RIALTO BRIDGE. *Built by* ANTONIO DA PONTE. A. D. 1590.

Early in the ninth century the first palace of the Doges was built, and from that period forward the new republic recognizing the importance of its position engaged, slowly at first, on a career of commerce and then of conquest; the whole strength of the Venetians being employed in achieving the greatness and prosperity of their commonwealth. Near the Rialto then was the real nucleus of the town, and the island of Rivo Alto or Rialto on which the bridge stands may thus be regarded as the mother city of the " Queen of the Adriatic, " the greatest of the maritime Republics of the Mediterranean.

Venice is built on a hundred islets formed of millions of piles partly of wood and partly of stone; the whole city is the most colossal edifice upon piles, that the world has ever seen. The streets are canals spanned by about four hundred bridges, the most remarkable of these is the Rialto (a single marble arch of ninety feet span), both for its simple beauty and for the interesting historical and romantic associations connected with it.

" This town resembles no other town, " writes Mauclair, " for here there are no horses, no carriages, no dust, no smoke; here one hears nothing but the human voice. The slender black gondola with its steel prow, shaped like the comb or some siren, glides smoothly along past great Palaces whose every name evokes tragic or glorious memories. "

The Grand Canal, the largest of the one hundred and fifty waterways which intersect Ve-

THE RIO DI PALAZZO.
In the distance is the Bridge of Sighs, on the right is the Eastern façade of the Doges palace.

— 82 —

VENICE — *VIEWS OF THE CITY.*

THE LIBRARY, THE PIAZZETTA DI SAN MARCO AND THE PALACE OF THE DOGES AS SEEN FROM THE GRAND CANAL.

The „Piazzetta," the little space between the Ducal Palace, the Library and the sea, is the principal entrance of Venice from the sea. Many historical reminiscences are connected with this, as it was from here that the armies of the Republic embarked for their expeditions to the East, and here, on their return home, they landed laden with the spoils of the conquered.

nice, is nearly two miles in length and traverses the city dividing it into two nearly equal portions. Along this triumphal thoroughfare the "finest street in the world," rise about two hundred marble palaces, patrician residences of those great old families whose names were written in the "Libro d'Oro"—the Golden Book—of the Republic.

The most conspicuous edifice at the mouth of the canal is the fine Church of S. Maria della Salute (p. 129), which with its gigantic dome forms one of the great landmarks of the city. The church was built by order of the Republic as a votive offering for escape from the pestilence which ravaged Venice in the year 1630.

VIEW OF THE GRAND CANAL AND THE DOME OF S. MARIA DELLA SALUTE.

Photo ALINARI, ANDERSON, BROGI.

VENICE — *VIEWS OF THE CITY.*

SAN MARCO AND THE DOGES' PALACE.

The two *Granite Columns* on the Molo between the Doges' Palace and the Library, were brought from Constantinople and erected here in the twelfth century. On one of the pillars is the Winged Lion of St. Mark holding the Gospel in his paw, on the other St. Theodore (the old patron of the Venetian republic) standing with sword and shield on a crocodile. St. Theodore, was a Syrian soldier who suffered martyrdom under Maximinian.

THE DOGES' PALACE AND THE PONTE DELLA PAGLIA.

On the right is the Carceri (Prisons), whence Casanova escaped, and where Silvio Pellico languished.

Photo ALINARI, ANDERSON, BROGI.

VENICE — *VIEWS OF THE CITY.*

THE BRIDGE OF SIGHS. As seen from the Ponte della Paglia.

  The Bridge of Sighs, built by ANT. DA CONTINO about 1600, served to unite the Criminal Courts in the Doges' Palace and the *Carceri* or criminal prisons (in the adjoining building) which were built by ANTONIO DA PONTE a few years before.
  The bridge spans the canal known as Rio della Paglia, its interior is converted into a double passage. Criminals, when taken out of the prisons to suffer death, were led across this bridge — hence its significant name — to hear their sentences and afterwards were executed.
  The Bridge of Sighs owes its celebrity principally to Byron's opening lines of „Childe Harold." as the present structure — that "pathetic swindle" as Mr. Howelles calls it — has probably never been crossed by any prisoner worthy of our sympathy.

Photo ALINARI, ANDERSON, BROGI.

PIAZZA AND BASILICA OF SAN MARCO.

The Piazza di San Marco, which Napoleon styled "le plus beau salon de l'Europe," surrounded on three sides by a continuous row of artistic buildings which seem to form one vast marble palace, is the most charming public square imaginable and the great gathering place of all Venice.

The Campanile of St. Mark's, built in the 14th century, is 325 feet high. In July 1902 it collapsed: but it was admirably rebuilt by a world-wide subscription between 1905 and 1911.

Photo ALINARI, ANDERSON, BROGI.

VENICE — THE LIBRARY OF ST. MARK.

VIEW OF THE OLD LIBRARY OF SAN MARCO. *Erected by* SANSOVINO. A. D. 1536-53.

THE OLD LIBRARY.
Erected by SANSOVINO.
A. D. 1536-53.

The *Library of San Marco* is perhaps the most magnificent civic building of the 16th cent. in Italy and the crowning triumph of Venetian art. The Library itself may be said to have been founded by Petrarch who, twelve years before his death settled in Venice and presented to the Senate his valuable collection of ancient manuscripts.

This Library was afterwards enriched by the addition of that of Cardinal Bessarion and others.

SAN MARCO, THE PIAZZETTA AND THE LIBRARY.

The principal entrance of Venice from the sea, is by the Piazzetta di San Marco shown here and opening into the great square illustrated on the following pages.

THE LOGGETTA. *Built by* SANSOVINO. A. D. 1540.

The Loggetta, at the foot of the Campanile, was the meeting place of the nobles and the seat of the military procurators during the deliberations of the Senate. It was greatly damaged by the fall of the Campanile, but has been carefully rebuilt with the old stones. This small marble building is a real gem. Its beauty is further enhanced by statues, bas-reliefs, bronzes, and all that art can offer. The façade with the four bronze statues of Peace, Mercury, Apollo, and Pallas are by SANSOVINO, and the bronze gate by ANTONIO GAI. In the interior is a group of the Virgin, the Infant Jesus, and the little St. John, by SANSOVINO, which is a masterpiece of grace and life.

BRONZE DOORS OF THE LOGGETTA. *By* A. GAI. 1734.

MADONNA. *By* SANSOVINO.

— 87 —

Photo ALINARI, ANDERSON, BROGI.

VENICE — ST. MARK'S SQUARE.

The Bronze Giants. *By* Antonio Rizzo a. d. 1497.   **The Clock Tower.**

The *Clock Tower* was erected in 1496-99 from designs by Coducci. It has a dial of blue and gold adorned with the signs of the zodiac. On a platform on the top are two gigantic figures in bronze which strike the hours on a bell.

The Piazza di San Marco.

The Piazza is enclosed by the most magnificent and striking buildings in Venice. On the left of the picture given here are the *Procuratie Nuove*, originally erected for the accommodation of the procurators of St. Mark; on the right stand the *Procuratie Vecchie*, a range of buildings erected in 1500; in the far end of the piazza is the *Nuova Fabbrica* erected in 1810 by order of Napoleon I.

Photo Alinari, Anderson, Brogi.

VENICE — *PIAZZA OF SAN MARCO.*

VIEW OF THE PIAZZA AND BASILICA OF SAN MARCO AND THE CAMPANILE.

PEDESTAL of a Flagstaff.
Bronze by A. LEOPARDI.

The focus of Venice is the Piazza of San Marco which Napoleon styled "le plus beau salon de l'Europe." It is the spot most frequently visited by the tourist who returns to it again and again. Deprived as Venice is of any other considerable portion of the "terra firma" the piazza is the only place in which the population can assemble for the purposes of public festivities and enjoyment. Here were celebrated all the great triumphs of the state; and here were represented those characteristic national ceremonies with which the Venetian government was accustomed to stimulate the energies of its citizens. The piazza forms an oblong rectangle, 576 ft. in length and 269 ft. in its greatest width. On three sides it is surrounded by imposing buildings, which appear to form one vast marble palace, on the east side it is bounded by the Basilica di San Marco, one of the most celebrated temples in the Christian world. This was the state church of the Republic, in which the newly-elected doges were presented to the people, and in which the authorities attended service on festivals in full state. San Marco was also the spot which hallowed every enterprise of whatever nature, and it blended in a peculiar way the civil and religious character with which every act of the Republic was imbued.

The PIGEONS OF SAN MARCO which enliven the Piazza are an entertainment of never failing interest to the tourist. They were formerly maintained by a provision of the Republic.

— 89 —

Photo ALINARI, ANDERSON, BROGI.

12. - *WONDERS OF ITALY.*

VENICE — ST. MARK'S. *The Western Façade.*

FAÇADE OF THE BASILICA OF SAN MARCO. *Completed in 1094. Byzantine architecture.*

The BASILICA OF SAN MARCO, the patron saint of Venice, is celebrated as being the repository of the Evangelist's body. The edifice was modelled on the Church of the Holy Apostles in Constantinople. It is built in the shape of a Greek cross (with nearly equal arms), covered with Byzantine domes in the centre and at the end of each arm. Round the western arm runs an atrium or narthex covered with a series of eight smaller domes, and its western exterior forms the lower part of the façade of the church with its five great portals, whose recesses are enriched with rows of marble columns of rich and varied materials and with capitals in an exuberant variety of styles. The main portal, richly ornamented, is spanned by an inner triple archivolt and an outer main one.

4. Translation of the body into the Church of St. Mark. (*First arch on the left*).

3. The Veneration of the saint by the Doge and Senators. (*Second arch on the left*).

In this mosaic we see the façade of San Marco as it was in the 13th century (without the Gothic additions). At that date the central lunette over the main portal contained a colossal mosaic figure of Christ in the act of blessing.

Saint Mark had been adopted as the Patron and Protector of the Republic early in the ninth century, when the Evangelist's body was stolen (p. 102) and brought from Alexandria to Venice. The foundations of a church in which to enshrine the precious relic were laid by Doge Giovanni Partecipazio in the year 830 on the site of a chapel of S. Teodoro (the old Patron of Venice). This first church was rebuilt after a fire in 976 in the Romanesque style, but in the year 1065 it was resolved to raise a much larger basilica for so great a Saint, and a reconstruction was begun in a Byzantine style and decorated with lavish and truly Oriental magnificence. The building is two hundred and fifty feet long, one hundred seventy wide.

LUNETTE with the symbols of the Evangelists. (*First portal on the left*).

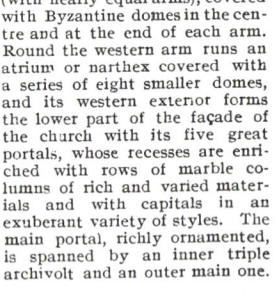

GREAT CENTRAL PORTAL. In the lunette is the "Last Judgment."

Photo ALINARI, ANDERSON, BROGI.

VENICE — ST. MARK'S

The famous bronze horses, 5 ft. in height, probably belonging to Nero's arch in Rome from whence Constantine the Great removed them to *Byzantium*, were brought to Venice in 1204 by the Doge E. Dandolo after the conquest of Constantinople. Napoleon carried them to Paris in 1797 but they were restored to Venice.

TWO OF THE FOUR BRONZE HORSES over the principal façade.

The gable of the central arch is crowned by a statue of St. Mark bearing his Gospel. Beneath is the emblem of the Evangelist in relief: a winged lion holding a book inscribed with the motto, *Pax tibi, Marce, Evangelista meus*. On the face of the arch are stories from Genesis in relief, on the under side are figures of Patriarchs and Evangelists.

CENTRAL ARCH of the Façade and the bronze horses.

URN-BEARERS SERVING AS RAINSPOUTS.

The lunettes of the five portals are filled with mosaics of various periods. Over the main entrance is the « Last Judgment » executed in 1836. The lunettes and soffits of the remaining four portals contain the story of the translation of the body of St. Mark. From right to left: 1. The removal from the church in Alexandria, the concealment in the basket, the authorities examine it but turn away in disgust on being told that it is pork; 2. Arrival of the ship at Venice, the body received with religious processions, the body is carried ashore; 3. Reception of the body in state and devotion of the Doge and Senators; 4. The body is carried into St. Mark's. The Doge and all the nobility are present.

2. **ARRIVAL** of the body of St. Mark at Venice. (*Second arch on the right*).

1. **EMBARKATION** of the body of St. Mark at Alexandria. (*First arch on the right*).

The main fabric of St. Mark's dates from the 11th century, the walls are of brick, but they are coated or incrusted throughout with slabs of marble, alabaster and other rare stones, and the whole is enriched with hundreds of pillars and a profusion of gold and mosaics. The ruined cities of Altinum and Aquileia were ransacked to ornament and enrich this church; for centuries the captain of every ship that traded in the Orient was ordered to bring marbles or fine stones for the builders; wherever the Venetian fleets went they brought home costly marble pillars, Byzantine sculptures, trophies, precious stones. Thus the great sanctuary was slowly elaborated till it became the marvellous *Chiesa d'Oro* which all the world admires today.

SIDE PORTAL.
On the right of main entrance.
Note the fine bronze gates and its reliefs.

BYZANTINE RELIEF over the minor left arch.

Photo ALINARI, ANDERSON, BROGI.

VENICE — ST. MARK'S. Central Doorway.

MAIN PORTAL.
First and second archivolts.

The relief in the lunette above the door represents St. Mark and the Angel.

The medieval reliefs on the soffit of the *first archivolt*, a man with serpents coming from his mouth, symbolises Heresy; a woman suckling serpents, the Church. Those on the face of the archivolt representing a woman seated on a lion and a man seated on an ox are of Byzantine invention.

The reliefs on the under side of the *second archivolt* represent the "labours" of the twelve months. Each month consists of a figure engaged in an occupation suitable to the season, and an appropriate zodiacal sign or symbol. 1) January, a man carrying a tree; 2) February, a man warming himself in front of a fire; 3) March, a warrior with lance and shield; 4) April, a youth carrying a lamb; 5) May, a man holding a rose and crowned with flowers by two maidens; 6) June, a man reaping; 7) July, a farmer mowing hay; 8) August, a slumb-

The " VIRTUES "
second archivolt.

RELIEFS on soffit
of *first archivolt.*

The " HANDICRAFTS
OF VENICE "
(*third archivolt*).

SECOND ARCHIVOLT.   FIRST ARCHIVOLT (left).

The " LABOURS
OF THE MONTHS "
(*second archivolt*).

Photo ALINARI, ANDERSON.

VENICE — ST. MARK'S.   *Central Doorway.*

LAST JUDGMENT.
Third or main archivolt.

RELIEFS on soffit of *first archivolt*.

The "BEATITUDES" *second archivolt*.

ering young man seated on a chair; 9) September, a man gathering grapes; 10) October, a man with a spade digging; 11) November, a man catching birds; 12) December, a man in the act of killing a pig. On the outer face of this archivolt are represented the Virtues and the Beatitudes.

On the under side of the *third* or *main archivolt* are reliefs representing the 14 *Arti* or Handicrafts of Venice: A) Architecture, an old man, — the architect of the façade (?); B) Boat-building; C) Wine-selling; D) Baking; E) Butchery; F) Milk and Cheese-selling. [Then follow: G) Masonry and Brick-laying and H) Shoemaking on either side of the figure of Christ on the keystone, — omitted here]. I) Barber-Surgery; J) Cooperage or Cask-making; K) Carpentry; L) Wood-sawing; M) Smithing; N) Fishing. The outer face of this archivolt contains figures of Prophets with their scrolls.

The "LABOURS OF THE MONTHS" *(second archivolt)*.

FIRST ARCHIVOLT (right).   SECOND ARCHIVOLT.

The "HANDICRAFTS OF VENICE" *(third archivolt)*.

— 93 —

Photo ALINARI, ANDERSON.

VENICE — ST. MARK'S.

THE NORTHERN FAÇADE.

THE DOMES AND THE UPPER PART OF NORTH AND WEST FRONT.

The lunettes in the arches of the upper (western) façade are filled with 17th century mosaics of the life of Christ. The subjects begin at the extreme left with the Descent from the Cross, then follow Christ in Hades, the Resurrection and the Ascension. The upper part of the western, northern and southern façades were further embellished in the 15th century with canopied pinnacles and gables which reflect the Gothic period of the city. The central gable on the western front is surmounted by a statue of St. Mark bearing his Gospel with three angels swinging censers in adoration on either side.

PINNACLES on west façade, and mosaic of Descent from the Cross.

DOOR ON NORTH FRONT, with relief of the Nativity.

PINNACLES on west façade, and mosaic of the Resurrection.

The four gables (right and left of the central one) on the western front are crowned by statues of warrior saints; while the six canopied pinnacles between the gables contain statues of the Evangelists, the Archangel Gabriel (on the extreme left), and the Blessed Virgin, kneeling (on the extreme right). The two latter form an Annunciation. On the northern façade are Romanesque sculptures of prophets, saints and angels, and several Byzantine reliefs of a symbolical character. The gables on this façade are crowned with figures of Virtues. From left to right: Hope, Temperance, Faith, Prudence and Charity

THE TWELVE APOSTLES AND THE LAMB.
Symbolical Greek relief.

ALEXANDER THE GREAT ascending to heaven.
Relief on north front.

(the figures of Justice and Fortitude are on the southern façade). In the pinnacles are statues of the Archangel Michael and the four Latin Doctors: St. Gregory, St. Ambrose, St. Augustine, and St. Jerome.

Photo ALINARI, ANDERSON.

VENICE — ST. MARK'S. The Atrium.

ST. MARK. *Mosaic after a cartoon by* TITIAN. A. D. 1545.

BRONZE DOORS in the atrium adorned with figures in niello.

The ATRIUM or Vestibule of St. Mark's runs round two parts of the church, —the front or western end, and the northern side. Its roof is divided into six cupolas, all of them, with their spandrels, arches and separating vaults, are covered with 13th century mosaics representing the chief facts of Old Testament Scripture (from the Creation to the Fall of the Manna); the New Testament is represented within the church itself. The 3 slabs of red marble on the pavement near the entrance, commemorate the scene of the reconciliation between Pope Alexander III. and the Emperor Frederick Barbarossa in 1177. According to tradition, the emperor, when in the presence of the Pope, uncovered his head, flung himself on the floor to kiss the Holy Father's feet and murmured, " it is not to thee, but to St. Peter," that I kneel," to which the pope replied, " both to *me* and to St. Peter."

MAIN INNER DOORWAY in the vestibule.

THE ATRIUM. Looking south. *Showing mosaics of the Creation.*

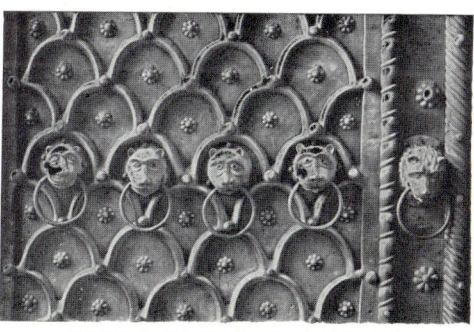

DETAIL OF BRONZE GATE. (Main Portal).

DETAIL OF BRONZE GATE. (Door to the right).

Photo ALINARI, ANDERSON.

VENICE — ST. MARK'S. *Atrium, First cupola.*

The Mosaics in the first cupola of the atrium are the most interesting; they represent the history of the Creation till the Fall. The figures of angels in white, varying in number, symbolise the days.

In the compositions, which were suggested by a 5th century Greek Bible in the Cottonian collection of the British Museum, Our Saviour is represented throughout as "the Lord" of the Old Testament, distinguished by the triple-rayed nimbus or glory.

"There is no likeness of God the Father in any of the mosaics. The Byzantine workers did not dare to attempt to make a figure of Him who is invisible: 'whom no man hath seen or can see,' but always in His stead put Jesus Christ, 'He whose goings forth have been from of old, from everlasting.' And Christ is so brought before us

HISTORY OF THE CREATION. *Mosaic in the first cupola.*

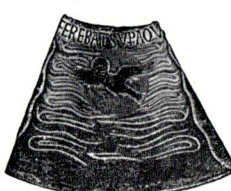

1. The Spirit of God moves upon the face of the waters.

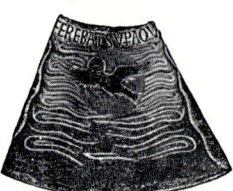

2. The partition of light from darkness.

3. The Lord makes a firmament *(second day).*

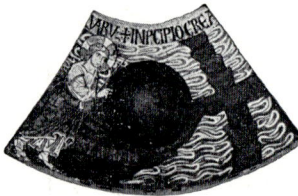

4. The Lord divides the waters above from the waters below.

5. The Lord makes dry land and plants *(third day).*

6. The Lord makes lights in the firmament of heaven. creates the Sun and the Moon *(fourth day).*

7. The Creation of Birds and Fishes.

8. The Lord makes living things *(fifth day).*

9. The Creation of Quadrupeds.

10. The Lord models man, a small figure not yet living *(sixth day).*

11. The Lord rests on the seventh day and blesses it.

Photo ALINARI, ANDERSON.

VENICE — ST. MARK'S. *Mosaics in the Atrium.*

in various aspects: as 'the visible image of the invisible God,' as he through whom God manifests Himself and works, every act of creation being here represented as wrought by Christ, 'by Him all things were made;' as He through whom every communication between God and man took place; and as the great Archetype of man, wearing, before time began, that image after the pattern of which man was made." (A. Robertson, *The Bible of St. Mark*).

The space in the pendentives below the cupola is filled by four large seraphs represented merely as heads with six wings. This emblem of the celestial hierarchy,—intended to represent a pure spirit glowing with love and intelligence, in which all that is bodily is put away, and only the head, the seat of soul, and wings, the attribute of spirit and swiftness, retained,—is of Greek origin (p. 98).

12. The Lord breathes into man the breath of life, represented by a little winged soul clinging to him.

13. The Lord takes Adam into the Garden of Eden; the rivers of which are symbolized by figures lying at the foot of the Tree of Life.

14. Adam names the animals.

15. The Lord puts Adam into a deep sleep, and draws Eve from his side.

16. The Lord presents Eve to Adam.

17. The serpent tempts Eve.

18. Eve plucks the apple and gives it to Adam.

19. Adam and Eve clothe themselves with foliage.

20. The Lord questions Adam, who exculpates himself by "the woman Thou gavest unto me...."

21. The Lord reproves Adam and Eve.

22. Adam and Eve hear their sentence of punishment.

23. The Lord clothes Adam and Eve (!).

24. The Lord expels Adam and Eve from Eden; they labour outside the garden.

WONDERS OF ITALY. — 97 — Photo ALINARI, ANDERSON

13.

VENICE — ST. MARK'S. Mosaics in the Atrium.

ABRAHAM and the Three Angels.

On the left Abraham receives the Angels; *in the centre* he ministers to them at table, while Sarah behind smiles at the prediction that she should bear a son.

SCENES FROM THE HISTORY OF NOAH.

Beginning above from left to right: the Deluge; Noah sends the raven and the dove; the return of the dove; exit from the Ark; Noah's sacrifice; the dispersal of the animals.

BUILDING OF THE TOWER OF BABEL.

Above on the left the Lord looks down while the building goes on; *on the right* the Lord descends in a glory of angels to confound the languages. The Dispersion is here represented by four groups of men moving in all directions.

STORY OF ABRAHAM.
Mosaic in the second cupola.

The mosaics in the second cupola (to the left of the main entrance) represent the History of Abraham: 1. The calling of Abraham; 2. His preparation for the journey; 3. Abraham accompanied by his wife, and his nephew Lot removes to Haran; 4. There he receives the divine command to remove to Canaan; 5. Lot is made prisoner by the King of Sodom; 6. The meeting of Abraham and Melchizedeck; 7. Abraham treats with the King of Sodom for the deliverance of Lot: God again appearing to Abraham; 8. Abraham and Sarah being childless Sarah brings her handmaid Hagar to Abraham; 9. Sarah, however, becomes jealous and Hagar flies from the home of Abraham; 10. Hagar is conforted by an angel and advised to return to Abraham; 11. Hagar becomes a mother (birth of Ishmael); 12. Thirteen years after the birth of Ishmael the divine promise is repeated (a son, the founder of the Israelite nation promised to Sarah); 13. Institution of circumcision; 14. The rite of circumcision. (*The story is continued in two lunettes below*).

THE ATRIUM. Looking Northwards showing mosaics of History of Noah.

Photo ALINARI, ANDERSON.

VENICE — ST. MARK'S. Mosaics in the Atrium.

The compositions in the fourth cupola (northern section of the atrium) are a continuation of the History of Joseph which begins in the corner cupola.

1. Joseph is sold to Potiphar. 2. Joseph is made overseer in Potiphar's house. 3. Joseph is tempted by Potiphar's wife. 4. He runs away leaving his garment in her hands. 5. The woman shows the coat and accuses Joseph. 6. Joseph is arrested and cast into prison. 7. Pharaoh on a throne orders the imprisonment of his chief butler and chief baker. 8. They have dreams while in prison. 9. Joseph interprets their dreams.

The story is continued in the pendentives: 10. Pharaoh recalls the chief butler. 11. The chief baker is hung and birds devour him. 12. Pharaoh asleep, he dreams of the seven lean kines devouring the seven fat ones. (*The story is continued in the arch to the right*).

HISTORY OF JOSEPH.
Mosaic in the 4th cupola.

HISTORY OF JOSEPH.

On the left Jacob sends Benjamin with his brothers to Egypt to buy corn; *right* Benjamin is received by Joseph who reveals himself to his brethren; *above* the brethren are emptying their sacks.

The Atrium was exclusively reserved for those not yet baptised and those about to be converted. Here they could meditate on the great events of the Old Testament: the story of the downfall of Man, and the lives of the Patriarchs until the time when the Law was given by Moses. The niches in the wall have been used as tombs for the Doges. To the right of the main entrance, there is the tomb of Vitale Falier, who solemnly consecrated the basilica in 1085; to the left, that of Felicita, wife of the unfortunate doge Vitale Michiel, who was assassinated in 1101. On the north are the urns of other doges.

THE ATRIUM. Showing the third (corner) cupola with story of Joseph.

THE ATRIUM. Looking Eastwards showing the fourth, fifth and sixth cupolas.

Photo ALINARI, ANDERSON.

VENICE — *ST. MARK'S.* The Interior.

CHRIST, THE VIRGIN, AND ST. MARK.
Mosaic above the main entrance (10th cent.).

In the book which Christ holds upon His knee is written : " I am the door, by me if any man enter in, he shall be saved... " The figure of Christ is robed in royal purple and blue, behind His head the nimbus is marked with the shadow of the cross, and the monogram I·C X·C (Jesus Christ). On the red marble moulding which surrounds the mosaic is written : " I am the gate of life ; let those who are mine enter by me. "

DESCENT OF THE HOLY GHOST. *First dome* (Western).

INTERIOR OF THE BASILICA OF SAN MARCO. *Completed* A. D. 1094.

The interior is magnificently decorated. The walls gleam with rare marbles ; the vaulting is adorned with splendid mosaics; the floor is inlaid with a variety of stones: jasper, porphyry, agate, etc., while all around are columns of precious marbles.

Photo ALINARI, ANDERSON.

VENICE — ST. MARK'S. The Interior.

The mosaics in St. Mark's occupy 40.000 sq. feet of walls. Those in the main body of the church are arranged in a chronological sequence of Christ's history and the chief facts of the New Testament: they form an epitome of the Christian faith. The Gospel story commences in the cupola over the High Altar, and is continued in the next two cupolas (and the arches between them) towards the main entrance, where it ends with the Last Judgment. The mosaics in the aisles represent the acts and martyrdoms of the Apostles and stories of St. Mark the patron.

In the cupola near the entrance or Western dome is represented the *Descent of the Holy Ghost*. In the centre is the Dove enthroned with its wings **expanded**, symbolising the Holy Spirit, from which twelve rays terminating in tongues of fire descend on the twelve Apostles, seated in a circle around the dome; below them, between the windows, are distributed groups (one man and one woman) of the various races: Hebrews, Egyptians, Parthians, Medes, etc., all the nations mentioned in the second chapter of Acts, as assembled at Jerusalem at the day of Pentecost, and to whom the newly inspired Apostles preached "in their tongues the wonderful works of God." In the pendentives are four angels singing 'Holy, Holy, Holy.'

The second cupola or Central dome is entirely occupied by the subject of the *Ascension*. In the centre, Christ in

THE ASCENSION. *Mosaic in the central dome.*

the act of benediction, is seen as rising into a blue heaven, borne aloft by angels and throned upon a rainbow, the symbol of reconciliation; all around are the twelve Apostles, divided by trees, typifying the Mount of Olives, while beneath Christ is the Madonna, attended by two angels. Beneath the circle of Apostles, between the windows, are the Theological and Cardinal Virtues. In the pendentives are the four Evangelists writing their Gospels, because on their evidence our assurance of the fact of the Ascension rests. Finally, beneath the Evangelists, as symbols of the sweetness and fulness of the Gospel which they declared, are figures pouring water from their urns of the 4 rivers of Paradise: Gyon, Fison, Euphrate, and Tygre.

FRAGMENTS OF THE MOSAIC PAVEMENT. *12th century*

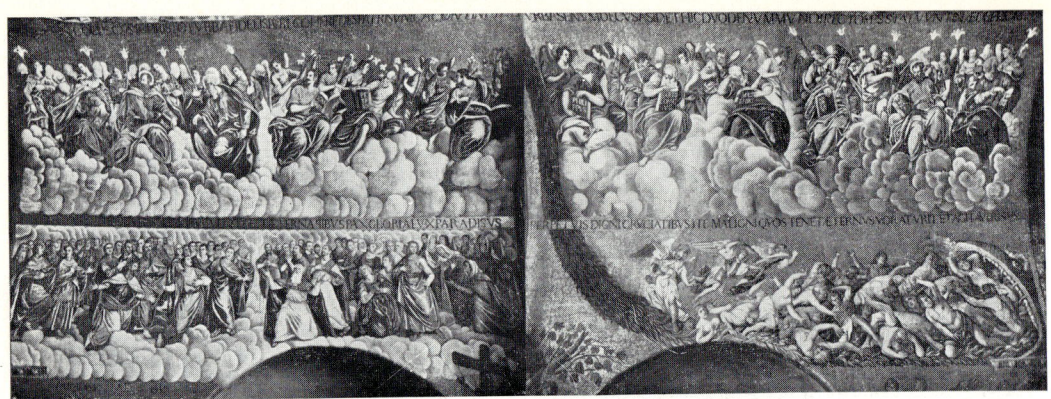

VENICE — *ST MARK'S.* *The Interior.*

THE LAST JUDGMENT. *Mosaic from a cartoon by* TINTORETTO.

THE CRUCIFIXION. *Mosaic of the 13th cent.*

STORIES OF ST. MARK. *Byzantine mosaics.*

In the vaulting above the organ to the right of the choir the history of the body of St. Mark after his death is portrayed in a series of Byzantine mosaics which are among the oldest and most interesting in the church. The story is most quaintly told in the following scenes: 1) Tribunus and Rusticus, Venetian merchants at Alexandria, with the assistance of the priest Theodore and the monk Stauracius, steal the body of the saint from the sarcophagus; 2) they carry the body in a basket for embarkation and cry "Kanzir, kanzir" (Pork, pork), to warn off Mohammedan officials; 3) the Venetians hide the body in a sail of the ship: the deluded Custom-house officials are departing; 4) the departure of the ship from Alexandria and its voyage: the miracle of the storm, St. Mark prevents the ship's destruction; 6) the arrival in Venice: the Doge, the clergy, and the people in procession joyfully receive the body on the arrival of the ship at Venice. (For the story of St. Mark see p. 91, 110).

VIEW OF THE NAVE. *From north aisle.*

BYZANTINE CAPITALS.

St. Mark's is a triumph of Byzantine architecture, the most splendid of any ecclesiastical interior in Christendom.

Photo ALINARI, ANDERSON.

VENICE — ST. MARK'S. The Interior.

PARADISE. *Mosaic from a cartoon by* TINTORETTO.

BIRTH OF THE VIRGIN. PRESENTATION.
Mosaic by MICHELE GIAMBONO. (*Cappella dei Mascoli*).

BYZANTINE BRONZE CANDELABRA.

The *Cappella dei Mascoli* in the north transept of the church was built in 1430 by Doge Francesco Foscari and dedicated to the Madonna. The roof of this beautiful chapel is covered with fifteenth century mosaics by *Michele Giambono* representing five scenes from the life of the Virgin. The series begins with: The Annunciation; The Birth of Our Lady; The Presentation of the Virgin in the Temple (both given here); The Meeting of Mary and Elizabeth at the Gate, The Death of Our Lady.

All the compositions in the Cappella dei Mascoli are conventional in style, but they are highly interesting as they belong to the period of transition and form a sort of connecting link between the Byzantine mosaics and those of the seventeenth century.

HOLY WATER STOUP.

VIEW OF THE NAVE. *From south aisle.*

The five domes, as well as the intervening vaults and walls, down to the triforia, are entirely incrusted with mosaics.

Photo ALINARI, ANDERSON.

VENICE — ST. MARK'S. The Interior.

VIEW OF THE GALLERIES AND THE MOSAICS. (Left aisle).

CHOIR AND TRANSEPT. (North).

On either side of the approach to the high-altar is a pulpit fixed to the northern and southern piers which support the central cupola. The pulpit on the left is in two storeys and has a canopy in the Byzantine style. The lower storey is used for the reading of the Epistle, while the upper one for the reading of the Gospel. Upon this pulpit and upon the piers supporting the central dome are richly-gilt figures of angels, said to be the work of Byzantine sculptors, and to have been brought to Venice at the same time as the bronze horses on the façade. The pulpit on the right was used by the church choir as a singing gallery, and in time of national crisis for addressing the people. Here the newly-elected doge presented himself to his subjects and promised them good government.

ONE OF THE MARBLE PARAPETS OF THE UPPER GALLERIES.

The chapel of St. Isidore, built to house the tomb of the saint, is an artistic gem. It contains his tomb and some rich mosaics of the 14th century, showing episodes of the saint's life.

St. Isidore suffered martyrdom on the island of Chios, under the emperor Gallus about the year 250. The doge Domenico Michiel brought his body to Venice in 1125, the sanctuary and the tomb and the commemorative statue date from 1350. On the front of the sarcophagus are represented episodes in the life of St. Isidore.

The mosaic on the arch behind represents the Saviour on a throne between St. Mark and St. Isidore.

THE CHAPEL OF ST. ISIDORE.

THE PULPITS AND THE ROOD SCREEN.

— 104 —

Photo ALINARI, ANDERSON.

VENICE — ST. MARK'S. The Interior.

CHOIR AND TRANSEPT (South).

VIEW OF THE GALLERIES AND THE MOSAICS (Right aisle).

"Under feet and over head," writes Ruskin, "a continual succession of crowded imagery, one picture passing into another, as in a dream.... the passions and the pleasures of human life symbolised together, and the mystery of its redemption; for the mazes of interwoven lines and changeful pictures lead always at last to the Cross, lifted and carved in every place and upon every stone; sometimes with the serpent of eternity wrapt round it, sometimes with doves beneath its arms and sweet herbage growing forth from its feet; but conspicuous most of all on the great rood that crosses the church before the altar, raised in bright blazonry against the shadow of the apse."

ONE OF THE MARBLE PARAPETS OF THE UPPER GALLERIES.

Fragment of column supporting the canopy of the high altar. The symbolical treatment of the reliefs, the costumes and other particulars presupposes the carvings to be of the 6th-11th cen.

ROOD SCREEN WITH STATUES OF THE VIRGIN, ST. JOHN, ST. MARK AND THE APOSTLES.
Executed by JACOBELLO and PIER PAOLO DELLE MASSEGNE (1394).

— 105 —

Photo ALINARI, ANDERSON.

14. - WONDERS OF ITALY.

VENICE — ST. MARK'S. The Choir.

The Eastern dome or choir cupola is decorated with Byzantine mosaics. In the centre is a half figure of Christ (beardless), in the act of blessing; beneath Him is a figure of the Madonna, having on her right the kings David and Solomon, followed by figures of the prophets who prophesied of Christ— Malachi, Zechariah, Haggai, Zephaniah, Jonah, Hosea, Habakkuk, Abdias, Daniel, Jeremiah, and Isaiah, all named in the inscriptions, and each holding a scroll on which the words of their prophecies are inscribed.

CHRIST SURROUNDED BY OLD TESTAMENT SAINTS, and symbols of the Evangelists. *Mosaics of the 13th cent. in the Eastern dome.*

CHRIST BLESSING. *Mosaic in the apse* A. D. 1506

The large mosaic in the apse representing Christ enthroned, holding a closed book on His knee and blessing with His right hand, dates from 1506. The High Altar covers the remains of St. Mark, which disappeared during the fire of 976 but were miraculously recovered in the year 1094. It stands beneath a canopy of *verde antico* supported by four columns of Greek marble most elaborately sculptured with 6th-11th century reliefs representing scenes from the life of Mary, and from the life of Christ. These columns are supposed to have been brought from the old Roman town of Pola in Istria. The altarpiece here is formed by the famous *Pala d'Oro* given on the opposite page.

VIEW OF THE HIGH ALTAR AND THE CHOIR.
On the altar is seen the famous "Pala d'Oro," the Golden Altar-Piece.

Photo ALINARI, ANDERSON.

VENICE — ST. MARK'S. *The Pala d'Oro.*

THE PALA D'ORO. THE GOLDEN ALTAR-PIECE. *Originally executed at Constantinople in* A. D. 976.

The famous *Pala d'Oro*, at the back of the high altar, is a marvel of gold, silver, enamel and innumerable gems, the masterpieces of Byzantine goldsmiths. Originally executed at Constantinople in the year 976, it was restored in Venice in 1105 and again under Doge Andrea Dandolo in 1345. "There are twenty-seven squares in the inner border alone, each of which contains a scene from Scripture. Every separate figure and morsel of *smalto* is separated from the surrounding ones by a fine line of filigree gold, so that the effect is more like that of a coloured glass window than a painting in enamel. The dividing lines and open spaces are covered with jewels, pearls, and even cameos, and the centre is divided into forty-three arches and five circular medallions, each of which contains a picture in *smalto* ". Leader Scott, *Renaissance of Art in Italy.*

CENTRAL PART OF THE "PALA D'ORO".

Photo ALINARI, ANDERSON, BROGI.

VENICE — ST. MARK'S. *Sacristy, Baptistery.*

The story of St. John the Baptist is shown in a series of ten mosaics on the walls of the Baptistery: 1) the Angel appears before Zacharias in the Temple and announces to him the birth of his son; 2) the birth of St. John the Baptist, Zacharias names the child; 3) St. John leaves for the desert; 4) An Angel gives him a cloak; 5) Preaching in the desert; 6) his discussions with the Pharisees; 7) St. John baptises Christ in the Jordan; 8) the banquet of Herod; here may be seen Salome dancing holding in the air the head of the Precursor; the king is horrified, while Herodias is triumphant; 10) the funeral; the disciples after having buried the body, bring his head for burial.

RENAISSANCE MOSAICS
on the vaulting of the Sacristy.

BRONZE DOOR of the Sacristy
by SANSOVINO, 1556.
Below the Entombment; *above* the Resurrection.

The bronze door behind the high altar leading to the sacristy was executed by Jacopo Sansovino in 1556. It has two large reliefs of the Entombment and the Resurrection of Christ, surrounded by admirable figures of Evangelists and Prophets which recall the work of Ghiberti on the gates of the Florentine Baptistery.

CHRIST commanding His disciples to baptize the Gentiles in His name. *Mosaic in the dome of the Baptistery.* A. D. 1300.

The BAPTISTERY and the adjoining Zeno Chapel, formed originally a portion of the (southern) Atrium. The mosaics here representing events in the life of Christ and St. John the Baptist date from about 1300. Those in the cupola over the font represent Our Lord (in the centre) sending His Apostles to preach to the Gentiles. Beneath, in a circle, are the Apostles, each baptizing a naked convert in a font, while a sponsor in the costume of the country where the apostle preached, stands by. The inscriptions above their heads mention the name of the apostle and the country where he preached and baptized. Thus, St. Mark baptises in Alexandria; St. John the Evangelist in Ephesus; St. James Minor in Judea; St. Philip in Phrygia; St. Matthew in Ethiopia; St. Simon in Egypt; St. Thomas in India; St. Andrew in Achaia; St. Peter in Rome; St. Bartholomew in India (India superior); St. Thaddeus in Mesopotamia; St. Matthias in Palestine. In the pendentives are the Four Greek Fathers of the Church—SS. Athanasius, John Crysostom, Gregory Nazianzen, and Basil; each holding a scroll inscribed with a Latin sentence relating to the rite of Baptism.

VIEW OF THE BAPTISTERY.

Photo ALINARI, ANDERSON.

VENICE — ST. MARK'S. The Baptistery.

THE FONT. The bronze lid is adorned with reliefs from the life of the Baptist; the bronze statue of the saint is by *Francesco Segala* 1565.

THE CRUCIFIXION. *Byzantine mosaic.*

On the left of the cross is the Virgin Mary and St. Mark, on the right St. John the Evangelist and St. John the Baptist. At the foot of the cross kneels the Doge Andrea Dandolo' on either side, also kneeling, his Grand Chamberlain and a Senator.

THE DAUGHTER OF HERODIAS DANCES BEFORE HEROD. *Mosaic.*

MONUMENT OF DOGE ANDREA DANDOLO († 1354).

SCENES FROM THE LIFE OF ST. JOHN THE BAPTIST. *Mosaic.*
Left Martyrdom of the saint; *centre* Salome presents his head to her mother; *right* Burial of the saint.

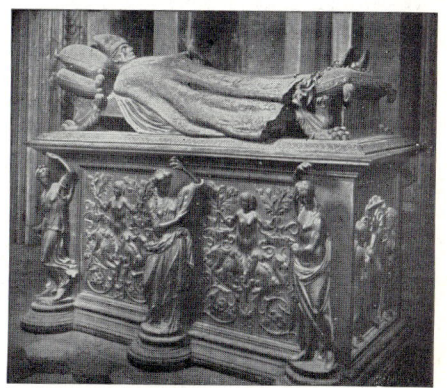

MONUMENT OF CARDINAL G. B. ZENO († 1501). By ALESSANDRO LEOPARDI and A. LOMBARDO. (*Cappella Zeno, p. 110*).

Photo ALINARI, ANDERSON.

VENICE — ST. MARK'S. The Cappella Zeno.

The little *Cappella Zeno*, adjoining the baptistery, contains the monument of Cardinal Gian Battista Zeno (given on the preceding page), and an interesting series of thirteenth century mosaics illustrating the legend of St. Mark, whose body rested first in this chapel after its arrival in Venice.

The story of the Evangelist is thus pictured: 1. St. Mark writes his Gospel at the request of his disciples; 2. St. Mark followed by his disciples submits his gospel to St. Peter, who approves of it and orders it to be read in the Church; 3. St. Mark baptizing at Aquileia in front of the Patriarchal church: the convert is seen in the font, and two brethren stand by with towels; 4. St. Mark falls asleep in his boat while sailing from Aquileia to Rome: the boat is driven by a storm amongst the reeds of the Venetian lagoons where an angel announces to St. Mark that after his death his body shall be honoured on that spot; 5. St. Mark's companion St. Hermagoras is appointed Bishop of Aquileia by St. Peter; 6. St. Mark leaving Rome for Egypt (his departure is symbolised by a gate surmounted by houses and towers); 7. St. Mark enters Egypt, preaches there, and expels demons from a maniac who stands in a cleft of a rock; 8. St. Mark in a dream at Pentapolis is ordered by an angel to sail to Alexandria; 9. St. Mark arrives at Alexandria, which is represented by the famous Lighthouse; 10. St. Mark heals the shoemaker Ananius of a wound made by an awl; 11. St. Mark is arrested by the Saracens while celebrating Mass at the altar; one man hits with a club, while another strangles him with a chain; 12. St. Mark's body maltreated, and dragged through Alexandria to the shambles; 13. St. Mark's body is buried in a sarcophagus by the disciples and the faithful. (For the story of St. Mark after his death *see* p. 102).

1. ST. MARK writes his Gospel.
2. He presents it to St. Peter who approves.
3. ST. MARK baptises at Aquileia.

4. ST. MARK sails from Aquileia to Rome.
5. ST. PETER ordains St. Hermagoras.
6. ST. MARK leaving Rome for Egypt.
7. ST. MARK enters Egypt and preaches there.

8. An angel orders him to sail to Alexandria.
9. ST. MARK arrives at Alexandria.
10. He heals the cobbler Ananius.

11. ST. MARK is arrested while celebrating Mass.
12. He is dragged through the city.
13. He is buried by his disciples.

Photo ALINARI, ANDERSON.

VENICE — *ST. MARK'S*. *The Treasury*.

SILVER GILDED AND ENAMELLED BYZANTINE MISSAL COVERS *in the Treasury of San Marco*.

BYZANTINE ENAMELS BELONGING TO THE "PALA D'ORO."

The TREASURY contains a most valuable collection of vessels in gold, silver, rock-crystal and other precious stones; Byzantine book-covers, reliquaries, and church furniture brought (1204) from St. Sophia, Constantinople.

SWORD of Franc. Morosini (1688).    ENAMELLED CHALICE. *11th cent.*    SILVER RELIQUARY. *12th cen.*

SILVER GILDED ALTAR FRONT with reliefs of Christ, the Virgin, the Apostles, and stories of St. Mark. *14th cent.*

— 111 —   Photo ALINARI, ANDERSON.

VENICE — ST. MARK'S.

WESTERN FAÇADE OF SAN MARCO AND THE DOGE'S PALACE.
In the distance is seen San Giorgio Maggiore.

SOUTHERN FRONT OF SAN MARCO.
In the foreground is the *Pietra del Bando*.

BYZANTINE RELIEF.

GRIFFIN WITH A CHILD.

UPPER GALLERY:
in the lunette
is the famous Madonna.

Beneath the famous lunette mosaic of the Virgin (given on the right) two lamps are nightly lit in memory of an act of injustice perpetrated on an innocent youth.

The southern façade, looking as it does towards the Molo, is most lavishly decorated with reliefs and costly marbles. The two beautiful square pillars with Byzantine reliefs placed exactly in front of the wall of the Baptistery of St. Mark's, were brought in 1256 from the church of St. Saba at St. John of Acre. The exquisite carving of the monograms and the quaint arabic inscriptions show that they are good examples of ornamental Greek sculpture of the 6th century. They have been put there as if in an open air museum.

.*.

Set in the corner pillar are two quaint groups in porphyry, brought to Venice from St. John of Acre, each representing two warriors embracing one another. At first these personages, in the act of giving the kiss of reconciliation, were thought to be four emperors of the time of Diocletian, but there have been many other interpretations.

THE "PIETRA DEL BANDO" AND
THE PILLARS OF ST. JOHN OF ACRE.

From the *Pietra del Bando*, the short porphyry pillar at the corner, the decrees of the Republic were promulgated to the people.

THE FOUR EMPERORS (?)
Greek porphyry reliefs.

Photo ALINARI, ANDERSON.

— 112 —

VENICE — *PALACE OF THE DOGES.*

PALACE OF THE DOGES. PORTA DELLA CARTA.
Erected by Giov. *and* Bart. Buon *in* 1438-43.

This magnificent doorway giving access to the interior court was at first called *Porta Dorata* because the sculptures and the ornaments were gilded; later its name was changed to *Porta della Carta* because the public decrees were posted here. Over the portal is a relief of the Doge Francesco Foscari kneeling before the Lion of St. Mark. On each side are statues of Fortitude, Prudence, Hope and Charity.

VENICE — *PALACE OF THE DOGES.* *Sculptures.*

THE JUDGMENT OF SOLOMON. ADAM AND EVE. THE DRUNKENNESS OF NOAH.

The groups in relief at each of the three angles of the palace and the statues of archangels above each group are intended respectively to inculcate a moral: Justice, Obedience, and Temperance. The Judgment of Solomon, on the angle next the portal, and the figure of Gabriel above, symbolises Justice; the group of Adam and Eve on the S. W. angle, and the archangel Michael above, is a warning against disobedience; the Drunkenness of Noah on the S. E. angle and the archangel Gabriel above, is an admonition against intemperance.

Numa building temples. Capital of the Lawgivers. The Emperor Trajan and the widow.

Aristotle. Capital of the Wise Men. Moses.

Capital of the « Virtues » (Left). Capital of the « Months » (Right).

The capitals of the thirty-six columns supporting the building are exquisitely carved with symbolical figures of virtues, vices, planets.

— 114 —

Photo ALINARI, ANDERSON

VENICE — *PALACE OF THE DOGES.*

THE PALACE OF THE DOGES. *Western and Southern Façades.*

THE PALACE OF THE DOGES, this magnificent political and civic monument, reflecting the glory and greatness of the Republic, embraces the whole history of Venice. It was first built in A. D. 820 for the first Doge of Venice. After a conflagration it was rebuilt and enlarged in the twelfth century under Doge Ziani. From the fourteenth century onwards many important additions were made to the old building; thus, the southern wing facing the Grand Canal was built by BASEGGIO in 1309-40; the western wing opposite the Library was erected by the architects GIOVANNI

BALCONY OF THE WESTERN FAÇADE.

ANGLE OF THE DOGES' PALACE
with the relief of Adam and Eve. 15th cent.

and BARTOLOMEO BUON in 1424-38; the eastern wing towards the Bridge of Sighs was begun by ANTONIO RIZZO in 1484, continued by PIETRO LOMBARDO and completed by SCARPAGNINO in 1549. The two façades overlooking the Piazzetta and the Molo are lightened by a lower arcade of 36 pillars whose stumpy appearance is due to the raising of the pavement of the piazza; and by an upper gallery or loggia of 71 elegant columns. It is said that at the time of the Republic sentences of death were proclaimed from between the 9th and 10th columns (of red marble) from the principal portal. The palace was not only used as the official residence of the Doge, but as the seat of government of the Republic and the place where all the councils of state were held.

Photo ALINARI, ANDERSON, BROGI.

VENICE — *PALACE OF THE DOGES. The Court.*

COURT OF THE PALACE OF THE DOGES.

THE SCALA D'ORO.

The court of the Doges' Palace is a very ornate and costly example of Venetian Renaissance. It was commenced by ANTONIO RIZZO, continued by PIETRO LOMBARDO, and completed by A. SCARPAGNINO.

The façades of the court are faced with marble and richly ornamented with friezes, reliefs, scrolls and devices bearing witness to the originality of design and beauty of execution of Venetian art. In the centre of the court are two richly sculptured well-heads dating from 1556-59.

In this court the Doge Marino Faliero (p. 124) was beheaded in 1355. Faliero was a passionate, ambitious old man; irritated against the nobles by an insult received from one of them, he organized a conspiracy against the Republic, by which all the principal citizens were to be slaughtered and he himself proclaimed sovereign. The plot was discovered on the eve of its execution and Faliero was degraded and decapitated.

The *Scala dei Giganti*, the «Giants' Staircase», from the colossal statues of Mars and Neptune standing above (representative of the military and naval supremacy of Venice) executed by SANSOVINO in 1554 is beautiful in every detail.

Every Doge was crowned on the top of the landing; the electors standing around him while the people acclaimed him from below, in the courtyard; a line of ducal guards kept the staircase.

The Scala dei Giganti leads into the palace by the *Scala d'Oro*, the «Golden Staircase», so called from its richness of the golden stucco decorations executed on the vault by Alessandro Vittoria; it was erected by SANSOVINO in 1556. It is built of marble and gold and in the days of the Republic, only those nobles whose names were written in the Golden Book were allowed to use it.

STATUE OF EVE.
By A. RIZZO.

THE SCALA DEI GIGANTI (Giants' Staircase).
Designed by A. RIZZO A. D. 1485-89.

STATUE OF MARS.
By SANSOVINO.

Photo ALINARI, ANDERSON.

STATUE OF EVE (*detail*), *by* A. RIZZO.   *Grimani Room.*

Two statues, of Adam and Eve respectively, formerly stood on the Foscari arch in the Palace court-yard. They have now been replaced by copies in bronze and Antonio Rizzo's marble originals, executed in 1464, are at present in the Grimani room. Both statues holds the fatal apple, but whille Eve looks down as if convicted of sin, Adam places one hand upon his breast, and raises his eyes to heaven as if seeking to justify himself.

Photo ALINARI, ANDERSON,

VENICE — *PALACE OF THE DOGES.* Vestibule.

VESTIBULE TO THE STATE APARTMENTS.

The *Vestibule* or Atrio Quadrato, has a fine gilded wooden ceiling with a painting by JACOPO TINTORETTO representing Venice and Justice presenting the Sword and the Scales to Doge Girolamo Priuli (see illustration).

On the walls of this hall are several admirable portraits of Procurators also by Tintoretto.

DOGE GIROL. PRIULI BEFORE VENICE. By JACOPO TINTORETTO. (*Detail of the ceiling*).

NICCOLÒ PRIULI.    PAOLO PARUTA.    VINCENZO MOROSINI.
Portraits of Procurators painted by JACOPO TINTORETTO.

ENTRY OF HENRY III. OF VALOIS INTO VENICE. By A. VICENTINO. (*Hall of 4 Doors*).

This picture commemorates the King's visit (1574) to the Republic on his way from Poland to assume the crown of France.

Photo ALINARI, ANDERSON.

VENICE — *PALACE OF THE DOGES.* *Hall of the 4 Doors.*

CEILING DECORATIONS. *By* PALLADIO, TINTORETTO and other masters. (*Sala delle Quattro Porte*).
The paintings represent allegorical scenes in honour of Venice.

The architectonic decorations of the *Sala delle Quattro Porte* are the work of PALLADIO. The magnificent ceiling with stucco-work has paintings by TINTORETTO and TIEPOLO.

NEPTUNE STREWING THE TREASURES OF THE DEEP AT THE FEET OF VENETIA.
Painting by TIEPOLO.
On the right Venice, leaning against a lion, watches Neptune pouring out riches from a shell, his trident being held by a Triton.

PERSIAN ENVOYS OFFERING GIFTS to the Doge Grimani. *By* G. CALIARI.

MARS AND NEPTUNE. *Allegory by* P. VERONESE. (*Sala del Collegio*).

DOGE GRIMANI KNEELING BEFORE RELIGION.
By TITIAN. A. D. 1555.
The doge is kneeling before the allegorical figure of Faith, seen holding up in one hand a chalice and leaning on a big cross. To the left, St. Mark is holding the Gospels, with the customary lion at his feet.

— 119 —

Photo ALINARI, ANDERSON.

VENICE — *PALACE OF THE DOGES.* Sala dell'Anticollegio.

CHIMNEY PIECE. *By* SCAMOZZI.

SALA DELL'ANTICOLLEGIO. (Waiting Room).

The decorations of the *Sala dell'Anticollegio*, were executed by SCAMOZZI who also designed the fine chimney-piece. All the pictures in this room are masterpieces of art.

RAPE OF EUROPA. *Painted by* PAOLO VERONESE.

Veronese's « Rape of Europa » is one of the master's most celebrated pictures. Jupiter, enamoured of Europa, a Phoenician princess, transformed himself into a white bull, and mingled with her father's herds whilst she was gathering flowers with her attendants. Europa, struck by the beauty and gentle nature of the beast, caressed him, and even mounted on his back. Two of her attendants are assisting her, while the amorous bull, is licking her foot. Above are little cupids scattering flowers. In the middle distance Europa and the bull appear again, about to enter the sea; whilst farther on, the bull is swimming with her towards the land. For the story goes that as soon as Europa had seated herself on his back Jupiter crossed the sea and carried her safely to Crete, and from this rape of Europa comes the name of the continent to which she was carried. 'For brilliancy, fancifulness, extraordinary refinement and invention in color it has no equal.... one has to look at it and keep silent.'

MINERVA DRIVING AWAY MARS. *By* J. TINTORETTO.

Tintoretto's mythologies in this room painted about 1578 are the loveliest poesies of the Venetian school. The picture of « Ariadne and Bacchus », has been styled 'the most beautiful oil-painting in the world.' On a strand, Ariadne receives the ring from Bacchus, while Venus, with a diadem of stars, approaches in the air to honor their nuptials. The goddess of love is the sublime beauty of immortal youth.... her full forms palpitate half enveloped in a white gauze. 'A poem of feeling and romance.... a symphony of delicately blended hues....'

« The interlocking of the superb forms »…. writes F. J. Mather Jr., « the technical miracle of Venus's easy turn in the air »…. « the hesitating hand of Ariadne and her almost resigned and reluctant acceptance of a new love, being mindful of love once betrayed. Also the delicacy of Bacchus's ardent gesture, as knowing himself to be not only wooer but consoler, is purest Tintoretto ».

MERCURY AND THE GRACES.

MARRIAGE OF ARIADNE AND BACCHUS.

Painted by JACOPO TINTORETTO.

Photo ALINARI, ANDERSON, BROGI.

VENICE — *PALACE OF THE DOGES.* Sala del Collegio.

"INDUSTRY" or "DIALECTIC".

CEILING PAINTINGS *by* P. VERONESE.

VENICE honoured by Justice and Peace.
Ceiling painting.

The superb ceiling, heavily carved and gilded, contains eleven beautiful allegorical paintings by PAOLO VERONESE and his assistants.

The *Sala del Collegio*, was destined to the audiences which the doge and his privy council granted to the ambassadors of foreign states. The walls are richly decorated with paintings in which portraits of Doges have been introduced. Over the throne is a Memorial picture of the Battle of Lepanto (1571), painted by *Paolo Veronese*, above is the Saviour in Glory in the act of blessing, below is Doge Sebastiano Venier rendering thanks to the Lord for the victory of Lepanto. The paintings on the side walls are by *Tintoretto*. Over the door: Doge Andrea Gritti praying to the Virgin; Nuptials of St. Catherine (with Doge Franc. Donato); opposite, Adoration of the Saviour (with Doge Alvise Mocenigo); Virgin in Glory (with Doge Nicolò da Ponte).

SALA DEL COLLEGIO.
This room was used for the meeting of the Collegio which consisted of the Doge and his councillors.

NUPTIALS OF ST. CATHERINE. *By* TINTORETTO.

DOGE MOCENIGO before the Saviour. *By* TINTORETTO.

Photo ALINARI, ANDERSON.

— 121 —

16. - WONDERS OF ITALY.

VENICE — *PALACE OF THE DOGES.* Senate Hall.

THE DEAD CHRIST supported by angels and worshipped by the Doges P. Lando and M. A. Trevisan and their patron saints.
By JACOPO TINTORETTO. (The chiaroscuro panels beneath are by Tiepolo).

HALL OF THE SENATE OR «SALA DEI PREGADI». (*The Invited*).
This hall was formerly decorated by TITIAN and PORDENONE, but their work was destroyed by the fire of 1577.
It is now adorned by paintings executed by TINTORETTO and PALMA GIOVANE.

— 122 —

Photo ALINARI, ANDERSON.

VENICE — *PALACE OF THE DOGES.* Senate Hall.

ALLEGORY OF THE LEAGUE OF CAMBRAI.
By PALMA " Il Giovine."

Palma's "Allegory of the League of Cambrai" symbolises the resistance of Venice to the famous league formed in order to crush her power. In the center of the picture is Doge Leonardo Loredan, crowned by angels; to the left, Venice, with the Lion of St. Mark and the sword of Justice, is attacking Europe on a bull. Europe's shield is blazoned with the various arms of the allied States. On the extreme left are two allegorical figures bringing corn to Venice.

The League of Cambrai was formed in the year 1508. Louis XII. of France, Ferdinand the Catholic of Spain, the Emperor Maximilian, and Pope Julius II. combined in an attempt to reduce the Venetians, and to divide their territories among themselves. Julius II. declared that he meant to cut the claws of the Lion of St. Mark. The Republic suffered serious losses, and though she made a heroic, and, for a while, successful effort to hide her exhaustion, she never recovered from the blow. 'In one day the Venetians lost all they had acquired in 800 years.'

DOGE LOREDAN IMPLORING the aid of the Virgin. *By* TINTORETTO.

VENICE " QUEEN OF THE SEA."

This fine allegorical picture is notable for the daring character of its entire conception. Above, Venice in silken robes, with crown and sceptre, sits enthroned among the gods of Olympus, while Tritons and Nereids rise from the blue sea-depths below bearing their tribute of coral and pearls from the ocean.

DETAIL OF THE DECORATIONS.
By C. SORTE.

THE DOGE CICOGNA adoring Christ to whom he is presented by St. Mark.
By PALMA " Il Giovine."

— 123 —

Photo ALINARI, ANDERSON.

VENICE — PALACE OF THE DOGES. Hall of the Great Council.

HALL OF THE GREAT COUNCIL: PARADISE (*Detail*) by JACOPO TINTORETTO.

Tintoretto's "Paradise," seventy-four feet long and twenty-four feet high, the largest picture in the world, contains some five hundred figures. Though blackened by age, this work reveals Tintoretto's wonderful imagination and his extraordinary power and daring in throwing such "a tempest" of human figures about in space. The general motif follows the medieval conception of circle beyond circle, centring round the figures of Christ and His Mother. Around and about them are the hierarchies of angels, of archangels, Biblical personages, Evangelists, Fathers of the Church, Saints, and Martyrs, all filled with a heavenly ecstasy. Many of the figures display much skill; some of the heads are admirable.

HALL OF THE GREAT COUNCIL *adorned with paintings by* P. VERONESE, J. TINTORETTO, BASSANO, PALMA GIOVANE, etc.

The Great Council, possessing supreme authority, was composed of the nobles whose names were inscribed in the Golden Book. The walls of this hall are covered with huge pictures recalling the military triumphs of the Venetian republic. On the frieze are the portraits of 76 doges. Amidst these is a black space with the inscription: "Hic est locus Marini Faletri decapitati pro criminibus" (length of the hall 59 yds., breadth 26 yds., height 49 feet).

— 124 —

Photo ALINARI, ANDERSON.

VENICE — DOGES' PALACE. Hall of the Great Council.

VENETIAN AMBASSADORS before Frederick Barbarossa at Pavia. By JACOPO TINTORETTO.

In the *Sala del Maggior Consiglio*, the Great Council held its sittings. Here the die was cast for war or peace, for honour or disgrace. The walls and roof of this sumptuous hall are covered with masterpieces in painting representing scenes from the history of the Republic; the apotheosis of the splendour of Venice, the might and triumphs of her arms. The north wall is decorated with scenes in the story of Pope Alexander III. and the Emperor Barbarossa; on the south wall are depicted the exploits of Doge Enrico Dandolo and the epic story of the conquest of Constantinople. Everywhere coronations, victories, sea-fights, doges, generals, heroes, allegories recalling the story of Venetian greatness, the vigour and patriotism of her citizens... The wall over the throne is occupied by Tintoretto's World of the Blessed! Venice dreamt only of Paradise! While on the ceiling are two stupendous works representing Venice crowned by Glory (p. 126), and Venice receiving the homage of conquered cities. The latter picture illustrated below is one of Tintoretto's famous allegories. In the upper part of the composition is a symbolical figure of Venice crowned and with the lion beside her. Just below, the Doge Niccolò da Ponte surrounded by Senators and Councillors presents to Venice the homage of the nobles and the citizens of the subject cities. Lower still are grouped the handicrafts soldiers and flags of the territories.

VENICE CROWNED BY VICTORY. Allegory by PALMA " Il Giovine."

BARBAROSSA AT THE POPE'S FEET. By F. ZUCCARI. (See p. 95).

THE DOGE DA PONTE offers to Venice the homage of the conquered cities. By TINTORETTO.

THE POPE PRESENTING A SWORD TO DOGE ZIANI. By FRANCESCO BASSANO.

VENICE — *PALACE OF THE DOGES.* Hall of the Great Council.

VENICE CROWNED BY GLORY or APOTHEOSIS OF VENICE. *Painting by* PAOLO VERONESE.

The celebrated allegorical picture « Venice crowned by Glory » on the ceiling of the *Sala del Maggior Consiglio* is a composition of the highest poetry and a perfect symphony of colours. It represents the glorification of the Venetian State and symbolizes the might and power of the Republic. The allegorical and historical part is depicted in the upper group; on the balustrade in the middle, are bishops, knights and beautiful ladies; below, soldiers keeping watch, prisoners with booty, military trophies and crowds of people witnessing the heavenly ceremony.

Photo ALINARI, ANDERSON.

VENICE — *PALACE OF THE DOGES.*

SALA DELLO SCRUTINIO. Election Hall.    SALA DEL CONSIGLIO DEI DIECI (Council of Ten).

The *Sala dello Scrutinio* was built and adorned with paintings after the famous fire of 1577. In this Hall were counted the votes for the 41 nobles who in turn had to elect the Doge, and the votes for the holders of the important offices of the state. At the end of the Hall is a triumphal arch of marble erected by the Senate in honour of the doge Francesco Morosini, the conqueror of Morea and victorious over the Turks in more than a hundred battles. On the ceiling are paintings representing the victories of the Venetians over the Pisan fleet in 1098, and over the Genoese in 1258. On one of the walls is the "Last Judgment" by PALMA, similar to the "Glory of Paradise" by Tintoretto (page 124); on the other walls are scenes from the history of the Republic; the battle of Lepanto, 1571; the victory of the Venetians over the Turks at the Dardanelles, 1658; the capture of Zara in 1346; the capture of Cattaro in 1378, etc. On the frieze, the same as in the Hall of the Grand Council, there are the portraits of the last thirty-nine doges, up to Luigi Manin, who abdicated in 1797.

The *Sala del Consiglio dei Dieci* was decorated by PAOLO VERONESE, BASSANO and other famous Venetian masters. The Council of Ten was first instituted in 1310. It acted in conjunction with the Doge and his councillors. Its business was to judge all political offence and the ill-doings of the patricians: it controlled the lives and fortunes of all Venice. In secrecy and silence the witnesses were examined; in secrecy and silence the sentence was carried out.

THE LAST JUDGMENT. By PALMA "Il Giovine." *Sala dello Scrutinio.*

YOUTH AND OLD AGE. By PAOLO VERONESE. *Sala dei Dieci.*

ADORATION OF THE MAGI.   By PAOLO VERONESE. (*Now in the Academy*).

SALA DELLA BUSSOLA. Voting Hall.
This room leads to the *Sala dei Capi*. (The 3 Inquisitors).

There is an opening in the wall here, once covered by a lion's head, into the mouth of which (called *Bocca di Leone*) secret charges against supposed enemies of the state were placed, from the outside.

Photo ALINARI, ANDERSON.

VENICE — *PALACE OF THE DOGES.*

HALL OF THE STATUES.
Archeological Museum.

DOGE LOREDAN BEFORE THE VIRGIN.
By PIETRO LOMBARDO.

The *Archeological Museum* occupies that part of the palace which was once set apart for the private apartment of the Doge. The collection includes many Greek and Roman sculptures in marble formerly the property of Cardinal Domenico Grimani, and bequeathed to the Venetian Republic in 1523. (The *Museum* has been transferred in the Royal Palace).

LOGGIA OF THE DOGES' PALACE
overlooking the Piazza San Marco.

THE ISLAND OF SAN GIORGIO
seen from the Loggia of the Doges' Palace.

The two magnificent bronze well-heads in the courtyard of the Doges' Palace were executed by ALBORGHETTI and NICCOLÒ CONTI in 1556-59.

BRONZE WELL-HEAD. A. D. 1556.

Photo ALINARI, ANDERSON.

VENICE — THE CHURCHES.

ISLAND AND CHURCH OF SAN GIORGIO. A. D. 1566-1610.

The Church of *San Giorgio Maggiore* was begun in 1566 by PALLADIO, but he did not live to finish it and the work was continued by *Antonio Palliari*, who designed the façade. The simple interior is remarkable for its austere beauty and noble proportions. The church possesses several good paintings. A fine view of Venice may be enjoyed from the top of the campanile (195 ft.).

SANTA MARIA DELLA SALUTE. Erected A. D. 1632-56.

Santa Maria della Salute was erected in 1632-56 by the architect LONGHENA, by order of the Senate, as a votive offering to the Virgin for having stayed the plague which devastated the city in the year 1630.

The interior is circular with rectangular altar-recesses and contains excellent paintings by eminent masters. In the sacristy is *Titian's* " St. Mark with four other saints," and *Tintoretto's* " Marriage at Cana," both illustrated here. The latter an immense picture painted for the refectory of the Brotherhood *dei Crociferi*, is one of the few which the master signed.

GATHERING OF THE MANNA. By TINTORETTO. (S. Giorgio).

Here the scene is laid in a spacious and beautiful landscape, in which many details of a domestic character have been introduced. In the centre are groups of women sewing, washing clothes, spinning and grinding manna, on the left a man is making shoes, while others are forging; in the right foreground Moses is seated; in the distance is the Israelite host.

ST. MARK AND FOUR SAINTS. Painting by TITIAN.

THE LAST SUPPER. By TINTORETTO. (S. Giorgio).

This work, remarkable for its effects of light and shade, is as far removed as possible from the solemn conception of Leonardo's composition in Milan. The company (except for Judas) is all seated on one side of the table. In the foreground kneels a comely serving-woman taking out dishes from a basket; round about are servants busy bringing more food.... It is a supper, a veritable repast !

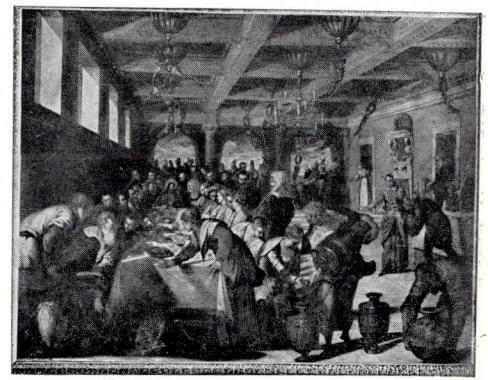

THE MARRIAGE AT CANA IN GALILEE. By TINTORETTO. (Santa Maria della Salute).

— 129 —

Photo ALINARI, ANDERSON, BROGI.

17. - WONDERS OF ITALY.

VENICE — SANTA MARIA GLORIOSA DE' FRARI.

Church of Santa Maria Gloriosa dei Frari (1330-1417).    St. Jerome. By A. Vittoria.

The *Church of Santa Maria Gloriosa dei Frari* (or simply " I Frari ") is a Franciscan Gothic church, built in 1330-1517, regarded as the *Pantheon* of Venice; many famous Venetians, — painters, sculptors and a few eloges — were buried within its walls. The " Frari " is also celebrated for the magnificent altarpiece presented by wealthy and noble families, either in devotion or self-glorification.

As in the church of SS. Giovanni e Paolo, there are at the " Frari " a considerable number of tombs of all periods. The simplest type of monument (early 14th century) consists of an effigy of the departed one with his hands crossed over breast, nearly always lying on a sarcophagus, supported by consols or placed in a niche.

Towards the end of the 14th century, the sarcophagus has additional decorations; a canopy, an alcone with curtains held apart by angels (see page 109); a small vault. The tomb of the unfortunate doge Francesco Foscari (15th cent., is a work of art which represents a period of transition between the Gothic and the Renaissance styles (see illustration on following page).

But as time went on and from the beginning of the 16th cent. the small vault was enlarged more and more until it formed a vast façade or a colossal triumphal arch.

The tomb changes to heroic pomp; vanity of man has no limits, he wants babylonian mausoleums and the architect puts his talent at the disposal of the noble families who think more of the glory of their grandsons than that of their ancestors and give them a tomb of very rare and precious marbles. The history of the Venetians might be illustrated by the aid of these monuments, which from the early simplicity pass on to increasing splendour and then to extravagance.

Madonna and Saints.
By Bartolommeo Vivarini.   Madonna and Saints. By Giovanni Bellini. A. D. 1488.

Altarpiece *Madonna and Saints*, Known as the " Frari Madonna ", is one of the most delightful works of Bellini. In a gilded niche, Our Lady rich blue robes, sits enthroned with the Infant standing on her knee. Below are two charming little angels, one plucks the strings of a lute, while the other blows a pipe. In the side panels are four noble figures of saints. The color is rich and mellow and the whole work impresses alike for its mystical feeling and for its grave beauty.

Photo Alinari, Anderson.

VENICE — SANTA MARIA GLORIOSA DE' FRARI

TOMB OF DOGE F. FOSCARI.
By A. e P. BREGNO.

TOMB OF CANOVA († 1822).
Executed by the master's pupils.

MONUMENT OF TITIAN († 1576).
By LUIGI and PIETRO ZANDOMENIGHI.

The *Madonna of the Pesaro Family* is the most celebrated altarpiece by Titian. It was presented to the "Frari" by Jacopo Pesaro, Bishop of Paphos in Cyprus, and commander of the Papal fleet, as a thanksgiving for his successfull expedition against the Turks.

The Virgin sits on her throne, bending down and gazing with benevolence at the donor himself kneeling at the foot of the steps. Just below her sits St. Peter holding a book, he interrupts his reading and turns to look down at the bishop. Behind the latter is a knight in armour (St. George?), holding a banner on which the arms of Alexander VI. (Borgia) are blazoned; the captive Turk beside the knight symbolises the victory of Jacopo Pesaro over the Infidel. On the right of the picture is seen St. Francis commending to the Virgin the other members of the Pesaro family kneeling humbly.

The composition and the coloring are masterly, the portrait faces admirable.

Altarpiece *Assumption*, by Titian, formerly in the Venice Academy, represents the culmination of Venetian art both for its dramatic movement and for the richness of color. The Virgin here is a powerful figure, borne upwards as if divinely impelled; her face is transfigured with gladness as she ascends into the presence of the Almighty to whom an angel brings the crown to be placed on the Madonna's head. In the terrestrial and lower part of the picture stand the Apostles, with uplifted heads and arms indicating with their passionate gestures various degrees of admiration and astonishment.

MADONNA OF THE PESARO FAMILY, *by* TITIAN (*1526*).

THE ASSUMPTION OF THE VIRGIN, *by* TITIAN (*1518*).

Photo ALINARI, ANDERSON, BROGI.

VENICE — SS. GIOVANNI E PAOLO.

ST. AUGUSTINE. *By* VIVARINI.

ST. ANTONINUS. *By* LORENZO LOTTO.

MONUMENT TO COLLEONI.

This most admirable monument was exposed to public view on the 21st of March 1496.

Bartolommeo Colleoni, the famous *condottiere* in the service of Venice, on his death, in 1475, bequeathed a large portion of his immense wealth to the Republic on condition that his statue should be erected on horseback in the Piazza di San Marco. An ancient law, however, forbade the erection of monuments in St. Mark's Square, and the Senate, by an ingenious quibble, evaded the condition by erecting it in the *Piazza* of the Scuola *di S. Marco.*

The monument was first designed (1481) by ANDREA VERROCCHIO, the Florentine painter and sculptor, pupil of Donatello and master of Leonardo da Vinci. The example of the Gattamelata monument at Padua (p. 155), inspired the conception of Andrea's model. Andrea died before the work was completed, and the task of finishing it was given to the Venetian sculptor ALESSANDRO LEOPARDI. To Verrocchio is due the general conception of the statue; but the breath of life that animates both horse and rider, the energy and the fiery spirit of the mighty soldier it commemorates, the richness of detail that enhances the massive grandeur of the group is to be assigned to Leopardi. The Venetian artist also designed the very elegant pedestal, and his name is inscribed on the statue.

"The stalwart figure of Colleoni, clad in armour, with a helmet upon his head, is the most perfect embodiment of the idea which history gives us of an Italian Condottiere. As his horse, with arched neck and slightly bent head, paces slowly forward, he, sitting straight in his saddle, turns to look over his left shoulder, showing us a sternly-marked countenance, with deep-set eyes whose steady intensity of expression reveals a character of iron which never recoiled before any obstacle." (Perkins, *Tuscan Sculptors*).

The Church of *SS. Giovanni e Paolo*, next to St. Mark's, the most important in Venice, is a Gothic edifice begun in 1234, but not finished and consecrated till 1430. The interior, in the form of a Latin cross, produces a great impression both by the vastness of its dimensions, and by the numerous works of art it contains. Like the "Frari," the walls of the church are adorned with sumptuous monuments of Doges, patricians, admirals, generals and artists (the Bellini brothers and Palma Giovane are interred here). These were the two churches in which patricians desired to be buried, and glorified in the minds of the public. "To give posterity an impressive and durable likeness of their heroes," writes Mauclair, "was a characteristic trait of Venetian psychology. Moreover, such a likeness lent itself better than any other, to that intimate fusion of architecture and statuary which corresponded with the taste of the race. These ornamental combinations, seen against the walls of their basilicas, presented in their special light, participating in rich surroundings of mosaics and colored marbles, appealed to the Venetian imagination very differently from isolated statues seen against the sky. These tombs are moreover splendid conceptions, which create a noble and opulent impression a true setting for the apotheosis of the great dead."

BARTOLOMMEO COLLEONI. *By* VERROCCHIO *and* LEOPARDI.

MONUMENT OF DOGE MOROSINI. (Gothic).

— 132 —

Photo ALINARI, ANDERSON, BROGI.

VENICE — CHURCH OF SS. GIOVANNI E PAOLO.

THE DOMINICAN CHURCH OF SS. GIOVANNI E PAOLO,
and (left) the « Scuola di San Marco ».
In the square is the Colleoni monument (p. 132).

ALTARPIECE OF ST. MAGDALENE.

TOMB OF DOGE A. VENDRAMIN.
By A. LEOPARDI and T. LOMBARDO (*XV cent.*).

TOMB OF DOGE P. MONCENIGO. (*Detail*.)
By LOMBARDO. (*VX cent.*).

TOMB OF DOGE M. COSNER.
After NINO PISANO. (*XIV cent.*).

PORTAL. SCUOLA DI SAN MARCO.

The building adjoining the church is the *Scuola di San Marco*, now the city hospital. Its rich façade is justly termed one of the triumphs of Venetian early Renaissance. In the lunette over the portal is a relief of St. Mark surrounded by his fraternity; the two reliefs below representing miracles of St. Mark, and the lions in feigned perspective, are by *Tullio Lombardi.*

SCUOLA DI S. MARCO (Ospedale Civico). *Rebuilt in 1485 by the* LOMBARDI.

Photo ALINARI, ANDERSON, BROGI.

VENICE — THE CHURCHES.

THE SUPPER AT EMMAUS. By GIOV. BELLINI.
(Church of S. Salvatore).

MADONNA AND CHILD. By A. VIVARINI.
(Church of the Redentore).

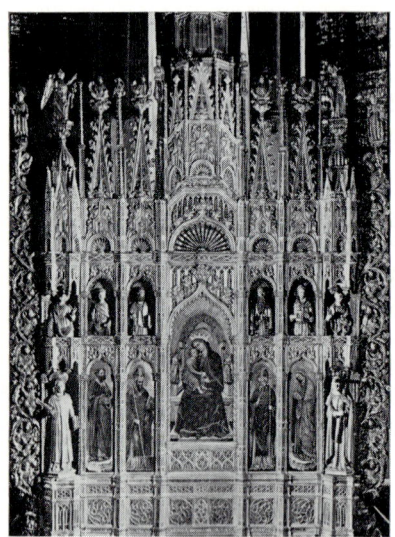

GREAT ALTARPIECE.
By A. VIVARINI - G. D'ALEMAGNA.
(Church of S. Zaccaria).

Nearly every church in Venice is rich in art treasures, both in painting and in sculpture, but it is impossible to do more than indicate a few of them here. *Titian's* famous « Martyrdom of St. Lawrence », in the church of *I Gesuiti*, is one of the most impressive compositions in spite of the darkening of the picture. It seems a fantasy of some Italian Rembrandt, a vision in gloom. The scene is laid in a wide street with an architectural background. It is night; at first nothing is distinguishable but a great blackness vaguely spotted with two or three lights coming from lanterns of burning fuel held at the end of a stick, and from a break in the clouds through which a luminous flame descends like a glory on the figure of the martyr who lies on a brazier surrounded by executioners. This fine altarpiece was painted in 1558, and together with many other works of art was taken to Paris in 1797.

MARTYRDOM OF ST. LAWRENCE.
By TITIAN. (Church of I Gesuiti).

CHURCH OF SAN ZACCARIA.
Erected in 1458.

MADONNA. By PALMA VECCHIO.

MADONNA. By GIOV. BELLINI.

Paintings in the Church of San Zaccaria.

— 134 —

VENICE — THE CHURCHES.

ST. FRANCIS.
Marble by T. LOMBARDI.
Church of S. M dei Miracoli).

Interior.   CHURCH OF SANTA MARIA DE' MIRACOLI.   Façade.
The church of *Santa Maria dei Miracoli*, designed by *Pietro Lombardo* (1481-89), is a gem of Renaissance architecture. On the façade are charming marble incrustations.

THE FEAST IN THE HOUSE OF LEVI.
By MORETTO DA BRESCIA. (*Church of the Pietà*).

THE NUPTIALS OF ST. CATHERINE.
By PAOLO VERONESE. (*S. Caterina*).

Near the church of St. Giovanni Grisostomo is the so-called *Corte del Milione*, the home of the Polo family which Marco, while a mere youth, left in 1271, with his father and his uncle Matteo, for the East. After crossing Asia, Marco arrived at the court of the Great Khan, the Tartar emperor of China, by whom he was received with favour and employed on several embassies. A quarter of a century later the three wanderers, dressed in coarse garb and speaking broken Venetian with a Tartar accent arrived in Venice (1295) laden with fabulous wealth: precious stones, gold, brocaded silks and velvets which had been given them. Having fallen into the hands of the Genoese at the disastrous battle of Curzola, Marco Polo was carried to Genoa and kept a prisoner for three years. It was during his captivity there that he wrote a story of his travels, his errands and his embassies undertaken at the order of the Khan; the first account, it seems, that opened up to wondering Europe the magnificence of the Eastern world. The *Travels of Marco Polo*, a delightful reading, fired the imagination of the people with tales of wonderful cities and the millions of treasure he had seen—Messer Marco *Milione*, they called him.

ST. CHRISTOPHER AND SAINTS.
By SEB. DEL PIOMBO. (*S. Giovanni Grisostomo*).

— 135 —

Photo ALINARI, ANDERSON, BROGI.

VENICE — THE CHURCHES.

Palma Vecchio's "Santa Barbara," the central panel of a large altarpiece, is probably the finest thing the master ever painted. The saint was the patroness of artillery and fortifications, and the picture was executed for the altar of the Venetian "Bombardieri." She is represented standing on a pedestal flanked by two cannons, a majestic and beautiful queen-like woman, crowned and holding her martyr's palm 'like a field marshal's baton.'

CHURCH OF SANTA MARIA FORMOSA.

The church of *Santa Maria Formosa*, consecrated to the Feast of the Purification or Candlemas, is one of the oldest in Venice, but was entirely restored in the 16th century. In the interior is *Palma Vecchio's* grandiose "St. Barbara."

SANTA BARBARA
By PALMA VECCHIO, ca. 1561.
(*Church of S. Maria Formosa*).

MADONNA AND CHILD.
By NEGROPONTE. (*S. Francesco*).

BAPTISM OF CHRIST. *By* CIMA.
(*Church of S. Giovanni in Bragora*).

THE INSTITUTION OF THE ROSARY.
Ceiling fresco by TIEPOLO. (*I Gesuati*).

Giovanni Battista Tiepolo (1695-1770), distinguished himself as a great draughtsman and a splendid colorist. Gifted with a brilliant fancy, and master of all the resources of his art, he was the Paolo Veronese of the 18th century,—the last of the old painters and the first of the moderns. The churches and palaces of Venice are full of the fairy-like creations of this master who excelled principally in fresco and ceiling decorations. (*See also*, pp. 144, 145).

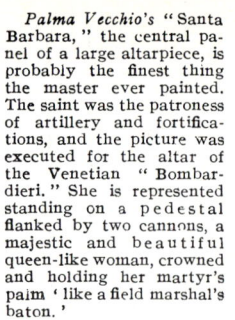

MADONNA AND SAINTS.
By TIEPOLO (*Church of I Gesuati*).

CHURCH DEGLI SCALZI.
By LONGHENA. (*16th cent.*).

— 136 —

VENICE — THE CHURCHES.

SANTA MARIA DELL'ORTO. *Gothic façade, 1460.*

PRESENTATION OF THE VIRGIN (detail), *by* TINTORETTO. (*Santa Maria dell'Orto*).

MARTYRDOM OF SS. MARCUS AND MARCELLINUS.
Painted by PAOLO VERONESE. (*Church of San Sebastiano*).

APOTHEOSIS OF ST. SEBASTIAN.
By PAOLO VERONESE.

The *Church of San Sebastiano* erected early in the 16th century, contains numerous admirable paintings of *Paolo Veronese*, as well as the sepulture of the master himself.

The picture given above is considered one of Veronese's best works. The scene is laid upon a flight of steps before a Renaissance palace. The two saints, Marcus and Marcellinus, with their hands and feet bound, are being led to martyrdom. Their sorrowing mother gesticulating, entreats them to save their lives by renouncing their faith. On the right the grey-headed father also implores them, women and children endeavour to persuade the martyrs to desist. But St. Sebastian, a fine powerful figure in armour, bearing a standard, encourages his fellow-sufferers by pointing towards heaven with an inspired look. The dramatic action and the expressions of the onlookers' faces is masterful.

The "Apotheosis of St. Sebastian," in the choir of the church, is another masterpiece of art. Here the saint is seen bound to the pillar at which he was shot with arrows. On the right is St. Mark, patron of Venice with his gospel, and St. Francis of Assisi with the cross and showing his stigmata; on the left is St. John the Baptist, St. Catherine of Alexandria and St. Elizabeth; above is the Virgin and Child surrounded by angel musicians, assisting the martyr in his last moments.

FINAL MARTYRDOM OF ST. SEBASTIAN.
By PAOLO VERONESE.
(*Church of San Sebastiano*).

Photo ALINARI, ANDERSON.

— 137 —

VENICE — ACCADEMIA DI BELLE ARTI. (Academy).

The *Accademia di Belle Arti* is one of the great sights of Venice: 'a feast of color, and a dream of artistic beauty.'

The Collection comprises about 800 pictures—chiefly by Venetian masters—brought here from suppressed churches, monasteries, and charitable guilds (Scuole). The gallery occupies the site of the old church, monastery and Scuola della Carità; some of the halls still retaining their old shape and primitive splendid ceilings.

GILDED WOODEN CEILING with portraits of painters. Guest chamber of the *Scuola della Carità*.

MADONNA OF THE TREES. By GIOVANNI BELLINI, 1487.

This immense ceiling is the work of MARIO COZZI a famous wood-carver of the 15th century. Each panel has a cherub with eight wings, and tradition has it that in these figures there is an allusion to the name of Aliotti, (ali-otto = eight wings), a member of the Congregation of Charity and donor of the decoration. The small arches have portraits of Venetian painters.

ST. GEORGE. By ANDREA MANTEGNA.

THE ANNUNCIATION. By PAOLO VERONESE.

This picture by JACOBELLO DEL FIORE, painted in 1432 for the cathedral of Ceneda, has such a wealth of figures that it was called the « Painting of Paradise ».

In the centre, on a raised throne below which are the four Evangelists and seven Angels, Christ is crowning the Virgin. At each side a crowd of angels and saints, the latter displaying scrolls on which their names are written.

In the foreground is kneeling the donor, the Bishop Antonio di Carrero. On the extreme left are four nuns, and on the extreme right four monks, each accompanied by an Angel.

CORONATION OF THE VIRGIN. Paradise. By JACOBELLO DEL FIORE. Early fifteenth century.

CORONATION OF THE VIRGIN. By G. D'ALEMAGNA and A. VIVARINI.

Photo ALINARI, ANDERSON.

VENICE — ACCADEMIA DI BELLE ARTI. (Academy).

THE FEAST IN THE HOUSE OF LEVI. *Painted by* PAOLO VERONESE. A. D. 1573.

Paolo Veronese's "Feast in the House of Levi" is one of the most famous works of the master, who has used (as was habitual to him), the biblical incident as a pretext for grouping richly dressed patricians in a most gorgeous imaginary architecture. Beneath the central portico Christ is seated at the table between SS. Peter and John. Among the lordly guests dressed in Venetian costume are many contemporary portraits, and the figure of the gallant nobleman in the left foreground giving orders to the attendants, is a portrait of Veronese himself.

This huge canvas (40 ft. by 19 ft.) was painted for the Refectory of the Dominican monastery of SS. Giovanni e Paolo. Such subjects—like the Last Supper, and the Marriage at Cana, were usually selected for the decoration of refectories.

The sense of space in this composition is boundless and it somewhat dwarfs the figures which are painted dark against the luminous sky, thus giving a new effect in painting.

So many secular episodes have been introduced by the master that he was exposed to the censure of the Inquisitors, who were especially scandalised at the introduction of a Disciple picking his teeth with a fork.

The "Madonna of St. Job," made for the church of that name about 1480, is one of the finest works of Giovanni Bellini. The Virgin's face noble and sweet has the sentiment of the Venetian school. "How admirably," writes F. J. Mather, Jr. "the strict symmetry of the group is relieved by varying the postures of the six saints and by contrasting the sober garb of the monkish saints with the superb nudity of Saints Job and Sebastian and the shimmering silks of the playing angels below."

MADONNA *by* BELLINI.
Detail of the San Giobbe altarpiece.

ALTARPIECE from the Church of San Giobbe.
By GIOVANNI BELLINI (ca. 1480).

ALLEGORIES. *By* GIOVANNI BELLINI.

These charming little pictures are panels from the lid of a *cassone*. On the left is «Knowledge» in a boat; in the centre "Fortune," a harpy-like blindfolded female with bird's feet and wings; on the right "Truth" holding a mirror.

MADONNA with St. Paul and St. George. *By* GIOV. BELLINI.

Photo ALINARI, ANDERSON, BROGI.

« Corpus Christi » Procession in the Piazza of St. Mark. *Painted by* Gentile Bellini. a. d. 1496.

This picture illustrates a miracle of the True Cross. « While a relic of the Cross was being carried in procession on St. John's Day, a merchant of Brescia whose son lay dying prayed fervently to the Relic and the youth was saved ». The merchant is seen kneeling behind the baldacchino under which the reliquary is borne; the baldacchino is decorated with the arms of the guilds of Venice. In the long procession to the right, the Doge is seen under the State umbrella with the Procurators of St. Mark, senators and chamberlains.

This composition is of a special interest as it portrays faithfully the Piazza and façade of St. Mark's as it was in 1496. The old mosaics on the façade are now in many cases replaced by modern ones (see p. 90); the Procuratie Vecchie are there but not the Clock Tower; houses then adjoined the Campanile; the façade of St. Mark's and the Porta della Carta are richly gilded,—the whole is a gorgeous piece of color.

Portrait of a Man.
By Antonello da Messina.

Miraculous Finding of a Fragment
of the « True Cross » which had fallen into the Canal.
Painted by Gentile Bellini. a. d. 1500.

Gentile Bellini (1429-1507) was fond of painting processions and crowded scenes. This and the picture given above show the master's "remarkable ability for treating historical subjects, his power of giving individuality of expression and action to the numerous figures he introduces into them, and of representing with correctness elaborate architectural backgrounds." (*See also* p. 60).

This work, like the one above, illustrates a miracle of the True Cross. « In crossing a bridge during a procession to the Church of San Lorenzo, a relic of the Holy Cross falls into the canal. Several persons plunge in to rescue it, but none succeed in recovering it except the chief of the Confraternity, Andrea Vendramin (afterwards doge) who is seen holding up the Relic miraculously buoyed up by it ».

The scene is treated with great *naïveté*. In the foreground to the right are seen the donors kneeling, to the left, at the head of the Venetian ladies along the quay witnessing the miracle a portrait of Caterina Cornaro, Queen of Cyprus, has been introduced.

Photo Alinari, Anderson, Brogi.

VENICE — ACCADEMIA DI BELLE ARTI. (Academy).

HISTORY OF ST. URSULA. *By* VITTORE CARPACCIO. A. D. 1490-96.
Left, Conon takes leave of his father; *right*, St. Ursula takes leave of her parents; *centre*, the meeting of Conon and his bride.

The *stories* of St. Ursula, monument of Christian art, were painted by *Vittore Carpaccio* in 1490-96 for the Chapel of the Scuola di Sant'Orsola. The compositions, based on the *Golden Legend* of Jacopo de Varagine, are the following: 1. The ambassadors of the pagan king of England, father of Prince Conon, arrive at the court of the Christian king Maurus to ask for the hand of his daughter Ursula; 2. Departure of the ambassadors with the answer that the bride desires to postpone the wedding in order to make a pilgrimage to Rome, accompanied by eleven thousand virgins; 3. Return of the ambassadors to England and delivery of their message; 4. Meeting of Conon and Ursula (see illustration); 5. Arrival in Rome: Ursula, her companions, and the prince receive the blessing of the Pope; 6. Dream of St. Ursula: an angel announces her martyrdom; 7. Arrival of St. Ursula at Cologne; 8. Martyrdom of the saint and her companions, Her funeral; 9. Apotheosis of St Ursula and her eleven thousand virgins.

The child-like legend of the young virgin is narrated in a simple but lively style, and the compositions are interesting on account of the picturesqueness of their settings, and the faithful rendering of the Venetian life of Carpaccio's time. The numerous figures are robed in costumes of infinite variety, the various embassies, the meetings and partings, the subordinate incidents are all treated with the most lively fancy.

MADONNA AND SAINTS.
By CIMA DA CONEGLIANO.

PRESENTATION OF JESUS AT THE TEMPLE
By VITTORE CARPACCIO. A. D. 1510.

ST. URSULA'S DREAM. ST. URSULA'S OBSEQUIES (detail).
Paintings by VITTORE CARPACCIO († 1525).

This altar screen, executed for the church of San Giobbe, was soon to rival the already famous one of Bellini in the same church (see p. 139). It is a masterpiece " of delicate and moral gentleness." To the right, St. Simon, clothed in a magnificent cloak, is advancing followed by two Levites and bowing to the Virgin who shows him the Infant Jesus. To the left are the Prophetess Anna and a woman who is carrying two turtle doves in a basket. "Never has Carpaccio come nearer to Bellini than in this painting, for if he has remained inferior to his rival in richness of colour, he has more than equalled him in the precision and severity of the figures. He did more; he surpassed him in the greatness of his composition and by the cleverness with which he combines the movements of the various characters of his subjects ». *Crowe and Cavalcaselle.*

— 141 —

ST. MARK RESCUING A CONDEMNED SLAVE.
By JACOPO TINTORETTO.

MADONNA AND SAINTS.
By PAOLO VERONESE.

The subject of this celebrated picture is taken from the Golden Legend. "A Christian slave, in the service of a certain nobleman of Provence, disobeyed the commands of his master and persisted in worshipping at the shrine of St. Mark, which was at some distance. On his return home, the master infuriated, ordered his eyes to be torn out. The instruments of torture, however, were miraculously blunted. The executioners then tried to cut off his legs, but the spade shattered." In the centre of the composition the tortured slave, unharmed, lies on the ground amid a crowd of spectators who look on animated by all the various emotions of sympathy, rage and terror. The executioners, holding up the broken implements are confounded, the oppressor on an elevated seat to the right bends forward amazed, while St. Mark rushes down like lightning from heaven to save his worshipper.

This is one of Tintoretto's masterpieces, a work of skilful foreshortenings and brilliant color.

THE INCREDULITY OF ST. THOMAS.
By CIMA (Giovanni Battista da Conegliano)
(1459-1517).

THE VIRGIN, THE INFANT JESUS, AND THE DOCTORS OF THE CHURCH.
By GIOVANNI ALEMANNO *and* ANTONIO VIVARINI.

The "Incredulity of St. Thomas" painted for the Oratory of the Guild of Masons, is a work of striking effect which unites a great richness of colour with a great clearness of contour. "The beauty of this painting," writes Gino Fogolari, "lies above all in the art of making the figures stand out against a very clear sky.... the naked Christ in this clear light is a miracle of clearness and beauty."

Painted for the hall of the "Albergo"—*Scuola della Carità*—where it may still be seen, this painting is the work of two masters who worked together from 1445. The Virgin, seated on a throne surmounted by a canopy, the columns of which are supported by four angels, is holding the Infant Jesus who is handing her a pomegranate : the large number of its seeds symbolises how the Word of Christ will spread throughout the world. On the left is St. Jerome in cardinal's robes, and St. Gregory the Great with the Dove representing the Holy Ghost on his shoulder. On the right is St. Augustine holding a book, and St. Ambrose Archbishop of Milan with a whip in his hand. The wealth of ornament and the magnificent robes give a great charm to this work of art.

Photo ALINARI, ANDERSON.

VENICE — ACCADEMIA DI BELLE ARTI. (Academy).

PRESENTATION OF THE VIRGIN IN THE TEMPLE. *Painted by* TITIAN *in* A. D. 1534-38.

PIETÀ. *By* TITIAN A. D. 1576. (*The master's last work*).

This pathetic picture begun by Titian for his own tomb and left unfinished at his death, was completed by *Palma Giovane*. On the right is Joseph of Arimathea, on the left the Magdalene; in the niches are statues of Moses and a Sibyl.

In this exceedingly beautiful picture, now restored to its original place, Titian has treated its subject as a domestic pageant of his own time. At the top of the grand staircase the High Priest, attended by a Levite, awaits Our Lady, who ascends the steps of the temple in a halo of radiance. Below, at the foot of the stairs, are her parents amid an assembly of stately beautiful Venetian ladies and gentlemen, obviously portraits, who look on with wonderment at the brave child. She pauses on the first landing, and with daintily gesture gathers up her pretty blue skirts before proceeding. In the foreground to the right sits an old peasant woman with a basket of eggs, gazing at the scene with evident curiosity. (This is said to be a portrait of Titian's mother). In the distance is an excellent view of Titian's own country of Cadore.

ST. JOHN THE BAPTIST. *By* TITIAN. (1477-1576).

THE RICH MAN'S PEAST OR DIVES AND LAZARUS.
Painted by BONIFAZIO VERONESE.

Bonifazio's " Lazarus and Dives " is a picture of the most exquisite sentiment, — the work of a man of poetic mind, who had observed keenly, and felt and thought deeply. Dives (a portrait of Henry VIII. of England) sits at table, richly clad, between two courtesans in gorgeous costume. The wealthy voluptuary is exchanging some words with his companion while he clasps the hand of the other, younger and more beautiful woman who listens to music in a pensive attitude, as if recalling the days of her innocence. The trio of musicians and the page holding the book of music, also deserve close study. To the right, Lazarus is seen begging, while a dog licks his sores. In the distance, several domestic episodes are represented: horses are being exercised, hawks trained, peacocks, etc.

The picture is said to have been painted by the order of Cardinal Grimani who wished to have thus portrayed Henry VIII. and Anne Boleyn, as a reflection on the king's antipapal policy. But in recalling the two famous personages, the artist only painted Venetian refinement; the introduction of Lazarus is a mere pretext for depicting a splendid lordly entertainment on the terrace of one of those beautiful marble palaces on the Grand Canal.

Photo ALINARI, ANDERSON.

VENICE — ACCADEMIA DI BELLE ARTI. (Academy).

PORTRAIT OF THE DOGE MOCENIGO.
By TINTORETTO.

THE FISHERMAN PRESENTING ST. MARK'S RING TO THE DOGE. By PARIS BORDONE.

Bordone's « Consignment of the Ring », is justly considered one of the most beautiful ceremonial pictures in existence. It is the masterpiece of the painter and commemorates the following legend : « One winter night in the year 1340, Venice was visited by an awful tempest which threatened to destroy the city. A poor fisherman, who with difficulty had reached the molo near St. Mark's, was making fast his boat when a grave old man accosted him and offered a large sum to be ferried over to San Giorgio Maggiore. The fisherman, fearful of the storm, would not venture, but finally rowed him over to the island. Here a knight in armour entered the boat and commanded that they should be rowed to San Niccolò di Lido. The fisherman remonstrated the danger of going with a single oar, but being urged and reassured by the strangers, went on, and though the storm was at its highest it seemed to him as if the waters were smooth. Arrived at San Niccolò, a third person, a venerable old man, joined them and the fisherman was ordered to make for the open sea. When they reached the Adriatic they beheld a ship filled with devils sailing swiftly forward to wreak destruction on Venice.

The three strangers rose, made the sign of the cross, and immediately ship and devils vanished, the storm ceased, and Venice was saved. The three strangers then revealed themselves as St. Mark, St. George and St. Niccolò, and asked the fisherman to be rowed back each to the place where he had embarked. When at last he had landed St. Mark at the molo, the fisherman, not satisfied with the honour of taking part in the miracle, demanded the promised payment.

" Thou art right, " answered the saint taking his ring from his finger and handing it to the fisherman, " go to the Doge with this ring, tell what thou hast seen, and ask thy reward. " The fisherman was persuaded and presented himself before the Doge next morning with the ring. The Procurators having sent for the sacred ring which was usually kept in a locked sanctuary in the treasury of St. Mark's church, found it missing, though the lock had not been tampered with. Thereupon they knew that this was a great miracle and the fisherman spoke the truth. A solemn procession was ordained, giving thanks to God for the averted danger, and the fisherman rewarded with a pension for life.

In his composition, Bordone has chosen the moment when the old fisherman, escorted by a chamberlain, mounts the steps and humbly presents to the Doge the sacred ring. The scene is laid in a magnificent marble hall. The Doge sits enthroned in his state robes, on either side of him are dignified Senators, at the foot of the stairs is another chamberlain and a group of Venetian gentlemen : all portraits. In the foreground the fisherman's lad sits carelessly on the steps near his grand-father's gondola; the building in the background is reminiscent of Sansovino's Library (p. 87).

In Bordone's composition the sumptuous architecture, the luminous colours the numerous figures with their gorgeous costumes, give a vivid idea of the magnificence and luxury of Venetian painting.

THE CALLING OF THE SONS OF ZEBEDEE.
By MARCO BASAITI.

THE PURIFICATION.
By JACOPO TINTORETTO.

PORTRAIT.
By ROSALBA CARRIERA.
Pastellist (1676-1758).

What strikes one in Basaiti's painting, "The calling of the Apostles," is the picturesqueness of composition "so full of religious tenderness." On the shore of the Lake Tiberias, Christ between St. Peter and St. Andrew is raising His hand to bless the three people who are stepping on shore. The first, James, is kneeling, and John, his brother, is advancing reverently, while their father gets out of the boat, where the fishermen's nets are piled. Fishing boats are crossing the lake, and in the background is the town of Zabulon.

Photo ALINARI, ANDERSON.

THE VIRGIN AND CHILD
WITH SS. LIBERALE AND FRANCIS.
BY GIORGIONE. (*Church of Castelfranco*).

APOLLO AND DAPHNE. BY GIORGIONE. (*Seminario Patriarcale*).

Giorgione's famous altarpiece, painted about 1504 for the cathedral of Castelfranco, where it remains to day, is composed in Bellini's style, but the landscape in the background with an effect of distance is delightful.

"LA TEMPESTA."
THE STORM, or THE PAINTER'S FAMILY.
BY GIORGIONE. (*Academy*).
Once in the Palazzo Giovanelli.

This little "genre" picture is the most beautiful work of Giorgione. The subject is mysterious: it is supposed that the young shepherd is the painter himself, and the woman nursing a fine baby, his wife; for this reason, this composition resembling a domestic scene is called "The Painter's Family". The storm, in a landscape full of freshness, with its shadows, its flashes of lightning and its thunder, is strikingly effective. In the background is Castelfranco, the native town of Giorgione.

INVENTION OF THE
HOLY CROSS.
BY TIEPOLO.
(*Academy*).

ANGELS RESCUING SOULS FROM PURGATORY. BY TIEPOLO. (*Scuola dei Carmini*).

Photo ALINARI, ANDERSON, BROGI.

VENICE — SCUOLA DI SAN GIORGIO DEGLI SCHIAVONI.

The *Scuola* or Brotherhood of St. George of the Slavonians, was established in 1452, by a few wealthy Dalmatian merchants, for the relief of old and poor Dalmatian sailors and for the education of the needy children of thei race. The small oratory of this confraternity, the only place in the city that retains its primitive paintings still set in the original carved and gilded wainscoting, is the most fascinating Renaissance chapel in Venice. These paintings which illustrate the lives of St. George, St. Tryphonius and St. Jerome, the patron saints of the Guild, are among the most exquisite works of Carpaccio who executed them about 1502-1511. The finest of the scenes are those of St. Jerome in his sumptuous studio, and the three scenes relating to the chivalric legend of St. George. The latter Saint was born of Cristian parents in Cappadocia, and was an officer in the Roman army. One day in travelling to join his legion he came to a town in Libya whose inhabitants were terrorized and destroyed by a monstruous dragon which infested the neighbouring desert. The people had given him all their flocks and herds, and when these were exhausted, they were daily forced to bribe him with two of their children and young people taken by lot. The day St. George rode into the town the lot had fallen upon the king's daughter and she was being led forth to her fate amid wailing and lamentation; but the Saint having heard the cause of all this grief, declared he would deliver her and the city through the power of Jesus Christ. As soon as the dragon appeared St. George spurred intrepidly his horse and immediately pierced the throat of the monster with his lance. Then he took the maiden's girdle, tied it round the creature's neck, and gave the girdle to her hand, and the conquered and crestfallen dragon crawled after them like a dog. In this guise

ORATORY OF THE SCUOLA DI SAN GIORGIO.

ST. JEROME IN HIS STUDY. *By* CARPACCIO.

ST. GEORGE VANQUISHING THE DRAGON.

ST. GEORGE LEADING THE DRAGON INTO THE CITY.

they entered the Pagan city. The people were terrified and fled, but St. George reassured them and promised that if they would be baptized and believe in the God through whose power he had wrought the deed, he would slay the beast in their

ST. GEORGE BAPTIZING THE KING AND PRINCESS,

ST. TRYPHONIUS SUBDUES A BASILISK.

presence. The Kind and all the inhabitants, to the number of twenty thousand, were at once converted, and were baptized in one day. Then St. George smote off the dragon's head, and the King loaded him with gifts, but he gave them all to the poor and went his way.

Photo ALINARI, ANDERSON.

VENICE — SCUOLA DI SAN ROCCO.

The *Scuola di San Rocco* is celebrated for the numerous works of Tintoretto it contains. The name *scuola* means a religious fraternity or charitable guild, and St. Roch's wealthy fraternity was instituted in 1478, for the purpose of tending the sick and poor, and particularly those attacked by the plague. The building (p. 153) erected in 1524-60 was designed by Bartolommeo Buon of Bergamo. The interior is a perfect gallery, the walls of the lofty halls being decorated with a series of fifty-six large paintings by Tintoretto. Like Masaccio's frescoes in the Brancacci Chapel, and those of Michelangelo in the Sistine, these works were a source of inspiration to contemporary and later students.

In the lower hall are scenes from the early life of Christ and his Mother, in the upper hall scenes from the Old and the New Testament. All these admirable paintings are fully and enthusiastically described by Ruskin in "Stones of Venice."

Tintoretto from the rapidity of his execution, received the nickname of *il Furioso*, and his connection with the Scuola illustrates his manner.

The Great Hall or «Sala dell'Albergo». *Scuola di San Rocco.*

Vasari relates that in the year 1560 the fraternity having determined to decorate their beautiful halls on a grand scale, they commissioned some of the best artists to prepare sketches before giving the order. The subject for competition was to be a cartoon of St. Roch in glory. On the day appointed, while the other artists displayed their designs, Tintoretto uncovered not a cartoon but the finished picture which he had secretly placed on the wall. That was his way of drawing he said, and he could do no other. In the end Tintoretto received the commission to paint the whole Scuola and he worked here during eighteen years.

The celebrated *Crucifixion* rivals in size and dramatic power Michelangelo's far more famous Last Judgment in the Sistine Chapel at Rome.

The composition is conceived with consummate skill and the contrasts of light and shade are superb. Eighty moving figures, — executioners, soldiers, populace, horsemen, disciples, women — with all imaginable expressions of hate, love and indifference, mingle and unite in a wealth of episodes.

This unique painting, executed in 1565, Tintoretto considered his masterpiece.

Christ before Pilate. Tintoretto.

Annunciation. *By* Tintoretto.

Crucifixion or «Calvary». *Painting by* Jacopo Tintoretto. A. D. 1565.

— 147 —

Photo Alinari, Anderson.

VENICE — THE ROYAL PALACE. Old Library.

MAIN SALOON OF THE LIBRARY OF ST. MARK.

On the walls are paintings by Tintoretto and Schiavone; on the ceiling are 21 medallions painted by Paolo Veronese.

ALLEGORY OF WISDOM. By TITIAN.

TRANSLATION OF ST. MARK FROM ALEXANDRIA. By TINTORETTO.
(Now in the Academy).

THE WOMAN TAKEN IN ADULTERY. By ROCCO MARCONI.

Tintoretto's painting represents the legendary scene of the Venetian merchants carrying off the body of St. Mark from the tomb at Alexandria, during a storm. In the right foreground the nude body of the saint is borne away; on the left the two Egyptians who tried to prevent the transport are seen lying on the ground, struck by lightning, while others are flying from the storm which is raging overhead. (*The picture is now displayed in the Academy*).

PROCURATORS OF ST. MARK. By J. TINTORETTO.

PROCURATORS OF ST. MARK. By J. TINTORETTO.

Photo ALINARI, ANDERSON.

VENICE — MUSEO CORRER, THE PALACES.

The Rezzonico Palace on the Canal Grande, rich with sumptuous halls and adorned with large frescoes by Jacopo Guarana, Giovanni Crosato and G. B. Tiepolo, contains the *Museo del Settecento Veneziano*, which is composed by furniture and paintings coming mostly from the Museo Correr.

Some of the paintings and two allegories, one of which represents the "Fortitude and Wisdom" and has been situated as a ceiling in one of the halls, are of Tiepolo; other paintings are by Longhi, Rosalba Carrera, Canaletto, G. B. Piazzetta and by Guardi. At the third floor the Hall of the Costumes, where we can see dresses in the eighteenth century fashion, and the puppet theatre are very interesting.

THE PARLOUR OF A CONVENT.
By F. GUARDI. (*Museo del '700*).

The "Parlour of a Convent" by *Guardi* is a valuable painting which shows us one of the aspects of the private life of Venice in the 18th century. " There were in the town at that time about 30 monasteries; in some of them the nuns led a pious and secluded life, but in others many of the nuns who were of noble birth and who had been compelled to enter the monastery, followed their religious rule less strictly and even passed their hours of solitude according to their pleasure. The conversation in these parlours rivalled that heard in the fashionable salons; there was music and refreshments, and the young nuns, laughing and talking (even with gentlemen), showed off their youth and beauty." (P. Molmenti. *Private Life in Venice*).

The *Museo Civico Correr*, formerly situated in the Fondaco dei Turchi; was moved in 1922 to the Royal Palace, where there is also the *Museo del Risorgimento*. The museum possesses important historical and artistic collections, paintings, statues, illuminated manuscripts, medals, armour, trophies, robes and other objects of the glorious past of Venice.

SAINTS AND MARTYRS.
(*Breviarium Grimani*).

VENETIAN COURTESANS, by CARPACCIO.
(*Museo Correr*).

The '*Breviarium Grimani*' now preserved in the Library of St. Mark, executed in the latter part of the 15th century, was the property of Cardinal Grimani. It contains nearly 800 vellum pages beautifully illuminated with ornaments and exquisite miniatures by *Memling* and other Flemish artists. The velvet cover enriched with gilded silver ornaments and the portrait of Cardinal Domenico Grimani on one side, and that of Doge Antonio, his father, on the other, was designed by *Alessandro Vittoria*.

SCHEME OF WALL DECORATION.    BANQUET OF CLEOPATRA AND MARK ANTONY.    EMBARKATION OF CLEOPATRA.
Frescoes by TIEPOLO (1696-1770), *in the Palazzo Labia*.

Photo ALINARI, ANDERSON.

VENICE — *THE PALACES.*

PALAZZO CORNER-SPINELLI.
Early Renaissance style.

PALAZZO GRIMANI.
By SANMICHELI *(16th cent.).*

PALAZZO MINELLI (Bobolo).
Staircase of the 15th cent.

PALAZZO VENDRAMIN-CALERGI.
Richard Wagner died here in 1883.

PALAZZO LOREDAN *or* AMBASCIATORI.
(15th century).

DOGANA DI MARE.
CUSTOM-HOUSE AND S. M. DELLA SALUTE.

THE ARSENAL.
FOUNDED IN 1104.

The Venetian palaces, remarkable for elegance of construction and decorative detail, confer a peculiar air of splendour and magnificence to the city and bear witness to the early civilization and peace of Venice. Protected as she was by her lagoon and waterways, and firmly ruled by her strong government the houses of Venice, unlike those of other cities, are built for pleasure and for state, with free means of access and a general air of peace and security.

Photo ALINARI, ANDERSON, BROGI.

VENICE — THE PALACES.

VIEW OF THE GRAND CANAL ON A FETE DAY. THE "SPOSALIZIO DEL MARE" OR NUPTIALS OF THE SEA.

The ceremony of the *Sposalizio del Mare* which the Doge annually celebrated in order to renew his marital authority on the Adriatic was istituted in 1173 (or perhaps earlier), to proclaim the naval supremacy of Venice to the world. The solemnity was performed with immense pomp and magnificence. On Ascension day the Doge in his robes of state, attended by the Senators in their gowns, the Papal Nuncio and the foreign ambassadors, embarked on the glorionsly painted, carved and gilded Bucentaur, and followed by innumerable gondolas filled with all the nobility of the state, and gaily dressed spectators, made for the open sea wherein he dropped a consecrated ring pronouncing the traditional words: *Desponsamus te, Mare*, etc. ("We espouse thee, sea, in sign of true and lasting dominion.") This nuptial ring had been given to the Republic in 1172 by Pope Alexander III. and the wedding ceremony was enjoined by his gratitude for the help and hospitality which the Republic had extended to him in his quarrel with Frederick Barbarossa. The ceremony was discontinued for the first time in 1797 when Napoleon Bonaparte entered the city of the Doges, and the symbolical Bucentaur was solemnly burnt down as a sign of the abolition of the Venetian power.

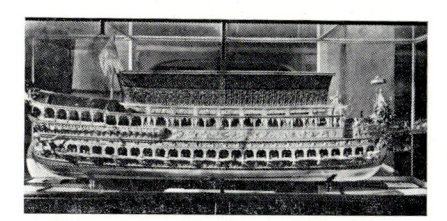

THE BUCENTAUR. Model of 1728. (*Arsenal Museum*).

This world-renowned vessel, the emblem of the maritime power of Venice, was propelled by eighty-four golden oars manned by 168 rowers. It was gloriously painted, carved and gilded; all overhung with gold and velvet, and had a deckinlaid with ebony and mother-of-pearl.

CA' D'ORO. The "Golden House". *About 1450.*

The "Ca' d'Oro" is a real masterpiece of grace. Baron Giorgio Franchetti, the last owner after having restored it, bequeathed it to the State together with its works of art. It is now a museum and has works of Vivarini, Carpaccio, Bordone, Mantegna, Titian, etc.

Photo ALINARI, ANDERSON, BROGI.

VENICE — *THE PALACES.*

PALAZZO GIOVANELLI.
Erected in the 14th cent.

PALAZZO CONTARINI-FASAN.
So-called "House of Desdemona".

PALAZZO DARIO.
Erected about 1480.

PALAZZO REZZONICO (MUSEO DEL SETTECENTO).
Here Robert Browning died in 1889.

PALAZZO PESARO (Galleria d'Arte Moderna).
Erected in 1679 by LONGHENA.

PALAZZO FOSCARI. *Erected i the 15th cent. Got hic style.*

FONDACO DEI TURCHI. *Late-Romanesque style (13th cent.).*

The *Palazzo Foscari*, one of the most beautiful in Venice, is interesting for its historical memories. Here lived Francesco Foscari who was elected Doge in 1423, and after 34 years' rule, during which time he had enlarged the Republic, fell under the suspicion of the Council of Ten. He saw his only son, Jacopo, suspected, arrested, tortured and exiled; the unfortunate father himself signed the sentence. Nevertheless, he was forced to abdicate at the age of 84 and died of grief the next day as the bell of St. Mark's proclaimed the election of his successor. An impressive monument was erected to his memory at the Frari. Henry III. of France stayed in this palace in 1574 on his return from Poland (see also p. 118).

— 152 —

Photo ALINARI, ANDERSON

VENICE — THE CANALS.

CANNAREGIO AND CHURCH OF S. GEREMIA.

THE GRAND CANAL. (On the right: the Cà d'Oro).

RIO SAN POLO.

RIO DEI MENDICANTI.

RIO DI SAN CANCIANO.

It is pure joy to glide swiftly and noiselessly down the Grand Canal or wander in and out among the quiet streets.

SCUOLA DI SAN ROCCO. *Designed by* BUON. A. D. 1517. (*See* p. 147).

PORTICO OF THE CÀ D'ORO.

"The word *Venetia*," it is said, "is interpreted by some to mean VENI ETIAM, which is to say, 'Come again and again'; for how many times soever thou shalt come, new things and new beauties thou shalt see."

Photo ALINARI, ANDERSON.

VENICE — *THE ENVIRONS.*

MURANO.
APSE OF SS. MARIA AND DONATO (*11th cent.*).
Since 1292 Murano has been the chief centre of the
Venetian glass industry.

TORCELLO.
THE DUOMO, *founded 850.* SANTA FOSCA (*12th cent.*).
Torcello was the refuge of the people of Altinum
and the residence of the first Doge.

THE VIRGIN IN PRAYER.
Byzantine mosaic of the 12th cent.
(Church of SS. Maria and Donato).

TORCELLO. THE DUOMO. A. D. 1008.
Early-Christian basilica
containing important mosaics.

THE VIRGIN AND THE APOSTLES.
Byzantine mosaic of the 12th cent.
(Duomo of Torcello).

FISHING BOAT ON THE LAGOONS.
In the distance the Palace of the Doges.

Photo ALINARI, ANDERSON, BROGI.

PADUA. CHURCH OF SANT' ANTONIO (Il Santo).
Erected in honour of the Saint. A. D. 1232-1307.

BRONZE STATUE OF GENERAL GATTAMELATA († 1443).
*Erected by the Venetians in honour of their hero.
A masterpiece of* DONATELLO. A. D. 1447.

PADUA

PADUA, the former capital of ancient *Venetia*, is monumental at every turn. On its piazzas rise the chief civic buildings of medieval times: the Loggia Amulea, the Palazzo della Ragione, known as « Il Salone », the Palazzo del Capitano. The chief attraction of Padua, however, is the Church of St. Anthony, « Il Santo », whose name is inextricably connected with that of the city.

The colossal Church, crowned by its Oriental pointed domes, is surprisingly impressive; the vast nave, supported by mighty stone pillars, contains the famous treasure-laden « Cappella del Santo », where the bones of the saint are preserved in a consecrated shrine.

St. Anthony of Padua was born at Lisbon in 1195. From his childhood his thoughts turned to self-sacrifice and religious zeal. In 1221 he joined the Franciscans and preached with a fervour that converted great multitudes of heretics and sinners, and so moved the vast audiences assembled around him, that the bitterest enemies fell upon each other's necks and swore ever after to live like brothers. Many legends are told of his numerous miracles. He died at Padua in 1231.

PALAZZO DELLA RAGIONE (Il Salone). (A. D. 1172-1219).

LOGGIA AMULEA (Palazzo Comunale).

Under the arches of the Loggia Amulea are statues of Dante and Giotto who met at Padua in 1306.

Photo ALINARI, ANDERSON, FOTOCELERE.

PADUA — *MADONNA DELL'ARENA.* *Scrovegni Chapel.*

CHAPEL OF THE MADONNA DELL'ARENA. *Erected in* A. D. 1303 *by order of Enrico Scrovegno.*

THE BIRTH OF THE VIRGIN.  THE PRESENTATION IN THE TEMPLE.
Frescoes by GIOTTO A. D. 1305.

THE ADORATION OF THE MAGI.  THE FLIGHT INTO EGYPT.
Frescoes by GIOTTO. A. D. 1305.

— 156 —

Photo ALINARI, ANDERSON.

PADUA — *MADONNA DELL'ARENA.* *Scrovegni Chapel.*

The interior decorations of this chapel were executed by GIOTTO and his pupils about 1304.

The frescoes represent scenes from the history of the Virgin and Christ and the New Testament and end with the Last Judgment, painted on the entrance wall.

The ornamental bands which separate some of the compositions, are adorned with figures of Saints, Prophets and Doctors. On the lower part of the walls are allegorical figures of the seven Virtues and their opposite Vices.

Though not a square foot of wall space has been left uncovered, yet the effect is perfectly harmonious.

In this 'noblest cycle of pictures known to Christian art,' Giotto appears as a great innovator and a master of high dramatic power and profound feeling.

It was during the execution of these works that the exiled Dante visited Padua (1306), when he is said to have been hospitably lodged by his friend the great painter, whose fame is celebrated in the «Divina Commedia» (Purg., XI, 94).

THE LAST JUDGMENT. *Fresco by* GIOTTO.

Judas Betrayal. 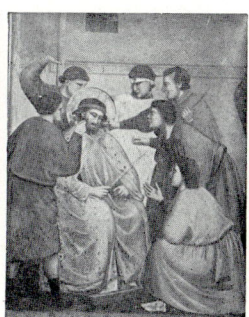 — Scourging of Christ.  — Christ. (Last Judgment).  — "Infidelitas."

THE BETRAYAL OF JUDAS.  — THE ENTOMBMENT. "PIETÀ."

Frescoes by GIOTTO. A. D. 1305.

Photo ALINARI, ANDERSON.

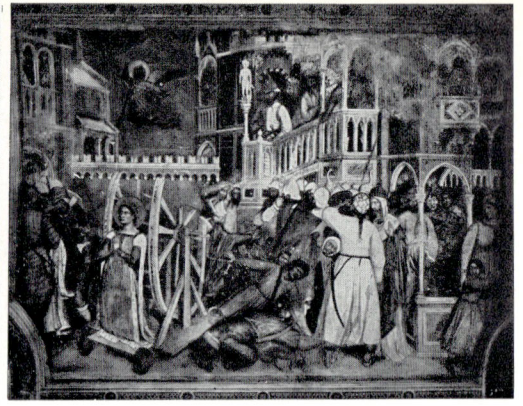

PADUA.

MARTYRDOM OF ST. GEORGE.   MARTYRDOM OF ST. CATHERINE.
Frescoes by ALTICHIERO *and* JACOPO AVANZO A. D. 1377. *(Cappella di San Giorgio).*

The *Cappella di San Giorgio*, erected about 1377, contains a series of twenty-one large frescoes, representing the youthful history of Christ, the Coronation of the Virgin, the Crucifixion, and the Legends of St. George, St. Catherine, and St. Lucy of Syracuse. Of these admirable pictures Dr. Burckhardt writes: « The composition shows throughout the good qualities which distinguish the best followers of Giotto; besides the telling clearness of the action, the grouping is beautiful in itself, but the principal point is that here, in hundreds of figures, the character of the individual.... is made real. In the beauty of single heads, the masters surpass most Giottesque painters ».

ST. JAMES BAPTIZING.   ST. JAMES BEFORE THE EMPEROR.   ST. JAMES BLESSING
Frescoes by MANTEGNA. A. D. 1455. *(Eremitani Chapel).*   A CONVERT ON HIS WAY TO MARTYRDOM.

ANDREA MANTEGNA (1431-1506) was an artist of unsurpassed originality. His style was sculpturesque and abstract, combining classic and Gothic reminiscences. He was the scholar of Squarcione, the founder of the Paduan school of painting.

COURT OF THE UNIVERSITY. A. D. 1552. *By* DELLA VALLE.   PALAZZO DEL CAPITANO. *Restored in 1532.*
Reginald Pole, was among the students here in 1519.   *Formerly the seat of the Venetian governor.*

Photo ALINARI, ANDERSON.

VIEW OF THE CITY AND THE RIVER ADIGE. (In the foreground the Church of S. Anastasia).

VERONA

VERONA is one of the largest and most beautiful towns of Venetia. It was here that the deepest of all love tragedies began and ended;—where Romeo and Juliet loved. Of great importance under imperial Rome, in medieval times it was regarded by the German emperors as the key to the mastery of Northern Italy. In 1227 Verona fell under the domination of the terrible Ezzelino da Romano, vicar of Frederick II. From the end of the 13th cent. it was ruled over by the *Scaligers* (the princes della Scala) and in the 15th cent. it became part of the republic of Venice.

Verona was the birthplace of the poet Catullus († B. C. 47); the Roman architect Vitruvius; and the physician G. Fracastoro († 1553).

MONUMENT OF CAN SIGNORIO DELLA SCALA († 1375). By BONINO DA CAMPIONE ca. 1374.

MONUMENT OF MASTINO II. DELLA SCALA († 1351).

TOMB OF CAN GRANDE I DELLA SCALA († 1329).

Gothic monuments to members of the House Della Scala (*Churchyard of S. Maria Antica*).

Photo ALINARI, ANDERSON, BROGI, FOTOCELERE.

VERONA — CHURCH OF SAN ZENO.

CHURCH OF SAN ZENO MAGGIORE. *Begun in the 10th cent.* The square tower on the left was part of a famous Benedictine convent, in which medieval German emperors sojourned on their way to Rome.

PORTAL OF SAN ZENO.

FRAGMENT OF ROMANESQUE RELIEFS ON THE FAÇADE.

The portal has slender columns supported by antique red marble lions and on the sides is adorned with reliefs of Old and New Testament subjects by NICOLAUS and WILIGELMUS (ca. 1139).

PART OF THE BRONZE DOORS with reliefs representing scenes from the Bible. 11th-12th cent.

Photo ALINARI, ANDERSON, BROGI.

VERONA — THE CHURCHES.

INTERIOR OF SAN ZENO MAGGIORE.

CRYPT OF SAN ZENO MAGGIORE.

San Zeno is the finest Romanesque ecclesiastical edifice in Northern Italy and the greatest church of the city. Begun about 900 it was completed about 1138. The impressive interior, contains a great many works of art.

MADONNA ENTHRONED. *Painted by* MANTEGNA. A. D. 1459.
On the left, SS. Peter, Paul, John and Augustine: *on the right,* SS. John the Baptist, Gregory, Laurence and Benedict.

CHURCH OF SAN FERMO MAGGIORE.
Romanesque style (11th cent.).

San Fermo Maggiore consists of two churches, one above the other. The lower church, erected in the Romanesque style in the year 1065 (?) by the Benedictines; the upper church, originally also Romanesque, was rebuilt in the Gothic style about 1313.

The interior, formed of a single nave, has a beautiful wooden roof, finely decorated. Among the numerous works of art here, the most remarkable is the monument of the physician Girolamo della Torre. It is of marble, and is adorned with fine bronze reliefs (most of the original ones are now in the Louvre).

MONUMENT OF G. DELLA TORRE.
By A. RICCIO. (San Fermo).

Photo ALINARI, ANDERSON. BROGI.

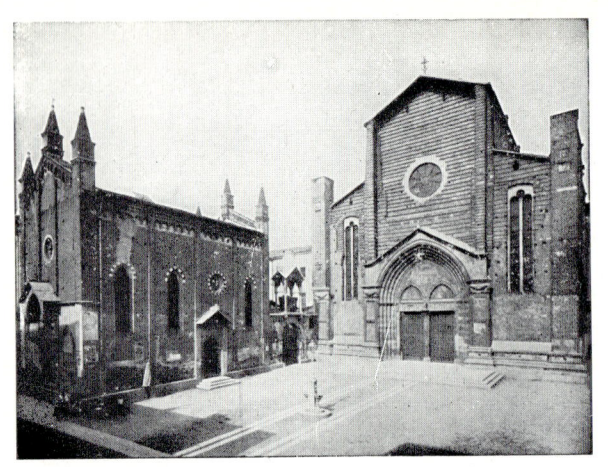

VERONA — CHURCH OF SANT'ANASTASIA.

Church of Sant'Anastasia. *Erected in 1290-1442. On the left is the tomb of Guglielmo da Castelbarco, and the church of S. Pietro Martire.*

Church of Sant'Anastasia. *Gothic style.*

St George and the Dragon. *Fresco painting by Pisanello (1380-1451).*

Knights Kneeling before the Virgin Enthroned. *Fresco by Altichiero (Church of Sant'Anastasia).*

Tomb of General Sarego. *(Church of S. Anastasia).*

Holy Water Basin. So-called "Il Gobbo di S. Anastasia."

Tomb of F. Cavalli. († 1396). *(Church of S. Anastasia).*

Photo Alinari, Anderson, Brogi.

VERONA — THE CHURCHES.

INTERIOR OF THE CATHEDRAL.

THE CATHEDRAL. (The Duomo).
Erected in the 12th cent. Romanesque-Gothic style.

INTERIOR OF THE BAPTISTERY.
The reliefs on the font date from 1200.

PORCH OF THE CATHEDRAL.

There is a tradition that the *Cathedral* was erected on the site of a temple of Minerva, but its reconstruction, begun in 1139, was not completed till 1514. The magnificent porch, dating from the 12th century, has, among others, sculptured figures of the Paladins Roland and Oliver, the warrior guards of Charlemagne, well known in story and legend.

The interior is spacious and lofty; the marble rood-screen in front of the high altar was designed by *Sanmicheli* and bears a bronze Crucifixion executed by *Giambattista da Verona*; in the right aisle is the Gothic shrine and tomb of St. Agatha, in red and white marble.

Near the Duomo is the *Baptistery* (Church of S. Giovanni in Fonte), remarkable for its huge font, a single block of marble, decorated with humorous and quaintly primitive reliefs depicting the early life of Our Saviour.

Opposite the Duomo is the *Biblioteca Capitolare*, the Chapter library, founded by the archdeacon Pacificus (778-846), containing most precious manuscripts and works of the Roman classic authors, including the famous palimpsest of the « Institutes of Gaius, » which was discovered by Niebhur in 1816.

MADONNA ENTHRONED.
By G. DAI LIBRI. (*S. Anastasia*).

VIRGIN AND CHILD.
By CRIVELLI. (*Museo Civico*).

MADONNA ENTHRONED.
By G. DAI LIBRI. (*S. Giorgio Maggiore*).

Photo ALINARI, ANDERSON, BROGI.

VERONA — THE PALACES.

The *Piazza delle Erbe*, the focus of Verona, where the city life flows in the most varied stream, is one of the most picturesque squares in Italy. In the time of the Romans, this was the Forum, and before the amphitheatre was built chariot races and gladiatorial fights were also held here. Now the Piazza is surrounded by fine medieval and Renaissance buildings, and is used as a fruit and vegetable market.

In the centre of the square rises the *Capitello* or Tribune, set up in 1207, a sort of marble canopy from which public decrees and sentences of death were delivered; near by is the fountain, built, according to tradition, by King Pepin, or Alboin, crowned by an ancient figure symbolising « Verona ». At the south end is the ancient Gothic tabernacle, and at the north end is a marble column, erected in 1524, bearing the Lion of St. Mark.

PIAZZA DELLE ERBE (*vegetable market*).

The *Piazza dei Signori* (or Piazza Dante, from the statue of the Poet in the centre), teems with associations relating to the *Scaligers*: here they dwelt and ruled the city and from them it received its original name and beauty. On the right of the Piazza is the beautiful Renaissance Palazzo del Consiglio « La Loggia », and next to it is the Prefettura, originally the private palace of Mastino I., built by him in 1272, and inhabited by him and his descendants. This was the residence which Giotto decorated, and where Dante spent many months, during his exile, as the honoured guest of the Scaligers. On the left is the old Palazzo del Capitano, now the law courts, and a wing of the Palazzo Comunale with its glorious tower (272 feet), erected in the twelfth century.

Not far from the Piazza delle Erbe is the medieval palace of the Cappelletti (the Capulets), the home of Juliet, for whom so many gentle hearts have wept and poets have sung. The Tragedy of the two lovers is said to have occurred about 1302, at an epoch when nearly every town in Northern Italy was rent by the fighting factions of Guelph and Ghibelline. In Verona, the former were favored by the Cappelletti family of nobles, the latter were supported by the Montecchi. In his play of « Romeo an Juliet », Shakespeare chose an episode in the feuds of these powerful rival houses, and has presented them to us under the names of *Capulets* and *Montagues*.

The « Tomb of Juliet », the sarcophagus which once contained her body and that of Romeo, her lover, stands in a garden formerly belonging to a convent of Franciscan nuns.

PALAZZO BEVILACQUA. *Designed by* SANMICHELI.

PALAZZO DEL CONSIGLIO. (La Loggia).
Designed by FRA GIOCONDO. *Erected in 1476-93*.

JULIET'S TOMB.

Photo ALINARI, ANDERSON, BROGI.

VERONA — THE PALACES.

PALAZZO DELLA RAGIONE. (Palazzo del Comune). *Founded in 1193.*

The superb Gothic processional staircase, dating from 1446-50, is one of the most imposing in all Italy.

Photo ALINARI, ANDERSON, BROGI.

CASTELVECCHIO. *Built by Can Grande II. della Scala.* A. D. *1358.*
It contains the "Museo Civico d'Arte".

PALAZZO DELLA GRAN GUARDIA VECCHIA.
Built in 1610, for public meetings.

PONTE PIETRA AND CASTELLO S. PIETRO.

THE ARENA. THE ROMAN AMPHITHEATRE. A. D. 290.

The *Ponte Pietra*, is partly supported by Roman piers. The Castello San Pietro which stands on top of the hill, occupies the site of the Palace of Theodoric, who lived alternately at Verona and at Ravenna. In that same palace lived afterwards Alboin, King of the Lombards (561-573), and here he forced his wife Rosamund to drink wine out of a cup which was formed from the skull of her father whom he had killed with his own hand. Rosamund, revenged herself by having Alboin assassinated.

The *Arena*, originally built at the end of the first century, is the largest amphitheatre after the Colosseum at Rome. The interior with seats for 25.000 spectators has been restored and is occasionally used for lyrical performances.

ARQUÀ. PETRARCH'S HOUSE.

ARQUÀ. TOMB OF PETRARCH († 1374).

ARQUÀ, a charming little village a few miles south of Padua, was the final residence of Petrarch. The house in which the great poet spent the four last years of his life is beautifully situated on the hill-side. It has painted wooden ceilings and frescoes illustrating the story of Petrarch and Laura, the chair in which the poet died and other mementoes of him. The visitors' book bears illustrious signatures, including those of Byron, Mozart, Queen Margherita, King Umberto, etc. For many weeks previous to his death, Petrarch was in a state of languor, and on the morning of his seventieth birthday, July 20, 1374 he was found dead in his library chair with his head resting upon an open book on the desk before him.

The tomb of the Poet, 'the great awakener of Europe from mental lethargy,' stands in the open on the little square before the church-door, a head of the poet in bronze surmounts the red marble ark. (*See also p. 253*).

Photo ALINARI, ANDERSON, BROGI.

VICENZA.

LOGGIA DEL CAPITANO.
(Pal. Comunale). By PALLADIO, 1571.

BASILICA PALLADIANA (Palazzo della Ragione). By ANDREA PALLADIO.
Begun in 1549, completed in 1614 and reconstructed in 1949.

VICENZA, the ancient *Vicetia* of the Romans, was an indipendent republic during the middle ages, but in 1405 was subdued and taken by the Venetians. In the 15th century Vicenza had a School of Painting strongly influenced by Mantegna, who was born here in 1431 but worked in Padua and Mantua. In the 16th century the town attained a high reputation having given birth to the last great architect of the Renaissance, ANDREA PALLADIO (1518-1580) who practically undertook the rebuilding of the town. He studied ancient Rome and was able to effect a revival of the ancient language of forms. The *Basilica Palladiana*, with its grand colonnade in two stories, is Palladio's greatest creation and may be considered the culminating point of pure Renaissance architecture.

TEATRO OLIMPICO. *Designed by* PALLADIO. *Completed by* SCAMOZZI *in 1584.*

This remarkable building with a magnificent stage representing a piazza and streets in perspective, was inaugurated in 1585 by the Accademia of Vicenza with the performance of Sophocles' " Ædipus Tyrannus ". The auditorium rises in thirteen semi-oval tiers.

Photo ALINARI.

TRENTO.

MONUMENT TO DANTE ALIGHIERI († 1321).
Executed by C. Zocchi 1896.

On the pedestal are three series of bronze figures representing personages of the "Divine Comedy." Below, Satan sits on a dragon; higher up, scenes from Purgatory; above Beatrice and angels in glory. *Height of the monument 57 ft.*

PANORAMIC VIEW OF TRENTO.

THE CATHEDRAL. *Consecrated A. D. 1145.*

CASTELLO DEL BUON CONSIGLIO. *13th-15th cent.*
This castle, the medieval stronghold and residence of the Prince Bishop and his Chapter, was rebuilt in the Renaissance style in the 16th century. It was in this castle, that Italy's 'greatest martyr of the great war,' Cesare Battisti, was executed.

TRENTO (Trent), the ancient *Tridentum*, belonged to Austria since 1814, but the entry of the Italian armies on Nov. 3rd 1918 marked the end of the Austrian rule, and by the Treaty of Versailles the whole province was incorporated with Italy.

The city, with its numerous towers, palaces and broad streets, is thoroughly Italian in character and historic traditions. The Romanesque Cathedral, built entirely of marble, was founded early in the eleventh century, but not completed till 1515. In the interior are many frescoes and tombs of bishops who for centuries ruled the city. Not far from the cathedral is the church of S. Maria Maggiore, in which the famous Council of Trent held its sittings for 17 years, from 1545 to 1563.

— 168 —

Photo ALINARI, FOTOCELERE.

GENERAL VIEW OF TRIESTE.

THE CATHEDRAL OF S. GIUSTO.

INTERIOR OF THE CATHEDRAL OF S. GIUSTO.
Twelfth century mosaics in the apse.

THE CASTLE OF MIRAMAR. *Built in 1854.*

TRIESTE is of very ancient origin, and was the battle-ground of Illyrian and Celtic tribes long before the Romans subjugated it about 177 B. C. It rose in importance under the Empire and became a prosperous seaport. The rulers of Trieste during the Middle Ages were the patriarchs of Aquileia, but in the 13th century Venice became all-powerful and the commune was compelled to pay a yearly tribute of ships and to swear allegiance to the Venetian Republic. Eventually the Kaiser came forward and the Venetian supremacy was gradually changed into an Austrian supremacy.

The Chief points of interest in the town are the harbour, and the Piazza dell' Unità, on which front the attractive Palazzo Comunale (Municipio), the Prefettura, and the Palazzo Lloyd Triestino. On an eminence, in the old part of the town, stands the Duomo or Cathedral di S. Giusto, built in the 5th century on the ruins of a Roman temple. Near by is the Arco di Riccardo, named after Richard " Cœur de Lion," who is said to have been confined here on his return from Palestine.

The *Castle of Miramar*, a few miles from Trieste, was built in 1854-56 for the unfortunate Prince Maximilian, the ill-fated Emperor of Mexico.

Photo ALINARI, FOTOCELERE.

PALAZZO SACRATI.   PALAZZO SCHIFANOIA.   PALAZZO. SCOTTI.
Portals of Renaissance palaces in Ferrara.

EMILIA, the region extending between the Po and the Apennines, derives its name from the *Via Æmilia*, that magnificent road, straight as an arrow, built as far back as two thousand years ago, and which traverses it for a length of more than two hundred miles, from Rimini to Piacenza. In medieval times, the southern districts of Emilia formed part of the Romagna and the Marches, but afterwards the whole region was divided between the duchies of Parma, Modena, the Papal territories which included Bologna and the Legations, and a number of petty principalities, the result of centuries of complicated development and foreign invasion.

Emilia is now divided into the eight provinces of Piacenza, Parma, Reggio, Modena, Bologna, Ferrara, Ravenna and Forlì. These glorious cities, for long the cradle of Italian prowess, the birth place of great men who cultivated art and sciences, teem with historical associations and monuments of art.

This church built in the 10th century belonged to the famous Benedictine abbey founded in the 6th century. In the year 1000 the monastery, declared free and independent by Otho III., reached its highest prosperity under the great Abbot, Guido da Ravenna, who held jurisdiction over territories stretching far and wide round Pomposa. At that time there was no other monastery (except Monte Cassino) in Italy so rich or so famous for virtue and scholarship; the noblest youth of Italy were sent there to be educated; its library was of wide celebrity and contained many treasures of ancient literature. Guido Monaco (d'Arezzo), the inventor of the musical scale, was a monk here at the end of the 10th century.

POMPOSA. ABBEY AND CHURCH OF SANTA MARIA.
The Campanile (163 ft.) dates from 1063.

Photo ALINARI.

RAVENNA. LA PINETA DI CLASSE.

La Pineta di Classe, the celebrated Pine forest of Ravenna which lies two miles from the town, dates from the sixth century. It has been extolled by Dante, who loved to wander through the long alleys of majestic pines; by Boccaccio who chose it as the scene of one of his tales; by Dryden and by Byron who was profoundly impressed by it. Here, in a peasant's hut, Garibaldi's wife, the brave and devoted Anita, died in 1849.

EMILIA - THE MARCHES

BOLOGNA

PIACENZA RAVENNA RIMINI
FERRARA MODENA PARMA
ANCONA LORETO URBINO

RIMINI. — Arch of Augustus. Erected in 27 B. C. marking the junction of the Via Æmilia with Via Flaminia.

PANORAMIC VIEW OF BOLOGNA

BOLOGNA

BOLOGNA is a city of great antiquity, known in history successively as an Etruscan colony, Gallic capital, a Roman colony, and, finally, a strategic point of importance throughout the struggles of the Middle Ages. Its celebrated university, founded by Irnerius, in 1070-1100, is the oldest in Europe, and in the 13th century it assembled as many as 10.000 students. One of its remarkable features is the fact that the university has numbered many women among its professors, one of whom was Novella d'Andrea (14th cent.), whose personal attractions were so great that she was made to lecture from behind a curtain, in order that the attention of the students might not be distracted by her charms. The anatomy of the human frame was first taught here in the 14th century, and galvanism was discovered here (1789) by Luigi Galvani.

The influence of the ecclesiastical power in Bologna is displayed in the numerous churches which were erected in the thirteenth and fourteenth centuries, and are distinguished not only by important works of art, but also by their enormous dimensions. The Picture Gallery and the Museo Civico, containing an important collection of antiquities, are of great interest.

Bologna was the home of Giosuè Carducci, who died here in 1907, and of Card. Mezzofanti, who spoke 50 languages.

FOUNTAIN OF NEPTUNE. *By* GIAMBOLOGNA. A. D. 1566.

GIAMBOLOGNA'S *great fountain* is one of the most striking ornaments in Italy. Above is a superb bronze figure of Neptune, " not an antique god, calm and worthy of adoration, " remarks Taine, " but a mythological god serving as an ornament, naked and displaying his muscles. " Below are four joyous children seizing leaping dolphins, and at the base as many sirens, 'displaying the magnificent nudity of their bending forms, the open sensuality of their bold heads and closely clasping their swollen breasts to force out the jutting water.'

Photo ALINARI, ANDERSON, BROGI.

PALAZZO DEL PODESTÀ. *Rebuilt in 1492.*

PALAZZO COMUNALE. *Begun 1292.*

The *Mercanzia* or *Loggia dei Mercanti* was erected about 1382. Its façade is adorned with images of patron saints and the arms of the city and of the Bentivoglio family who ruled Bologna in the 15th cent. From the balcony in the center sentences were passed, and bankruptcies proclaimed.

In the massive Gothic palace given below the young and unfortunate King Enzo († 1272), son of Frederick II. was kept a prisoner for 25 years by the Bolognese. His captivity is said to have been solaced by the affection of the beautiful Lucia Viadagola, from whom the Bentivoglio family claim descent.

THE MERCANZIA. *Erected in 1382.*

LEANING TOWERS. *(12th cent.).*

PALAZZO DI RE ENZO. *Erected early in the 13th cent.*

These leaning towers are perhaps the most singular structures in Bologna. The one on the right, the *Torre Asinelli*, erected about 1109 is 320 ft. in height and 4 ft. out of the perpendicular; it has a staircase of 447 steps leading to the summit. The *Torre Garisenda* (left) begun in 1110 and left unfinished, is 156 ft. high and 8 ft. out of the perpendicular. In medieval times every powerful family had a tower to which to escape in case of trouble. (See also *p. 304*).

Photo ALINARI, ANDERSON, BROGI, FOTOCELERE.

BOLOGNA — SAN PETRONIO.

CHURCH OF SAN PETRONIO. *Begun in the year 1390 in the Gothic style.*

San Petronio, the largest church of Bologna, was begun in 1390 in the Gothic style in emulation of the cathedral of Florence, but never finished in accordance with the original plans. The main portal of the half-finished façade is enriched with sculptures by JACOPO DELLA QUERCIA, the interior, of extremely beautiful proportions, contains numerous works of art, carved stalls and stained glass windows.

THE MAIN PORTAL.

DETAIL OF LEFT PORTAL.    VIEW OF THE INTERIOR.    DETAIL OF MAIN PORTAL.

It was in this church that Charles V. was crowned emperor of the Holy Roman Empire by Clement VII. in 1530, this being the last time that a German emperor was crowned by a Pope.

Creation of Adam.    Creation of Eve.    The Temptation.    The Expulsion.

Marble reliefs by JACOPO DELLA QUERCIA. A. D. 1425-28. (Main portal). "Superb figures, grand and vigorous nude bodies, pagan in action and in shape." (Cfr. Raphael's and Michelangelo's frescoes in the Vatican, pp. 470-478).

Photo ALINARI, ANDERSON, BROGI.

BOLOGNA — THE CHURCHES.

RELIQUARY of the 15th cent.
(*Church of San Paolo*).

BASILICA DI SANTO STEFANO.

Santo Stefano consists of eight different churches, the oldest being SS. Pietro e Paolo and dating from the 4th cent. In an open court here is "Pilate's Bowl" presented by King Liutprand. According to the pious legend, it is the basin in which Pilate washed his hands after surrendering Christ to the Jews.

ANNIBALE BENTIVOGLIO († 1445).
Attr. to NICC. DELL'ARCA. (*S Giacomo*).

SAN GIACOMO MAGGIORE.
Founded 1267.

TOMB OF ANT. GALEAZZO BENTIVOGLIO.
By JACOPO DELLA QUERCIA. (*S. Giacomo*).

CHURCH OF S. MARIA DEI SERVI. *Built in 1383.*

— 175 —

Photo ALINARI, ANDERSON, BROGI.

BOLOGNA — THE CHURCHES.

CHURCH OF SAN FRANCESCO. *Early Gothic style.*

CHURCH OF SAN DOMENICO. *Begun in 1235.*

The *Church of San Francesco* built in the thirteenth century on the model of French churches, was completely restored in 1887. The interior, in the form of a basilica, contains the tomb of Pope Alexander V. († 1410), and the large marble altar given below by JACOBELLO and PIERPAOLO DELLE MASSEGNE.

This church erected about 1235 in honour of S. Dominic, who died in Bologna in 1221 (see p. 223), contains many monuments and magnificent inlaid stalls. But the art-treasure of the church is the famous marble shrine called the *Arca di San Domenico* illustrated below.

GOTHIC MARBLE ALTAR. *By J. and P. DELLE MASSEGNE.*

ARCA DI SAN DOMENICO. Tomb of S. Dominic.

This great altarpiece executed in 1338 is the earliest known work of JACOBELLO and PIERPAOLO DELLE MASSEGNE, two Venetian brothers. It contains a central bas-relief representing the Coronation of the Virgin surmounted by a figure of the Almighty and a statue of the Madonna and Child. On either side are innumerable statues and statuettes in niches. The lofty pinnacle in the centre is crowned by the Crucifixion and two saints, while the lesser pinnacles support busts of saints. The reliefs on the predella represent episodes from the life of S. Francis.

The prominent features of the Arca are the six bas-reliefs by NICCOLÒ PISANO and FRA GUGLIELMO around the sarcophagus representing the principal events in the life of S. Dominic: Pope Honorius III. confirms the Order of S. Dominic, The appearance of the Apostles Peter and Paul to S. Dominic, The saint praying for the restoration to life of the young Lord Orsini who had been killed, S. Dominic's doctrine tested by fire, The miracle at S. Sabina (p. 248), S. Reginald of Orleans. The kneeling angel on the right is an early work of Michelangelo.

— 176 —

Photo ALINARI, ANDERSON, BROGI.

BOLOGNA — *PINACOTECA NAZIONALE.*

ST. CECILIA *By* RAPHAEL.

Raphael's "St. Cecilia," in the *Pinacoteca Nazionale*, was executed in Rome in A. D. 1513. In the centre, Santa Cecilia, radiant and ecstatic stands wrapt in listening to the choir of angels, only indicated above; she holds a small organ reversed, with its tubes falling out, scattered at her feet lie her other instruments, silent before the diviner music. On the left St. Paul, a noble figure in grand drapery, inwardly moved, leans on his sword and looks thoughtfully on the soundless instruments. Further back, St. John, in whispered conversation with St. Augustine, both listening, variously affected. On the right, the Magdalen, turns to the spectator directing his attention to the holy scene. St. Cecilia, a Roman lady, is said to have excelled so eminently in music, that an angel was enticed from the celestial regions by the fascinating charms of her melody; owing to this tradition she is considered the patroness of music and musicians.

Photo ALINARI, ANDERSON, BROGI.

BOLOGNA — THE PALACES.

PALAZZO BEVILACQUA (*14th century*).   PALAZZO FAVA.

Nearly every street in Bologna has its long arcades which enable pedestrians to pass from place to place in the shade, and confer to the city an air of old world picturesqueness.

PALAZZO BEVILACQUA. THE COURT. *Early Renaissance style.*

Photo ALINARI ANDERSON, BROGI.

PIACENZA. MODENA.

PIACENZA. PALAZZO MUNICIPALE. *Erected* A. D. 1281. *A fine example of Gothic architecture.*

PIACENZA was founded by the Romans as a stronghold to secure one of the passages of the Po. In the middle ages it was one of the first towns which organised itself into a Republic. Then it successively came under the domination of the Visconti, the Sforza, and the popes, and finally, in 1545 into the possession of the Farnese family. The Palazzo Municipale illustrated above is the most notable Gothic building in town. On the lofty campanile (300 ft.) of the cathedral hung the iron cage, the *gabbia*, in which criminals were exposed naked, to the mockery of mankind.

THE CREATION OF ADAM AND EVE. THE FALL. (12th cent.). *Reliefs by* NICOLAUS *and* WILIGELMUS. (*Modena Cathedral*).

MODENA, the ancient *Mutina* of the Romans possesses one of the most interesting cathedrals of the twelfth century. Its façade has a grand porch with pillars resting on the backs of colossal marble lions,—intended to tipify the strength and watchfulness of the Church. In the noble campanile (315 ft.) called *La Ghirlandina*, is preserved the famous bucket which the Modenese captured from the Bolognese in 1325 and which inspired Tassoni his celebrated poem "La Secchia Rapita."

PIACENZA. THE CATHEDRAL. *Lombard-Romanesque.* A. D. 1122.

MODENA. THE CATHEDRAL. *Founded by Matilda of Tuscany* (1099). (*Romanesque style*).

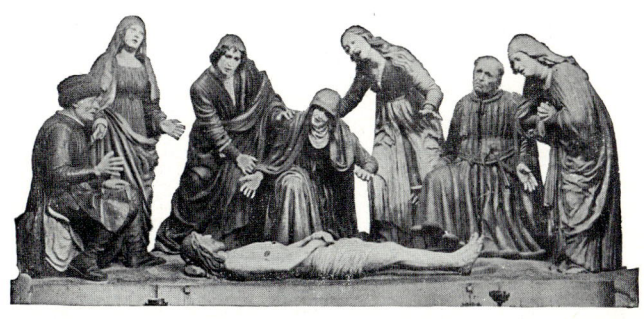

PIETÀ. *Coloured terracotta group by the ultra-realistic master* GUIDO MAZZONI (1450-1518), *who was the first to introduce this exaggerated mode of art at Modena.* The startling effect of these life-size figures robed in heavy but carefully arranged draperies, may easily be imagined. (*Church of S. Giovanni*, Modena).

Photo ALINARI, ANDERSON.

FERRARA.

FERRARA. THE CASTLE. 14th cent.
This is the most impressive fortress in Italy.

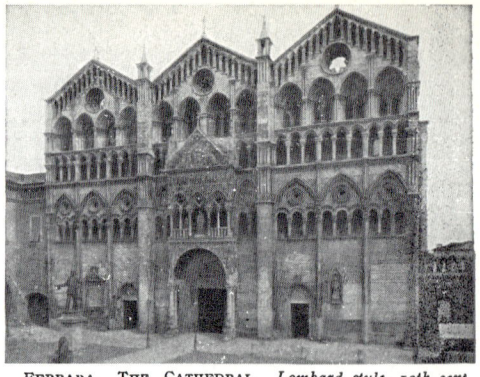

FERRARA. THE CATHEDRAL. *Lombard style. 12th cent.*
The façade is decorated with 14th and 15th cent. sculptures.

FERRARA has a romantic and sentimental interest all its own, and though now almost deserted, was in Renaissance times famous for its gayety and splendor. No city enjoyed more brilliant and more frequent public shows. Nowhere did the aristocracy maintain so much of feudal magnificence and chivalrous enjoyment. The great palace castle, the best preserved relic of princely feudal life in Italy, the noble Cathedral, the array of palaces and the tradition of her splendid and luxurious Court still recall the period of her Golden Age.

The magnificent halls of the huge castle, which is the center of everything in Ferrara, are redolent of the atmosphere of many social gatherings in which poets, players, court flatterers, knights, pages and fair ladies in rich brocades took part. But beneath the cube of solid masonry, the dungeons still recall the tragedies born of family feud and jealousy and of ducal tyranny. It was in one of these dungeons, shut from daylight by a seven-fold series of iron bars, that Niccolò III., Marchese d'Este, caused his wife Parisina, and her lover, who was his own natural son, to be beheaded, a story which Byron has made the subject of one of his poems. Niccolò's son Lionello (1441-1450), inaugurated the age of splendour that Borso (†1471) continued.

Under the great Duke Ercole I. (1471-1505), father of Isabella and of Beatrice d'Este, Ferrara became a center of intellectual and artistic life to which flocked some of the greatest men: Boiardo, (author « Orlando Innamorato ») Ariosto, Tasso, Guarini, invited by the duke.

Ercole's son and successor, Alphonso I., was the third husband of one of the most famous and inexplicable of women, Lucrezia Borgia, whose beauty and irresistible fascination subjugated every one. She amended her life while at Ferrara and died here in 1519, greatly beloved and respected.

Ercole II. (1534-58), son of Alphonso, was the husband of Renée, patroness of reformers Calvin and Marot.

The sights most worth seeing in Ferrara, besides the castle and the cathedral, are the church of Corpus Domini, containing the tombs of Alphonso I., and Lucrezia Borgia; the house of Ariosto, in which the poet died in 1533; the Hospital of Sant'Anna, where Tasso was kept in confinement for nearly seven years as a madman; the Palazzo dei Diamanti, now the picture gallery; the Palazzo Schifanoia (« Sans Souci »). This was built in 1391 as a summer palace and completed under Borso d'Este in 1469. Within, the walls of the principal saloon are adorned with the celebrated frescoes, executed between 1467 and 1470, by FRANCESCO COSSA, COSIMO TURA and their scholars. The scenes are divided into sections (three on each wall of the apartment), each representing a month of the year, and consisting of three superimposed zones. Above appear the deities of antiquity in triumphal chariots drawn by emblematical animals, surrounded by votaries; in the middle are the signs of the zodiac and symbolical figures appropriate to the month represented; beneath are scenes of Duke Borso's daily life, employments of men and women in the various months, popular festivals, etc. The whole series was devised as a pictorial glorification of Borso's just and benevolent rule. He is the central figure of the pageantry: we see him gorgeously attired, riding forth a-hunting or returning from the chase; conversing with his courtiers or administering justice; looking on at the races or interchanging courtesies with the Venetian Ambassador.

The frescoes have all the charm and thrilling interest of a historical picture book; in them the whole Italian life of the 15th century, in the country and in the city, the camp and the court, « surrounded with the pastoral and romantic atmosphere of a Boiardesque poem, » is vividly portrayed.

For a fuller account of these remarkable frescoes see « The Story of Ferrara », by Miss Ella Noyes (in the « Mediæval Town Series). »

ALLEGORY OF APRIL.
Fresco by FRANCESCO COSSA. *(Palazzo Schifanoia).*

The races on St. Georges' Day (Detail of above fresco).

— 178 —

Photo ALINARI, ANDERSON.

GENEALOGICAL TABLE OF THE HOUSE OF ESTE [I.]
Lords and Marquis of Ferrara.

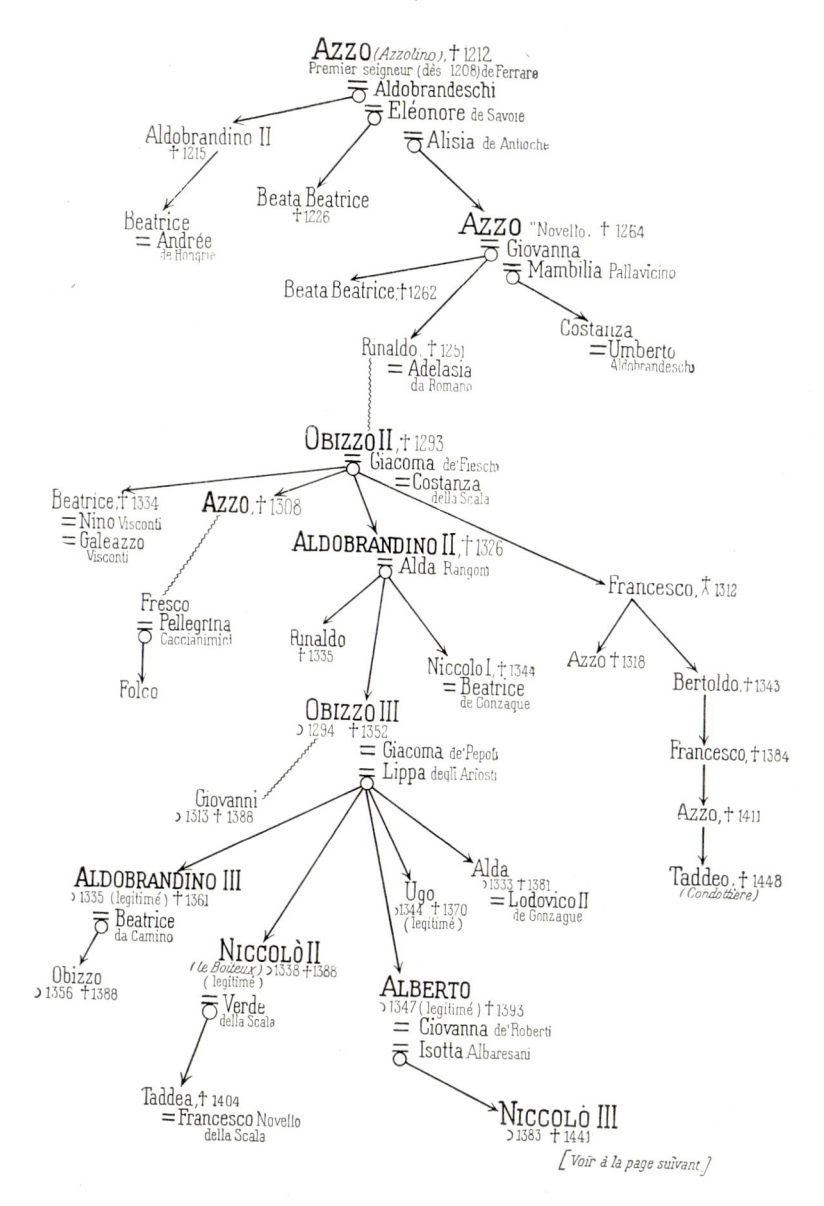

AZZO *(Azzolino)*, † 1212
Premier seigneur (dès 1208) de Ferrara
⚭ Aldobrandeschi
⚭ Eléonore de Savoie
⚭ Alisia de Antioche

- Aldobrandino II † 1215
- Beata Beatrice † 1226
- AZZO "Novello" † 1264
  ⚭ Giovanna
  ⚭ Mambilia Pallavicino

Beatrice = Andrée de Hongrie

Beata Beatrice † 1262

Rinaldo † 1251 = Adelasia da Romano

Costanza = Umberto Aldobrandeschi

OBIZZO II † 1293
⚭ Giacoma de'Fieschi
= Costanza della Scala

- Beatrice † 1334 = Nino Visconti = Galeazzo Visconti
- AZZO † 1308
- ALDOBRANDINO II † 1326
  ⚭ Alda Rangoni
- Francesco † 1312

Fresco = Pellegrina Cacciahimici
Folco

Rinaldo † 1335
Niccolo I † 1344 = Beatrice de Gonzaque
Azzo † 1318
Bertoldo † 1343

OBIZZO III ⟩ 1294 † 1352
= Giacoma de'Pepoli
⚭ Lippa degli Ariosti

Francesco † 1384
Azzo † 1411
Taddeo † 1448 *(Condottiere)*

Giovanni ⟩ 1313 † 1388

ALDOBRANDINO III ⟩ 1335 (legitimé) † 1361
⚭ Beatrice da Camino

Obizzo ⟩ 1356 † 1388

NICCOLÒ II *(le Boiteux)* ⟩ 1338 † 1388 (legitimé)
⚭ Verde della Scala

Ugo ⟩ 1344 † 1370 (legitimé)

Alda ⟩ 1333 † 1381 = Lodovico II de Gonzague

ALBERTO ⟩ 1347 (legitimé) † 1393
= Giovanna de'Roberti
⚭ Isotta Albaresani

Taddea † 1404 = Francesco Novello della Scala

NICCOLÒ III ⟩ 1383 † 1441

[Voir à la page suivante]

THE HOUSE OF ESTE, is one of the oldest of the former reigning families of Italy, whose members were at first supreme magistrates and afterwards hereditary princes. It was in all probability of Lombard origin, and descended from the margraves who governed Tuscany in Carolingian times.

Oberto, son of Count Azzo of Canossa, received the town of Este from the emperor Otho the Great in 961, whence the family derived its feudal name. In 984, Mantua, Modena and Ferrara were granted also as imperial fiefs. Azzolino or Azzo was imperial vicegerent and podestà of Verona, Padua and Ferrara.

Late in the 13th century they transferred their original residence from Este to Ferrara, when Azzo " Novello ", having annihilated the army of Ezzelino da Romano, the champion of the Hohenstaufen in Northern Italy, made Ferrara his official residence, and considerably extended the power of the house, which from an early period was a liberal patron of art and science.

GENEALOGICAL TABLE OF THE HOUSE OF ESTE [II.]
Marquis and Dukes of Ferrara and Modena.

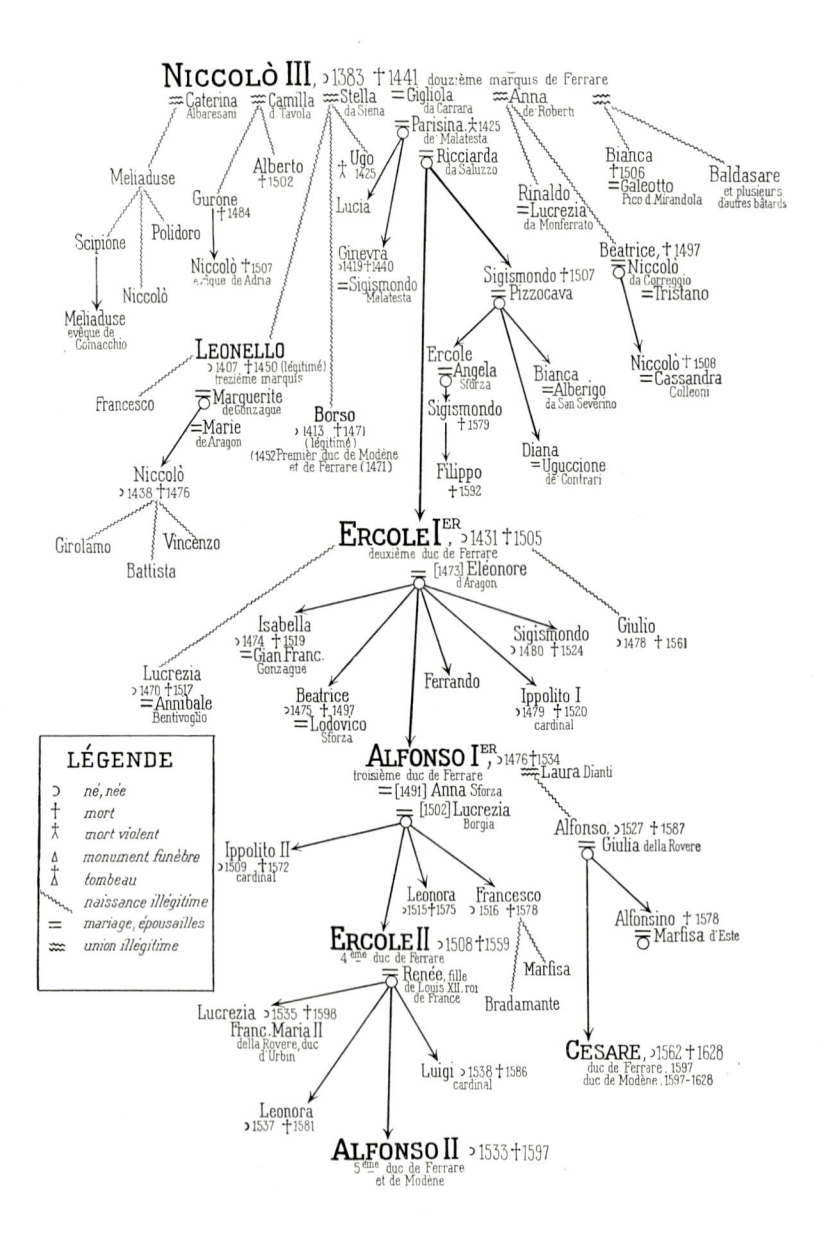

[Genealogical chart of the House of Este, descending from Niccolò III (1383–1441), twelfth marquis of Ferrara, through his wives and consorts: Caterina Albaresani, Camilla d'Tavola, Stella da Siena, Gigliola da Carrara, Anna de Robert, Parisina (1425) de Malatesta, Ricciarda da Saluzzo, and others. Descendants shown include Meliaduse, Scipione, Polidoro, Niccolò (évêque de Adria), Meliaduse (évêque de Comacchio), Francesco, Alberto (†1502), Gurone (†1484), Lucia, Ugo (†1425), Ginevra (1419–1440) = Sigismondo Malatesta, Ercole = Angela Sforza, Sigismondo (†1579), Diana = Uguccione de' Contrari, Filippo (†1592), Rinaldo = Lucrezia da Monferrato, Sigismondo Pizzocava (†1507), Bianca = Alberigo da San Severino, Bianca (†1506) = Galeotto Pico di Mirandola, Baldasare et plusieurs d'autres bâtards, Béatrice (†1497) = Niccolò da Correggio = Tristano, Niccolò (†1508) = Cassandra Colleoni.

Leonello (1407–1450, légitimé), treizième marquis, = Marguerite de Gonzague, = Marie de Aragon; their children: Niccolò (1438–1476), Girolamo, Vincenzo, Battista.

Borso (1413–1471, légitimé), 1452 Premier duc de Modène et de Ferrare (1471).

Ercole Ier (1431–1505), deuxième duc de Ferrare, = [1473] Eléonore d'Aragon; children: Isabella (1474–1519) = Gian Franc. Gonzague; Lucrezia (1470–1517) = Annibale Bentivoglio; Beatrice (1475–1497) = Lodovico Sforza; Ferrando; Sigismondo (1480–1524); Giulio (1478–1561); Ippolito I (1479–1520) cardinal.

Alfonso Ier (1476–1534), troisième duc de Ferrare, ≈ Laura Dianti, = [1491] Anna Sforza, = [1502] Lucrezia Borgia; children: Ippolito II (1509–1572) cardinal; Leonora (1515–1575); Francesco (1516–1578); Ercole II (1508–1559), 4ème duc de Ferrare = Renée, fille de Louis XII roi de France; Alfonso (1527–1587) = Giulia della Rovere; Alfonsino (†1578) = Marfisa d'Este.

Children of Ercole II and Renée: Lucrezia (1535–1598) Franc. Maria II della Rovere, duc d'Urbin; Luigi (1538–1586) cardinal; Leonora (1537–1581); Alfonso II (1533–1597), 5ème duc de Ferrare et de Modène; Marfisa; Bradamante.

Cesare (1562–1628), duc de Ferrare 1597, duc de Modène 1597–1628.

LÉGENDE

⊃	né, née
†	mort
✳	mort violent
△	monument funèbre
▲	tombeau
⟩⟩	naissance illégitime
=	mariage, épousailles
≈	union illégitime

Niccolò III., who ruled Ferrara, Modena, Parma, and Reggio, waged many wars, was made general of the army of the Church, and in his later years governor of Milan. His second son, Borso, received the title of Duke of Modena and Reggio from emperor Frederick III., and that of Duke of Ferrara from Pope Paul II.

FERRARA — *PALAZZO SCHIFANOIA.*

TRIUMPH OF MINERVA. *Allegory of* March. *By* FRANCESCO COSSA.

Minerva, whose festival in ancient times was celebrated in March, rides upon a triumphal car drawn by unicorns (Borso's badge). On the right are women engaged in needlework, weaving at the looms or looking on, on the left are groups of professors and jurists reading or discoursing. (The Ram is the zodiacal sign).

TRIUMPH OF VENUS. *Allegory of* April. *By* F. COSSA.

In April, the month sacred to Venus, the season of the renewal of life, Venus triumphs in her barge drawn by swans. In one hand she holds a flower and in the other the apple of Paris. An armed warrior (Mars?) chained to her car kneels before her. On either side, to the sound of lutes and viols, youths and maidens kiss and embrace, or linger in amorous dalliance. Rabbits, symbolising fertility, scamper about freely. In the background, standing upon a rock are the 3 Graces presiding over the lovers' joys. The whole scene is like a painted page of Boccaccio.

TRIUMPH OF APOLLO. *Allegory of* May. *By* F. COSSA.

VENUS AND MARS. *Triumph of Venus.*

For May we have Apollo, the god of song and music. He rides upon a car drawn by four horses which Aurora, seated in front, is guiding. On the left is a group of poets, on the right a host of children (symbolising the poets' inventions?), and behind the Nine Muses and their winged horse Pegasus standing at the fountain of Helicon.

The frescoes dealing with other months (omitted here), are ascribed to COSIMO TURA and other painters. For June we have Mercury riding upon a car drawn by four horses which Aurora, seated in front, is guiding. On the poet is the sign of this month. For July we have the Triumph of Jove, riding upon a car drawn by two lions. For August, Ceres, the protectress of agriculture, triumphs in her car drawn by two dragons; the Virgin stretched over the sun is the zodiacal sign of this month. For September, we have a female figure riding on a car drawn by two monkeys; the Scales is the sign of this month. The paintings devoted to the remaining months have perished.

Photo ALINARI, ANDERSON.

PARMA

PARMA is of Roman origin, but possesses few relics of antiquity, except the great Emilian way which passes through it. It is a mediæval city and famed in the history of art as the home of Antonio Allegri, surnamed CORREGGIO. The Cathedral, one of the finest examples of the Lombard-Romanesque style, was begun in A. D. 1058; its dome is adorned with paintings by Correggio and his followers. The Baptistery, of Veronese marble, was built in 1196-1322; its magnificent portals are embellished with important scriptural sculptures by Benedetto Antelami.

THE CATHEDRAL AND BAPTISTERY. *Lombard-Romanesque style, 11th-12th cent.*

Fragment from the ASSUMPTION, by CORREGGIO. (*In the dome of the cathedral*).

REST ON THE FLIGHT TO EGYPT. Madonna della Scodella. *By* CORREGGIO. 1528.

CORREGGIO (1494-1534), famous for his mastery of chiaroscuro, was above all things a *painter*, and his mode of execution and his colouring are peculiar to him alone. From Michelangelo he acquired his taste for aërial movement, for figures hovering in mid-air which amaze the onlooker by foreshortenings that seem impossible and yet are true to nature. " The cheerfulness of Raphael, " writes Symonds, " the wizardry of Lionardo, and the boldness of Michael Angelo, met in him to form a new style, the originality of which is undisputable, and which takes us captive—not by intellectual power, but by the impulse of emotion. "

The joyous creations of Correggio's sensuous nature fill the churches of Parma. (*See also* the Camera del Correggio or Refectory of the abbess of the convent of St. Paul).

MADONNA DI SAN GIROLAMO. "Il Giorno." Painted by CORREGGIO. *About* 1525.

DESCENT FROM THE CROSS. *By* BENEDETTO ANTELAMI. 1178. (*Relief in the cathedral at Parma*).

Photo ALINARI, ANDERSON, BROGI.

PALACE OF THEODORIC THE GREAT (restored).
This palace was ruined by Charlemagne who plundered it.

MAUSOLEUM OF THEODORIC († 526)
Built by his daughter Amalasuntha.

RAVENNA

RAVENNA is the richest treasure-house of early-Christian art. Her churches sparkling with a profusion of the richest ornaments, and her great monuments are such as the whole world cannot furnish elsewhere. From the fifth to the eighth century Ravenna was the capital of the ancient Western Roman empire; the seat of government of the Gothic Kings, and afterwards of the Exarchs or Viceroys of the Byzantine Emperors.

It was in Ravenna that Dante found rest for time and eternity; here Gaston de Foix (p. 63) fell in one of the bloodiest battles which Europe had yet seen; here Byron sought peace and repose beside the beautiful Countess Guiccioli.

MAUSOLEUM OF DANTE.

The tomb of Dante is the goal of many a pilgrimage. After spending the latter years of his life at Verona under the protection of Can Grande della Scala, in the year 1320 the exiled Poet found a last refuge at the court of Guido da Polenta, Lord of Ravenna and father of that unfortunate Francesca, whose story has been told by Dante (*Hell* V.) with such unrivalled pathos. The following year he undertook a mission to Venice and there contracted a fever which carried him off on Sept. 14th 1321, at the age of 56, shortly after he had completed his great epic. His remains were temporarily interred in a stone sarcophagus by his friend Guido in the portico of San Francesco. But the exile and death of Guido and political troubles delayed for 150 years the erection of a monument which in 1483 was raised by Bernardo Bembo, the father of the Cardinal, and by him decorated with an effigy of the Poet in bas-relief and with an epitaph. The mausoleum with the "little cupola, more neat than solemn," in which the Bembo monument stands was erected in 1780 by the Cardinal Gonzaga.

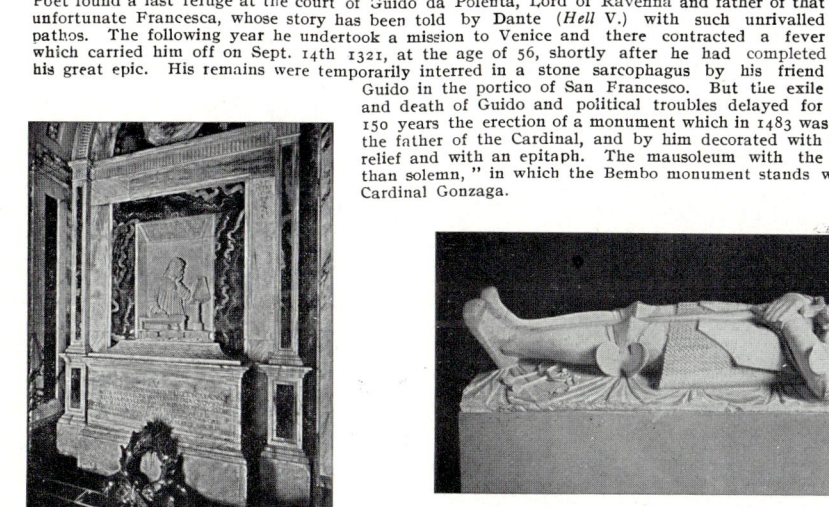

Colonna dei Francesi, commemorating the Battle of Ravenna, erected in 1557 on the spot where Gaston de Foix (p. 62) expired.

TOMB OF DANTE. († 1321).
By PIETRO LOMBARDI.

MONUMENT OF GUIDARELLO GUIDARELLI. *By* TULLIO LOMBARDI.
This is one of the most perfect representations of death ever given in sculpture.

Photo ALINARI, ANDERSON.

RAVENNA — *SANT'APOLLINARE NUOVO.*

Sant'Apollinare Nuovo was built by Theodoric the Great in A. D. 500, as the Arian Cathedral. After the fall of the Gothic Kingdom in 560, it was converted into a Catholic church. The glittering mosaics of the nave are very impressive and unique. On each side, above the arches, are two prodigious friezes with long processions of white robed Saints. On the left (the side of the church occupied by the women), is represented the town of Classis from which a solemn procession of twenty-two Virgin Saints headed by the Three Magi bearing gifts, advance towards the Madonna enthroned between angels. On the right side, we see a similar procession of twenty-six Saints all clad in white garments, with wreaths in their hands approaching Christ enthroned between angels. Higher up, between the windows, are single figures of the Apostles and Saints. Above the windows are interesting panels in mosaic representing the Life and Miracles of our Lord, down to the Resurrection.

INTERIOR OF THE BASILICA OF SANT'APOLLINARE NUOVO.

THE TOWN OF CLASSIS, APOSTLES, SAINTS.
Part of the mosaic frieze in the left side of the nave.

INTERIOR OF SANT'APOLLINARE NUOVO,
showing the left side of the nave.

THE MAGI FOLLOWED BY HOLY VIRGINS APPROACHING THE MADONNA ENTHRONED. (*Left wall of the nave*).

Photo ALINARI, ANDERSON.

RAVENNA — *SANT'APOLLINARE NUOVO.*

BASILICA OF SANT'APOLLINARE NUOVO.

SANT'APOLLINARE NUOVO.
Erected about A. D. 500.

Few of man's works are more striking than the long processions of virgins and martyrs on either side of the nave.

INTERIOR OF SANT'APOLLINARE NUOVO
showing the right side of the nave.

THE PALATIUM, THE PALACE OF THEODORIC.
Part of the mosaic frieze in the right side of the nave.

SAINTS WITH WREATHS IN THEIR HANDS APPROACHING CHRIST ENTHRONED. (*Right wall of the nave*).

Photo ALINARI, ANDERSON.

RAVENNA — *CHURCH OF SAN VITALE.*

The Emp. Justinian with the Archbp. Maximian and attendants. The Empress Theodora and her court.
Note the halos of Christian saints which the artist, in his courtly flattery, has placed on the heads of the emperor and of his domineering wife. *Sixth century mosaics in the apse of San Vitale.*

Abraham entertaining the three Angels. - Sacrifice of Isaac. Sacrifice of Abel. The offering of Melchisedek.
(*Sixth century mosaics in the choir of San Vitale*).

The *Church of San Vitale*, an octagonal domed structure representing the triumph of Byzantine architecture in the West was begun in A. D. 525, on the spot where St. Vitalis suffered martyrdom. In the interior the lower part of the walls are covered with rare marbles; the massive pillars are crowned by capitals sculptured in the Byzantine style; but the great feature of San Vitale is the brilliant mosaic work of the time of Justinian and Theodora with which the walls are encrusted.

View of the choir. Transversal view of the interior

— 184 —

Photo Alinari, Anderson.

RAVENNA. *Early Christian Art.*

MAUSOLEUM OF GALLA PLACIDIA. (A. D. 440).

THE GOOD SHEPHERD. *Fifth century mosaic.* (*Mausoleum of Galla Placidia*).

The *Mausoleum of Galla Placidia*, founded about A. D. 450, by that beautiful Empress, is a casket of jewels rather than a mere monumental chapel. Its interior, literally covered with splendid mosaics of the rarest colour and design, is a triumph of decorative art. In the lunette over the altar Our Saviour appears with a cross in his hand, standing beside a grate with burning coals, beyond which is seen an open book-case containing rolls of the Gospels, each marked with the Evangelists name. In the lunette over the entrance there is a representation of the « Good Shepherd » (symbolizing Christ, see p. 503). seated among his flock and caressing or feeding one of his sheep. In the lunettes, at the termination of the transepts, are seen stags (symbolising proselytes) quenching their thirst at the Fountain of Life. In the vaults of the arches are the Apostles, two by two, between and below each are pairs of doves sipping out of vases. Finally in the center of the dome, between large stars on a dark blue sky, a richly decorated cross glitters, surrounded by the symbols of the Four Evangelists.

The great sarcophagus in front is the tomb of Placidia, whose body, it is said, was placed in it clothed in her imperial robes and seated on a throne of cypress. The two sarcophagi on the right are those of Constantius and Valentinian III. her son.

THE BAPTISM OF CHRIST *and the 12 Apostles.* (*Sixth century mosaic. Baptistery of the Arians*).

BAPTISTERY OF THE ORTHODOX. A. D. 450.
The mosaics here are among the most ancient at Ravenna.

THE BAPTISM OF CHRIST *and the 12 Apostles.* (*Baptistery of the Orthodox*).

The Baptistery of the Orthodox, adjoining the cathedral, was converted from a bath-house by Archbishop Neon in the 5th Cent.

— 185 —

Photo ALINARI, ANDERSON.

RAVENNA. Early Christian Art.

THRONE OF THE ARCHBISHOP MAXIMIN (546-52).
(*Archiepiscopal Palace*).

The *Throne of the Archbishop Maximin (so-called)*, is considered the finest piece of ivory work in existence, both for its historical associations and for the quality of its decorations. The work was probably made in Alexandria, Egypt, in the 5th century, from whence it was taken to Grado and subsequently sent as a gift to Emperor Otho III. in 1001, who left it at Ravenna. The throne is adorned with reliefs in ivory representing scenes from the life of Christ and the history of Joseph. On the front of the seat is St. John the Baptist with the four Evangelists. All the scenes are framed by intertwining branches peopled with tiny animals.

Joseph's blood-stained tunic shown to Jacob.
Joseph is let down in the well.
(*Ivory reliefs on Maximin's throne*).

Meeting of Joseph and Jacob.
The Dream of Pharaoh.

"Christ between two Apostles." 5th cent.
Sarcophagus of Rainaldus.
(*Cathedral of Sant'Orso*).

"The Adoration of the Magi." 5th cent.
Sarcophagus of the Exharch Isaac. (Cfr. mosaic on p. 182).
(*Basilica of San Vitale*).

Photo ALINARI, ANDERSON.

RAVENNA — SANT'APOLLINARE in Classe.

Interior.   SANT'APOLLINARE IN CLASSE.   *Campanile and façade.*

Sant'Apollinare in Classe, begun in 534 and consecrated 15 years later by Archbishop Maximin, is the largest basilica at Ravenna. The interior rests on 24 columns of cipollino and has a wooden roof. In the aisles are several sarcophagi richly sculptured with early Christian reliefs and emblems, containing the remains of archbishops of the 5th and 8th centuries. The rich marbles that once encased the walls were taken off by Sigismondo Malatesta in 1449, but the tribune and triumphal arch, still retain their precious mosaics of the 6th and 7th centuries.

APSE AND TRIUMPHAL ARCH MOSAICS.

THE GRANDING OF THE "PRIVILEGES" to the Church of Ravenna.

The apse is adorned with a mosaic of the « Transfiguration ». Upon a blue ground, within a blue circle studded with gold stars and jewels, appears a gemmed cross, in the centre of which, the head of Our Saviour is inserted like a precious stone. Below the cross are inscribed the Latin words « Salus Mundi ». On each side of the circle are the half-length figures of Moses and Elias; lower down are three sheep which symbolize the Apostles on Mount Tabor; while at the top, the hand of God issuing from the clouds is seen pointing to the cross. Below the circle, upon a flowery meadow, stands a large figure of the martyr Apollinaris, his hands raised in the act of preaching, and on either side twelve sheep representing the faithful (?) listening to his words.

On the Great Arch is a bust of Christ, in the act of blessing, with the symbols of the Evangelists, and below them twelve sheep (symbolizing the Apostles) advancing towards Christ from the towns of Jerusalem and Bethlehem.

Sarcophagus of the Archbishop Theodore. A. D. 677.

« Christ handing the Law to Peter ».
Fifth century sarcophagus.

The church of Sant'Apollinare is 3 miles from Ravenna, it is the only relic left of the ancient town of Classis, the naval station of Imperial Rome whose port was capable of holding 250 war-galleys.

THE DUOMO. CHURCH OF SAN FRANCESCO, called "Tempio Malatestiano." A. D. 1447.

RIMINI, the ancient *Ariminum* founded by the Umbrians, became a Roman colony in 268 B. C. and was held as an outpost against the Gauls. Julius Cæsar held it in 49 B. C. after crossing the Rubicon. The singular edifice given above, originally a Gothic church, was entirely remodelled in 1447 by Sigismondo Pandolfo Malatesta from designs by LEON BATTISTA ALBERTI. All the Malatesta are buried here, and here, too, is the shrine dedicated to Isotta,— Sigismondo's mistress. For centuries the Malatesta ruled Rimini like tyrants, Sigismondo was perhaps the worst of the race. To enumerate the crimes which he committed would violate the rules of decency; he killed three wives in succession and committed outrages on his children. Yet, he united a romantic zeal for culture with the vices of a barbarian, he read books with patient care always encouraged literature, and delighted in the society of artists.

TOMB OF ISOTTA DEGLI ATTI.
Sigismondo's mistress.

SIGISMONDO MALATESTA KNEELING.
Part of a fresco by PIERO DELLA FRANCESCA.

THE ADORATION OF THE MAGI.
Romanesque relief. (San Mercuriale, Forlì).

On the left the Three Kings are seen in bed and the angel appears to them: in the centre they are portrayed taking off their cowns or kneeling to the Virgin.

FORLÌ. CHURCH OF SAN MERCURIALE. 12th c.

FORLÌ, where in 410 Galla Placidia married Athaulfus, King of the Visigoths, was an independent Guelfic city till 1315, when the sovereignty was usurped by the Ordelaffi, and afterwards by Girolamo Riario, the husband of Caterina Sforza. Forlì was the birth-place of the eminent painter Melozzo da Forli.

Photo ALINARI, ANDERSON, BROGI.

LORETO, ANCONA. [THE MARCHES].

GENERAL VIEW OF LORETO. On the right: the dome of the « Santuario ».

LORETO, about two miles from the Adriatic, is one of the most celebrated places of Christian pilgrimage in the world. According to the legend, the house of Nazareth in which the Holy Virgin was born and which was the home of the Holy Family after their return from Egypt, became an object of profound veneration after the Empress Helena, mother of Constantine went to worship there, and caused a church to be erected over it. In the thirteenth century, the church having fallen into decay and being threatened with desecration by the Saracens, the Holy House was miraculously transplanted by angels in 1291 from Nazareth to Tersatto in Dalmatia, where it remained for three years. But being again in danger, the angels once more took it up on the night of December 9th 1294, bore it over the Adriatic, and deposited it in a laurel-grove (*Lauretum*), near Recanati. The *Santa Casa* soon became an object of pilgrimage, and such offerings were made to the shrine that a church was soon erected over it. In the year 1586 Pope Sixtus V. surrounded the place with walls as a defence against the incursions of the Saracens, and accorded to Loreto the privileges of a town.

The present church or *Santuario della Santa Casa*, was begun on the site of the primitive church in 1465, and continued by GIULIANO DA MAIANO. The lofty dome was completed by GIULIANO DA SANGALLO, while the beautiful façade was erected in 1570-87 under Sixtus V., a colossal statue of whom stands at the entrance of the temple. The interior is very impressive and contains numerous works of art including paintings by MELOZZO DA FORLÌ and SIGNORELLI. Beneath the dome rises the Santa Casa (like St. Francis' Porziuncola at Assisi, p. 375), a simple rude stone edifice of 36 feet by 17; its walls externally cased in marble with admirable reliefs and statues of prophets and sibyls. On the little altar in the interior is a black figure of the Virgin and Child in cedar, said to be the first work of St. Luke. This highly revered image is richly adorned with jewels and precious stones and in front of it silver lamps are kept burning day and night. In 1797 it was taken to Paris, but restored to its place in 1801.

THE CASA SANTA, or "Holy House."

INTERIOR of the "Holy House."

ANGEL. *By* GUERCINO. (*Church of S. Agostino, Fano*). The 'Guardian Angel' of Browning's poem.

ANCONA. CATHEDRAL OF S. CIRIACO. A. D. 1150. Built in a mixed Byzantine and Romanesque style. Façade of the 13th cent.

THE ANNUNCIATION. *By* LORENZO LOTTO. (*S. Maria dei Mercanti, Recanati*).

Photo ALINARI, ANDERSON, BROGI.

THE DUCAL PALACE. (1465). COURT OF THE DUCAL PALACE.
Erected by order of FEDERICO DI MONTEFELTRO. *Designed by* LUCIANO LAURANA.

URBINO, lies on a hill between the Apennines and the Adriatic, amid scenery of austere grandeur. In the 13th century the town came into the possession of the Montefeltro family, and under Federigo Montefeltro (1444-82), it rose to great prominence and prosperity. Federigo was not only the most able general of his day, famous for his sincerity and plain dealing, but a generous patron of art and an accomplished ruler. He made Urbino the centre of cultivated society, and although his means were not great, he lavished them on the poet, the artist and the scholar, while he reared a palace, celebrated alike for the perfection of its internal arrangements and for the magnificence and beauty of its saloons, its doorways, windows and fire places rich in sculptured ornaments.

In 1474 Federigo was created Duke of Urbino by Pope Sixtus IV., and the following year he was made Knight of the Garter by Edward IV. of England. His Court was regarded as a model among the princely courts of that period. It was a school of military education to which princes sent their sons in order to learn manners and the art of war; his library containing copies of all the Greek and Latin authors then discovered, was filled with scholars. In his relations to his people he showed what a paternal prince should be, and he went about unarmed, receiving the blessing of his subjects, for each of whom he had some kindly word.

Federigo's son, Guidobaldo, zealously followed his father's example with the assistance of his wife, Elisabetta Gonzaga, one of the most distinguished women of her age. She was not so much celebrated for her learning, as for her virtue and amiability. She was devoted to her husband who was afflicted with gout and 'other misfortunes,' and her noble character character and serenity exercised a beneficial influence on all who approached her. A famous description of the Court of Urbino under Guidobaldo and his estimable Duchess, depicting it as the most refined social school and the resort of the first literary and political celebrities of the day, is given by Count Baldassar Castiglione in his work *Il Cortegiano* or « the mirror of a perfect courtier ».

In 1497, Guidobaldo was treacherously expelled from Urbino by Cesare Borgia, but after the death of Alexander VI. and the subsequent fall of Cesare, he returned to his duchy and was welcomed with enthusiasm and tears of joy by his subjects.

MADONNA AND SAINTS, *by* LUCA DELLA ROBBIA (1449). (*Church of S. Domenico*).

GENEALOGICAL TABLE OF THE HOUSE OF MONTEFELTRO
Dukes of Urbino

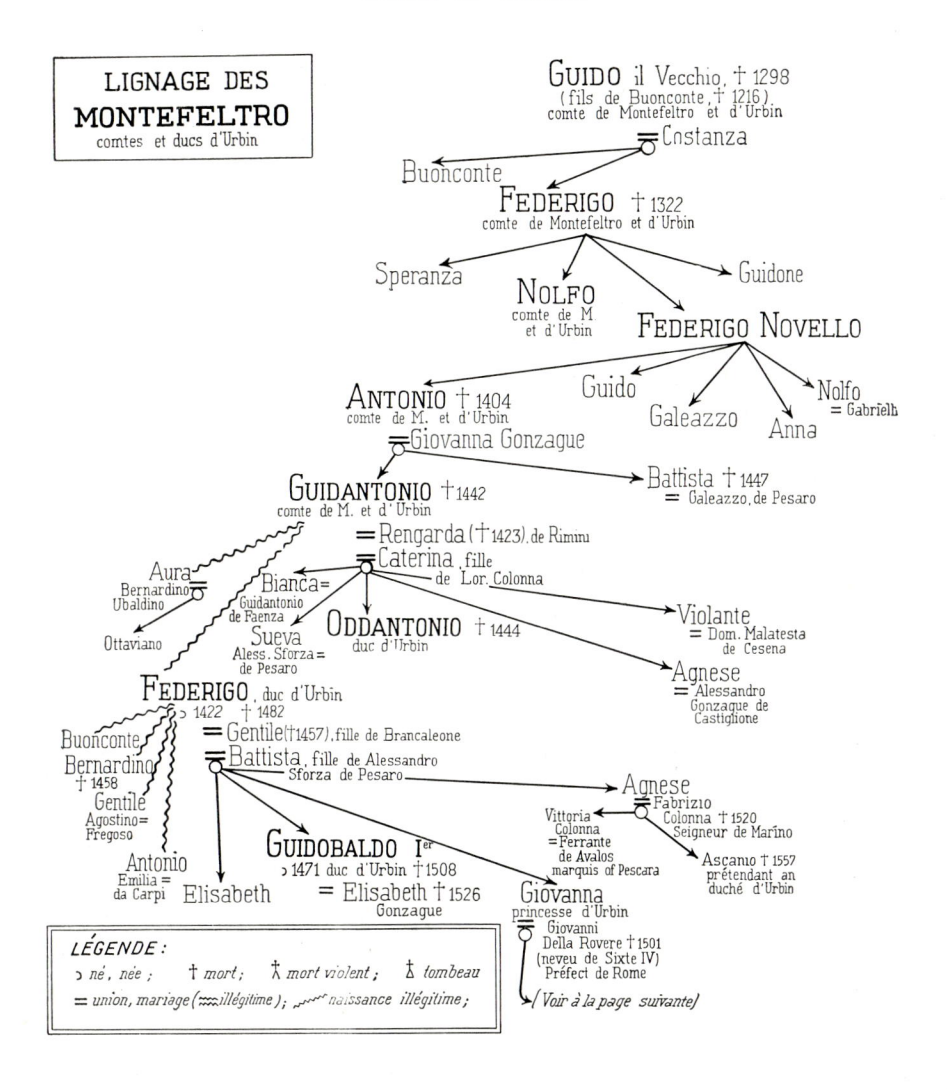

A distinguished Italian family of Montefeltro, a hill-town situated in the Apennines at the foot of which the Tiber takes its rise.

In 1268, Guido il Vecchio (d. 1298), Count of Montefeltro, and one of the most prominent figures in the time of Dante, great Ghibelline captain, was Conradin's vicar in Rome. In 1274, he was captain of Forlì, and in the next year was appointed captain-general of the Ghibellines in Romagna. The year after at the head of the combined forces of the Ghibellines in Romagna and Florence he won a decisive victory over the Guelfs. In 1292 he made himself master of Urbino, which he held and defended against the Malatesta of Rimini. Guido (whose son Buonconte was killed at the battle of Campaldino in 1289 while fighting on the Ghibelline side) died in 1298, in the Franciscan monastery at Assisi.

GENEALOGICAL TABLE OF THE HOUSE DELLA ROVERE

Dukes of Urbino

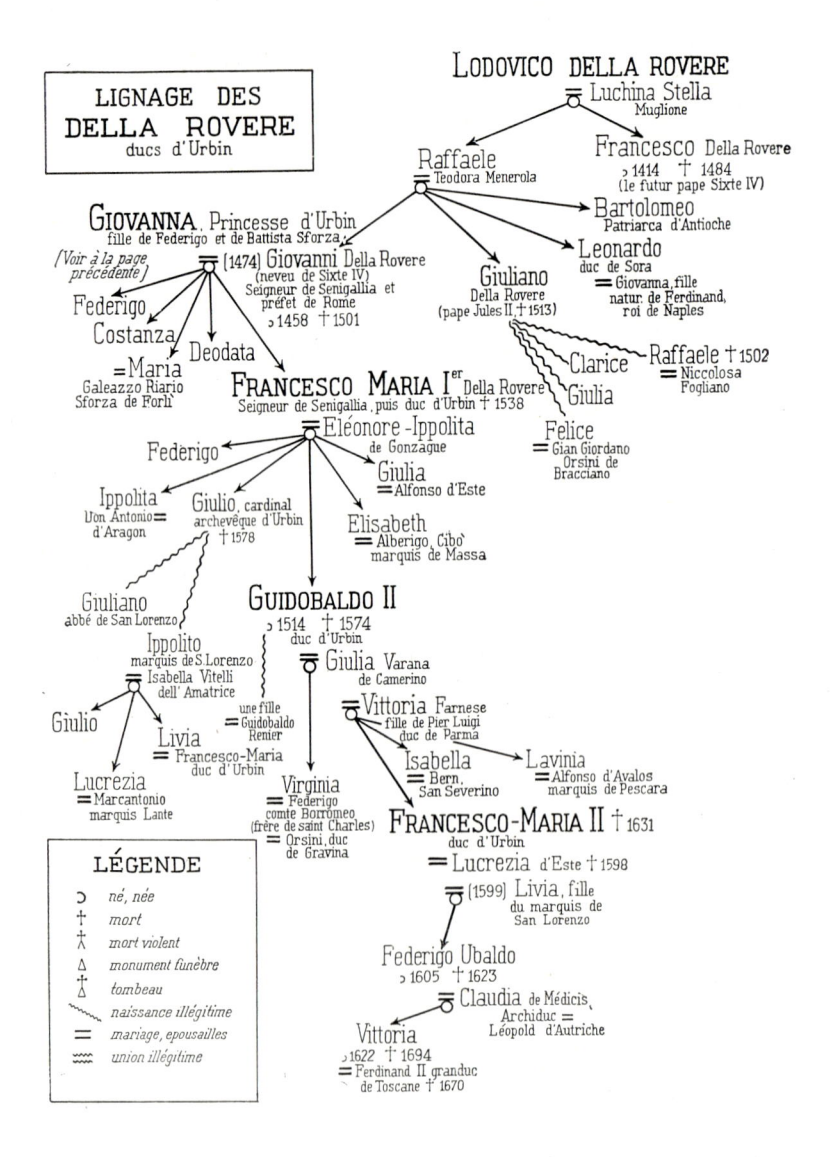

LIGNAGE DES DELLA ROVERE ducs d'Urbin

LODOVICO DELLA ROVERE = Luchina Stella, Muglione

- Raffaele = Teodora Menerola
- Francesco Della Rovere ⊃ 1414 † 1484 (le futur pape Sixte IV)
- Bartolomeo, Patriarca d'Antioche
- Leonardo, duc de Sora = Giovanna, fille natur. de Ferdinand, roi de Naples

GIOVANNA, Princesse d'Urbin, fille de Federigo et de Battista Sforza
(Voir à la page précédente)
= (1474) Giovanni Della Rovere (neveu de Sixte IV), Seigneur de Senigallia et préfet de Rome ⊃ 1458 † 1501

- Federigo
- Costanza = Maria, Galeazzo Riario Sforza de Forlì
- Deodata
- **FRANCESCO MARIA I**er Della Rovere, Seigneur de Senigallia, puis duc d'Urbin † 1538
  = Eléonore-Ippolita de Gonzague
- Giuliano Della Rovere (pape Jules II, † 1513)
- Clarice
- Giulia
- Raffaele † 1502 = Niccolosa Fogliano
- Felice = Gian Giordano Orsini de Bracciano

- Federigo
- Ippolita = Don Antonio d'Aragon
- Giulio, cardinal, archevêque d'Urbin † 1578
- Giulia = Alfonso d'Este
- Elisabeth = Alberigo Cibò, marquis de Massa

- Giuliano, abbé de San Lorenzo
- Ippolito, marquis de S. Lorenzo = Isabella Vitelli dell'Amatrice
- **GUIDOBALDO II** ⊃ 1514 † 1574, duc d'Urbin
  = Giulia Varana de Camerino
  = Vittoria Farnese, fille de Pier Luigi duc de Parma

- Giulio
- Livia
- une fille = Guidobaldo Renier
- Francesco-Maria, duc d'Urbin
- Lucrezia = Marcantonio, marquis Lante
- Virginia = Federigo comte Borromeo (frère de saint Charles) = Orsini, duc de Gravina
- Isabella = Bern. San Severino
- Lavinia = Alfonso d'Avalos, marquis de Pescara
- **FRANCESCO-MARIA II** † 1631, duc d'Urbin
  = Lucrezia d'Este † 1598
  = (1599) Livia, fille du marquis de San Lorenzo

- Federigo Ubaldo ⊃ 1605 † 1623
  = Claudia de Médicis, Archiduc = Léopold d'Autriche
- Vittoria ⊃ 1622 † 1694 = Ferdinand II granduc de Toscane † 1670

LÉGENDE
- ⊃ né, née
- † mort
- ☨ mort violent
- ∆ monument funèbre
- ☨ tombeau
- ∼ naissance illégitime
- = mariage, épousailles
- ≈ union illégitime

After Guidobaldo's death (1508), the duchy of Urbino was continued by the Della Rovere family, one of whom, Giovanni, nephew of Pope Sixtus IV., married the Duke's sister Giovanna, in 1474, and was created Duke of Sinigaglia and Prefect of Rome. This man, a plebeian, founded the second dynasty in the Dukedom of Urbino.

Throughout the 16th century the state of Urbino manufactured Majolica, especially at Gubbio and Castel Durante. Most of the finest pieces were made for the dukes.

EMILIA - THE MARCHES *Mediæval Strongholds.*

RIMINI. CASTLE OF THE MALATESTA.
Erected in 1446 by Sigismondo Malatesta.

CENTO. THE CASTLE.
Formerly belonging to the House of Este.

TOLENTINO. CASTELLO DELLA RANCIA. *Built in the 12th century.*
It was near this castle that Joachim Murat was defeated by the Austrians in 1815, taken prisoner, and shot.

FORLÌ. CASTLE OF CATERINA SFORZA.

Begun in 1359 by Cardinal Albornoz, in 1500 this stronghold was valiantly defended by the indomitable Caterina Sforza, against the soldiery of Cesare Borgia; and when the enemy had threatened to murder her children unless she surrendered she replied: "I am young enough to have more!"

GRADARA. THE CASTLE.

The Castle of Gradara built by the Malatesta, Lords of Rimini, is supposed to have been the scene of the tragedy of Francesca da Polenta and Paolo Malatesta (an event immortalised by Dante in the 5th canto of the Inferno).

Photo ALINARI, ANDERSON.

CASTLE OF SAN MARINO.

The REPUBLIC OF SAN MARINO, the smallest in the world, is one of the most curious places in Italy. Its foundation is ascribed to S. Marinus, a pious stonemason who fled to this mountain solitude at the time of the persecutions of the Christians (4th cent.) under Diocletian. This diminutive state has preserved its independence for fourteen hundred years, while all the other former states of Italy changed their masters and forms of government several times. The Republic has an area of 23 square miles with a population of 12.000 inhabitants; it is governed by two Capitani Reggenti, elected every six months from the sixty members of the Great Council, in which every house has its representative.

A few miles from San Marino is the old Castle of San Leo, where the notorious Count di Cagliostro died in confinement in 1795.

TUSCANY

FLORENCE. THE RIVER ARNO AND THE PONTE VECCHIO.

FLORENCE
PRATO PISTOIA LUCCA PISA SIENA
SAN GIMIGNANO VOLTERRA AREZZO

WONDERS OF ITALY.

FLORENCE. Sacristy of Santa Croce. *Michelozzo*

CHRONOLOGY OF FLORENTINE HISTORY

B. C.
200 Roman Camp of *Florentia*. The Flaminian Road from Rome to Northern Italy which crosses the Arno by the ancient Roman Bridge (*Ponte Vecchio*) encourages early development of Florence.

A. D.
488. Baptistery of S. Giovanni founded.
556. First Wall, *Primo Cerchio*, built.
786. Charlemagne visits the town.
852. Wool trade flourishing in Florence.
934. Medical faculty in practice.
990. Benedictines settle in Florence.
1063. Great Religious Revival.
1074. Second Wall begun, *Oltrarno* taken.
1076. Countess Mathilda of Tuscany encourages Crafts.
1080. Ancient Roman Bridge rebuilt in stone and called *Ponte Vecchio*.
1101. Consuls for the Crafts first appointed by Mathilda.
1115. Death of Mathilda. Birth of Commune; Florence declared independent of all external rule.
1138. City divided into Six Wards or *Sesteri*, *Buonuomini* elected for each.
1150. Silver Florin first used.
1154. First record of Florentine merchants trading with Great Britain, chiefly in wool.
1165. The "Society of Towers" for the *Grandi*, and "Corporations" for the *Popolani* established.
1183. The Peace of Constance confirms self-government to Florence and other Tuscan Communes.
1194. First record of Florentine Bankers.
1197. Legal Tribunals fully established. First distinct mention of Seven Greater Guilds. Tuscan League under lead of Florence established by pope Innocent III.
1199. First recorded mission of Florentine Bankers to London.
1200. Silk industry in a thriving condition. First mention of the Guild of Bankers.
1204. The Rectors of the Guilds styled "Priors." Census of the population and occupations.
1207. First *Podestà*, elected.
1215. Tragedy at the Buondelmonte-Amidei marriage originates the two great parties · the *Guelphs* and the *Ghibellines*. Wars with Pisa, Siena and other cities. Florence divided between two hostile camps.
1218. College of Doctors and Apothecaries in existence. The *Ponte alla Carraia* built in stone. Inhabitants of *Oltrarno* and the *Contado* required to take oath of allegiance to Florence.
1222. The first *Monte Comune* or Pawnshop opened. School of Medicine and Surgery founded.
1233. The *Podestà* orders every adult male to register his name, age and occupation. Mercantile Companies affiliated to the Guilds.
1237. The *Ponte alle Grazie*, Rubaconte, built. Streets of Florence paved with hard stone setts.
1247. Party feuds and the encroachments of Frederick II., of Hohenstaufen and of the Uberti retard trade and commerce.
1250. *Podestà* deposed, the *Capitano del Popolo* appointed instead. Popular government established. Pistoia, Volterra, San Gimignano under the authority of the Florentine. Foreign *Condottieri* first employed. Guelphs chased from Florence.
1252. The *Zecca*, Mint, established. The first Gold Florin is coined. The *Ponte Santa Trinita* built. Law made obliging patricians to reduce height of their towers. Guelphs recalled.
1258. The *Bargello*, Palazzo del Podestà built. Ghibellines expelled.
1260. Battle of Montaperti. Victory of the Ghibellines at Florence. *Lettere di Cambio*, Letters of Credit first issued by Bankers. The Ponte Vecchio rebuilt. Count Guido Novello assumes supreme authority. The Public Prison, *Stinche*, opened.
1266. The Guelphs regain power. A new government, *Signoria* formed.
1267. Charles of Anjou, Lord of Florence makes many knights.
1269. Disastrous floods destroy bridges.
1282. First *Signoria*, or presidents of trade-guilds assume office.
1285. Third Wall, or *Terzo Cerchio* built. Hospital of *Santa Maria Nuova* founded. Great Fire (1289) destroys many workshops. Battle of Campaldino (1289).
1295. Giano della Bella in power. The *Ordinamenti di Giustizia* promulgated, the noble are excluded from power.
1300. The First Jubilee of Pope Boniface VIII. Strife of the *Bianchi* and *Neri*, "Blacks" and "Whites," The Blacks victorious (1301). Dante banished and condemned to death, his property confiscated.
1305-1377. Papal Schism. *Piazza della Signoria* laid out and paved. Great scarcity and bad trade.
1313 King Robert of Naples appointed Lord of Florence. Trouble among the wool-workers.
1325. Charles of Anjou. Duke of Calabria, Regent of Florence. Failure of the Scali Bank, 400,000 florins.
1336. Alliance with Venice.
1340. Disastrous failure of the Bardi and Peruzzi Banks (see *p. 614*).
1342. Overthrow of the Constitution. Walter of Brienne, appointed

— 191 —

Conservator of the Peace and Lord of Florence is expelled (1343).
1343. Buonaccorsi Bank failure. Attack by *Popolani* on palaces of *Grandi*. Many *Grandi* families enrolled among *Popolani*.
1345. Butchers occupy the forty shops in the new Ponte Vecchio.
1348. The Black Plague ravages the country. Three-fifths of the inhabitants die.
1355. *Condottiere* system first created.
1378. Rebellion of the poorer classes (Tumulto de' Ciompi). Three years' anarchy follows.
1381. Rule of the aristocratic party, headed by the Albizi. Florence strong and prosperous.
1406. Florence takes Pisa, and purchases Cortona for 60,000 gold florins.
1419. Pope Martin V. resides at Florence, and gives the "Golden Rose" to the Government.
1422. Giovanni de' Medici (founder of the Medici dynasty) is elected *Gonfaloniere di Giustizia*. The *Spedale degli Innocenti* is founded.
1427. New system of taxation, the *Catasto*. Jews allowed to settle in the Ghetto (1429).
1429. Cosimo the Elder takes the government; but is overthrown by the Albizi in 1433.
1434. Cosimo returns from exile and resumes government.
1464. Piazza della Signoria completed.
1471. Bernardo Cennini's printing-press first in operation.
1475. Unwritten law affirmed: "Every Florentine-born adult is free to gain his living as he wills."
1478. Conspiracy of the Pazzi. Giuliano de' Medici is murdered in the cathedral.
1492. Savonarola begins his sermons on morality. Lorenzo de' Medici, styled *Capo della Repubblica*, dies
1495. Government Pawnshop, il *Presto*, opened. Piero, the feeble son of Lorenzo de' Medici is defeated by Charles VIII., of France and expelled with his brothers Giovanni and Giuliano. Florence becomes a Republic till 1512.
1502. Corruption creeps into Florentine Legal Tribunals. Piero Soderini elected *Gonfaloniere* for life.
1509. Florentine militia established by Macchiavelli.
1511. Great frost. *Il Calcio* (Florentine football), and other games, played on the frozen Arno river.
1512. The Medici brothers are recalled from exile, and reinstated by Spanish troops.
1527. Florence a prey to disorders and plague. The Medici are once more expelled, by a revolution lead by the Strozzi. Christ proclaimed (1529) King of Florence.
1528. Michelangelo fortifies the city.
1529. Siege of Florence by the Prince of Orange; famine and plague ravage the city.
1530. Florence is taken by the troops of Charles V. Alessandro de' Medici is created hereditary duke. The *Signoria* abolished.
1536. Charles V., visits Florence.
1537. Cosimo I., son of Giovanni delle Bande Nere, founds the Junior Branch of the Medici obtaining the title of Grand-Duke (ended 1737 when, with Giovanni Gastone, the House of Medici becomes extinct).
1547. Inundation and famine.
1737. Florence and Tuscany under Austrian rule, till 1801.
1801. Tuscany becomes a Republic, then Kingdom of Etruria.
1807. Tuscany is incorporated with France (Napoleonic Regime).
1814. Grand-Duke Ferdinand III., is reinstated.
1824. Grand-Duke Leopold II., son of Ferdinand III.
1860. Tuscany is united to the Kingdom of Italy, and becomes (1865) its capital, till 1871.

GENERAL VIEW OF FLORENCE IN THE YEAR 1450.
From a fresco of the fifteenth century in the Palazzo Vecchio.

VIEW OF FLORENCE AND THE HILL OF FIESOLE AS SEEN FROM THE VIALE DEI COLLI.

FLORENCE.

" Of all the fairest cities of the earth,
" None is so fair as Florence. 'Tis a gem
" Of purest ray; what a light broke forth
" When it emerged from darkness ! "

— ROGERS.

VIEW FROM SAN MINIATO.

FLORENCE is one of the world's handsomest cities and well deserves the touching epithet of " La Bella. " Its situation in the plain on both sides of the Arno, surrounded by hills whose slopes are adorned by nature and art, is one of exquisite beauty.

Of the ancient history of Florence little is known; originally a mere suburb of the Etruscan hill-town of Fiesole, in Roman times, thanks to its position on the great route from Rome to Northern Italy and Germany, which commanded the passage of the Arno (at the Ponte Vecchio), Florence grew rapidly. But its transformation from a comparatively small town, its prosperity and extraordinary political and artistic importance began in the 13th century during the lifetime of Dante.

Thenceforth, under the able government of the guilds and of the patrician families, the most brilliant period in the history of Florence was inaugurated. From the 13th to the 16th century the city was covered with monuments, churches and palaces erected and decorated by the greatest artists of Italy.

Florence, the city of Dante, Petrarch, Boccaccio and Galileo, the cradle of the Renaissance, is called the *Athens of the West*. Ancient Athens, however, is utterly ruinous compared with the so much younger Florence, where the development of art is still clearly to be seen. Here, everything — or nearly everything — remains unspoiled and unaltered, each work in the place it was originally destined for, and still instinct with the spirit of the ancient founders.

As we wander through her streets, the glorious past is vividly brought before our minds. The fortress-like appearance of the Palazzo Vecchio, the Bargello and other old palaces recall the frequent popular risings and the bitter fightings which these edifices have witnessed; the noble Loggia dei Lanzi, reminds us of Orcagna; the mighty dome of the Cathedral, bears record or

Photo ALINARI, ANDERSON, BROGI.

FLORENCE — *THE CRADLE OF THE RENAISSANCE.*

THE RIVER ARNO AND THE PONTE SANTA TRINITA, *built by* AMMANNATI. A. D. 1570.
(Destroyed by German mines on the night of Aug. 3-4, 1944, it has been rebuilt in 1958).

Brunelleschi; its impressive nave, re-echoes with the impassioned eloquence of Savonarola; its graceful Campanile, brings to our minds Giotto; the bronze doors of the Baptistery recall Ghiberti. We are shown the house where Dante lived, the spot where he sat and watched the building of the great Duomo; the square where Savonarola offered up his life in flame, — a martyr to political hatred and religious fanaticism; we pass the shops where Donatello, Verrocchio and Ghirlandaio worked; the house where Benvenuto Cellini cast his bronze Perseus. We stand before doorways made beautiful by the art of Della Robbia; we pace cloisters decorated by Fra Angelico and Andrea del Sarto; we see Michelangelo's masterpieces in sculpture, Raphael's most famous works in painting, we gaze at the old frescoes and the faces and costumes of the men and women of the fifteenth century are vividly brought before our eyes. We turn to another walk, and, in the presence or the magnificent tombs in San Lorenzo, are led to think of the Medici, the great family, who for over three hundred years ruled this illustrious city; whose care for the advancement of art and science produced such wide effects, and who preserved to the world many of the treasures of art which the fair city now possesses. What memories and what a series of names for any country to be proud of !

Hence, as Yriarte has well said : " We must dearly love Florence, for she is the mother of all those who live by thought; we must study her without ceasing, for she offers us an inexhaustible source of instruction. "

MICHELANGELO'S STATUE OF DAVID (*Bronze copy*).
PIAZZALE MICHELANGELO.

Photo ALINARI, ANDERSON, BROGI.

FLORENCE — VIEWS OF THE CITY.

VIEW OF THE CITY FROM THE PIAZZALE MICHELANGELO (San Miniato).

The beauty of Florence has been celebrated by many writers in prose and verse; and the visitor who views it from the Piazzale Michelangelo, will not dispute their praises. How glorious, how pleasant it is to stand there and look at the city spread at our feet! Yonder, the mighty dome of the cathedral rises in all its majesty; to the left, is Giotto's incomparable campanile; close to it, is seen the tower of the Badia and that of the Bargello; far away, the cupola of San Lorenzo. Farther on the left, is the slender tower of the Palazzo Vecchio; nearer to us, is the big church of Santa Croce; to the north-east, on the hill is Fiesole; further still are the Apennines.

Three-fourths of the town lies on the right bank of the Arno, the remaining fourth, with the Pitti Palace, lies on the left. Seven bridges cross the river; the finest, Santa Trinita, is given on the opposite page.

VIEW OF THE RIVER ARNO AND THE PONTE VECCHIO, *built by* TADDEO GADDI. *14th century.*

This is the oldest bridge in Florence, which carries across the river a large part of the city traffic; and this is not inconsiderable, for Florence has now a population of nearly two hundred and fifty thousand inhabitants. The bridge is flanked with goldsmiths' shops and houses, above which runs a corridor, built by VASARI, connecting the Uffizi and **Pitti Galleries**.
(The only bridge on the Arno spared by the Germans who, however, destroyed — Aug. 3, 1944 — all ways of access or approach thereto).

Photo ALINARI, ANDERSON, BROGI.

FLORENCE — PIAZZA DELLA SIGNORIA.

THE HISTORIC PIAZZA DELLA SIGNORIA.

THE PIAZZA DELLA SIGNORIA was once the Forum of the Florentine republic, the centre of its political and social life. Every great event in the history of Florence has taken place in this piazza; every name of distinction among her citizens is connected with the monuments that stand here, one may read the course of Florentine art by studying its architecture and sculpture.

GRAND-DUKE COSIMO I.
Bronze by GIAMBOLOGNA.

The historic square is dominated by buildings so bold and grandiose in conception as to recall the ancient Roman architecture. On the right is the Loggia dei Lanzi, where, in the presence of the people, the solemn acts of public life were performed; in front is the formidable rectangle of the Palazzo Vecchio.

Many tragical and cruel reminiscences are connected with this Piazza, and with the old Palace that stands here. First came the fierce struggle between the Guelphs and the Ghibellines, which lasted for centuries; then, at intervals, wild outbreaks of the old Florentine passion and vindictiveness; the tragedy of the Pazzi conspiracy; the execution of Savonarola.

FOUNTAIN OF NEPTUNE. *By* BARTOLOMMEO AMMANNATI. A. D. 1575.

The eastern side of the Piazza della Signoria is occupied by the *Mercanzia* (the old Chamber of Commerce), erected in 1559; and the *Palazzo della Condotta*, the former residence of the officials entrusted with the payment of condottieri (p. 74). In the 15th and 16th centuries the square was also used for public festivals, tournaments and even bull fights; and at this time it was adorned with numerous statues and monuments thus forming a veritable open-air museum. At the corner of the palace is the great fountain of Neptune with bronze figures of tritons and naiads; in front of the palace on the left is Donatello's Marzocco (original in the Bargello), and his group of Judith and Holofernes, which was regarded as symbolical of liberty, and placed here as a warning to tyrants of the fate which awaited them. The words inscribed on the base are, '*Exemplum Salutis Publicæ Cives posuere* MCCCCXCV.'

DONATELLO'S MARZOCCO (copy).
Heraldic emblem of Florence.

RELIEF ON THE BASE
of Donatello's "Judith."

JUDITH AND HOLOFERNES
Bronze by DONATELLO.

— 196 —

Photo ALINARI, ANDERSON, BROGI.

FLORENCE — *PALAZZO VECCHIO*

The PALAZZO VECCHIO was begun in the year 1298 and intended for the double purpose of a residence for the presiding magistrates, and a place of assembly for public deliberation. Its fortress-like appearance, is due to the fact that the edifice was reared in times full of danger, when the state was divided by factions, assailed by secret conspiracies, or treatened by popular tumult, and the imperious and warlike features of the building may be taken to represent the whole course of Florentine history.

From the lofty tower (308 ft.) still peals forth the deep-toned voice of the ancient bell, which, according to the manner of its ringing either summoned the officials to their duties, or called the citizens unarmed to the consideration of public affairs; or, with arms in hand, brought them together for the defense of their city.

On the walls, between the small arches supporting the external gallery, we still see the painted arms of the Commonwealth. The lily, emblem of the city; the cross, emblem of the people; " Libertas " emblem of the Priors; the eagle trampling on a dragon, emblem of the Guelphs; two golden keys, emblem of the Church; the pills, emblem of the Medici. While the Monogram of Christ and the inscription ' Rex regum et Dominus dominantium ' placed over its doorway in 1529, bears record to the election by the citizens of Christ for their King.

At the period of the erection of the palace the directors of the affairs of Florence were the members of a committee called *Signoria*. They were at first known as *Priori* (chief men or city fathers); later they received the title of *Signori*, or lords. The priori held office but two months, during which period they lived in the palace together; each had his own private quarters, but they ate at the same table, which was supplied at public expense. They were not allowed to leave the building on any pretext whatsoever. as they were supposed to be ready to transact the public business at any hour of the day or night.

In the tower of the Palazzo Vecchio Savonarola was confined for six weeks before his execution in 1498. The year before his martyrdom, on the last day of Carnival, the Friar had caused a huge pyramid to be erected on this Piazza. It consisted of the so-called « vanities » —masquerading costumes and masks, false hair and rouge pots, musical instruments and diceboxes, books of Latin and Italian poets, priceless parchments and illuminated manuscripts, works of art and paintings, especially such as represented feminine beauty. When this pile was set alight, the Signoria appeared on the balcony and the air echoed with song, the sound of trumpets and the pealing of bells. On the following year another pile stood in the Piazza, and with it the body of Savonarola burnt to ashes. On the pavement, in front of the palace, a bronze medallion marks the spot where the Dominican Prior of San Marco and his two companions, were hanged and burned May 23rd 1498.

Stupendous though the Palazzo Vecchio is, it would have been of vaster proportions but for the prohibition given to Arnolfo to make use of the site on which the houses of the Uberti—an exiled and hated Ghibelline family—had stood. To avoid this " cursed ground, " the palace stands for ever of an irregular shape. (Since 1871 it is used as the town-hall).

THE PALAZZO VECCHIO, OR DELLA SIGNORIA.
Begun in 1298 by ARNOLFO DI CAMBIO.

HERCULES AND CACUS. *Marble.*
By BANDINELLI. A. D. 1546.

Hercules is in the act of slaying a fabulous robber who had made the mistake of stealing some of his cattle. It is the poorest group in the piazza : a caricature of its model.

Bronze plate marking the spot where Savonarola's body fell.

MAIN ENTRANCE TO THE PALAZZO VECCHIO. *On the left is a marble copy of Michelangelo's* « David ». *(Original in the Academy, see p. 290).*

— 197 —

Photo ALINARI, ANDERSON, BROGI.

FLORENCE — *LOGGIA DEI LANZI.*

Hope. Faith. Temperance.

Figures by GIOVANNI D'AMBROGIO and JACOPO DI PIERO (*Loggia dei Lanzi*).

The "Perseus" is one of the famous statues of the world, and the most celebrated work of the Florentine sculptor Benvenuto Cellini. The noble figure of the hero stands magnificent as a type of calm strength, looking down upon the lifeless body of Medusa. The marble pedestal is adorned with marvellous richness, and contains bronze statuettes of Jupiter and Danaë, father and mother of Perseus, of Minerva and Mercury. On the parapet below is a poetical and picturesque relief of Perseus rescuing Andromeda.

In his autobiography Cellini gives us a vivid account of the casting of this masterpiece and of the terrible anxieties and dangers through which he passed before his efforts were rewarded with complete success. He first describes how he devised and built a special kind of furnace, made the mould and set it beneath the smelting pot which was filled with chunks of copper bronze and alloy, and was connected with the mould by canals properly arranged for conducting the molten liquid, and the assistants placed at

PERSEUS DELIVERING ANDROMEDA.
Bronze relief by B. CELLINI, *formerly on the pedestal of the* "Perseus," *and now in the Bargello.*

PERSEUS *with the head of Medusa.*
Bronze by CELLINI. A. D. 1553.

their posts; then, how, in the midst of the operation of fusing, overcome by fatigue and seized with the most terrible attack of fever he was obliged to betake himself to bed, and, while writhing upon his bed he was suddenly informed that the statue was irrevocably spoiled. With a scream, Benvenuto leaped from his bed, and dealing kicks and blows on all who offered consolation, rushed to the furnace and gave orders to feed the furnace with well-dried young oak-wood, and a block of tin added to the pot of metal. With the forced heat the furnace burst, but the metal was partly fused though not enough, more tin was wanting.... in he cast his pewter dishes and plates, about 200; and when the metal began to flow again and the mould was filling, he threw himself on his knees, praised God, returned to bed and soundly slept away his fever.... When in 1554 the "Perseus" was uncovered in the Loggia dei Lanzi where it now stands, it was received with expressions of admiration by the artistic, literary and fashionable classes of Florence. The pillars of the loggia were bedecked with odes and sonnets written in its praise, and Cellini, ruffling with hand on hilt in silks and satins through the square was flattered by being pointed out, as the great

THE LOGGIA DEI LANZI (*of the* 'lancers').
At first known as Loggia de' Priori or della Signoria. Designed by ORCAGNA.
Erected A. D. 1376-83 *by* BENCI DI CIONE *and* SIMONE DI FRANCESCO TALENTI.

artist who had made this wonderful statue, which he believed unsurpassed and unsurpassable. In the Bargello are two sketch-models of the statue, one in wax (p. 294) and one in bronze, — both show variations from the original, and are more graceful.

— 198 —

Photo ALINARI, ANDERSON, BROGI.

FLORENCE — *LOGGIA DEI LANZI.*

THUSNELDA.
Ancient marble.

MENELAUS *with the body of Patrocles*
Ancient sculpture.

HERCULES AND NESSUS.
Marble by GIAMBOLOGNA.

THE RAPE OF POLYXENA.
Marble by PIO FEDI (1866).

ANCIENT SCULPTURE.
From the Villa Medici, Rome.

Giambologna's "Rape of the Sabines," is considered the masterpiece of the artist, who modelled the group with no reference to subject. His composition was merely intended to be a skilful representation of a stalwart youth bearing away a struggling woman from a vanquished foe. The relief on the base representing the Rape of the Sabines was added by the sculptor as an interpretation to his newly found subject.

RAPE OF THE SABINES.
Marble group
by GIAMBOLOGNA A. D. 1583.

THE LOGGIA DEI LANZI, built as a place of assembly for the discussion of political or commercial matters in rainy weather, or for public ceremonies, contains many wonderful groups of statuary, including some of the finest creations of antique and modern art, such as the *Rape of the Sabines*, *Hercules slaying the centaur Nessus*, both by GIAMBOLOGNA; *Menelaus with the body of Patrocles*, an antique brought from Rome; the bronze *Perseus* by CELLINI; the *Rape of Polyxena*, a marble group by PIO FEDI (1866); and five antique portrait-statues of vestals or priestesses: Thusnelda, etc.

THE RAPE OF THE SABINES.
Relief by GIAMBOLOGNA
on the base of the above group.

— 199 —

Photo ALINARI, ANDERSON, BROGI.

FLORENCE — *PALAZZO VECCHIO.* First Floor.

ENTRANCE WALL OF THE GREAT HALL. *Frescoes* by VASARI.

HALL OF LEO X., with paintings from the life of the pope.

THE GREAT HALL or *Sala dei Cinquecento*.

The Great Hall or *Sala dei Cinquecento*, was built by the architect Cronaca in 1495 by the advice of Savonarola, to accommodate the popular Council, created on the expulsion of the Medici. The hall is 176 feet long 61 feet broad and 73 feet high. Here the grand-dukes received the homage of their subjects on their accession. In the year 1503 Leonardo da Vinci and Michelangelo prepared cartoons to decorate the hall with frescoes from Florentine history; but upon the return of the Medici in 1512, the cartoons were lost or destroyed. It is now adorned with frescoes by *Vasari* and his pupils, representing scenes from the wars against Siena and Pisa. Ranged along the walls are sculptures by Florentine artists, including a group by *Michelangelo*.

FOUNTAIN *by* VERROCCHIO.

COURT OF THE PALAZZO VECCHIO. By MICHELOZZO. A D. 1454.

The beautiful court of the Palazzo Vecchio was restored by Michelozzo in 1454. The elaborate stucco decorations of the pillars were added in 1565. Verrocchio's bronze statuette of the *Boy holding a Dolphin* on the fountain, is a gem of Florentine art.

Photo ALINARI, ANDERSON, BROGI.

FLORENCE.

THE PALAZZO VECCHIO OR DELLA SIGNORIA.

In the tower of the palazzo Savonarola, the Dominican preacher, was confined before his execution in the square in front of the palace. (*See p. 197*).

FLORENCE — *PALAZZO VECCHIO. First Floor.*

ENTRY INTO FLORENCE OF POPE LEO X.

POPE LEO X. appoints 31 Cardinals.

The scene represents the Piazza della Signoria: in the background is the Loggia dei Lanzi, on the left the Palazzo Vecchio, and, beyond, the church of S. Piero Scheraggio which stood on the site of the present Uffizi Palace. Among the crowd of mace bearers, in the left foreground, are the portraits of Francesco da Castiglione (carrying the great processional cross), Pietro Bembo, Ariosto, Sannazzaro, and Pietro Aretino.

In the background to the left are portraits of Giuliano de' Medici, Leonardo da Vinci and Michelangelo.

Frescoes by VASARI *in the Hall of Leo X.*

STUDY OF FRANCIS I. (Medici).

DOORWAY. *Sala dei Cinquecento.*

HALLWAY LEADING TO GREAT HALL.

PERSEUS AND ANDROMEDA.

A WOOLEN MANUFACTURE.

A GOLDSMITH WORKSHOP.

Wall decorations by GIORGIO VASARI, ANGELO BRONZINO, *and* FEI *in the Study of Francis I., de' Medici.*

— 201 —

Photo ALINARI, ANDERSON, BROGI.

26. - WONDERS OF ITALY.

FLORENCE — *PALAZZO VECCHIO. Second Floor.*

THE DINING ROOM.

CAMERA DI ESTHER *Quartiere di Eleonora di Toledo.*

CAMERA DI PENELOPE.

The so-called *Quartiere di Eleonora* is composed of a suite of four rooms originally occupied by the Signori, but assigned by Cosimo I. to his consort Eleonora di Toledo during their residence (1540-50) in the palace. The ceilings were decorated by *Stradano* with paintings illustrating the virtues of woman. Thus, in the Sala delle Damigelle the artist represented "The Rape of the Sabine Women;" in the Camera di Esther "Ahasuerus crowning Esther;" in that of Penelope "Penelope weaving"; in that of Gualdrada "Her refusal to kiss Otho IV." (*See* p. 389).

THE RAPE OF THE SABINES. *Ceiling painting by* STRADANO. *Sala delle Damigelle.*

THE 'GOOD GUALDRADA.' *Camera di Gualdrada.*

THE WARDROBE. *The presses are decorated with maps by* I. DANTI.

MARBLE DOORWAY. *By* BENEDETTO DA MAIANO.

CAPPELLA DEI PRIORI. *Decorated by* RIDOLFO GHIRLANDAIO.

The *Sala dei Gigli*, so-called from its wall decoration of golden flower-de-luce on a blue background has a splendid ceiling of gilded hexagonal panels, and frescoes by *Ghirlandaio*, representing the apotheosis of St. Zenobius, bishop of Florence, and figures of Roman heroes: Brutus, Mutius Scævola, Camillus, Decius, Scipio and Cicero.

SALA DEI GIGLI. *Frescoes, by* D. GHIRLANDAIO.

SALA D'UDIENZA DEI PRIORI. *Ceiling by* B. DA MAIANO

The *Sala d'Udienza dei Priori*, or Audience Chamber, is decorated with frescoes by *Cecco Salviati* representing the Story of Camillus. The beautiful marble portal surmounted by a figure of John the Baptist is the work of *Benedetto da Maiano*. The wooden doors with exquisite intarsiatura have portraits of Dante and Petrarch.

Photo ALINARI, ANDERSON, BROGI.

FLORENCE — *PALAZZO VECCHIO.* Quartiere degli Elementi.

SATURN MUTILATING URANUS. *Allegory of* AIR.
Ceiling fresco by VASARI.

TERRACE OF SATURN.

VULCAN'S FORGE. *Allegory of* FIRE.
Mural fresco by VASARI.

"SUMMER." Sala di Berecinzia.

THE BIRTH OF VENUS. *Allegory of* WATER.

SALA DEGLI ELEMENTI.
Decorated by GIORGIO VASARI.
The paintings on the walls and ceiling represent the Four Elements.

Allegory of THE EARTH.

SALA DI ERCOLE.

SALA DI CERERE.

The suite of rooms on the second floor known as the *Quartiere degli Elementi*, was occupied by the Grand Duke Cosimo I., whose name is inscribed on the tiled floors of the apartment. The principal room —Sala degli Elementi— derives its name from the paintings on the walls and ceiling representing the "Four Elements;" in the Sala di Ercole the paintings illustrate the "Labours of Hercules;" in the Sala di Berecinzia are allegories of the "Four Seasons;" in the Sala di Cerere are representations of the "Goddess of Plenty;" another room called Sala di Giove is decorated with scenes from the story of "Jupiter."

Photo ALINARI, ANDERSON, BROGI.

FLORENCE — THE BAPTISTERY.

The origin of the Baptistery is lost in almost mythical obscurity, early writers declare it to have been originally a temple dedicated to Mars, but Tuscan archeologists consider it to have been erected in the seventh or eighth century.

Until the erection of the Duomo it was the principal church of Florence and was dedicated to St. John the Baptist, the patron and protector of the city.

About 1200 the building was remodelled at the expense of the wool-merchants' guild, when the principal entrance which was originally on the west was closed and replaced by the square apse or tribune, and the present portals added. The dark-green and white marble stripes with which the edifice is encased inside and out are of a remarkable effect. The pavement is a marvel of intricate inlaying and mosaics including the signs of the Zodiac and a motto which may be read the same backwards and forwards, « En giro torte sol ciclos et rotor igne » (page 208). In this building Dante was baptized and even now all children born in Florence of Catholic parents are baptized here. Being a baptistery, the edifice is mainly decorated with works referring to the life of the Baptist; the chief ornament, however, are the celebrated bronze doors, in which a whole world of thought is fixed into exquisite forms.

THE BAPTISTERY (Church of San Giovanni Battista).
Tuscan-Romanesque style.

ANDREA PISANO'S DOOR. A. D. 1336.
Over the door: the Beheading of John the Baptist, by DANTI, 1571.

GHIBERTI'S SECOND DOOR. A. D. 1425-52.
Over the door: the Baptism of Christ, by SANSOVINO, 1560.

GHIBERTI'S FIRST DOOR. A. D. 1403-24.
Over the door: Preaching of John the Baptist, by RUSTICI, 1511.

Photo ALINARI, ANDERSON, BROGI.

FLORENCE — THE BAPTISTERY. The Bronze doors.

ANDREA PISANO'S DOORS.

GHIBERTI'S SECOND DOORS.

GHIBERTI'S FIRST DOORS

These doors, on the south side of the baptistery, were executed by Andrea Pisano who completed them after nine years' labour. The panels contain reliefs representing events in the life of St. John the Baptist, and allegorical figures of the Cardinal Virtues. They are : 1. The Angel appears to Zacharias. 2. Zacharias is struck dumb. 3. The Visitation of Mary to Elizabeth. 4. The Birth of John the Baptist. 5. Zacharias writes, « His name is John ». 6. John departs for the Wilderness. 7. John preaches to the Pharisee. 8. John preaches to the people. 9. John baptises in the Jordan. 10. The Baptism of Christ. 11. John reproves Herod. 12. John led to prison. 13. John questioned by the Jews. 14. John announces the advent of Christ. 15. The daughter of Herodias asks for John's head. 16. The Decollation of John. 17. Herod at supper receives the head of John. 18. The daughter of Herodias presents John's head to her mother. 19. The Disciples carry the body of John to burial. 20. Entombment of John. 21. Hope. 22. Faith. 23. Charity. 24. Humility. 25. Fortitude. 26. Temperance. 27. Justice. 28. Prudence.

These are the doors which Michelangelo declared fit for the gates of Paradise. They are a marvel of art and formed a source of inspiration to generations of successive artists. They occupied Ghiberti for twenty seven years (1425-52). Each panel represents various events from the Old Testament : 1. Creation of Adam, of Eve, Temptation, Expulsion. 2. Adam tilling the soil, Cain and Abel at their vocation, their sacrifices, the murder of Abel. 3. The Flood, Exit from the Ark, Noah's sacrifice, his Drunkenness. 4. Abraham entertains the Three Angels, Sarah at the tent, Hagar in the desert, the sacrifice of Isaac. 5. Esau with his dogs approaches Isaac, Rachel and Jacob, Isaac blessing Jacob. 6. Joseph and his brethren in Egypt, Finding of the cup in Benjamin's sack, Benjamin and his brothers take away the corn. 7. Moses receives the Law, the People are frightened by storm and the sound of trumpets. 8. The Ark carried round the walls of Jericho, Joshua crosses the Jordan on foot. 9. Battle against the Ammonites, David cuts off Goliath's head. 10. Solomon receives the Queen of Sheba in the Great Temple at Jerusalem.

These doors, on the north side of the baptistery, were executed in 1403-24 by Lorenzo Ghiberti, after a competition in which his design was preferred to those of Brunelleschi, Jacopo della Quercia and other famous artists of the time. The reliefs represent the principal events of the life of Christ, the Evangelists, and the Fathers of the Church. The subjects run as follows : 1. The Annunciation. 2. The Nativity. 3. The Adoration of the Magi. 4. The Dispute with the Doctors. 5. The Baptism of Christ. 6. The Temptation. 7. Christ drives the money-changers from the Temple. 8. Christ and Peter on the water. 9. The Transfiguration. 10. The Raising of Lazarus. 11. The Entry into Jerusalem. 12. The Last Supper. 13. The Agony in the Garden. 14. The Kiss of Judas. 15. Christ bound to the Pillar. 16. Christ before Pilate. 17. Christ bearing the Cross. 18. The Crucifixion. 19. The Resurrection. 20. The Descent of the Holy Ghost. 21. St. John. 22 St. Matthew. 23. St. Luke. 24. St. Mark. 25. St. Ambrose, bishop of Milan. 26. St. Jerome. 27. St. Gregory the Great. 28. St. Augustine, bishop of Hippo.

In the year 1401 the Signory of Florence, in concert with the Trade-Guilds, decided to complete the bronze gates of the Baptistery. They invited artists from all parts of Italy to prepare designs for competition. Six of the competitors, of whom Ghiberti was one, were selected, and requested to model and cast a single bronze panel representing the sacrifice of Isaac. A year later, when the trial-pieces were submitted for adjudication, the umpires held that those of Ghiberti and Brunelleschi were superior to the other four, but hesitated to decide which of the two was the best. The judges were extricated from this difficulty by Brunelleschi, who, with notable generosity, and conscious of his rival's superiority, withdrew from the contest.

A comparison of the two models, leaves no doubt of Ghiberti's superiority. « His composition », says Perkins, « is distinguished by clearness of narrative, grace of line, and repose, Brunelleschi's is melodramatically conceived, and awkwardly composed. In Ghiberti's Abraham we see a father who, while preparing to obey the Divine command, still hopes for a respite, and in his Isaac a submissive victim ; the angel who points out the ram caught in a thicket, which Abraham could not otherwise, and does not yet see, sets us at rest about the conclusion ; while the servants, with the ass which brought the faggots for the sacrifice, are so skilfully placed, as to enter into the composition without distracting our attention from the principal group ».

Lorenzo Ghiberti's.   Filippo Brunelleschi's.
THE SACRIFICE OF ISAAC.
Trial bronze panels in the National Museum (Bargello).

« Brunelleschi's Abraham is on the contrary, a savage zealot, whose knife is already half buried in the throat of his writhing victim and who, in his hot haste, does not heed the ram which is placed directly before him, nor the angel, who seizes his wrist to avert his blow ; while the ass, and the two servants, each carrying on a separate action, fill up the foreground so obtrusively, as to call off the eye from what should be the main point of interest ».

— 205 —   Photo ALINARI, ANDERSON, BROGI.

FLORENCE — THE BAPTISTERY. Details of the bronze doors.

[Above: "The Decollation of John".
Below: "The daughter of Herodias presents John's head to her mother".
Panels from ANDREA PISANO *doors* (1336).

Above: "Christ drives the money-changers from the Temple".
Below: "The Adoration of the Magi".
Panels from GHIBERTI'S *first doors* (1403-24).

"Stories of Esau and Jacob".

"Finding of the cup in Benjamin's sack".

Panels from LORENZO GHIBERTI'S *second doors* (1425-52).

— 206 —

Photo ALINARI, ANDERSON, BROGI.

FLORENCE — *THE BAPTISTERY.*

BRONZE DOORS. *Executed by* LORENZO GHIBERTI. A. D. 1425-52.
These doors, which Michelangelo declared were "worthy to be the gates of Paradise," occupied 27 years of Ghiberti's life.

Photo ALINARI, ANDERSON, BROGI.

FLORENCE — THE BAPTISTERY. Interior.

The mosaics in the cupola of the Baptistery were executed by ANDREA TAFI († 1320) and other artists. Above the high altar is a gigantic figure of Christ as Judge of the world. He is seated on the rainbow and stretches forth his hands, the palm of the right open towards the blest, the back of the left, repulsively, towards the condemned. Above the Saviour, in the space near and around the lantern, are the hierarchies of Angels, Thrones, Dominations, and Powers; below, on either side of our Lord are angels blowing the trumpets of the Last Judgment or displaying the instruments of the Passion; still lower, on His right, are the twelve Apostles headed by the Virgin; and to the left, the Saints of the Old Testament, headed by the Baptist. At the feet of Christ is the scene of the Last Judgment; the souls force the heavy lids of their sarcophagi, and rise from their graves, the just are received by angels, the unjust by devils, who lead them away respectively to paradise or hell. On the right of Christ, the three patriarchs, Abraham, Isaac and Jacob, seated side by side, within the gates of Paradise, hold several souls in their laps, whilst on the opposite side Satan, amidst the condemned, is devouring one of the lost souls.

THE MOSAICS IN THE DOME. *Executed by* ANDREA TAFI. *13th cent.*

The rest of the octagonal cupola is divided into four bands, each composed of fifteen panels: the uppermost contains the principal stories of the Old Testament, from the Creation to the Great Flood; the second band, the history of Joseph and his brethren; the third, the life of Christ; the fourth and lowest, the life of John the Baptist. The mosaics in the tribune were executed about 1225-28 by JACOPO TURRITA, a companion of St. Francis of Assisi.

The finest work in sculpture in the Baptistery is the tomb of John XXIII. who was deposed by the Council of Constance in 1414. The dethroned pontiff, after the Schism came to Florence and spent the rest of his life here. He left funds for his tomb which was erected by his friend Cosimo the Elder. The peacefully slumbering bronze figure of the Pope is the work of *Donatello*. Beneath the sarcophagus, between brackets, are the insignia of the bishop, Pope and Cardinal. In front of the pedestal stand the figures of Faith, Hope and Charity; the first is by *Michelozzo*, the two latter by *Donatello*.

TOMB OF POPE JOHN XXIII. († 1419). By DONATELLO *and* MICHELOZZO.

THE BAPTISTERY (A. D. 1200). Part of the pavement representing the Signs of the Zodiac. From this pattern Florentine weavers inspired themselves for the designs for their famous fabrics: velvets, brocades, damasks, etc.

Photo ALINARI, ANDERSON, BROGI.

FLORENCE.

GIOTTO'S CAMPANILE. *Begun* 1334, *completed* 1387.

In the year 1334 *Giotto*, architect of the cathedral, was asked to draw up the plan of a bell tower. After his plan was sanctioned, a decree was issued so that " the campanile should excel in splendour, height and perfection all what the Roman and the Greek had done in that field in the past."

WONDERS OF ITALY.

FLORENCE — *THE CATHEDRAL. S. Maria del Fiore.*

THE CATHEDRAL (Duomo) AND THE CAMPANILE.

The Duomo begun A. D. 1296 *by* ARNOLFO DI CAMBIO.
The Campanile begun in the year 1334 *by* GIOTTO.
The Façade designed by DE FABRIS, *completed* 1887.

THE APSES AND BRUNELLESCHI'S DOME. A. D. 1420-34.

PORTA DELLA MANDORLA (North side).
In the lunette is the "Annunciation" a mosaic by *Ghirlandaio*; in the archivolt is the "Madonna with the Girdle," a marble relief by *Nanni di Banco*, A. D. 1414.

The Cathedral of Santa Maria del Fiore (St. Mary of the Flower), so called in allusion to the lily in the city arms, which marks the tradition that Florence was founded in a field of flowers, was begun in 1296 by ARNOLFO DI CAMBIO, who was ordered « to raise the loftiest, most sumptuous, and most magnificent edifice that human invention could devise, or human labour execute ». After Arnolfo's death in 1301 the operations were successively directed by GIOTTO (1334-37) ANDREA PISANO (1337-49), FRANCESCO TALENTI (1351-69), and other architects. In 1417, a committee of architects and engineers was summoned to advise how best to construct a dome; a famous competition took place, resulting in the appointment of FILIPPO BRUNELLESCHI. The construction of the gigantic dome took fourteen years, and the church was finally consecrated in 1436. The building, larger than all previous churches built in Italy covers an area of 84.000 feet; being 555 ft. in length and 340 ft. in breadth. The height of the dome, including the lantern, is 350 ft. More than a century later, Michelangelo, when engaged on his design for the dome of St. Peer's at Rome, was told that he had now an opportunity of surpassing that of Florence; he replied: « I will make ther sister dome. Larger; yes, but not more beautiful ».

— 209 —

Photo ALINARI, ANDERSON, BROGI.

27. - *WONDERS OF ITALY.*

FLORENCE — *THE CATHEDRAL. S. Maria del Fiore.*

BRONZE SARCOPHAGUS.
By L. GHIBERTI.
A. D. 1440.

This sarcophagus contains the remains of St. Zenobius, the early bishop of Florence. The relief on it represents a miracle of the Saint, the restoration of a dead child to life. In the centre lies the body, over which the spirit hovers in the shape of a little child, between the praying Saint and the kneeling mother, around whom a crowd of spectators have gathered.

The interior of the cathedral is most impressive, and on first entering it the visitor's soul is filled with admiration by the immensity of its proportions, which seem to grow and grow in the dim, solemn, consecrated space. As we walk on the splendid marble pavement we cannot help recalling the scenes which took place here during the preaching of Savonarola. " People got up in the middle of the night, " says one writer, " to get places for the sermon, and came to the door of the cathedral, waiting for hours outside till it should be opened. " On some occasions the floor space was insufficient for the multitude assembled, and a lofty amphitheatre with seventeen rows of seats was erected against the wall of the nave. Then the people were packed so closely that no man could stir, and though many thousand — young and old, women and children — were thus collected together, no sound was to be heard, not even a "hush," until the haggard, pale, enthusiastic figure of the Friar of San Marco entered the pulpit, like a threatening prophet of old, full of dire forebodings. The vanity of this world, the seductions of the flesh, the immoral and enervating beauty of all arts and sciences, formed the theme of Savonarola's preachings. " These sermons, " writes Symonds, " caused such terror, alarm, sobbing, and tears, that every one passed through the streets without speaking, more dead than alive. "

BRONZE DOORS OF THE OLD SACRISTY.
By LUCA DELLA ROBBIA.

INTERIOR OF SANTA MARIA DEL FIORE.

Michelino's picture of Dante expounding his *Divina Commedia* presents a view of Florence with its 15th cent. turreted walls ; on the left is represented Hell ; behind are the seven circles of Purgatory, leading up to Paradise, symbolised by stars above. Inferno is conceived by Dante as in shape like an inverted cone. The apex of the cone which is composed of nine circles, is at the centre of the earth. Purgatory is formed of a mountain-island, which was thrown up, like a volcanic hill, by Satan when he fell from heaven and pierced the earth to the centre.

The great poem of Dante consists of three Cantiche each containing 33 Canti of about 145 lines, and the Inferno has an extra, introductory Canto. " Inferno, " " Purgatorio, " and " Paradiso " — three kingdoms.... Dante's World of Souls....— all three summing up the true Unseen World, as it figured in the Christianity of the Middle Ages ; a thing for ever memorable, for ever true in the essence of it, to all men.... but delineated in no human soul with such depth of veracity as in this of Dante's.... to the earnest soul of Dante it is all one visible fact — Hell, Purgatory, Paradise, with him not mere emblems, but indubitable awful realities.

The picture was hung here when the church was used for public lectures for the purpose of explaining the poem.

DANTE EXPLAINING THE DIVINE COMEDY. *By* MICHELINO.

Photo ALINARI, ANDERSON, BROGI.

FLORENCE — *THE CATHEDRAL. S. Maria del Fiore.*

RESURRECTION OF CHRIST.
The first terracotta reliefs executed by LUCA DELLA ROBBIA, A. D. 1443-46.

ASCENSION OF CHRIST.
(Over the doors of the sacristies).

VIEW OF THE CHOIR. *Showing the doors of the sacristies.*

The choir of the cathedral has an historical interest attached to it; for it was the scene of the frightful Pazzi conspiracy against the Medici, the rulers of Florence. This terrible affair originated at Rome, with the connivance of Pope Sixtus IV. The conspirators were Girolamo Riario, nephew of the Pope, whose aim was to become master of Florence; Francesco Salviati, Archbishop designate of Pisa, who expected to be made bishop of Florence, if the attempt succeeded; the young cardinal Raffaello Riario, the Pope's grandnephew; and the Pazzi family, who were not only opposed to the temporal power of the Medici, but were their rivals in the banking business. The first plan formed by the plotters, was to poison Lorenzo and Giuliano de' Medici at a banquet, but Giuliano being unable to attend the banquet, the scheme fell through. Whereupon, the conspirators determined that the murder should take place at the service in the cathedral, where it was known that there would be a great crowd, which would facilitate the escape of the murderers. On Sunday morning of the 26th of April 1478, Lorenzo (the Magnificent), together with his younger brother Giuliano went to the cathedral to attend mass; Lorenzo took his place at the south side of the choir, while Giuliano stood at the opposite side. At the moment when the officiating priest elevated the Host (the preconcerted signal for attack), and when at the sound of the bell all the congregation was bowing to the earth, Giuliano furiously attacked by the hired assassins, fell dead at once where he stood, his body being stabbed again and again. At the same time two priests attacked Lorenzo, who, though wounded in the neck, with much presence of mind, escaped assassination by fighting his way into the old sacristy closing the heavy bronze doors behind him.

STATUE OF POGGIO BRACCIOLINI.
Marble by DONATELLO.

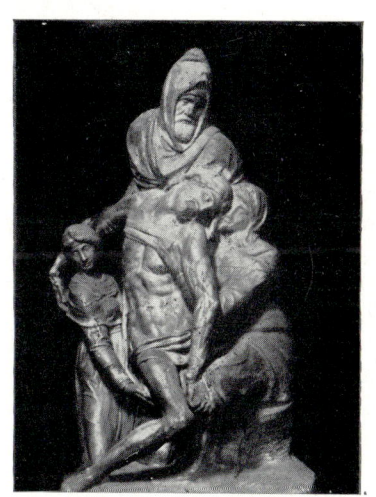

DEPOSITION. *By* MICHELANGELO. A. D. 1555.
The master's last work.

In December 1965 excavations under the Duomo floor were begun in order to find the remains of St. Reparata, the first cathedral of Florence already existing in the year one thousand. According to tradition, the church was dedicated to St. Reparata to remember the victory carried off by the Florentines and by the army of Honorius, emperor of the West, on the 8th of October, 405, day of the feast of St. Reparata, against the Ostrogothic king Radagasio. St. Reparata was still used as a church even after the beginning of the construction of the Duomo (1296) and was definitely interred only in 1375.

Actually it is possible to enter from the Duomo into some spaces of the ancient cathedral and to see all what has been recovered up to now: perimetrical walls of the church, tracts of mosaic flooring, grave-stones of figures in bas-relief, wall decorations and a fresco of Christ's Entombment attributed to an artist of the first half of the 14th cent.

Photo ALINARI, ANDERSON, BROGI.

This lovely Campanile, built to receive the Cathedral's bells, remains unique and unsurpassed in beauty after six centuries of existence. The perfect grace of its outlines, the wondrous charm of its proportions, and the loveliness of its traceried windows, which increase in size with the different stories, make the colossus marvellously light and elegant.

The Baptist. David (the «Zuccone»). Jeremiah.
Statues by DONATELLO. *Western side of Campanile.*
(*The originals are in the Cathedral Museum*).

In the year 1334 GIOTTO who had been appointed architect of the cathedral, received the commission from the Signory to prepare plans for a campanile or bell-tower adjoining the church; and when his design had been approved a decree was passed that " the Campanile should be built so as to exceed in magnificence, height and excellence of workmanship everything of the kind that had been achieved of old by the Greeks and Romans when at the zenith of their greatness. "

The foundation stone was laid with great ceremony on July 18th 1334 and the work made rapid progress. After Giotto's death in 1337 (he was buried in the cathedral at the corner nearest his campanile), the work was carried on by his successors *Andrea Pisano* and *Francesco Talenti* in strict adherence to the original plans, except for the spire, intended to be 150 feet high, which was never added.

This wonderfully simple structure, 276 feet in height, is richly adorned with marbles of most harmonious colouring, delicately cut ornaments, statues and a series of bas-reliefs which have been substituted in 1665 by casts. Their subjects are : the story of Genesis ; the invention of various arts, mechanical, intellectual, figurative ; the Planets ; the Virtues ; the Sacraments. "These subjects, " writes H. B. Cotterill, " form a cycle ; their connexion may be intimated somewhat as follows. Man is created and finds himself amidst the realm of nature. He devises means to satisfy first his bodily, then his intellectual, then his aesthetic needs. His innate character depends on heavenly influences transmitted by the planets (as taught by Dante and the schoolmen), but by devotion to the religious and ethical virtues, and by the aid of the Sacraments, he can rise above his inborn defects and realize the true life. "

The ascent of the campanile (by an easy staircase of 414 steps) commands a series of ever widening panoramas of the city and the neighbouring heights.

GIOTTO'S CAMPANILE. *Begun 1334. Completed 1387.*

PORCH OF THE CAMPANILE.

Photo ALINARI, ANDERSON, BROGI.

FLORENCE — CATHEDRAL MUSEUM.   Bas-reliefs of Giotto's campanile.

1. Conquest of the sea. *Navigation and colonisation.*
2. Conquest of the earth. *Hercules and Antæus.* 
3. Agriculture. *The reclaiming of the soil.* 
4. Trade, *or earthly prosperity.* 

The reliefs which adorned Giotto's Campanile form a most interesting series, exhibiting, in distinct compartments— on each side —an epitome of history, a chronicle of human progression, physical, intellectual, and moral, from the Creation till Giotto's day.

These admirable reliefs are fully described in *The Shepherd's Tower* by Ruskin. The best art critics in every age have agreed that Giotto 'soared above the conception of the most competent architects' in the model which he created; and that in the ornaments of bas-relief and sculpture the most perfect combination of subjects, the most admirable form, were happily brought together.

5. The Lamb of God. Christianity. *(Over the door).*
6. Architecture. 

THE SIX BAS-RELIEFS on the Eastern side of the Campanile representing the period of discovery and colonisation; the human intercourse between stranger nations and the introduction of Christianity. *Designed by* GIOTTO, *executed by* ANDREA PISANO.

1. Sculpture. (Phidias?).
2. Painting. (Apelles?). 
3. Grammar. 
4. Arithmetic. (Pythagoras?). 

THESE RELIEFS, on the Northern side of the Campanile, represent the period of intellectual and moral development: the Fine Arts, Philosophy, Poetry, and the Exact Sciences.

5. Music. (Orpheus?).
6. Logic. (Plato and Aristotle?). 
7. Harmony. (Tubalcain?). 

The last five reliefs executed in the middle of the 15th century are attributed to LUCA DELLA ROBBIA.

Photo ALINARI. ANDERSON, BROGI.

FLORENCE — CATHEDRAL MUSEUM. Bas-relief of Giotto's Campanile.

1. The Creation of Adam.
   Note the symbolical trees in these reliefs. 
2. The Creation of Eve.
3. Eve spinning, Adam delving.
   The first labour after the Fall. 
4. Jabal at his tent
   accompanied by his watch-dog.

5. Jubal
   inventor of the "harp and organ."
6. Tubal Cain 
   hammering on his anvil.
7. Noah 
   lying under the vine.

THE SEVEN BAS-RELIEFS on the Western side of the campanile representing the first stage of society: Patriarchal or Nomad life. Designed by GIOTTO, executed by ANDREA PISANO.

1. Astronomy.
   The first glance of the heavens. 
2. House-building.
   Providing a stationary home. 
3. Medicine,
   or the invention of pottery (?). 
4. Riding. *A symbol of the energy and enterprise of man.*

5. Weaving,
   expressive of female domesticity.
6. Legislation. 
   The giving of the "Book of Law."
7. Dædalus flying. 
   The dispersion of nations (?)

THE SEVEN BAS-RELIEFS on the Southern side of the Campanile representing the second stage of society: the State or Nation, the fixed home life developing race and country. *Designed by* GIOTTO, *executed by* ANDREA PISANO.

---

* See Lord Lindsay's *History of Christian Art*, and Ruskin's *Mornings in Florence*.

Photo ALINARI, ANDERSON, BROGI.

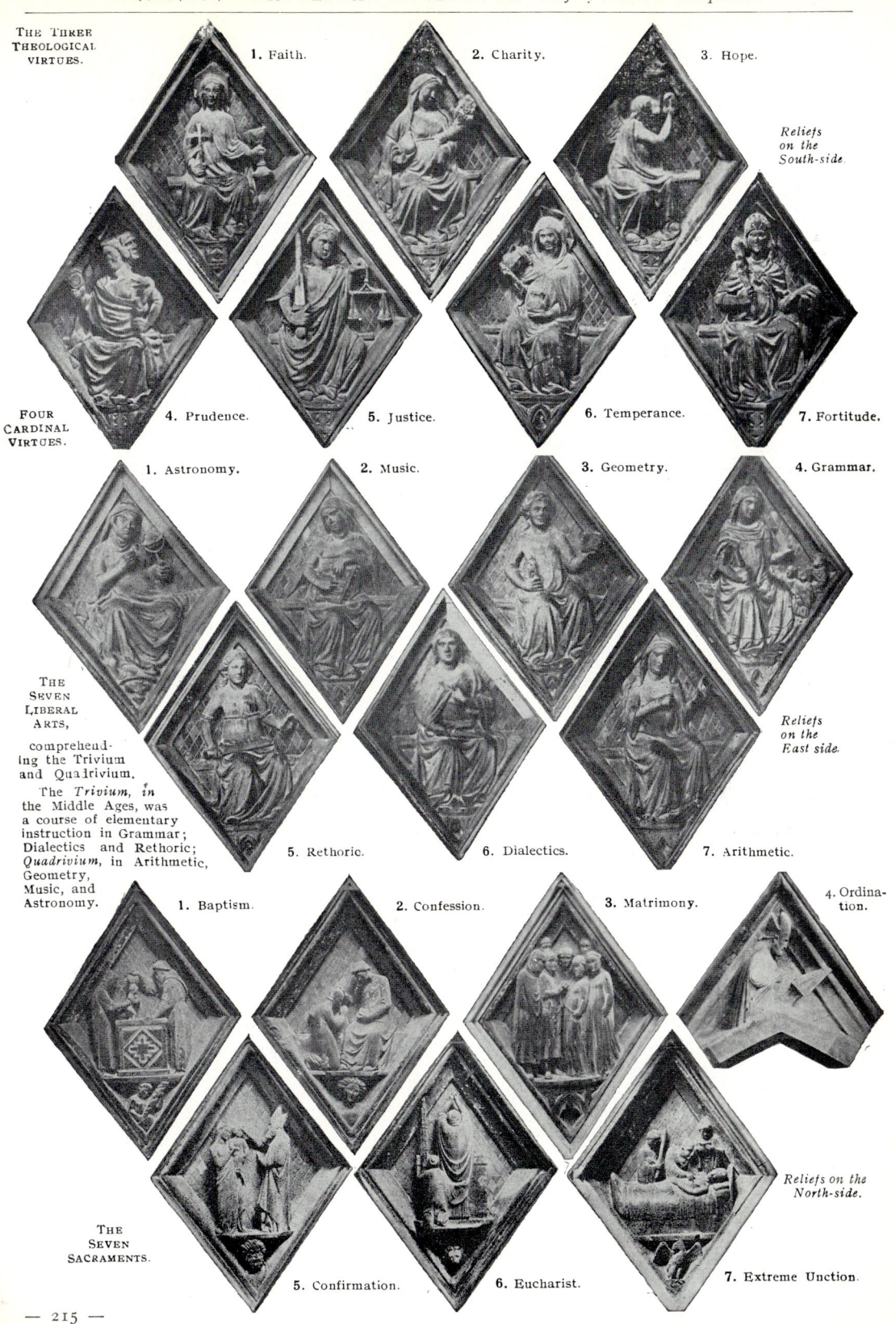

FLORENCE — CATHEDRAL MUSEUM. Bas-relief of Giotto's Campanile.

THE THREE THEOLOGICAL VIRTUES.

1. Faith.
2. Charity.
3. Hope.

Reliefs on the South-side.

FOUR CARDINAL VIRTUES.

4. Prudence.
5. Justice.
6. Temperance.
7. Fortitude.

1. Astronomy.
2. Music.
3. Geometry.
4. Grammar.

THE SEVEN LIBERAL ARTS,

comprehending the Trivium and Quatrivium.

The *Trivium*, in the Middle Ages, was a course of elementary instruction in Grammar; Dialectics and Rethoric; *Quadrivium*, in Arithmetic, Geometry, Music, and Astronomy.

5. Rethoric.
6. Dialectics.
7. Arithmetic.

Reliefs on the East side.

1. Baptism.
2. Confession.
3. Matrimony.
4. Ordination.

THE SEVEN SACRAMENTS.

5. Confirmation.
6. Eucharist.
7. Extreme Unction.

Reliefs on the North-side.

— 215 —

SINGING GALLERY (*Cantoria*). By DONATELLO. A. D. 1433-39. *Formerly in the Cathedral.*

In this work the master attained the highest point of grace and delicacy. The troop of merry children who go dancing and singing on their way, are varied with admirable effect. Donatello was the first to give the child a due place in sculpture, ' he composed whole works with motives of infants, and in nearly all his productions always a child appears in the most unexpected place. ' This Cantoria is considered the most popular work of the master. The motive is evidently classical, suggested by Roman reliefs in which cupids are represented ; the amphorae, the shells, the gold mosaic on the pillars and on the background have great decorative value in the general effect. Donatello's influence on art was enormous, and he is justly considered the greatest sculptor of the revival (*see* p. 301). Both Donatello's and Luca's Cantorie were originally placed above the doors of the sacristies in the Cathedral. But in the year 1688, on the occasion of the nuptials of Ferdinand de' Medici with Princess Violante of Bavaria they were removed as inadequate to the enlarged orchestra of the day and substituted with large galleries or balconies of carved and painted wood.

SILVER ALTAR or « DOSSALE ». *Formerly in the Baptistery.* The reliefs represent scenes from the life of the Baptist.

In a room adjoining to the one of the "Cantoria" is the High Altar or *Dossale* which formerly stood in the Baptistery. This exquisite work in silver dates from different periods : it was 114 years in perfecting, being placed successively in the hands of the best goldsmiths of the city. Thus, the main front dates from 1366-1402 ; the large central statue of St. John by *Michelozzo* is of 1451 ; the side reliefs : Birth of St. John by *A. Pollaiuolo*, and Death of the Baptist by *Verrocchio* are of 1477-80. Among those entrusted with work on it, was also *Tommaso Finiguerra*, who originated the art of engraving.

FLORENCE — CATHEDRAL MUSEUM. *Opera di S. Maria del Fiore.*

Boys with trumpets.
Sonum tubæ.

Singing with the psaltery.
Psalterium.

Girls with lutes.
Cithara.

Drumming and dancing.
Tympanum.

SINGING GALLERY (*Cantoria*). By LUCA DELLA ROBBIA. A. D. 1431-38. *Formerly in the Cathedral.*

This Cantoria executed for the Cathedral and taken down in 1688, is one of Luca's earliest and greatest works in marble.

The reliefs illustrate one of the most beautiful poems in the Book of Psalms. The groups of happy boys and girls dancing, playing on musical instruments, and singing are exceedingly lovely. Not a detail has been left out, not a touch forgotten. We see the motion of their hands beating time as they bend over each other's shoulders to read the notes, the rhythmic measure of their feet as they circle hand in hand to the tune of their own music, the very swelling of their throats as, with heads thrown back and parted lips, they pour forth their whole soul in song.

Like Donatello, Luca had the faculty of giving the loveliest presentment of children the world has ever seen.

Children dancing.
Choro.

Playing on organ and harp.
Chordis et organum.

Beating tambourines.
Cymbalis jubilationis.

Clashing cymbals.
Cymbalis benesonantibus.

The Psalm of David from which Luca borrowed the theme for his compositions has been copied on the frieze of the cantoria. The first two verses :

"Laudate Dominum in sanctis ejus : laudate eum in firmamento virtutis ejus "
"Laudate eum in virtutibus ejus : laudate eum secundum multitudinem magnitudinis ejus "

are inscribed on the upper frieze and form the subject of the two end panels. On the two lower friezes runs the remainder of the text:

"Laudate eum in *sono tubæ* : laudate eum in *psalterio* et *cithara*;"
"Laudate eum in *tympano* et *choro* : laudate eum in *chordis* et *organo*;"
"Laudate eum in *cymbalis benesonantibus*;"
"Laudate eum in *cymbalis jubilationis*; omnis spiritus laudet Dominum."

The words in italics refer to the eight front panels given above.

Never perhaps was the innocent beauty, the naïve charm of childhood so sympathetically and perfectly expressed than in these lovely bands of youths thrilled through and through with the power and the joy of their melody.

Singing boys. (*End panel*).

Singing boys. (*End panel*).

— 217 —

FLORENCE — SANTA CROCE (Church of the Holy Cross).

SANTA CROCE, begun by ARNOLFO DI CAMBIO in 1294. The Campanile by G. Baccani (1865), is in the 14th. century style.

INTERIOR OF SANTA CROCE. A Franciscan church.

This is the oldest and finest of all the churches belonging to the Mendicant orders. It is 460 ft. long and 134 ft. wide. Almost from its foundation this church became the favourite place of interment of the Florentines. In the colossal space of the nave, which is only the more impressive by reason of its extreme simplicity, are buried, under splendid monuments, some of the greatest Italians. Hence, the church is called the « Pantheon » or « Westminster Abbey » of Florence.

Santa Croce, contains, moreover, an exquisite marble pulpit, and many important frescoes by GIOTTO and his scholars.

The piazza in front of the church was the scene of tournaments and games.

MADONNA DEL LATTE. By A. ROSSELLINO.

MARBLE PULPIT. By B. DA MAIANO. A. D. 1475. With stories from the life of St. Francis.

BUST OF MICHELANGELO. By B. LORENZI.

Michelangelo died in Rome in his ninetieth year; during his illness, he had expressed a wish that his body should be taken to Florence, and buried at Santa Croce. After his death his remains were secretly transported to Florence, and a great funeral ceremony, in the presence of an immense number of artists and people took place in the church of San Lorenzo.

MONUMENT TO MARSUPPINI († 1455). By DESIDERIO DA SETTIGNANO.

TOMB OF MICHELANGELO († 1564). With the figures of Sculpture, Painting and Architecture. *Erected in 1570. Designed by Vasari.*

— 218 —

Photo ALINARI, ANDERSON, BROGI.

FLORENCE — SANTA CROCE (Church of the Holy Cross).

VIEW OF THE SACRISTY, *and the frescoes by* NICCOLÒ DI PIETRO GERINI (1400).

ANNUNCIATION. *By* DONATELLO. A. D. 1430.

THE ORDEAL OF FIRE.    ST. FRANCIS RECEIVING THE STIGMATA. 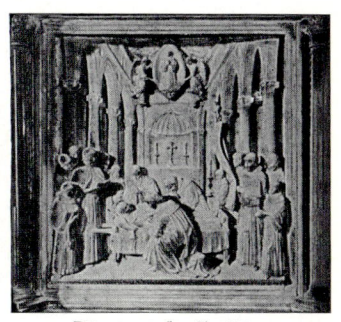   DEATH OF ST. FRANCIS.
Marble reliefs on the pulpit by Benedetto da Maiano, representing events from the life of St. Francis.

CENOTAPH OF DANTE († 1321).
By STEFANO RICCI. A. D. 1829.

Dante Alighieri, born in Florence in 1265, was the first great poet of modern times. His « Vita Nuova » is epochmaking in many ways; his « Divina Commedia » is a mirror of the whole Universe, a history of Humanity. He was unrighteously banished from Florence for political reasons and lies buried in his death city at Ravenna. The Florentines, having repented, begged back his body which the Ravenna people obstinately kept.

TOMB OF MACHIAVELLI († 1527).
By I. SPINAZZI.

Niccolò Machiavelli, born in Florence, was secretary of the Florentine Republic. Being opposed to the Medici was imprisoned and subjected to torture on their return to power. At last set at liberty, spent the last years of his life in literary labours, producing among other works a « History of Florence » and a treatise on government, entitled « The Prince ».

TOMB OF GALILEO († 1642).
By G. B. FOGGINI.

Galileo, born at Pisa, demonstrated the isochronism of the pendulum; constructed the first astronomical telescope, and proved the motion of the earth, thus provoking the hostility of the Church towards him. He was imprisoned and brought before the Inquisition where he was compelled to forswear himself; but he concluded his recantation with the exclamation: « but, it moves ! »

The church of Santa Croce is "the recognised shrine of Italian genius,"—Michelangelo, Machiavelli, Galileo, Alfieri, Ugo Foscolo, Leonardo Bruni, Marsuppini, Lanzi, Ghiberti, and many other famous men lie buried here. On the pavement are a large number of monumental tombstones of illustrious Florentine citizens: disciples of St. Francis, prelates, scholars, and warriors.

Photo ALINARI, ANDERSON, BROGI.

FLORENCE — *SANTA CROCE. Choir Chapel.*

LEGEND OF THE ORIGIN AND FINDING OF THE HOLY CROSS. *Frescoes by* AGNOLO GADDI (1380).

The traditional legend relates that: — « Adam, being sick, sent his son Seth at the Gates of Paradise to procure the oil of mercy to anoint him. **(1)** The archangel Michael **a p p e a r e d** and told Seth that the oil could only be obtained after 5500 years (the period corresponding with the interval from the Fall to the Atonement) had elapsed; meanwhile he gave him a branch of the tree whereof Adam had eaten, bidding him to plant it on Mount Lebanon, and that when it bore fruit his father would be healed. Seth returned and **(2)** finding his father dead, buried him and planted the branch on his grave, where it took root and flourished into a big tree till the days of Solomon, when it was cut down and used in building the Temple. The workmen, however, finding the " wood " unsuitable, rejected and threw it aside into a certain marsh, where it served as a bridge. But when the Queen of Sheba came to Jerusalem to visit Solomon, and was about to step upon the " wood " to cross the said marsh, she beheld in a vision how the Saviour of the world was to be suspended on it, and **(3)** forthwith she knelt down and worshipped the " wood; " at the same time informing Solomon that when this event should occur the kingdom of the Jews would come to an end. Solomon, alarmed, **(4)** causes the tree to be buried in the deepest bowels of the earth, on the spot whence afterwards arose the Pool of Bethesda. At the time of Our Lord's passion, the tree having been found floating on the surface of the water, **(5)** was taken out by the Jews and **(6)** used to construct the Cross of Christ.

After the crucifixion, the Cross lay buried for 300 years, until **(7)** the Empress Helena, mother of Constantine, discovered it together with the crosses of the two thieves. The difficulty of d i s t i n g u i s h i n g the Cross of Christ from the two pertaining to the robbers was solved by the bishop of Jerusalem, who **(8)** caused a dying woman to touch all three, and when she came to the True Cross she was **i m m e d i a t e l y** healed. Helena **(9)** caused the Cross of the Lord to be taken to Jerusalem and to be cut in halves; one half she carried away for her son, the other half she left, enclosed in a costly silver shrine, at Jerusalem.

After m a n y years, Chosroës, King of the Persians, subjugated all the kingdoms of the East, took Jerusalem, and **(10)** carried away the part of the True Cross left there by Helena. He **(11)** built a tower of gold and silver, in which he dwelt, and placing the Cross beside him, commanded a l l men to worship him as King of kings, and Lord of lords. This aroused the indignation of the Christian Emperor Heraclius **(12)** to whom an angel appeared bidding him to recover the Cross. Heraclius with a mighty army, came to the Danube to fight against the son of Chosroës, and the two princes agreed to settle their dispute **(13)**

(Continued on next page).

1. Seth receives a branch of the Tree of Knowledge;
2. Seth plants over Adam's grave the branch from which afterwards the " wood " of the Cross was to be taken.

9. The Empress Helena causes the Cross to be carried in procession amid adoring people to Jerusalem where she left half of it in a precious silver shrine.

3. *Centre*: The Queen of Sheba worships the sacred " wood "
4. *Right*: Solomon orders the burial of the sacred " wood."

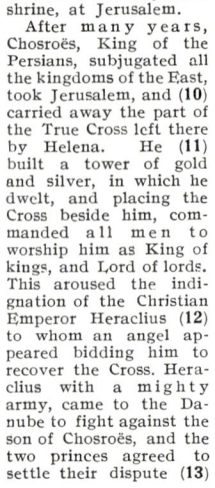

10. Chosroes, King of Persia, captures Jerusalem and carries off the portion of the Cross preserved there.

5. *Left*: The " wood " is taken from the pool of Bethesda, and
6. *Right*: is used to construct the Cross of Our Saviour.

11. *Left*: Chosroës in the tower; 12. *Centre*: Heraclius in his tent; 13. *Right*: Victory of Heraclius at the bridge.

7. *Right*: The Cross buried for 300 years is discovered;
8. *Left*: its authenticity is miraculously revealed.

14. *Left*: Death of Chosroës; 15. *Above*: Heraclius trying to enter Jerusalem on horse; 16. *Right*: he enters on foot.

— 220 —

FLORENCE — SANTA CROCE. Bardi and Peruzzi Chapels.

DEATH OF ST. FRANCIS. *Fresco by* GIOTTO ca. 1310 *(Cappella Bardi).*

THE BARDI AND PERUZZI CHAPELS.

THE BANQUET OF HEROD.
Fresco by GIOTTO ca. 1310 *(Cappella Peruzzi).*

The chapels belonging to the Bardi and Peruzzi, the two great banking families of Florence, were adorned with frescoes by Giotto (ca. 1310). In the Bardi, the chapel nearest the choir, the master painted seven scenes from the life of St. Francis; in the adjoining Peruzzi chapel, three scenes from the story of the Baptist (left wall), and three scenes from that of St. John the Evangelist. These paintings, the work of Giotto's ripest years, full of simplicity and sentiment, display great mastery and freedom of movement.

GIOTTO (1267-1337), was the first of the great Florentine painters who exercised the most influence on the development of Art. Filling the walls of churches and palaces in different parts of Italy with pictures of sacred history and the legends of saints, he depicted the whole range of human emotion. He worked for forty years not only creating but inspiring enthusiasm everywhere. His pupils and followers worked after his manner but, with one or two exceptions, none of them possessed extraordinary abilities, and, like all imitators, their work grew poorer as their distance from their master increased.

In the 14th century the religious sentiment dominated the plastic faculty. Under the influence of the two new religious orders—Franciscan and Dominican—numerous new churches and monasteries were being erected throughout Italy. There was a demand to decorate the internal walls of these edifices with such representations as the Life of Christ, of the Virgin Mary, and the stories of the favorite saints for the encouragement of piety or with Biblical stories,—the Last Judgment, Paradise, Inferno, etc., intended to teach and to impress on the minds of the people the doctrines of the Church. Thus, the aim of fourteenth century painters was to tell a story in a simple unaffected way; and as they were only required for the object itself, they seldom used their imagination or attempted *(Continued on next page)*

THE RAISING OF DRUSIANA.

ASCENSION OF ST. JOHN THE EVANGELIST.

Frescoes by GIOTTO ca. 1310, *in the Cappella Peruzzi.*

(Continued from preceding page) by single combat on the bridge, in which Heraclius defeated and killed the son of Chosroës. He (14) then went to Chosroës, seized him in his tower, beheaded him and carried off the Cross back to Jerusalem. But when, (15) mounted on his royal steed he was about to enter the city through the gate which the Lord had entered on an ass, the stones of the gate suddenly descended and closed themselves up like a wall. An angel appeared and reproved the emperor for his presumption. Then Heraclius shedding tears at once dismounted, and (16) stripped to his shirt, took the Cross and walked barefooted to the wall, which then parted giving him free admission, and he finally restored the Cross to its place ».

— 221 —

Photo ALINARI, ANDERSON, BROGI.

FLORENCE — *SANTA CROCE (Church of the Holy Cross).*

(*Continued from page 221*) to make an exhibition of their skill in portraying violent emotion or uncalled-for passion. This pictorial art, carried out in a given form, without essential advance or change in its method of representation, was called « Giottesque », and prevailed till the dawning days of the 15th century when an artist appeared —young Masaccio—who pointed the way with his frescoes in the church of the Carmine (p. 240).

A comparison of the two frescoes given here representing the « Presentation in the Temple », shows the close similarity of Giottesque work. In both pictures the treatment is very slightly varied. Almost every group is reproduced exactly, each figure is stereotyped ; in da Milano's picture pointed arches,—the new Gothic style of architecture,—replace the old Romanesque round ones of Taddeo's composition.

PRESENTATION IN THE TEMPLE.
Fresco by TADDEO GADDI (ca. 1335).
(*Pupil of Giotto, Baroncelli Chapel*).

PRESENTATION IN THE TEMPLE.
Fresco by GIOV. DA MILANO (ca. 1365).
(*Pupil of T. Gaddi, Rinuccini Chapel*).

MADONNA ENTHRONED with Saints.
Terracotta by LUCA DELLA ROBBIA.

When Donatello exhibited this crucifix, his friend Brunelleschi remarked that the figure of Christ looked like a peasant. Donatello, mortified, replied that it was easier to criticize than to make another as good ; to which his friend vouchsafed no reply, but practically answered him by modelling a crucifix more in harmony with his ideal, and then happening to meet him in the street one morning, invited him to breakfast at his studio. As they walked together, Brunelleschi, feigning a momentary engagement, begged Donatello to precede him with a supply of eggs, cheese, and fruit which he had just bought in the market ; and, following him unobserved to the door, saw him, as he caught sight of the crucifix, let go the corners of his apron (filled with eatables), and heard him, as he stood surrounded by the broken eggs, exclaim in an ecstasy of admiration : « By the side of this my Christ was indeed but a crucified peasant ». (*Brunelleschi's crucifix, is given on the opposite page*).

WOODEN CRUCIFIX,
by DONATELLO.

On the right side of the façade is the entrance to the 13th century cloister at the end of which is the *Cappella dei Pazzi*, founded by the ancient Florentine family whose name it bears. The chapel was built by Brunelleschi (1430-45) and is one of the most beautiful creations of the Renaissance period. In the vestibule is a charming frieze of angel's heads by Donatello and Desiderio da Settignano. The colonnade has a barrel-vault and a shallow cupola with terracotta decorations by Luca della Robbia; the carved wooden door is by Giuliano da Maiano (1472). The interior is very simple, with medallions of Apostles and Evangelists by Luca della Robbia; the small apse has decorations of the school of Donatello; the stained-glass window is attributed to Alessio Baldovinetti.

CAPPELLA DE' PAZZI. *Erected by* BRUNELLESCHI. A. D. 1430.

Photo ALINARI, ANDERSON, BROGI.

FLORENCE — SANTA MARIA NOVELLA.

SANTA MARIA NOVELLA. Begun A. D. 1278; completed A. D. 1357.
Façade by LEON BATTISTA ALBERTI. A. D. 1470.

INTERIOR OF THE CHURCH. *Gothic style.*

The Dominican Church of S. Maria Novella was the first important monumental church built at Florence. The interior design, in pure Tuscan-Gothic, was prepared by two Dominican friars FRA SISTO and FRA RISTORO. In order to give an impression of greater magnitude and perspective, the architects diminished the width of the arches dividing the nave from the aisles towards the transept and raised the pavement two steps half way up the whole width of the church. Thus, from the main entrance the nave appears longer than it actually is, owing to the decreasing distances of the pillars. The marble façade, begun in 1350 in the Gothic style, was completed in the Renaissance style from designs by LEON BATTISTA ALBERTI, at the expense of Giovanni Rucellai. The adjoining monastery was the residence of the popes and other distinguished guests of the city. The vast piazza in front of the church was frequently used for church festivals, and for chariot races, the two obelisks serving as goals.

St. Dominic was born in 1170 in Calaruga, Spain. He studied theology and became a canon in the diocese of Osma. While on a mission to France preached to the Albigenses and distinguished himself in the conversion of those heretics. In 1215 he founded a religious order of preaching friars at Toulouse. Soon after he visited Rome (where he met St. Francis of Assisi), and obtained the papal sanction for the foundation of his *Order of Preachers*. From this time St. Dominic was busily engaged all over Europe founding convents for his followers, the *Dominicans*, whose special charge was to guard the orthodoxy of the Church. In his zeal he sanctioned persecution when persuasion was of no avail; a practice relentlessly followed by the chiefs of the Spanish Inquisition. In 1220 he took up his residence in the principal convent of his Order at Bologna, making occasional journeys to superintend the more distant communities. But, fatigue, excitement and the extreme heat of the season brought on a raging fever, of which he died on 6th August 1221.

Upper part of a lavabo by G. DELLA ROBBIA (1497)

WOODEN CRUCIFIX. By BRUNELLESCHI.
(*See note on preceding page*).

MADONNA « RUCELLAI ».
Altar-piece attributed to CIMABUE.

This is one of the most famous works of Cimabue. The picture was so enthusiastically admired when it was first painted (1280), that it was carried in joyous procession from Cimabue's studio to this church.

THE HOLY TRINITY.
Fresco by MASACCIO.

Photo ALINARI, ANDERSON, BROGI.

— 223 —

FLORENCE — S. MARIA NOVELLA. Choir or Tornabuoni Chapel.

The choir chapel contains DOMENICO GHIRLANDAIO's most important frescoes, painted about 1490. This was the chapel of Giovanni Tornabuoni, chief of the Medici bank in Rome, in 1485. Giovanni had lost his wife, Francesca Pitti, in child birth (p. 300), and on his return signed a contract with Ghirlandaio to decorate the chapel in her honour with subjects from the *Life of the Virgin* and *St. John the Baptist*, his patron. The painter assisted by numerous pupils among whom was young Michelangelo, devoted four years to the undertaking. On the upper part of the window wall is a Coronation of the Virgin; on either side of the window are SS. Francis and Peter Martyr, the Annunciation and John the Baptist, and below these, kneeling, Giovanni Tornabuoni and Francesca Pitti, his deceased wife. On the left wall, beginning below from left to right: the Expulsion of Joachim from the Temple, Nativity of Mary, Presentation in the Temple, Nuptials, Adoration of the Magi, Massacre of the Innocents, and Death and Assumption. On the right wall, from right to left: Zacharias in the Temple, the Visitation, Nativity of John, Zacharias naming the child, the Baptist preaching in the desert, Baptism of Christ and the Feast of Herod.

The most striking feature of these frescoes is the modernizing of sacred history by the introduction of numerous contemporary portraits of eminent men and beautiful women making visits of ceremony; together with many details of every day life in Florence. Thus, in the *Nativity of the Virgin* Ghirlandaio gives us a portrait of Lodovica Tornabuoni and four noble ladies; in the *Nativity of the Baptist* that of Ginevra de' Benci, a celebrated beauty of her day; in the *Visitation* that of Giovanna degli Albizi who became the bride of Lorenzo Tornabuoni; in the scene of *Zacharias in the Temple* portraits of Marsilio Ficino, Cristoforo Landino, Angelo Poliziano, and members of the Tornabuoni family and their kinsmen the bankers Sassetti; in the *Expulsion of Joachim* we have the painters Baldovinetti, Mainardi, and Ghirlandaio himself.

SCENES FROM THE LIFE OF THE VIRGIN. *Frescoes on the left wall.*

SCENES FROM THE LIFE OF THE BAPTIST. *Frescoes on the right wall.*

THE BIRTH OF THE VIRGIN. *Frescoes by* GHIRLANDAIO. THE BIRTH OF JOHN THE BAPTIST.

EXPULSION OF JOACHIM FROM THE TEMPLE. (Life of the Virgin).  ZACHARIAS IN THE TEMPLE. (Life of the Baptist).

FLORENCE. UFFIZI GALLERY.

Federigo da Montefeltro, *by* Piero della Francesca (*see p. 258*).

FLORENCE — S. MARIA NOVELLA. *Filippo Strozzi's Chapel.*

The Chapel of Filippo Strozzi, to the right of the choir, contains the tomb of the founder who died in 1491, and frescoes by *Filippino Lippi* (1502) representing stories from the Lives of St. Philip and St. John the Evangelist. Right wall: *St. Philip exorcising the dragon*, which had been worshipped as the god Mars, by the inhabitants of Hierapolis. The dragon, at the saint's command, has crept from a hole beneath the altar, and while moving emits such dreadful odor that the son of the king has fallen dead in the arms of his attendants. But Philip restored him to life. *Martyrdom of St. Philip*: here the saint is crucified as the priests of the dragon were incensed against him. Left wall: *St. John resuscitating Drusiana* (comp. with Giotto, p. 221). *Martyrdom of St. John*, in a cauldron of boiling oil (omitted here). On the ceiling are represented the Patriarchs.

Filippino Lippi, the son of Fra Filippo and Lucrezia Buti, was born in 1457. His master was Botticelli, whose influence is very observable in many of his works. In 1484 he was charged with the completion of the frescoes in the Brancacci chapel which Masaccio had left unfinished sixty years before. On the whole his works show great skill in composition, and great refinement of feeling. But in these frescoes painted at the close of his career he spends himself in superfluous and ineffective inventions—violent gestures, strange attitudes, streaming draperies, archeological ornaments, which destroy all sense of beauty and repose.

MARTYRDOM OF ST. PHILIP APOSTLE.
Fresco by FILIPPINO LIPPI.

ST. JOHN RESUSCITATING DRUSIANA.  ST. PHILIP EXORCISES A DRAGON.
Frescoes by FILIPPINO LIPPI *in the Cappella Filippo Strozzi.*

1   2   3   4
1. Marsilio Ficino; 2. Cristoforo Landino; 3. Angelo Poliziano; 4. Genti'e de' Becchi, Bishop of Arezzo.

Domenico Ghirlandaio was born in Florence in 1449. He studied painting under the direction of Baldovinetti. At that time the Renaissance movement was in full swing at Florence, and he rose amidst the great influences around him. Fresco was his

Lodovica Tornabuoni. Ginevra de' Benci. Giovanna degli Albizi.
(*Birth of the Virgin*). (*Birth of the Baptist*). (*Visitation*).

favourite vehicle, and he is said to have declared that he would decorate the whole circuit of the walls of Florence with frescoes. He combined the art of distributing figures in a given space, with perspective and truth to nature, in greater perfection than any other painter of his times. He died of plague fever in 1494 and was buried in the church of Santa Maria Novella.

FLORENCE — S. MARIA NOVELLA. Capp. Strozzi.

The Strozzi Chapel is dedicated to St. Thomas Aquinas, the glory of the Dominican order, whose virtues are extolled in four allegorical medallions on the ceiling. On the altar wall is painted the Last Judgment, on the left wall Paradise, Inferno on the right. The whole is a rare example of a completely preserved mid-14th century chapel. After the lapse of five centuries these compositions bring us face to face with one of the greatest ideals of medieval times: Mysticism; when Christendom looked at the world through a fantastic veil of mystic illusions. In those days the painter who felt conscious of his high vocation considered himself as the auxiliary of the preacher. « His work », says Symonds, « was then a Bible, a compendium of grave divinity and human history, a book embracing all things needful for the spiritual and the civil life of man. He spoke to men who could not read, for whom there were no printed pages, but whose heart received his teaching through the eye ».

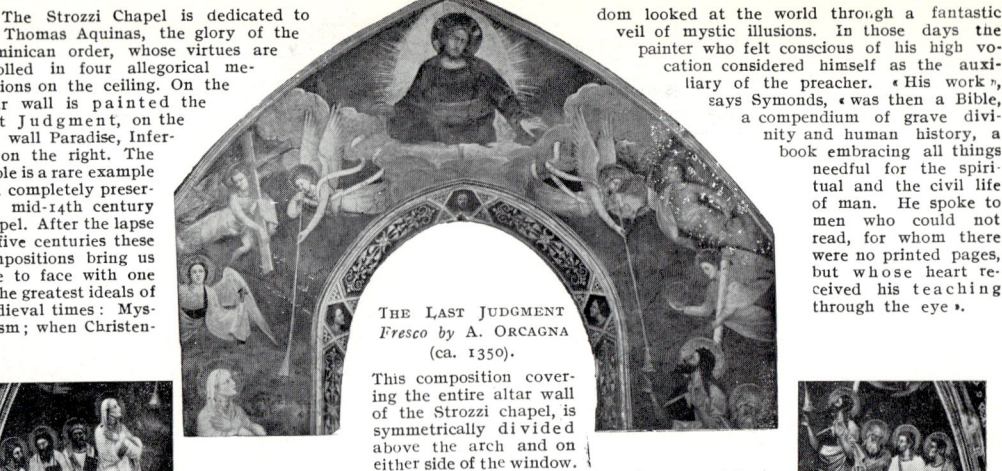

The Last Judgment Fresco by A. Orcagna (ca. 1350).

This composition covering the entire altar wall of the Strozzi chapel, is symmetrically divided above the arch and on either side of the window.

High up, the Saviour appears on a cloud and makes the sublime gesture that decrees the end of the world; he is accompanied by angels displaying the instruments of the Passion, and blowing the summons. The Apostles, equally divided on either side, sit as assessors, while the Virgin and St. John kneel between them and the Saviour.

The scene of the resurrection takes place below; on the left, beside a row of five saints, are grouped the Elect, all evidently portraits, in the costume of the time—here is seen Dante gazing up in fixed adoration, and Petrarch in priestly dress. On the right, beside a row of five heresiarchs, are crowded the Condemned. The faces in the first (left) group express the foretaste of celestial beauty, those in the second (right) are distorted by grief and despair. In the foreground angels help the Elect rising from their graves, while the Condemned are eagerly pulled out by devils

THE ELECT.

Altar-piece by Andrea Orcagna. A. D. 1357.

THE CONDEMNED.

Orcagna's predella picture given below represents the following quaint legend. « One night, a certain hermit sitting in his hut heard a sound as of a host rushing past. He opened his window, and called out to know who they could be, and a voice answered, ' We are demons; Henry the Emperor is about to die, and we go to seize his soul!' The hermit then requested that on their return they inform him of the result. This they promised, and after a time that same night they came again, and knocked at the window. When the hermit inquired of their success the fiends swore that all had gone ill, for they arrived, just

CHRIST giving the Keys to St. Peter (right) and the book to St. Thomas Aquinas, who is presented by the Madonna; behind them the Archangel Michael and St. Catherine of Siena; *On the right*, St. John the Baptist, St. Lawrence and St. Paul.

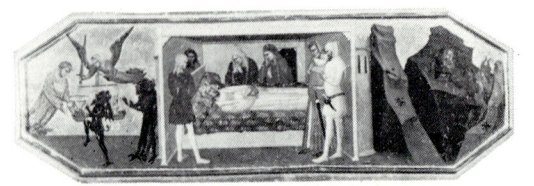

The contention for the soul of Emp. Henry II. († 1024). In the centre the emperor is seen dying; on the right devils go to seize his soul; on the left St. Michael holds the scales to weigh the souls.

as the emperor expired, and were about to seize his soul when, lo! his good angel came to save him. ' We disputed long, and at last the Angel of Judgment' (St. Michael) 'laid his good and evil deeds in the scales, and, behold! our scale descended and touched the earth ;—the victory was ours! when all at once the *roasted fellow* ' (St. Laurence) ' appeared, and flung a gold cup ' (which the emperor had presented to the Church) ' into the other scale, which changed the balance, and we were forced to withdraw in a hurry. ' And having said these words, the whole company of demons vanished ». (See Jameson's *Sacred and Legendary Art*).

— 226 —

Photo Alinari, Anderson, Brogi.

FLORENCE — S. MARIA NOVELLA. Cappella Strozzi.

Andrea Orcagna's " Paradise " is a work of singular grandeur in conception and stateliness in arrangement.

Above, between bands of Angels and Apostles, the figures of the Saviour and the Virgin are seated on a magnificent throne, under which are two angels, one singing praises on his viol, the other kneeling in prayer, typifies the worship of eternity.

Right and left is an immense company of saints, martyrs, virgins, prophets, patriarchs,—all absorbed in vision and love of God. They are ranged side by side in unbroken lines extending from top to bottom 'like lilies in a garden border.'

The intermediate space below is occupied by groups of the Elect, the new comers, in the dress of the artist's time. Among the figures is Dante himself, the inspirer of this pictorial poem. Conspicuous in the foreground, is a woman (the donor) in a black dress introduced by an angel to Paradise.

The wonderful beauty of the faces, beaming with rapture and beatitude can only be discovered after long study.

Orcagna's " Hell " is divided in accordance with Dante's first *cantica* ; hence, the successive circles or regions,—each with its appropriate horrors—are more easily followed it compared with the various episodes commemorated by the great Poet.

Beginning from the top :

1. The *Gloomy Forest*, where Dante lost his way (*Inf.*, I, II).
2. *Vestibule of Hell.* Here are punished those who had passed their time (for living it could not be called) in a state of apathy and indifference both to good and evil (*Inf.*, III).
3. The old ferryman Charon crying, « Woe to you wicked spirits ! hope not ever to see the sky again » (*Inf.*, III).
4. *First circle.* Limbo wherein are the souls of those, who, although they have lived virtuously, nevertherless, for lack of baptism, merit not the bliss of Paradise (*Inf.* IV).
5. *Second circle.* Here in the presence of Minos, the Infernal Judge, the carnal sinners are tossed about ceaselessly by the most furious winds : on this side and on that (*Inf.*, V).
6. *Third circle*, wherein the gluttonous are punished. Cerberus with his threefold throat barks at them, flays them, and their limbs piecemeal disparts. Their torment is to lie in the mire (*Inf.*, VI).

PARADISE. *Fresco by* ANDREA ORCAGNA.

7. *Fourth circle*, guarded by Plutus. Here the prodigal and the avaricious are condemned to the same torment; which is, to meet in direful conflict, rolling great weights by main force against each other with mutual upbraidings (*Inf.*, VII).
8. *Fifth circle.* The Stygian lake, wherein the wrathful and the gloomy, all naked, are sunk (*Inf.*, VII).
9. The iron ramparts encircling the fiery city of Dis guarded by throngs of angry devils (*Inf.*, VIII).
10. Gateway to the city of grief domineered by the three hellish Furies with serpents twined in their hair (*Inf.*, IX).
11. *Sixth circle.* The city of Dis, wherein the arch-heretics are interred in sepulchres burning with intense fire (*Inf.*, XI).
12. *Seventh circle* A. River of hot blood wherein are tormented those who committed violence against their neighbour. On the banks a troop of Centaurs armed with keen arrows chase them whenever they attempt to emerge from the blood (*Inf.*, XII).

13. *Seventh circle* B. Marsh which contains both those who have done violence on their own persons and those who have violently consumed their goods ; the first changed into rough and knotted trees whereon the harpies build their nests, the latter chased and torn by black female mastiffs (*Inf.*, XIII).

14. *Seventh circle* C. Plain of arid and hot sand where the self-slayers and those who committed violence against God, Nature and Art, are tormented by dilated flakes of fire, which are eternally showering down upon them (*Inf.*, XIV).

15. *Eighth circle* A. Gulf containing those who, either for their own pleasure, or for that of another, have seduced any woman from her duty ; these are violently scourged by demons (*Inf.*, XVIII).

16. *Eighth circle* B. Foss of ordure in which the flatterers are condemned to remain immersed in filth (*Inf.*, XVIII).

17. *Eighth circle* C. Lake of fire with apertures from which emerge the legs of those who have been guilty of simony (*Inf.* XIX). *

18. *Eighth circle* D. Gulf containing those who practised the arts of divination and astrology. They have their faces reversed and set the contrary way on their limbs ; thus, unable to see ahead they are compelled ever to walk backwards (*Inf.*, XX).

19. *Eighth circle* E. Pool of boiling pitch in which are plunged the barterers or public peculators (*Inf.*, XXI).

20. *Eighth circle* F. The hypocrites, condemned to pace continually under pressure of heavy leaden bonnets, Caiaphas is seen fixed to a cross on the ground ; he lies transversally on the way, so that all have to tread on him in passing (*Inf.*, XXIII).

21. *Eighth circle* G. The robbers : these sinners are tormented by venomous and pestilent serpents (*Inf.*, XXIV).

22. *Eighth circle* H. The evil counsellors ; here each flame envelops a sinner (*Inf.*, XXVI).

23. *Eighth circle* I. The slanderers, the schismatics, and the heretics ; they endure their penal tortures by having their limbs miserably maimed or divided in different ways. One is seen carrying his severed head like a lantern (*Inf.*, XXVIII).

24. *Eighth circle* J. The alchemists, forgers and impostors ; these are afflicted by divers horrible diseases. Two, covered from head to foot with tetter, are seen propped against each other (*Inf.*, XXIX).

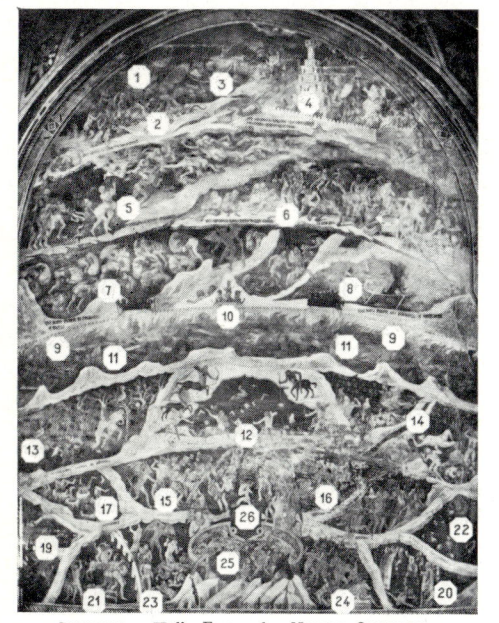

INFERNO. Hell. *Fresco by* NARDO ORCAGNA.

25. *Ninth and last circle.* Frozen circle guarded by Giants, wherein the traitors and the ungrateful are covered with ice (*Inf.*, XXXI).
26. Lucifer in the frozen circle gnawing sinners with each of his three mouths (*Inf.*, XXXIV). (*See also p.* 210).

The whole of this composition bears the impress of that mystical terrorism which burdened the mind of medieval **Christianity**.

* In this region called " Malebolge " Dante trusts the simonist popes Clement V., Boniface VIII., and Nicholas III. On the soles of their feet are seen burning flames.

— 227 —

FLORENCE — S. MARIA NOVELLA. Cappella degli Spagnuoli.

The Cappella degli Spagnuoli, formerly the chapter-house of the Dominican monastery, was erected about 1340, at the expense of a rich citizen of Florence, for the purpose of celebrating the newly instituted annual *Festival of Corpus Christi*. It bears its present name because assigned to the Spanish residents of Florence in 1566. The chapel is the most remarkable example of a completely decorated Giottesque interior. The frescoes, formerly attributed to Taddeo Gaddi and Simone Martini, are now supposed to be the work of ANDREA DA FIRENZE (ca. 1370). Fra Jacopo Passavanti, a Dominican, is said to have selected the theme of the pictures. « Each composition », writes Lord Lindsay, « derives significance from juxtaposition with its neighbour, and one idea pervades the whole, the Unity of the Body of Christ, the Church, and the glory of the Order of St. Dominic as the defenders and preservers of that Unity. This chapel, therefore, is to the Dominicans what the church of Assisi is to the Franciscans, the graphic mirror of their spirit, the apotheosis of their fame ». The vaulted roof of the chapel is divided into four triangular compartments, and the picture in each compartment has reference to the larger composition on the wall below it. The series in its march of thought commences on the altar wall (opposite the entrance) with a representation of the Passion of our Lord, rises to its climax in the compartment of the roof with the Resurrection of Christ, continues with the Ascension on the opposite compartment, and leads to the stories from the lives of St. Dominic and St. Peter Martyr on the entrance wall. Contiguous to these, in the left compartment of the roof is represented the Descent of the Holy Spirit on the Apostles, and beneath it, on the wall, the Triumph or Glorification of St. Thomas Aquinas, the mouth-piece of that Spirit, the supreme medieval exponent of the Holy Roman Church. In the right compartment of the roof is represented the Ship of Peter—symbolical of the Church—and on the wall below, the Church Militant and Triumphant,—her Unity on earth defended, and her individual members guided on the heavenward path, by the Dominicans.

VIEW OF THE CAPPELLA DEGLI SPAGNUOLI.

Descent of the Holy Spirit. The Pentecost.

The Virgin and Apostles are gathered on the upper floor of a building closed by folding doors. High up is seen the Celestial Dove in a glory of light ; rays proceed from the centre on every side, « And there appeared unto them cloven tongues, like as of fire, and sat upon each of them, and they were all filled with the Holy Ghost, and began to speak with other tongues as the Spirit gave them utterance » (*Acts*, 11). Below are several persons from every nation, listening with amazement to the Apostles talking in their different languages.

GLORIFICATION OF ST. THOMAS.

This fresco is an allegorical representation of the « Wisdom of the Church ».

On a lofty throne, St. Thomas sits in state, displaying an open book bearing the following Latin words from the Book of Wisdom : « Wherefore I prayed and understanding was given me : I called upon God, and the spirit of Wisdom came to me. I preferred her before sceptres and thrones ». At his feet the discomfited heretics Arius, Sabellius and Averrhoes ; while the three Theological and the four Cardinal Virtues with their symbols float gracefully above his head. Right and left of St. Thomas are prophets and saints (from left to right) : Job, David, St. Paul, St. Mark and St. John, St. Matthew, St. Luke, Moses, Isaiah, Solomon. Beneath are seated fourteen female figures symbolizing the Arts and Sciences ; at the feet of each, is a male figure, representing various personages, celebrated for excellence in that particular art or science. The following is their order from left to right : *Civil Law*, with Justinian ; *Canon Law*, with Pope Clement V.* ; *Practical Theology*, with Peter Lombard ; *Speculative Theology*, with Dyonisius Areopagita ; *Demonstrative Theology*, with Boëthius ; *Mystic Theology*, with St. John Damascene ;

THE TRIUMPH or GLORIFICATION OF ST. THOMAS AQUINAS.

Scholastic Theology, with St. Augustine ; *Arithmetic*, with Pythagoras ; *Geometry*, with Euclid ; *Astronomy* with Ptolemy ; *Music*, with Tubalcain ; *Dialectic*, with Aristotle ; *Rethoric*, with Cicero ; and *Grammar*, with Priscian.

« It will be seen », writes Symonds, « that the whole learning of the Middle Age—its philosophy as well as its divinity—is here combined as in a figured abstract, for the wise to comment on and for the simple to peruse. None can avoid drawing the lesson that knowledge exists for the service of the Church, and that the Church, while she instructs society, will claim complete obedience to her decrees. The *ipse dixit* of the Dominican author of the "Summa" is law ».

* Clement V. removed the Papal Seat to Avignon in 1309, where it remained till 1377 see note on p. 227).

FLORENCE — S. MARIA NOVELLA. Cappella degli Spagnuoli.

The « Passion of Our Lord », the great event upon which the Christian Church is especially founded, is here represented in one continuous picture on the altar wall, facing the entrance to the chapel.

Below on the left is the *Procession to Calvary*—our Saviour in the midst preceded by the soldiery on horseback, and followed by the Virgin and the other women of Galilee, winds round the walls of Jerusalem and ascends to the hill, on the summit of which is the *Crucifixion*. The sky is peopled with angels coming from every direction to witness the great sacrifice. On the left, a group of three angels carry away the soul of the penitent thief, while devils take that of the obdurate one on the right; here in the extreme corner a group of soldiers part the garments of the Saviour. Finally, low down is the *Descent of Christ in Limbo*: Our Saviour, standing on the broken door, beneath which Satan lies crushed, takes Adam by the hand to lead him out; Eve with clasped hands kneels beside Adam, behind is seen Abel bearing the lamb; Noah, between his wife and his son, follows with the ark; behind these is Abraham with Isaac on his right and Ishmael on his left, followed by Moses holding the tables of the Law, his brother Aaron and David with the lyre. Other Saints of the Old Testament kneel (Methuselah kneels behind Eve) or press forward with rapture, while devils lurk in a cavern powerless and with every sign of fear.

PROCESSION TO CALVARY.   THE CRUCIFIXION.   CHRIST IN LIMBO.

THE CHURCH MILITANT AND TRIUMPHANT. — This strikingly original composition is a living picture of the world of Christendom during the Middle Ages. In the lower part, to the left, is represented the Cathedral of Florence symbolizing the Church militant. Before it, the dual earthly powers,—Spiritual and Temporal, Pope and Emperor—enthroned equally; the Pope, a portrait of Benedict XI., is attended by church dignitaries, and representatives of the various monastic orders; the Emperor, Henry VII. (?), by diverse temporal authorities, besides burghers, pilgrims, beggars and women.* At the feet of the Pope, repose a flock of sheep, figurative of the faithful, guarded by two dogs, symbolizing the Dominicans, and painted black-and-white, in allusion to the particoloured habit of the order. Further, to the right, the dogs are represented killing the wolves who have been worrying the sheep of Christ,— figurative of the Inquisitors hunting out and destroying heresy; St. Dominic directing attention to them. Next to him St. Peter Martyr is arguing and expostulating with heretics while St. Thomas exhibits a controversial treatise to a similar group of opponents: one, struck by conviction, tears up his heretical book. Higher up, are represented the pleasures and vanities of this life; four careless men and women at dalliance in an orange grove, they are guilty of no dogmatic heresy, but indifferent to the duties of the time and the prospects of eternity. To the left a Dominican monk absolves a repentant sinner, and St. Dominic points the way to paradise.

The goal of all earthly endeavour: Paradise, symbolizing the Church Triumphant, is represented immediately above the roof of the Cathedral, and the gate of entrance (with St. Peter in charge), above the front portal; within the gate are seen Saints and Martyrs, each recognizable by his emblem. On the top of the picture, is Christ in Glory, with the symbols of the Evangelists beneath. « What the painters of these frescoes undertook to delineate for the Dominicans of Florence, was the fabric of society sustained and held together by the action of in-

THE CHURCH MILITANT AND TRIUMPHANT. Paradise obtained by devotion.

quisitors and doctors issued from their order. The Pope with his Cardinals, the Emperor with his Council, represent the two chief forces of Christendom, as conceived by the medieval jurists and the school of Dante. Seated on thrones, they are ready to rise in defence of Holy Church, symbolized by the picture of S. Maria del Fiore » (Symonds, *Renaissance in Italy*).

---

* Among the Emperor's attendants several illustrious personages are pointed out by tradition. Thus, the figure of the King on the Emperor's left is supposed to be Philip le Bel of France; the one in front wearing a white hood and short cloak is Cimabue; beside whom, in a red dress stands Taddeo Gaddi, while Giotto's head in profile is between them. At Cimabue's right is Simone Martini. Next to Philip le Bel is the Captain of the People, on whose left, a little lower, stands Petrarch in white hood and cape, and beside him, lower still, is Boccaccio, full face with a white cap and a book. Fiammetta, Boccaccio's sweetheart, is the middle one of three kneeling females; a flame appears above her garment; behind her, is seen the profile of Petrarch's Laura.

FLORENCE — OR SAN MICHELE (Church of the Trade Guilds).

(Statues on the Western side).

S. MATTHEW.
Money-Changers).
By Ghiberti-Michelozzo 1422.

S. STEPHEN.
(Wool-Weavers).
By Ghiberti 1428.

S. ELOY. (Farriers).
By Nanni di Banco
1415.

S. PETER.
(Butchers).
By Donatello
1408.

S. PHILIP.
(Shoemakers)
By Nanni di Banco

FOUR SAINTS.
(Masons, Bricklayers, Carpenters, Smiths).
By Nanni 1408.

(Statues on the Northern side).

One of the traceried windows.
Italian-Gothic architecture.

The Church of Or San Michele, the shrine of the Arts and Crafts of Florence, was originally a grain market or loggia, and the upper part a granary. On one of the pilasters of the old building was a painted figure of the Holy Virgin which in the early part of the 14th century acquired the character of a miraculous image, crowds reverted to it for devotion, and it was determined to convert the loggia into a church by filling up the arches with a continuous wall. This was done under the superintendence of TADDEO GADDI who began the work in 1337.

Soon after work was begun the city magistrates granted a petition of the Silk Weavers' Guild, that they should be allowed to decorate one of the exterior pilasters with a niche containing the statue of their patron saint; an example which was followed by several other guilds, and led to the external decoration of the edifice with statues of saints before which it was customary for each of the guilds to come in state to make offerings on the feasts of their proper patrons. These statues are among the best productions of the Florentine school of sculpture.

When it was decided to transform the old grain market into a church a Company or fraternity of lay men was formed in honour of the Madonna of Or San Michele ; it soon rose into the highest veneration for charity and benevolence ; legacies and offerings pouring in from every side. In the following year (1348), Florence suffered from a great plague ; many citizens, after seeing the whole of their family die, bequeated their all to

S. GEORGE (Copy).
(Armourers).
DONATELLO.

CHURCH OF OR SAN MICHELE. Erected in 1337-1404. On the right is the old Guild House of the wool weavers.
The statues on the exterior were each given by one of the Arts or Guilds of Florence.

charitable institutions. On this occasion the Company of Or San Michele received considerable sums of money for distribution among the poor, but the latter having been almost exterminated by disease, the Company resolved to expend a portion of the money in erecting a tabernacle to enshrine the miraculous picture of the Madonna, which had been the cause of their association. The commission to execute the tabernacle was given to Andrea Orcagna.

Photo ALINARI, ANDERSON, BROGI.

FLORENCE — OR SAN MICHELE (Church of the Trade Guilds).

(Statues on the Southern side).

S. JOHN BAPTIST. (*Cloth-Dealers*). By Ghiberti 1414.

CHRIST AND S. THOMAS. (*Merchants*). By Verrocchio.

S. LUKE. (*Judges and Notaries*). By Giambologna 1602.

(Statues on the Eastern side).

S. MARK. (*Flax Merchants*). By Donatello 1413.

S. JAMES. (*Furriers*). By Ciuffagni.

MAD. AND CHILD. (*Physicians and Apothecaries*).

MADONNA. By Luca della Robbia (*Physicians and Apothecaries*).

S. JOHN EV. (*Silk-Weavers*). By Montelupo 1515.

In the thirteenth century all business and even professional life in Florence centered in the Trade Guilds, or *Arti*, as the Florentines called them. They were divided into Greater or Lesser Guilds—*Arti Maggiori*, and *Arti Minori*. The number of the former was generally seven and comprised: the Guild of Judges and Notaries (*Arte dei Giudici e dei Notai*), the Guild of Dressers and Dyers of Foreign Cloth (*Arte di Calimala*), the Guild of Wool Manufacturers (*Arte della Lana*), the Guild of Silk Manufacturers (*Arte della Seta* or *di Por S. Maria*), the Guild of Bankers and Money Changers (*Arte del Cambio*), the Guild of Physicians and Apothecaries (*Arte dei Medici e Speziali*), the Guild of Furriers (*Arte dei Vajai*). The number of the minor guilds (usually fourteen) varied at different times according to the fluctuations of politics, and consisted of Butchers (*Beccai*), Shoemakers (*Calzolai*), Tanners (*Galigai*), Masons (*Muratori*), Oil-merchants (*Oliandoli*), Linendrapers (*Linaiuoli*), Locksmiths (*Chiavaiuoli*), Armourers (*Corazzai*), Saddlers (*Correggiai*), Carpenters (*Legnaiuoli*), Innkeepers (*Albergatori*), Blacksmiths (*Fabbri*), Wine merchants (*Vinattieri*), Bakers (*Fornai*). The wealthiest of the Greater Guilds was the *Arte della Seta*; the most important the *Calimala* which dealt in Transalpine fabrics and had no less than twenty warehouses; and the *Arte della Lana* which had two hundred workshops with 30.000 workmen.

The Guild of Bankers and Money Changers, however, is the one which history most closely identifies with Florentine enterprise. The Florentines were the great bankers of the age, and made their city the chief money market of the then civilized world. In the 13th, 14th and 15th centuries the most prominent members of the guild had earned a world-wide reputation for their sagacity and integrity, and the financial transactions of kings, of the popes, and of the business world generally, at home and abroad, were entrusted to their care. The Bardi, Peruzzi, Pitti, Medici, della Gherardesca, and other great banking families were the Rothschilds of their time; they owned banks in all countries and frequently made large loans to foreign princes. It is said that Edward III. of England, would hardly have been in a position to have won Cressy without the enormous sums which the Peruzzi and the Bardi had advanced to him at the beginning of his war with France. The widespread trade of the three great manufacturing guilds—*Calimala, Wool* and *Silk* and the consequent banking operations involved, at a time when the transmission of bullion became more and more risky, gave rise to the *Lettere di Cambio*—Letters of change, or credit. And to this admirable and convenient system of exchanging cash values against paper, due to the initiative of the Florentines, we owe the origin of our present system of banking, which has done so much for the increase of wealth and the advancement of civilization.

Only members of the guild were recognized by the State, and they were generally assigned positions in the Mercato Nuovo (p. 308). This privilege gave the right to a table, covered with green cloth—*tavola di contanti*,—and a chair conveniently placed for the transaction of business. The "Bank" consisted of a leather pouch or bag of gold money, a wooden or metal bowl full of small coins for change, a Day Book and a sheet of clean parchment for entries of the day's business.

In 1338 there were about eighty money-changers' stalls in the Mercato Nuovo, which did a business of two million gold florins yearly. The big guilds governed the city, while the minor had political privilege. Only guild members were allowed to vote for city officers.

INTERIOR OF OR SAN MICHELE.
Orcagna's tabernacle is given on following page.

Photo ALINARI, ANDERSON, BROGI.

FLORENCE — *CHURCH OF OR SAN MICHELE.*

This celebrated tabernacle rising in stately beauty to the roof of the church is the masterpiece in sculpture of Orcagna, and one of the finest works of its kind in Italy. It is entirely of marble, inlaid with mosaic, gold and *lapis lazuli*; enriched with numerous pinnacles, columns, and sculptures in lavish profusion. All round the base are reliefs representing scenes from the life of the Virgin, the Apostles, the Christian Virtues, the Sciences and the Arts. At the back of the shrine is a large relief, of the Death and Assumption of the Madonna. The old, miraculous image destroyed by fire, was replaced by the present picture of the Madonna and child by Bernardo Daddi.

DEATH AND ASSUMPTION OF THE VIRGIN.

GOTHIC TABERNACLE *by* ANDREA ORCAGNA. A. D. 1349-59

The large relief at the back of the tabernacle. "The Death of the Madonna and her Assumption," or rather, Our Lady of the Girdle, is one of Orcagna's great works. In the lower compartment the Madonna lies upon her death bed surrounded by the Apostles; Our Saviour appears on the further side with the soul in his arms. Among the Apostles the artist has introduced his own portrait. In the upper compartment the Madonna is being carried up to heaven by angels, and dropping her girdle to St. Thomas who had doubted her Assumption (*See* p. 277).

1. Birth of the Virgin.   2. Presentation in the Temple.   3. Marriage of the Virgin.

7. The Purification.

4. The Annunciation.   5. The Nativity.   6. Adoration of the Magi.

Of the above reliefs that of the Marriage of the Virgin is distinguished by its simple grace and dignity. But in The Warning of Death, Orcagna shows his high powers of dramatic expression. Here the Virgin appears as an old woman, touched but not defaced by age; she gazes wistfully and submissively at the celestial messenger announcing her approaching death.

8. The Warning of Death.

— 232 —

Photo ALINARI, ANDERSON, BROGI.

FLORENCE.

THE CHURCH OF OR SAN MICHELE. (*Erected in 1337-1404*).

FLORENCE — CHURCH OF SAN LORENZO.

The Church of San Lorenzo, by Brunelleschi. *The Façade is unfinished.*
The Statue of Giovanni delle Bande Nere is by Bandinelli (1540).

The church of San Lorenzo, famous all over the world on account of its memorial chapels of the Medici family, was consecrated by St. Ambrose in 393. Early in the 15th century, ruin menacing it, the Medici and other Florentine families undertook to rebuild it. The present church, begun in 1419, is one of the masterworks of Brunelleschi († 1446), who did not live to complete the building. The interior, noble and harmonious, is in the form of a Latin cross, with columns of *pietra serena* and a gilded ceiling. The inner wall of the façade was designed by Michelangelo; the cupola was decorated by *Meucci*; the high altar is inlaid with rich Florentine mosaics representing stories from the old Testament.

San Lorenzo having been built by the bounty of the Medici became the parish church and the family vault of the race. Here they were baptized as children, married as young men and girls, and buried when their lives came to an end. The church has witnessed many an event of historical interest, — the splendid marriage of Lorenzo the Magnificent with Clarice Orsini, when the whole city was feasted by the Medici for three successive days and nights; the solemn funereal service performed in 1564 over the earthly remains of Michelangelo before the body was borne to its last resting place in the church of Santa Croce, etc.

The façade of the church is still wanting. In 1515 Leo X. gave the commission for its building to Michelangelo, who was greatly interested in the scheme; the proposition offered to him the possibility of combining masses of sculpture and architecture on a large scale, with a definite calculation of effect. But the scheme fell through and the front of the church remains to this day unfinished. Michelangelo's design is preserved in the Casa Buonarroti (Michelangelo's museum pag. 307).

The two pulpits in the nave of the church are highly interesting as being Donatello's latest work. The great sculptor died (1466) before the work was finished and the pulpits were completed by his pupils Bertoldo and Bellano (Bertoldo became the master of Michelangelo). The wonderfully wrought reliefs, representing scenes from the Passion, display originality in design and a grand passionate style. The first pulpit which Donatello executed was placed on the left side of the nave; the second on the right side. They were placed opposite one another, that they might be used by theological disputants, and for reading the gospel and the epistle. From these pulpits the great Dominican Girolamo Savonarola delivered some of his most stirring sermons, even against the Medici, the patrons of the church.

The Crucifixion. *Bronze by* Donatello.

View showing Donatello's bronze Pulpits.

Photo Alinari, Anderson, Brogi.

FLORENCE — CHURCH OF SAN LORENZO (Old Sacristy).

BUST OF S. LORENZO.
Terracotta by DONATELLO.

Bronzino's "Martyrdom of St. Lawrence" belongs to the period when Art had become absolutely formal. The composition exhibits nothing but anatomical pedantry, not a trace of unsophisticated vision.

In the centre of the picture the saint is seen lying on the gridiron; around him the executioners are busy kindling the fire; in the foreground are several women symbolizing the Virtues; on the right, seated on a throne, the prefect of Rome with outstretched arm points to the martyr. The drawing is skilful but the arrangement defective from the multiplicity and confusion of twisted arms and legs in a variety of forced attitudes. Standing in front of it the visitor has the impression of looking at an anatomical museum rather than at a religious picture.

MARTYRDOM OF ST. LAWRENCE. (*Left aisle*).
Fresco painting by ANGELO BRONZINO. (1502-72).

Bronzino, a scholar of Pontormo, was an admirer of Michelangelo and like the great master he delighted in the display of his knowledge of anatomy; on some occasions, however, he excited even disgust by his want of taste and his faulty perspective.

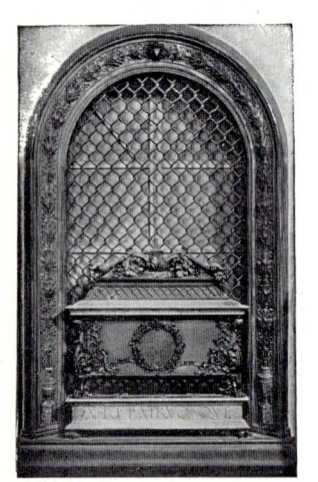

TOMB OF PIERO
AND GIOVANNI DE' MEDICI.
By VERROCCHIO.

THE OLD SACRISTY. Founded by Giov. de' Medici.
Erected by BRUNELLESCHI. 1421-38.

The Old Sacristy of San Lorenzo is an excellent example of Brunelleschi's style and one of the earliest achievements of Renaissance architecture. Everything here refers either to St. Lawrence or to the Medici and their patron saints. Near the entrance is the monument of Giovanni and Piero de' Medici, sons of Cosimo, erected by order of Lorenzo the Magnificent; it is the earliest important work of Verrocchio, who began his career as a goldsmith. A striking feature of this beautiful monument is the absence of religious symbols or figures conveying the idea that it was destined to receive the mortal remains of a Christian soul. The admirable plastic decoration of the sacristy is by Donatello. On the walls are stucco medallions of the Four Evangelists; in the spandrels are circular stucco reliefs with scenes from the life of John the Baptist: the Raising of Drusiana, St. John in the desert, his Martyrdom, and his Ascension; below these runs a frieze of small medallions with beautiful cherubs; on a sideboard is a charming bust of the young S. Lorenzo, one of the most attractive creations of Donatello.

BRONZE DOORS. (Sacristy).
By DONATELLO.

The two pairs of bronze doors on the sides of the altar were likewise executed by Donatello, by order of Cosimo the Elder. The simple treatment of the low reliefs on these doors, with two figures of dignified Saints moving or writing, discussing or converting each other, reveals the genius of the artist who repeated the simple theme twenty times without breaking the laws of harmony.

TOMB OF GIOVANNI DI BICCI DE' MEDICI AND HIS WIFE.
Designed by DONATELLO (Old Sacristy).

— 234 —

Photo ALINARI, ANDERSON, BROGI.

FLORENCE — CHAPEL OF THE PRINCES (Medici Chapel)

The Chapel of the Princes, situated behind the choir of San Lorenzo was begun as a family mausoleum by the Grand Duke Ferdinand I. in 1604. The edifice was designed by *Prince Giovanni de' Medici* and erected by the architect Nigetti; its construction occupied more than a hundred years, and was not brought to its present state (it is yet unfinished) until after the death of the last of the Medici.

The building is octagonal in design and surmounted by a dome; the walls are covered throughout with highly polished marbles, " the richest crust of ornament that was ever lavished on so large a surface. "

Round the chapel are huge Oriental porphyry sarcophagi of the six grand-dukes, surmounted by their gilded bronze statues representing them clad in their robes of state, with crown and sceptre, and on each sarcophagus a jewelled cushion in granite and a gilded and jewelled crown. Slabs of porphyry below each monument bear the names of the defunct in letters of jasper.

The lower part of the walls is lined with a variety of rare marbles,—African marble, Siena marble, Carrara marble, verde antico, petrified wood, Sicilian asper, white and yellow Corsican granite, etc.,—and decorated with coats-of-arms of Tuscan towns in a kind of mosaic of inlaid marbles and precious stones,—lapis lazuli, jasper, chalcedony, agate, mother of pearl, coral, amber, etc., for which a manufactory was founded in Florence (and still exists) under royal patronage. The dome was intended to be lined with lapis lazuli, to harmonize with the walls, but the idea was rejected on account of the enormous cost and labour it involved. It was finally decorated with paintings in 1830. The grand-dukes with their wives and children are interred in the crypt below the chapel. The grand-dukes were buried in their regalia, with crown and sceptre, the princes and princesses in their wonderful clothes and jewels. In 1857 the Government ordered an examination of the coffins which numbered forty-nine and it was then discovered that most of them had been broken open and pilfered. The chapel is said to have cost about one million pounds sterlings.

The Nativity. Crucifixion. Noah's sacrifice. The Resurrection. Cain and Abel. Last Judgement. Adam and Eve. The Fall.

Ceiling of the Chapel. *Frescoes by* P. Benvenuti.

Chapel of the Princes or Mausoleum of the Grand-Dukes. *Begun in 1604.*

| Cortona | Pisa | Florence | Fiesole | Siena | Pistoia |

Armorial Bearings of the various cities formerly ruled over by the Medici.

— 235 —

FLORENCE — CHURCH OF SAN LORENZO (Medici Chapel).

This famous chapel was entirely designed by Michelangelo to receive the sculptures he intended to place there ; hence, as Symonds said, « it may be looked on either as the masterpiece of a sculptor who required fit setting for his statues, or of an architect who designed statues to enhance the structure he had planned ». The whole work is a blending of marvellous beauty and harmony, a triumph of architecture and sculpture.

The chapel, a quadrangular edifice, surmounted by a dome, was planned in 1520 in the time of Leo X. and completed in 1524 under Clement VII. When the building was ready, Michelangelo commenced the famous tombs, upon which he was occupied more or less incessantly, for the next ten years. There were to be three tombs or monuments, but only two were executed : one to *Giuliano, Duke of Nemours* ; the other to *Lorenzo, Duke of Urbino*. Through an irony of fate the third monument intended for Lorenzo the Magnificent and his brother Giuliano, the fathers of the two Medici popes, was never commenced, and they lie here unrecorded and forgotten.

The scheme of the tombs is novel and arbitrary. Each tomb consists of three colossal statues : the deceased, represented as living, and, on the sloping lids of the sarcophagus two recumbent allegorical figures in attendance, chosen in place of the customary mourning Virtues. The whole conception is symbolical and its inner meaning can only be in part with certainty interpreted. The figure of Giuliano typifies energy and leadership in

The New Sacristy (Medici Chapel). *By* Michelangelo. A. D. 1520-34.

Tomb of Giuliano de' Medici († 1516).

Tomb of Lorenzo de' Medici († 1519).

repose ; below, the male figure typifies Day, the female Night, or the man Action and the woman the sleep and rest that produce Action. The figure of Lorenzo typifies Contemplation ; below, the female figure typifies Dawn, the male figure Twilight, the states which lie between light and darkness, action and rest. The figures are indeed beyond all description noble and beautiful ; there is something of mysterious and superhuman grandeur about them. Here is revealed to us the whole titanic nature of Michelangelo, the greatest of the Moderns, with its enormous creative force, and fiery aspirations.

— 236 —

Photo Alinari. Anderson, Brogi.

FLORENCE — CHURCH OF SAN LORENZO (Medici Chapel).

The figures on the Medici tombs represent the culminating point of Michelangelo's art. The statue of Lorenzo is, by common consent, considered one of his greatest achievements in sculpture. The duke is represented in profound meditation, hence called " Il Pensieroso " (the Thinker); he sits with one finger pressed upon his lips, as if forbidding interruption, and with a mysterious depth of expression in his face, which is shaded by the peak of the helmet ' it fascinates and is intolerable. '

Giuliano, represented as a Roman general with the commander's baton in his hand, sharply turns his head to the side, as if to watch some distant evolutions of his troops.

The two pairs of figures reclining on the sarcophagi are characterised by audacious attitudes and violent play of muscle which evoke at once admiration and stupefaction. Here Michelangelo displays a consummate knowledge of the human body, and a mastery of the chisel, such as none have attained since, and such as were only attained before him by the Greeks in their greatest period of art. The male figures are unfinished; the " Day " a giant, in an attitude of irritation, rises wearily from his mask of rock; " Twilight, "

MADONNA AND CHILD.
By MICHELANGELO.

FIGURE OF LORENZO DE' MEDICI (the Thinker).
By MICHELANGELO.

THE FIGURE OF " NIGHT. " *By* MICHELANGELO.

THE FIGURE OF " DAWN. " *By* MICHELANGELO.

leaning upon his elbow sinks gently to repose. The colossal female figures, are completed, and are praised in prose and verse J. A. Symonds writes: " 'Dawn' starts from her couch, as though some painful summons has reached her sunk in dreamless sleep, and called her forth to suffer. Her waking to consciousness is like that of one who has been drowned and who finds the return to life agony. Before her eyes, seen even through the mists of slumber, are the ruin and the shame of Italy. Opposite lies ' Night, ' so sorrowful, so utterly absorbed in darkness and the shade of death, that to shake off that everlasting lethargy seems impossible. Yet she is not dead. If we raise our voices, she too will stretch her limbs and, like her sister, shudder into sensibility with sighs. Only we must not wake her; for he who fashioned her, has told us that her sleep of stone is great fortune. "

— 237 —

Photo ALINARI, ANDERSON, BROGI.

FLORENCE — BIBLIOTECA MEDICEO-LAURENZIANA.

THE LAURENTIAN LIBRARY. *Designed by* MICHELANGELO.

One of the 88 "plutei" or presses containing illuminated manuscripts. *Designed by* MICHELANGELO.

The MEDICEO-LAURENTIAN LIBRARY, the first Public Library to exist in Europe, is a noble monument of the zeal of the Medici in the advancement of learning.

Founded in 1444 by Cosimo the Elder in his private residence, it was considerably increased by his son Piero and his grandson Lorenzo the Magnificent, whose wealth gave him the means of gratifying his passion for collecting books and manuscripts all over Europe and the East. When the Medici were expelled from Florence, the library was confiscated to the State and the Republic deposited it with the Dominicans of San Marco. In 1508, the great-grandson of Cosimo, Cardinal Giovanni de' Medici (afterwards Leo X.) purchased it and brought it to his private palace in Rome. Later, Clement VII. (another Medici pope) having determined to restore the collection to Florence, commissioned MICHELANGELO to prepare plans for the present building which was begun in 1523. Michelangelo built the beautiful, effective vestibule and left designs for the rest of the building which was completed by VASARI and others. The great hall, is over 160 feet long. Its fifteen windows, are of coloured glass and were designed by GIOVANNI DA UDINE. The wooden ceiling and the eighty-eight "plutei," a combination of benches

Portrait of Petrarch.
Miniature attributed to SIMONE MARTINI.

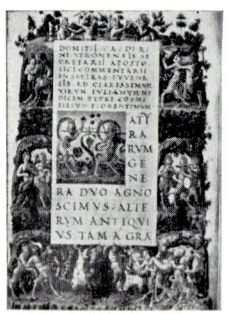

The Satires of Juvenal.
Page from an old codex.

Consecration of the Duomo.
Page from an old missal.

Petrarch's Laura.
Miniature attributed to SIMONE MARTINI.

and cabinets containing most precious manuscripts, were designed by MICHELANGELO. The terracotta pavement designed by TRIBOLO is an imitation of the ceiling. The celebrated library contains some 10.000 manuscript books and illuminated works of Greek, Hebrew, Arabic, Syriac, Coptic, Latin and Italian classical authors. It includes an original manuscript of *Virgil* (4th cent.); two fragments of *Tacitus*; *Terence*, from the hand of *Politian*; the *Divina Commedia*, transcribed a few years after Dante's death; copy of the celebrated letter of *Dante* in which he rejects the conditional permission to return to Florence; original letters of *Petrarch*; portraits of Laura and Petrarch; Benvenuto Cellini's holograph autobiography; the *Decameron*, transcribed in 1343 from *Boccaccio's* autograph; the famous original copy of the *Pandects of Justinian* (A. D. 533) discovered by the Pisans when they captured Amalfi in 1137, the finding of which caused so great an influence on the civilization of Europe.

CLOISTERS OF SAN LORENZO leading to the Laurentian Library. These cloisters formerly afforded an asylum for homeless cats. The ancient custom, of feeding them when the clock struck twelve noon was a most curious sight.

THE VESTIBULE AND STAIRCASE. *Designed by* MICHELANGELO.

Photo ALINARI, ANDERSON, BROGI.

— 238 —

FLORENCE — OGNISSANTI, SANTO SPIRITO.

[CORONATION OF THE VIRGIN. *Terracotta by* LUCA DELLA ROBBIA *over the portal of the Franciscan church of Ognissanti.*

THE MADONNA OF MERCY protecting the Vespucci family. *Fresco by* GHIRLANDAIO. (*Church of Ognissanti*).

The Church of Ognissanti, erected in 1554 was remodelled in the 17th century in the Baroque style. The only works of real artistic merit in the interior are the frescoes illustrated here. Sandro Botticelli and Amerigo Vespucci (born in a house near by) are buried in the crypt. The old refectory of the suppressed Minorite monastery adjoining the church, contains a fine « Last Supper » painted by Ghirlandaio in 1480.

The monastery and church of Ognissanti originally belonged to the Lombard Order of the Humble Brothers, the *Frati Umiliati*, who settled here in 1251. These gifted and industrious monks did much to promote and improve the woollen-manufacture in Florence. They filled with their carding, weaving and dyeing houses the whole region around now occupied by the present Piazza in front of the church, and by the hotels and shops in the neighborhood.

ST. JEROME. (*Church of Ognissanti*). *Fresco by* GHIRLANDAIO.

This is one of the master's early works. St. Jerome is represented in a thoughtful attitude at his scriptorium.

ST. AUGUSTINE. *Fresco by* BOTTICELLI.

The saint's face seems burdened by the life long meditation on the terrible mysteries of God's eternal decrees.

Ghirlandaio's « Madonna of Mercy » (della Misericordia) contains several portraits of the Vespucci family which are thus identified by Miss Cruttwell in her book *Florentine Churches*: « Amerigo Vespucci, the discoverer of America, is the youth with dark hair whose head is seen next the Madonna on the left. The old man in the foreground is probably his father Anastasio, donor of the painting. The monk behind may be his brother, Fra Antonio, a friend and follower of Savonarola; and the young man between him and the bishop, Guidantonio Vespucci, Ambassador to the Court of France, to whom Amerigo acted at one time as secretary. The lady kneeling below the Virgin's hand to the right may possibly be Simonetta Cattaneo, known as « La Bella Simonetta » married to a Vespucci, mistress of Giuliano de' Medici, since her features bear some resemblance to Pier di Cosimo's portrait of her as Cleopatra in the Museum of Chantilly ».

CHURCH OF SANTO SPIRITO. *Designed by* BRUNELLESCHI. *Begun in 1436. Completed in 1487.*

SACRISTY OF SANTO SPIRITO. *Erected by* G. DA SANGALLO, CRONACA, *and* ANT. POLLAIUOLO.

This magnificent church built in the form of a Latin cross, is a fine example of early Renaissance architecture. Here may be perceived the spirit of a new, and reforming time which strove after the noble simplicity of early Christendom and the return towards the forms of the ancient Christian basilicas.

Photo ALINARI, ANDERSON, BROGI.

FLORENCE — S. MARIA DEL CARMINE: Brancacci Chapel.

S. Maria del Carmine, the church of a Carmelite monastery, was burned down in 1771, and entirely rebuilt. But the Brancacci chapel with its frescoes, painted about 1423 and following years by Masaccio and Masolino, and completed in 1484, by Filippino Lippi, escaped destruction. The chapel was dedicated to St. Peter and the prescribed subjects were drawn from the « Acts of the Apostles », and « The Golden Legend ». These celebrated frescoes were a source of inspiration and a school where all succeeding artists studied, and whence Raphael deigned to borrow the composition and the figures of a portion of his cartoons. It was in this chapel that Michelangelo while studying the frescoes in 1492 had a quarrel with young Torregiano, when the latter, losing all self control, struck Michelangelo such a blow upon his nose that the great sculptor was disfigured for life.

THE TRIBUTE MONEY. *Fresco by* MASACCIO.

This composition, painted entirely by *Masaccio*, is divided into three parts : in the centre, the tax-gatherer demands payment of the poll tax when there is not any money in the company ; Christ, calm and majestic, turns to Peter and commands him to find the coin in the mouth of a fish. In the left background, Peter is seen catching the fish. On the right again, Peter, with an air of mingled dignity and contempt, delivers the coin to the tax-collector. « Masaccio has formed a group of potent and formidable individuals », writes F. J. Mather Jr., « these simple men are fit to shake a world. He has shown them in a moment in which discouragement and determination blend. A technicality threatens to check the salvation of the world. He has discriminated between the assured authority of the Christ and the wrathful energy of St. Peter. He has invested the majestic forms with massive draperies grandly disposed in simple folds. He has given even the tax-gatherer the grace of a Roman athlete ». This fresco forms an epoch in the history of painting.

Masaccio (1401-1428), was one of the greatest painters of the Renaissance. While still a youth he became the pupil of Masolino. But he really owed much to Brunelleschi, the inventor of perspective drawing, to Ghiberti, and to Donatello whom he wished to emulate in painting. In his representation of the nude he is a realist who models like a great sculptor. He understood how to subordinate the unimportant figures in his compositions to the principal actors, and to distribute color and light and dark so as to give the swiftest and truest representation of mass and distance.

« What above all renders his style attractive », writes Symonds, « is the sense of aërial space. For the first time in art the forms of living persons are shown moving in a transparent medium of light, graduated according to degrees of distance, and harmonised by tones that indicate an atmospheric unity ». Gifted with exceptional powers, Masaccio revolutioed art by his vigorous initiative, and arrived intuitively at results whereof as yet no scientific certainty had been secured.

ST. PETER RESUSCITATING THE SON OF THE KING OF ANTIOCH. *Fresco by* MASACCIO *and* FILIPPINO LIPPI.

This fresco represents a miracle said to have been worked by the Apostles Peter and Paul in resuscitating a youth, when Simon Magus, the magician, had failed. St. Peter is in the act of bidding the youth arise, in the presence of his father, who sits on a throne to the left. On the extreme right St. Peter is enthroned and receiving the homage of the king and a Carmelite monk. The central portion of the composition and the Apostle enthroned were painted by *Masaccio*; the nude boy and about ten of the spectators behind him were added by *Filippino Lippi* some sixty years later, evidently from Masaccio's designs. Many of the personages, especially the group of five on the extreme left, are portraits of distinguished Florentines.

Photo ALINARI, ANDERSON, BROGI.

FLORENCE — S. MARIA DEL CARMINE. *Brancacci Chapel*

THE EXPULSION.
By MASACCIO.

S. PETER BAPTIZING. *By* MASACCIO.
Note the shivering youth to the right.

SS. PETER AND JOHN GIVING ALMS.
Fresco by MASACCIO.

S. PETER IN PRISON.
By FILIPPINO.

SS. PETER AND JOHN HEALING THE SICK
WITH THEIR SHADOWS. By MASACCIO.

ADAM AND EVE.
By MASOLINO (?).

DELIVERANCE OF
PETER. By FILIPPINO

SS. PETER AND JOHN HEALING THE CRIPPLE AT THE BEAUTIFUL GATE. THE RAISING OF TABITHA.
Fresco by MASACCIO, according to F. J. Mather Jr. But attributed to MASOLINO by Vasari, Layard and B. Berenson.

— 241 —

Photo ALINARI, ANDERSON, BROGI.

31. - WONDERS OF ITALY.

FLORENCE — SS. ANNUNZIATA. *Frescoes in the Atrium.*

1. INVESTITURE OF S. FILIPPO BENIZZI. *Fresco by* COSIMO ROSSELLI (1476).

ATRIUM OF THE SANTISSIMA ANNUNZIATA adorned with the celebrated frescoes by ANDREA DEL SARTO and other artists.

2. GAMBLERS STRUCK BY LIGHTNING. *Fresco by* ANDREA DEL SARTO.

The church of the « Annunziata » was originally founded in 1250 at the period of extraordinary religious enthusiasm for the Blessed Virgin. It was dedicated to the « Vergine Annunziata » by seven Florentine nobles who, twenty years earlier had resolved to forsake the world, and, distributing their wealth to the poor, retired to a contemplative life on Monte Senario, some six miles from Florence. There they devoted themselves to the perpetual service of the Virgin and instituted the order of the *Servi di Maria*, under the rule of St. Augustine.

The principal saint of the order is S. Filippo Benizzi (1234-1285), who became noted as a preacher and exerted himself to the utmost to reconcile the opposing factions which at that time distracted Florence. In 1516 Pope Leo X., allowed his festival to be celebrated as a *Beato*, and it was on this occasion that the Atrium of the church was decorated with a series of frescoes representing episodes from the saint's life. These are :

1. *Investiture of S. Filippo Benizzi.* Right : the saint divests himself of his worldly clothing ; left : he assumes the habit of the Order.
2. *Gamblers struck by lightning.* One day S. Filippo and two of his brotherhood were ascending to their monastery of Monte Senario ; some gamblers and profligate youths were playing cards under a tree ; the saint rebukes them ; they mock and insult him ; a thunderbolt falls, the tree is struck, two scoffers are killed, the others rush away, while the monks quietly pursues their way.
3. *Cure of a possessed girl*, who is supported by her parents during a paroxism of madness, while the demon is flying out of her mouth. S. Filippo stands before her blessing with his uprised hand.
4. *Death of S. Filippo.* The dead saint lies on a bier ; groups of monks and spectators are gathered on either side ; in the foreground a child is lying dead on the floor but, by touching the saint's bier, arises restored to life.
5. *Children healed by the Saints' robe.* Women bring their sick children to touch the saint's garments which are held by a priest. Among the

3. CURE OF A POSSESSED MAIDEN.  4. DEATH OF S. FILIPPO.  5. CHILDREN HEALED BY THE SAINT'S ROBE.

Incidents in the Life of S. Filippo Benizzi, founder of the Order of the Servites. By A. DEL SARTO. A. D. 1510.

— 242 —

Photo ALINARI, ANDERSON, BROGI.

FLORENCE — SS. ANNUNZIATA. *Frescoes in the Atrium.*

BIRTH OF THE VIRGIN. By ANDREA DEL SARTO (1514).

MARRIAGE OF THE VIRGIN. By FRANCIABIGIO (1513).

spectators on the right of the altar are several individual portraits. Thus, the woman kneeling in front of the priest is supposed to be the portrait of Lucrezia del Fede, whom Andrea del Sarto married a few years after the picture was painted ; the man standing, second from the altar, is Andrea himself ; the aged man leaning on a staff approaching from the extreme right, is Andrea della Robbia, who was a personal friend of the master.

On the opposite side of the atrium is another series of frescoes from the life of the Virgin. The first, representing the *Birth of the Virgin*, is one of Andrea del Sarto's finest works. The composition swells in a magnificent curve from left to right ; the action is varied and expressive ; the figures singularly graceful and dignified ; the faces of exquisite beauty ; the scheme of colouring more than ever faultless. The woman in the centre, looking out of the picture, is Lucrezia del Fede, Andrea's wife. (*See note on p. 263*).

Andrea del Sarto's grave is in this same courtyard.

The church was restored by *Michelozzo* in 1444, and the interior redecorated in the Baroque style in the 17th century. Among the many chapels which it contains, one is of especial interest, the chapel of the "Annunziata" built in 1448 at the expense of Piero de' Medici. Here, above the gorgeous silver altar, is a 'miraculous' 14th cent. picture of the *Annunciation*, of which the Virgin's head is said to have been painted by an angelic hand, while the artist slept. This precious image is exhibited only on great festivals, on which occasion multitudes of people flock to worship it.

THE VISITATION. By PONTORMO. A. D. 1516.

THE MADONNA DEL SACCO. By ANDREA DEL SARTO. A. D. 1524.

This fresco, in the cloisters of the adjacent Servite monastery, represents the Repose on the Flight into Egypt. The picture takes its name from the sack of hay on which St. Joseph leans. The figures are disposed in simple and admirable attitudes ; the colouring, and the balance of light and shade is perfect.

THE ASSUMPTION. By ROSSO FIORENTINO (1517).

Photo ALINARI, ANDERSON. BROGI.

— 243 —

FLORENCE — *SANTA TRINITA. Sassetti Chapel.*

SANTA TRINITÀ. *Attributed to* N. PISANO (1250).    DEATH OF ST. FRANCIS. *Fresco by* GHIRLANDAIO.

The Sassetti Chapel in the church of Santa Trinità is adorned with some of the most beautiful frescoes of DOMENICO GHIRLANDAIO, which he executed in 1485 for his patron Francesco Sassetti. The series, comprising six large compositions representing scenes from the life of St. Francis, is arranged in double rows on three walls. Beginning with the *upper row* on the left : 1. St. Francis banished from his father's house, renounces the world. 2. Pope Honorius III. confirms the rule of the Franciscan order. This fresco is remarkable for the nobility of space composition and for portraiture. In the distance is a view of the Palazzo Vecchio and the Loggia dei Lanzi; on the right is an excellent portrait of Lorenzo the Magnificent and Francesco Sassetti; in front, coming up from a lower level, only their heads emerging are portraits of: Angelo Poliziano the great humanist and tutor of Lorenzo's youthful sons, one of whom, Giuliano—future Duke of Nemours, is coming up beside him; they are followed by Piero—who succeeded his father in the rule of Florence; and Giovanni—the future Pope Leo X.; Luigi Pulci and Matteo Franco, poets and personal friends of Lorenzo. 3. St. Francis in presence of the Sultan. *Lower row*: 1. St. Francis receiving the stigmata. 2. Resuscitation by St. Francis of a child of the Spini family : here the scene takes place outside the church of S. Trinità, on the left is seen the Palazzo Spini (now Ferroni) in the distance the Bridge of S. Trinità. 3. Death of St. Francis. This composition, the most remarkable of the series, is strictly imitated from one of the same subject by Giotto in Santa Croce (p. 211). Several citizens in the costume of Ghirlandaio's day, appear as spectators. On the left is a bishop chanting litanies for the dying, with spectacles on his nose—the earliest known representation of those useful instruments. Immediately behind the bishop is Ghirlandaio himself. On either side of the altar are the donors—Francesco Sassetti, who was confidential treasurer to Lorenzo the Magnificent, and Nera Cosi, his wife. The altarpiece is given below.

POPE HONORIUS III. confirms the Rule of the Order of St. Francis.   Lorenzo the Magnificent and Francesco Sassetti.

This altarpiece is a typical work of the Renaissance period. The scene is laid amid classical ruins, a poetical and symbolical way of representing the triumph of Christianity over Paganism. The Virgin kneels with a sweet smile, in prayer, her whole soul absorbed in the contemplation of her child, who lies on the hem of his mother's garment ; the traditional goldfinch, the scarlet of whose head is the symbol of sacrifice, stands perched on a stone near. The shepherds of sacred history, conversing together, are portraits of the donors,—the Sassetti. Joseph shades his eyes from the light, and looks up at the angel who is descending with the good tidings to another group of shepherds, who are seen on a distant hill tending their flocks. The Magi approach through a triumphal arch.

Adoration of the Shepherds. *By* D. GHIRLANDAIO. (1485).    Francesco Sassetti.

— 244 —

FLORENCE — LA BADIA (The Abbey).

MADONNA AND CHILD AND ANGELS. *Terracotta relief by* LUCA DELLA ROBBIA *over the portal of the Badia.*

The Church of La Badia was founded in 978 by Ugo, Marquis of Tuscany and his mother Willa. In the 13th century both church and convent were enlarged by *Arnolfo di Cambio*, but in 1665 the church was entirely rebuilt and very little left of the original edifice.

MONUMENT TO COUNT HUGO († 1006). By MINO DA FIESOLE. A. D. 1481. (*In the Church of La Badia*).

This monument, a typical example of Renaissance Tuscan tombs, is one of Mino's most important works.

Count Ugo, *il gran barone*, as he is called by Dante, governed Tuscany as Viceroy of the Emperor Otho II., during the latter part of the 10th century. He and his mother were the founders of seven Benedictine monasteries in Tuscany, one of the first being the Abbey or Badia of Florence, of which the present church is the only relic.

APPARITION OF THE VIRGIN TO ST. BERNARD. By FILIPPINO LIPPI. A. D. 1480. (*In the Badia*).

STREET SHRINES AND TABERNACLES.

A very noticeable feature of Florentine streets is the existence of large numbers of shrines and tabernacles intended to inspire the faithful to prayer. Many still bear their pendant lamps which were kept burning day and night before them, — a most useful practice in old times when the modern idea of lighting the streets had not received attention. These objects of art varying in size and elegance from the most ordinary plaster cast of the Madonna to the beautiful works of Donatello, Mino da Fiesole, the Della Robbias, etc., are now considered public ornaments of the city, and under the law, even the owner of the building to which they are attached, is not permitted to remove them, without special license of the authorities.

TABERNACLE OF THE MADONNA in the Via Nazionale.

TABERNACLE OF ST. AMBROSE in the Piazza S. Ambrogio.

Filippino's « Apparition of the Virgin to St. Bernard », is a work full of naïve beauty and one of the most religious pictures.

St. Bernard († 1153), the founder of the Order of the Cistercians, was remarkable for his devotion to the Blessed Virgin ; one of his most celebrated works was composed in her honour as Mother of the Redeemer. His health was extremely feeble ; and one day, while writing his homilies, it is said the Virgin graciously appeared to him, and comforted and restored him by her divine presence.

This is the moment the painter has chosen to represent. The saint seated at a rude desk out of doors near his convent seems entranced, and looks with ecstatic veneration at the Virgin who, attended by angels, stands before him, one hand resting lightly on his book. On the rock behind, just above St. Bernard's head, is inscribed his famous motto, — *Sustine et abstine* (Bear and forbear). The portrait of the donor, Piero del Pugliese, appears below on the right.

Photo ALINARI, ANDERSON, BROGI.

FLORENCE — *SPEDALE DEGLI INNOCENTI (Foundling Hospital).*

LOGGIA OF THE FOUNDLING HOSPITAL. (*Spedale degli Innocenti*). *Designed by* BRUNELLESCHI. A. D. 1419 ? In the spandrels are the original terracotta medallions of swaddled infants, varied in form and expression, by A. DELLA ROBBIA.

The *Spedale degli Innocenti* (Foundling Hospital), the earliest institution of the kind in Europe, was founded in 1421 by Giovanni de' Medici and liberally endowed by succeeding members of the family. Thousands of foundlings are annually maintained within the building. The larger number, soon after admission, are dispersed among the peasantry living round Florence, who are paid for their maintenance until they are old enough to return to the institution within the city.

This admirable altar-piece painted in 1488 for the Foundling Hospital dedicated to the Massacred Innocents of Bethlehem, stands in its original altar in the chapel of the Innocenti. The Virgin, calm and dignified, holds the Child tenderly on her knee; close by sits St. Joseph in silent admiration. The two Elder Kings kneel reverently, the Eldest, a noble figure, is just about to kiss the foot of the divine Infant, whilst the third King, young and beautiful, is standing on the left and holds a jewelled glass cup in his hand.

Among the crowded groups of adorers are many portraits of contemporary Florentines, including Ghirlandaio's own, by the pillar behind the youthful king. In the far distance, on the right, is seen the Annunciation to the Shepherds; the Murder of the Innocents is represented on the left. By a touching and appropriate invention, the master has placed two of the martyred Innocents kneeling in the foreground; they are presented to the Saviour by St. John the Baptist and St. John the Evangelist and are clothed in white and with bleeding wounds on their shoulders and arms. The composition is masterly and exquisite

ADORATION OF THE MAGES.
By D. GHIRLANDAIO, 1488.

FLORENCE — THE MONASTERIES.

THE CRUCIFIXION. *Fresco by* PERUGINO. A. D. 1495. (*Convent of S. Maria Maddalena de' Pazzi*).

This noble picture occupies the entire wall of the chapter-house of the convent. In the centre is the Crucifixion, and the Magdalen gazing adoringly at the Saviour. On the left, stands the Virgin with clasped hands, the image of resignation and deep, speechless grief; St. Bernard, the founder of the Cistercian branch of the Benedictines, kneels beside her. On the right, is St. John, the Apostle of Love, standing, whilst St. Benedict robed in the habit of the Order is kneeling. The life-size figures, set in a simple, spacious landscape, are remarkable for their abstractness and isolation, which is accentuated by the introduction of the three solitary trees on the hill. The whole composition is full of pathos and harmonizes with the solemnity of the scene represented.

MATERNAL LOVE.   THE HEAD OF ST. JOHN PRESENTED TO HEROD.   ALLEGORY OF HOPE.
Frescoes in monochrome from the history of John the Baptist. By ANDREA DEL SARTO. ca. 1520. (*Chiostro dello Scalzo*).

The *Misericordia*, whose members in their mysterious black dominoes are familiar to almost every visitor to Florence, is the greatest of the benevolent societies of old Florence. The organisation has remained in active existence uninterruptedly for more than six centuries, and has relieved numberless cases of suffering, and, during calamitous times, performed the last offices for innumerable dead.

Its origin dates from about 1240, when business being very active in Florence, many porters were employed in carrying merchandise from one place to another. Whilst looking for jobs they were generally congregated in the cathedral square, and, in bad weather, they took shelter in an open cellar near by, where they spent their leisure in gambling, and profane swearing. One of their number, Pietro Borsi, a pious man, was greatly shocked by the oaths and vices of his comrades; he reproved them and proposed that they provide a box in which, for every offense against good morals, the offender should deposit a *crazia* (about ½ penny). His proposition was received seriously and after some money had been thus collected, he suggested that the men should form themselves into a society and devote the proceeds of their fines to the purchase of six litters, one for use in each ward of the city and that they serve alternately in turns for one week in transporting victims of street accidents, and sick-persons to the hospitals or to their homes, and the dead to burial.

Oratory and Office of the MISERICORDIA or Company of Brothers of Mercy. *Founded in* 1240 (*Piazza del Duomo*).

From these humble beginnings the company gradually received the support of the principal citizens, who associated according to the plan of the original institution, and by degrees attained to its present important proportions.

— 247 —

Photo ALINARI, ANDERSON, BROGI.

FLORENCE — *MONASTERY OF SAN MARCO*. Museo di San Marco.

CLOISTERS OF THE DOMINICAN MONASTERY OF SAN MARCO. *Erected from 1437 to 1443 from designs by* MICHELOZZO.

The *Monastery of San Marco* is a perfect museum of the works of Fra Angelico, who passed nine years of his life within its walls. Originally built for Silvestrine monks, in the year 1430, through the instrumentality of Cosimo de' Medici, it was transferred to the Dominicans. The edifice being in a state of dilapidation the monastery and the adjoining church were rebuilt at Cosimo's expense who entrusted the work to his friend, the architect Michelozzo, and at the same time commissioned Fra Angelico to decorate the walls with those incomparable frescoes which all the world now comes to see. From 1490 to 1498 San Marco was also the home of the great prior and Dominican preacher, Girolamo Savonarola, many memorials of whom exist within the building.

« La PROVVIDENZA ». The Supper of St. Dominic. *Fresco by* SOGLIANI *in the Large Refectory*.

Sogliani's fresco of « La Provvidenza » represents an episode in the life of St. Dominic. « It happened that when he was residing with his friars in the convent of S. Sabina at Rome, the brothers who had been sent to beg for provisions had returned without bread, and they knew not what they should do, for night was at hand, and they had not eaten all day. Then St. Dominic ordered that they should seat themselves in the refectory, and taking his place in their midst offered a prayer to heaven : and behold ! two beautiful ethereal angels, clad in white and shining garments, appeared amongst them and distributed from the folds of their drapery the *bread of paradise* ». The meaning of this appropriate subject for a refectory is obvious : « The Dominican Order receives its sustenance from the Divine Bounty ».

The upper part of the fresco (omitted here) representing the Crucifixion with the Virgin Mary and St. John and two saints kneeling on either side, was painted by *Fra Bartolommeo*.

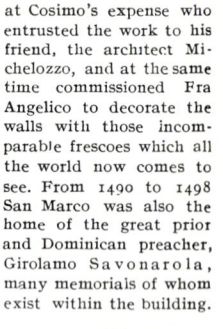

ST. PETER MARTYR imposing silence. Symbolical of the Sanctity of the Dominican Order. *By* FRA ANGELICO.

S. DOMINIC embraces the Cross: symbolical of the Devotion of the Dominicans. FRA ANGELICO.

Photo ALINARI, ANDERSON, BROGI.

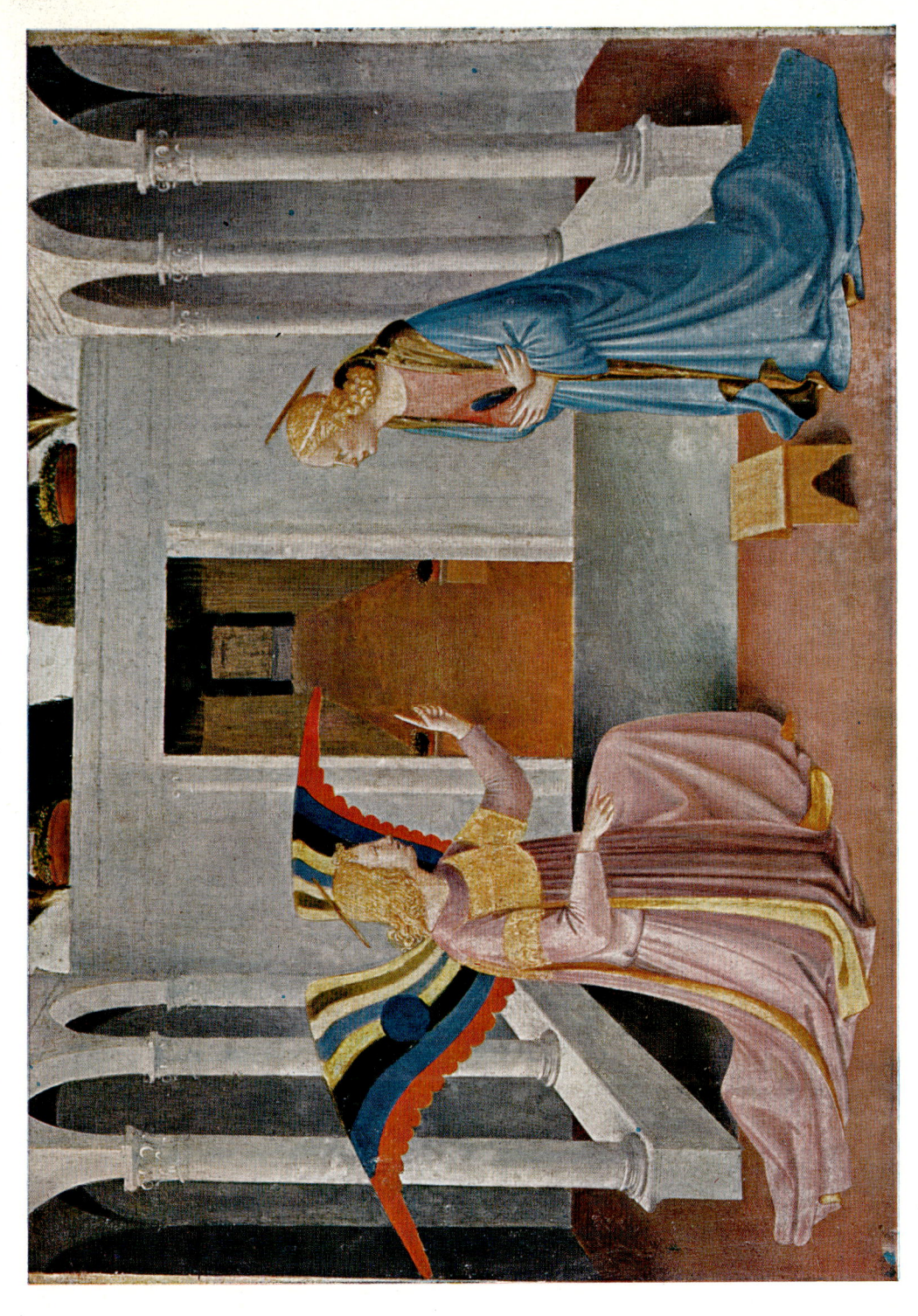

FLORENCE. MONASTERY OF S. MARCO. THE ANNUNCIATION (*detail*). Panel by FRA ANGELICO.

FLORENCE — MONASTERY OF SAN MARCO. *Museo di San Marco.*

THE ANNUNCIATION. *Fresco by* FRA ANGELICO.

Here the scene is laid under the portico of the Annunziata church. Beneath there is a Latin inscription inviting all passers-by to say an Ave to the Blessed Virgin.

CORONATION OF THE VIRGIN. *Fresco in the Dormitory.*

In the cells of distinguished members of the Order Fra Angelico and his assistants painted a little picture intended for the private devotion of the brother occupying the cell.

THE CRUCIFIXION or ADORATION OF THE CROSS. *Fresco by* FRA ANGELICO. A. D. 1440. *(Chapter-House).*

This « Crucifixion » is one of Fra Angelico's noblest compositions. Here the death of Christ on the cross is represented as a sacred mystery ; and its spiritual meaning is emphasized by the insertion, above the head of Christ, of the white pelican. The pelican is the ancient symbol of Our Saviour.

On the left of the cross stands the traditional group of the fainting Virgin, supported by the Maries and St. John the Evangelist ; next is St. John the Baptist standing and St. Mark kneeling, patrons of the city and of the monastery, then St. Lawrence, St. Cosmo and St. Damian, the three patrons of the Medici. On the right is the group of the founders of all the various Monastic Orders : nearest the cross St. Dominic kneels in ardent adoration ; behind him, also kneeling, St. Jerome, the father of all monks ; between them, standing, St. Albert the founder of the Order of the Carmelites, and next St. Augustine the founder of the Austin Friars. Behind St. Jerome kneels St. Francis of Assisi with the crucifix, followed by St. Bernard founder of the order of the Cistercians ; in the background, between the last two saints, stands St. Benedict representing the Benedictines, next again, also standing and holding a crutch, is St. Romualdo founder of the Camaldolese (reformed Benedictines), beside whom kneels St. Giovanni Gualberto, founder on the Vallombrosans. Finally, near the arch is St. Peter Martyr kneeling, and behind him, standing, St. Thomas Aquinas, the « Angelical Doctor » ; the last two saints represent the Sanctity and Learning of the Dominican Order.

CHRIST WELCOMED AS A PILGRIM BY TWO FRIARS.
" Inasmuch as ye have done it unto one of the least of these my brethren, ye have done it unto me." Symbolical of the Hospitality of the Dominicans.

Photo ALINARI, ANDERSON, BROGI.

FLORENCE — *MONASTERY OF SAN MARCO. Museo di San Marco.*

MADONNA DELLE STELLE.
By FRA ANGELICO.

ST. DOMENICO. *By* FRA ANGELICO.
Detail of the Jesus Christ's story in the Praetorium.

Fra Giovanni da Fiesole, commonly called, from his great piety, *L'Angelico*, was born in 1387 and died in Rome in 1455. He joined the order of the Dominicans at Fiesole in 1407, and seems to have begun his career in art as an illuminator of manuscripts. He was truly the painter of Christianity as preached by St. Francis of Assisi. His works are exclusively religious or ecclesiastical; his suave virgins and angels breathe the purest piety and humility; the brilliancy of colour and richness which he gives in his pictures of angels and heavenly scenes are marvellous. Painting in him served as a formulary to express the emotions of faith, hope and charity. His contemporaries gave him, even during his life-time, the title of *Beato*, Blessed; and in truth, in looking upon the glorified faces he painted, we feel something of that peace which passeth understanding. Some say that he never took up his pencils without imploring the blessing of Heaven before he began his work; and remained in a kneeling position the whole time he was occupied in painting the figures of Jesus and the Virgin Mary. Every time that he painted Christ on the cross, tears flowed as abundantly from his eyes as if he had assisted on Calvary at this last scene of the passion of Our Lord.

ANGEL, *by* FRA ANGELICO.    THE MARRIAGE OF THE VIRGIN. *Painted by* FRA ANGELICO.    ANGEL, *by* FRA ANGELICO.

Photo ALINARI, ANDERSON, BROGI.

FLORENCE — MONASTERY OF SAN MARCO. *Museo di San Marco.*

The "Last Judgment" is one of Fra Angelico's most celebrated easel paintings. In the upper part of the picture the Saviour is enthroned amid a garland of adoring angels. He turns the back of His left hand to the condemned, whilst extending towards the blessed the open palm of His right hand. On the left is the Virgin bending towards her Son, opposite is St. John, his hands clasped reverentially. Beneath, is seen the Archangel Michael bearing the Cross on his shoulder, whilst attendant angels arouse the dead with their trumpets. On either side are patriarchs, prophets and saints, with their symbols, among whom may be seen St. Dominic on the extreme left and St. Francis on the extreme right (the Inferno side). The lower, central part of the composition is occupied by a long pavement of open, empty tombs, from which the dead have risen. To the right the condemned, huddled together, are hurried to the torments of hell by demons with long, grappling-hooks; among the damned are kings, queens, cardinals, bishops and false monks who loved money better than their mission.

THE LAST JUDGMENT. On the left is Paradise, on the right, Inferno. *By* FRA ANGELICO. A. D. 1440 (*Early Renaissance*).

Hell is divided into compartments, in accordance with the orthodox medieval conception; in the centre sits Satan crunching sinners. To the left of the picture are gathered the blessed; some are embraced by their guardian angels, others look up with grateful love to the Saviour, or embrace each other. Angels crowned with roses move in a mystic dance amidst flowers, whilst others float onwards in a stream of golden light, towards the gates of Paradise. « One almost fancies one hears the 'bells ringing and the trumpets sounding melodiously, within the golden gates,' 'as if heaven itself were coming down to meet them,' in the Jubilee of welcome ».

This highly coloured altarpiece representing the « Descent from the Cross » was painted for the church of Santa Trinita. In the centre St. John and other saints are removing from the cross, with reverent hands, the lifeless body of Christ. On the left the Magdalene on her knees is kissing the feet of the Saviour with passionate grief. Near by stand the Madonna, St. Veronica and the Maries. On the right, St. Nicodemus, with a compassionate face holds the crown of thorns and displays pathetically the three nails which pierced the feet and the hands of Our Lord. This painting of singular beauty and finish, rouses in the spectator's mind the profoundest feelings of sympathy and devotion.

On the frame are figures of saints; in the *cuspidi* are three panels by *Don Lorenzo Monaco*, master of Fra Angelico.

DESCENT FROM THE CROSS. *Altarpiece by* FRA ANGELICO. A. D. 1435.

Photo ALINARI, ANDERSON, BROGI.

This "Last Supper," one of *Ghirlandaio's* best works, is composed in the traditional form: the table with the return at either end, Judas sitting in front by himself, the Apostles and Christ in a row behind, St. John asleep by the side of the Lord,— the whole is a well ordered group, but pathos, not to say tragedy, is entirely lacking in this the most solemn of scenes. Judas is the only one of the Apostles not crowned with a nimbus, while behind him sits an ill-omened cat, probably, intended for the fiend. Observe how the arched structure of the room has been carried out into the upper part of the composition, producing a most effective semblance of continued vaulting; and also the orange trees, the flying birds, the peacock perched on the window sill, the border of the table cloth, the decanters and dishes, the cherries and loaves of bread, the salt cellars

THE LAST SUPPER. *Fresco by* D. GHIRLANDAIO (ca. 1480). *Small Refectory.*

and other minutiæ so frequent with Ghirlandaio, who delighted in ornaments. Another Last Supper by the same artist and very similar to this exists in the refectory of the monastery of the church of Ognissanti.

Scene of Savonarola's execution—May 23, 1498— in the Piazza della Signoria.

SAVONAROLA'S CELL, containing relics of the great preacher: including fragments of his garment, his hair shirt, his rosary, and some of his books.

Girolamo Savonarola, born at Ferrara in 1452, was in his youth of a studious and ascetic turn. At 24 he became a Dominican monk and took up as a special mission the task of recalling the inhabitants of the cities of Italy from their luxurious and profligate ways. In 1490 he was elected Prior of the monastery of San Marco and he began that career which, eight years later, ended with his martyrdom. At first from the pulpit of San Marco, and later from that of the cathedral he fulmined period after period of impassioned oratory. The subject of his preachings was invariably: the loss of religious faith, the unworthiness of the Holy See, the shameless intrusion of Paganism under the cloak of the humanities, the Roman scandals of Papal elections contrived by a most cynical simony. He dared to stand against the power of Lorenzo de' Medici, and the reigning pontiff Alexander VI., predicting the downfall of the various states of Italy before a foreign conqueror, unless a general reformation of morals took place. The theme on which he loved to dwell was this: Repent! A judgment of God is at hand! A sword is suspended over you! "During these sermons ", writes a contemporary, " the walls of the church re-echoed with sobs and wailings dominated by the Friar's ringing voice which paralysed the hearts of all his hearers." For a while he swayed the people according to his will, and by the power of his magnetic eloquence made himself almost a god in the eyes of the Florentines. They accepted him as their political leader and moral reformer; but in time a combination of enemies headed by Alexander VI. who had excommunicated him, succeeded in subverting his influence. On the 9th April 1498 Savonarola was arrested and imprisoned in the Palazzo Vecchio. There he was frequently subjected to agonizing torture in order to wring something from him which his judges could twist into an admission of either treason or heresy. Nothing could be elicited from him proving his guilt, nevertheless, on the 23rd May 1498 the Great Prior, together with two of his disciples, Fra Domenico and Fra Silvestro, was hanged and burned in presence of the whole city.

PORTRAIT OF SAVONAROLA († 1448). *Painted by* FRA BARTOLOMMEO.

Savonarola's efforts were limited pretty much to his own day and generation. Had he abjured politics and cultivated the personal good will of the hated and vile pontiff, he might have risen to the places of highest dignity in the Church.

— 252 —

THE LAST SUPPER (the upper part omitted). *Fresco by* ANDREA DEL SARTO. A. D. 1527. *Convent of San Salvi.*

In this painting, which resembles Leonardo's renowned fresco at Milan (p. 58), though not to be compared with that work in the profound conception of the subject, Andrea has chosen the self-same moment, « One of you shall betray me ». The reality of the scene represented is most striking, and the picture deserves its high celebrity. The single figures are finely characterized, having the aspect of portraits. The work is treated with simplicity, directness, and great dignity.

THE LAST SUPPER. *Fresco by* ANDREA DEL CASTAGNO. A. D. 1450. *Monastery of Sant'Apollonia.*

This work, one of the most important and representative of the artist, is highly interesting for it exhibits the painter as a strict realist, devoid of all feeling for beauty and grace, but not without a sense of rugged grandeur.

Francesco Petrarca, the great lyric poet, was born (1304) at Arezzo in Tuscany, and spent his youth at Avignon studying law. In 1327 he met for the first time the mysterious Laura, a lady of surpassing beauty, in the church of St. Claire; conceived a great passion for her which she could not return and wrote sonnets in praise of her which immortalised both himself and her. In 1341 he was crowned laureate in the Capitol of Rome and loaded with honors. His numerous Latin works had a great and purifying influence in the classical revival. He preached the attractiveness of liberal studies, and was the inaugurator of a literature which was obedient to the great longing of man to be free from authority and from a mystic terror, and to enjoy the beauty of life. He was one of the first to advocate public libraries; discovered important ancient manuscripts, formed collections, and employed scribes to transcribe and translate classical authors. He died in 1370 at Arquà near Padua.

Giovanni Boccaccio (1313-1375), was born probably at Certaldo near Florence. When still young his father sent him to Naples to pursue a mercantile career. He studied hard and discovered his literary vocation. At Naples he fell in love with Maria, a beautiful woman, whom he afterwards immortalised as *Fiammetta*. His amorous romances, with their beautiful gardens and sunny skies, fair women and luxurious lovers are written with consummate art and won for himself the reputation of being the first modern novelist. His chief work, the Decameron, consists of a collection of a hundred tales not of moral tendency, which are supposed to be related by ten persons during the space of ten days. It describes the life of a company of seven « gentle ladies » and three noble youths who in 1348 fled from the horrors of plague-stricken Florence to a country-house near Fiesole and in the gardens of that delightful retreat passed their time in pleasure, in gallantry, and in comic or licentious tales. « The whole book », says Symonds, « glows with the joyousness of a race discarding dreams for realities, scorning the terrors of a bygone creed, revelling in nature's liberty ».

PETRARCH. BOCCACCIO.
Frescoes by A. DEL CASTAGNO, *in Sant'Apollonia.*

FLORENCE — *MUSEO ARCHEOLOGICO.*

COLOURED ALABASTER SARCOPHAGUS FROM CHIUSI.
The figures of the deceased are represented as lying on a bed. 2nd cent. B. C.

ALABASTER SARCOPHAGUS.

The ARCHEOLOGICAL MUSEUM is of the greatest interest as it contains a magnificent and varied collection of Greek, Roman and Etruscan bronzes, including pottery and other objects found in ancient Etruria, and probably of Etruscan manufacture. The works of art of this singular people prove them to have attained a high degree of civilization, but nothing remains of their history beyond a few inscriptions, difficult to decipher, in an extinct language, and the scanty records, or references made to them by Roman authors. They appear to have been a mixed race of colonists from Asia, Egypt and Greece, who had intermarried with the Italian aborigines.

THE "IDOLINO." *Bronze Greek original. 5th cent.* B. C.

SARCOPHAGUS OF LARTHIA SEIANTIA.
Etruscan Sarcophagus with traces of painting found at Chiusi.

THE ORATOR. *Bronze from Lake Trasimene.*

THE FRANÇOIS VASE. *6th cent.* B. C.

The François Vase found in 1845 is perhaps the finest Greek vase in existence. The decorations represent: the Calydonian Hunt: Theseus and Ariadne. Funeral games, the Marriage of Peleus and Thetis, the Death of Troilus, Battles of Pigmies, etc. *6th cent.* B. C. The museum has a rich collection of painted vases, dating from the 7th, 6th, and 5th cent. B. C. Their decoration is highly interesting, as they belong to the period of great archaic painting, when vase painters imitated their great contemporaries.

CHIMÆRA.
It is expressive of pain. Greek bronze. 5th cent. B. C. *(Found in 1553).*

— 254 —

Photo ALINARI, ANDERSON, BROGI.

FLORENCE — UFFIZI GALLERY.

PORTICO DEGLI UFFIZI

THE PALACE OF THE UFFIZI was erected by order of the Grand Duke Cosimo I. to house the government offices (hence the name). The building was begun by Vasari in 1560, and completed in 1574. The edifice now contains the National Library, the State Archives, and, on the upper floor, the Picture Gallery. This famous gallery originated with the Medici collections, to which numerous additions have been made down to the most recent times; its collection of paintings, lately re-organized by its eminent Director, is the richest and most varied in the world, and of great interest to students of the history and evolution of Italian painting, the pictures being now wisely arranged according to school and order of time in the various rooms.

Beginning with a collection of early Giottesques and Sienese altar-pieces, it gradually leads on to the early 15th century: Fra Filippo Lippi, Verrocchio, Pollaiuolo, Lorenzo di Credi and Ghirlandaio: culminating with the glorious group of Florentine masters Botticelli, Filippino Lippi and Andrea del Sarto. The Umbrian and Venetian schools as well as the foreign schools are also well represented.

The Gallery contains also valuable tapestries and a large number of antique marble sculptures, besides drawings, etc. Beneath, is the Portico degli Uffizi, a narrow oblong space opening on to the Piazza della Signoria. Outside the arcade, which extends along the whole length of the ground floor, are niches at regular intervals, and in these niches stand marble statues of the most famous Tuscans. Here are Nicolò Pisano, Giotto, Orcagna, Donatello, Leonardo da Vinci, Michelangelo, Dante, Petrarch, Boccaccio, Machiavelli, Amerigo Vespucci, Galileo, Benvenuto Cellini, Cosimo the Elder, Lorenzo the Magnificent and many others; truly a series of names for any country to be proud of!

DANTE 1265-1321.

The first great poet of modern times. His *Vita Nuova* is epochmaking in many ways; his *Divina Commedia* is a mirror of the whole Universe, a history of Humanity. He was unrighteously banished from Florence and lies buried in his death-city Ravenna.

PETRARCH 1304-74.

The great lyric poet whose Latin works had a great and purifying influence in the classical revival.

GIOTTO 1267-1337.

The leading spirit of numerous artists.

DONATELLO † 1466.

Great Florentine sculptor of the 15th cent.

LEONARDO DA VINCI 1452-1519.

Painter as well as sculptor, poet, moralist, philosopher, civil and military engineer etc.

MICHELANGELO 1475-1564.

The greatest sculptor, painter and architect of modern times. His position among artists is so unique as to place him almost outside the pale of ordinary criticism. He " saw nothing, felt nothing, interpreted nothing, on exactly the same lines as anyone who had preceded or followed him. "

Photo ALINARI, ANDERSON, BROGI.

FLORENCE — *UFFIZI GALLERY. Ancient Sculptures.*

THE WRESTLERS. B. C. 350.

CORRIDOR OF THE UFFIZI GALLERY.

The splendid group of the « Wrestlers » is considered to be the masterpiece of the Greek realistic school. The strain and muscular action of the two athletes is well displayed. When found the head of the victor was missing and it was replaced with another antique head altogether lacking in expression.

The *Hall of Niobe*, contains the famous group of statues of Niobe and her children struck by the arrows of Apollo and Artemis. These are believed to have been executed in ancient Rome from originals by *Scopas* (B. C. 4th cent.) and brought to Florence in 1775. Niobe, in Greek mythology, had seven sons and seven daughters; proud of her children she boasted of her superiority over Leto, the mother of only two children, Apollo and Artemis. As a punishment, Apollo slew her sons and Artemis her daughters. This tragic story was a favourite subject in Greek literature and art.

HALL OF NIOBE. *Erected in the year 1775.*

THE "GRINDER". *Greek marble. Found in Rome in the 15th cent.*

NIOBE WITH HER DAUGHTER. B. C. 295.

THE MEDICI VENUS.

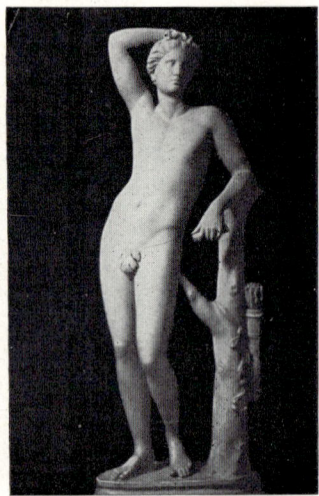

YOUNG APOLLO. *Attributed to* CLEOMENE.

The celebrated *Venus of the Medicis*, a Greek work of the 5th cent. B. C. was found in Hadrian's Villa, near Rome, and brought to Florence in 1680. Of all the statues of ancient times this is undoubtedly one of the finest. The right arm and the lower half of the left have been restored, the inscription on the base is modern.

— 255 —

Photo ALINARI, ANDERSON, BROGI.

FLORENCE. UFFIZI GALLERY.

Madonna adoring the Child. By Correggio (see p. 269).

FLORENCE — UFFIZI GALLERY. Italian Painting.

ITALIAN PAINTING begins at **Florence**, with Cimabue and Giotto. Cimabue was the first to slacken the fetters of Byzantine mannerism in which Art was bound; Giotto, his pupil, burst them and cast them off for ever. **Siena**, the rival city of Florence, a little earlier produced a remarkable master, Duccio, who was the leading spirit of numerous artists; but it was Giotto, who showed himself as one of those liberating geniuses in whom the aspirations of a race are suddenly crystallized. He worked for forty years, not only creating but inspiring enthusiasm everywhere. His pupils and followers extended throughout Italy; unfortunately their works degenerated into mere mechanical labous and with Spinello Aretino († 1410) closes the first period of painting. During this period, called the " Giottesque, " the religious sentiment dominates the plastic faculty and artists decorate the walls of churches and public edifices with divine images, legends of saints, symbols and subjects conveying moral precepts.

At the beginning of the fifteenth century, an artist appeared who revolutionized art by his vigorous initiative. It was Masaccio (1401-28), in whom art found a great pictorial interpreter. During this second period termed the age of " Realism, " painters no longer confined themselves to a fixed cycle of religious or allegorical subjects represented with the traditional surroundings, but began to look freely around them and took to the study of nature and the human form. The artists of this period are usually grouped under three heads, according to the main tendencies

Fragment from the Cartoon of the Bathing Soldiers, by MICHELANGELO. (Uffizi).

THE LIFE LED BY THE FIRST HERMITS IN THE DESERT OF EGYPT. *Painting of the 14th cent.*

The desert is peopled with hermits leading a life of solitude and self-imposed penances. St. Paul, the first hermit, is seen visited by St. Anthony (high up on the right); the death of the former, and the lions digging his grave; demons in the disguise of women tempting St. Anthony; hermits fishing. weaving baskets, carving wooden spoons, etc.

which they severally exibit. Action, movement, space, and the expression of strong and intense passion are the characteristics of the *first group* represented by Masaccio, Fra Filippo Lippi, Botticelli, Filippino Lippi. The *second group*: Piero di Cosimo, Ghirlandaio, Andrea del Sarto, Fra Bartolommeo, remarkable for their power of illustration, colour and expression, gives to the representation of the sentiments and affections the utmost ideal grace and beauty. The *third group*: Paolo Uccello, the brothers Pollaiuolo, Verrocchio, Lorenzo di Credi, belong to a school produced by the efforts of sculptors; their aim is accurate delineation of actual things, problems of science, and laws of perspective. Fra Angelico is a marked exception; coming from a school of miniaturists, he successfully resisted the persuasions of the times, and sought to express the inner life of the adoring soul.

In the first decade of the sixteenth century painting in Florence reached its zenith. The great Florentine masters of this culminating period are Leonardo da Vinci, perhaps the most gifted man that ever lived and Michelangelo. The latter was a complete personality. Poet, architect, sculptor and painter, he felt himself, and claimed to be, exclusively a sculptor. He enriched art with unsuspected new effects, but his style was pernicious to art and led to mannerism and decline.

Photo ALINARI, ANDERSON, BROGI.

FLORENCE — UFFIZI GALLERY. The early masters.

MADONNA. By CIMABUE (1240-1303).

The history of early Italian art is the history of the effort to escape from the swaddling clothes of the rigid Byzantine school.

Between the fall of the Roman empire to the birth of Cimabue lie centuries of obscurity, terror, devastation and barbarism. During this long period which we call the middle Ages, the plastic arts had degenerated into a barren and meaningless scholasticism, a mere handicraft practised by Greek or Byzantine artificers who absolutely copied from one another in the most slavish manner. This degraded style of painting generally known as *Byzantine art* continued to be pursued whith care and industry till into the thirteenth century when with the re-civilization of the West a national art awoke in Italy. Yet, it is not at Florence that the great story first opens; it is at Pisa with Niccolò Pisano, at Siena, with Ugolino and Duccio. But, nevertheless, it is really Cimabue born at Florence in 1240 from whom we must date the true beginning of Italian Art.

The changes which he introduced into the art of painting were an increase of pictorial skill and an attempt to substitute for the conventional image of an ideal personage the representation of real humanity. His greatest work is the Madonna in the Rucell a chapel in the church of Santa Maria Novella. It is in the Byzantine style from which Cimabue did not free himself; but we see here a distinctly fresh endeavour to express emotion and to depict life. From the date of this altarpiece the preeminence of the Florentine school begins to develop itself, expands later in the person of Giotto, to reunite in Ghirlandaio all the branches of its progress, and finally to culminate in the greatness of Michelangelo, Raphael, and Leonardo da Vinc

This altarpiece resembling the picture in S. Maria Novella, is an early work of the master. The figure of the Virgin is over life size, the Child is a little adult. The composition is treated in the hieratic Byzantine manner and reveals the docility of the master but only partially his power. The three adoring angels on each side show his faithfulness to the old rule of precise bilateral symmetry. Beneath are four Prophets holding their prophetic scrolls.

MADONNA. By GIOTTO (1267-1337).

In this altarpiece the great advance in art made by Cimabue's pupil is distinctly evident. The Virgin is stately and the face is not conventional but is painted from the living model. The Child looks more like a child; the old simmetrical arrangement of the side figures is still maintained, but with much added charm in composition. The colouring is rich and the composition of an imposing character though the gigantic figure of the Madonna is unhappily crowded by the canopy.

SCENES FROM THE LIFE OF ST. NICCOLÒ DA BARI.
Painted by AMBROGIO LORENZETTI.

On the left: T. S. *Niccolò resuscitating a Child strangled by the devil*. This story is represented nto three episodes; on the staircase the devil is seen insnaring the child, below the devil strangles the child, on the right the child is seen lying dead on a bed and again restored to life in an attitude of adoration towards his benefactor who appears through a window. T. S. *Niccolò prevents the famine at Myra by begging grain from passing ships*. Here a number of men discarging corn are seen alongside the ships, while angels from above pour out sacks of wheat in the ships to make up for the quantity delivered to S. Niccolò, who stands on the dock directing operations.

On the right: T. S. *Niccolò prevents the prostitution of three Maidens by throwing them gold*. A nobleman who had three daughters was so poor that he could not provide them with food except by sacrificing them to an infamous life Nicholas head of this and for three successiv nights he took a handful of gold, and tying i up in a handkerchief, threw it in the dwelling of the poor man. T. *The Consecration of S. Niccolò as Bishop of Myra*.

Photo ALINARI, ANDERSON, BROGI.

FLORENCE — UFFIZI GALLERY. Early Sienese and Florentine School.

This famous *Annunciation*, the joint work of Simone Martini and Lippo Memmi, is one of the finest productions of the early Sienese school. The whole panel is entirely painted on gold-leaf which accounts for the brilliancy and lustre. It is thus described by the art critics Crowe and Cavalcaselle : " The Virgin, in the act of receiving the Angel, and shrinking with a side-long action and with affected softness of motion from him, is rendered with an exaggeration of tenderness in the close lids and hardly apparent iris of the eyes. The Angel is presented kneeling in a dress and stole, all engraved with embroidery in relief and the words *Ave Gratia plena Dominus tecum* issuing from his mouth are given in a similar manner. This is a picture whose affected tenderness might well have had influence on the school of mystic painters." Above is the dove, symbolic of the Holy Spirit, circled by winged cherub heads. Right and left are two patron saints of Siena, Sant'Ansano and Saint Juliet, with their palms of Martyrdom.

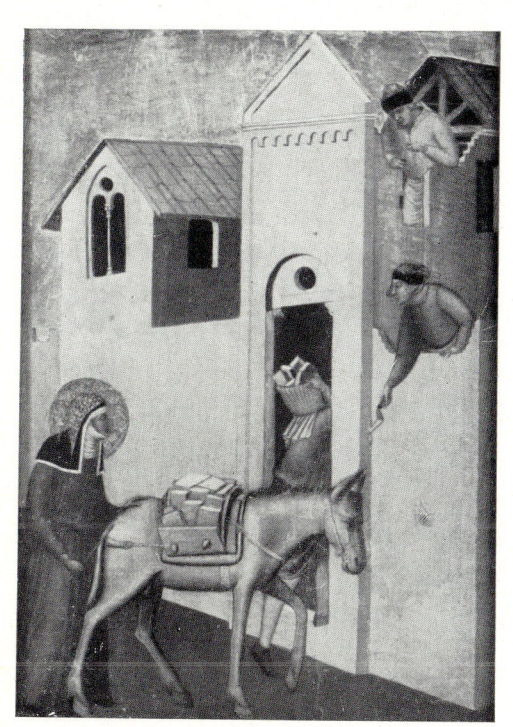

ANNUNCIATION, WITH SANT'ANSANO AND SAINT JULIET,
by SIMONE MARTINI and LIPPO MEMMI, 1333.

THE BLESSED HUMILITY BUILDS A CONVENT
by PIETRO LORENZETTI.

This is one of the scenes of a polyptych, dated 1316, illustrating the episodes of the Blessed Humility's life.

DEPOSITION. By GIOTTINO († 1369).

The dead Christ is extended on a white shroud, and embraced by the Virgin ; at his feet kneels the Magdalena ; Mary Salome kisses his right hand and Martha the other ; the third Mary is seated in the corner to the right. In the background at the foot of the Cross is St. John, on his left hand, Joseph of Arimatæha and Nicodemus. On the right of St. John kneels a young girl in a rich Florentine costume, and beside her, also kneeling, a Benedictine nun ; these two formale, the donors, are presented by their respective patron saints.

— 256B —

Photo ALINARI, ANDERSON, BROGI.

FLORENCE — UFFIZI GALLERY. Gothic flamboyant.

This magnificent altarpiece, the most important work of Don Lorenzo, a Camaldolese monk, was executed in 1413 for the high altar of the (now suppressed) artist's own Monastery degli Angeli at Florence.

In the central arch in front of a canopy is the crowning of the Virgin. Our Lady attired in a white robe, symbolic of her purity, is bending her head to receive the jewelled diadem which the Saviour is placing on her head. On the sides and behind the throne are numerous lovely angels, symbolic of the monastery *degli Angeli*; in front two other angels swing censers, while a third in the centre playing an organ has been almost destroyed by a reliquary which formerly was attached there.

On either side of the altarpiece, standing or kneeling on the symbolic star-lit arch of heaven are groups of saints witnessing the scene of the coronation. In the group to the left, nearest the throne, St. John the Baptist, patron of Florence; next in St. Peter with the keys; then St. Benedict, with the scourge and an open book; behind him St. Stephen with the stones on his head; next St. Paul with the sword; then St. James the Greater with his staff; and St. Anthony Abbott. Behind are St. Louis of France, St. Louis of Toulouse and another saint. In the opposite group, on the extreme right to balance St. Benedict, is St. Romuald, founder of the Camaldolese Order (a branch of the Benedictines); next him, St. Andrew with the symbol of his cross; and St. John the Evangelist; behind the last is St. Laurence with the gridiron; then St. Bartholomew with the knife; St. Zenobius (?), and St. Francis with the crucifix.

The six panels in the *predella* represent scenes from the Bible and Stories from the Life of St. Benedict. 1, Death of St. Benedict: a monk reads the service over his body, others are gathered round it mourning or kissing the saint's hands while St. Maurus gazes upwards where the soul is seen ascending to heaven; 2. St. Benedict teaching in his monastery, a young monk tempted by the devil, St. Benedict in a cave near Subiaco receives food from brother Romanus; 3. the Nativity; 4. the Adoration of the Magi; 5. St. Benedict in his cell sends St. Maurus to rescue St. Plaicdus from drowing, and St. Benedict paying a visit to his sister St. Scholastica and her community of nuns; 6. St. Benedict restoring to life a novice who had been killed by a wall falling on him at the convent of Monte Cassino. The frame of this noble altarpiece is richly decorated and gilt; in the pilasters are beautifully executed miniature figures of the Prophets and other Old Testament characters.

CORONATION OF THE BLESSED VIRGIN.
Great Altar-piece by DON LORENZO MONACO. A. D. 1413.
In the predella: the Nativity, Adoration of the Magi, and stories of St. Benedict.

Gentile da Fabriano's "Adoration of the Magi," was executed in 1423, for the church of Santa Trinita. The picture is painted on gold leaf, the profuse gilt relief ornaments, the fullness of the composition, the delicacy and minuteness of treatment are all indicative of the poetic naïveté with which the religious feeling of the period invested this exceedingly popular event.

Contrary to custom, the Holy Family occupies the left of the picture; the Three Kings, the eldest of whom is kneeling, have robes of gilded and exquisite decorative effect; they are followed by a great train of attendants (among whom the artist has portrayed himself,—the man full face in a red turban behind the younger King), and by horses, camels, dogs, monkeys, falcons, etc. In the background above are three separate scenes referring to the subject of the picture. On the left, the Magi behold the Star from the summit of a hill; in the centre, they ride in procession to enter Jerusalem; on the right, they are seen approaching the gateway of Bethlehem.

In the predella are three panels representing: The Nativity, The Flight into Egypt, and The Presentation in the Temple.

THE ADORATION OF THE MAGI. FLIGHT INTO EGYPT. A. D. 1423.
By GENTILE DA FABRIANO (1360-1440).

Photo ALINARI, ANDERSON, BROGI.

FLORENCE — *UFFIZI GALLERY.* *Florentine School.*

CORONATION OF THE VIRGIN, *by* FRA ANGELICO A.D. 1435.

THE NATIVITY, *by* PISELLINO.

SELF-PORTRAIT, *by* FILIPPINO LIPPI.

Photo ALINARI, ANDERSON, BROGI.

FLORENCE — UFFIZI GALLERY. *Florentine School.*

This painting is an interesting specimen of the master's earliest attempts at foreshortening and perspective. " His real passion," says the art critic Berenson, " was perspective, and painting was to him a mere occasion for solving some problem in this science, and displaying his mastery over its difficulties."

In vain did his wife in the long winter nights, moved by tenderness or compassion, often rouse herself from her slumbers and entreat him to put aside his works till the morrow. The enthusiastic artist only replied, " Anima mia ! if you could but understand the delights of perspective ! " and she could never draw from him any other answer.

BATTLE OF SAN ROMANO *by* PAOLO UCCELLO (1397-1475).

MADONNA ENTHRONED AND SAINTS.
Altarpiece by DOMENICO VENEZIANO (1400-1461).

BATTISTA SFORZA.   FEDERIGO DA MONTEFELTRO.
Portraits painted by PIETRO DELLA FRANCESCA 1466.

This altarpiece is the only extant work of Domenico Veneziano. Painted for the church of Santa Lucia de' Magnoli it was taken to the gallery in 1862.

The saints have strong figures and large heads ; the peculiar scheme of colour, pale pink and green is due in part to restorations.

" It is a first commencement of oil painting, and the search for the transparent effects produces a result quite different from any contemporary painting".

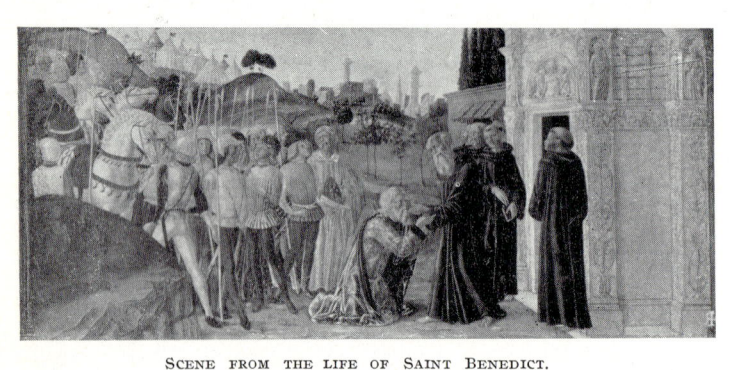

SCENE FROM THE LIFE OF SAINT BENEDICT.
Predella by NEROCCIO DI BARTOLOMEO LANDI (1447-1500).

ST. ANNE enthroned with the VIRGIN and the INFANT CHRIST.
By MASACCIO (1402-1482).

Photo ALINARI, ANDERSON, BROGI.

FLORENCE — UFFIZI GALLERY. Filippo Lippi.

Fra Filippo Lippi, was born in Florence. Left an orphan at the age of 15 he was induced to take the vows and became a monk in the Carmelite convent close to the Church del Carmine. He probably assisted Masaccio in his works in the Brancacci Chapel and eventually became his pupil. Later, he was influenced by Fra Angelico, and his style showing vigour blended with tenderness, represents the synthesis of Masaccio and Fra Angelico. He died in 1469.

THE VIRGIN ADORING THE CHILD. By FRA FILIPPO LIPPI (1406-1469).

THE NATIVITY. By FRA FILIPPO LIPPI.

In the distance is presented a rocky land-scape with an attempt at a night effect; on the left kneels St. Ilarione, on the right the Magdalen.

THE CORONATION OF THE VIRGIN. By FRA FILIPPO LIPPI (A.D. 1447). On the right, the kneeling figure of the painter.

THE ANNUNCIATION. By ALESSIO BALDOVINETTI.

MADONNA WITH CHILD AND TWO ANGELS. By FRA FILIPPO LIPPI.

The Virgin adoring her Child supported by two Angels was at first in the villa of the Poggio Imperiale, so that it is supposed to have been painted for the Medici family. The Virgin sits just near the window forming the frame of the picture and showing a large and deep landscape. She has no mantle; her blue dress is more low-necked than the one of the *tondo* in the Pitti Gallery (see p. 285) and her coiffure is still more refined. The veil is so transparent that through it can be seen the ear. On the top of the head is a big pearl; other pearls smaller and smaller until they become tiny go, forming the two sides of a triangle, from the veil up to the front of the Virgin.

The features of the face are the same of the *tondo* in the Pitti Gallery; the inner life seems ever deeper. Two little angels support the Child; the one on the shoulder of which he leans his little foot has a rather forced smile. The Infant Jesus lifts up his hand towards his mother's neck. Not being obbliged to sustain him, She can join her hands to adore Him.

THE ANNUNCIATION. By FRA FILIPPO LIPPI.

— 259 —

Photo ALINARI, ANDERSON, BROGI.

MADONNA WITH ANGELS AND SIX SAINTS.
By SANDRO BOTTICELLI (1447-1510).

On the left: St. Catherine, St. Augustine and St. Barnabas. On the right: the Baptist, the Archangel Michael and St. Ignatius.

THE BIRTH OF VENUS.
By SANDRO BOTTICELLI.

The *Birth of Venus*, very similar in design and conception to the "Primavera" given on the opposite page, was probably painted for Giuliano de' Medici, and the Venus herself is supposed to be a portrait of the beautiful Simonetta Vespucci, mistress of that prince.

The newly-born goddess standing on a shell is wafted to shore by the breath of the Zephyrs. Her figure has a strange elusive beauty. On the flower-strewn shore the figure of Spring dressed in a white robe with blue corn-flowers holds out an embroidered mantle sown with daisies in which to wrap the nude form of the goddess. « Venus comes to earth » writes F. J. Mather, Jr., « with no joyous expectation. She glimpses unfulfilled desires, the eternally deferred goal of earthly love. She obeys a destiny with resignation and a pensive humility — almost asks pardon for the confusion she is fated to produce among mortals ».

MADONNA AND CHILD WITH POMEGRANATE.
By BOTTICELLI. *Painted about* A. D. 1470.

CORONATION OF THE VIRGIN
"THE MAGNIFICAT". By BOTTICELLI.

Painted about 1466 for Piero de' Medici and his wife Lucrezia. The two angels on the left, holding the inkstand and the book, are portraits of their children Lorenzo and Giuliano.

PALLAS AND THE CENTAUR.
By BOTTICELLI.

MADONNA AND CHILD.
By BOTTICELLI.

THE ANNUNCIATION.
By BOTTICELLI. A. D. 1490.

— 260 —

Photo ALINARI, ANDERSON, BROGI.

FLORENCE. UFFIZI GALLERY.

THE VIRGIN MARY ADORING THE INFANT CHRIST.
By FILIPPINO LIPPI (1457-1504).

FLORENCE — UFFIZI GALLERY. Paintings by Botticelli.

This, perhaps the most important of Botticelli's pictures, was painted for Lorenzo the Magnificent to commemorate the tournament of Giuliano de' Medici, held in honor of the beautiful Simonetta Vespucci in 1475.

The *Return of Spring* to earth is an allusion to the reign of Lorenzo, and the new era of youth and joy which the "Magnificent" had inaugurated.

In the centre of a grove of orange trees Venus (Simonetta !) stands presiding the scene. On the right from out a laurel grove the spring months come bearing flowers : March, cold and blue, blowing wind on to April represented by a transparently draped female figure who proceeds towards May (Flora) ; the latter, tall and erect, fully clad in a robe embroidered with flowers, scatters blossoms as she advances from a fold of her garment.

On the left is the group of the Three Graces, representing the joy and freshness of spring-time, on whom the little god of Love aims his arrows—spring being the period of courtship and mating. Next is Mercury (a portrait of Giuliano?) dispelling the clouds and gathering fruit.

THE RETURN ON SPRING. "PRIMAVERA". *By* BOTTICELLI.

This is one of Botticelli's finest works painted after the description of a picture of Apelles.

In the middle is the figure of Calumny, richly attired, attended by Treachery and Malice, both busy dressing her hair. She holds a torch in her left hand, while with her right she is dragging a nude youth, the innocent victim of calumny. A ragged man representing Envy precedes the group, leading Calumny before the tribunal of the Unjust Judge who has ass' ears. The Judge sits on a throne listening to two female figures: Ignorance and Suspicion, who whisper their insidious advice into his ears.

On the left a hideous figure attired in black, symbolizing Remorse, turns round to look at the naked figure of Truth, who is invoking heaven against the fearful scene of violence and injustice enacted.

THE CALUMNY APELLES *by* BOTTICELLI, 1499.

Pietro (il Gottoso) de' Medici as a votive offering to be placed in S. Maria Novella in gratitude for his escape from assassination in the conspiracy of Luca Pitti in 1466.

The picture is a glorification of the House of the Medici, and shows us three generations of the elder branch of the family surrounded by their friends including many eminent literary men.

Cosimo, Piero and Giuliano (father, son and grandson) represent the three kings (one old, one middle-aged and one young). Cosimo kneels at the feet of the Child-Christ, in the centre Piero kneels with his back to the spectator, to his right Giuliano also kneeling, in a robe of white and gold. On the extreme left of the picture is Lorenzo the Magnificent at the age of 17, standing and holding a sword (which explains the meaning of the whole picture). The figure in yellow on the extreme right is supposed to be a portrait of Botticelli himself.

ADORATION OF THE KINGS. *By* BOTTICELLI. A.D. 1467

Judith with the head of Holofernes.
Painted by BOTTICELLI.

34. - WONDERS OF ITALY.

— 261 —

FLORENCE — *UFFIZI GALLERY.* *Florentine School.*

TOBIA AND THE ARCHANGELS.
By BOTTICELLI (1466-1498).

The subject of the "Adoration of the Magi." is very frequently represented in sacred art. Magi, in the persian tongue, signifies "wise men"

The prophecy of the Syrian seer Balaam had been kept as a tradition among his people, who waited with faith and hope for its fulfilment. when, therefore, their sages (the Magi) beheld the long expected star of beatitude, they at once knew its import, and three of them hastened to follow its guidance.

Taking leave of their relations and firends, they journeyed for the space of two years, the star going before them, and arrived at length at Jerusalem. There they asked at once: "Where is He who is born King of the Jews?" On hearing this question King Herods was troubled, and he inquired of the chief priests where Christ should be born. And they said: "in Bethlehem of Judea." So the Magi departed, and the star which had so miraculously guided them proceeded before them and stood over the place where the Infant was. "And when they were come into the house, they saw the young Child with Mary his mother, and fell down and worshipped Him: and when they had opened their treasures, they presented unto Him gifts: gold (emblem of Royalty), and frank incense (emblem of Deity), and myrrh (emblem of humanity)".

MADONNA AND CHILD AND SAINTS.
By FILIPPINO LIPPI. A. D. 1485.

ADORATION OF THE MAGI.
By D. GHIRLANDAIO. A. D. 1487.

ADORATION OF THE KINGS.
By FILIPPINO LIPPI (1457-1504).

ADORATION OF THE SHEPHERDS.
By LORENZO DI CREDI (1459-1537).

Photo ALINARI, ANDERSON, BROGI.

FLORENCE — UFFIZI GALLERY. *Florentine School.*

THE FOUR SAINTS by ANDREA DEL SARTO, 1528.
(*The Archangel S. Michael, S. John Gualbert, John the Baptist, St. Bernard of the Uberti*).

Albertinelli's "Visitation", the masterpiece of the master, is a remarkable example of the way in which mediocre artists, inspired by the teachings and companionship of the giants of the High Renaissance, often produced noble works.

Albertinelli born in 1474 was first apprenticed to Cosimo Rosselli and later became a pupil and friend of Fra Bartolommeo, who is said to have designed the original cartoon from which this work was painted.

The exceeding simplicity of the composition is its great charm. The group is arranged with masterly skill, the earnest reverential gaze of Elizabeth, as she bends forward to salute the future mother of the Saviour, is full of feeling and tenderness. Elizabeth's face is in deep shadow, her subordination to Mary is further accentuated by the slight inclination of her head. The blending of the colours and the drapery are managed with simplicity and great skill. The grandeur, power and grace, and depth of expression in the two figures are quite extraordinary.

THE VISITATION.
By MARIOTTO ALBERTINELLI. A. D. 1503.

ANDREA DEL SARTO was one of the most distinguished painters of the Renaissance. He composed skilfully and gave movement to his figures bathing them in a soft and luminous light. He painted also many extensive works in fresco which placed him in the foremost rank amid his contemporaries. Chaste and severe in style, masterly in design, clear and well ordered in composition and arrangement, these frescoes unite some of the best qualities of the art of the fifteenth century with the larger aims of thet of the sixteenth.

The subject of the picture is taken direct from the actual gospel narrative. It is Luke who tells us the episode of the Visitation or Salutation of Elizabeth. "And Mary arose and went up into the hill country in haste, to the house of the cousin Elizabeth, and saluted her ". And there- upon Elizabeth exclaimed, "Whence is this to me, that the mother of my Lord should come to me ?" And Mary broke forth into the wonderful hymn of the Magnificat, which has been sung ever since in the churches throughout Christendom.

The moment chosen by artists for the representation of the episode is always the one when Elizabeth steps forward to greet and embrace the Blessed Virgin.

DECOLLATION OF ST. JOHN THE BAPTIST.
By ANDREA DEL SARTO.

PERSEUS LIBERATING ANDROMEDA FROM THE SEA MONSTER.
Painted by PIERO DI COSIMO (1462-1521).

Pietro di Cos mo took his name by Cosimo Rosselli whom he helped in the decoration of the Sixtine Chapel in Rome ; in his first mithological paintings can be recognized the style of Botticel l.

THE MADONNA DELLE ARPIE.
By ANDREA DEL SARTO, 1517.

This Madonna, called of the *harpies* from the figures at the corners of the pedestal, is the masterpiece of Andrea del Sarto, the greatest colourist of the Florentine school.

— 263 —

FLORENCE — UFFIZI GALLERY. Leonardo and Umbrian School.

ANNUNCIATION. By LEONARDO DA VINCI.
(an early work)

With this *Annunciation* Leonardo deviates from the traditional scheme used by the other painters for the same subject. His *Annunciation* takes place in the open air, on the flowery meadow of a Florentine villa and in the background we can see that fantastic scenography of the landscape which will be typical of Leonardo. In this poetical painting, we see the Virgin with her noble bearing and the Archangel with his shining face, sure of himself.

It is a work dating back to Leonardo's youth, executed when he was a pupil of Andrea Verrocchio. In fact, the stump's technique, created by him, is not yet here completely realised and the outlines are still of clear-cut drawing.

Leonardo da Vinci born in 1452, died at Amboise in 1519. Of noble physical type, he was endowed with a combination of intellectual qualities such as probably no other man possessed. Besides being a painter, he was likewise sculptor, poet, musician, moralist and philosopher *(See page 58)*.

HOLY FAMILY *by* LUCA SIGNORELLI (1441-1523).

BAPTISM OF CHRIST. *By* VERROCCHIO.
The left Angel is attributed to LEONARDO.

ADORATION OF THE MAGI *(unfinished)*.
By LEONARDO DA VINCI. A. D. 1481.

Photo ALINARI, ANDERSON, BROGI.

FLORENCE — UFFIZI GALLERY. Umbrian School.

THE ASSUMPTION WITH SAINTS.
By PERUGINO. A. D. 1500.

MARTYRDOM OF ST. SEBASTIAN.
By GIROLOMO GENGA of Urbino (1476-1551).

St Sebastian, was born in the third century and served in the Roman army. He was secretly a Christian, and comforted Christian prisoners ; converted the prefect of the city and many others, and was condemned to be shot to death by Diocletian. The arches having pierced him with many arrows left him for dead, but a devout widow, who came to bury his body, found that life had not departed. She tended him and when he recovered he confronted the emperor and denounced his gods and was thereupon beaten to death with clubs.

PERUGINO (Pietro Vannucci) was born in 1446 and died 1524. He owed much of the excellence of his works to the Florentine painters (Verrocchio?). He had an instinct for large airy compositions, and golden transparent colours, an exquisite sense of reverie and ecstasy, but could not represent movement.

This noble altarpiece is one of Perugino's finest and most characteristic works. The composition according to the conventional idea of the subject, is divided into two parts,—the heaven above and the earth beneath. The Virgin is represented in a *mandorla*, surrounded by cherubs and angels. Her attitude and expression of ecstatic adoration as well as the pose of her hands, are all characteristic of Perugino. Above is the Almighty in a circle with adoring angels. In the lower portion of the picture are four Vallombrosan saints, as spectators of the celestial mystery above. These are (from left to right) : the Cardinal Saint Bernard degli Uberti ; Saint Giovanni Gualberto, the founder, represented with a cross and a crutch ; Saint Benedict, the patriarch, holding the rod ; the Archangel Michael. The latter's face is one that often recurs in Perugino's pictures and is said to be a portrait of the master's wife. The work executed in oil on wood was painted for the high altar of the suppressed monastery of Vallombrosa. The artist has inscribed his name below, with the date : PETRUS PERUGINUS PINXIT AD MCCCCC.

THE ARCHANGEL.
By MELOZZO DA FORLÌ.

FRANCESCO DELL'OPERA.
By PERUGINO.

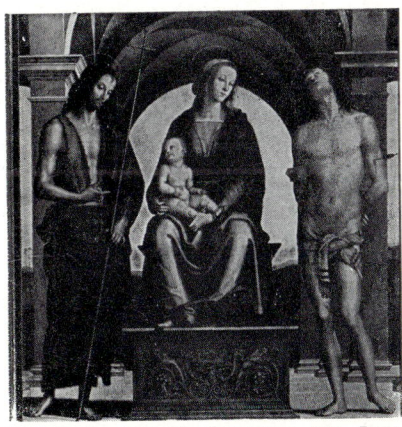

THE VIRGIN WITH SS. SEBASTIAN AND JOHN THE BAPTIST. *Painted by* PERUGINO. A. D. 1493.

FLORENCE — UFFIZI GALLERY. Tribune.

"Il Magnifico" (the Magnificent) is the title given to this most illustrious member of the Medici. He ruled with almost regal power 22 years, and his encouragement made Florence the centre and focus of the arts for the whole world. After his death "The Splendour, not of Tuscany only, but of all Italy disappeared".

Cosimo de' Medici also called Cosimo the Elder. He was a successful financier and was known as "The Great Merchant of Florence." His immense wealth he spent liberally for the advancement of art and science. He built the Medici Palace (now Riccardi); helped in rebuilding San Lorenzo and San Marco; founded the Medici Library, and enriched Florence with numerous churches and monuments. The people acclaimed him "The Father of his Country".

LORENZO THE MAGNIFICENT.
Grand-son of Cosimo the Elder. By VASARI.

COSIMO THE ELDER. *Surnamed "Father of his Country." By* PONTORMO.

GRAZIA DE' MEDICI  — ELEONORA OF TOLEDO.  — MARIA DE' MEDICI.
Portraits of members of the House of Medici by BRONZINO.

THE VIRGIN AND ST. ANNE.
After the original by Leonardo in the Louvre.

MADONNA ENTHRONED.
By ROSSO FIORENTINO († 1541).

ADORATION OF THE SHEPHERDS.
By HONTHHORST *(Gherardo delle Notti)*.

— 266 —

Photo ALINARI, ANDERSON BROGI.

THE MADONNA DEL CARDELLINO (of the Goldfinch). *By* RAPHAEL. Painted A. D. 1506. (*Florentine period*).

The *Madonna del Cardellino*, is one of Raphael's most charming compositions, and belongs to his Florentine period. Our Lady, with Jesus and the child Baptist is full of simplicity and divine grace. The pyramidal grouping is superb, the well proportioned figures are so delicately painted, and with such accuracy that "they seem of living flesh rather than drawn and coloured."

Raphael's works are generally divided into three periods or "manners." The first, or Umbrian manner, acquired when a pupil of Perugino, was characterized by careful, minute, clear handling, and golden transparent colours. The second, or Florentine manner, began with his first visit to Florence, and his intercourse with the great artists there, who awakened new ideas in him of the wider boundaries of Art ; it was a development of his early style, which put him on a parity with older contemporaries. The third, or Roman manner, developed after he went to Rome (1509), was a complete reconstruction of his style, almost a new school of painting, so powerful and broad did it became. Abandoning the tender smoothness of the early work, he took that grandeur of outline and composition, and richness of colour which characterize all his works of this last period.

LEO X. († 1522) WITH TWO CARDINALS. *By* RAPHAEL. A. D. 1519.

The *Holy Family* is the only existing easel painting which Michelangelo finished. It was painted for the marriage of Angelo Doni with Magdalene Strozzi.

" The Madonna "—writes the art critic Wölfflin—" is a masculine woman with mighty bones, her arms and feet bare. Her legs bent under her, she crouches on the ground and reaches over her shoulder for the Child, whom Joseph, seated in the background, hands to her—a tangle of figures, curiously crowded in action." The drawing, however, displays Michelangelo's complete knowledge of anatomy, and the artist's thorough mastery of his favourite method : how to express the greatest amount of action in a very limited space.

The figures are skilfully conceived while the sharply defined outlines give to the picture the aspect of a painted relief. " Michelangelo saw nothing, interpreted nothing on exactly the same lines as anyone who had preceded or followed him."

Raphael's " Portrait of Pope Julius II " is considered as one of the great historical portraits in the world. The original cartoon, drawn by Raphael's own hand, is now in the Corsini Palace in Florence. The original, which for more than half a century adorned the favourite church of Julius II. (S. Maria del Popolo) at Rome, has perished. Vasari who saw that original there, describes it as a marvel, " the sight of which madeo ne tremble."

In this picture the powerful pontiff sits in state, a long white beard. It is said that when he arrived at Bologna in 1510, he dismissed his barber and resolved that his beard should remain uncut until the French hand been expelled from Italy), descends on his breast : his face is wrinkled, the eyes are deep set, the lips compressed, the whole attitude is that of a man bending under cares. The French were driven out in 1512.

HOLY FAMILY. *By* MICHELANGELO. A. D 1504

PORTRAIT OF POPE JULIUS II. († 1513). *After the original by* RAPHAEL. A. D. 1510.

JOSEPH PRESENTS TO THE PHARAOH HIS FATHER AND BROTHERS. *By* FRANCESCO GRANACCI.

Photo ALINARI, ANDERSON, BROGI.

FLORENCE — UFFIZI GALLERY.

MADONNA WITH THE LONG NECK.
By PARMIGIANINO.

THE "MADONNA DEL POPOLO".
By FEDERIGO BAROCCIO. A. D. 1579.
Painted for the Fraternità di Arezzo.

EVANGELISTA SCAPPI.
By FRANCESCO FRANCIA.
(*Bolognese School*).

This self-complacent gentleman of Bologna, quantly holding a scroll upon which his name is inscribed, is the masterpiece of the painter.

PORTRAIT OF A LADY.
By ANTONIO DEL POLLAIOLO.

SALOME. By BERNARDINO LUINI.

PORTRAIT OF G. G. SFORZA.
By AMBROGIO DE PREDIS (?)
(*Lombard School*).

The picture of Salomè is one of the best works of Luini who has constantly used this face with its seductive beauty to represent equally the perversion of Salomè, or the purity of the Virgin. Painters seldom have more than one type of female beauty. Bernardino Luini was the most popular of Leonardo's disciples. So much of the latter's characteristics appear in this picture that it was at one time attributed to him.

BACCHANTE. By ANNIBALE CARACCI (1560-1609).

MEDUSA by CARAVAGGIO.

— 268 —

Photo ALINARI, ANDERSON, BROGI.

"Bacchus Adolescent" *Painting by* Caravaggio.

FLORENCE — UFFIZI GALLERY. *Venetian School.*

*Repose on the flight into Egypt.
By Correggio.*

Correggio's "Madonna adoring the Child" is one of the master's most exquisite works. It was presented by the Duke of Mantua to Cosimo II. de' Medici and placed in the gallery in 1617. While having the semblance of a devotional picture there is nothing to mark the scene as a religious one, — it is simply a mother enraptured in the contemplation of a playful child. However, the delicate grace of execution, the mastery in the treatment of color and light and shade is so incomparable that the artist well deserves the title given him of "il re della luce."

Correggio (Antonio Allegri), so named from his native village near Modena, was born in 1494. Very little is known of his early life, he probably was influenced by Titian and the painters of Mantua and Modena. He soon gave proof of very great technical ability. His works are distinguished by the most beautiful handling of chiaroscuro; by means of ingenious contrasts he creates effects of the most dazzling brilliance and the darkest shadow; his flesh tones are rich and warm, or cool and opalescent, with infinitely subtle modulations.

*Madonna adoring the Child
or ,, Nativity."
By Correggio (1494-1534).*

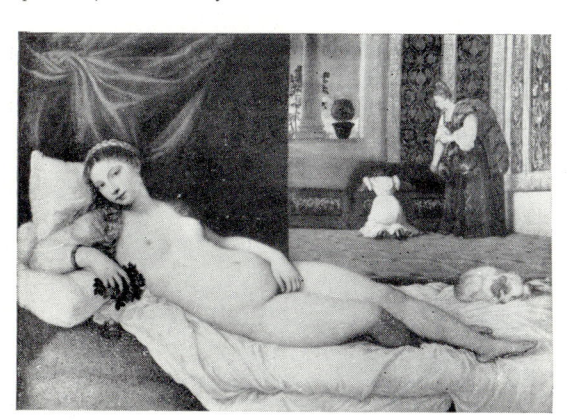

Titian's "Reclining Venus" painted about 1538 for Francesco Maria I. Duke of Urbino, is believed to be an idealized portrait of his wife, the Duchess Eleonora Gonzaga. This superb painting recalling Giorgione's *Sleeping Venus* now in the Dresden Gallery, is described by Crowe and Cavalcaselle thus: "We may fancy her to have bathed and to be waiting for her handmaids, who are busy in the room, one of whom removes a dress from a chest....

Reclining Venus. By Titian. A. D. 1538.

Nature, as Titian represents her here, is young and lovely, but conscious and triumphant without loss of modesty. The flesh is not marbled or cold, but sweetly toned. Perfect distribution of space, a full harmony of tints, atmosphere both warm and mellow."

*Portrait of Catherine Cornaro
Queen of Cyprus.
Painted by Titian.*

Titian Vecellio was born at Pieve di Cadore in 1477. In his youth he was placed in Giovanni Bellini's studio to study painting; there he met Giorgione with whom he associated and from whom he inherited his splendour of colour, while surpassing him in fertility of invention. This greatest of Italian painters combined in himself the multiple pictorial gifts of the Venetian school, and in his long career essayed every class of subjects pagan mythology and sacred pictures, while in his portraits, he presents to us humanity in its noblest and most beautiful forms. He died in 1576.

*"La Flora." By Titians.
Painted about 1516.*

*Leda with the Swan.
By Tintoretto (1518-92).*

— 269 —

35. - WONDERS OF ITALY.

Photo Alinari, Anderson, Brogi

FLORENCE — UFFIZI GALLERY. Venetian School.

ALLEGORY OF THE CHURCH. By GIOVANNI BELLINI.

PIETÀ. By GIOVANNI BELLINI.

Bellini's « Allegory of the Church » is an illustration of a 14th century French poem entitled « Man's Pilgrimage ». To the extreme left of a quadrangular space, paved with fine marbles and surrounded by a railing, is the Madonna enthroned, without the Infant Saviour. Beside her kneels St. Catherine of Alexandria, crowned, and on the left St. Catherine of Siena. Behind the railing, as though guarding the enclosure, are St. Paul with his sword, and, near the open gate, St. Peter.

In the centre of the enclosure is the Tree of Life from which nude children, symbolic of human souls, pluck fruit. To the extreme right stand St. Job and St. Sebastian, the two great plague saints. Beyond stretches a poetical landscape with opalescent lake and steep mountains, buildings and woods, apparently symbolic of the world and its difficulties. Here are seen a centaur symbol of vicious inclination ; a hermit in his cell, indicating the best refuge for such temptations. This enigmatical picture, remarkable for the depth and richness of colouring, is unique among Bellini's numerous works.

A KNIGHT. By GIORGIONE.

THE DEATH OF ADONIS. By SEB. DEL PIOMBO.

PORTRAIT OF A MAN. By G. B. MORONI († 1577).

MOSES : The Ordeal of Fire. By GIORGIONE.

ENRICHETTA, Princess of Modena. By ROSALBA CARRIERA.

PORTRAIT OF A LADY. By SEBASTIANO DEL PIOMBO.

The subject of the above picture is taken from an old Rabbinic legend which goes as follows. When Moses was 3 years old Pharaoh's counsellors advised that he should be slain. The King objected that the baby was too young and innocent, and to decide the point a ruby ring and burning coals were set before the child. If he should take the ring it was an omen that he knew right from wrong and should be slain ; but if the coals, his life would be spared. When the child saw what was set before him he reached out for the ring, but the Angel Gabriel, present in disguise, turned his hand aside and Moses took a hot coal and put it into his mouth. His tongue was so burnt that while he lived he never was able to speak distinctly.

Sebastiano del Piombo's fine portrait of a lady, dated 1512 was formerly erroneously attributed first to Raphael then to Giorgione. It is now believed to be a likeness of Beatrice of Ferrara a popular "improvvisatrice," distinguished for her mental powers. The colouring is warm and pleasing.

Photo ALINARI, ANDERSON, BROGI.

FLORENCE — UFFIZI GALLERY. Venetian School.

ESTHER IN PRESENCE OF ASSUERUS
Painting by PAOLO VERONESE.

MARTYRDOM OF ST. JUSTINA. *By* PAOLO VERONESE.

THE ASCENSION. THE ADORATION OF THE MAGI. THE CIRCUMCISION.
Triptych painted about 1464 by ANDREA MANTEGNA (1436-1506). *(Paduan School).*

This magnificent triptych, is one of the finest and most carefully executed works of Mantegna. Painted about 1461 for the chapel of the Ducal Palace of the Gonzagas at Mantua, it was sold to the Medici and placed in this gallery in 1632. The scenes are most exquisitely painted and finished throughout like a miniature ; in the 'Adoration' the perspective is cunningly enhanced by the curved shape of the panel ; the scene of the 'Circumcision' is treated with great feeling and realism, — the little St. John, who sympathetically averts his head, is of special charm and truth to nature ; the 'Ascension' is less perfect.

LANDSCAPE. *By* FRANCESCO GUARDI.

VIEW OF VENICE. *By* CANALETTO (ANTONIO CANALE).

Photo ALINARI, ANDERSON, BROGI.

FLORENCE — UFFIZI GALLERY. Flemish School.

Tommaso Portinari. THE ADORATION OF THE SHEPHERDS. Maddalena Portinari.
Triptych by HUGO VAN DER GOES († 1482). (Flemish School).

Hugo van der Goes' magnificent triptych, undoubtedly the finest Flemish work in the gallery, was painted in 1476, at Bruges, for Tommaso Portinari agent of the Medici Bank in that city.
In the main panel kneels the Virgin with St. Joseph, the adoring shepherds and several angels robed in rich vestments; the Child lies on the ground emanating supernatural light in the foreground are two vases with exquisite flowers and a wheat-sheaf: symbolic of the " bread of life." In the left panel, the donor Tommaso Portinari, kneels with his two sons, presented by their patron name-saints Thomas and Antony Abbot. In the right panel, the kneeling figures of the donor's wife Maddalena and her daughter Margherita, presented by the Magdalen and Saint Margaret. This great altarpiece was one of the first works in oil that made their appearance in Italy.

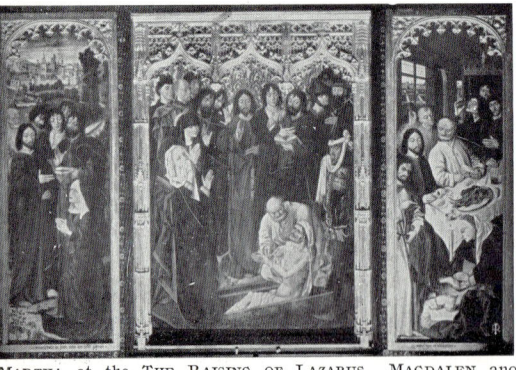

MARTHA at the THE RAISING OF LAZARUS. MAGDALEN anoints Christ's feet.
feet of Christ. By NICHOLAS FROMENT.

THE MORNING MEAL.
By JAN STEEN.

In the central panel is depicted the Raising of Lazarus, whose features have the most ghastly expression of death and returning life ever given to a man's face. Christ, in the middle of the picture is uttering the words: " Loose him, and let him go ; " with his right hand Jesus points to heaven, as if he said : " I have raised thee by the power of Him who sent me." To the left, is Lazarus. sister Martha, holding her nose ; the bystanders are conventional. In the left panel, Martha, kneeling, meets Jesus on his arrival at Bethany, saying : " Lord, if thou hadst been here, our brother had not died." In the right panel is represented the supper in the house of Levi, and the Magdalen is seen anointing the feet of the Saviour.
Little is known of the painter of this curious work, except that he was patronized by King René of Anjou, which may account for the introduction (in the right corner of the central scene), of a court jester holding his nose. Froment a painter of the 15th century, belonged to the School of Aix-en-Provence.

ST. BENEDICT.
By HANS MEMLING.

DEPOSITION or PIETÀ.
By ROGER VAN DER WEYDEN.

— 272 —

Photo ALINARI, ANDERSON, BROGI.

FLORENCE — UFFIZI GALLERY. French, Dutch and German Schools.

PORTRAIT OF MARIE ADELAIDE (as Diana).   PORTRAIT OF ANNA HENRIETTE (as Flora).
The daughters of Louis XV. of France painted by JEAN MARC NATTIER.

Nattier (1685-1766) was a favourite court portrait painter. The palace at Versailles is filled with his portraits of the daughters of Louis XV. and though, perhaps, a little monotonous in his grace, he has left us many delicious portraits of royal dames and court beauties.

ADORATION OF THE KINGS.   EMPEROR CHARLES V.   ISABELLA BRANT, by RUBENS.
By ALBERT DÜRER.   By VAN DYCK.   (Rubens' first wife).

PORTRAIT OF RICHARD SOUTHWELL.   ST. PETER PREACHING.   PORTRAIT OF AN OLD MAN.
By HOLBEIN the Younger.   By HANS VON KULMBACK.   By REMBRANDT.

The Uffizi Gallery has a large collection of admirable paintings of Flemish, Dutch, French, and German masters. Conspicuous among these are works by Hugo van der Goes, Roger van der Weyden, Memling, Rembrandt, Rubens, Metsu, Jan Steen, Albrecht Dürer, Holbein, Watteau, Boucher, Nattier, Claude Lorrain, Kulmback and others.

— 273 —

Photo ALINARI, ANDERSON, BROGI.

FLORENCE — UFFIZI GALLERY. Tapestries.

Tapestry, being easily moveable was greatly in vogue in medieval times for the ornamentation of dwelling-houses. They were used as wall-hangings and curtains in the homes of the rich, and in the churches to preserve people against wintry weather and cold drafts. However large these textiles could be easily rolled up and taken along by travellers on their journeys and even by soldiers during wars.

The art of weaving tapestry was introduced from the East, and spread through Europe at the time of the Crusades. A fine silk-tapestry hanging with an equestrian portrait of an Emperor of the East was found in the tomb of Bishop Gunther, who died in the year 1064 on his way home from an embassy to Constantinople and was buried, enwrapped in this hanging, in Bamberg cathedral.

How this great industry first arose we do not precisely know, but

FESTIVAL ON OCCASION OF THE MARRIAGE OF HENRY II. OF FRANCE with Catherine de' Medici.

it has been conjectured that the election of Baldwin of Flanders as emperor of the East in the year 1204, may have familiarized the Flemings with Byzantine work like that brought home by Bishop Gunther. However, shortly afterwards the Flemings established factories in several of their cities; their industry as it developed was characteristically Flemish, and in its turn it exerted a very wide in-

DEPARTURE OF CATHERINE DE' MEDICI WITH HER COURT FROM ANET.
(Anet : the château or mansion built by Henry II. for Diana of Poitiers).

Henry II., second son of Francis I. of France, married Catherine de' Medici in 1533 ; became heir apparent at the death (1536) of Francis, dauphin of France. Largely under the influence of his mistress Diane of Poitiers, he died of a wound received in a tournament. Of his seven children three became kings of France.

Catherine de' Medici, became Queen of France in 1547, began to assert herself in government when her eldest son, Francis II. became king in 1559 ; regent during the minority of CharlesIX. (1560-1573), she had complete control during his entire reign ; exerted some influence over her third son Henry III. Stirred up wars between Catholics and Huguenots, and planned the Massacre of St. Bartholomew (1572).

Henry III., married (1575) Louise of Lorraine, daughter of Nicholas, Count of Vaudemont. Aided his mother in plotting Massacre of St. Bartholomew ; His indolence and corrupt life scandalized everyone in his court ; his reign was marked by continuous civil conflicts between Catholics (Holy League) and Huguenots. Had Henry, Duke of Guise, and his brother the cardinal (Louis II, of Lorraine) murdered. He was murdered by a fanatic monk, Jacques Clément.

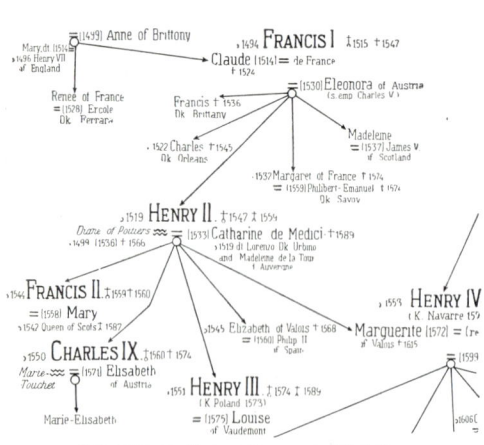

LINEAGE OF VALOIS-ORLEANS. (Detail).
(See explanation of symbols on pp. 179, 190, 518).

FEAST GIVEN BY CATHERINE DE' MEDICI
IN HONOR OF POLISH AMBASSADORS.

— 273B —

Photo ALINARI, ANDERSON, BROGI.

fluence upon the rest of Europe, bringing the art to great perfection.

Already in the 14th century the tapestries of Bruges, Brussels, and other Flemish towns, including Arras, were as famous as were later the French Gobelins. To that time may be traced the origin of those large pictorial tapestries which soon brought the weaver into successful rivalry with the painter in the decoration of churches, halls, palaces and dwelling-houses. In the dukes of Burgundy, who acquired the Flemish provinces by marriage, the weavers found patrons of almost unlimited wealth and luxury. In the year 1479 Arras was captured by Louis XI. king of France, and the industry which had brought the city so much fame suffered a check from which it never recovered. Thenceforth Brussels began to take the place that Arras had lost, and from the early years of the 16th century until the end of the 18th it was the leading tapestry-weaving centre in the Low Countries. The best known and the most frequently repeated of the tapestries woven at Brussels was the famous set of the "Acts of the Apostles," designed by Raphael which when hung in their destined position round the walls of the Sistine chapel (p. 472) evoked the greatest enthusiasm.

Tapestry weaving in Italy began about the 15th century, when a number of weavers from Flanders crossed the Alps, either driven from their country on account of their religious or political scruples, or attracted by the sums offered by some of the cities and princes of Italy. Establishments for weaving were planted at Ferrara, Venice, Mantua, Siena, Bologna and elsewhere. But in spite of the real beauty of much Italian work, the craft has never become entirely acclimatized in a country where fresco-painting is more suited to the climate and the national genius.

When Cosimo I. de' Medici became Grand-Duke of Tuscany, he determined to establish a manufactory for tapestry in Florence that should excel all other establishments of the same kind in Italy; in 1545, therefore, he induced two Flemings, *Nicholas Karcher* and *Jean Van der Roost*, to come to Florence and take the direction of the establishment, which finally was placed in the via degli Arazzieri, on this account so named. The painters chiefly employed for the cartoons were Agnolo Bronzine, Francesco Salviati, Jacopo da Pontormo and Francesco Ubertini, also called *Il Bachiacca*; they were succeeded by Jean Stradano, Alessandro Allori and Bernardo Poccetti. When the Grand-Duke FerdinandII. ascended the throne he invited *Pierre Fevère* from Paris, who produced magnificent works closely resembling oil paintings. But the industry created by the Medici continued to flourish until the death of Gian Gastone (1737), the last Medici Grand-Duke, when it was decided to close the establishment.

AN AQUATIC FEAST PRESIDED BY HENRY III. OF FRANCE AND HIS CONSORT LOUISE OF LORRAINE.

Nevertheless, there had been time to produce an enormous quantity of tapestries; the villas and the palaces of the grand-dukes were abundantly supplied; there were enough works to adorn the *Loggia dei Lanzi* and the façade of the *Palazzo della Signoria*. The greater part of the tapestries are now in the Palazzo Vecchio and in the Uffizi and Pitti galleries-where there are also ma: gnificent Gobelins (p. 286).

FESTIVAL ON THE OCCASION OF THE MARRIAGE OF KING HENRY II. OF FRANCE WITH HIS CONSORT CATHERINE DE' MEDICI. *Tapestry by* KARCHER (*Uffizi, Florence*).

Photo ALINARI, ANDERSON, BROGI.

FLORENCE — UFFIZI GALLERY. *Portraits of Painters.*

LEONARDO DA VINCI.
Painted by himself.
(1452-1519).

RAPHAEL OF URBINO.
Painted by himself.
(1483-1520).

MICHELANGELO BUONARROTI.
Born at Caprese, died at Rome.
(1475-1564).

ANDREA DEL SARTO.
Painted by himself.
(1487-1531).

TITIAN VECELLIO.
Painted by himself.
(1477-1576).

ELISABETH VIGÉE LE BRUN.
Painted by herself.
(1755-1842).

The Uffizi Gallery possesses a large, unique collection of portraits of distinguished artists from all countries, from the fifteenth to the twentieth centuries. These remarkable works, chiefly painted by the artists themselves whose names they bear, constitute one of the attractions of the gallery.

PORTRAIT OF RUBENS.
Painted by himself.
(1577-1640).

PORTRAIT OF REMBRANDT.
Painted by himself.
(1606-1669).

PORTRAIT OF VAN DYCK.
Painted by himself.
(1599-1641).

Photo ALINARI, ANDERSON, BROGI.

FLORENCE — PITTI PALACE.

The Palazzo Pitti. Begun by Luca Pitti in 1440 from designs by BRUNELLESCHI.

Staircase leading to the Picture Gallery. *The marble fountain is by* DONATELLO.

THE PITTI PALACE, was occupied by the King of Italy when Florence was the capital of the kingdom (1865-71). The edifice was begun in 1440 by Luca Pitti, a wealthy citizen of Florence, who at that date was one of the chief rivals of the Medici. After the failure of the conspiracy against Piero in 1466 (page 261), Luca lost his power and influence and the building remained unfinished till 1549 when it was sold to the Medici Grand-dukes who gradually completed it and made it their residence.

To Brunelleschi, a creator and originator in architecture, is due the design of this splendid palace which represents the first and most colossal attempt on record, to construct an artistic façade out of unhewn blocks of stone. The huge masses of stone are only cut at the corners, and the rest of them being left rough give an increased effect of vastness and ruggedness: they recall the Cyclopean walls which surrounded the cities of the Etruscans.

Only the central part of the palace dates from the 16th century, the wings were added in the 17th century. The whole front as it stands to day is 672 feet long and 119 feet high, each storey is 49 feet in height. At the time of the Medici the palace was called the Grand Ducal Palace and later the Royal Palace.

The Boboli Gardens, extending on the hillside behind the palace, were planned in the 16th century. A cypress alley leads right through these gardens, and as it rises, a beautiful and widespread view of Florence is obtained. Cypresses, laurels, stone pines, oleanders, myrtle, ilex, flowers.... bloom everywhere. Beautiful marble fountains, where colossal river-gods let the water drip gently from their urns, rise from the midst of artificial lakes. The luxuriant growth and bloom, the stillness of the place, the pure, perfumed air,—all these lend to the Boboli Gardens an atmosphere of delight and beauty which fills and soothes the soul unspeakably.

Fountain. *By* TADDA.    Fountain in the Boboli Gardens.    The Grotto. *By* BUONTALENTI.

In the back of the Pitti Palace is a great courtyard surrounded on three sides by the building, while on the fourth side is a stone terrace one storey high on which is a beautiful fountain by *Tadda*. Next to this is the so-called Amphitheatre, an open space enclosed by oak-hedges and six rows of seats. This Amphitheatre, large enough to accommodate four thousand spectators, was used for open air festivities of the court.

— 275 —

Photo ALINARI, ANDERSON, BROGI.

36. - *WONDERS OF ITALY.*

FLORENCE — PITTI GALLERY.

HALL OF THE ILIAD.

HALL OF SATURN.

"OLYMPUS." *Fresco by* SABATELLI. A. D. 1819.
Ceiling of the Hall of the Iliad.

The PITTI GALLERY, located in the left wing of the palace, contains about five hundred paintings most of which are masterpieces by the greatest masters in painting. This invaluable collection was (like the Uffizi's) formerly the property of the Medici who, for hundreds of years, devoted much time and money to it.

The pictures are arranged in a suite of six halls and several smaller rooms, all splendidly adorned with allegorical ceiling-paintings, whence their names are derived.

The ceiling of the first apartment, the Hall of the Iliad, was painted by *Sabatelli* in 1819, and represents « Olympus ». Here the gods are gathered around Jupiter who forbids them to mingle in the fight between the Greeks and the Trojans. In the lunettes is represented the story of Juno : the goddess visiting Venus ; Juno awakening Morpheus ; Juno in the presence of Jupiter ; Neptune rising from the waves ; Jupiter conversing with Juno ; Hector carried from the battlefield is being revived by Apollo ; the burning of the Greek fleet.

The ceilings of the next five rooms denominated from the planet which, according to the fancy of the artist was to denote one of the virtues or excellences of Cosimo I., were painted by Pietro da Cortona about 1640. Thus, Saturn—symbolizes the duke's prudence and sagacity ; Jupiter—his majesty and powers of government ; Mars—his energy and successes in war ; Apollo — his splendour and patronage of the Arts ; Venus—his loving and lovable nature.

The gods of Olympus are gathered around Jupiter, enthroned, who forbids them to mingle in the fight between the Greeks and the Trojans. On the right of Jupiter is Aurora, flying, and beneath her Juno, sitting ; lower down is Pluto and Proserpine, Apollo, Diana and Vesta, a flame issuing from her head; lower still Hercules conversing with Hebe.

On the left of Jupiter is Ganymede, Minerva, Mercury with the caduceus, then Vulcan, Venus (with Cupid in her lap), and Mars in armour; behind these, Bacchus, Morpheus and the Three Graces. Beneath the throne is Neptune, Destiny and the Three Fates; lower down is Thetis facing Cybele, Ceres and Pan.

LA DONNA GRAVIDA.
By RAPHAEL.

PHILIP II. OF SPAIN.
By TITIAN.

PORTRAT OF
By RIDOLFO GHIRLANDAIO.

Photo ALINARI, ANDERSON, BROGI.

Andrea del Sarto's «Assumption of the Virgin», a noble example of the master's beautiful colouring, was painted for the cathedral of Cortona and brought to Florence in 1639.

The Virgin is seated amid vapoury clouds above, her hands joined in adoration. She is borne up towards heaven by most lovely angels who proclaim the glad tidings to the Apostles below.

The Apostles, gathered round the Virgin's tomb, are looking up in wonder and astonishment. Conspicuous among them is S. Thomas in the centre holding up his left arm as if in expectation of the Virgin's Sacred Belt. In the foreground, kneeling, are S. Margaret of Cortona on the right, and S. Niccolò of Bari with his three golden balls on the left. The face of the Virgin is a likeness of Andrea del Sarto's wife whom the master painted again and again in all his Madonnas.

The subject of this picture, presenting the final scene of the Virgin's life on earth, is very frequently represented in sacred art. According to the old legend, while Mary was living in the home of John on Mount Sion, an angel appeared to her and told her, on the part of her son, that after three days her soul should depart from the flesh and reign with the Lord for ever. And Mary gave thanks to God and begged that the Apostles might be assembled at her death. And thus it happened. Just before the death of the Virgin, the Apostles were miraculously transported in clouds from the various places where they preached and collected before the door of Mary. And towards nightfall, on the third day, Jesus appeared and the soul of Mary left her body, and was received into the arms of her Son, and together they ascended into heaven. But the body remained upon the earth and the Apostles reverently laid it in a tomb in the valley of Jehoshaphat and watched beside it for three days, until the Lord appeared with a multitude of angels, raised up the Virgin Mary, and she was received, body and soul, into heaven.

But the Apostle Thomas had been delayed and was not present at the Virgin's Assumption, and when he arrived would not believe in the resurrection of the Virgin. He desired that the tomb should be opened before him, and when this was done it was found to be full of lilies and roses. Then, looking up to heaven, he beheld the bodily form of the Virgin, in a glory of light, slowly mounting towards heaven. To confirm his faith, the Virgin loosened her girdle and dropped it into the arms of Thomas. After many vicissitudes this same girdle was eventually brought to the Cathedral of Prato where it is now preserved and venerated.

ASSUMPTION OF THE VIRGIN.
Altarpiece by A. DEL SARTO. A. D. 1526.

The Angel refusing the Gifts of Tobias.
By BILIVERTI.

Tobias had been sent on a mission by his father Tobit who was afflicted with blindness. He was accompanied by a stranger who, it transpired, was the Archangel Raphael disguised. Under his direction, the mission of Tobias was an entire success, and he returned home with the heart, the liver and the gall of a fish which miraculously healed his father's blindness. The artist has chosen the moment when the stranger reveals his identity, and explains to them his great message.

The VIRGIN appearing to St. Philip.
By CARLO MARATTA.

PHILIP IV. OF SPAIN.
By VELASQUEZ.

A PRINCE OF DENMARK.
By SUSTERMANS.

Photo ALINARI, ANDERSON, BROGI.

FLORENCE — PITTI GALLERY. *Sala di Saturno.*

VIEW OF THE HALL OF SATURN.

Raphael's « Madonna della Sedia », is the most popular picture of the Pitti Gallery. The Virgin, seated on a low chair, whence the name, holds the Child on her lap; the little St. John at her side folds his hands in prayer. « Its chief charm », says Hilliard, « is in its happy blending of the divine and the human elements. Some painters treat this subject in such a way that the spectator sees only a mother caressing her child : while by others the only ideas awakened are those of the Virgin and the Redeemer. But heaven and earth meet on Raphael's canvas, the purity of heaven and the tenderness of earth. The round, infantile form, the fond, clasping arms, the sweetness and the grace belong to this world ; but the faces, especially that of the Infant Saviour, in whose eyes there is a mysterious depth of expression..., are touched by the light from heaven, and suggest something to worship as well as something to love ».

The colouring is warm and beautiful ; the composition drawn with great freedom, notwithstanding the compression of the group, which is adapted to a closely fitting frame.

MADONNA DELLA SEDIA (of the Chair.).
By RAPHAEL
A. D. 1512.

PORTRAIT OF ANGELO DONI.
Painted by RAPHAEL.

VISION OF EZEKIEL.
Painted by RAPHAEL.

MADDALENA DONI.
Painted by RAPHAEL.

Photo ALINARI, ANDERSON, BROGI.

FLORENCE. PITTI GALLERY.

THE MADONNA DEL GRANDUCA. *By* RAPHAEL. A. D. 1505. (*Florentine period*).

 This is one of the master's most exquisite pictures. It speaks to the heart and captivates us chiefly by the half-concealed beauty of the Madonna who holds the Child tranquilly in her arms, and looks down in deep thought. Painted in light colours and modelled with extraordinary delicacy, the Virgin has all the pensive sweetness and reflective sentiment of the Umbrian school, while the Infant is loveliness itself.

 This picture was kept in the private appartment of the Grand-Duke Ferdinand III, who so esteemed in that he carried it whith him wherever he travelled. Hence the name.

FLORENCE — *PITTI GALLERY.* Sala di Saturno.

THE DEPOSITION FROM THE CROSS.
By PERUGINO. A. D. 1495.

MARY MAGDALENE.
By PERUGINO.

GROUP OF SAINTS (DISPUTA).
Painted by ANDREA DEL SARTO. A. D. 1518.
From left to right: St. Augustine, St. Laurence, St. Peter Martyr *and* St. Francis; *left* St. Sebastian, *right* Mary Magdalene *kneeling.*

Perugino's « Deposition from the Cross » is justly considered one of the noblest works of the master. The composition is truly fine and simple, and the whole treatment of the subject is deeply sympathetic and sincerely human. The figures collected round the Saviour are gracefully drawn; their mournful faces varying in intensity of grief, the poses of the heads, the distant, lovely landscape are all characteristic of Perugino.

The dead body of Christ lying on a white cloth is sustained by Joseph of Arimathea while the Magdalene supports his head. The Virgin mother holds his left arm and wistfully gazes into her son's face. Behind the Magdalene, standing, is Mary Cleophas with raised hands; behind the Virgin, kneeling, is Mary Salome, and next to her, also kneeling, is Nicodemus holding the lower part of the shroud. On the extreme left, standing, are St. John and the wife of Zebedee, and on the extreme right are three figures, one of whom holds the three nails of the Passion in his left hand.

The picture was painted in 1495 for the nuns of the convent of S. Chiara. A rich Florentine merchant so admired the work that he offered the nuns three times what they had paid for it if they would sell it to him, at the same time promising them a replica by Perugino himself. The offer was refused; at the suppression of the convent the picture was eventually brought to the Pitti.

ANNUNCIATION. *By* A. DEL SARTO.

THE RISEN CHRIST WITH THE FOUR EVANGELISTS. *By* FRA BARTOLOMMEO.

Portrait of CARDINAL INGHIRAMI.
By RAPHAEL.

MADONNA DEL BALDACCHINO.
Altar-piece by RAPHAEL.

Portrait of CARDINAL BIBBIENA.
By RAPHAEL.

Photo ALINARI, ANDERSON, BROGI.

FLORENCE — PITTI GALLERY. Sala di Giove.

CEILING FRESCO. By P. DA CORTONA. (Sala di Giove).

The ceiling fresco represents: Hercules and Fortune leading Cosimo I. into the presence of Jupiter to receive the crown of Immortality.

THE THREE FATES.
By FRANCESCO SALVIATI.

This picture was formerly attributed to Michelangelo and later to Rosso Fiorentino.

ST. JOHN THE BAPTIST.
By ANDREA DEL SARTO.

Fra Bartolommeo's « Deposition » was painted for the Augustinian convent outside the Porta San Gallo. This noble work, the masterpiece of the artist, is one of the most impressive Depositions in the world of Art. The lifeless form of Christ, supported by St. John, is drawn with perfect anatomical accuracy. The expression of the Saviour's face, is touchingly sad and dignified. The gentle resignation of the sorrowing Virgin, tenderly holding the head of her dead Son while she stoops to kiss his forehead, and the passionate grief of the Magdalene, who has thrown herself at the feet of the Lord, are given with simple truth of nature.

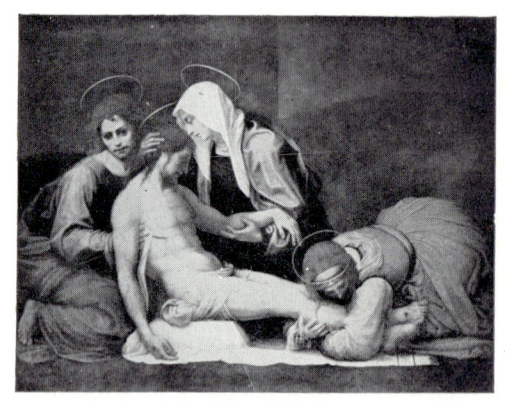

DEPOSITION or PIETÀ.
Painted by FRA BARTOLOMMEO (1475-1517).

THE THREE AGES OF MAN.
Venetian School of the XVI century.
This picture was formerly attributed to Lorenzo Lotto.

PORTRAIT OF ANDREA DEL SARTO AND HIS WIFE.
This is the only real portrait of the master's wife.
By ANDREA DEL SARTO (?).

Photo ALINARI, ANDERSON, BROGI.

FLORENCE — PITTI GALLERY. Sala di Giove.

ANNUNCIATION. By A. DEL SARTO (1511).

Andrea del Sarto's "Annunciation" given above is the best of the many pictures of the same subject painted by the master. The position of the Virgin here is reversed from familiar usage. She stands at the left and is separated from Gabriel by a little *priedieu* upon which is an inscription which may be thus translated: 'Andrea del Sarto has painted thee here as he carries thee in his heart and not as thou art Maria to propagate thy glory and not his fame." The face of the Virgin, as usual, is a likeness of the master's wife. In the background is seen the portico of a Renaissance house, on the balcony above are two figures watching a youth bathing (?).

ST. JEROME. By P. POLLAIUOLO.

NYMPHS AND SATYRS. By RUBENS.

A crowd of satyrs and nymphs are seen in violent struggle. "All laws are disregarded, and the satyrs are capturing any one whom they can." On the ground lies a dead deer, from which may be inferred that the satyrs were returning from a hunting expedition and have fallen in with the nymphs.

"The Donna Velata," the lady with the veil, whose luminous eyes seem to sparkle with vitality, is said to be a portrait of the "Fornarina," (?) the woman Raphael loved, and to whom he addressed his sonnets.

The resemblance between this portrait and the Virgin in the Sistine Madonna at Dresden, justifies the surmise that the same model sat for both pictures. The beauty of the woman is great, but it is not the beauty of a courtesan. Her bearing is dignified and her eyes are not searching, but firm and clear. She wears a beautiful gown over a shirt of fine white linen, a necklace made of a set of oval medallions, and a pendant fastened to her brown hair. The richness of her costume, however, is subdued by the solemn simplicity of the enframing veil.

THE "DONNA VELATA." By RAPHAEL.

HOLY FAMILY. By RUBENS.

Photo ALINARI, ANDERSON, BROGI.

FLORENCE — PITTI GALLERY. Sala di Marte.

CARDINAL BENTIVOGLIO.
By A. VAN DYCK.

DANIELE BARBARO.
By PAOLO VERONESE.

MADONNA AND CHILD (Detail).
By MURILLO (1617-82).

CONSEQUENCES OF WAR. *Allegory by* RUBENS. A. D. 1625.

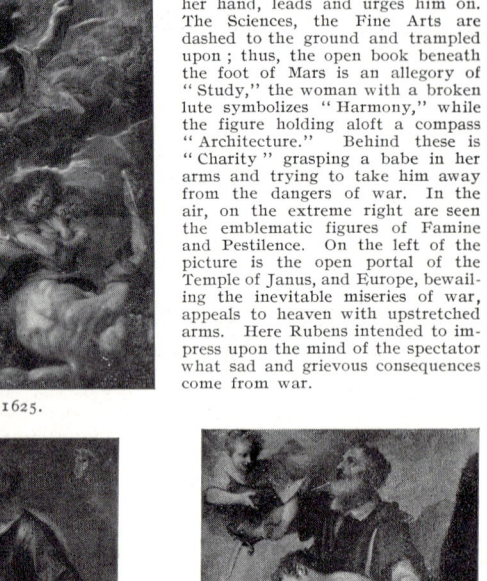

This picture, one of Rubens' masterpieces, exhibits nearly all the qualities peculiar to the master's style. In the centre Mars, clad in armour unheeding the prayers of Venus, tears himself away from her and follows Alecto, who with the torch of Discord in her hand, leads and urges him on. The Sciences, the Fine Arts are dashed to the ground and trampled upon; thus, the open book beneath the foot of Mars is an allegory of "Study," the woman with a broken lute symbolizes "Harmony," while the figure holding aloft a compass "Architecture." Behind these is "Charity" grasping a babe in her arms and trying to take him away from the dangers of war. In the air, on the extreme right are seen the emblematic figures of Famine and Pestilence. On the left of the picture is the open portal of the Temple of Janus, and Europe, bewailing the inevitable miseries of war, appeals to heaven with upstretched arms. Here Rubens intended to impress upon the mind of the spectator what sad and grievous consequences come from war.

FOUR PHILOSOPHERS.
By RUBENS.

ST. PETER WEEPING.
By GUIDO RENI.

THE SACRIFICE OF ISAAC.
By CIGOLI.

Rubens' celebrated picture of the « Four Philosophers », is a portrait of himself — the figure standing to the left —, that of his brother Philip — sitting next him and holding a pen —, Lipsius, the philosopher, — seen full face with his forefinger upon a book, — and Hugo Grotius, the Treasurer of Holland and Zeeland, — seen in profile. In a niche in the wall is a bust of Seneca with a vase of tulips before it.

Photo ALINARI, ANDERSON, BROGI.

FLORENCE. NATIONAL MUSEUM.

Palazzo del Podestà or Bargello.

FLORENCE — *PITTI GALLERY.* Sala di Apollo.

APOLLO, the tutelary deity of Poetry and the Fine Arts, points to Cosimo I. — who is guided by Virtue—the way to Immortality. *Ceiling fresco begun by* P. DA CORTONA, *completed by* C. FERRI.

PORTRAIT OF VINCENZO ZENO. *By* TINTORETTO.

This very living portrait of a Venetian nobleman, is one of Tintoretto's best works. Through the window is a view of the lagoons. Inscribed : VINCENTIUS ZENO ANNO ÆTATIS SVE LXXIIII.

HOLY FAMILY. *By* ANDREA DEL SARTO.

PORTRAIT OF THE DUKE OF NORFOLK. *By* TITIAN (detail).

THE DEPOSITION. *By* ANDREA DEL SARTO.

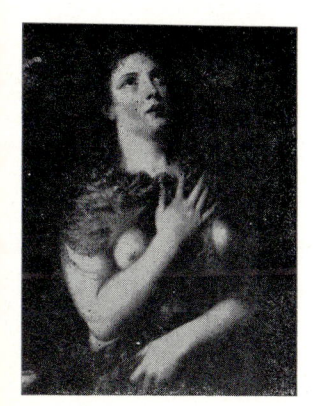

THE MAGDALENE. *By* TITIAN. A. D. 1552.

CHARLES I. OF ENGLAND. HENRIETTA MARIA. *Portraits by* ANTON VAN DYCK.

VITTORIA DELLA ROVERE *by* SUSTERMANS.

Titian's " Magdalene," regarded as a work of art, is a triumph of technical skill. Face, hair, and arms are exquisitely rendered. But the master here chose to represent the Penitent's first state rather than her last. He simply paints a beautiful Venetian woman, with rich golden hair, covering her just enough to salve her modesty, but not to conceal her shape. The upturned face and eyes, streaming with tears, the alabaster pot of precious ointment serve merely to indicate that the picture is meant for a Mary Magdalene. The master's signature is inscribed on the pot.

— 283 —

37. - WONDERS OF ITALY.

FLORENCE — *PITTI GALLERY*. *Sala di Venere.*

CEILING FRESCO. *By* P. DA CORTONA (*Sala di Venere*).

Minerva rescues from the arms of Venus a young man (Cosimo I.) and conducts him to Hercles. An allusion meaning the triumph of Reason over Pleasure.

TRIUMPH OF DAVID. *By* MATTEO ROSSELLI. A. D. 1621.

David is carrying the head of Goliath in one hand and the giants' sword in the other. This picture is distinguished for its freshness of life and beauty and for its richness of colour.

HARBOUR AT SUNRISE. *By* SALVATOR ROSA.

Titian's "La Bella," is one of the finest portraits ever produced. It was painted about 1536 and is probably a likeness of the Duchess Eleonora of Urbino, whose features can also be recognised in Titian's Venus in the Uffizi (p. 269). "The eye is grave, serene, and kindly, the nose delicate, the mouth divine." The picture was taken to Paris in the 18th century when the background was entirely repainted.

LA BELLA. *By* TITIAN. A.D. 1536.

PIETRO ARETINO. *By* TITIAN ca. 1546.

This portrait, which Aretino himself called a "hideous marvel," is a fine example of what the paint-brush of an artist can do to arrest the soul in the features of a man. Aretino was a celebrated pamphleteer and a slanderer by profession; his services were bought by anyone who wished for them. "He spoke evil of every one except Christ, and for that he excused himself saying that he did not know him".

Aretino died in 1556, after an uncontrollable fit of laughter.

The *Concert* is considered one of the most important masterpiece of the Italian painting, but after having been considered, up to the end of the 19th century, a work by GIORGIONE, it was definitively attributed to TITIAN and precisely to his first manner (giorgionesca).

The principal figure, an Augustine monk with the face of an ascetic, has evidently struck a rich chord on the harpsichord and turns to his companion. His gesture and expression tell an entire tale... The modelling of his face is masterful; the two figures on the side are but accessories to the central musician. "The whole interest of his face," writes Symonds,

A MUSICAL CONCERT *By* TITIAN. *Formerly attributed to Giorgione.*

"lies in its concentrated feeling—the very soul of music, as represented in Robert Browning's 'Abt Vogler,' passing through his eyes."

— 284 —

Photo ALINARI, ANDERSON, BROGI.

Allori's picture of "Judith with the head of Holofernes", is the best known and most highly finished work of the master. Here the Hebrew heroine is no imaginary person: it is the portrait of the painter's mistress—La Mazzafirra,—to whom he was devoted, and for whom he spent the greater part of his farings, eventually ruining himself. The slave in the background is La Mazzafirra's mother, while the head of Holofernes is the artist's own portrait. "He intended to indicate in this allegory," says Viardot, "the torture he constantly experienced from the capricious pride of the daughter and the greedy rapacity of the mother." The colouring is rich, the beauty and splendid attire of the young woman very striking, the expression of simple piety and wonder of the old one well rendered.

PORTRAIT OF TOMMASO MOSTI.
Painted by TITIAN.
(*Sala della Giustizia*)

JUDITH with the head of Holoferne.
By CRISTOFANO ALLORI.
(*Sala dell'educazione di Giove*)

Fra Filippo Lippi's "Madonna," is one of the finest works of the master.

The Virgin's face, of great beauty and refinement, is said to be a portrait of Fra Filippo's mistress Lucrezia Buti. In her right hand the Virgin holds a party open pomegranate. The pomegranate is supposed to show by the multiplicity of its seeds how widely the word of Christ would be propagated throughout the world. In the background, on the right is the meeting of Joachim and Anna; on the left is represented the birth of Mary.

The face of Lucrezia Buti often appears in Fra Filippo's paintings. She was the daughter of a Florentine merchant. Left an orphan she was placed as a novice in the Convent of S. Margherita at Prato, here she met Fra Filippo, who at that time was painting a picture for the Convent chapel, and became his mistress.

HOLY FAMILY or "MADONNA DELL'IMPANNATA". *By* RAPHAEL.
(*Sala di Ulisse*)

MADONNA. *By* FRA FILIPPO LIPPI.
(*Sala di Prometeo*)

The incident represented by *Raphael*'s picture of the "Holy Family», is most charming: the Virgin is in the act of receiving the Infant from St. Anne and St. Elizabeth, and while the child turns, still laughing, after them, he takes hold of his mother's dress. St. Elizabeth with her left fore-finger shows to the Saviour the little St. John, who is seated on a skin with one hand raised and the other holding a cross. In the background is seen a window covered with a linen pane, a custom called in Florence *impannata*, hence the name of the picture. The work originally sketched a circular picture, was executed about 1518 for a Florentine banker living in Rome. It subsequently came into the collection of the Grand-Duke Cosimo I. who placed it in the chapel of his apartment in the Palazzo Vecchio.

SAINT SEBASTIAN.
By SODOMA. A. D. 1515.
(*Sala del Castagnoli*)

TABLE IN FLORENTINE MOSAIC.

The bronze pedestal is by G. DUPRÈ.

This table costs 40.000 pounds sterling and 14 years' labour.

MICHELANGELO'S BOYHOOD.
(*Sala delle Allegorie*)

Photo ALINARI, ANDERSON, BROGI.

FLORENCE — *PITTI PALACE*

SCENES FROM THE LIFE OF JOSEPH. *Painted by* ANDREA DEL SARTO.

VENUS. *By* CANOVA.

These panels were the lids of two marriage chests, painted for the nuptial chamber of Margherita Borgherini and each panel represents different scenes which may be considered as one picture. In the first, on the left, Joseph relates his dreams to his parents Jacob and Rachel, and his brethren; in the centre, Jacob and Rachel send Joseph to his brethren; farther back, the brethren let Joseph down in the well; to the right, Joseph is sold to the merchants; in the foreground, Reuben is showing Joseph's blood-stained tunic to Jacob. In the second panel, Joseph is in Egypt. On the left, Pharaoh is seen asleep; behind the bed are seen the fat and lean kine, and in the front the full and empty ears of corn; on the staircase Joseph is led to prison by two guards; below he is brought before Pharaoh; on the extreme right, Pharaoh listens to Joseph's interpretation of his dreams; in the centre, Pharaoh, surrounded by his court, names Joseph governor and bestows on him a gold chain. Lovely landscape in the background.

STORY OF ESTHER: THE BANQUET.    ESTHER CROWNED BY AHASUERUS.

Two of a series of six Gobelin tapestries executed about 1737-40 by JEAN AUDRAN from cartoons by JEAN FRANÇOIS DE TROY.

The Royal Apartments are luxuriously furnished and contain many interesting pictures: a Madonna by Carlo Dolci with a gorgeous marble frame; pictures and portraits of various members of the House of Medici, including the notorious Catherine; exquisite Gobelin tapestries; very rich and beautiful tables and cabinets in *pietra dura*, alabaster and ivory.

Among the treasures of the Pitti Palace the famous series of Gobelin tapestries illustrating the History of Esther is not the least important. This very interesting story of the deliverance of the Jews from the brink of universal destruction is represented in six large compositions: 1. *The Toilet.* Esther from her beauty is chosen by the Persian King Ahasuerus: her preparation

THE BANQUETING OR BALL ROOM.
State Apartments.
This remarkable hall was designed by G. M. PAOLETTI.

before her presentation to the King. 2. *The Coronation.* Esther is made Queen. 3. *The Meeting of Haman and Mordecai.* Mordecai refuses to pay homage to Haman (omitted here). 4. *The Decree.* The reading of the decree ordering the extermination of "a certain evilly disposed people." Esther overwhelmed with grief: she petitions the King: her swoon. 5. *The Triumph of Mordecai.* Haman's mortification: he leads Mordecai's horse through the city (omitted here). 6. *The Banquet.* Haman is accused and sentenced to death: his plot to ruin the Jews is defeated: Ahasuerus favours Esther: Mordecai is exhalted: the Jews slay their enemies: the feast of Purim is instituted to commemorate their deliverance from Haman.

— 286 —

FLORENCE — *PITTI PALACE. Museo degli Argenti.*

Silver-gilt salver attributed to BENVENUTO CELLINI.

THE TRIUMPH OF ALEXANDER THE GREAT. *Ceiling fresco.*

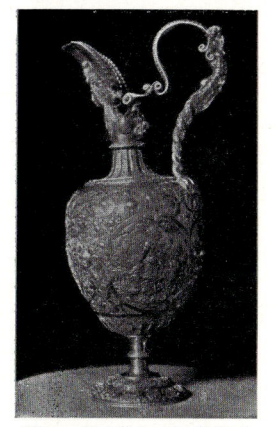

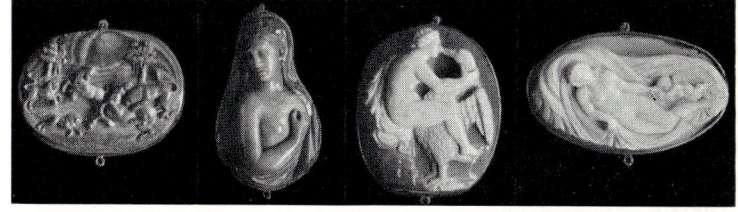

CAMEOS, INTAGLIOS AND ENGRAVED STONES.

Silver-gilt Pitcher *by Cellini.*

The MUSEO DEGLI ARGENTI—Silver Museum—located on the ground floor, contains a splendid collection of old plate and goldsmith work; ivory carvings; rock crystal gobelets; vases, cups, tables, cabinets, etc. in *pietra dura*; Limoges enamels; crucifixes and reliquaries; ecclesiastical vestments and tapestries; jewellery, cameos, intaglios and other curios formerly owned by the Medici. There is besides a collection of porcelain including specimens from China and Japan, Capodimonte, Sevres, Dresden and Vienna.

The great hall (fourth room) was decorated with frescoes in 1633 by *Giovanni da San Giovanni* and his scholars. On the ceiling is an allegory a propos of the nuptials of Grand-Duke Ferdinand II. and Vittoria della Rovere,—the alliance of the oak (*rovere*) leaves with the Medici balls; on the walls are allegorical compositions presenting the most important acts in the life of Lorenzo the Magnificent and his patronage of the Arts.

ROCK CRYSTAL PITCHER.

Enamel work is an art of a difficult technique and emploies precious materials; it is a painting where the colours are obtained by baking. The history of enamel work goes from the 11th to the 15th century. In the Middle Age its most important art center of production was Bisanzio and his enamellists were called all over Europe to execute enamel works of goldsmith's art. The *Pala d'Oro* in the St. Mark's church at Venise (*see p.* 107), the finest and most important monument of the enamel art in the Middle Age, is the work of the artists of Constantinople.

During the Renaissance wonderful enamel works were produced by Limoges enamellists.

PIETRA DURA CABINET. Gian Gastone de' Medici.

JEWEL CASKET sourmounted by a miniature tree in enamel.

— 287 —

Photo ALINARI, ANDERSON, BROGI

Genealogy

HISTORICAL SKETCH.

1. The son of Averardo and the founder of the Medici dynasty. In his lifetime served as Prior and Gonfaloniere, and was looked upon as the first banker in Italy.

2. Also called Cosimo the Elder. He was a successful financier and was known as « The Great Merchant of Florence ». His immense wealth he spent liberally for the advancement of art and science. He built the Medici Palace (now Riccardi); helped in rebuilding San Lorenzo and San Marco; founded the Medici Library, and enriched Florence with numerous churches and monuments. The people acclaimed him « The Father of his Country ».

3. Being an invalid he was surnamed the Gouty. Unambitious and of little power as a politician, he was unable to maintain the popularity his father had won, and, after a brief exercise of authority made way for his brilliant son Lorenzo.

4. Il Magnifico (The Magnificent) is the title given to this most illustrious member of the Medici. He ruled with almost regal power 22 years, and his encouragement made Florence the centre and focus of the arts for the whole world. After his death « The Splendour, not of Tuscany only, but of all Italy, disappeared ».

5. Lorenzo's younger brother murdered by the Pazzi in the Cathedral of Florence. He left a natural son, Giulio, who in 1523 became Pope Clement VII.

6. The eldest son of Lorenzo. He had an impetuous temperament and pretended to rule despotically. Having surrendered the frontier-fortresses to Charles VIII. of France, was expelled with his brothers Giovanni and Giuliano, and ended his days in exile. He ruled two years.

7. Ruled from 1512 to 1513.

8. A natural son of Giuliano brought up by Pope Leo X. and created cardinal by Clement VII. He was poisoned by order of Duke Alessandro.

9. Ruled from 1513 to 1519. His daughter Catherine became Queen of France.

10. He was surnamed the « Moor ». His parentage is uncertain; some historians assert that he was the natural son of Giulio (Clement VII). He was the worst tyrant Florence ever endured. He was created hereditary Duke in 1532 by Charles V. and married the Emperor's natural daughter in 1536. The following year he was assassinated by his own cousin Lorenzino.

11. He was a great soldier of extraordinary bravery and the greatest commander produced by Italy in the 16th century.

12. He was the founder of the junior branch of the Medici and reigned from the death of Alessandro in 1537 to 1574. He combined the various territories belonging to Florence into a single monarchical state and obtained from Pope Pius V. the title of Grand Duke.

13. He was a natural son of Cosimo I. and Eleonora degli Albizi, born after the death of Eleonora of Toledo. To him is due the design of the Medici Mausoleum.

14. Ruled from 1574 to 1587. He married Joanna of Austria, the sister of Emperor Maximilian. After the death of his wife he married the celebrated beauty Bianca Cappello, whose fascination and romantic history is related in every chronicle of the time. Maria, his second daughter, became Queen of France. He died without heirs and the throne passed to his brother Ferdinand I.

15. He reigned from 1587 to 1609. At 14 he had been created a cardinal and resided in Rome. He married the daughter of Catherine de' Medici.

16. Reigned from 1609 to 1620. He succeeded his father at the age of 19 and was the last of the Medici to be a ban his protection and supplied him with the means to effectuate his discoveries (telescope etc.).

17. Reigned from 1620 to 1670. He was only ten years when his father Cosimo II. died, and at first the government He made new additions to the Pitti Palace, and enlarged the façade to its present size. With his two brothers, Leopoldo

18. Reigned from 1670 to 1723. Weak and tyrannical he was noted for his superstitions and bigotry.

19. The last Grand-Duke. He married Anna Maria of Saxe Lauenburg, but owing to her extremely jealous disposition s

20. The last member of the Medici. Before her death she bequeated to Tuscany the whole, immense and invaluable collec their history: thus acquiring an imperishable title to the gratitude of Italy.

* In 1594 Henry of Navarre became King of France (Henry IV.). Having divorced his wife Marguerite of Valois, he married (16

NOTE. — A broken line indicates illegitimate parentage. An ✠ appended to a name indicates a violent death.

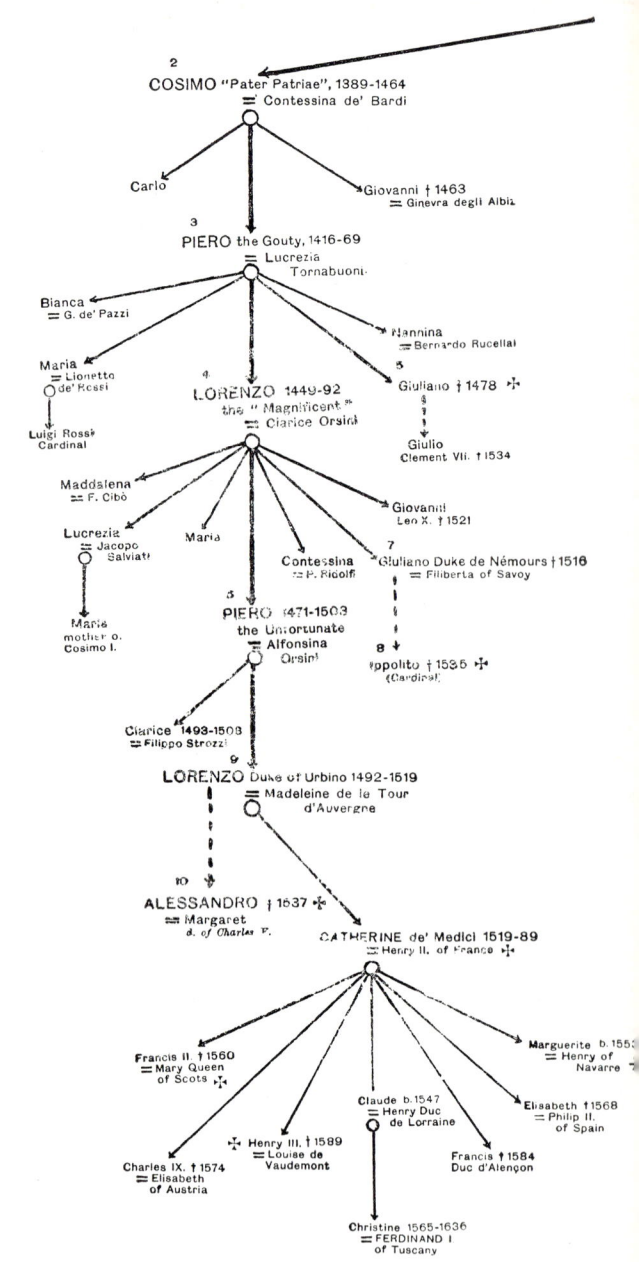

---

2 COSIMO "Pater Patriae", 1389-1464 = Contessina de' Bardi

— Carlo
— Giovanni † 1463 = Ginevra degli Albizi
— **3 PIERO the Gouty, 1416-69** = Lucrezia Tornabuoni

  — Bianca = G. de' Pazzi
  — Maria = Lionetto de' Rossi
    — Luigi Rossi Cardinal
  — Nannina = Bernardo Rucellai
  — **4 LORENZO 1449-92 the "Magnificent"** = Clarice Orsini
  — **5 Giuliano † 1478 ✠**
    — Giulio Clement VII. † 1534

    — Maddalena = F. Cibò
    — Lucrezia = Jacopo Salviati
      — Maria mother o. Cosimo I.
    — Maria
    — Contessina = P. Ridolfi
    — Giovanni Leo X. † 1521
    — **7 Giuliano Duke de Nemours † 1516** = Filiberta of Savoy
    — **6 PIERO 1471-1503 the Unfortunate** = Alfonsina Orsini
      — Clarice 1493-1508 = Filippo Strozzi
      — **9 LORENZO Duke of Urbino 1492-1519** = Madeleine de la Tour d'Auvergne
        — **10 ALESSANDRO † 1537 ✠** = Margaret d. of Charles V.
        — **CATHERINE de' Medici 1519-89** = Henry II. of France ✠
          — Francis II. † 1560 = Mary Queen of Scots ✠
          — Charles IX. † 1574 = Elisabeth of Austria
          — Henry III. † 1589 ✠ = Louise de Vaudemont
          — Claude b. 1547 = Henry Duc de Lorraine
          — Marguerite b. 1553 = Henry of Navarre
          — Elisabeth † 1568 = Philip II. of Spain
          — Francis † 1584 Duc d'Alençon
          — Christine 1565-1636 = FERDINAND I of Tuscany
    — **8 Ippolito † 1535 ✠ (Cardinal)**

of the Medici

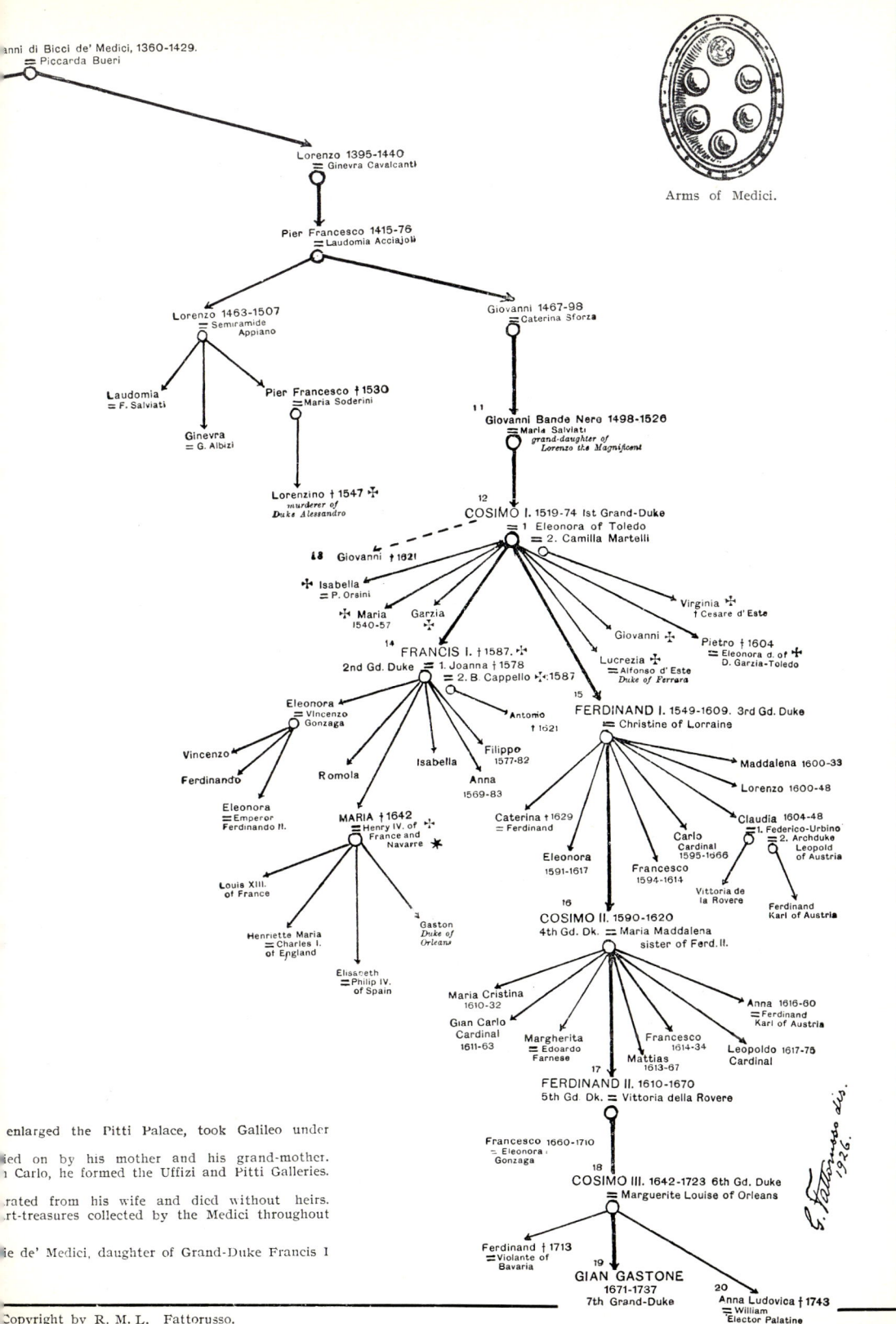

Arms of Medici.

anni di Bicci de' Medici, 1360-1429.
= Piccarda Bueri

Lorenzo 1395-1440
= Ginevra Cavalcanti

Pier Francesco 1415-76
= Laudomia Acciajoli

Lorenzo 1463-1507
= Semiramide Appiano

Giovanni 1467-98
= Caterina Sforza

Laudomia
= F. Salviati

Pier Francesco †1530
= Maria Soderini

Ginevra
= G. Albizi

11
Giovanni Bande Nere 1498-1526
= Maria Salviati
grand-daughter of Lorenzo the Magnificent

Lorenzino †1547 ✠
murderer of Duke Alessandro

12
COSIMO I. 1519-74 1st Grand-Duke
= 1 Eleonora of Toledo
= 2. Camilla Martelli

13 Giovanni †1621

✠ Isabella
= P. Orsini

✠ Maria 1540-57

Garzia ✠

Virginia ✠
† Cesare d' Este

Giovanni ✠

Pietro †1604
= Eleonora d. of ✠
D. Garzia-Toledo

14
FRANCIS I. †1587. ✠
2nd Gd. Duke = 1. Joanna †1578
= 2. B. Cappello ✠ 1587

Lucrezia ✠
= Alfonso d' Este
Duke of Ferrara

15
FERDINAND I. 1549-1609. 3rd Gd. Duke
= Christine of Lorraine

Eleonora
= Vincenzo Gonzaga

Antonio
† 1621

Vincenzo

Filippo 1577-82

Maddalena 1600-33

Ferdinando

Romola

Isabella

Anna 1569-83

Lorenzo 1600-48

Eleonora
= Emperor Ferdinando II.

MARIA †1642
= Henry IV. of ✠
France and Navarre ✱

Caterina †1629
= Ferdinand

Claudia 1604-48
= 1. Federico-Urbino
= 2. Archduke Leopold of Austria

Louis XIII.
of France

Eleonora 1591-1617

Carlo
Cardinal
1595-1666

Henriette Maria
= Charles I.
of England

Gaston
Duke of
Orleans

Francesco
1594-1614

Vittoria de
la Rovere

Ferdinand
Karl of Austria

Elisabeth
= Philip IV.
of Spain

16
COSIMO II. 1590-1620
4th Gd. Dk. = Maria Maddalena
sister of Ferd. II.

Maria Cristina 1610-32

Anna 1616-60
= Ferdinand
Karl of Austria

Gian Carlo
Cardinal
1611-63

Margherita
= Edoardo
Farnese

Francesco
1614-34

Leopoldo 1617-75
Cardinal

Mattias
1613-67

17
FERDINAND II. 1610-1670
5th Gd. Dk. = Vittoria della Rovere

enlarged the Pitti Palace, took Galileo under
ied on by his mother and his grand-mother.
1 Carlo, he formed the Uffizi and Pitti Galleries.
rated from his wife and died without heirs.
rt-treasures collected by the Medici throughout

ie de' Medici, daughter of Grand-Duke Francis I

Copyright by R. M. L. Fattorusso.

Francesco 1660-1710
= Eleonora
Gonzaga

18
COSIMO III. 1642-1723 6th Gd. Duke
= Marguerite Louise of Orleans

Ferdinand †1713
= Violante of
Bavaria

19
GIAN GASTONE
1671-1737
7th Grand-Duke

20
Anna Ludovica †1743
= William
Elector Palatine

— 287B —

FLORENCE — *PITTI PALACE.* *Museo degli Argenti.*

MADONNA AND CHILD and scenes from the life of the Virgin and our Lord. *Silver niello by* POLLAIUOLO?

ROCK CRYSTAL CASKET executed for Pope Clement VII. (Medici).

This is the rarest work in the collection. The casket is lined with silver, thus giving the illusion of relief to the engraving which was executed by the celebrated gem-cutter *Valerio Belli.* There are 24 panels representing stories in the life of Christ. This treasure of art was presented to Francis I. in 1533 upon the marriage of Catherine de' Medici with the king's son afterwards Henry II. The framework is by *Benvenuto Cellini.*

GRAND-DUKE COSIMO II. *Florentine mosaic.*

CRUCIFIXION with six scenes from the life of Christ. *Limoges enamel.*

The head of the grand-duke, the hands, the legs, and lining of the mantle and ermine are in Volterra jasper, the hair in Egyptian flints, the rest of the dress in oriental chalcedony, red jasper, gold and enamel. Through the window is seen the dome of the cathedral and the campanile. The work is ornamented with about three hundred diamonds.

Jasper Cup with a Hercules in gold and encrusted pearls.

Mitre and infulae with miniature embroideries in peacock's feathers representing scenes in the life of our Lord. It belonged to Cardinal Giulio dei Medici.

Lapis lazuli vase formerly the property of the Medici.

Photo ALINARI, BROGI.

ADORATION OF THE SHEPHERDS. By LORENZO DI CREDI.
(detail of the picture on page 262).

FLORENCE — GALLERIA DELL'ACCADEMIA.

A MARRIAGE BETWEEN THE ADIMARI AND RICASOLI FAMILIES. (On the left the Baptistery).
Painting from a cassone of the fifteenth century, used to hold the bride's trousseau.
(See page 298 for the use of the cassone in medieval times).

APPARITION OF THE VIRGIN TO ST. BERNARD.
Painted by ANDREA ORCAGNA (1308-1368).

APPARITION OF THE VIRGIN TO ST. BERNARD.
Painted by FRA BARTOLOMMEO (1475-1517).

"SLAVE." *By* MICHELANGELO.

FIRST CORRIDOR OF THE ACADEMY. In the distance is Michelangelo's "David," transferred here in 1873 from the door of the Palazzo Vecchio. Ranged along the walls are several unfinished statues by Michelangelo and casts of other works by him. Among the latter are those of the two famous *Slaves* (originals in the Louvre) which were intended for the Tomb of Pope Julius II. "They are two marvellous examples of the variations on the human body to which the genius of Michelangelo devoted itself;" writes Professor Hourticq, "two splendid athletic figures, of which the one is straining to break his chains, while the other seems to have given up in desperation: effort and lassitude, action and exhaustion, these are the constant themes of the Florentine master." These "slaves" or "prisoners" are said to be 'symbols of the imprisoned human souls.'

— 289 —   Photo ALINARI, ANDERSON, BROGI.

38a. - WONDERS OF ITALY.

COLOSSAL STATUE OF DAVID. "Il Gigante." *Executed by* MICHELANGELO. A. D. 1501-1503.

This celebrated statue, the first great work in sculpture of Michelangelo, was modelled by the youthful artist in 1501-1503 out of a gigantic block of Carrara marble, which had been abandoned as spoiled. When the David was finished it was decided to place it in front of the Palazzo Vecchio. Accordingly the marble colossus was moved out from the wooden construction (where it was executed) near the Cathedral square, whence it took about forty men four days to drag it to the Piazza della Signoria. As soon as it was set upon its pedestal the chief member of the Signoria came to see it, and after expressing his great admiration for the marvellous work, remarked that the nose seemed to him too large, whereupon Michelangelo gravely mounted on a ladder, chisel in hand, and after pretending to work for a few moments, during which he left fall some of the marble dust which he had taken up in his pocket, turned with a questioning face to the critic, who responded, « Bravo ! Well done ! you have given it life ».

« Michelangelo's David », says the art critic Springer; « is vastly superior to all ancient and modern statues whatever. The boldness and assured touch of the great sculptor certainly awake our admiring astonishment. Not only the subject was prescribed to him, but also its size and proportions, added to which he was confined to the narrowest limits for the development of the attitude and motion. Yet this constraint is not perceptible, and the history of the statue could by no means be divined from its appearance. Outwardly the demeanour of the young hero is composed and quiet; but each limb is animated by a common impulse from within, and the whole body is braced up for one action. The raised left arm holds the sling in readiness, the right hand hanging at his side holds the handle of the sling, next instant he will make the attack ».

Photo ALINARI, ANDERSON BROGI.

FLORENCE — *PALAZZO del PODESTÀ. BARGELLO. National-Museum.*

DAVID (*unfinished*) (1529). By MICHELANGELO.

The Bargello contains several youthful works of Michelangelo. The Faun's Mask given here was chiselled by him when a boy of 15, while studying in the gardens of Lorenzo de' Medici. The work attracted the notice of Lorenzo, who took Michelangelo into his house and treated him as one of the family.

FAUN'S MASK. By MICHELANGELO.

PALAZZO DEL PODESTÀ OR BARGELLO.

BRUTUS. By MICHELANGELO A. D. 1538.

The bust of Brutus, said to have been modelled from an ancient intaglio, is one of the finest specimens of Michelangelo's creative genius.

This, like so many other of the master's works, is unfinished, but the fine-toothed marks of the chisel in the style peculiar to him are very visible. " We must regard this Brutus," writes Symonds, " as an ideal portrait, intended to express the artist's conception of resolution and uncompromising energy in a patriot eager to sacrifice personal feelings and to dare the utmost for his country's welfare. Nothing can exceed the spirit with which a violent temperament, habitually repressed, but capable of leaping forth like sudden lightning; has been rendered."

MADONNA WITH THE BOOK (*unfinished*). By MICHELANGELO (1503).

In *Michelangelo's* tondo of the " Madonna with the Book," left in a state of incompleteness, we have the beauty and tender pathos which distinguish some of the master's early sculptures.

BACCHUS (ca. 1496). By MICHELANGELO.

— 291 —

Photo ALINARI, ANDERSON, BROGI.

83. - WONDERS OF ITALY.

FLORENCE — PALAZZO del PODESTÀ. BARGELLO. National Museum.

CARVED STONE ESCUTCHEONS OF FORMER « PODESTAS ».

WROUGHT IRON LANTERN.

The *Palazzo del Podestà* is a remarkable specimen of an urban fortress of the 13th century. No other building of Florence possesses a more solemn interest than this palace, commonly known as the Bargello. Its construction was begun in 1255 as the residence of the Capitano del Popolo and later the Podestà, or chief magistrate of the city, who according to the Statutes was always a foreigner of noble birth.

During the 14th century the building was repeatedly damaged by fire and riots; within its walls some of the most violent scenes in Florentine history were enacted. In 1574, the palace was converted into a prison and place of execution for criminals, and assigned to the head of police, the Bargello, from whom it derives its usual present name. Terrible have been the scenes which its walls have witnessed. The dark vaulted hall (now the armoury) giving access to the courtyard, was the torture chamber, here was an *oubliette* or pit, out of which, some years ago, have been taken several basketfuls of human bones. The scaffold was near the well in the centre of the courtyard, here, during stormy days, many notable Florentine patriots have been beheaded. The scaffold and all the instruments of torture were burned in 1782.

COURTYARD OF THE PALAZZO DEL PODESTÀ, BARGELLO.
The interior of the palace is now fitted up as a museum of plastic and minor arts : *Museo Nazionale.*

Photo ALINARI, ANDERSON, BROGI

FLORENCE — *PALAZZO del PODESTÀ. BARGELLO. National Museum.*

VIEW OF THE COURTYARD AND THE GRAND STAIRCASE
leading to the *Salone di Donatello*.

ARMOUR OF EMPEROR CHARLES V.
Milanese work. 16th cent.

TABLEAU IN THE COURTYARD. Costumes of Dante's times. (*Photo Alinari*).

From 1857 to 1865 the building was again admirably restored to its present condition and fitted up as a museum of arts and crafts. The picturesque courtyard, partly surrounded by open arcades and richly adorned with coats-of-arms in carved stone-work of former *podestas*, is an eloquent picture of the city and age of Dante. A noble processional staircase leads from this courtyard to the upper loggia and halls, which are now filled with an array of artistic treasures including the best examples of Renaissance plastic

This magnificent collection comprises sculptures in marble and in bronze, some executed by the most notable Florentine artists; a series of Della Robbia ware from suppressed churches and monasteries; and a valuable assortment of ivories, enamels, medals, seals, tapestries, majolicas, etc., all deserving the closest attention.

In the chapel, on the first floor (p. 298) is to be seen a fresco portrait of Dante attributed to Giotto (*An exterior view of the building is given on page* 304).

THE ARMOURY. *Formerly the torture-chamber.*

Photo ALINARI, ANDERSON, BROGI.

FLORENCE — BARGELLO. National Museum.

Allegory of ARCHITECTURE.
By GIAMBOLOGNA.

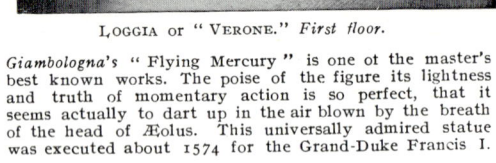

LOGGIA or "VERONE." First floor.

Giambologna's "Flying Mercury" is one of the master's best known works. The poise of the figure its lightness and truth of momentary action is so perfect, that it seems actually to dart up in the air blown by the breath of the head of Æolus. This universally admired statue was executed about 1574 for the Grand-Duke Francis I.

MERCURY. Bronze.
by GIAMBOLOGNA.

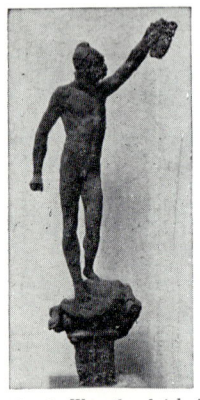

PERSEUS. *Was the sketch for the bronze statue* (p. 198).

BUST OF COSIMO I. DE' MEDICI.
Bronze by BENVENUTO CELLINI.

HERCULES AND ANTÆUS.
Small bronze by A. POLLAIUOLO.

CRUCIFIXION. *Bronze relief.*
By DONATELLO.

CRUCIFIXION. *Bronze relief.*
By BERTOLDO.

THE "MARZOCCO."
By DONATELLO.

Formerly in the Piazza now replaced by a bronze copy.

— 294 —

Photo ALINARI, ANDERSON, BROGI.

BARGELLO — *Salone di Donatello.*

The great Hall on the first floor of the Bargello is fitted up as a museum of the works of Donatello. Many of his most important sculptures are here collected; among these are the St. George, the two St. Johns and the bronze David given here.

The " David " was the first nude statue executed since classic times. It was made for Cosimo the Elder and originally placed in the courtyard of the Medici Palace. The boy-shepherd, a delightful expression of youth and vigour, is here represented standing on a circular garland, with one foot on the head of Goliath, on whose helmet are reliefs of cupids drawing a chariot.

This wasted figure of the Baptist, with head bent in study of the scroll he holds, displays wonderful skill and knowledge of anatomy. The effect of long fasting is given by the pinched nostrils, the large eyes, the half open lips and the contracted brow. As patron of Florence the Baptist was more frequently represented in Tuscan art than any other saint.

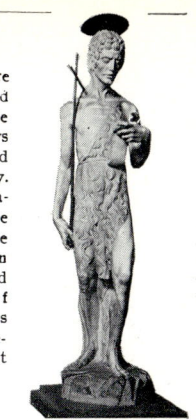

Verrocchio's ' David ' in contrast to Donatello's version, is full of life and movement. " The stripling who left his few sheep in the wilderness, " writes Hyett, " and faced single-handed the giant from whom an army had fled, has never been more truthfully imagined. "

ST. JOHN THE BAPTIST *By* DONATELLO.

ST. GEORGE. *Marble* by DONATELLO. A. D. 1416.

ST. JOHN THE BAPTIST. *By* DONATELLO.

DAVID. *Bronze* by DONATELLO. A. D. 1430.

DAVID. *Bronze* by VERROCCHIO. A. D. 1476.

Donatello's " St. George, " brought hither from Or San Michele (page 230), is generally considered to be the masterpiece of the artist. The statue was made in 1416 for the Guild of Armourers and placed in the tabernacle on the north side of the church, but in 1866 was removed to the Bargello and replaced by a bronze copy.

The brave and bold soldier saint stands with erect head and piercing glance, as if about to turn upon a deadly enemy. " Every line, " writes Perkins, " is indicative of the cool resolve which ensures triumph ; every portion of his body, even to the slightly compressed fingers of the right hand full of a dominant thought. " The relief beneath the statue (original still at Or San Michele), representing St. George and the Dragon, with the exposed princess looking on in the background, is one of the most exquisite and poetic of the master's sculptures, a triumph of technical skill in the *stacciato* or flat relief.

Donatello's bust of « Niccolò da Uzzano » deserves notice as the first essay in Renaissance portraiture. Anatomically the work is a masterpiece, executed with marvellous care and attention to details. The modelling of the skull and the neck, the receding forehead, the cavernous eye sockets and the peaked nose, the projecting jaw and the peculiar form of the ear, the wrinkled skin, the whole face is full of life and truth. It is a remarkable work and one of the most lifelike and dramatic portraits in existence.

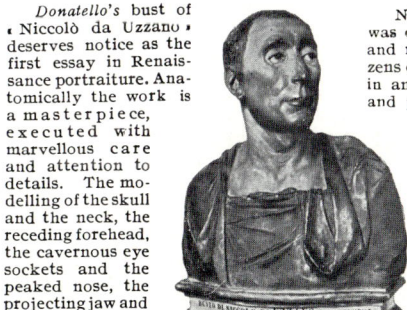

Niccolò da Uzzano was one of the wisest and most upright citizens of Florence, living in an age of intrigues and petty rivalries, when the Medici and the Albizi were struggling for power. A defender of the liberty of his country, he took a large and sane view of every situation; the soundness of his judgment gave him a vast influence, which he consistently used in checking party passions and in opposing unjust wars. He died in his palace (Via de' Bardi) in 1433.

THE YOUTHFUL ST. JOHN. *Relief by* DONATELLO.

BUST OF NICCOLÒ DA UZZANO. *Coloured terracotta by* DONATELLO.

MADONNA AND CHILD. *By* MICHELOZZO (1396-1472).

— 295 —

Photo ALINARI, ANDERSON, BROGI.

FLORENCE — *PALAZZO del PODESTÀ. BARGELLO.*

CRUSADER. *Small bronze of the fifteenth century.*

KNIVES AND FORKS. 16th cent.

HELMET AND SHIELD. *Formerly belonging to Francis I. of France.*

TWO IVORY COMBS. *Fifteenth century.*

Forks came into use during the Renaissance, — down to the 15th century people still ate with their fingers out of a common dish. Before the meal everyone would wash his hands at the table and openly, so as to give assurance of his cleanliness to the other guests. At the end of the meals, the washing again took place.

Being articles of luxury, forks were often made of precious metals and kept in cases, each person carrying his own outfit.

IRON KEYS of the 8th—17th cent

CHIMNEY-PIECE. *Fifteenth century.*

PAX. Niello of the 15th cent.

Credences were primarily used for testing food. For fear of being poisoned, high personages caused the eatables and beverages which were going to be served them, to be tested in their presence. This testing, which enabled them to have confidence (in latin, *credere*) took place on a special piece of furniture: a *credence* table.

CREDENCE TABLE AND DRESSER.

Photo ALINARI, ANDERSON, BROGI.

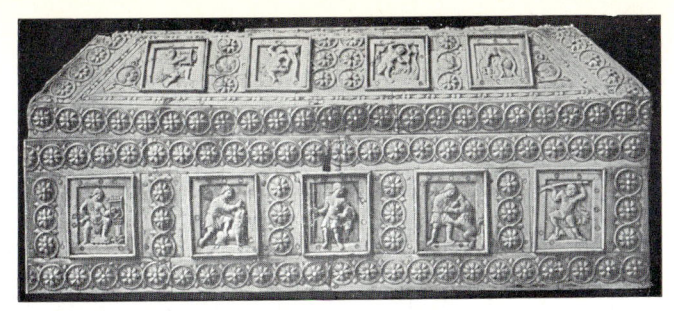

FLORENCE — *PALAZZO del PODESTÀ. BARGELLO.* National Museum (First floor).

IVORY CASKET, with reliefs representing the Labours of Hercules.
Italo-Byzantine work of the 9th cent.

CRUCIFIXION.
French ivory of the 9th cent.

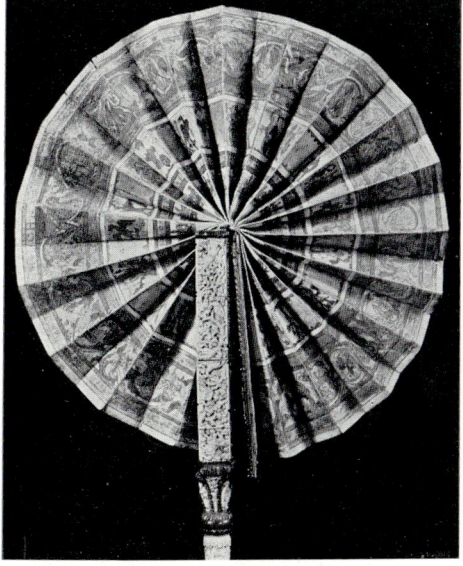

FLABELLUM from Tournus, 9th cent.

This beautiful fan made of richly carved ivory and illuminated parchment is probably the rarest piece in the museum. Fans were carried before the Pope on state occasions; they were of delicate colours, and sometimes of costly and splendid materials. In ancient times they were used to chase flies from the altar during mass.

ALLEGORY OF THE TRIUMPH OF LOVE. Ivory.
Italian Art of the 15th cent.

IVORY SADDLE. *Italian Art, circa 1400.*

IVORY CHESS-BOARD. *French Art, 15th cent.*

Photo ALINARI, ANDERSON BROGI.

FLORENCE — PALAZZO del PODESTÀ. BARGELLO. National Museum (First floor).

DUKE FRANCIS I. DE' MEDICI.
Wax portrait by CELLINI.

ENTRANCE TO THE CHAPEL OF THE PODESTÀ
containing frescoes attributed to GIOTTO.

PORTRAIT OF DANTE (1265-1321).
Painted about 1300 *by* GIOTTO.

The ancient chapel of the *Podestà*, at one end of the audience chamber, is decorated with (now ruined) Giottesque frescoes from the history and legends of Mary Magdalene, St. Nicholas of Bari, the Last Judgment, etc. In the fresco on the wall facing the entrance representing Paradise, is the famous portrait of Dante ascribed to Giotto. The great Poet stands there full of dignity wearing the graceful falling cap of his times. In a glass case below is a mask of Dante's face made at Ravenna in 1321.

A CAVALCADE ON ST. JOHN'S DAY NEAR THE BAPTISTERY. *Painted Cassone or Wedding Chest. Florentine work of the 15th century.*

Throughout those war-like times of the Middle Ages, the chest, being easily moveable, played a preponderant part amongst the household furniture. It was taken on campaigns and crusades and appeared under tents as well as in rooms, where it was put alongside beds to be used as footsteps or placed against the wall and used as a bench.

They were given as wedding presents to newly married couples who were setting up house and, on that account, acquired almost a symbolical character when they were solemnly carried through the streets to the new abode. A luxurious ornamentation was the outcome of this practice and, from the 14th century, this luxury became such that sumptuary laws were often necessary to control their richness.

MADONNA AND CHILD. *Marble relief.*
By DESIDERIO DA SETTIGNANO (1428-1464).

HOLY FAMILY.
Coloured terracotta reliefs of the fifteenth century (second floor).

MADONNA AND CHILD.

— 298 —

Photo ALINARI, ANDERSON, BROGI.

FLORENCE — *PALAZZO del PODESTÀ. BARGELLO. National Museum (Second floor)*.

BUST OF A BOY (Cast).
From the original by DONATELLO.

SANTA CECILIA (Cast).
From the original by DONATELLO.

MADONNA AND CHILD.
Marble relief by VERROCCHIO.

Donatello (1383-1466), was undoubtedly the greatest Florentine sculptor before Michelangelo. His works were exceedingly numerous; he was gifted with a facility of production as astonishing in its degree as was the greatness of his genius, and he never refused the humblest commission. One of his rare faculties was that of calculating effect in proportion to distance, and of judging the amount of finish necessary for a figure destined to be seen at a certain height. He was an innovator in every sense: to him is indubitably due the invention of that peculiar and most beautiful method of low or flat relief (*stiacciato*) which had no prototype in antiquity.

THE VIRGIN ADORING. *Marble relief by* ANTONIO ROSSELLINO (1427-1479).

MADONNA AND CHILD.
Marble relief by MINO DA FIESOLE (1431-1484).

Verrocchio (1435-1488), the pupil of Donatello, began his career as a goldsmith, but he gradually abandoned his minuter labours in the preciou metals for the wider field of sculpture. He was also a painter, and, above all, a great draughtsman. His reputation was greatly enhanced by his having been the master of Lorenzo di Credi, Perugino, and Leonardo da Vinci.

THE DEATH IN CHILD-BED OF FRANCESCA PITTI TORNABUONI. *Marble relief by* VERROCCHIO. A. D. 1477.

This relief was part of a monument made for a church at Rome. « Around the couch upon which the dying woman sits, supported by her attendants, stand her relatives and friends, one of whom tears her hair in an agony of grief, while another, in striking contrast, crouches in silent despair upon the ground, her head enveloped in the folds of a thick mantle ». *Perkins*.

Photo ALINARI, ANDERSON, BROGI.

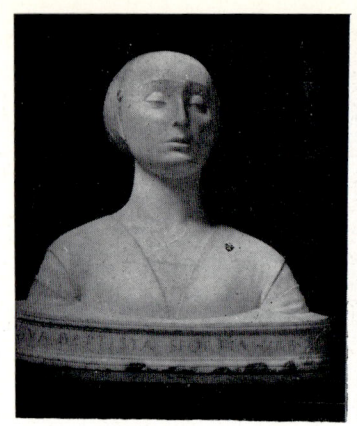

FLORENCE — *PALAZZO del PODESTÀ. BARGELLO. National Museum (Second floor).*

BATTISTA SFORZA.
Marble by F. LAURANA. († 1490).

BUST OF A YOUNG WOMAN.
Marble by VERROCCHIO.

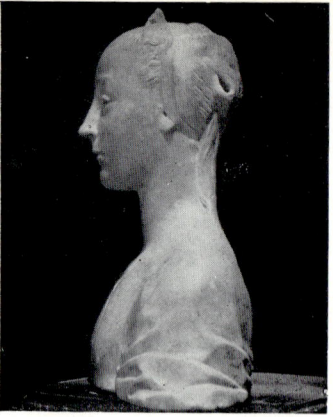

BUST OF A YOUNG WOMAN. *Marble by* DESIDERIO DA SETTIGNANO. (1428-1464).

MADONNA AND CHILD.
Terracotta relief by VERROCCHIO.

MADONNA AND CHILD.
By AGOSTINO DI DUCCIO (1418-1481).
Coloured terracotta.

FAITH. *Marble relief.*
By MATTEO CIVITALI.
(*Formerly in San Michele at Lucca*).

HALL OF THE MAJOLICAS
and of the DELLA ROBBIA WARE.

The Bargello possesses numerous admirable coloured terracotta reliefs of the Virgin and Child, executed as aids to private devotion. The colouring of sculpture was freely and extensively practised by Florentine artists of the 15th and 16th centuries, and almost every work in terracotta or gesso was so embellished, — the natural surface of terracotta being deemed insufferably crude and unseemly.

FRANCESCO SASSETTI.
Marble by ANTONIO ROSSELLINO.

Photo ALINARI, ANDERSON, BROGI.

FLORENCE — PALAZZO del PODESTÀ. BARGELLO. National Museum (Second floor).

PIERO DE' MEDICI. The Unfortunate.
(Son of Lorenzo the Magnificent).
By VERROCCHIO.

PIERO DE' MEDICI. The Gouty.
(Father of Lorenzo the Magnificent).
Marble by MINO DA FIESOLE (1453).

GIULIANO DE' MEDICI (?) († 1478).
(Father of Pope Clement VII.).
Terracotta by A. POLLAIUOLO (ca. 1470).

Among the numerous busts of noted personages to be found in the Bargello, that of Charles VIII. of France is of high historical value.

In the year 1494, at the request of Lodovico Sforza of Milan (p. 73), Charles with a large army entered Italy and passing rapidly through Lombardy advanced upon Tuscany by way of Sarzana and Pietrasanta. Here, however, the frontier fortresses stopped his march: further progress might have been impossible had Piero de' Medici («the Unfortunate») possessed more courage. But he had the incredible folly to deliver up the forts to the French, who lost no time in taking possession of them. The Florentine were furious; the Medicean palace was pillaged; Piero and his family fled to Venice; the rule of the Medici, so artfully built up, was overthrown in a day.

On November 17 Charles clad in black velvet with mantle of gold brocade and splendidly mounted entered Florence in the style of a victorious monarch entering a conquered city. By his side was the Cardinal Giuliano della Rovere (afterwards Julius II.), the Cardinal of St. Malo and a few marshals. They were followed by the royal body-guard composed of the flower of the French aristocracy with splendid dress and equipments; then came the fierce Swiss infantry, the light Guascon skirmishers, the gigantic Scottish archers, — in all about 12.000 men. The streets of Florence were draped with tapestries and gay flags, and the people shouted « Viva Francia ». The procession marched over the Ponte Vecchio, wound across the Piazza della Signoria and then round the Duomo, halting before its great door. Here the King descended, entered the cathedral and was met by the Signory. After joining in prayers with their royal guest they escorted him to the Medici Palace where he took up his abode, and the soldiers quartered about the city. That night and the next day the city was a blaze of illuminations, the intervening day was spent in feasting and pageantry. But when Charles' pretensions were known, there were signs of an outburst of popular fury, and he had to modify his proposals. At last the monarch summoned the Signory before him and ordered his secretary to read his *ultimatum*, and then an ever memorable scene occurred. The members of the Signory deemed the terms of the treaty insulting to the Republic and refused to accede to the King's demands. Whereupon he flew into a rage and swore that if the treaty he had dictated were not forthwith signed he would order « his trumpets to be sounded »

BUST OF CHARLES VIII.
of France.
Terracotta of the 15th cent.

meaning he would call out his troops and sack the city. At this Piero Capponi, one of the Florentine commissioners, sprang to his feet, snatched the paper on which the conditions were written from the hand of the secretary and tore it in the King's face, exclaiming. « If you sound your trumpets we will ring our bells ». The King reflected: an incident which occurred after his entry had taught him that his men had no chance in a city which at the first stroke of the alarm bell could be converted into a menacing stronghold, and an army destroyed in its narrow streets; he had the good sense to laugh the matter off, gave in and Florence was saved. A less humiliating treaty was drawn up and its terms solemnly sworn to in the Duomo on Nov. 25th 1494. A few days after the French departed for Rome (carrying off many of the valuables that Cosimo and Lorenzo de' Medici had gathered in their palace).

Charles' invasion of Italy formed a turning point in the history of Italy, as it opened her gates to foreign despotism.

PIETRO MELLINI. *Marble*
by BENEDETTO DA MAIANO. (1442-97).

GIOVANNI DELLE BANDE NERE.
Marble by F. DA SANGALLO. (1494-1576).

Photo ALINARI, ANDERSON, BROGI.

FLORENCE. — *PALAZZO del PODESTÀ. BARGELLO. National Museum (Second floor).*

MADONNA AND CHILD. *Relief by* LUCA DELLA ROBBIA. (1400-82).

MADONNA AND CHILD AND ANGELS. *By* LUCA DELLA ROBBIA.

MADONNA AND CHILD. *Relief by* LUCA DELLA ROBBIA.

Luca della Robbia (1400-1482), commenced as a goldsmith but soon devoted himself to sculpture in bronze and marble. This great artist, however, is better known for his labours in a different and peculiar direction. He was undoubtedly the original founder or inventor of what may, in a certain sense, be termed a new art—that of enamelled sculpture; in other words, he first put into practice the method of applying a vitrified enamel glaze, similar to that of the Majolica ware, to works in relief on a large scale. This mode of art he greatly developed in his lifetime, and left as a specialty to his descendants, who, for nearly a century carried on the fabrication on an extensive scale. The process was kept secret by the family, and its history has died with them.

His principal assistant was his nephew *Andrea* (1435-1525), himself a great artist. Andrea's sons, *Giovanni, Girolamo*, and *Luca* continued the fabrication in the early part of the 16th century.

Luca was not the discoverer of the peculiar enamel glaze which he applied to his works. Enamel glaze was known and applied to pottery many centuries before Luca's time. His real discovery was the having succeeded in applying the enamel covering to the great surfaces of massive terracotta sculptures; a process involving an infinity of conflicting technical difficulties impossible to be here described in detail; and to have reconciled and overcome them so perfectly as he speedily did, will ever remain a marvel of skill.

The enamel first used by Luca upon figures was pure white, and that upon his backgrounds and accessories blue and green. But the introduction of other tints, though sparingly used at first, very soon followed, and afterwards a full system of chromatic decoration was introduced which little by little degraded the originally pure marble-like surface to the level of waxworks.

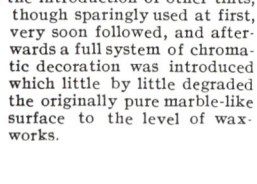

ADORING MADONNA. *Coloured terracotta relief by* ANDREA DELLA ROBBIA. (1435-1525).

MADONNA AND CHILD. *By* LUCA DELLA ROBBIA.

THE ANNUNCIATION. *By* GIOVANNI DELLA ROBBIA. (1469-1529).

— 302 —

FLORENCE — *PALAZZO del PODESTÀ. BARGELLO. National Museum (Second floor).*

ISOTTA DA RIMINI.

SIGISMONDO MALATESTA, Tyrant of Rimini

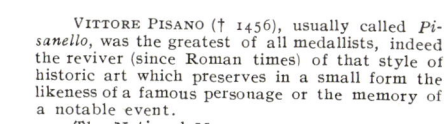

Medals by VITTORE PISANO.

NICCOLÒ PICCININO.

VITTORINO DA FELTRE.

VITTORE PISANO († 1456), usually called *Pisanello*, was the greatest of all medallists, indeed the reviver (since Roman times) of that style of historic art which preserves in a small form the likeness of a famous personage or the memory of a notable event.

The National Museum possesses a very rich collection of medals from all parts of Italy, besides a very interesting set of dies and punches attributed to Benvenuto Cellini, and other celebrated artists. "Where indeed," writes Perkins " can we find more delicate shades, of modelling, greater truth to nature more exquisite taste in the use of costume and arrangement of drapery than in the profile heads upon Pisanello's medal's, or bolder foreshortening than in those groups of mounted cavaliers with which he adorned their reverses?"

GIULIANO DE' MEDICI. The Pazzi Conspiracy.

BRONZE MEDALS BY BERTOLDO, struck in memory of the tragedy.

The "choir" and the high altar of the cathedral was at that time surrounded by a wooden screen (shown in the medal) designed by Ghiberti. See p. 211.

LORENZO DE' MEDICI. The Pazzi Conspiracy.

CHIMNEY-PIECE *from the Palazzo Rosselli del Turco.*
By BENEDETTO DA ROVEZZANO.

The largest proportion of the medals in the National Museum are by *Pisanello* and his school. These miniature works of art are highly interesting on account of the portraits which they exhibit, and the events they commemorate. The finest medals are those of Vittorino da Feltre, who spent his life in teaching youths; Sigismondo Malatesta, the tyrant of Rimini, and Isotta, his wife; Niccolò Piccinino, the famous condottiere; Savonarola, Filippo Visconti of Milan, Lodovico Gonzaga of Mantua, Giovanni delle Bande Nere, Duke Cosimo I. with the Golden Fleece, Eleonora of Toledo; and many famous Italian beauties, such as Lucrezia Tornabuoni, Costanza Rucellai, Leonora Altoviti, Maria Poliziano....

THE YOUNG BACCHUS.
Marble by SANSOVINO.

Photo ALINARI, ANDERSON, BROGI.

FLORENCE — THE PALACES.

The character of Tuscan architecture is that of simple grandeur; imposing in its aspect, its principle is one of power and security. The ancient dwellings of the nobles at least, were frowning fortresses, with deep massy walls in which, at a great height, a few windows were sparingly introduced. Every patrician house had a tower (there were about 150 towers in Florence, a great many of them may still be seen in the old part of the city); the possession of a tower was the great distinction of the nobles. The tower served as a castle to which the household could retire in case of danger or siege, and breathe the free air above the reach of the lances and staves of the assailants, and from which they could fling down stones and heavy missiles on them. These towers, which rose in grandeur above the city walls, were formidable weapons of war in medieval times, when cities were divided by factions; their appearance must indeed have been singularly striking and grand. But in order to lessen the temptation to civil broils a law was made obliging all towers to be reduced to the height of fifty braccia (about 90 ft.). To day only S. Gimignano pag. 352 gives an idea, on a reduced scale, of a city of towers.

PALAZZO DEL PODESTÀ (BARGELLO).
Begun in 1255 for the residence of the Captain of the People.

PALAZZO FERRONI.
Formerly Spini. Erected about 1400.

ARTE DELLA LANA.
Old guild house of the wool-weavers. Erected in 1308. Restored in 1905.

THE HOUSE AND TOWER OF DANTE. Here was born the Divine Poet Alighieri in the year 1265. In a neighbouring street lived Dante's first love, Beatrice Portinari.

PALAZZO DAVANZATI.
14th century. Refitted with antique furniture.

Lanterns and torch holders of wrought iron which still adorn the lower stories of Florentine palaces, were a distinguishing mark of the dwellings of the noble Florentines. The two very beautiful specimen given here were made by *Niccolò Grosso* (1455-1509) who was the most renowned metal-worker of the 15th century. His specialty was *fanali*, or lanterns, handirons, torch-holders and rings knockers, etc. Niccolò was a man of humorous independence and bluntness, and refused money that was not earned honourably. «First come, first served», was his rule, whether the 'comer were a prince or a peasant. But in making contracts he always insisted that a portion of the sum agreed upon should be paid before the work was begun and the whole when it was completed, and no credit allowed. This practice of demanding *caparra*, or earnest-money, earned for him the nickname of «Il Caparra».

Iron Gothic Lantern.
By NICCOLÒ GROSSO
(Palazzo Guadagni).

Arms of the Silk-weavers' Guild.
School of Donatello.
(Palazzo Arte della Seta).

Iron Ring and Torch Holder. By N. GROSSO.
(Palazzo Strozzi).

Photo ALINARI, ANDERSON, BROGI.

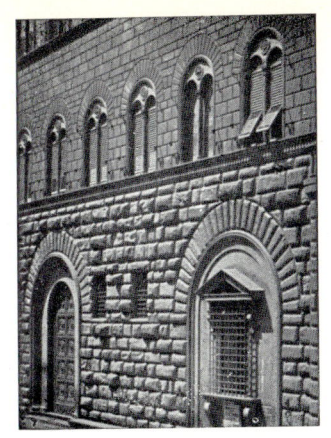

FLORENCE — THE PALACES.

PALAZZO MEDICI-RICCARDI.
Detail of the Façade.

One of the most difficult tasks which the Florentine builders of the Renaissance had to cope with was the transforming the old fortress type of dwelling occasioned by necessity, into a noble city palace. This work was done by Filippo Brunelleschi, who, after a close study of the antiquities of Rome evolved something entirely new and original. The Medici-Riccardi, the Strozzi, the Rucellai, are typical of the new style originated by him in the Pitti palace (p. 275) and developed by his successors. These palaces consist of massive buildings surrounding a square courtyard with arcades all round, the exterior still preserves the character of a medieval fortress, while the decoration of the interiories essentially classic. There is an air of grandeur and stateliness about these palaces that is found nowhere else, and their artistic charm consists in the simplicity of proportions, the just relation in the height of the stories, and the tasteful adjustment of the windows in the vast surface of the façades. The architecture though wanting in elegance and variety is highly impressive from its massiveness. The use of huge, dark grey stones gives an effect of rugged strength; this ruggedness, however, was somewhat softened in the Medici and other more recent palaces, where the roughly hewn blocks,—*rustica* work—is limited to the lower stories, but in the successive ones recedes in gradations.

THE PALAZZO STROZZI.
Begun in 1489 by BENEDETTO DA MAIANO.
Completed 1536.

COURT OF THE MEDICI PALACE. By MICHELOZZO.

COURT OF THE STROZZI PALACE.

THE PALAZZO GUADAGNI.
Erected by CRONACA (1506).
(*Early Renaissance*).

THE PALAZZO RUCELLAI.
By BERNARDO ROSSELLINO and
LEON BATTISTA ALBERTI (1460).

THE PALAZZO BUTURLIN.
Designed by DOMENICO
DI BACCIO D'AGNOLO.

Photo ALINARI, ANDERSON, BROGI.

FLORENCE — PALAZZO MEDICI (Riccardi).

THE GALLERY. *Ceiling fresco by* LUCA GIORDANO (1684).

PALAZZO MEDICI-RICCARDI. *By* MICHELOZZO. (15th cent.).

The *Palazzo Medici*, sometimes called *Riccardi* after its later owners, was the original home of the great Medici family who occupied it for a hundred years. This noble building, a model of Renaissance architecture, was erected by order of Cosimo the Elder, about 1444-52 by the architect MICHELOZZO. A world of interest gathers round this palace, from the many important events with which it is associated. Here Lorenzo the Magnificent maintained his brilliant establishment; here the future Pope Leo X. was brought up; here Catherine de' Medici was born and lived as a girl; and here have been entertained emperors, popes, kings, and most of the distinguished men of the 15th and 16th centuries.

Of all the art treasures which the palace formerly contained, one alone now remains: the private chapel, decorated in 1469 by BENOZZO GOZZOLI, for Piero de' Medici, surnamed the Gouty.

The Chapel is gorgeously decorated with frescoes by B. Gozzoli, pupil of Fra Angelico. These pictures painted in 1469 are considered the masterpiece of the artist, who painted them by means of lamplight as there was originally no window to the chapel.

The three walls of the tiny chapel are occupied by one magnificent picture illustrating the second episode connected with the Nativity: the *Journey of the Three Kings to Bethlehem*, which is represented as a pompous medieval processional pageant, with knights, squires, and pages in sumptuous array, dogs and hunting leopards. The stately retinue moving from a castle-crowned hill-top (Vincigliata, near Fiesole), winds its way in regal pomp through delightful woodland scenery to Bethlehem.

The whole work is a pictorial version of an historical event which, through the instrumentality of the Medici, took place in Florence thirty years earlier: the great Episcopal Council of 1439, which met for the purpose of uniting the Eastern and Western branches of the Christian Church. The Council (which failed in its purpose), was attended by the Pope Eugenius IV., the Emperor of the East, the Patriarch of Constantinople, and a vast concourse of nobles, church dignitaries, and Greek scholars, all hospitably entertained by Cosimo *Pater Patriae*. In 1439 Gozzoli was only twenty, but, no doubt, the young artist retained a deep impression of the splendid processions and the gorgeous costumes he saw at the functions which took place in the summer of that year, and he has reproduced in this picture persons, dresses, and customs of which

THE JOURNEY OF THE MAGI. *Fresco by* BENOZZO GOZZOLI (Chapel of the Palace).

LORENZO THE "MAGNIFICENT."

Photo ALINARI, ANDERSON, BROGI.

FLORENCE — *PALAZZO MEDICI (Riccardi)*.

FRESCO ON THE LEFT OF THE ALTAR.    INTERIOR OF THE CHAPEL.    FRESCO ON THE RIGHT OF THE ALTAR.

we should otherwise have but little idea. For the Eldest King Benozzo chose the Patriarch of Constantinople, Joseph, who died in Florence and is buried in S. Maria Novella; he is the old man on a mule, of which half has been cut to make a new door in the chapel. The second or Middle-aged King is a portrait of John Paleologus, Emperor of the East. The Youthful King is none other than the young heir of the Medici family: Lorenzo, wearing a crown. Behind him, come various members of the family leading a gathering of all the most learned men of the time. In the front line is Cosimo *Pater Patriae*, in an embroidered coat, mounted on a white horse with trappings adorned with the Medici arms; on his right, his brother Lorenzo,

John Paleologue.    Patriarche Joseph   Castruccio.

THE JOURNEY OF THE THREE KINGS. *Fresco by* BENOZZO GOZZOLI (Chapel of the Palace).

mounted on a quiet mule; on the extreme left of the picture, is Piero (the Gouty), bare-headed; and next to him, his second son, Giuliano, on a white horse, preceded by a negro with a bow. The throng behind comprises Florentine and Greek scholars, the latter distinguished by their beards. Amidst the crowd Benozzo has portrayed himself, with his name plainly inscribed on his red cap.

Over the altar, where the window now is, there was originally a picture of the Nativity by Fra Filippo Lippi. On the walls on either side of the altar, Gozzoli painted the world on that night of the Nativity of Christ referred to in the picture which was over the altar. The scenes are laid amidst delicious landscapes of roses and pomegranates, peopled with groups of most exquisite and most sympathetic angels flying, standing or kneeling in adoration, and singing their song of « Glory to the God in the highest, and on earth peace ».

Photo ALINARI, ANDERSON, BROGI.

FLORENCE — MINOR MUSEUMS.

THE VIRGIN MARY. *Painted terracotta.*
Sienese art, 15th century.

ENTRANCE HALL. Museo Bardini.
Gothic architecture.

CHIMNEY-PIECE with the arms
of the Este family. *15th cent.*

The *Museo Bardini*, contains several important sculptures of the 14th-17th centuries, valuable tapestries, furniture, etc.

The *Casa Buonarroti*, which once belonged to Michelangelo and was bequeathed by his family to the city, is one of the most interesting dwellings in Florence. The rooms are decorated with scenes and allegories of the great master's life, and contain a collection of memorials of Michelangelo including manuscripts, drawings, architectural sketches, models, and the two reliefs given here. These works, executed when he frequented the house and garden of Lorenzo the Magnificent, are wonderfully modelled. In the *Battle of the Centaurs* Michelangelo's early tendency toward bold movements and the representation of vehement passion is very evident.

BATTLE OF THE CENTAURS. (Unfinished).

MADONNA ON THE STEPS.

Marble reliefs by MICHELANGELO *in the* Casa Buonarroti (*Michelangelo's Museum*).

VIEW OF THE VILLA STIBBERT.

GREAT HALL OF THE MUSEO STIBBERT.

Formerly the property of Mr. Frederick Stibbert, *an Englishman.*

The *Museo Stibbert* contains one of the most remarkable exhibits of armour in existence. The collection, recently reorganized by Prof. A. Lensi, includes numerous valuable and curious specimen of European, Oriental, and Japanese weapons and armour representing different periods of history; and many bronzes, majolicas, textiles, costumes, artistic furniture and pictures.

FLORENCE — VIEWS OF THE CITY.

THE « SCOPPIO DEL CARRO » or Explosion of the Car.

THE LOGGIA DEL BIGALLO.
A Gothic building erected in 1353, for the exhibition of foundlings to the charitable public (opposite the Baptistery).

This is a medieval ceremony still performed in Florence in front of the Duomo on Holy Saturday in presence of a large concourse of people from all parts of the world. As midday strikes and the choir in the cathedral chants the *Gloria in Excelsis*, the *Colombina*, or dove—a mechanical device fitted with a slow fuse—is lighted by the Archbishop upon the high altar and despatched along a wire to the ancient car shown in our illustration and which is stationed outside the church. The car is richly adorned with fireworks and at the contact of the Colombina these are ignited and explosion follows on explosion to the great delight of the spectators. The origin of this ceremony dates from the First Crusade.

It is related that at the capture of Jerusalem in 1099 a Florentine warrior, an ancestor of the Pazzi, was the first to plant the Christian banner on the walls of that city. For this deed of valour he was rewarded by Godfrey de Bouillon with three bits of flint from the Holy Sepulchre. On his return home he presented the flints to the Signory, who ordered that the new fire on Easter Eve should be struck from them. The precious stones are preserved in the Church of SS. Apostoli, and ever since, on Saturday morning in Passion week fire is struck from them and a taper lighted, and from it the candle in the *portafuoco* which is borne to the cathedral in solemn procession. It is from this portafuoco that the Colombina is lighted, and if, after having ignited the fireworks on the car, it returns without a hitch to the altar it is accepted as a good omen for the success of the year's crops.

THE BRONZE BOAR.

THE MERCATO NUOVO, or Flower Market.

In ancient times the Mercato Nuovo was the headquarters of the Guild of Bankers and Money Changers (p. 231). The present building built in 1547-51 by *Battista del Tasso* for Cosimo I. is adorned with a good bronze copy of the antique marble boar in the Gallery of the Uffizi. The market is now used for the sale of flowers, straw and linen wares.

The Palazzo di Parte Guelfa and the adjacent church of San Biagio (now Vieusseux's Library) illustrated here, were the headquarters and meeting place of the Guelf Party.

In the great Papal and Imperial quarrel that shook Italy in the 12th century the parties of *Guelf* and *Ghibelline*, of the Papacy and the Empire, took shape and acquired an ineradicable force. The Guelfs, friends of democratic expansion, maintained, against the claims of the Emperor, the independence of Italy and the supremacy of the Pope. The Ghibelline party, which included naturalized nobles, men of arms, and advocates of feudalism, supported the authority of the German emperors over the Italian States. Out of the innumerable contentions of the two factions, which were divided by irreconcilable ideals, in 1267 there arose at Florence the so-called *Parte Guelfa*,—a miniature republic within the republic. This organization consisted of a committee of six officers or Capitani, a secret council of fourteen

PALAZZO DI PARTE GUELFA
on the left the suppressed church of S. Biagio.

members, and a great council of seventy members. Its professed activity was to watch over the interests of the Guelf cause, which the city had finally embraced. To this organization was given one-third part of the property which was confiscated from the Ghibellines. It had a special officer for hunting up and accusing those whom it suspected of Ghibelline sentiments, and the punishment was at the discretion of the Capitani. For a long time the Guelf party remained a dangerous unconstitutional organization and exercised a more or less pernicious influence on Florentine affairs. As its power increased, the pride of the party leaders waxed apace and their insolence towards the remainder of the citizens became almost intolerable. « This Parte Guelfa », says Machiavelli, « abused its powers exceedingly for party purposes, and the Captains became more feared than the Signoria itself, and behaved most insolently towards it ». The organization was dissolved in the 15th century.

— 309 —

Photo ALINARI, ANDERSON, BROGI.

39A. - *WONDERS OF ITALY.*

FIESOLE. CHURCH OF ST. FRANCIS.

THE CATHEDRAL. FIESOLE.
Tuscan-Romanesque style.

BUST OF BISHOP SALUTATI († 1466).
By MINO DA FIESOLE. (Cathedral).

BADIA DI FIESOLE (11th cent.).
Tuscan-Romanesque style.

Fiesole is situated on a hill to the north of Florence, and overlooks the valley of the Arno. When Rome was a mere village, Fiesole was already a flourishing Etruscan town, the cyclopean walls of which are still to be seen. Then gradually the Romans obtained the supremacy and Fiesole became their colony.

From a terrace or *belvedere* just below the little Franciscan monastery which crowns the hill, a striking, unrivalled distant view may be enjoyed. At our feet lies the city of Florence, shut in by hills of varied outline, and beyond, long drawn lines of mountains stretching out far and wide in the distance. The well preserved Roman theatre, which was situated within the ancient city walls was discovered in 1809.

Among the many beautiful villas situated on the hill-side of Fiesole, one possesses a more romantic interest than all others: the Villa Palmieri, which now belongs to an American gentleman. According to tradition, this is the place where Boccaccio's gay company of young ladies and gentlemen met when they fled from the horrors of plague-stricken Florence in 1348 and spent their time telling stories for ten consecutive days.

RUINS OF THE ROMAN THEATRE. FIESOLE.

Photo ALINARI, ANDERSON, BROGI.

FLORENCE — THE ENVIRONS. San Miniato.

INTERIOR OF SAN MINIATO.

CHURCH OF SAN MINIATO AL MONTE. *Begun in 1013.*

TOMB OF CARDINAL JACOPO OF PORTUGAL. *By* A. ROSSELLINO.

THE APSE. Mosaic of 1297.
The windows of the apse are closed by translucent slabs of alabaster. 

THE MARBLE PULPIT. *11th cent.*

The *Church of San Miniato* is one of the finest examples of the Tuscan-Romanesque style. Both interior and exterior are incrusted with coloured marble, the 11th cent. marble pavement is very similar to that of the Florentine baptistery. At the end of the nave is an exquisite Renaissance chapel by *Michelozzo*, which formerly contained Gualberto's miraculous Crucifix (now at S. Trinita); in the left aisle is the beautiful Chapel of S. Jacopo, containing the tomb of Cardinal Jacopo of Portugal († 1459), and a fresco of the Annunciation by *A. Baldovinetti*, on the ceiling are terracotta medallions of the Cardinal Virtues and the Holy Ghost by *Luca della Robbia*; the pulpit and screen of incrusted marble in the choir dates from the 11th cent. In the sacristy are frescoes from the life of St. Benedict by *Spinello Aretino*.

The old fortifications surrounding the church and the adjoining monastery were erected (1529) by *Michelangelo*: it was from these ramparts that the master distinguished himself for his stout defence of the city against the Imperial troops during the siege of Florence in 1530.

Not far from San Miniato is the *Torre del Gallo,* "Galileo's Tower." Here Galileo invented his telescope, and from its tower "in the still midnight of far-off time" he made his astronomical observations.

HALL IN THE TORRE DEL GALLO.

TORRE DEL GALLO.

Photo ALINARI, ANDERSON, BROGI.

— 311 —

FLORENCE — THE ENVIRONS.

The Certosa or Carthusian Monastery of Florence, was founded in 1341 by Niccolò Acciaiuoli, a Florentine, Grand Seneschal of Queen Giovanna of Naples, who employed ANDREA ORCAGNA to prepare the design. The building, which stands on an abrupt eminence covered with olive trees and vines, has more the aspect of a medieval fortress than of a sacred edifice. Formerly women were not admitted beyond the *hospitium* or guest-house, which is on one side of the anterior court, but since 1865, when the government took possession of the place, it has been thrown open to visitors of both sexes. The main church has a richly ornamented pavement and fine carved stalls of 1590; over the altar is represented the Death of San Bruno, founder of the Order a fresco by POCCETTI. In the crypt are well preserved Gothic tombs of the Acciaiuoli. The large cloister, which serves also as a burial ground, is surrounded by a portico adorned with heads of saints in Robbia ware, the well-head in the centre is said to have been designed by MICHELANGELO. Around the cloister are 18 apartments for the monks, each of which consists of a sitting and a bedroom, a small studio, a covered terrace and a small garden. From the cell usually shown to visitors, an enchanting view of Florence and the surrounding district is obtained. Excellent *chartreuse* is made by the monks, on the premises. The Order of the Carthusians was founded in 1084, by Bruno, a monk of Cologne, and the first seat of the Order was the famous monastery at Chartreux, near Grenoble, known as *la grande Chartreuse*. Of all the reformed Benedictine congregations, this is the most austere. To the ordinances of St. Benedict, which commanded poverty, chastity, obedience and daily labor, was added almost perpetual silence. Only once a week they were allowed to walk and discourse together; flesh was absolutely forbidden at all times; of pulse, bread and water to which they were confined, they made but one meal a day, and that was eaten separately in their cells, except on certain festivals, when they were allowed to eat together, but in silence. They were enjoined to study, to cultivate their fields and to transcribing books (when these were more costly than fine raiment), by which at first, they supported and enriched their community. Their habit is white, they wear sandals and have their heads closely shaven.

WELL. By MICHELANGELO (?).

CLOISTERS OF THE CERTOSA.
(the garden serves as a burial ground).

MEDICI VILLA OF CAREGGI.

This, the most famous of the Medici Villas, was built by Cosimo the Elder from the designs of MICHELOZZO. It was the favorite residence of Lorenzo the Magnificent, and in it the meetings of his Platonic academy were held. Here Lorenzo loved to gather in *symposium* his chosen friends—Pico della Mirandola, Angelo Poliziano, Marsilio Ficino, and other literary spirits; on which occasions the works of the Greek were discussed, and expounded. Cosimo the Elder and Lorenzo the Magnificent both died here.

MEDICI VILLA OF POGGIO A CAIANO.

Built about 1480 for Lorenzo the Magnificent by GIULIANO DA SANGALLO, this villa is surrounded by a fine old park. Here Lorenzo came frequently, and composed his poem entitled « Ambra », and here it was that the Grand Duke Francis and the beautiful Bianca Cappello died in 1587. The main saloon is adorned with frescoes by Andrea del Sarto, Franciabigio and Alessandro Allori: the subjects are all classical, and typify events in the history of the Medici. The Loggia has a ceiling richly decorated with stucco, and a fine Della Robbia frieze.

The sons of Lorenzo the Magnificent
(*Fragment from the fresco on p. 244*).

— 312 —

Photo ALINARI, ANDERSON, BROGI.

PISA — ROMANESQUE ARCHITECTURE.

PISA. THE CAMPANILE AND APSE OF THE CATHEDRAL.

The Campanile, or bell-tower of Pisa, was begun in 1174 by the architect BONANNO of Pisa, continued (about 1260) by William of Innsbruck, and completed in 1350. It is built entirely of white marble and owing to its remarkable oblique position, 14 feet out of the perpendicular, it is usually known as the *Leaning Tower*. It is generally believed that some imperfection of the foundations caused the edifice to lean on one side before the building had reached the third storey, and that the architects tried to correct this deficiency by giving an inclination in the opposite direction to the upper part of the construction.

A staircase of 293 marble steps leads to the summit whence a very beautiful view embracing land and sea is obtained. Looking out from the top gallery the sensation of falling over is very curious and startling.

Galileo availed himself of the oblique position of the campanile in making his experiments on the laws of gravity.

Photo ALINARI, ANDERSON, BROGI.

THE CATHEDRAL. PORTALE DI SAN RANIERI. *Bronze doors* by BONANNO. ca. 1180.

BONANNO DA PISA, the architect of the Campanile, was also eminent as a bronze-caster. Of two pairs of bronze doors he executed for the cathedral of Pisa, only those illustrated here remain *in situ*; the others made for the main portal, were lost (now replaced by Giambologna's work) together with other works of art in the great fire of 1596. These doors, of marked Byzantine sentiment, have a series of reliefs representing incidents in the life of Christ, each subject being explained by Latin inscriptions. Beginning from below from left to right : A) 1. the Annunciation ; 2. the Visitation ; 3. the Nativity and the Announcement to the shepherds ; 4. the Journey of the Magi ; B) 1. the Purification and Presentation of the Infant Christ in the temple ; 2. the Flight into Egypt ; 3. Herod and the Massacre of the Innocents ; 4. the Baptism of Christ ; C) 1. The Temptation ; 2. the Transfiguration ; 3. the Raising of Lazarus ; 4. the Entry into Jerusalem ; D) 1. the Washing of the feet ; 2. the Last Supper ; 3. the Kiss of Judas ; 4. the Crucifixion ; E) 1. Christ in Limbo ; 2. the Three Marys at the Tomb ; 3. the Ascension ; 4. the Death of the Virgin Mary (cfr. p. 232). The compartments on the top represent : *left* Adoring Angels approaching Christ seated on a throne ; *right* the Virgin enthroned surrounded by four angels. In the compartments below are figures of Prophets amidst palm-trees. The whole composition has analogies with the only other extant work by the same master : the bronze doors executed in 1174-86, for the cathedral of Monreale (p. 575)

— 313* —

BAPTISTERY. A. D. 1153-1278.	CATHEDRAL. A. D. 1063.	CAMPANILE. 1174-1350.
Built of marble by DIOTISALVI.	*By* BUSKETUS *and* RAINALDUS.	*Begun by* BONANNO.

PISA

Pisa, is one of the oldest cities of Italy. Originally an Etruscan town it became a Roman colony in 180 B. C. with the name of *Colonia Julia Pisana*. Little is known of Pisa's progress during the barbarian invasions, but in the eleventh century it was a busy city and enjoyed the proud position of being one of the chief commercial ports of the Mediterranean, a rival of Genoa and Venice. Her military development and flourishing trade is to be attributed to her zeal in waging incessant war against the Saracen invaders and depriving them of Sardinia (1025), and, for a short period, of the Balearic Isles. The greatest victory of the Pisan navy was achieved in 1063 near Palermo against the Saracens, when they captured six vessels laden with rich merchandise and which they brought home in triumph. In 1099, the Pisans joined in the first Crusade, took a considerable part in the capture of Jerusalem, and reaped many commercial advantages from it, combining war and trade in the East. Towards the close of the 12th century Pisa had reached the zenith of her power and prosperity as a republic. The greatness and wealth of the Pisans at this period of their history is proved by the group of noble buildings illustrated above; Pisa was the first Italian city that took a pride in architectural magnificence.

But the Ghibelline sympathies of the Pisans involved them in terrible struggles with the Guelph republics surrounding them; the battle of Benevento (1266), where King Manfred fell, and the rout of Tagliacozzo (1268), which marked the downfall of the Hohenstaufen in Italy, were fatal to Pisa. Her power was broken at the battle of Meloria in 1284 when the whole Pisan navy was destroyed by the Genoese. Henceforth except for brief intervals of fortune she was compelled to submit to a succession of Lordships: Uguccione della Faggiuola (1311), Castruccio Castracani (1326), Gian Galeazzo Visconti (1396). The Florentines gained possession of Pisa in 1405. On the arrival of Charles VIII. of France (he had married Anne of Brittany) the king granted (1494), the Pisans their liberty, but he broke his promise, and in 1509 their city was again besieged and fell finally in the power of the Florentines.

PALAZZO DELL'OROLOGIO.

The building illustrated here restored by VASARI in 1560, is situated in the Piazza dei Cavalieri, — formerly the centre of Pisa. Here, until 1655, stood the ill-famed « tower ot hunger » Torre dei Gualandi, in which Count Ugolino della Gherardesca with his sons and two grandsons was starved to death in 1288 (DANTE, *Inferno*, XXXIII).

PISA — THE BAPTISTERY.

John preaches to the people — Baptism of Christ. — John reproves Herod.
STORIES from the Life of St. John the Baptist. *Main portal.*

MAIN PORTAL of the Baptistery.

The *Baptistery*, constructed almost entirely of marble, was begun in 1153 by DIOTISALVI but not completed till about 1278; the Gothic gables and pinnacles were added in the 14th cent. It is a circular building covered by a dome 187 ft. high; there are four entrances, and the main portal facing the cathedral has elaborately carved columns and 13th cent. sculptures from the life of the Baptist over the doorway. The impressive interior measuring 100 ft. in diameter has a singular echo which converts the notes of a simple scale into the most wonderful harmonies, when sung by a simple voice (the lightest whisper is reflected and prolonged in the whole building). The most striking features of the interior are the beautiful octagonal marble font (similar, probably, to that, no longer existing, in the baptistery at Florence) originally intended for adult immersion, and Niccolò Pisano's hexagonal pulpit. This famous pulpit executed in 1260 is the masterpiece of the artist. Three of its seven columns are supported upon the backs of lions, the central column rests on a group of men and animals. The reliefs on the five panels above represent the Nativity, the Adoration of the Magi, the Presentation, the Crucifixion and the Last Judgment. Figures of Evangelists, Prophets and Virtues are in the spandrels of, and between the arches.

INTERIOR OF THE BAPTISTERY. *In the centre a marble font by* GUIDO BIGARELLI A. D. 1246. *On the left is the famous pulpit by* NICCOLÒ PISANO A. D. 1260.

In Pisa, as in many other cities of Italy, all christenings are performed in the baptistery, as there are no fonts in parish churches.

THE NATIVITY. *Marble reliefs on Niccolo's pulpit.* ADORATION OF THE MAGI.

— 314 —

Photo ALINARI, ANDERSON, BROGI.

PISA — THE CATHEDRAL.

INTERIOR OF THE CATHEDRAL.

THE CATHEDRAL. A. D. 1063-1118. *Pisan style.*

THE VIRGIN, CHRIST AND ST. JOHN.
Mosaic by CIMABUE (1302) *in the dome.*

The *Cathedral*, commenced in 1063, after the great naval victory of the Pisans in Sicily, was designed by the architects BUSKETUS and RAINALDUS, and consecrated by Pope Gelasius II. in 1118. The building — the most magnificent example of the Pisan style — is constructed almost entirely of white marble, ornamented with alternated courses of black and coloured marbles. The beautiful façade adorned with columns and open galleries served as a model of architecture for the cathedrals of Lucca, Pistoia and other cities throughout the Pisan archbishopric. The ancient bronze doors of Bonanno, destroyed in the great fire of 1596, were replaced in 1602 by the present doors executed by *Giovanni da Bologna*, representing scenes from the Life of the Virgin and of Christ. (The old bronze doors of the south transept which escaped the fire are illustrated on p. 313*).

MAIN DOORWAY OF CATHEDRAL.
Bronze doors by GIOV. DA BOLOGNA.

The interior borne by sixty-eight ancient columns is 311 ft. long and 106 ft. wide. The harmonious majesty of all its details give it an appearance of much greater magnitude. Besides Giovanni Pisano's famous pulpit illustrated on the following pages, the cathedral contains many works of art. The large bronze lamp which hangs in front of the choir is the work of *Lorenzi*; its swaying is said to have suggested to Galileo the idea of the pendulum.

ABRAHAM'S SACRIFICE. *By* SODOMA.

BRONZE LAMP, *by* LORENZI, A. D. 1587.

ST. AGNES. *By* A. DEL SARTO.

40. - WONDERS OF ITALY.

PISA — THE CATHEDRAL. Gothic sculpture.

MARBLE PULPIT. *Executed by* GIOVANNI PISANO. A. D. 1300-10. (Cathedral of Pisa).

  This magnificent pulpit, one of the most important works of Giovanni Pisano, was partly destroyed in the burning of the cathedral in 1595, and the parts dispersed. For a long time many unsuccessful attempts were made at reconstruction. Finally, after patient work the restoration of the pulpit and its reconstruction on the original design, introducing Giovanni's remaining sculptures, was brought to completion, and once more replaced (1926) in the Cathedral.
  The pulpit is supported by six porphyry columns, and five pillars with marble figures representing; *a)* The *City of Pisa* with two sucklings as a symbol of fertility, supported by the Four Cardinal Virtues. *b)* The *Imperial Majestas* impersonated by a Rector (?), with scales in his left hand, symbolizing Justice and Truth, supported by the Four Evangelists. *c)* The *Archangel Michael. d) Hercules* (?). *e)* (In the centre) Group of the *Theological Virtues* upon a base with reliefs of the Seven Liberal Arts.
  The pulpit itself is octagonal with slightly curved panels, and a platform enclosed by two plane panels. The reliefs on the panels represent: the « Birth of the Baptist and the Visitation », the « Birth of Christ » and « Announcement by an Angel to the Shepherds », the « Adoration of the Magi », the « Presentation in the Temple, with the Flight into Egypt », the « Massacre of the Innocents », the « Betrayal, and the Passion of Christ », the « Crucifixion », the « Last Judgement, divided into the Blessed and the Condemned ». Between the panels are figures of Prophets, in the spandrels figures of Sibyls.

— 316 —

Photo ALINARI

PISA — *Details from Giovanni Pisano's pulpit.*

THE ADORATION, *relief of the Pulpit by* GIOVANNI PISANO.

The City of Pisa, the Cardinal Virtues.    The Theological Virtues.    The Imperial Majestas.

Photo ALINARI, ANDERSON, BROGI.

PISA — THE CHURCHES.

CHURCH OF SAN MICHELE IN BORGO (1304).
The upper part of the façade is by FRA GUGLIELMO.

SANTA MARIA DELLA SPINA. *French-Gothic style.*
This exquisite little church erected in 1230 as an oratory for sailors about to go to sea, was so called from its possession of a fragment of the veritable « Crown of Thorns ». The statues on the exterior are by Pisan artists. Restored in 1872 it offers an interesting example of early imported Gothic in Italy.

MADONNA AND CHILD. *by* DON L. MONACO.

MADONNA. *partly gilded,* *by* NINO PISANO (*S. M. della Spina*).

SANTA MARIA DELLA SPINA.

INTERIOR OF SAN PIERO A GRADO.

APSES OF SAN PIERO A GRADO.

The ancient port of Pisa was located at *San Piero*, where, according to tradition, St. Peter first landed in Italy. This very ancient basilica (4 miles west of Pisa) was formerly much frequented as a pilgrimage church. The present edifice dates from the end of the 11th cent. and contains beautiful antique columns and interesting frescoes illustrating scenes from the lives of SS. Peter and Paul.

— 317 —

Photo ALINARI, BROGI.

CHURCH OF SAN PAOLO A RIPA D'ARNO.
Romanesque façade of the 12th cent. (Compare with Duomo).

CHURCH OF SANTA CATERINA.
Erected ca. 1253. Pisan-Gothic style.

CHURCH OF SAN FREDIANO.
Built in the 12th cent. Romanesque style.

ST. THOMAS AQUINAS. *By* TRAINI.

This remarkable picture painted for the church of Santa Caterina represents S. Thomas Aquinas enthroned, surrounded by a golden sphere or disc. Our Saviour in glory appears in the sky blessing him and sending down on his head inspiration in the shape of three rays. Single rays descend in like manner on the heads of Moses, S. Paul and the Four Evangelists ranged in a semicircle below Christ. They, like Plato and Aristotle who are standing to the right and left of S. Thomas, hold the volume of their writings open in their hands; and rays of light from these eight volumes converge upon the head of the *angelic doctor*, who becomes the focus, as it were, of the inspiration sent forth from Christ and from the classic teachers. The whole sum of inspiration thus communicated and concentrated in his person is gathered into form in the book, the «Summa Theologiæ», held by S. Thomas in his hands, and from which the rays of light re-issue and are shed upon two groups of ecclesiastics, chiefly Dominicans, in the lower part of the picture. Between these groups Averrhoes lies prostrate and discomfited beneath the feet of S. Thomas, with his book face downwards, struck by a shaft from the volume in the saint's hands

ST. FRANCIS. *Church of S. Francesco.*

MADONNA. *By* N. PISANO.

ST. MARTIN parting with his cloak. *Church of S. Martino.*

Photo ALINARI, BROGI.

PISA — THE CAMPOSANTO.

VIEW OF THE CAMPO SANTO.

ROMAN SARCOPHAGUS

with reliefs relating to the myth of Hippolytus and Phaedra, from which, according to Vasari, Niccolò Pisano drew inspiration, and copied various figures for his pulpit. This ancient sarcophagus is interesting on account of having served as a tomb of Beatrice († 1076), mother of Matilda of Tuscany.

EASTERN GALLERY OF THE CAMPOSANTO.
On the background: the wall-painting "Triumph of Death" (damaged).

Photo ALINARI, ANDERSON, BROGI.

PISA — THE CAMPOSANTO.

VIEW SHOWING THE FAMOUS CHAINS *that once defended the ancient harbour of Pisa at the mouth of the Arno.*

These chains captured by the Florentines in 1315, remained suspended in front of their baptistery until 1848.

MADONNA, *by* GIOVANNI PISANO.

The *Campo Santo* was begun about 1270 from plans by GIOVANNI PISANO and consecrated in 1278. Its architecture originates from the cloisters of the churches. It has an area of four hundred feet in length, and one hundred and twenty in width. On the east side is a large chapel with a dome. The quadrangle in the centre is said to have been filled with earth brought from the Holy Land. The whole of the interior walls, from top to bottom, are adorned with large frescoes by painters of the 14th and 15th centuries. They represent scenes from the Old and New Testaments and allegories of a peculiarly grand and imaginative character. Ranged along the walls are many tombs and an important collection of Etruscan, Roman and medieval sculptures. The building was much damaged during the war in 1943.

The Campo Santo is only one of the teeming interests of the city; everything in Pisa tells of a glorious past and of departed splendour; its greatness left a stamp for all time on the glorious cluster of marble buildings comprising the Cathedral, the Baptistery and the Leaning Tower.

MONUMENT OF EMPEROR HENRY VII. OF LUXEMBOURG who died at Buonconvento in 1313.
By TINO DI CAMAINO. A. D. 1315.

The effigy of the emperor is robed in a mantle decorated with the eagles of the Ghibellines. The front of the sarcophagus has figures of saints; at each end stand mourning genii.

THE TRIUMPH OF DEATH. *Attributed to C*

The group of beggars and cripples.

This immense fresco is composed of four scenes. In the foreground on the left, a gay hunting party of richly attired princes and ladies with a train of cavaliers suddenly comes face to face with Death in the form of three open coffins each containing the body of a king, in different stages of decay. In the corner, close by, stands a monk, St. Macarius, who by means of an inscription reminds the party of the evanescence of human pleasures.

In the centre a crowd of beggars and cripples with outstretched arms call upon Death to end their misery, but she heeds them not, hastens on flying and swinging her scythe, — mows down the life of people of every condition — and directs herself towards an orange-garden on the right where a company of young ladies and society men, splendidly dressed, are conversing and enjoying themselves with song and music.

PISA — THE CAMPOSANTO.

FRANCESCO TRAINI. *Painted about 1350.*

On the right, the angels ascend to heaven with those they have saved; while the demons drag their prey to a fiery mountain on the left, and hurl the souls down into the flames.

« In those piles of the promiscuous and abandoned dead », writes Symonds, « those fiends and angels poised in mid-air struggling for souls, those blind and mutilated beggars vainly besieging Death with prayers and imprecations for deliverance, while she descends in her robe of woven wire to mow down with her scythe the knights and ladies in their garden of delight; again in those horses snuffing at the open graves, those countesses and princes face to face with skeletons, those serpents coiling round the flesh of what was once fair youth or maid, those multitudes of guilty men and women trembling beneath the trump of the archangel — tearing their cheeks, their hair, their breasts in agony, because they see Hell through the prison-bars, and hear the raging of its fiends, and feel the clasp upon their wrists and ankles of clawed hairy demon hands; in all this terrific amalgamation of sinister and tragic ideas, vividly presented, full of coarse dramatic power, and intensified by faith in their material reality, the Lorenzetti brethren, if theirs be indeed the hands that painted here, summed up the nightmares of the Middle Age and bequeated an ever memorable picture of its desolate preoccupations to the rising world ».

In contrast to the followers of the joys of the world, in the upper left part of the composition is represented the calm and happy life of the hermits, who in contemplation and abstinence have attained the highest term of human existence.

Beneath Death human corpses are closely pressed and heaped: from their insignia they may easily be identified as former kings, queens, princes, cardinals, bishops, etc. Their souls raise from them in the form of infants whom a crowd of angels and demons above contend for the possession of them. The souls of the Pious fold their hands in prayer; those of the Condemned shrink back in horror.

Angels and demons take possession of the souls of the deceased.

Photo ALINARI, BROGI.

— 321 —

41. - WONDERS OF ITALY.

THE LAST JUDGMENT AND HELL (Left half).
Attributed ORCAGNA *or to* FRANCESCO TRAINI. *Painted about 1350.*

Above, sits Christ in glory, raising, according to traditional usage, His outspread right hand to show His wound, and pointing with his left to the wound in His side, as signs of mercy to the rising Dead. The Virgin is seated in glory on the right of the Saviour. On either side sit the Apostles and above hover the Angels holding the instruments of the Passion. In the centre, under Christ and the Virgin is a group of Angels in symmetrical arrangement: two of them blow their trumpets to summon the dead from their graves, while a third kneeling partly conceals his face, apparently shuddering at the terrible spectacle.

All the lower part of the composition is occupied by the two great gatherings of the Blessed (left), and the Condemned (right), while in the centre the archangel Michael with unsheated sword presides at the separation of the worthy from the unworthy. The men are rising from their graves: armed angels directing them to the right and left, Solomon is seen emerging from his tomb, doubtful, undecided as to which side he should turn; an Angel grasps by the hand a monk and is in the act of dragging him towards the group of the Condemned, while on the right another Angel leads away from this last group a youth in secular costume and gently conducts him towards the Blessed. The Blessed and the Condemned emerge on both sides, — the gestures of the latter show all the torments of despair, the flames of hell rage around them, and demons already seize them by their vestments.

COSIMO DE' MEDICI WATCHING THE BUILDING OF THE TOWER OF BABEL. *Fresco by* BENOZZO GOZZOLI.

PISA — THE CAMPOSANTO.

THE LAST JUDGMENT AND HELL (Right half).

This composition is a continuation of the Last Judgment. Inferno is represented as divided into four compartments rising one above the other according to Dante's conception. In the centre sits Satan, a hideous monster, — himself a fiery furnace in which sinners are consumed; here, according to the inscriptions, we see Julian the Apostate, Attila the scourge of God and Simon Magus. The Condemned are distributed into various groups or sections. Beginning on the top from left to right: 1) the heretics, the diviners, the simoniacs and the prophets of false dogmas (here may be seen Arius, Mohamed, the Antichrist and Averrhoes); 2) the lazy and the envious; 3) the hot-tempered, the self-murderers and the gluttous; 4) the misers and the carnal sinners. The lower part of the fresco has been repeatedly restored. (See also p. 227).

NOAH'S VINTAGE.   *Fresco by* BENOZZO GOZZOLI A. D. 1470.   NOAH'S DRUNKENNESS.

One of the first Italian painters to take part in the revival of art in Italy was GIUNTA of Pisa. Few works exist of him, the *Crucifix of San Ranieri* illustrated here, signed by Giunta, is a typical example of the numerous crucifixes produced in the 13th cent. by Pisan artists who were fond of representing the crucified Redeemer dead and with signs indicative of the convulsions of agony.

It must be observed that the figure of Christ on the Cross has not always occupied a preponderant position in churches and religious ceremonies; the acceptance of this symbol was slow and laborious. The early Christians impelled by a sense of caution in the midst of persecutions abstained from all direct representations of the Lord. They evoked him symbolically with some sign or figure intelligible to the initiated alone. Later, in order to represent the death of Christ, the mystic image of the Lamb was placed at the foot of the cross. As for reproducing the scene of the crucifixion, the idea would have caused horror, it seemed irreverent to portray the Son of God submitting to His infamous punishment. Not until the sixth century do we find figures of Christ on the Cross appearing in manuscripts and very rare church pictures, but in 705 Pope John VII. officially permitted such representation and a mosaic crucifixion was placed in the Vatican. Yet, several centuries were required to overcome the feelings of hereditary reluctance. From the end of the 11th cent. the use of crucifixes tended to become general; until that period the Saviour was only seen clothed in a long robe with sleeves down to his feet. At the same time it seemed indecorous to show the Lord in physical grief or in humility, hence we see the crucified One shown as living with his head upright, his body straight and his feet in juxtaposition. Towards the end of the 12th cent. the sleeves disappeared; successively the trunk was bared and a sort of skirt covered the lower limbs, soon the skirt was shortened and from the 13th cent. it no longer was but a cloth tied around the loins. Thenceforth, crucifixions became more realistic; the crucified One, who up to this time had remained living, now stood dead; his head bowed down, his limbs and bust showed the yielding of a corpse, artists sought to represent the most painful postures and endeavoured to show all the cramping signs of agony; they also added small scenes on the sides representing incidents from the life of Christ. (A practice applied also to primitive pictures of Saints).

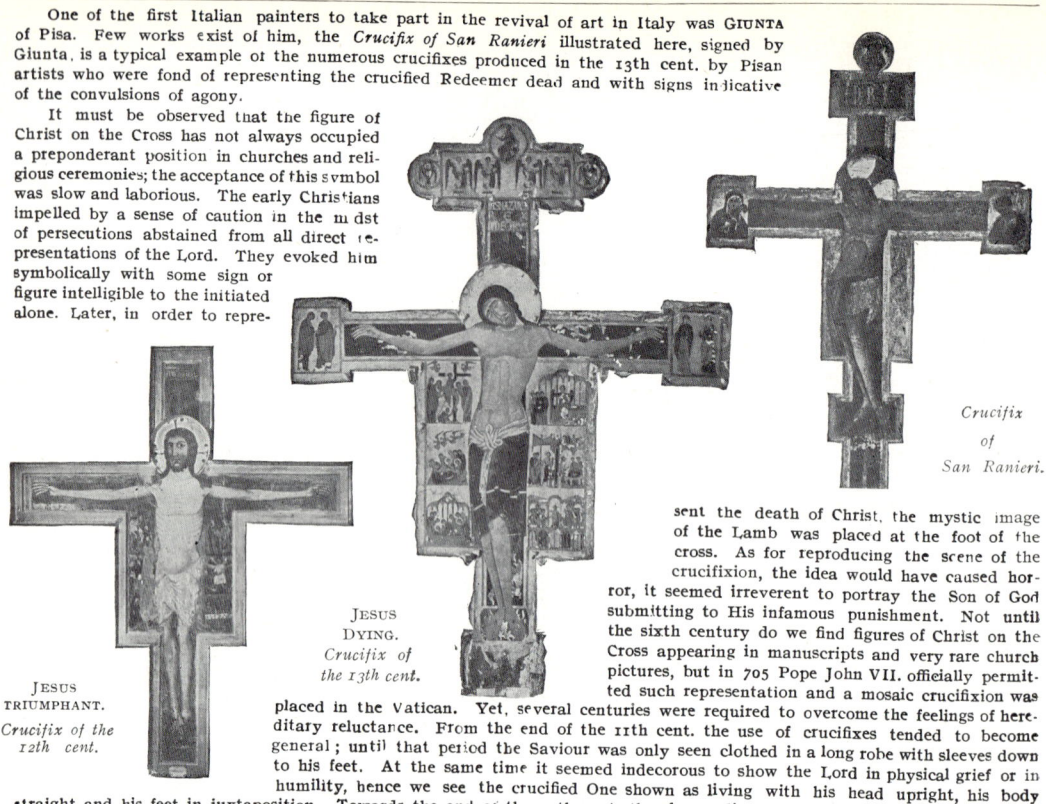

Crucifix of San Ranieri.

JESUS DYING. *Crucifix of the 13th cent.*

JESUS TRIUMPHANT. *Crucifix of the 12th cent.*

MADONNA. By N. PISANO.

THE ANNUNCIATION. By NINO PISANO.

NINO PISANO († 1368), son of Andrea, was the last noteworthy representative of the Pisan school and occupies a special place in the history of art. His style was more *genre* in character, his productions were impressed with originality. His "Annunciations" consisting of two separate statues of the Archangel and the Virgin are prototypes of an exquisite and refined grace, perfectly modelled and enriched by gilding or colouring.

CRUCIFIXION. By LUCA TOMMÈ. (*Sienese 14th cent.*).

CHURCH OF SAN MICHELE. *Romanesque style.*
Founded in the 8th cent. This church was re-erected in the 12th cent. The gorgeous façade was in part rebuilt in the 19th cent.

MADONNA AND CHILD.
By MATTEO CIVITALI (1436-1501).

MATTEO CIVITALI, a native of Lucca, is one of the most pleasing sculptors. His charming works captivate us by their exquisite semplicity and suavity.

LUCCA has a very ancient origin. It first belonged to Etruria and then became a Roman colony. Successively it was ruled by the Ostrogoths, Longobards and the Franks. In 1314 it was subdued by Uguccione della Faggiuola, Lord of Pisa, with whom Dante resided here. Later it fell into the hands of Castruccio Castracane (1322), and Mastino II. della Scala (1328) and, in turn, ruled by Florence and Pisa until 1369 when it purchased its freedom from the emperor Charles IV. for 100.000 gulden and remained a republic till the French invasion of 1799. In 1805 Napoleon I. gave Lucca as a Duchy to his sister Elisa Baciocchi, but in 1814 it fell to the Bourbons, Dukes of Parma, by whom it was ceded to Tuscany in 1847.

Lucca possesses numerous churches of the early medieval period, built or restored on the plans of the Pisan cathedrals, besides having many important sculptures and paintings by great masters.

MADONNA ENTHRONED with St. Stephen and John the Baptist.
By FRA BARTOLOMMEO (1508).

MONUMENT OF ILARIA DEL CARRETTO.
By JACOPO DELLA QUERCIA. A. D. 1406.
At her feet a dog: symbol of faithfulness.

CATHEDRAL OF SAN MARTINO.
Founded in the 6th cent. Rebuilt in the 11th cent. in the Romanesque style. The façade is by GUIDETTO, *about 1210.*
Note the crenate Ghibelline merlons on the Campanile.

(Lucca is the birthplace of the musicians Boccherini † 1805, and Giacomo Puccini † 1924).

Photo ALINARI, BROGI.

PISTOIA.

THE CATHEDRAL. *Begun in the 12th cent.* THE CAMPANILE, *dating from 1200.*
THE PALAZZO PRETORIO, *formerly Palazzo del Podestà.*

THE BAPTISTERY. A. D. 1316-59.
Designed by ANDREA PISANO.

PISTOIA, the Roman *Pistoria*, where Catiline was defeated and slain in 62 B. C., became a republic in the 12th century, but the character of the people made the career of the commune stormy and disastrous. For nearly two centuries the city was the scene of the fiercest struggles between the Guelphs and Ghibellines. In the year 1300, the members of two rival branches of the same family started a great quarrel which in time spread until the whole city was involved. The adherents of the opposing parties were distinguished by the names of *Bianchi* and *Neri* (White and Blacks), and they caused so much disorder and bloodshed that the government of Pistoia appealed to Florence for aid. The Signory took up the management of Pistoian affairs and thenceforth the town existed under the protection of Florence, whose fortunes it shared.

PART OF THE SILVER ALTAR in the Cappella San Jacopo.
Executed in the 13th-15th cent. (Cathedral).

The Church of Sant'Andrea, a Romanesque edifice of the 12th century, contains the famous pulpit of *Giovanni Pisano*, executed in imitation of his father's pulpit (p. 314) at Pisa. It rests on seven red marble columns supported by lions and human figures. The reliefs on the sides represent the Nativity, the Adoration of the Magi, the Massacre of the Innocents, the Crucifixion, and the Last Judgment. On the angles are noble figures of prophets and sibyls.

MARBLE PULPIT.
By GIOVANNI PISANO (1298).
(Church of Sant'Andrea).

MASSACRE OF THE INNOCENTS.
(*Panel from* G. *Pisano's pulpit*).

ADORATION OF THE MAGI. *By* GRUAMONS *and* ADEODATUS. A. D. 1166. (*Church of Sant'Andrea*).

— 326 —

Photo ALINARI, BROGI.

PISTOIA.

CHURCH OF SAN GIOVANNI FUORCIVITAS. *Pisan style 1200.*

MARBLE PULPIT *by* FRA GUGLIELMO OF PISA. 1270 (S. *Giov. Fuorcivitas*).

THE LAST SUPPER, *by* GRUAMONS. (*San Giovanni Fuorcivitas*).

THE VISITATION. *Terracotta.* By L. DELLA ROBBIA. (*S. Giov. Fuor.*).

NURSING THE SICK.

The *Ospedale del Ceppo*, so named from the hollow-stump (*ceppo*) in which alms were collected, was founded in the year 1277. On the portico is the famous coloured terracotta frieze executed in 1514-25 by GIOVANNI DELLA ROBBIA and his assistants, representing the Seven Works of Mercy: clothing the naked, receiving strangers, nursing the sick, visiting prisoners, burying the dead, feeding the hungry, and comforting the mourners.

FEEDING THE HUNGRY. *Terracotta reliefs.*

OSPEDALE DEL CEPPO. *Founded in 1277.* Showing reliefs of the seven works of mercy.

— 327 —

Photo ALINARI, BROGI.

PRATO.

THE CATHEDRAL. *Begun in the 12th cent., and remodelled by* GIOVANNI PISANO *in 1318. Gothic style.*

PULPIT *on the façade of the Cathedral. Reliefs by* DONATELLO *and* MICHELOZZO.

THE DANCE OF SALOME. *By* FRA FILIPPO LIPPI (1460).
One of a series of remarkable frescoes in the choir of the Cathedral.

MADONNA AND CHILD. *By* FILIPPINO LIPPI.

The Cathedral contains the highly-revered *Sacra Cintola*, or "girdle of the Virgin," which is annually exhibited from Donatello's pulpit outside the church. (*See* pag. 277). The choir is decorated with a series of frescoes depicting stories from the lives of St. John the Baptist and St. Stephen by *Fra Filippo Lippi*, the finest work of the master.

PULPIT. *By* MINO DA FIESOLE.

THE VIRGIN. *By* G. PISANO (1317).

PALAZZO PRETORIO (*13th cent.*).

Photo ALINARI, BROGI.

— 328 —

VIEW OF SIENA. *On the center, the cathedral's campanile; on the left, the Mangia Tower.*

SIENA

OF ALL the towns of Southern Tuscany none is more famous or pleasanter than Siena. Attractive and gay, with serene skies and a soft climate, it offers visitors a pleasant and interesting sojourn, welcoming them with the friendly motto inscribed upon its gate : COR MAGIS TIBI SENA PANDIT. Moreover, the harmonious Italian language is heard here to perfection; the inhabitants are as refined and agreeable as their speech; their manners pleasing and prepossessing.

The city is built on three hills or ridges, high above the green, fruitful plain of the Chianti district. Its plan is like a three pointed star, radiating from the *Piazza del Campo*, — that explains why at first the town was divided into three quarters or *Terzi*. To a greater extent than most cities in Italy, Siena has preserved its medieval aspect; it is still surrounded by its old walls and gateways, — too extensive for a town whose population is now only about one third of its heyday. The tourist entering Siena for the first time is struck by the character of its constructions; the streets are not merely tortuous and narrow, rising and descending constantly; but are often superposed the one over the other by flights of steps. The numerous feudal palaces, marvellous time-darkened buildings of the old nobility of Siena, seem to bend towards each other, as if for mutual support; the houses crowded together in picturesque disorder in the little ravines between the hills and on the slopes, are full of charm.

THE ARMS OF SIENA.

Among the noblest fruits of Sienese art are the public buildings adorning the city. The dazzling marble *Duomo*, is one of the finest examples of Italian Gothic architecture; the *Palazzo Pubblico*, in the Piazza del Campo, a fine specimen of pointed Gothic, has one of the noblest towers in Italy. Siena possesses an archiepiscopal see, and a university, founded in 1203, which was in high repute as early as the 14th century.

PORTA CAMOLLIA. *16th century.*
It bears the inscription *Cor magis tibi Sena pandit.*
" Siena opens her Heart still wider to thee."

— 328* —

42. - WONDERS OF ITALY.

VIEW OF THE CITY FROM THE CAMPANILE OF THE CATHEDRAL.
In the centre, is seen the *Piazza del Campo*, and the *Palazzo Pubblico*; on the left the Palazzo Sansedoni.

CHRONOLOGY OF THE PRINCIPAL EVENTS

The origin of Siena is little known; scarcely any traces of Etruscan antiquity have been left in the city, which is considered as having been founded in the early days of Rome by *Senus*, the son of Remus, whence the place obtained its name and emblem. Legend has it that Siena was evangelized by Ansanus, the courageous young Roman noble, who was martyrised (303) under Diocletian.
It was during the middle ages that Siena began to acquire prosperity and grandeur; in the eighth century Siena was governed by *Gastaldi* and had already become a centre of importance. Under the Carolingians it was ruled by Counts. They were men of noble rank, some of whom the descendants of the foreign invaders, the counts and barons of the Frankish and German Emperors; their aim naturally was to make Siena throw in its lot with the Ghibellines. In time five noble families came to stand out pre-eminently, with special privileges from the Republic and influence in the State: the *Piccolomini*, the *Tolomei*, the *Malavolti*, the *Salimbeni* and the *Saracini*. These families of various tendencies were divided against themselves, and battle feuds arose. After 1050, the Emperor Henry III. granted and confirmed to the Bishops of Siena many rights and privileges temporal as well as spiritual.

1115. Death of the Countess Matilda of Tuscany; her extensive dominions are dismembered, and the citizens of Florence, Lucca, Pisa and Siena establish their independence.

1125-1170. Siena becomes a Republic. At first the government is in the hands of the nobility; soon after it is wrested by the people. A few years later it is composed of 100 nobles and 50 plebeyans. Gradually the government of the city extended its sway over the neighbouring townlets of the *contado*, whose feudal lords were forced to reside in the city for some months in the year, to fight for the Commune in war. In spite of internal factions and dissensions Siena is prosperous, its commerce extends greatly; fugitives from Milan, flying from the Teutonic hordes of Barbarossa settle in the city and introduce the Art of Wool; Sienese nobles sail in Pisan galleys to take part in the Crusades and the capture of Acre. In 1159, Siena gave to the Church the " great Pope of the Lombard League," Alexander III., who for twenty years upheld the rights of Italy against Barbarossa.

1170-1200. The Duomo is consecrated (1179), by Alexander III. In the great struggle against Frederick Barbarossa, Siena, believing that he meant to deprive them of her *contado*, closes her gates against the troops of the emperor and hurles back his son Henry discomfited from the Porta Camollia. The Ghibellinism of the Sienese was always of a patriotic type, and Siena, with the election of a foreign *podestà*, became the partisan of the Italian movement.

1200-1230. Siena is the banking-house and trade-capital of Italy; a growing commercial rivalry arises between the Sienese and the Florentine republics: Siena was *Ghibelline* Florence *Guelph*, each had need of expansion. Florence desiring also a commercial supremacy becomes Siena's natural enemy, each especially striving to get into the hands of its own merchants and bankers the increasingly lucrative affairs of the Roman Curia. Henceforth Siena's history is one of futile and in the end hopeless wars with the rival city; each striving to extend its own *contado* at the expense of the other. Poggibonsi, Colle di Val d'Elsa, Montalcino, Montepulciano were perpetual sources of contention, and the Sienese suffered severe defeats time after time; her territory horribly devastated; the insolent invaders made inroads up to the very gates of the city, hurling from catapults " asses " and other *brutture* over the walls. Grosseto was the first place of importance that fell (1224) permanently into the hands of the Sienese. It had been previously swayed by those most potent Counts Aldobrandeschi di Santa Fiora, recorded by Dante.

1230-1260. By an apparently peaceful revolution (1233), the people attained an increased share in the government, a supreme magistracy of " The Twenty-Four," *I Ventiquattro*, was created. But their rule became irksome to the nobles, who formed a rival party and strove to oust the *popolani* from power. In 1240, the opponents rose in arms; the battle began in three places in the city, the palazzo Tolomei and the palazzo Malavolti were burned, and after much devastation and bloodshed the Twenty-four got the upper-hand, drove out a number of nobles and appointed a new podestà, who reconciled the leaders of either party. In the comparative tranquillity that followed (1240) the streets and squares of the city were paved for the first time. In 1254, a treaty

Photo ALINARI, ANDERSON, BROGI.

SIENA — THE PALACES. History.

PIAZZA AND PALAZZO SALIMBENI.
Gothic style, 14th cent.
In the centre, statue of Sallustio Bandini, the promoter of the draining works of the Sienese Maremma.

Three sides of the *piazza* are taken by three palaces reproducing three styles of Sienese architecture. The medieval is represented by the *Palazzo Salimbeni*, in the centre; the Renaissance by the *Palazzo Spannocchi*, on the right, which in 1554 was the residence of Piero Strozzi, when he held the command of the Sienese militia; the Baroque is represented by the *Palazzo Tantucci*, on the left, the work of Riccio (1546). At the rear of the palazzo Salimbeni is the *Rocca Salimbeni*, a very fine example of the turreted-palace-residence of one of the most powerful Sienese families of the 13th century.

PALAZZO SPANNOCCHI.
Built for Ambrogio Spannocchi, treasurer of pope Pius II.
By GIULIANO DA MAIANO, *1473*.

BANNER-HOLDER 14th c.
(*piazza di Postierla*).

An incident which took place on the eve of the Battle of Montaperti, described below, brings to our minds the small painting given on page 347, the "Presentation of the Keys of Siena to the Virgin." — Arrived at Siena, the Florentine ambassadors were received by the Sienese magistrates; " We request, " they said, " that this city be immediately dismantled. But if you refuse to surrender, you may be assured that our powerful Commune of Florence will attack you and in this case we will show you no mercy. We desire, therefore, to know your intentions this instant." Certain members of the Council desired to temporise, a great majority, however, would only hear of immediate resistance. After a brief deliberation, to the arrogant ultimatum of the Florentines, " The 24 " gave this short answer: " We have understood your demands and we order you to return to the chiefs of your Commune and to tell them that we will give them an answer directly." The Sienese hastened their preparations for the conflict, the great bell was rung to gather the clergy and the people inside the Duomo where mass was celebrated and the *Priori* or *Signoria* took communion; the Bishop then ordered the people to take off their shoes, and walk bare-foot in procession within the church singing loudly and praying the Virgin that the city might be liberated from the violence of the Florentines, and during this appeal the keys of the city were solemnly presented to the Holy Virgin's image.

ROCCA SALIMBENI, on rear of palazzo Salimbeni.

was concluded between Siena and Florence, but in 1257 the latter found a pretext of war in the fact that Siena had given shelter to Ghibellines she had expelled. Siena appealed to King Manfred for military assistance, while Florence equipped a large citizen army. The Sienese, led by their podestà Provenzano Salvani and by Farinata degli Uberti, with the help of Manfredi's troops inflict a terrible defeat upon the Florentine Guelphs at the battle of Montaperti, on the Arbia river. It was one of the most bloody and fiercest battles recorded in the history of Tuscany. Ten thousand Florentines were killed, fifteen thousand taken prisoners; the Florentine flag attached to the tail of a donkey was dragged through the streets of Siena; the Florentine *carroccio* remained in the hands of the Sienese, who, out of gratitude for the victory, dedicated the city to the Virgin Mary, attributing to her their success.

1260-1320. The victorious Republic distinguishes itself for its splendid activities and soon reaches the height of her power and prosperity; new coins are struck on which, to the old inscription of *Sena Vetus*, is added that of *Civitas Virginis*. But with the death of King Manfred (son of the emperor Frederick II.), at the Battle of Benevento (1267); and the death (1268) of Conradin of Hohenstaufen, at Tagliacozzo, Charles of Anjou was successful in gaining a preponderant influence in the affairs of Siena, and in 1270 he caused her to join the League of the Guelph Cities of Tuscany. The old discords were renewed within the city and in the following century Siena was obliged to plead for the protection of the German Emperor Charles IV., who had entered Italy. A protection which fourteen years later was repressed by a popular revolt. Then the conflicts with Florence, the rival city, continued; the internal faction-fights recommenced resulting in ruthless, implacable bloody executions, in banishments, not of hundreds but of thousands of persons.

1320-1400. Nevertheless, for a time Siena acquired a relative peace, during which the building of palaces in the new *Trecento* style of architecture was resumed. It was during the years 1320-1340 that the Republic reached the culminating point of her splendour. The *Palazzo Pubblico* was finished, new city gates were opened, beautiful new fountains erected, magnificent private palaces rose to embellish the city. At this time it was also decided to build a cathedral of imposing grandeur and magnitude; unfortunately, the plan had to be abandoned owing to the great epidemic — the Black Plague — of 1348, which ravaged the city. Chroniclers relate that 80,000 perished in Siena and its neighbourhood, and that only 15,000 souls remained alive there. All activities and energies suffered greatly, and this proved to be the beginning of the city's slow decadence. A successful revolu-

— 329 —

Photo ALINARI, ANDERSON, BROGI.

PALAZZO DEL CAPITANO.
Gothic style, Early 14th century.

PALAZZO PICCOLOMINI 1470.
Designed by BERNARDO ROSSELLINO.

PALAZZO SARACINI. *Gothic style. Erected in the 14th century.*

At first inhabitated by the Captain of War or military commander, and the Captain of Justice or chief judiciary functionary, and afterwards passed in turn into the possession of the Grottanelli, the Pecci and now the Piccolomini Clementini. Like the earlier palaces, it is of a severe type of beauty. In the 15th century the edifice was considerably altered but was restored in its original form in the 19th century.

The building in Gothic style seen in the distance at the end of the street is the Archiepiscopal palace.

Built for Nanni Piccolomini, father of pope Pius III., probably from a design from Bernardo Rossellino, this palace is reminiscent of the palazzo Rucellai (p. 305), and affects the imagination in the same way as do some of the Florentine palaces. On the principal façade adorned with tasteful decorations in wrought-iron, are the arms on the popes Pius II., and Pius III., of an austere stately beauty it was a fitting dwelling-place for the heads of a great house that for generations had done noble service to the State.

Built in the latter part of the thirteenth century, this palace was also at one time the seat of the Republic. Formerly the property of the Marescotti, then of the Piccolomini del Mandolo and finally of the Saracini, who had the façade reconstructed in the 17th century. According to tradition, a sentinel was placed on the tower of this building to watch the various phases of the battle of Montaperti, which he described and announced to the anxious people beneath, awaiting the results of the conflict.

The streets of old Siena were, without doubt, very narrow, and some rather dirty according to our modern notions. The rain and the swine were their chief cleansers. At night they were dark and deserted, no one walking through them after 9 o'clock; only here and there a small yellow flame was kept burning before a shrine or the image of the Virgin Mary. In Siena, as in Paris in the 18th century, it was normal for the housewife to throw her slops out of the window, a practice which must have seriously annoyed some of the night-roving dandies of Dante's *brigata spendereccia* or spendthrift brigate (*Inf.* xxix, 130). But here this practice was only permitted at night-time, and in certain streets.

tion was concluded in 1385, and resulted in the expulsion of many families on whose industry and experience in trade the prosperity of Siena largely depended. In 1387 there was a renewal of war with Florence and Siena, who called to her aid Gian Galeazzo Visconti, duke of Milan, who made himself master of Siena for twenty years.

1400-1500. Another affray with Florence (1454), and a plot to hand over Siena to Alphonso of Naples is discovered. When Aeneas Sylvius Piccolomini was elected (1455) pope, Sienese nobles are readmitted to a share in the government. After the conclusion of the war (1480) of Milan and Florence against Naples and the pope, Alphonso, Duke of Calabria tried to obtain suzerainty of Siena. The Neapolitan royal family, however, fell out of favour; and in 1487, Pandolfo Petrucci, a returned exile succeeds in getting hold of the government until his death in 1512. He was a thoroughly sensible tyrant and held complete sway on the exhausted people; encouraged the arts and sciences, and was surnamed *il Magnifico*; but he was merely a politician, quick at devising temporary expedients without being able to establish a dynasty. No sooner he was dead the city returned to its previous state of turbulence; the people again took control.

1500-1900. In 1522 Siena became a "free city," under the protection of the Emperor Charles V. But in the year 1531, the Emperor made an end of her independence and Siena became a vassal of the empire. Soon after, however, the city revolted and gave herself up to France, out of gratitude for assistance received from King Henry II. At that time the old towers of the nobles of Siena were still standing in every quarter of the city, as thick as trees in a forest. The revenge of Charles V. however, was not long delayed. An army composed of Spanish, German and Italian troops soon brought destruction (1554) to the territory of the Re-

A STREET OF OLD SIENA.

public, and the following year Siena sustained a formidable siege, celebrated in the annals of warfare by the heroic resistance of the inhabitants, especially the women. The city which before this last war had a population of one hundred thousand souls, was reduced to forty thousand; half of the people perishing from famine, sufferings, tortures or banishments. With the help of King Philip II., of Spain, Cosimo I. de' Medici, after a long siege and when all eatables within the city had been consumed, brought Siena to definite submission and annexed it to Tuscany (1559); Pius V., on this occasion conferred on him the title of Grand-Duke. From this time onwards the history of Siena ceases as a city-state, though she retained a separate administration for another two hundred years. In 1807, Siena with Tuscany was annexed to France by Napoleon Bonaparte; but in 1859, she once more took a leading part in the politics of Italy, for she was the first Tuscan city to vote for the annexation of Piedmont and the monarchy of King Victor Emmanuel II.

Photo ALINARI, ANDERSON, BROGI.

SIENA — THE PALACES.

There is perhaps no other city in Italy so rich in secular Gothic architecture as Siena. Following upon the rapid growth of trade in the 13th and 14th centuries, wealthy trading families like the Tolomei, the Salimbeni, *et al.*, early in the thirteenth century built for themselves palaces in the heart of the city.

After the completion of the large brick palazzo Pubblico, a new fashion arose in architecture; no man of wealth and position was content unless he had a gracefully-designed brick palace with rows of pointed and cuspid windows on the second and third storeys.

Thus the larger Gothic palaces in the city belong for the most part to one brief period of about sixty years: from the foundation of the palazzo pubblico or *della Signoria* 1289, and the Great plague 1348, when all Siena's activities and energies suffered greatly.

As at Florence, the walls of the ground floor are adorned with fine wrought-iron lanterns, torch-holders and banner supports

BANNER HOLDER on the *Palazzo Grisoli*.

The inhabitants of Siena were divided into two distinct classes, the soldiers and the people; on the one side were the Knights, or the aristocratic party, on the other side were the People, who were destined to become the supreme rulers of the State. The city was divided in three parts, or *Terzi* (see p. 349); each *terzo* divided into wards or *contrade*, which were originally 35 in number. These divisions were made in the beginning, for military purposes, the men of each *contrada* forming a society of arms. Each *terzo* had its own gonfalonier, and the hosts of the three *terzi* formed the citizen army. The sacred symbol of civic unity was the *carroccio*, or war-chariot, before which each loyal Sienese took his oath to defend, and if necessary shed his life-blood to the last drop for the community. The Knights were similarly organized, and either their *terzi* or their *contrade* were alike to those of the people. They also had their standard-bearer for each *terzo*, but they had no *carroccio*. This was a low, heavy waggon drawn by oxen and surmounted by a lofty pole bearing either the image of the Virgin Mary or a large Crucifix, while the standard of the city floated from a yard arm. In the interior of the car was an altar. From the car or from another that followed it, resounded the bell that gave signals to the fighters; near it was the commander; around it the priests and monks praying for the success of the city arms. The *carroccio* was the rallying-point of the soldiers, its surrender was considered as the final defeat and humiliation of the army.

PALAZZO TOLOMEI. *Gothic style. Early 11th cent.*

The *palazzo Tolomei* is the oldest secular building in Siena. Originally built in the year 1203, before the creation of the palazzo Pubblico, although burned down by the people on two occasions and rebuilt in 1247, it still retains its aspect of a typical Sienese mansion. In 1310, it was the residence of Robert of Anjou, king of Naples.

Near by, stands the ancient church of *San Cristoforo*, built about 1100, where the General Council of the " Twenty-Four," assembled, before the palazzo Pubblico was built.

PALAZZO BUONSIGNORI. *Gothic style.*

The *Palazzo Buonsignori*, one of the most elegant specimen of civic architecture, was built of brick in the 14th cent. and sold for 3000 golden florins to the Benassai. The palace on the right of which the doorway and two windows are shown here was the residence of the unfortunate Pia de' Tolomei.

COURTYARD OF THE PALAZZO BUONSIGNORI.

PALAZZO POLLINI. *An original edifice by* B. PERUZZI.

Photo ALINARI, ANDERSON, BROGI.

SIENA — VIEWS OF THE CITY.

The great *Piazza del Campo*, mentioned by Dante (*Purg.* xi, 134), has at all times been the heart and centre of Siena, for here, whether for pleasure of for war, for councils good or evil, have her people always assembled.

It is semicircular in form and depressed towards the centre, resembling an ancient theatre. It is here that the popular festivals, sports and tournaments took place, and even now the Palio horse-races (p. 350) are held.

On the south side of the piazza is the stately palazzo Pubblico; opposite is the Gothic palazzo Sansedoni and the celebrated *Fonte Gaia*, the "joyous fountain," with charming reliefs in marble, which Jacopo della Quercia finished in 1419. The fountain is a large rectangular basin enclosed on three sides by a low wall covered on its interior face with sculptured figures of the Madonna, the Virtues and other Biblical scenes placed in niches. The original panels now replaced by reproductions were removed in the palazzo Pubblico.

THE PIAZZA DEL CAMPO. *On the left marked X is the* "Fonte Gaia."

FONTE GAIA.
Copy, executed in 1868, of the fomtain built by JACOPO DELLA QUERCIA.

The *Loggia di Mercanzia* or *dei Nobili* (now the *Casino degli Uniti*), was built for the Guild of Merchants. The statues on the pillars of SS. Ansano, Savino, Victor, etc. are by *Antonio Federighi* and *Vecchietta*; the marble benches beneath the portico are adorned with sculptured figures of philosophers, ancient heros, generals, the Cardinal Virtues, etc.; on the back are wreaths enclosing the Lion and Balzana shields and a pair of scales and a bale : the seal of the merchants. Here formerly sat the commercial tribunal ; regarded as the most impartial of the kind, to which even foreign states resorted

STATUES OF SS. PETER AND PAUL.
By VECCHIETTA. *Loggia Mercanzia*.

LA "LOGGIA DI MERCANZIA."
Built in 1417-38 from designs by SANO DI MATTEO.

MARBLE BENCH with reliefs of philosophers, generals of antiquity. (on the back are the devices of the *Consoli di Mercanzia*).

Photo ALINARI, ANDERSON, BROGI.

SIENA — PALAZZO PUBBLICO.

This slender, graceful tower, has a height of 304 ft., and is the noblest tower in Italy: a staircase of 360 steps leads up to the summit, whence a magnificent view may be had on the surrounding Tuscan countryside.

The *Mangia Tower* obtained its name in this way: long before there were public clocks, certain of the bells of the city were struck at fixed hours to advise the inhabitants of the time. At the head of the men appointed to this office, a certain Giovanni Ducci, was nicknamed *Mangia*, or *Mangiaguadagni*. His place was taken by an automaton to whom the same nickname was given. For centuries this figure was called the Mangia, and in time the tower generally styled the *Torre del Mangia*.

The *Palazzo Pubblico*, a huge edifice built of brick and travertine, was erected between the years 1289 and 1305, to house the *Podestà* with his family and household, and the members of the *Signoria*. Over every door and window is the *balzana*, the black and white shield of the Commune; on the column marking the entrance to the right wing of the palace, is the *Lupa* of gilded bronze (the she-wolf with Romulus and Remus), the arms of the city of Siena. In her best days, the merchants of Siena had others than merely personal aims. They wished to make their city great and prosperous. The citizens combined to found and to develop important public institutions (p. 342), which became inseparable parts of the structure of the Commune.

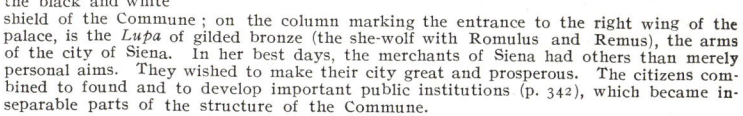

At the foot of the tower is the *Cappella di Piazza*, in the form of a loggia, begun in 1352, after the cessation of the great plague of 1348, which is said to have carried off more than 30,000 persons. The fresco on the altar wall is by *Sodoma*.

In 1425, in front of the *Cappella di Piazza* was set up a pulpit, whence Fra Bernardino the great preacher of his age delivered one of his first sermons (see p. 336). He denounced the factions of the Sienese, and exhorted them to put an end to the discords that for so long had disturbed the city; he thundered against the excesses of their luxurious living; their love of gambling, their lasciviousness and the obstentation of the prevailing fashions, for in this the ladies outshone all competitors. Like the Florentine women censured by Dante, the Sienese, not content with heightening the attractiveness of their charms by cutting their splendid dresses very low, made an extravagant use of paints and powders. So powerful was the effect of St. Bernardino's words that a pyre was erected in this piazza and there was a great burning of vanities, cards, dice, false hair, cosmetics, and obscene books and pictures were thrown into the fire.

TORRE DEL MANGIA.
Erected 1338-1349.

THE PALAZZO PUBBLICO. *Built from 1289 to 1309.*

CAPPELLA DI PIAZZA, or *del Voto*.
In memory of the Plague of 1348.

CORONATION OF THE VIRGIN, by SANO DI PIETRO. (*Sala della Bicchernа*).

On the ground floor, in the *Sala dei Signori di Bicchernа*, is a "Coronation", by *Sano di Pietro*, and other works by various masters. At the back of the palace is the market-place which leads to the Via de' Malcontenti and the Via di Porta Giustizia, through which, in ancient times, condemned prisoners were led to the place of execution beyond the city-walls.

The interior of the palace contains a series of magnificent apartments embellished with numerous mural paintings by Sienese masters.

COURT OF PALAZZO PUBBLICO.

Photo. ALINARI, ANDERSON, BROGI.

SIENA — *PALAZZO PUBBLICO.* Sala della Pace. Mural Frescoes.

ALLEGORY OF THE GOOD GOVERNMENT OF SIENA. *Fresco by* AMBROGIO LORENZETTI. A. D. 1337-1343.

The *Sala della Pace,* Hall of Peace, is thus named owing to the figure representing Peace in the centre of the principal fresco, facing the window. This hall was first called *dei Nove,* having been formerly used by a wardrobe-room of the Commune. Upon its three walls, AMBROGIO LORENZETTI painted in 1338 the great allegorical paintings of the Good and the Bad Government. The Good Government bears this signature : AMBROSIUS LAURENTII DE SENIS HIC PINXIT UTRINQUE.

On the right an enthroned majestic male figure, clothed in robes of black and white—the colours of the city, symbolizes the Good Government. In his left hand he bears a shield on which is painted the Blessed Virgin—the city's protectress, in the right he holds a sceptre and two ropes which are connected with the scales of Justice at the other end of the picture. Above him float the three Theological Virtues : *Faith,* with her cross, *Charity,* with her burning heart, and *Hope* gazing upwards. Various Virtues, his attributes and coadjutors, are seated on either side of Good Government. To his right are Prudence, Fortitude and Peace ; to his left Magnanimity, with a plate of money, Temperance, with the hour glass, and Justice, with the sword in one hand, a crown in the other, and a human head in her lap. Beneath his foot-stool are Romulus and Remus suckled by the she-wolf (the emblem of Siena in medieval times). Right and left are men-at-arms, horse and foot, keeping guard over malefactors and political prisoners.

On the left of the picture are symbolized Justice and Concord : the supporters of a well ruled state. Justice, a superb female figure is enthroned, above her is Wisdom holding a pair of scales in each of which is a winged figure or genius. The one on the left symbolizing Distributive Justice, beheads a malefactor with one hand and crowns a just one with the other ; the one on the right—Commutative Justice, administers the civil law. Below Justice sits Concord, a heroic figure with her smoothing plane in the right hand while in the left she holds two cords, one of which is attached to each of the scales and the other passes through the hands of a long procession of citizens (the twenty four councillors who formed the government) on to the right hand of the principal figure in the composition—the *Good Government of Siena.* The figure of "Peace," reclining upon her pillow, with her foot on a helmet and shield, is remarkably beautiful ; the folds of her white dress suggest an ancient sculpture.

THE RESULTS AND BLESSINGS OF THE GOOD GOVERNMENT OF SIENA. *By* AMBROGIO LORENZETTI.

The town of Siena is seen with her towered palaces and her Duomo ; her streets are crowded with people working at their trades. They are building and manufacturing, buying and selling, intent on business or pleasure ; girls are seen dancing and children playing in the square ; the shops are filled with craftsmen occupied at their various callings ; through the gates stream merchants and country people with laden mules bringing the produce of their farms into the town. All indicates prosperity and peace.

And the same outside the city : hunting proceeds with animation ; the fields are being worked, grain beaten ; cavaliers ride about.

— 332 —

Photo ALINARI, ANDERSON, BROGI, LOMBARDI.

SIENA — *PALAZZO PUBBLICO.* Sala della Pace, di Balìa, Council Chapel.

ALLEGORY OF THE BAD GOVERNMENT, or TYRANNY.
Fresco by AMBROGIO LORENZETTI.

On the wall facing the "Blessings of Good Government," *Lorenzetti* painted an "Allegory of the Bad Government," conceived as a complete antithesis. Here, the onlooker is confronted by the hideous figure of a *Tyrant*, mail-clad and wearing a blood-red mantle, enthroned beneath a trinity of evil: *Tyranny, Avarice* and *Vainglory*. Three vices sit on either side of the monster; right: *Cruelty, Treachery* and *Fraud*; left: *Wrath, Dissension* and *War*. *Justice* in the shape of a woman, captive, tear-stained, desolate, lies prostrate at the feet of Tyranny. In town and country are scenes of disorder, cruelty, and oppression. Panic reigns in the place of Security. Nobles and men-at-arms are riding forth to kill and to plunder; conflagrations and massacres break out and looting takes place.
[This fresco is much damaged and many details are no longer visible].

TRIUMPHAL ENTRY OF POPE ALEXANDER III.
Painting by SPINELLO ARETINO.

The *Sala di Balìa*, where in the early days of the Republic *balìe* or temporary committees of the Sienese Constitution used to gather, was decorated in 1407 by Spinello Aretino with frescoes from the history of Pope Alexander III. (Bandinelli).
There are 16 scenes representing the great struggle between the Papacy and the Empire. The story begins with the Coronation of a Pope, Adrian IV. 1154, or Alexander III. 1159, and the investiture of Frederick Barbarossa in 1155 at Rome. This is followed by the Quarrel of Barbarossa with the Pope; the siege of Milan in 1158; and continued round through a number of scenes to the famous *Triumphal entry of Alexander III. into Rome in 1177*,

SALA DELLA BALÌA. *Frescoes by* SPINELLO ARETINO, 1407.

after his reconciliation with, or rather victory over Barbarossa. Pope Alexander III. rides first, the Emperor leading the Pope's horse and the Doge Ziani walk beside him; cardinals and citizens follow. For the Sienese the interest in the struggle lay in the fact that Alexander III. was a native of Siena, and in the support accorded him by the Sienese throughout the contest.
The pictorial decorations of the *Sala di Balìa*, were commissioned by the Signoria. The scenes are not arranged in chronological order; on the entrance wall are represented the Capture of an Italian town by the imperialists, anp the Naval Victory of the Venetians in 1176, in which the emperor's son Otto was taken prisoner. The latter scene is a splendid rendering of medieval warfare.

BURIAL OF THE VIRGIN. *By* TADDEO DI BARTOLO.

COUNCIL CHAPEL, on the right a holy-water basin by TURINO.

The altar-piece is a Holy Family by *Sodoma*; the Choir-stalls carved by *Dom. di Niccolò*; mural frescoes by *Taddeo di Bartolo*.

— 333 —

Photo ALINARI, ANDERSON, BROGI.

43. · WONDERS OF ITALY.

SIENA — *PALAZZO PUBBLICO.* Sala del Mappamondo.

MAJESTAS. MADONNA AND CHILD surrounded by Saints. *Painted by* SIMONE MARTINI in A. D. 1315.

The *Sala del Mappamondo*, so named owing to a large circular map, now lost, hanging on its walls and representing the Sienese territory painted there by Ambrogio Lorenzetti. Here at one time the Council of the Bell or Senate of the State met. The whole of one wall is occupied by a "celestial vision" or *Majestas*, painted by Simone Martini. Our Lady enthroned is holding up the Divine Infant on Her knees to bless the deliberations of the Council; Saints and Apostles, Virgin Martyrs and Angels stand in attendance while two kneeling Angels offer baskets of flowers to the Divine Mother and Child. The four saintly protectors of the city, — Ansanus, Savinus, Crescentius and Victor, are represented kneeling in the foreground.

On the opposite wall, also painted by Simone Martini in 1328, is the equestrian portrait of Guidoriccio da Fogliano, a medieval captain of war, riding, fully armed, his baton of command in his hand, his horse gorgeously caparisoned. It was painted in commemoration of his brilliant capture of Montemassi, the castle seen on the left of the picture, from which the banner of the Commune floats; on the right foreground are preparations for storming the castle-town which had rebelled against Siena, further back is seen the *Battifolle*, — the name given to a *wooden* fortress with towers and ramparts, usually constructed whenever it was necessary to maintain a long siege.

ST. BERNARDINO, *by* SANO DI PIETRO.

ST. BERNARD TOLOMEI, *by* SODOMA.

ST. CATHERINE, *by* VECCHIETTA.

Beneath Guido's portrait is the Virgin enthroned by *Guido da Siena* (1221); right and left Sant'Ansano and San Vittore, by *Sodoma* ; and on the other wall, San Bernardo Tolomei, San Bernardino and Santa Caterina illustrated above. The upper part of the wall is decorated with paintings representing the victories of the Sienese over the Florentine at Torrita (1363), and at Poggibonsi (1479).

PORTRAIT OF GUIDORICCIO DA FOGLIANO, *by* SIMONE MARTINI (1328).

Photo ALINARI, ANDERSON, BROGI.

SIENA — THE CATHEDRAL.

THE CATHEDRAL. *Façade by* GIOVANNI PISANO. *Completed* A. D. 1380.

This magnificent cathedral, built wholly of marble and adorned inside and outside with ornaments of exquisite beauty occupies the highest ground in the town and stands on the site of an ancient temple of Minerva. The building as it now stands was begun in A. D. 1229 and completed about the middle of the fourteenth century. In 1331, when the church was yet unfinished, the Sienese got the notion that it was too small for the importance of their city; thereupon they resolved to erect a grander, new edifice surpassing in magnificence all other churches in Italy. Accordingly plans were laid by LANDO DI PIETRO and construction was begun of a huge nave of which the present cathedral was to form the transept only. But soon after, a plague swept over Italy (1348) and the city was so depopulated that such ambitious plan was abandoned and the old construction brought to completion. Part of this grand nave is still standing and it enables us to judge of its vastness. The *façade* was completed in 1380 from designs by GIOVANNI PISANO. It is composed of red, white and black marble and, like that of Orvieto, is adorned with sculptures and mosaics. A comparison of the two façades proves their similarity. Orvieto is more varied, although not more harmonious in its parts : a greater richness and grandeur are given to it in the enlarged size of the central doorway. At Orvieto the effect is due to the mosaic ; at Siena to the use of polychrome marbles.

Photo ALINARI, ANDERSON, BROGI.

SIENA — THE CATHEDRAL.

INTERIOR OF THE CATHEDRAL. *Gothic architecture.*

The pavement has a surface of nearly 30000 square yards.

The pavement has more than 50 "graffiti" designs.

Most of the pavement is generally protected by a wooden-floor, removed on special occasions.

In the right transept is the *Cappella del Voto* belonging to the Chigi family of Siena.

PLAN OF THE MARBLE PAVEMENT ADORNED WITH GRAFFITI.

On entering the duomo we are amazed from the beauty of its proportions, the intricacy of its ornaments, and the interlacing of its columns. The stained glass of the circular window in the entrance wall was designed by *Perin del Vaga*.

One of the most peculiar features of the interior decoration is a row of terracotta-busts of the Popes, carried all round the church above the great arches. These imaginary portraits, larger than life, lean, each from its separate niche crowned with the triple tiara. Their accumulated majesty reminds us of the whole past history of the Church.

Faith.   Religion   Charity.
         Hope.

HISTORY OF FORTUNE.
By PINTORICCHIO 1506.

Fortune is represented as a nude female figure holding a sail above her head and standing with one foot on a globe and the other on a storm shattered bark. She has landed ten of her subjects on a rocky island, the stony path of which leads up to a hill surmounted by a flowery garden where Wisdom sits enthroned. Two of the men start on the upward path to seek wisdom, others, undecided, gaze longingly back, one, with a discontented look, sinks down to rest, waiting for Fortune to come to him, while another shakes his fist at her. But she heeds him not and steps off again into her bark to fetch new votaries. On the right of Wisdom Socrates receives the palm, on her left Crates empties a basket of jewels into the sea.

Sibilla Albunea Tiburtina	La Fortuna con 4 Filosofi	Sibilla Persica
Sibilla Samia	La Fortuna	Sibilla Eritrea
Sibilla Frigia	L'Aquila imperiale	Sibilla Cumana
Sibilla Ellespontina	Stemma di Siena Pisa, Lucca, etc.	Sibilla Cumea
Sibilla Libica	Hermes Trimegisto	Sibilla Delfica	Statua del Papa Paolo V

Lower part of the pavement.

Photo ALINARI, ANDERSON BROGI.

SIENA — THE CATHEDRAL.

Niccolò Pisano's Sienese pulpit is on a larger scale than that of the Pisan baptistery (p. 316), and octagonal instead of hexagonal. It is supported by pillars of oriental marble resting upon the backs of lions, and a central column the base of which is adorned with allegorical figures representing the Liberal Arts: Grammar, Dialectics, Rethoric, Philosophy, and Music. The panels are divided by beautiful statuettes of Saints, Apostles, the Madonna and Child, Angels, and other symbolical figures; the admirable reliefs represent: The Visitation and The Nativity, The Adoration of the Magi, The Presentation in the Temple and Flight into Egypt, The Massacre of the Innocents, The Crucifixion, The Last Judgment. The elaborately ornamented staircase in the style of the Renaissance, is by *Bartolommeo Neroni* and was added in 1543. In the reliefs of this pulpit the scriptural subjects are almost similar to those of the Pisan pulpit by the same artist. The Nativity and the Adoration of the Magi are finer than at Pisa. The story

MARBLE PULPIT. *By* NICCOLÒ PISANO *his son* GIOVANNI, *and* ARNOLFO DI CAMBIO (1266-68).

begins with the Visitation, and to the right of this the Madonna is seen lying on a couch, rising herself on her arm to watch the women who wash the Child. In the Adoration, the whole circumstance of travel is represented in the lower part of the panel, winding up to the upper part in order to bring the kings before the Child. Here one of the Magi is for the first time shown kissing the Child's foot, a detail often repeated. The horses, camels, dogs are all realistically rendered, the landscape is indicated by the two trees introduced in the background. To the right of this panel, at the corner, is a Madonna and Child, one of the finest figures carved since classic times.

Il is impossible to mention here the numerous works of art which this admirable edifice contains. Over the highaltar, designed by Baldassarre Peruzzi, is the grand bronze tabernacle given on p. 337, brought here in 1506, to replace Duccio's famous altarpiece "Majestas," now in the cathedral museum (p. 340). The finely carved choir-stalls and the reading desk are by Bartolomeo Neroni (*il Riccio*). By the pillars supporting the dome are two flag-staffs from the *carroccio* used at Montaperti, in 1260 (p. 329), by the victorious Sienese.

TOMB of the CARD. PETRONI († 1314). [*By* TINO DI CAMAINO.]

ÆOLUS (*The god of wind*).

JOSHUA'S VICTORY AND HANGING OF FIVE AMORITE KINGS by PAOLO DI MARTINO, 1426.

INTERIOR OF THE CATHEDRAL.

Photo ALINARI, ANDERSON, BROGI.

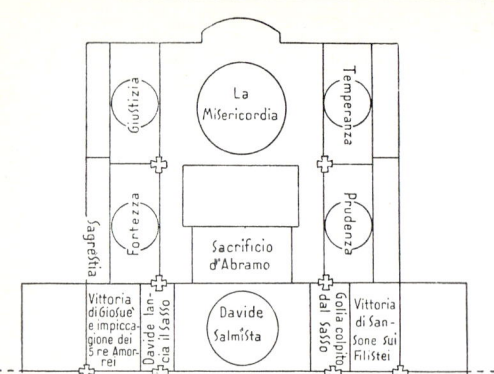

SIENA — THE CATHEDRAL.

Upper part of the pavement.

ALBERTO ARRINGHIERI.
Fresco by PINTORICCHIO (1504).

MARBLE FONT with reliefs representing scenes from Genesis.
(*School of* JACOPO DELLA QUERCIA)

MASSACRE OF THE INNOCENTS, *Graffito*
by MATTEO DI GIOVANNI. (1435-1495).

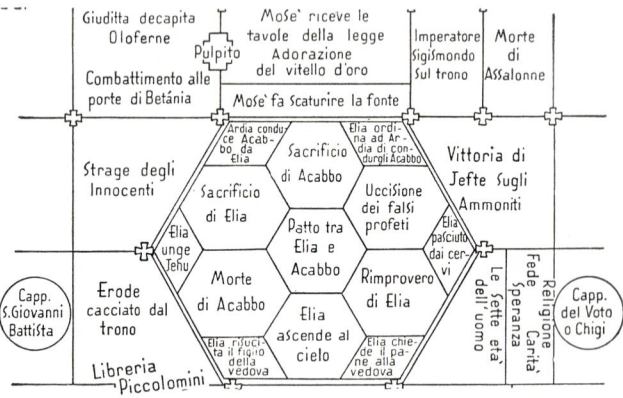

PLAN of the central part of the pavement.

Matteo's "Massacre of the Innocents" is perhaps the most successful of his various representations of this painful but seemingly favoured subject (he painted it three times). The son of Giovanni di Bartolo, a mercer, Matteo was the chief Sienese painter of his time. His works show a decided advance upon those of his immediate predecessors in vitality, grace, drawing and the handling of drapery.

THE DEATH OF ABSALOM.
By PIERO DEL MINELLA.

The *graffito*, above on the right, representing Absalom's tragic fate is highly interesting. He was his father's David favourite. Having rebelled against his parent he was defeated in "the wood of Ephrain", and killed by Joab, who found him caught by the hair in an oak-tree.

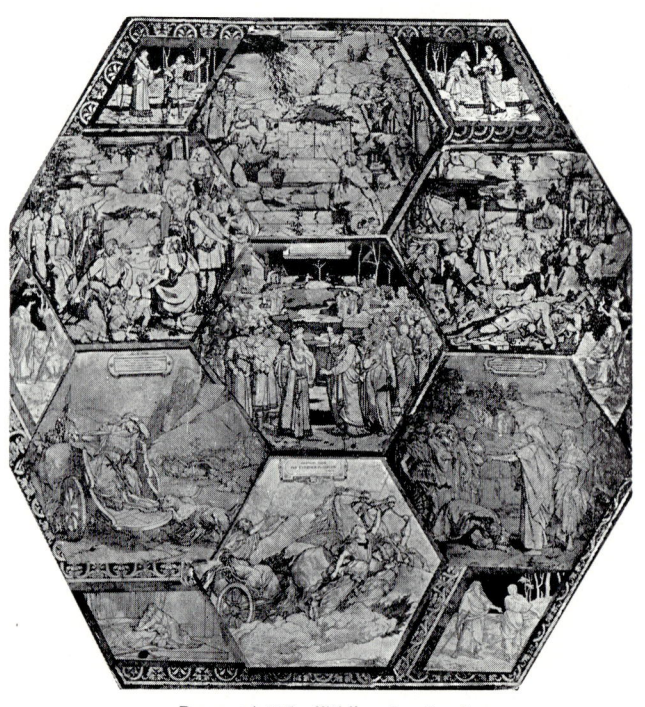

Pavement "Graffiti," under the dome.

— 336 —

SIENA — THE CATHEDRAL.

ST. JOHN THE BAPTIST. *Bronze by* DONATELLO, of the year 1457.

BRONZE TABERNACLE *by* VECCHIETTA (1472). The angels are by GIOVANNI DI STEFANO and FRANCESCO DI GIORGIO.

ST. BERNARDINO preaching in the Piazza del Campo. *by* SANO DI PIETRO.

HOLY WATER BASIN. *By* ANT. FEDERIGHI (1462).

THE PICCOLOMINI ALTAR (1481-85) with sculptures by ANDREA BREGNO and five statues of saints, SS. Peter, Pius, Gregory, James and Francis.

ALBERTO ARRINGHIERI. *By* PINTORICCHIO (1504).

ENTRANCE TO THE LIBRARY. *Sculptures by* L. DI MARIANO, " Il Marrina." (1497). Above is the Coronation of Pope Pius III., by *Pintoricchio*.

Another of the most remarkable feature is the marble pavement, inlaid and covered entirely with a variety of pictures in " Graffito " (a kind of *tarsia* work). Some of these compositions are as old as the cathedral; others are the work of Matteo di Giovanni, Beccafumi, *Pintoricchio*, and other eminent artists. They represent in the liberal spirit of medieval Christianity, the history of the Church before the Incarnation. Hermes Trimesgistus and the Sibyls meet us at the entrance...; in the centre of the church we see the mighty deeds of the old Jewish heroes : Moses, Samson, Joshua, Judith, Elias..., the five kings of the Amorites, and the Deliverance of Bethulia. The grandest compositions are : the Sacrifice of Isaac, the Massacre of the Innocents, the Seven Ages of Man ; the Symbols of Siena and her allied cities, etc. The execution varies : the oldest scenes are simple outlines engraved on the white marble and filled with black stucco. Later, sabling was introduced by the use of grey and also of coloured marble.

Conspicuous among the art treasures of the interior is the well-known octagonal pulpit of Niccolò Pisano ; the numerous statues, sepulchral monuments, and bas-reliefs by Renaissance artists adorning the various altars and chapels, the *cappella del Voto*, the *cappella Chigi*, the *Libreria Piccolomini*. The choir stalls dating from the 16th century, were carved from Riccio's designs.

Photo ALINARI, ANDERSON, BROGI.

SIENA — *LIBRARY OF THE CATHEDRAL.* Scenes from the life of Pius II.

The *Library* of the cathedral, one of the finest and best preserved creations of the Renaissance, was erected at the expense of Cardinal Francesco Piccolomini, afterwards Pope Pius III., to receive the books and manuscripts that his uncle, Pius II., had left him. The interior is a marvel of harmonious decoration. The large frescoes on the walls represent scenes from the life of Pius II. (Æneas Sylvius Piccolomini), whose career had been connected with all the great events of the period.

1. Æneas Sylvius Piccolomini sets out for the Council of Bale.

Æneas, a youth of twenty-five, is seen riding a white horse, starting for the Council of Bale, in company with Cardinal Capranica who heads the cortège. In the background is the bay of Genoa; the youth on the horse to the left is supposed to be a portrait of Raphael

LIBRARY OF THE CATHEDRAL.
Built in 1495, by order of Cardinal Francesco Piccolomini. Decorated by PINTORICCHIO, *in 1503.*

2. Æneas at the court of King James I. as ambassador of the Council. 1435.

After the Council of Bale, in which Æneas took a notable part, he was sent as ambassador by the Cardinal Albergato to the court of King James of Scotland. [James VI., of Scotland, on the death of Elizabeth, in 1603, succeeded to the throne of England as James I.].

3. Æneas crowned poet laureate by the Emperor Frederick III. at Frankfort. 1442.

In 1439, having entered the service as papal secretary of the Antipope Felix V. (Amadeus of Savoy), a new period of his career opened and he was sent on a mission to Frederick III., Emperor-elect, who bestowed upon him the Laureate crown, and made him one of his imperial secretaries and historians.

4. Æneas in the presence of Eugenius IV. as the envoy of the Emperor. 1445.

In 1445, Æneas, created prince of the empire, was sent by Frederick III., to Pope Eugenius IV., whose cause he had now determined to adopt. Soon after he became private secretary of Pope Nicholas V., who made him Bishop of Trieste (1447), and later of Siena (1450).

Photo ALINARI, ANDERSON, BROGI.

SIENA — LIBRARY OF THE CATHEDRAL. Scenes from the life of Pius II.

5. Æneas, Bishop of Siena, at the meeting of the Emperor and his bride Eleonora. 1452.

6. Æneas receives the Cardinal's hat from Pope Calixtus III. 1456.

7. Æneas is elevated to the Pontificate and becomes Pope Pius II. 1458.

As Bishop of Siena, he presided at the meeting of Frederick III., and his bride-elect Eleonora of Portugal, outside the Porta Camollia, where a column still records the event. [The beautiful and youthful Eleonora, born in 1434, daughter of King Edward of Portugal, after a most unpleasant voyage of 104 days, landed at Leghorn and a little later arrived at Siena, and was met by her fiancé outside the city gate. Her irresistible charm awakened to enthusiasm that great connoisseur of feminine beauty, Æneas, who so strongly influenced the monarch that, as a consequence, Frederick forgot all traditional etiquette of royalty, took Eleonora in his arms and embraced her without ceremony; and not long afterwards the wedding was celebrated at Rome. This was followed by the act of coronation in St. Peter's. It was the last coronation of a German Holy Roman Emperor, that was ever performed in the old Constantinian basilica of St. Peter's].

Calixtus III. (Alfonso Borgia, the successor of Nicholas V., and the uncle of Alexander VI.), was elected pope at the age of eighty. It was under his pontificate that the revision of Joan of Arc's unfair trial took place (1455), and her innocence proclaimed.

In 1458. Æneas was elected Pope and took the name of Pius II. In the picture he is seen carried in procession by prelates, while the Master of Ceremonies burns a piece of tow before him, with the traditional warning: *Sancte Pater, sic transit gloria mundi*.

"All the charm of the Italian Renaissance," writes Gabriel Faure, " all that is meant in the two words, breathes from these paintings which sing of the joy of living. Handsome cavaliers, ladies in sumptuous gowns, fine landscapes, love-poetry, what a pleasure for the eyes and the spirit ! "

8. Pius II. presides a Congress at Mantua to promote a crusade against the Turks. 1459.

9. Pius II. canonizes St. Catherine of Siena. (Portraits of Raphael and Pintoricchio).

10. Pius II. arrives at Ancona to incite the Crusaders and dies there. 1464.

In 1459, Pius II. opened a Congress at Mantua to proclaim a crusade against the Turks; but he received little support from the French and the Germans. [The fall of Constantinople (1453) had made a deep impression upon him, and he never ceased to preach against the infidels].

Pius II. canonizes St. Catherine of Siena, whose crusading zeal had anticipated his own. The corpse of the saint is seen lying at the Pope's feet. Below, among the crowd, the two most conspicuous figures on the left, are Raphael and Pintoricchio. [The Saint died 1380].

Pius II. is at Ancona, whither he had gone to head the crusade against the Turks. He was seriously ill of fever, and died soon after, gazing across the sea towards that promised land which he had vainly longed to conquer.

All around the library is exhibited a very valuable collection of Choir Books, with exquisite miniatures by Liberale da Verona, Girolamo da Cremona, Sano di Pietro and others. The celebrated antique marble group of the Three Graces, found at Rome and used as a model by Raphael, Pintoricchio, and Canova, which for many years stood in the centre of the hall, was removed (1857) at the desire of Pope Pius IX., who deemed it an unfit ornament for a Christian church, and is now preserved in the cathedral museum or *Opera del Duomo*.

Photo ALINARI, ANDERSON, BROGI.

SIENA — THE CATHEDRAL MUSEUM. Opera del Duomo.

MADONNA AND CHILD, ANGELS AND SAINTS (Majestas). *Great Altar-piece by* DUCCIO DI BUONINSEGNA. (1310).

Duccio di Buoninsegna. (1260?-1320), was the first great painter at Siena and the founder of the Sienese school. His greatest work was the famous "Majestas" illustrated here, which he painted about 1310. The work, richly covered with ornaments in gold, consisted of many parts forming one great altar-piece, 14 ft. long by 7 ft. in height and painted on both sides. On the front, the Madonna enthroned holding the infant Saviour, with Angels, Saints and Apostles surrounding the throne, and four bishops, tutelaries of Siena, kneeling in front.

On the reverse, a series of twenty-six panels depicting the life and passion of the Lord (the Entry into Jerusalem and the Crucifixion are larger than the rest). These compositions, with figures about nine inches high, bear the impress of a vigorous reform in art, and embody principles of dramatic action and expression which were adopted by several generations of Duccio's followers.

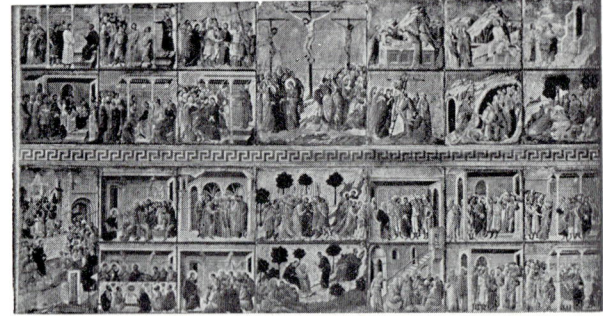

SCENES FROM THE LIFE AND PASSION OF CHRIST. *By* DUCCIO.

GILT WOODEN CRUCIFIX.
Attributed to
GIOVANNI PISANO.

THE FOUR SAINTS, *by* AMBROGIO LORENZETTI (1340).

SIENA — *CHURCH OF SAN GIOVANNI. The Baptistery.*

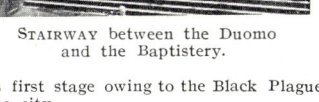

The *Church of San Giovanni*, the old baptistery of Siena, and forming a sort of crypt to the cathedral, was begun about 1317. The unfinished Gothic façade erected in 1382 is from a design ascribed to *Mino del Pellicciaio*.

The interior is adorned with paintings by *Vecchietta, Benvenuto di Giovanni*, and other artists. But the chief ornament of the church is the hexagonal marble font, designed by *Jacopo della Quercia* and executed in 1425-32. This masterpiece of the Italian Renaissance is adorned by six beautiful bronze-gilt reliefs from the history of John the Baptist executed by various artists : 1. The Angel appearing to Zacharias in the Temple, is by *Jacopo della Quercia* ; 2. The Birth of the Baptist, by *Giovanni di Turino* ; 3. The Preaching of St. John in the Desert, by *Giovanni di Turino* ; 4. Baptism of Christ, by *Lorenzo Ghiberti* ; 5. St. John brought before Herod, by *Lorenzo Ghiberti* ; 6. The Head of St. John presented to Herod, by *Donatello*.

Between the panels, at the corners of the font, are statuettes of the Virtues : Charity (on the left

CHURCH OF SAN GIOVANNI. *Baptistery.*
Façade by MINO DEL PELLICCIAIO.

MARBLE FONT.
Designed by J. DELLA QUERCIA.

of the first panel), Justice, Prudence, Fortitude, Faith, and Hope, The last two are by *Donatello*

The tabernacle above, and the statuette of John the Baptist on the summit, is attributed to *Jacopo della Quercia*.

Jacopo della Quercia (1374-1438), the author of the Fonte Gaia (p. 331), born at Siena, must be considered as one of the chief masters of the great Tuscan school, rather than a local Sienese artist. His principal works were executed at Florence, Lucca (p. 325), Bologna (pp. 174, 174), as well as at Siena. Vasari says : " He was the first after Andrea Pisano, Orcagna and others, who, working in the art of sculpture with more earnest study, showed what a much nearer approach could be made to Nature than had before been achieved ; so that it was by his example that others were taught to turn their attention towards rivalling her works."

Zacharias in the Temple. By J. DELLA QUERCIA.

DOORWAY of the unfinished grand nave.

The Sienese wished to build one of the greatest temple of the world. The nave was to be colossal, and the actual church would have served as a transept only. The first arcades constructed give the visitor an idea of the magnificence of the monument had it been completed. But it remained unfinished in its first stage owing to the Black Plague of 1348, which devastated the city.

STAIRWAY between the Duomo and the Baptistery.

The head of John brought before Herod. DONATELLO.

Donatello (1384-1466), the author of exceedingly numerous works executed at Florence *et al.*, was gifted with a facility of production as astonishing in its degree as was the greatness of his genius and he never refused the humblest commossion. He was an innovator in every sense. Whilst Christian art in the 15th century culminated in Lorenzo Ghiberti, Donatello commenced and indeed almost carried to perfection the " new manner," as it was soon expressively designated ; to him is due the invention of that peculiar and most beautiful method of low or flat relief (*stiacciato*).

— 341 —

Photo ALINARI, ANDERSON, BROGI.

SIENA — CHURCH OF SAN DOMENICO.

CHURCH OF ST. DOMENICO, *gothic style.* (*13th cent.*).

The church of San Domenico is intimately connected with the story of St. Catherine of Siena, for it was the scene of many of her visions and ecstasies. It not only possesses a contemporary portrait of her painted by her friend and correspondent Andrea Vanni, but her head also, which was embalmed immediately after her death and is preserved in a shrine over the altar of the saint. The admirable frescoes on either side of it given below were painted by Sodoma (Bazzi) in 1526. In conception and execution alike, they are considered marvels of art.

The group to the left representing the *Svenimento* is full of grace and pathos; the expression of tender anxiety and reverence, of the nuns, the sweetness, the languor, the beauty of the pallid features of St. Catherine falling exausted in the arms of her attendant nuns render this composition justly celebrated.

THE FONTEBRANDA.
It is at the feet of the hill where is built the church of St. Domenico.

The picture given on the right is a fresco in the chapel of S. Maria sotto le Volte (Hospital of S. Maria della Scala). It represents the return of Pope Gregory XI. from Avignon to Rome in 1377. St. Catherine and another nun is conspicuous in the assemblage of cardinals, prelates, and princes who form the triumphal procession.

THE POPES' RETURN FROM AVIGNON.
By MATTEO DI GIOVANNI.

PORTRAIT OF ST. CATERINE of Siena.
By ANDREA VANNI.
It's the only real portrait of the Saint.

ALTAR OF ST. CATHERINE. *Fresco by* IL SODOMA. A. D. 1526.
Left, "Svenimento" of St. Catherine; right, the Saint in ecstasy.

Photo ALINARI, ANDERSON, BROGI.

SIENA — THE CHURCHES.

The great Gothic *church of San Francesco*, was built by the Franciscans in the latter part of the 13th century. It was outside the wall and there was a gate of S. Francesco. When pope Pius II. came to Siena, he stayed in the convent. The vast interior is the most typical and austerely Franciscan of all the Gothic churches of Tuscany.

The preaching Orders required churches capable of holding large congregations at small cost. In these churches there were to be if possible, no detached supports to the roof, which might prevent the preacher from being seen by a portion of his congregation. Its architect succeeded in doing what was required of him, but he did not produce a beautiful church.

In the following centuries the interior of San Francesco was richly adorned by some of the great Sienese masters. The church is adjoined by two fine early-Renaissance Cloisters, with remains of 14th century tombs of nobles.

CRUCIFIXION. *By* AMBROGIO LORENZETTI.
(*Church of San Francesco*).

MADONNA. *By* MINO DEL PELLICCIAIO
(*Church of the Servi*).

MADONNA DEL LATTE. *By* A. LORENZETTI.
(*Church of San Francesco*).

ST. AUGUSTINE *and Episodes from his life.*
Painted by SIMONE MARTINI (*Church of S. Agostino*).

THE HIGH ALTAR *by* L. DI MARIANO
in the Church of Fontegiusta.

FONTEGIUSTA. *Built 1484.*
Early Renaissance.

MADONNA. *By* SANO DI PIETRO.
(*Oratorio di San Bernardino*).

— 343 —

SIENA — PINACOTECA. Picture Gallery.

MADONNA AND CHILD, and Saints.
Altar-piece by DUCCIO (op. 1278-1320).

ANNUNCIATION.
By A. LORENZETTI (1344).

The Picture Gallery possesses a valuable extensive collection of pictures chiefly by native masters. Duccio, the contemporary of Cimabue, is the first great name in Sienese Art; his works (see also p. 341) far surpass those of his predecessors in tender beauty and sentiment. An equally important master was Simone Martini (pp. 258, 333, 368), who followed worthily in Duccio's footsteps. Ambrogio Lorenzetti, the third of the greater men, was the most imaginative painter of the early school; his allegorical frescoes in the Palazzo Pubblico (p. 332) are justly famous. Ambrogio perished in the great plague of 1348, and for a time all artistic progress seemed at an end. For a century the painters of Siena followed the traditions, and generally clung to the limited methods of their predecessors, from whose influence they were unable to emancipate themselves. Their works had an affected simplicity, and were executed with religious care. In the works, for instance, of Matteo and Benvenuto di Giovanni (ca. 1470), there is still the same expression of religious ecstasy, and the same prodigal use of gold in the background, as marked the works of the preceding century: yet they were contemporaries with Botticelli, who introduced many new motives into art.

At the close of the 15th century, owing to contact with other schools, whose representatives were frequently invited to Siena, the tide of progress at length began to set in. The great innovators were Baldassare Peruzzi and Giovanni Antonio Bazzi, surnamed "il Sodoma". The latter, a pupil of Leonardo, possessed an innate sense of youthful beauty and grace; while his technical skill in fresco painting and his fertility are marvellous. By his example the languishing school of Siena received a new impulse, but the style of this period shows no affinity with the true Sienese school.

ANNUNCIATION AND DEATH OF THE VIRGIN.
By TADDEO DI BARTOLO.

ADORATION OF THE MAGI.
By BARTOLO DI FREDI (1330-1410).

PARADISE. Fragment of altarpiece by GIOVANNI DI PAOLO.

Photo ALINARI, ANDERSON, BROGI.

SIENA — *PINACOTECA.* Picture Gallery.

MADONNA AND SAINTS. ENTOMBMEMT. By AMBROGIO LORENZETTI (OP. 1324-1348).
St. John the Evangelist (*left*) and ST. John the Baptist (*right*) are attributed to the Lorenzetti's school.

MADONNA AND CHILD.
(Neroccio di Bart. Landi).

"Sienese painting in the 15th cent.", says Edmund G. Gardner in *The Story of Siena*, " is distinguished by its mystical tone and its exceedingly conservative, not to say retrogressive, spirit. No preoccupation with scientific researches, no problems of movement or anatomy, disturbed the calm of the Sienese painters; we meet with hardly any portraiture in their work, and even less mythology. The most turbulent of Italian people chose that their painters should give them art that was exclusively the handmaid of religion. While foreign sculptors, such as Donatello and Ghiberti, were welcomed and employed in Siena, foreign painters were practically excluded until the last two decades of the century."

"Great spiritual beauty in faces, accuracy of drawing within certain limits, with a profusion and a lavishness in the use of gold and the brilliant colours (this the Sienese particularly demanded of their painters), characterise the school of this epoch."

The religious feeling was a passion with the Sienese; their art reflects this spirit. It is like the religion of their St. Catherine rapt and ecstatic. Their prevailing characteristics are a peculiar beauty and tenderness of expression, inspired by devotional enthusiasm, differing altogether from that style which classical study had introduced in the northern schools of Italy.

ST. ANNE, with the Virgin and Child on her lap.
Painted by LUCA TOMMÈ. (1347).

MADONNA, *by* DUCCIO.

MADONNA, *by* LORENZO MONACO.

MADONNA, *by* MATTEO DI GIOVANNI.

— 345 —

Photo ALINARI, ANDERSON, BROGI.

THE ANNUNCIATION, by GIROLAMO DA CREMONA.

HOLY FAMILY WITH ST. JOHN.
By PINTORECCHIO.

SODOMA (Antonio Bazzi) was born in Lombardy, in his youth came within the sphere of the powerful influence of Leonardo da Vinci and he brought to Siena the knowledge of that great master. The most popular of the master's works in the Pinacoteca are the "Christ bound to the column," and the "Descent of Christ into Limbo." The latter famous for the figures of Adam and Eve, is a fine example of his power as a colourist, and of giving expression to his figures.

DESCENT FROM THE CROSS, by SODOMA.

CHRIST IN LIMBO, by SODOMA.

From Lombardy, *Sodoma* was brought to Siena in 1501, by some agents of the wealthy Spannocchi family. Here his artistic gifts and his youth gained him friends, and within the six years that followed his arrival he found ample employment. In 1505 he commenced the series of 25 great frescoes in the Benedictine convent of Monte Oliveto Maggiore (p. 351). Hence he was invited to Rome by the Sienese banker Agostino Chigi, and was employed by pope Julius II., in the Vatican (p. 458); in the Villa Farnesina, his patron's summer residence, he painted the "Nuptials of Alexander and Roxana" (p. 493). Back in Siena, in 1525, he painted the famous frescoes in San Domenico (p. 344). Afterwards he visited Pisa, Volterra and Lucca returning to Siena not long before his death (1549).

SIENA. CHURCH OF ST. FRANCIS.

Detail of the fresco, by AMBROGIO LORENZETTI, *given on the following page.*

St. Ludovic of Anjou kneeling before the pope Boniface VIII.
Fresco by Ambrogio Lorenzetti in the church of St. Francis.

SIENA — ARCHIVIO DI STATO. Painted Tavolette.

Allegory of the Government of Siena.

"The central figure is clad in black and white. He holds in his hand a black and white sphere; above his head is the word LIBERTAS which forms the inscription upon one of the shields of the Commune; and starting from his face, as if issuing from his mouth, is the legend KI BEN MINISTRA REMGNA. To his left sits the Camarlingo; to his right the Scrittore. The latter is making an entry in the book before him, while the former turns his head to listen to the words spoken by the allegorical figure."
William Heywood, *A Pictorial Chronicle of Siena.*

Allegory of the Government of Siena. *Benv. di Giovanni* (1474).

Marriage of Count San Severino and Lucrezia Malavolti. *Sano di Pietro* (1473).

The Virgin recommending the city of Siena to Christ. *Sano di Pietro* (1480).

Allegory of Peace and War.

"To the left we see a group of citizens who receive money from the public treasury, while above them hovers Peace, a nude female with an olive bough in her hand and the legend HÆC (*pax*) CIVES DITAT. To the right are soldiers of fortune to whom the Camarlingo tenders their pay. Over head is War armed with a sword, and the motto HOC (*bellum*) EXTEROS."
William Heywood, *A Pictorial Chronicle of Siena.*

Allegory of Peace and War. *Giov. Martini* (1468).

San Galgano and the Camarlingo Don Stefano. *Guido Cinotti* (1320).

The Virgin protecting Siena in the time of the earthquakes. *Benv. di Giovanni* (1467).

Presentation of the Keys of Siena to the Virgin (1483).

Madonna guiding into port the ship of State. *Bernardino Fungai* (1487).

Battle of Porta Camollia. *Giovanni Cini* (1526).

The Archivio di Stato possesses a valuable collection of painted *Tavolette*, or covers of the Municipal Tax Registers from the *Biccherna* (office for the receipt and disbursement of revenues) and the *Gabella* (tax collector's office). These Tavolette, painted by well known artists and dating from the 13th down to the 16th cent. are important from an historical point of view as they constitute a pictorial chronicle of the Medieval Commune. Upon the lower part were inscribed the names both of the Camarlingo (chief officer) and of the Provveditori, the rest of the surface was used for decorative purposes, — portraits of officials, scenes from sacred and profane history, etc. Members of religious orders — usually a monk of San Galgano — were invariably placed at the head of the Biccherna, because they were not likely to fall into corrupt practices, having no family interest to serve, and being prohibited from accumulating private property.

Photo ALINARI, ANDERSON, BROGI.

HORSE-RACES IN THE PIAZZA DEL CAMPO ON A PALIO DAY.

THE "PALIO" OF SIENA

THE "PALIO" is the most popular festival in Siena. It is held in connection with the Feast of the Assumption, and takes place in the square of the Campo on July 2nd and August 16th. It consists of a great procession of young men of the town in 15th century costumes, and of a horse race. It is a very picturesque sight which attracts a crowd of spectators from all countries.

From time immemorial the town has been divided into 17 *Contrade*, or wards (p. 330), each forming a self-contained unit, with its own name, its leaders, Church, traditions, flag and colours. The colours of the contrada of the She-Wolf are black and white which happen to be also the colours of Siena. The *Wave* has white and blue; the *Tower* has amaranth; the *Goose* has the three Italian colours (red, white and green). One can easily recognise from their coats-of-arms the *contrade* of the *Forest*, the *Sheep*, the *Tortoise*, the *Eagle*, the *Dragon*, the *Unicorn*, the *Giraffe*, the *Panther*, the *Shell*, the *Snail*, the *Owl* and the *Caterpillar*. Each of ten *contrade*, chosen by lot, enters in the race a horse, previously blessed in the Church of the district.

SHE-WOLF  WAVE  OWL  GOOSE

The winner of the race receives a banner, the palio (pallium) with the image of the Virgin. On the day of the race the Campo presents an impressive scene, reminiscent of a square in the Middle Ages. The Town Hall, the balconies and the windows of the houses display draperies in which red and yellow predominate; at the head of the procession on a prancing horse appears the standard-bearer of the Commune in a historic costume displaying the great standard of Siena, the glorious *Balzana*, half white, half black; behind this personage come the musicians in green livery, blowing their long trumpets; then the Captain of Justice, preceded by a page, followed by constables, all magnificently clothed. The *comparse*, or representatives of the ten districts who are going to take part in the race, appear in gala costumes; tight breeches with many coloured stripes: green, orange, blue, black or red doublets; with a purse or a dagger hanging from

TOWER 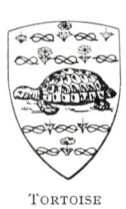 TORTOISE  EAGLE  GIRAFFE

Photo ALINARI, ANDERSON, BROGI.

SIENA — THE PALIO. Arms of the "Contrade."

1. TERZO DI CITTÀ.    2. TERZO DI SAN MARTINO.    3. TERZO DI CAMOLLIA.

From an early date Siena was divided into three districts: the *Terzo di Città* on the S. W., the *Terzo di San Martino* on the S. E., and the *Terzo di Camollia* on the N.

In early days the *Palio* was not run in the Piazza del Campo, as it is to-day; it probably took place on the public highway outside one of the city gates. It was not until 1603 that it was run in the Great Piazza del Campo.

the belt. At the head of each group a drummer beats his drum, followed by the *Alfieri* who wave their many-coloured flags with unrivalled skill. In their hands these flags are now still, now waved round and round, twirled round the body under their legs, over their heads; they pass from one hand to the other, then, cutting the air with the swiftness of an arrow, they are cleverly caught as they descend. This flag throwing affords many thrilling moments during the procession. In the rear comes the *Carroccio*, the old battle-car of the town, splendidly draped with red velvet edged with gold, surmounted by the Lion and the She-Wolf, the heraldic emblems of Siena; and finally come the guards of the commune led by their captain armed with helmet and breastplate on horse-back; the arquebusiers and the halberdiers close the pageant, which is watched with great interest

SHELL    WOOD    SNAIL    DRAGON

[In Italy, in the middle ages, many pastimes were indulged in besides running the Palio. Pisa had her *Giuoco del Ponte*, Arezzo her *Giuoco del Saracino*, Perugia her *Battaglia de' Sassi*, Gubbio the *Festa dei Ceri*; while in Florence, until the beginning of the 17th century, the youth of the city were wont to divert themselves with the *Giuoco del Calcio*, — the prototype of the modern foot-ball, and which probably bore a certain similitude to the *Pallone* of Siena. Another popular game played throughout Tuscany during the 13th - 14th centuries was the *Elmora*, for which the Sienese in particular displayed an extraordinary predilection; those who took part in it being armed with lances and swords of wood; their heads were protected by caps or helmets made of rushes, and they carried leather shields. It was, in fact, a mimic battle].

PORCUPINE    UNICORN    CATERPILLAR    PANTHER

VAL MONTONE

The word *Palio* itself simply means a banner; and a banner was the trophy presented to the victor of horse races in Siena.

GROUP OF "COMPARSE" WAVING THEIR FLAGS.

— 349 —

Photo ALINARI, ANDERSON, BROGI.

SIENA — VIEWS OF THE CITY.

On the left is the cathedral's campanile.

Descending the hill on which the cathedral stands, the tourist reaches a valley lying between the ancient part of the city and a western eminence crowned by the church of San Domenico (p. 342); in this depression, a kind of suburb of the poorer people, not far off the fountain of Fontebranda, is the very House of St. Catherine, in which she lived, her father's workshop, and the chapel which has been erected in commemoration of her saintly life. Over the entrance is written in letters of gold "Sponsæ Christi Katherinæ domus." The different rooms in the building have been converted into small chapels or oratories. Visitors are shown the room she occupied, and the stone on which she placed her head to sleep; the bag in which her alms were placed, the sack-cloth that she wore beneath her dress, the Crucifix from which, according to the legend, she received the *stigmata* at Pisa, in the year 1375.

From the little loggia which runs along part of the house the campanile and dome of the cathedral may be seen; on the opposite side rises the huge church of San Domenico, in which Catherine spent the long ecstatic hours that won for her the title of Christ's spouse. In a chapel attached to the big church she watched and prayed; there Christ appeared to her and gave her his own heart, there she assumed the robe of poverty, and gave her Lord the silver cross and took from Him the crown of thorns.

St. Catherine was one of twenty-five children born in wedlock to Jacopo and Lapo Benincasa, citizens of Siena. Her father exercised the trade of dyer and fuller. In the year of her birth, 1347, Siena was at the height of her power and splendor, soon after (1348) the great plague or Black Death began to rage, which swept off eighty thousand citizens,

HOUSE OF ST. CATHERINE.   PORTA ROMANA.

Palazzo Bandini Piccolomini.

and interrupted the building of the great cathedral. In the midst of so large a family, and during these troubled times, Catherine grew almost unnoticed; but it was not long before she manifested her peculiar disposition; at six years old she already saw visions and longed for a monastic life. As she grew, her wishes became stronger; she refused the proposals which her parents made that she should marry, and so vexed them by her obstinacy that they imposed on her the most servile duties in their household. These she patiently fulfilled, pursuing at the same time her own vocation with unwearied ardor; at length the firmness of her character won the day. Her parents consented to her assuming the Dominican robe, and at the age of thirteen she entered the monastic life.

From this moment till her death we see in her the ecstatic, the philanthropist, and the politician combined to a remarkable degree. For three years she never left her cell. Yet when she returned to the world, convinced at last of having won by prayer and pain the favor of her Lord, it was to preach to infuriated mobs, to toil among men, to execute diplomatic negotiations, to harangue the republic of Florence, to correspond with queens, and to interpose between kings and popes... The domestic virtues and the personal wants and wishes of a woman were annihilated in her; she lived for the Church, for the pope, and for Christ. J. A. SYMONDS, *Sketches in Italy.*

PALAZZO DEL CAPITANO. *Gothic style. Restored in* 1854.    THE "LOGGIA DEL PAPA." *Designed by* A. FEDERIGHI. 1432.

Photo ALINARI, ANDERSON, BROGI.

SIENA — THE ENVIRONS.

CORONATION OF THE VIRGIN.
By A. della Robbia.

MADONNA AND CHILD.
By Sassetta.

CHURCH AND FRANCISCAN CONVENT OF 'L'OSSERVANZA'.

The environs of Siena afford many delightful drives and excursions to points of interest. The church of the Franciscan *Convento dell'Osservanza*, was founded by S. Bernardino in 1423, and enlarged by Giacomo Cozzarelli in 1489 by order of Pandolfo Petrucci, tyrant of Siena. Among the many works of art which the church contains is the Coronation of the Virgin, one of the most beautiful works of ANDREA DELLA ROBBIA. In the upper part of the altarpiece sits the Virgin surrounded by angels with instruments of music in their hands; below, from left to right are the Baptist, S. Bernardino, St. Catherine of Siena and St. Francis standing, in front of the latter a donatrix kneeling. The reliefs in the predella represent the Annunciation, the Assumption, and the Nativity: simple in composition and full of sentiment as a Fra Angelico!'

VIEW OF BELCARO.

Belcaro occupies the site of a medieval castle of the early days of the Republic. Towards the end of the 14th century, it was much damaged and was given to St. Catherine as the seat of a convent of "religious women who shall continually pray for the city and inhabitants of Siena." Later, the convent became a fortress once more, and in 1525 it came into the possession of the Turamini, a rich family of bankers, who had the present edifice rebuilt from the designs of Baldassare Peruzzi, and employed the master himself to decorate it with frescoes. During the siege of Siena, in 1554, Belcaro became the head-quarters of the Marquis of Marignano, commander of the troops of Cosimo I. de' Medici.

The chief charm of Belcaro is its noble view, upon all sides the mountains and the valleys of the Sienese territory lie outstretched before the visitor's eyes.

TEMPTATION OF THE FASTING MONKS. *Fresco by* SODOMA.
(*Benedictine convent of Monte Oliveto Maggiore*).

About six miles south of Siena is the famous Benedictine convent of Monte Oliveto Maggiore, founded (1313) by Bernardo Tolomei of Siena, for the new "Olivetan" order. Pope Pius II., and the emperor Charles V., sojourned here; the monastery was suppressed by Napoleon I., in 1810; some of the monks remain as caretakers and gardners. The walls of the cloisters are adorned with celebrated paintings by *Luca Signorelli*, and *Il Sodoma*, representing forty-one scenes from the life of St. Benedict, explained by inscriptions beneath the pictures: St. Benedict's departure from home, Totila kneeling to the Saint, Soldier in disguise attempting to deceive the Saint, Punishment of two monks addicted to dainties, Resuscitation of a dead man whom Satan had thrown from a well, Exorcism of Satan, Temptation of the fasting monks, etc.

ABBEY OF LECCETO.
Founded in the 4th cent.

ABBEY OF SAN GALGANO.
Founded in 1201. Cistercian style.

— 351 —

Photo ALINARI, ANDERSON, BROGI.

SAN GIMIGNANO — *The Town of the Beautiful Towers.*

GENERAL VIEW OF SAN GIMIGNANO.

SAN GIMIGNANO is perhaps the only town in Italy which presents to us so faithful a picture of Medieval Italy. Its frowning walls and towers (whence the name of San Gimignano delle Belle Torri), its narrow streets and mysterious alleys all carry us back to Dante's time. In 1300 Dante was sent hither as envoy of Florence when he delivered a speech in the newly built Palazzo del Podestà inviting the Commune to send representatives to an assembly of Guelphs, but in spite of his eloquence democratic liberty was ruined by the dissensions of the leading families of the Salvucci (Ghibellines) and Ardinghelli (Guelphs).

In the old Piazza della Pieve, now called *Piazza del Duomo*, are several important buildings. The cathedral, usually called « *La Collegiata* » dates from the 11th century, and the whole of its walls are covered with 14th century frescoes. In the right aisle is the chapel of Santa Fina

PORTA SAN MATTEO.
San Gimignano is still surrounded by its old walls, and its three gates.

MAJESTAS. THE VIRGIN AND CHILD SURROUNDED BY SAINTS.
Fresco by LIPPO MEMMI, *pupil of Simone Martini,*
(*In the Sala di Dante, Palazzo Comunale*).

NUPTIALS OF CANAAN, *by* BARNA DA SIENA (1380).
Frescoes in the Cathedral (*La Collegiata*).

BURIAL OF SANTA FINA, *by* D. GHIRLANDAIO (1470)

Photo ALINARI, ANDERSON, BROGI.

SAN GIMIGNANO — *The Town of the Beautiful Towers.*

PALAZZO COMUNALE. *13th cent.*    TOWERS OF THE ARDINGHELLI.    PIAZZA DELLA CISTERNA.

with a marble altar by B. da Maiano and admirable frescoes by Ghirlandaio; in the sacristy (Museo dell'Opera) are several important works of art besides a number of devotional objects. Adjacent to the Collegiata is the Gothic *Palazzo Comunale* or *del Podestà*, containing a famous fresco by Lippo Memmi and a picture gallery. At the north end of the town is the church of *Sant' Agostino* in which are the famous frescoes by Benozzo Gozzoli and an exquisite marble altar by Benedetto da Maiano.

MARBLE ALTAR OF SANTA FINA.
By BENEDETTO DA MAIANO. A. D. 1468.
(*Cathedral La Collegiata*).

MARBLE ALTAR OF ST. BARTOLDUS.
By BENEDETTO DA MAIANO. A. D. 1494.
(*Church of Sant'Agostino*).

Photo ALINARI, ANDERSON, BROGI.

SAN GIMIGNANO — *Frescoes in the Church of Sant'Agostino.*

S. MONICA PRESENTS HER SON TO THE SCHOOLMASTER

ST. AUGUSTINE AS TEACHER OF RETHORIC IN ROME.

Frescoes by BENOZZO GOZZOLI. A. D. 1463-67.

St. Augustine, the third Doctor of the Church, was born in Northern Africa in A. D. 354. His father was a heathen, his mother Monica a Christian. He spent his youth in dissipation but soon afterwards he went to Rome where he gained fame and riches by his eloquence at the bar. From Rome he went to Milan and falling under the influence of St. Ambrose

ST. AUGUSTINE DEPARTS FOR MILAN.

ST. AUGUSTINE ARRIVES IN MILAN.

Frescoes by BENOZZO GOZZOLI (*Pupil of Fra Angelico*).

he was converted to the faith and baptized in presence of his mother. After some time he was ordained priest and later bishop of Hippo. The rest of his life was spent in the practice of every virtue; his writings in defence of Christianity are numerous and his controversies of various heresies celebrated; and he is regarded as the patron saint of theologians.

DEATH OF SANTA MONICA.

ST. AUGUSTINE ON THE BIER.

Frescoes by BENOZZO GOZZOLI.

St. Augustine took an active part in the Church controversies of his age, opposing especially the Manichæans, the Donatists, and the Pelagians; his principal works are his "Confessions," his "City of God," and his "Letters."

Photo ALINARI, BROGI.

PIENZA, VOLTERRA.

PIENZA. PALAZZO PICCOLOMINI.
Designed by ROSSELLINO (1462).

VOLTERRA. THE CATHEDRAL.
Façade by N. PISANO (?).

In ancient times Volterra was a strongly fortified town and one of the twelve confederate cities of Etruria. A free town in the Middle Ages, in 1361 it was annexed to Florence. Volterra possesses to-day many interesting remains and monuments of two thousand years — gateways and walls — and a museum filled with relics of Etruscan Civilization. In the palazzo de' Priori is a fine picture gallery; the cathedral, has a beautiful pulpit and sculptures by Mino da Fiesole.

VOLTERRA. PALAZZO DEI PRIORI (1208-57).

VOLTERRA. THE ETRUSCAN TOWER.

VOLTERRA. MUSEO GUARNACCI. *Founded in 1781.*

The Museum contains a valuable collection of Etruscan antiquities found in Volterra and its environs, such as Cinerary Urns in alabaster, terracotta and sandstone dating from the 2nd and 3rd cent. B. C. On the cover of these urns is the reclining figure of the deceased, while on the sides are represented scenes from Greek mythology and Etruscan life.

Photo ALINARI, ANDERSON, BROGI.

AREZZO.

THE ANNUNCIATION.
By P. della Francesca.

SANTA MARIA DELLA PIEVE.
Founded about 1050. Façade of 1216.

DEFEAT OF CHOSROES (fragment).
By P. della Francesca (1420-92).

THE QUEEN OF SHEBA adoring the miraculous beam.   SOLOMON'S RECEPTION of the Queen of Sheba.
Scenes from the Legend of the Holy Cross, by PIERO DELLA FRANCESCA. A. D. 1450 (Church of S. Francesco).

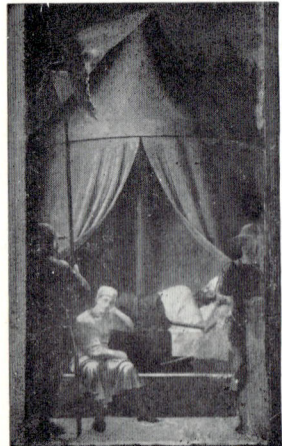

DREAM OF CONSTANTINE    MADONNA DELLA MISERICORDIA    RESURRECTION OF CHRIST. (Borgo San Sepolcro).

Piero's figures are finely constructed and beatifully placed, but passionless and almost motionless coldly impressive. Some 20 miles south of Arezzo, on a hill-top is *Cortona*, the belvedere of Umbria, Tuscany and lake Trasimene.].

— 356 —

Photo ALINARI, ANDERSON, BROGI.

VIEW OF ASSISI AND THE MONASTERY OF ST. FRANCIS.

ITALY bright and beautiful as it is, has few regions supplying more absorbing subjects for the eye and the soul of the tourist, than Umbria,—this wonderful district of luxuriant valleys, rivers and mountains on whose lofty summits were perched the chief cities of ancient Etruria. Umbria includes not only Perugia, the cradle of Umbrian art, and Assisi, the hallowed abode of St. Francis, but it includes also numerous medieval towns such as Orvieto, Foligno, Spoleto, Spello, Montefalco, Terni, Trevi, Todi, Gubbio, etc., all admirably situated on the most picturesque points.

UMBRIA

PERUGIA
ASSISI ORVIETO
SPOLETO GUBBIO
TODI

STREET OF PERUGIA.

PERUGIA — THE PALACES.

PALAZZO COMUNALE. *Begun* **A. D. 1281.**
It contains a fine picture gallery of Umbrian art.

FONTANA MAGGIORE. *Erected* **A. D. 1280.**
NICCOLÒ *and* GIOV. PISANO *and* ARNOLFO.

The façade of the palazzo Comunale towards the Duomo is adorned with the armorial bearings of the towns which were allied with Perugia ; over the portal are a griffin, the emblem of the town, and a lion in bronze (14th cent.) ; below are iron chains and bars of city gates, commemorating the victory gained by the Perugians in 1358, over the Sienese. In the 14th century many towns had their streets and piazzas *incatenate*, or furnished with chains, to the end that they might be barricaded at a moment's notice against feudal cavalry. In the 15th cent. power was concentrated in the Baglioni family, lords of Spello, etc., who had defeated the Oddi. But their tyrannical rule came to an end when Gian Paolo Baglioni was lured to Rome, in 1520, and beheaded.

ENTRANCE TO PALAZZO COMUNALE.
In the lunette are the patron saints of Perugia.

PALAZZO DEL CAPITANO DEL POPOLO.
Erected A. D. 1472.

OLD GATEWAY
and remains of the Palazzo del Popolo.

THE **PORTA AUGUSTA** or **ARCO DI AUGUSTO**. An ancient town-gate whose foundations date from Etruscan times.

Photo ALINARI, ANDERSON, BROGI.

GENERAL VIEW OF PERUGIA.

PERUGIA

THE GRIFO.
relief in the Church della Luce (Perugia).

PERUGIA, situated in the heart of Umbria, is the empress of hill-set cities. From its high-built battlements and church towers, the enraptured eye can sweep a circuit of the Apennines unrivalled in its width ; Assisi, Spello, Spoleto, Trevi.... are within range of vision, while the beautiful Umbrian plain spreads at the spectator's feet. Each point of vantage carries a bastion or tower of Etruscan, Roman, or medieval architecture marking the limits of the town upon its mountain plateau. Everywhere art and nature lie side by side.

In the neighborhood of the town itself there is plenty to attract the traveller of archeological bent. In the piazza there is one of the most perfect Gothic palaces to be found in Italy. The space in front of this palace was the scene, in medieval times, of all the bloodiest tragedies in the annals of Perugia. Here also the people of the surrounding district gathered to hear the sermons of St. Bernardino of Siena who, from the open air pulpit of the cathedral, preached peace in vain.

The name of Perugia suggests at once the painter who, more than any other, gave expression to devout emotions in consummate works of pietistic art. It was the adopted home of the great Pietro Vannucci, surnamed Perugino, in whose studio the young Raphael worked.

Photo ALINARI, ANDERSON.

PERUGIA — THE CHURCHES.

ORATORIO DI SAN BERNARDINO.

Lunette of the Façade by AGOSTINO DI DUCCIO. *A polychrome work of 1460.*

This is a beautiful specimen of Renaissance decoration. An infinite variety of reliefs, arabesques and ornaments cover the whole façade. Over the door are reliefs representing scenes from the life of S. Bernardino. In the lunette, the Saint appears in a glory of flaming tongues, attended by angels playing on instruments.

CHURCH OF THE MADONNA DI MONTE LUCE.
The church possesses a fine ciborium dating from 1483.

THE CATHEDRAL OF SAN LORENZO.
A Gothic edifice of the 15th century. (Façade unfinished).

CAPPELLA DEL ROSARIO. A. D. 1459.
(*Church of San Domenico*).

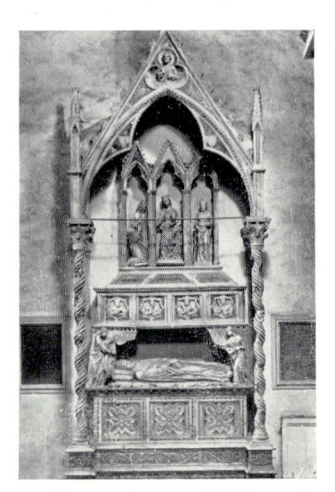

TOMB OF BENEDICT XI. † 1304.
General of the Dominicans.

CHURCH OF S. ERCOLANO. *13th cent.*
A Perugian street.

The *Church of San Domenico*, erected in the Gothic style about 1304 and almost entirely rebuilt in 1632 by *Maderna*, contains the tomb of pope Benedict XI., one of the best works of *Giovanni Pisano*, executed by order of cardinal Acquasparta. Pope Benedict's rule lasted only eight months. He was a loyal supporter of his predecessor, Boniface VIII., at the time of the conspiracy of Anagni, and died, it is said, from poison administered by the partisans of Philip le Bel of France.

Photo ALINARI, ANDERSON.

PERUGIA — THE CHURCHES. San Pietro de' Cassinensi.

CHURCH OF SAN PIETRO DE' CASSINENSI. *Erected in the year 1000.*   PANEL from the choir stalls.
This church, adjoining the old Benedictine monastery, is a veritable picture gallery. It contains works by Perugino, Pontormo, Sassoferrato, Caravaggio, Lo Spagna, Masolino and others.

READING DESK.   CHOIR-STALLS by STEFANO DA BERGAMO. A. D. 1535.
The choir-stalls in walnut, executed from designs by Raphael, are exquisitely carved and inlaid.

ST. MAURO.    ST. SCOLASTICA.    ST. ERCOLANO.
Panels from an altar-piece by PERUGINO.

Photo ALINARI, ANDERSON.

PERUGIA — COLLEGIO DEL CAMBIO.

Decoration on the ceiling of the Collegio del Cambio, with medallions of the seven planets.
These admirable arabesques were executed by the pupils of Perugino.

PORTRAIT OF PERUGINO. († 1523).
Painted by himself.
Born at Città della Pieve 1446.
Founder of the Perugian School of Painting.

Above: THE ALMIGHTY IN GLORY. *Fresco by* PERUGINO.
Beginning from left to right: Isaiah, Moses, Daniel, David, Jeremiah, Solomon; the Erythrean, Persian, Cumean, Libyan, Tiburtina and Delphic Sibyls.

THE BAPTISM OF CHRIST. THE ANNUNCIATION. *By* PERUGINO.

ADORATION OF THE MAGI. *By* PERUGINO.

— 362 —

Photo ALINARI, ANDERSON.

PERUGIA — *COLLEGIO DEL CAMBIO.*

SALA DI "UDIENZA DEL CAMBIO."  SALA DEL COLLEGIO DELLA MERCANZIA.

The *Collegio del Cambio*, the old Exchange and chamber of commerce, contains a series of frescoes considered among the noblest works of Perugino. Here, amidst rich designs, the Umbrian master portrayed the philosophers of Greece and Rome, the kings and generals of antiquity, the prophets, the sibyls, and the Virtues. These compositions, masterful in drawing and colour, breathe the spirit of the Renaissance and throw important light on the tendency of thought of that period.

Above: Prudence and Justice. *Frescoes by* PERUGINO. A. D. 1500. *Above*: Fortitude and Temperance.
Fabios, Socrates, Numa, Furius, Pittacus, Trajan.   Lucius, Leonidas, Horatius, Scipio, Pericles, Cincinnatus.

TRANSFIGURATION. *By* PERUGINO.    THE TRINITY. *By* RAPHAEL. 1505. (*Church of San Severo*). (Cfr. "Disputa" Vatican).

— 363 —

Photo ALINARI, ANDERSON.

47. - WONDERS OF ITALY.

PERUGIA — GALLERIA NATIONALE UMBRA.

BURIAL OF ST. HERCULANUS.   *Frescoes by* BENEDETTO BONFIGLI.   BURIAL OF ST. LOUIS OF TOULOUSE.

The Umbrian National Gallery, situated in the Palazzo Comunale, contains principally a collection of Perugian painters of the 15th and 16th centuries, centering around Perugino (1446-1628) who was the chief of the Umbrian school. This school of painting rose as early as the time of Dante, but did not produce such masters as Gentile da Fabriano, Benedetto Bonfigli, Fiorenzo di Lorenzo and Perugino until the 15th century.

The Umbrian painters lived in a country cut-off from contacts with the great outside world of the Middle Ages. Such a life led them to a certain exclusiveness and exaltation, depending on a keen sensibility, combined with an arrow mental horizon. Umbrian art aims not at suggesting a situation, but at creating a state of feeling PERUGINO is the most widely known for his colours.

MADONNA, *by* PERUGINO.   THE NATIVITY, *by* PERUGINO.

ADORATION OF THE SHEPHERDS. *By* FIORENZO DI LORENZO.    ADORATION OF THE MAGI. *By* B. BONFIGLI.

PERUGIA — GALLERIA NAZIONALE UMBRA.

MADONNA with SS. Catherine, Agnes, Elizabeth, Anthony, Louis, etc. *Altar piece by* TADDEO GADDI.

ST. FRANCIS trampling upon Haughtiness, Wantonnes and Avarice. *Altar-piece by* TADDEO DI BARTOLO (1362-1422).

DESCENT OF THE HOLY GHOST. *By* TADDEO DI BARTOLO.

MADONNA AND CHILD. *By* GENTILE DA FABRIANO.

MADONNA AND ANGELS. *By* FRA ANGELICO.

MADONNA WITH CHILD AND SAINTS. *By* BENOZZO GOZZOLI.

MADONNA ENTHRONED. *By* B. MARIOTTO. (Late 15th cent.).

Photo ALINARI, ANDERSON

PERUGIA — *PINACOTECA VANNUCCI*. *Altarpiece by Pinturicchio.*

Pietà. Entombment.

The Virgin and Child with St. John.

St. Augustine
Above: the Angel Gabriel

GREAT ALTARPIECE *by* **PINTURICCHIO**.

St. Jerome.
Above: the «Annunziata».

This beautiful Altarpiece was painted by PINTURICCHIO in 1495-96, for the Convent of S. Maria dei Fossi.

PINTURICCHIO (Bernardino di Betto), was born at Perugia in 1454 and studied under Fiorenzo di Lorenzo. Later in life he probably entered into partnership with Perugino, whose influence his works display. He was one of the best Umbrian painters, and his productions, though always showing Umbrian peculiarities, are more truly naïve, and less open to the charge of mannerism and affectation, than are too often those of Perugino. Pinturicchio died at Siena, 1513, where some of his finest mural paintings may be seen in the Cathedral.

St. Augustine by the sea.

St. Jerome in the Desert.

— 365* —

Photo ALINARI, ANDERSON.

VIEW OF ASSISI. *On the right, the* CASTLE OF ROCCA MAGGIORE. *(14th cent.).*

ST. FRANCIS. *By* SIMONE MARTINI,
Lower church of St. Francis. Fresco in the right transept.

ASSISI

THE CITY OF MYSTICISM.

ASSISI, the birthplace of St. Francis who founded the religious order, is deservedly the popular shrine that it is. The city of mysticism is loved by men of all creeds, who recall the story of the holy man, who, with poverty as a garment trod his long way succouring the poor.

The town is picturesquely situated on the slopes of Monte Subasio and commands charming views of the delightful Umbrian valley. Immense antiquity is suggested by everything around Assisi : Etruscan tombs, Roman temples, medieval castles, convents, churches. But the great sight of Assisi is the celebrated basilica of St. Francis, one of the most remarkable edifices in Italy. It is built over the tomb of the Saint who left such sweet odour of sanctity in the middle ages. The great veneration in which this church was held is evinced by the amount of fresco paintings with which the walls were covered in the thirteenth and fourteenth centuries.

Photo ALINARI, ANDERSON.

ASSISI — *SAN FRANCESCO.*

THE PORTICO AND THE LOWER AND UPPER CHURCH OF ST. FRANCIS.

ST. FRANCIS OF ASSISI was born in 1182. His father was a rich merchant who traded in silk and wool. In his youth, Francis delighted especially in gay and sumptuous apparel and led a life of pleasure and frivolity. In a quarrel between the inhabitants of Assisi and Perugia in 1201 he was captured and imprisoned when he was seized with a dangerous fever. It was on this occasion that his thoughts turned towards God and to higher things; a consciousness of his sins, a feeling of contempt for the world and its vanities, sank deep in his mind, and after a year of imprisonment he returned home and devoted himself to a life of poverty and self-denial. Followers soon collected round him, and in 1210 he founded his famous Order of Mendicanti Friars, the *Franciscans*. Poverty and self-abnegation were the essential characteristics of the order, which under different designation — Minorites, Capuchins, Observatens — soon spread all over Europe. During his prayers, St. Francis was frequently favoured with visions of the Virgin and the Saviour; the most important being the one experienced in his solitary cell on Mount Alvernia in 1224, when Christ impressed upon him the marks of his wounds (stigmata). In the last years of his life he suffered from the loss of his sight and broken in health through a life of hard work and privations he died on 4th Oct. 1226, and was canonized two years after.

TOMB OF ST. FRANCIS, with the stone coffin of St. Francis hidden here by Frate Elia and discovered in 1818.

Photo EDITRICE FRANCESCANA.

ASSISI — SAN FRANCESCO.

UPPER CHURCH OF SAN FRANCESCO. *Completed* A. D. 1253. (Gothic style).

The Upper Church, built in the form of a Latin cross, is important in the history of architecture, having been erected by foreign architects at a time when the Gothic style was foreign in Italy. Its walls are entirely covered with large frescoes executed in the 13th and 14th centuries by CIMABUE, GIOTTO and their followers. These compositions must, likewise, be regarded as one of the most important event in the historical development of modern painting.
The upper part of the walls of the nave is adorned with scenes from the Old Testament; the lower part with 28 scenes from the life of St. Francis painted by Giotto and his scholars in the last decade of the thirteenth century.

VESTIBULE OF THE LOWER CHURCH. *On the end wall is the* Cappella del Crocifisso.

The interior of the church was decorated by predecessors of Cimabue and the best artists of the Florentine, Sienese and Umbrian Schools of painting.

ASSISI — *SAN FRANCESCO. Cappella di San Martino.*

1. ST. MARTIN PARTING WITH HIS CLOAK.   2. DREAM OF ST. MARTIN.   3. ST. MARTIN RECEIVES KNIGHTHOOD.

The Chapel dedicated to St. Martin is adorned with frescoes of scenes from the life of the saint by SIMONE MARTINI (ca. 1326). Those reproduced here are: 1. and 2. represent the legend of St. Martin's youth,—his bestowal of the half of his cloak on the beggar, at the gate of Amiens, and the appearance of Our Saviour to him in a dream wearing the cloak he had bestowed on the beggar.

4. ST. MARTIN BEFORE THE EMPEROR.   5. ST. MARTIN CELEBRATES MASS.   6. VISION OF ST. MARTIN.

3. represents St. Martin's investiture with his sword and spurs, by the emperor Julian. 4. the saint is seen in his interview with the emperor when he renounced his service and offered to encounter the enemy armed only with the Cross. 5. one day, as he went to church to celebrate mass, St. Martin met a naked beggar and gave him his inner robe, accepting from the archdeacon a miserable narrow vestment which he placed under his cope. But, when he elevated the host, his arms being exposed by the shortness of the sleeves, angels appeared and covered them with golden bracelets. 6. St. Martin, now Bishop of Tours, has fallen into a reverie; a priest tries to rouse him while another kneeling waits patiently. 7. the saint is on his death-bed, expiring, surrounded by priests and monks, while his soul is carried up by angels to heaven. 8. shows the funeral ceremony.

SIMONE MARTINI (1283-1344), a contemporary of Giotto and the friend of Petrarch, was the most important painter of the Sienese school.

7. DEATH OF ST. MARTIN.   8. FUNERALS OF ST. MARTIN

Photo ALINARI, ANDERSON.

St. Francis, *detail of a fresco by* Cimabue *in the lower church.*

ASSISI — SAN FRANCESCO. Lower Church.

A MIRACLE OF ST. FRANCIS.   *Frescoes by* GIOTTO.   **ST. FRANCIS RESUSCITATES A CHILD.**

A child of the Spini family having fallen from a tower of the Palazzo Spini, was being carried to the grave, when the intercession of St. Francis was invoked and he appeared among the bewailers and restored the child to life.

A boy had been killed by the fall of a house; the mother, full of faith, vowed a new *sindon*, or linen cloth, to cover St. Francis' altar if he would restore her son to life. (The figure on the extreme left is a portrait of Giotto).

THE LOWER CHURCH.   *Begun in 1228. Completed in 1253.*

The high-altar stands above the tomb of St. Francis. It is formed by a slab brought from Constantinople, resting on twenty Gothic columns. On the vaulting above are the famous allegorical frescoes painted by GIOTTO (ca. 1302-1305), illustrative of the vows of the Franciscan order. From the middle of the nave two flights of steps descend to the *Crypt* where the remains of St. Francis, concealed there by Brother Elias, were discovered in 1818, after fifty-two nights of hard work. Around this spot a shrine was erected soon after the discovery. Here enclosed by a grille is seen the piece of solid rock in which were secreted the bones of the saint and the stone sarcophagus which now preserves them.

Photo ALINARI, ANDERSON.

ASSISI — *SAN FRANCESCO.* Lower Church. *Giotto's Allegories.*

Sancta Castitas.

From the tower of a fortress surmounted by the white banner of Purity, through a window appears "Chastity," as a young maiden praying: two angels floating in the air present to her the palm-branch and the Book of the Scriptures. Below are seen two bearded warriors ready to defend the fortress. In the centre of the composition, a youth receives the baptism emblematical of his vow of purity. In the left angle, St. Francis welcomes three disciples ascending the hill, ambitious of leading the *angelical life*; in the right angle, assisted by three angelic figures, "Penance," winged, but in an hermit's robe, puts to flight the Flesh and the Devil.

REPRESENTATION OF CHASTITY. *Fresco by* GIOTTO. A. D. 1305.

Sancta Paupertas

On a rocky wilderness, Christ is seen uniting St. Francis in marriage with "Lady Poverty," who stands in the midst of the picture emaciated, in a tattered robe, her bare feet among thorns, which a boy is trusting against her with a staff, while another youth throws stones, but roses and lilies flower behind her. She is attended by Hope and Charity as brides-maids, herself being thus substituted for Faith. In the left angle a man is giving his cloak to a beggar; in that on the right are two figures richly attired: one holds a falcon while the other is clutching a (money?) bag. The subject of this picture was probably suggested by a passage in Dante's *Paradiso*.

ST. FRANCIS WEDDED TO POVERTY. *Fresco by* GIOTTO. A. D. 1305.

— 370 —

Photo ALINARI, ANDERSON.

ASSISI — SAN FRANCESCO. Lower Church. Giotto's Allegories.

REPRESENTATION OF OBEDIENCE. *Fresco by* GIOTTO. A. D. 1305.

Sancta Obedientia.

Under the porch of a church, "Obedience," who is figured as an angel dressed in the Franciscan garb, puts the yoke over the head of a kneeling monk who bends his head devoutly to receive it. On his right is the double faced figure of Prudence; on his left Humility. On each side of the porch are groups of angels kneeling, one of whom (in front) seems to repulse Satan figured by a centaur. On the roof of the porch, attended by two kneeling angels, stands St. Francis in his monastic habit, a yoke upon his shoulders, a cross in his left hand. Above his head the hands of the Almighty appear coming from heaven, holding (or dropping?) the knotted cord of the Franciscans.

Gloriosus Franciscus.

Saint Francis is seated on a gorgeous throne, wearing the rich gold-embroidered robe of a deacon; in one hand he holds the cross, in the other the rule of his Order. On every side are choirs of jubilant angels celebrating his praises, some with hymn or song, others with trumpets or flutes. Above the saint's head, suspended from heaven, hangs a banner on which is depicted the Cross surrounded by seven stars. The whole cortege floating on clouds is apparently rising to heaven. This composition represents the glorification or apotheosis of St. Francis.

ST. FRANCIS IN GLORY. *Fresco by* GIOTTO. A. D. 1305.

— 371 —

Photo ALINARI, ANDERSON.

ASSISI — SAN FRANCESCO. *Giotto's frescoes in the Upper Church.*

St. Francis renounces the world.
St. Francis and his father renounce each other in presence of the Bishop of Assisi. Francis divests himself and hands back the garments to his father.

St. Francis receives honour.
from a simpleton of Assisi who, whenever met Francis, took off his own mantle and spread it for him to walk over, prophesying that he was worthy of reverence.

St. Francis appears to Innocent III.,
who, in a dream sees the falling Church supported by Francis. Thus, discovering he was the one who, by his works, would sustain the Church of Christ.

St. Francis in ecstasy.
One night, while St. Francis was in divine communion with God, his brethren saw him lifted from the ground and surrounded by a shining cloud.

Institution of Christmas Feast.
In order to commemorate Christ's nativity, St. Francis devoutly prepared a *manger* at Greccio and summoned the people to celebrate the joyful event.

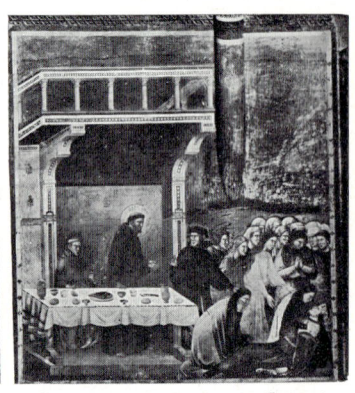

Death of the Knight of Celano.
St. Francis being invited to dine with a devout nobleman, warned him of his approaching death and exhorted him to confess and make peace with God.

St. Francis appears to Gregory IX.,
who hesitated before canonizing St. Francis, doubting the celestial infliction of the « stigmata ». The saint appeared to him in a dream, and exposing the wound in his side filled a vial with the blood that flowed from it, and gave it to the Pope.

Cures the wounded man.
A certain Catalonian who had been mortally wounded by robbers, and given over by his physician, invoked St. Francis, who appearing, attended by two angels, touched his wounds and healed him.

The Miraculous spring.
St. Francis and his companions, in journeying over a mountain on a hot day were exhausted by fatigue and thirst. The saint, kneeling down prayed and caused a spring of water to well forth.

— 372 —

Photo ALINARI, ANDERSON.

ASSISI — SAN FRANCESCO. Giotto's frescoes in the Upper Church.

ST. FRANCIS IN THE CHARIOT OF FIRE.

One night, during his absence from his brethren they beheld a fiery chariot with a dazzling globe resting upon it, which they knew to be the spirit of St. Francis.

VISION OF BROTHER PACIFICO.

who having entered a deserted church with the holy man, while the latter was praying fervently, saw the thrones richly adorned prepared in heaven for St. Francis.

EVIL SPIRITS EXPULSED FROM AREZZO.

The city was distracted by factions; in order to disperse these seditious powers of the air, St. Francis sent Fra Sylvester to command them in his name to depart.

ST. FRANCIS PREACHES TO THE BIRDS.

.... Near Bevagna, St. Francis came to a place where numerous birds of different kinds were assembled together, which, seeing the holy man, turned towards him, saluted him and bent their heads in attentive expectation.

THE BODY OF ST. FRANCIS

being carried to Assisi, the bearers halt before the porch of the Church of St. Damian, and are received by St. Clara and her nuns. St. Clara leans over the holy body and mourns, while a nun kisses his hand.

ST. CLARA of Assisi († 1263), under the influence of St. Francis, and against her parents' will, at the age of 13 became a nun. She founded the Order of the *Poor Clares*.

THE VIRGIN WITH ANGELS AND ST. FRANCIS. *Fresco painting by* CIMABUE.

" To this day, " says Ruskin, " among all the Mater Dolorosas of Christianity, Cimabue's at Assisi is the noblest; nor did any painter after him add one link to the chain of thought with which he summed the creation of the earth, and preached its redemption."

— 373 —

ASSISI — *CHURCH OF SANTA CHIARA.*

CHURCH OF SANTA CHIARA. *Erected in* A. D. 1257.

CHOIR OF ST. CLARA. *(Church of San Damiano).*

CRUCIFIX of the 12th cent. (See also page 324).

St. Clara of Assisi was born in 1194 of noble family, her uncommon beauty and the great wealth of her parents exposed her to many temptations and offers of marriage. But she had heard of St. Francis and was burning with the desire to follow his example. In 1212, under the influence of the holy man and much against her parents' will she entered a Benedictine nunnery and later founded, and was first abbess of the *Order of Poor Clares* (Clarisse). The rule was as austere as

ST. CLARA. *By* LIPPO MEMMI.

that of St. Francis. Voluntary poverty, abstinence and silence were strictly ordained. They were to exist literally upon charity,—when nothing was given to them, they fasted. The extreme austerity of her life wasted her health, and after acute bodily sufferings at the age of 60 she died and was canonized two years after. She is buried in her church.

CATHEDRAL OF SAN RUFFINO. *Completed* A. D. 1140.

CRUCIFIX *of the 13th cent.*

PORTICO OF THE TEMPLE OF MINERVA. *Now Church of Santa Maria della Minerva.*

— 374 —

ASSISI — CHURCH OF SANTA MARIA degli ANGELI.

INTERIOR OF SANTA MARIA DEGLI ANGELI.
Designed by VIGNOLA. A. D. 1569.

THE CELL WHERE ST. FRANCIS DIED. Oct. 4, 1226.
On the exterior: Death of St. Francis, *by* D. BRUSCHI. 1886.

The vast church of Santa Maria degli Angeli, erected on the site of the first oratory of St. Francis, is one of the great works of VIGNOLA who begun its construction in 1569. Under the lofty dome of the church stands the little chapel of the *Porziuncola*, the cradle and nucleus of the Franciscan Order.

The name of Porziuncola « small portion » was given to a slip of land of a few acres in extent, at the foot of the hill of Assisi, and on which stood a little chapel. Both belonged to a community of Benedictines, who afterwards bestowed the land and the chapel on the brotherhood of St. Francis. Here, the first disciples of the saint gathered around him, and round this chapel he built individual cells or huts for the brothers to whom he gave the name of *Fratres Minores*, to signify the humility and the submission enjoined them. It was at the Porziuncola that St. Francis had his first vision of the future greatness of his order, and where S. Clara was received by the holy man and made her profession. In the fourteenth century, particular indulgences were granted to those who visited it for confession and repentance on the 5th of August, and it became a celebrated place of pilgrimage and veneration.

CHAPEL OF THE "PORZIUNCOLA."
On the front, St. Francis receiving the indulgence (il Perdono) of the Porziuncola, *by* OVERBECK.

INTERIOR OF THE "PORZIUNCOLA."

In the right transept of the church is a beautiful altar with terracotta reliefs executed by LUCA DELLA ROBBIA. Behind the chapel of the Porziuncola is the cell in which St. Francis lived and died. It has frescoes of the companions of the saint by LO SPAGNA and a terracotta statue of St. Francis by L. DELLA ROBBIA. Beyond the sacristy is the celebrated little garden of thornless roses. Once they were mere thorns, but after St. Francis rolled his naked body upon them to mortify the flesh, these blossomed and ever since fresh leaves and blossoms come forth every year.

Photo ALINARI, ANDERSON.

ASSISI — *San Francesco.*

ST. FRANCIS PREACHES TO THE BIRDS. (*See page 373*).

GENERAL VIEW OF ORVIETO.

THE NATIVITY.
Relief on the façade of the Cathedral.

ORVIETO

ORVIETO occupies the site of *Volsinii*, one of the twelve capitals of ancient Etruria, destroyed by the Romans in 280 B. C. Its origin and importance has been proved by the discovery of numerous tombs outside the city walls, in which many valuable vases and trinkets were found.

Orvieto is one of the most remarkable towns in Italy. It is built upon the platform of a huge tufa rock emerging from the plain like an island with ramparts of cliff on every side. In medieval times Orvieto was a stronghold of the Guelphs, and many a pope, flying from rebellious subjects or foreign enemies, sought refuge within its walls.

The town, however, is chiefly celebrated for its magnificent Cathedral, a fine example of Italian Gothic architecture, and one of the most interesting ecclesiastical edifices in Italy.

Photo ALINARI.

ORVIETO. THE CATHEDRAL. *Begun* A. D. 1285.

The upper part of the façade is adorned with beautiful mosaics shining like gems or pictures on enamel.

in the left triangles:	in the central triangles:	in the right triangles:
on top, Marriage of the Virgin	*on top*, Coronation of the Virgin	*on top*, Presentation of the Virgin.
below the Baptism of Christ	*below*, Assumption of the Virgin	*below*, the Birth of the Virgin.

Around the Rose-window: the Church-Fathers; *above*: statues of the Apostles; *on the sides*: statues of Prophets.

The bas-reliefs on the lower part of the pilasters represent scenes from the Old and New Testament:

first pilaster,	*second pilaster*,	*third pilaster*,	*fourth pilaster*,
from the Creation down to Tubal Cain.	Abraham; genealogy of the Virgin.	History of Christ and of the Virgin.	Last Judgment and Hell.

Photo ALINARI, ANDERSON, BROGI.

INTERIOR OF THE CATHEDRAL.

THE CATHEDRAL OF ORVIETO, erected in commemoration of the « Miracle of Bolsena », is one of the greatest works ever achieved by the hand of man. The building was begun about 1285, perhaps by Arnolfo di Cambio. The construction of the edifice progressed so rapidly that some twenty years later the first mass was celebrated in the church.

The design of the cathedral is very simple; it consists of a nave and aisles, with transept and rectangular choir. The interior is austere and depends on surface decoration: statues, fresco paintings and woodwork. The chief treasures are Luca Signorelli's paintings in the Chapel of San Brizio (p. 382 *sq?.*).

The façade was begun in 1310 under the supervision and according to the plans of LORENZO MAITANI, the great Sienese architect. It is a triumph of decorative art; on every square inch of it have been lavished invention, skill, and precious material.

The lower part of the façade is adorned with reliefs representing scenes from the Scriptures. They were executed in A. D. 1320-30 by LORENZO MAITANI and other Sienese artists followers of the Pisani. These sculptures are characteristic of the transitional style which preceded the Renaissance; for nearly a century they were a source of inspiration to all successive masters.

« Willingly would I descant on the matchless façade of Orvieto, similar in style, but more chaste and elegant than that of Siena — on the graces of its Lombard architecture — on its fretted arches and open galleries — its columns varied in heu and form — its aspiring pediments — its marigold window with the circling guard of saints and angels — its quaint bas-relief — its many-hued marbles — its mosaic gilding, warming and enriching the whole, yet imparting no meretricious gaudiness — the entire façade being the petrifaction of an illuminated missal — a triumphant blaze of beauty obtained by the union and tasteful combination of the three Sister graces of Art ». — *Crowe and Cavalcaselle.*

THE ROSE-WINDOW.

The Rose-window is a work of great beauty; the square panel enclosing it is adorned with mosaics of the Fathers of the Church; the frame, with sculptured heads; the niches around contain marble statues of the Apostles and Prophets.

Photo ALINARI, ANDERSON.

ORVIETO — THE CATHEDRAL. *Reliefs on the Façade.*

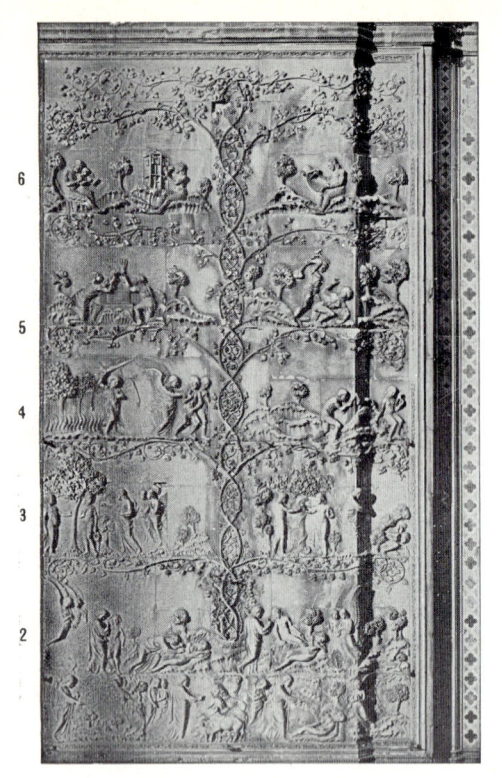

THE GENESIS. *First pilaster to the left.*

Six series of reliefs divided by the curves of the wild ivy that trails all over represent scenes from the creation of the world down to Tubal Cain. Beginning from below and from the left: **1.** God creates the Fishes, the Birds and the Trees; Creation of the animals; Creation of Man. **2.** God instils the breath of life into Adam; God removes the rib from the side of sleeping Adam; Creation of Eve. **3.** Earthly Paradise,—the Tree of Knowledge is forbidden; the Tasting of the Forbidden Fruit; Adam and Eve hide among the trees. **4.** Adam and Eve driven out of Paradise (flames of fire encircle the Tree of Life); Adam tilling the soil, Eve sits spinning. **5.** The Offerings of Cain and Abel; Cain kills Abel. **6.** Noemi teaches a child to read; her brother Tubal Cain inventor of musical instruments sits before his bells; and draws with a compass.

THE PROMISE OF REDEMPTION. *Second pilaster.*

Two vertical series of reliefs separated by the coils of the acanthus. **1.** Abraham reposing and in the central division rising directly from Abraham, the Kings of Judea (lineage of Christ): David, Solomon, Rehoboam, Abijah, Asa, Jehoshaphat, the Virgin Mary and Christ. **2.** A coffin with the skeleton of Abraham. **3.** Samuel anointing David; Gideon squeezing out the fleece; Balaam consults God; Balaam driving. **4.** Moses returning thanks for the liberation of the Israelites from Egypt; Moses presented to Pharaoh's daughter (?). **5.** Abraham leaves Ur; Melchizedek meeting Abraham. **6.** Vision of Ezekiel; Josiah's nurse suckling him. **7.** Abijah quieting the conspiracy of Jeroboam; Heliodorus driven from the Temple. **8.** Judith in Betulia; Daniel explains the fateful writing. **9.** The Angel Gabriel announces the birth of the Baptist to Zacharias; the Crucifixion.

SCENES FROM THE CREATION. *Lower part of the first pilaster.*

Photo ALINARI, ANDERSON.

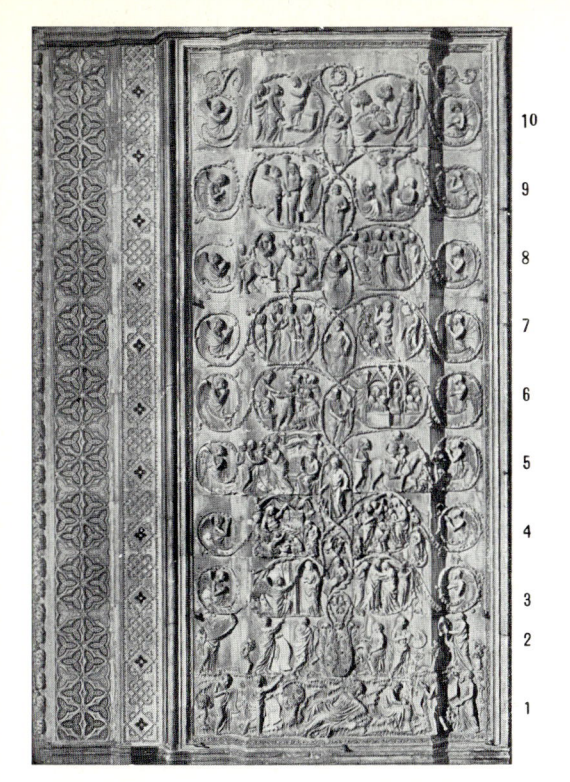

THE REDEMPTION. History of Christ. *Third pilaster.*

Two vertical series of reliefs enclosed between the acanthus' trails. Below, **1.** and **2.** Adam or Jacob with the four greater Prophets. In the central division rising directly above Jacob are the minor prophets holding a scroll. **3.** (from left to right). Annunciation; Visitation. **4.** Nativity; Adoration of the Magi. **5.** Presentation in the Temple; Flight into Egypt. **6.** Massacre of the Innocents; Christ among the Doctors. **7.** Baptism of Christ; Temptation or Miracle of Christ. **8.** Entry into Jerusalem; the Betrayal. **9.** Scourging of Christ; Crucifixion. **10.** The Three Marys at the Sepulchre; Christ appearing to the Magdalen (*Noli me tangere*). The extreme right and left are occupied by adoring angels.

THE LAST JUDGMENT. *Fourth pilaster.*

Five series of reliefs divided by the slender stems of the vine. Beginning from above: **1.** Christ as Judge in a mandorla of angels; on the sides Apostles, Saints, the Virgin Mary, John the Baptist, Instruments of the Passion and groups of angels summoning the dead with their trumpets. **2.** Cortege of Popes, Bishops, Friars (left), Nuns (right) and those who devoted themselves to Christ and a life of celibacy. **3.** The Blessed directed by angels. **4.** The Just awaiting to be taken upward; the Wicked driven downward. **5.** The Resurrection: all are intent on forcing the heavy lids of their sarcophagi; Inferno: the agonies of the Condemned, who are tortured by monsters and horrible demons with snaky legs.

THE RESURRECTION OF THE DEAD.   HELL. THE AGONIES OF THE CONDEMNED.

— 381 —

Photo ALINARI, ANDERSON.

ORVIETO — THE CATHEDRAL. Chapel of San Brizio.

HISTORY OF ANTICHRIST. *Fresco by* LUCA SIGNORELLI. A. D. 1499-1502.

ANTICHRIST.

The scene is laid in a valley near Jerusalem. In the front of the picture the Antichrist, a travesty of Christ, is represented standing on a pedestal, beside which are scattered the golden vessels taken from the temple. A demon is wispering into his ear. Around the false prophet are gathered all sorts of men: the pure and the dissolute, the reckless and the thoughtful, knights, friars, old men and women. Amongst them are the portraits of Dante, Boccaccio, Petrarch, Raphael, Pintoricchio, Cesare Borgia, Christopher Columbus, and members of the Vitelli, Petrucci, Malatesta, Baglioni, and Bentivoglio families. Behind, a group of friars and men are gathered round a monk, who reads the gospel of St. Matthew and foretells the coming of the true Messiah. Further back, the profaned temple guarded by soldiers; here and on the left of the picture acts of violence and murder prevail: the ground is strewn with corpses. In the centre are depicted the miracles of Antichrist, who is seen resuscitating a dead man, to the surprise of all spectators. While higher up, he is seen hurled down from heaven by the Archangel Michael. The two devout figures, in the corner to the left, are supposed to be portraits of Luca Signorelli and Fra Angelico.

RESURRECTION OF THE DEAD.

This is the most important of Signorelli's frescoes. Here the master has introduced a great number of naked figures in which a perfect drawing of the nude is observable.

« Two angels of the judgment—gigantic figures, with the plumeless wings that Signorelli loves—are seen upon the clouds. They blow trumpets with all their might; so that each naked muscle seems strained to the blast, which bellows through the air, and shakes the sepulchres beneath the earth. Thence rise the dead. All are naked, and a few are seen like skeletons. With painful effort they struggle from the soil that clasps them round, as if obeying an irresistible command. Some have their heads alone above the ground. Others wrench their limbs from the clinging earth; and as each man

RESURRECTION OF THE DEAD. *Fresco by* LUCA SIGNORELLI. A. D. 1499-1502.

rises it closes under him. One would think that they were being born again from solid clay and growing into form with labour. The fully risen spirits stand and walk about, all occupied with the expectation of the judgment; but those that are in the act of rising have no thought but for the strange and toilsome process of this second birth. » J. A. Symonds, " *Sketches in Italy.* "

— 382 —

Photo ALINARI, ANDERSON.

ORVIETO — THE CATHEDRAL. Chapel of San Brizio.

"Castarum Virginum Cohors" (*Choir of the Virgins*).   "Doctorum Sapiens Ordo" (*Church Fathers*).
Frescoes by LUCA SIGNORELLI, on the ceiling of the chapel.

The "Fulminati."

THE END OF THE WORLD.
By SIGNORELLI.

This fresco painted on the entrance wall of the chapel, is divided into two sections.

All around are signs of the end of things: the sun and moon are darkened, the sun sheds sparks of fire, stars fall from the sky, temples and palaces are overturned by earthquake, and mankind destroyed by fire. Below, on the right, a sibyl turns over the books of prophecies, while a prophet gesticulates and points to the event of the great drama. On the left side of the picture are the Fulminati. «Look at the *Fulminati*—so the group of wicked men are called whose death precedes the judgment. Huge naked angels, sailing upon van-like wings, breathe columns of red flame upon a crowd of wicked men and women. In vain they fly from the descending fire. It pursues and fells them to the earth. As they fly, their eyes are turned toward the dreadful faces in the air. Some hurry through a portico, huddled together, falling men, and women clasping to their arms dead babies scorched with flame. One old man stares straight forward, doggedly awaiting death. One woman scouts defiance as she dies. A youth has twisted both his hands in his hair, and presses them against his ears to drown the screams and groans and roaring thunder. They trample upon prostrate forms already stiff. Every shape and attitude of sudden terror and despairing guilt is here.» J. A. Symonds, "*Sketches in Italy.*" (*Fresco by* SIGNORELLI).

Death of the Three Witnesses.

Photo ALINARI, ANDERSON, BROGI.

ORVIETO — THE CATHEDRAL. Chapel of San Brizio.

OUR SAVIOUR SITS IN JUDGMENT amidst angels.
Fresco by FRA ANGELICO A. D. 1447. (Above the Altar).

THE GOODLY FELLOWSHIP OF PROPHETS.
Fresco by FRA ANGELICO A. D. 1447.

THE BLESSED ASCENDING INTO HEAVEN.
Scenes from the Last Judgment.

THE CONDEMNED DESCENDING INTO HELL.
Scenes from the Last Judgment.

These compositions, painted on the altar wall of the chapel, are a continuation of the corresponding ones given on the following page and painted on the side walls. The one on the left is a scene from Paradise. Angels above make sweet melody with their instruments, while below other angels direct the ways of the elect. The picture on the right shows the entrance to hell. The scene is dark and gloomy; in the centre is the ferry-boat of Charon, with the old boatman coming to take souls across the Styx. On the banks of the river the Condemned crowd themselves to be taken in, in the distance others, terror-stricken and with uplifted arms, run hither and thither, threatening or invoking aid from above.

Photo ALINARI, ANDERSON.

PARADISE.

This composition, and the one on the left of the altar, illustrated on the preceding page, represent scenes from the antechamber of Paradise. The attitude and expression of the figures betokens the most unspeakable bliss.

« Signorelli has contrived to throw variety and grace into the somewhat monotonous groups which this subject requires. Above are choirs of angels, not like Fra Angelico's, but tall male creatures clothed in voluminous drapery, with grave features and still, solemn eyes. Some are dancing, some are singing to the lute, and one, the most gracious of them all, bends down to aid a suppliant soul. The men beneath, who listen in a state of bliss, are all undraped. Signorelli, in this difficult composition, remains temperate, serene, and simple; a Miltonic harmony pervades the movement of his angelic choirs. Their beauty is the product of their strength and virtue. No floral ornaments or cherubs, or soft clouds, are found in his Paradise; yet it is fair and full of grace.... » J. A. Symonds, " Sketches in Italy."

PARADISE. *Fresco by* LUCA SIGNORELLI. A. D. 1499-1502. (Left wall).

HELL.

The representation of Hell is replete with vehement and fantastic action; the misery and suffering of the souls is so vividly and powerfully depicted, that it seizes upon our imagination and makes us shudder.

« This is a complicated picture, consisting of a mass of human beings entangled with torturing fiends. Above hover demons bearing damned spirits, and three angels see that justice takes its course. Signorelli here degenerates into no medieval ugliness and mere barbarity of form. His fiends are not the bestial creatures of Pisano's bas-reliefs, but models of those monsters which Duppa has engraved from Michael Angelo's " Last Judgment "—lean, naked men, in whose hollow eyes glow the fires of hate and despair, whose nails have grown to claws, and from whose ears have started horns. They sail upon bats' wings; and only by their livid hue, which changes from yellow to the ghastliest green, and by the cruelty of their remorseless eyes, can you know them from the souls they torture.... » J. A. Symonds, " Sketches in Italy."

HELL. THE PUNISHMENT OF THE WICKED. *By* L. SIGNORELLI. A. D. 1499-1502. (Right wall).

ORVIETO — THE CATHEDRAL. Chapel of San Brizio.

Scenes from LUCA SIGNORELLI's fresco of "Antichrist."

LUCA SIGNORELLI (1441-1523), was the most distinguished painter of his time. To him is due the inauguration of the study of the human form for its own sake. The mural paintings illustrated in these pages are the master's chief works. These compositions, executed ten years before the ceiling of the Sistine Chapel by Michelangelo, and about forty years before the completion of the "Last Judgment" by the same master, show how powerfully Michelangelo was influenced by Signorelli's productions.

Adam and Eve. "Paradise."  — Groups from "Resurrection."  — Groups from "Hell."

"Purgatory"

The lower part of the walls of the chapel is adorned with "tondi" in chiaroscuro, representing scenes from Dante's *Divina Commedia*, mythological subjects, and the portraits of Dante, Virgil, etc. They are surrounded by the most exquisite arabesque decorations.

PORTRAIT OF DANTE. — PORTRAIT OF VIRGIL.

Photo ALINARI, ANDERSON.

ORVIETO — THE CATHEDRAL. Interior.

SILVER-GILT RELIQUARY OF THE SANTO CORPORALE.
Executed by UGOLINO DI VIERI *of Siena.* A. D. 1337.

BAPTISMAL MARBLE FONT. A. D. 1403.
By PIERO DI GIOVANNI *and* JACOPO DI PIERO.

The Reliquary of the Santo Corporale contains the blood-stained chalice (corporale) connected with the Miracle of Bolsena. It is a work of great beauty and resembles in form the cathedral. The Miracle of Bolsena occurred in 1263. A young Bohemian priest who doubted the dogma of transubstantiation, was celebrating mass in the church of Santa Caterina at Bolsena, when, in elevating the host, blood issued from five gashes in the wafer, resembling the five wounds of

MARBLE ALTAR OF THE VISITATION.
By SAMMICHELI *and* MOSCA. A. D. 1425.

ALTAR OF THE ADORATION OF THE MAGI.
By SAMMICHELI *and* MOSCA. A. D. 1425.

our Saviour and stained the corporal. Thereupon, the priest seeing the blood fall on the linen of the altar, was convinced of the truth. The occurrence was announced to Pope Urban IV., then at Orvieto, who requested the Bishop to go and fetch the "Corporale" and bring it to Orvieto. The events of the miracle are represented on the reliquary in pictures of transparent enamel; the miraculous Santo Corporale is shown to the public on Corpus Christi and on Easter Day every year.

Photo ALINARI, ANDERSON.

ORVIETO — *MUSEO DELL'OPERA.*

ST. PETER AND THE MAGDALENA, *by* SIMONE MARTINI.

The Museo dell'Opera, near the Cathedral, contains a very interesting and valuable collection of antiquities. It comprises the famous Græco-Etruscan sarcophagus (4th cent. B. C.) discovered near Orvieto in 1912, numerous ancient painted vases and glass-ware, mosaics, marble and wooden sculptures, Sienese and Umbrian paintings, carved choir stalls and reading desk, and the colossal marble statues of the Apostles (15th-17th cent.) which formerly stood at the base of the pillars in the nave of the cathedral.

MADONNA AND CHILD.	THE VIRGIN.	THE ANNUNCIATION.	MADONNA AND CHILD.
Attrib. to L. MAITANI.	*Wooden statues of the fourteenth century.*		*Attrib. to* FRA GUGLIELMO.

On the first floor, are several wooden statues of the Virgin Mary, produced by 13th-14th century artists. As in the case of Saviour (*see Crucifix*, p. 324) representations were gradually transformed and, after being hieratic and almost incorporeal till the 13th cent., artists began to give to figures real human forms; instead of a seated posture the Madonna rose and bore the Infant Christ on her arm. Finally, with the Renaissance, she was represented in the tender attitudes of her maternal rôle.

Photo ALINARI, ANDERSON, BROGI.

ORVIETO — *MUSEO DELL'OPERA.*

NEOPTOLEMUS SACRIFICING POLYXENA ON THE TOMB OF ACHILZES. (*Græco-Etruscan sarcophagus of the 4th cent. B. C.*).

This sarcophagus, found in 1912, is very important in the history of archeology. Each side has sculptures still bearing traces of painting; the reliefs representing scenes of the Homeric legend are harmonious and well balanced, the heroic figures noble and severe. These compositions are regarded as fine examples of early Greek art.

ETRUSCAN SARCOPHAGUS.

ETRUSCAN VASE WITH SPHINX.

ETRUSCAN VASE.

VASE WITH RELIEFS.

ULYSSES AND THE SORCERESS CIRCE.
Græco-Etruscan sarcophagus.

— 387 —

Photo ALINARI.

ORVIETO — *THE PALACES*.

MEDIÆVAL TOWER in the Via del Duomo.

PALAZZO MARSCIANO. *By* A. DA SANGALLO *and* SCALZA.

PALAZZO DEL POPOLO *or* DEL PODESTÀ. *12th cent.*

PALAZZO COMUNALE. *By* SCALZA.

WELL OF SAN PATRIZIO.

ETRUSCAN TOMBS.

The Well of San Patrizio, begun by A. da Sangallo junior in 1527 and completed by Mosca in 1540, is a marvellous piece of engineering. It is a sort of hollow tower 200 ft. deep; the upper part being hewn in the tufa rock while the lower part, which touches the tertiary marl of the tufa rock, is built of masonry. Two separate spiral staircases of 248 steps circling one above the other, wind round the shaft, one was used for the descent one for the ascent of the water-carrying beasts.

— 388 —

Photo ALINARI, ANDERSON, BROGI.

UMBRIA — Città di Castello. Spoleto.

CITTÀ DI CASTELLO. Silver Altar front presented to the Cathedral, by Pope Celestine II. (1144).
The side panels represent: the Nativity, the Adoration of the Magi, Entry into Jerusalem, and the Crucifixion. In the centre: Our Saviour, and the symbols of the Four Evangelists.

HALL OF THE PALAZZO COMUNALE. CITTÀ DI CASTELLO.

GREAT HALL OF THE CASTLE OF POPPI. (*Restored in 1907*).

SPOLETO: THE CATHEDRAL. *12th cent.*
It contains frescoes by FRA FIL. LIPPI.

The Castle of Poppi was originally built by Guido Guerra, the first Count of Poppi. On the upper floor a chamber is shown as that of "la bella Gualdrada," the beautiful daughter of Bellincion Berti, mentioned by Dante (*Paradise* XV.). In the year 1209, the emperor Otho IV. being at a festival in Florence, where Gualdrada was present, was struck by her beauty; and inquiring who she was, was answered by Bellincion that she was the daughter of a man who, if it was his Majesty's pleasure, would compel her to embrace him. On overhearing this, she arose from her seat, and blushing, in an animated tone of voice said, " No man shall ever be allowed that freedom, unless he is my husband." The emperor was no less delighted by her resolute modesty than he had before been by the loveliness of her person; and calling to him Guido, one of his barons, gave her to him in marriage; at the same time raising him to the rank of a count, and bestowing on her a large extent of territory around Poppi as her portion.
From the tower there is a fine view of the famous plain of Campaldino.

THE CASTLE OF POPPI (*Tuscany*).
Built by ARNOLFO DI CAMBIO, 1274.

Photo ALINARI, ANDERSON, BROGI.

TODI: S. M. DELLA CONSOLAZIONE.

This pilgrimage church, remarkable for its symmetrical proportions, was erected from 1508 to 1524. It is a beautiful example of Bramante's style of architecture.

SPOLETO: TEMPLE OF THE CLITUMNUS.

This little temple, now turned into a church, dates from the 4th cent. It stands near the *Sources of the Clitumnus*, so glowingly described by Pliny and Byron.

TERNI: CASCATA DELLE MARMORE.

The waters dash on the rocks with so much impetuosity, that a great part, being reduced almost to vapour, re-ascends once more to the top. (Height 650 ft.).

GUBBIO: PALAZZO DE' CONSOLI.

Gubbio still preserves its medieval character. The Gothic Palace of the Consuls, loftily situated on the slope of the mountain, is one of the stateliest City Halls in Italy. The whole town is full of specimens of medieval architecture; it is also famous for its school of majolicas. The "Festa dei Ceri," is the most popular festival in Gubbio; it is held on the eve of St. Ubaldo's feast, on May 15 of every year; three colossal heavy wooden pedestals, each over 30 ft. high, and crowned by wax statues of SS. Ubaldo, Antonio and Giorgio, are borne in procession through the town, and then, in a wild race, rushed up to the old convent of St. Ubaldo. In visiting Gubbio tourists are reminded of the miracle wrought by St. Francis when he converted a very fierce wolf who appeared in the territory and which not only devoured animals but also men and women. (*Fioretti*, xxi).

VIEW OF NARNI.

Narni, half way between Rome and Perugia, is picturesquely situated on an eminence which overhangs the brink of a luxuriant valley. Not far from the town is the *Bridge of Augustus*.

TOMB OF THE VOLUMNII. About 300 B. C. *Discovered in 1840 (near Perugia).*

The Tomb of the Volumnii is the most interesting of the sepulchres of ancient Etruria, and one of the sights which, when once seen, is not likely to be forgotten. The visitor descends a long flight of steps to the entrance, formerly closed by a huge slab of travertine, and finds himself in a sort of mysterious cavern, a spacious oblong chamber, on which open nine smaller ones, all hewn in the rock. All around are several cinerary urns, some of which with recumbent figures of the deceased lying on the lid. From the roof still hang the genii of death; on the walls and on the vaulting are carved the heads of the sun-god and of the ever-recurring Medusa with her glaring eyes.

Photo ALINARI, ANDERSON, BROGI.

THE ROMAN CAMPAGNA: RUINS OF THE AQUEDUCT CONSTRUCTED BY APPIUS CLAUDIUS, 313 B. C.

LATIUM

ROME
TIVOLI FRASCATI SUBIACO ANAGNI
VITERBO CAPRAROLA TOSCANELLA
FOSSANOVA OSTIA

PORTA MAGGIORE,
formed by the arches of two aqueducts buit by Claudius in 52 A. D.

PONTE MOMENTANO. *Ancient bridge restored in the 13th cent.* TOMB CÆCILIA METELLA. *1st. cent.* A. D.

CHRONOLOGY OF THE PRINCIPAL EVENTS IN THE HISTORY OF ROME.

B. C.
753. — Foundation of Rome (Legend of Romulus and Remus).
716-509. — Mythical period of the Kings.
509. — Downfall of the monarchy. — Rome is a Republic.
390. — Invasion of the Gauls. Rome is sacked and burned by Brennus.
295. — Rome extends authority over the countries bordering the Mediterranean.
266. — Rome is supreme in Italy. The Etruscans totally lose their independence.
264. — The Carthaginians declare war against the Romans. First Punic War.
234. — Ravenna founded by Greek colonists. Is annexed to Rome.
219-202. — Second Punic War. Hannibal conducts a remarkable expedition from Africa to Italy through Spain. Battle of Lake Trasimene.
205. — Spain is regarded as a Roman province.
168. — Egypt formally acknowledges the suzerainity of Rome.
146. — Macedonia is made the eighth Roman province. Carthage destroyed.
146. — Carthage with the north coast of Africa becomes a Roman province.
143-31. — The universal power of Rome is firmly established.
60. — The first triumvirate is formed by Pompey, Julius Cæsar and Crassus.
44. — Julius Cæsar is assassinated.
27. — Octavius Augustus, the first of the Roman emperors rules the Roman world.
27 B. C. to 476 A. D. — The Roman Empire.

A. D.
64. — Rome is burned by Nero who accuses the Christians of the crime.
64. — First persecution of the Christians.
64-78. — Rome is rebuilt on a grand scale. Nero erects his magnificent Golden Palace.
97-117. — Trajan reigns. The Empire is extended to its largest limits and comprises Arabia, Armenia, Asia Minor, Britain, part of the Caucasus region, Corsica, Crete, Cyprus, Cyrenaica, Dacia, Dalmatia, Egypt, Gaul (France), Greece, Italy, Macedonia, Mauretania, Moesia, Noricum, Numidia, Pannonia, Rhætia, Sardinia, Sicily, Spain, Syria, Thrace, Tunis, Western Germany.
312. — Constantine defeats Maxentius near Rome. He accords to Christianity equal rights with all other religions.
330. — Rome ceases to be the capital. The seat of the empire is transferred to Byzantium.
410. — Sack of Rome by Alaric. By the Vandals in 455.

476 — Romulus Augustulus, last emperor. About twelve centuries after the founding of Rome, the empire falls in consequence of domestic revolutions and not by conquest.
590-604. — Gregory the Great is enthroned and assumes the title of Sovereign Pontiff.
754. — The Frankish king Pepin marches into Italy against the Lombards and Byzantines. The temporal power of the Popes begins.
774. — Charlemagne conquers Lombardy and annexes it to the dominions of the pope.
800. — Charlemagne is crowned in St. Peter's by Leo III. The Holy Roman Empire.
1073-85. — The investiture dispute. Gregory VII., struggles for supremacy with the emperors.
1143-55. — Arnold of Brescia attempts a revolution.
1309. — Clement V., leaves Rome for Avignon, which becomes the official seat of the Holy See until 1377. The papal absence was a period of great misery; the population of the City being reduced to less than 20.000 souls.
1377. — Return to Rome of Gregory XI. The pope first resides at the Vatican.
1413. — Rome is sacked by Ladislas, King of Naples.
1447. — Nicholas V., pope. He commences a new St. Peter's.
1471. — Sixtus IV., pope. He erects the Sistine Chapel.
1503. — Julius II., pope. He founds the Vatican Museum and gives fresh impulse to the Arts.
1511. — Martin Luther visits Rome.
1513-21. — Leo X., pope. The Golden Days of Rome.
1527. — Sack of Rome by the troops of Charles of Bourbon who fell in the attack.
1572. — Gregory XIII., pope. He institutes the Gregorian calendar. Ten days are dropped out of 1582. Oct. 5 becomes Oct. 15.
1626. — The new Basilica of St. Peter is consecrated.
1809. — The States of the Church are annexed to France. Abolition of the temporal power of the popes.
1814. — Fall of Napoleon. Rome and the Papal States restored to the popes.
1846. — Pius IX., pope. He institutes political reform and aims at the unification of Italy under papal supremacy.
1848. — A republican insurrection breaks out in Rome Pius IX., escapes in disguise to Gaeta. A provisional government is formed. A republic is established.
1849. — Rome restored to Pius IX., by the French.
1860. — The States of the Church are annexed to Sardinia.
1870. Sept. 20 — Italian troops enter Rome, the city is incorporated with the Kingdom (now Republic) of Italy. Rome is the capital of Italy.

PIAZZA NAVONA
Fountain of the Rivers. *By* Bernini.

MONUMENT TO KING VICTOR EMMANUEL II., AND THE FORUM OF TRAJAN.

ROME

> " 'Tis the centre
> " To which all gravitates. One finds no rest
> " Elsewhere than here. There may be other cities
> " That please us for a while, but Rome alone
> " Completely satisfies. It becomes to all
> " A second native land by predilection,
> " And not by accident of birth alone. "
>
> —LONGFELLOW.

THE " VIA DEI FORI IMPERIALI "
AND THE MONUMENT TO VICTOR EMMANUEL II.

The *Imperial Way* (Via dei Fori Imperiali) was opened recently: it goes in a straight line from Piazza Venezia to the Colosseum and passes through the various ancient Forums.

ROME, for many centuries the undisputed mistress of the world, the supreme and eternal city, the seat of Empire and Christendom, and since 1870 the capital of the Kingdom of Italy, is a world in itself. Whatever has possessed greatness —art, religion, history—has left its traces in this city. Pagan antiquity, the origin of Christianity and of the Byzantine civilization, the struggles and the transformation of the early Middle Ages, the ecclesiastical supremacy of the thirteenth century, the Renaissance of the fifteenth and sixteenth—all these epochs had Rome for centre; they covered it with their works, and they live again it it in a multitude of monuments and ruins which still reflect the glory and splendour of her past.

The history of no country in the world is so fraught with interest as that of Rome : from a sheepfold it grew into a town, from a town to a walled city, then to a little nation, a kingdom, a republic, an empire... Legend ascribes its foundation to Romulus in 753 B. C.; the first nucleus of

— 393 —

Photo ALINARI, ANDERSON, BROGI.

houses or huts were built on the Palatine, afterwards the town gradually crept up the sides of the now world-famous « seven hills »—the Palatine, Capitoline, Quirinal, Cœlian, Aventine, Viminal and Esquiline. Already in the 6th cent. B. C. under the kings of the Tarquinian family it was a flourishing town. After the expulsion of the kings (509 B. C.) the efforts of republican Rome were directed in conquering her rivals the Etruscans and in establishing her supremacy over Sicily, Greece and the countries bordering the Mediterranean. Thenceforth too the city began to assume an aspect more worthy of its proud dignity as capital of the civilized world;

VIEW OF THE CASTEL SANT'ANGELO, THE RIVER TIBER AND THE BRIDGES UMBERTO I., SANT'ANGELO, AND VICTOR EMMANUEL II.

VIEW OF THE " VIA DEI FORI IMPERIALI, " AND THE COLOSSEUM.

stately buildings were erected, walls, highways and works of public utility constructed. With Augustus (30 B. C.) began the long line of famous emperors under whose auspices the city was completely transformed, enlarged and embellished with new temples and magnificent buildings.

After the fall of the Roman Empire (A. D. 476) and throughout the Middle Ages Rome experienced a period of great misery; being several times sacked and devastated both by Goths and Saracens and shaken by revolutions and internecine wars. But after the return of the Papal Court from Avignon (1377), out of the ruins of the empire a new Rome rose and under the patronage of the Popes a revival of the arts and sciences began. Popes, cardinals and patrician families vied with each other in repairing the old churches, erecting new ones, restoring the monuments of antiquity and raising magnificent palaces which form the pride of modern Rome.

These were truly the golden days of Rome, resulting in the noble works of art and the array of objects which, on every side, call the attention and excite the admiration of the visitor to the Eternal City.

* * *

Rome, capital of the ancient world, guardian of civilization, centre of the Christian world, has everything that is great and remarkable. Here, everything has the air of ancient dignity and power.... Art is everywhere; so great is the number of monuments of all ages that it would require a century to know them well. To be able to study its history, to describe its beauties, to stir up all the memories that belong to it, an entire library would be needed. « There is something here », writes Camille Mauclair, « that does not exist in any other part of the world, five or six civilizations superimposed and merged during twenty five centuries ».

FOUNTAIN OF THE PIAZZA DELLE TERME.

This fountain is remarkable for its powerful jet. The four bronze groups of Naiads and sea-monsters are by RUTELLI (1900).

Photo ALINARI, ANDERSON, BROGI.

ROME — VIEWS OF THE CITY.

THE TIBER, CASTEL SANT'ANGELO AND THE DOME OF ST. PETER'S.

The *Castel Sant'Angelo*, erected in A. D. 136 by the emperor Hadrian as a tomb for himself and the succeeding Cæsars of his family, was in origin entirely encrusted with white marble and surmounted by statues and a bronze quadriga on the summit.

The present name of the building is due to a miraculous event which occurred in 590. Legend relates that Pope Gregory the Great while conducting a penitential procession through the streets of Rome to pray for the cessation of the plague then ravaging the city, he beheld above the mausoleum the Archangel Michael sheating his sword.

Its history is almost the history of Rome. Converted into a fortress in the 5th cent. it was always used by the party in power as a stronghold. Belisarius held the castle against Totila in 548, and used its statues as missiles from the parapets. Later the citadel passed into the hands of Narses. It kept out the Lombards in 755, and the Saracens in 846. In the 10th century it was the headquarters of Marozia and her mother Theodora, so celebrated in the history of that lawless period. Here in 928 Pope John X. was suffocated in a dungeon by her order, and here in 974, Crescentius, the son of Theodora murdered in the same manner Benedict VI. Gregory VII. held it in 1084 against Henry IV In the 15th cent., Alexander VI., added the superstructure (further extended by later popes: p. 499) which crowns the ancient edifice, and completed the covered passage leading from the Vatican. Thenceforth, it was used by the popes as a place of safety in times of danger.

VIEW OF THE VIA DELLA CONCILIAZIONE LEADING TO ST. PETER'S.

The *Column of Marcus Aurelius*, was erected about A. D. 176, to commemorate his victories over the Germanic tribes and the Sarmatians. It is an imitation of the column of Trajan (p. 401), and has about the same height and proportions.

COLUMN OF MARCUS AURELIUS.
Erected about A. D. 176.

The reliefs of the spiral band around it are inferior in execution to those of Trajan's column.

The statue of St. Paul on the summit of the column replaced (1589) the bronze statues of the emperor Marcus Aurelius and his wife Faustina which have disappeared.

Photo ALINARI, ANDERSON, B ROGI.

ROME — THE ROMAN FORUM.

Amid the thousand romantic associations with which Rome teems, there are none possessing a deeper or more engrossing interest than those which fill the heart of the traveller as he gazes upon the Roman Forum, the space extending between the Capitoline and the Palatine. Tradition makes this the scene of the battle between the Romans and the Sabines after the rape of the Sabine women, and the central point of the life of the new community. At first a market place and centre of trade, it became later the focus of Roman life religious and political. In it were the Temple of Vesta and the house of the Pontifex Maximus. It was here that the Senate had its assemblies, where the rostras were placed and the destinies of the world discussed. The entire history of the most renowned of all peoples, worked itself out in this little space. Constantly adorned under the Republic and the Empire, the Forum was resplendent with most magnificent monuments, basilicas, triumphal arches, statues, memorial columns, costly marbles and gilded bronzes, and, until the 6th cent., it remained practically intact. Then followed a period of vandalism, when it was used as a quarry; churches and palaces alike derived not only their columns and stones from the Forum, but even their lime by the burning of marble. Abandoned for many centuries, it was gradually buried in rubbish, its desolate area became a cattle market and the glorious name of *Forum Romanum* was changed into that of Campo Vaccino, the "cow pasture." But since the 19th cent. systematic explorations have been made culminating in the recent discoveries and restorations. To-day the tourist can marvel at and enjoy a most unusual sight ; at every turn he finds glorious remains, at each step he sees history written in marble.

VIEW OF THE FORUM FROM THE TABULARIUM LOOKING TOWARDS THE COLOSSEUM.
ARC OF SEPTIMIUS. TEMPLE OF VESPASIAN. TEMPLE OF SATURN.

Before entering the Forum the visitor will do well to prelude by a survey of its topography and (see illustration above) to identify its principal monuments from the terrace at the rear of the Senatorial Palace ; a building erected on the foundations of the *Tabularium*.
In the foreground are the three columns of the temple of Vespasian, the open space beyond was the original *Forum Romanum*, bounded on either side by the *Sacra Via*.
On the left is the Arch of Severus, and behind, partly hidden, the ruins of the Basilica Emilia. On the right are the eight columns of the temple of Saturn, and the ruins of the Basilica Julia ; farther off are the three columns of the temple of Castor and Pollux on the right of which rises the Palatine hill, and the House of the Vestal Virgins. In the distance is the Arch of Titus and the Colosseum.

THE CURIA. *Restored* 1933.

The *Curia*, on the right of the arch of Severus, erected by Julius Cæsar, was connected with the Secretarium and used as a council room by the Senate.

ARCH OF SEPTIMIUS SEVERUS A. D. 203.

The *Arch of Severus*, erected in honour of the emperor and his two sons Caracalla and Geta, was originally surmounted by a bronze chariot, in which the emperor was seen seated between his two sons. It is covered with reliefs of their victories over the Parthians.

COLONNADE OF THE TWELVE GODS OR DII CONSENTES. A. D. 367.

The *Dii Consentes*, whose images were represented at public festivals, and who had to be consulted previously to every grave undertaking. Rebuilt in A. D. 367, this is perhaps the latest monument of the pagan religion.

Photo ALINARI, ANDERSON, BROGI.

THE ROMAN FORUM.

The *Temple of Saturn*, originally built in 497 B. C. is one of the oldest sanctuaries in the Forum. The eight granite columns now standing belong to a reconstruction of the 4th cent. A. D., after the empire had become Christian. In early times the edifice was the depository of the *Ærarium Publicum*, the state treasury, and as such it was maintained by the Senate long after Saturn had been disestablished. The *Saturnalia*, or dedication feast of this temple, is the origin of the modern Carnival.

TEMPLE OF VESPASIAN.

The *Temple of Vespasian*, was erected in honour of that deified emperor and of his son Titus in A. D. 79-96. The columns and entablature are of the best Roman period; on the frieze are carved, the sacrificial implements, the knife, axe, flamen's mitre.

The *Basilica Julia*, first planned and built by Cæsar in 46 B. C. and rebuilt after a fire by Augustus, was a vast magnificent structure with two stories of open arcades and a flat panelled wooden ceiling over the central space. It contained four law courts, which carried on their proceedings without mutual disturbance, and many small chambers or *tabernæ* for commercial uses. In this basilica the principles of Roman law were first formulated.

The *Column of Phocas*, 56 feet high, is the last monument erected in the Forum. It is constructed of ancient fragments and was dedicated in 608 A. D. to the Byzantine emperor Phocas whose gilded statue stood on the summit. Between the column of Phocas and the arch of Severus, are the remains of the *Rostra*, a platform for speakers. Here, it is believed, Mark Antony appealed to the Romans for vengeance on Cæsar's murderers, while the dead Cæsar lay at his feet.

The *Plutei of Trajan* or Anaglypha Traiani, the two finely-sculptured marble panels standing isolated near the column of Phocas, once stood on the parapets or side balustrades of the Rostra. They are sculptured on both sides, on the inner side of both are depicted the boar, the ram and the bull; their joint sacrifice called *Suovetaurilia*, was performed at public ceremonies. On the outer sides are represented famous deeds of the emperor and interesting architectural backgrounds showing the Forum.

COLUMN OF PHOCAS and Plutei of Trajan.

ROME — THE ROMAN FORUM.

The *Temple of Castor and Pollux* dates from the early days of the Republic. It was dedicated to the Dioscuri in 484 B. C. in memory of their aid which enabled the Romans to defeat the Tarquins and their Latin allies at the battle of Lake Regillus in 496 B. C. According to tradition on the night of the battle the twin gods were seen watering their horses at the spring of Juturna at the foot of the Palatine, and from them the citizens received the news of the victory. The existing columns belong to a restoration of the reign of Trajan or of Hadrian.

The *Temple of Julius Cæsar*, of which only the concrete substructures remain, was built by Augustus in the year 29 B. C. on the site where the body of the murdered dictator was burnt in 44 B. C. amid signs of public grief, and where Mark Antony pronounced the famous funeral oration which so deeply impressed the multitude. This was the first temple dedicated to the worship of a mortal.

THE FORUM AS SEEN FROM THE HOUSE OF THE VESTALS.
CASTOR AND POLLUX. NOVA VIA. TEMPLE OF J. CÆSAR. TABULARIUM.

SHRINE OF JUTURNA.

Close by the temple of Castor is the spring associated with the beautiful legend of the Dioscuri and the *Shrine of Juturna*, the goddess of fountains. Recent excavations have brought to light a quadrangular basin with a pedestal in the middle, and some fragments of antique statues of Esculapius and of the Dioscuri; a puteal and a marble altar with reliefs of Castor and Pollux, Jupiter, Leda with the swan and Diana Lucifera holding the symbolic torch.

Sancta Maria Antiqua the oldest Christian basilica in the Forum, was erected in the 6th cent. probably in the Library attached to the temple of Augustus (*Bibliotheca Templi Divi Augusti*) of which only massive and very high walls remain. The church was several times restored and richly adorned with frescoes between the years 600 and 845. The frescoes (a unique example of church iconography of that period) executed by Byzantine artists, are of great interest to students of early Christian art. The building was abandoned in the 9th century owing to disasters by earth-quakes and collapse of neglected walls overhanging it on the Palatine hill.

COURT OF THE HOUSE OF THE VESTAL VIRGINS.

The *House of the Vestals*, dates from several rebuildings and restorations made in the reigns of Augustus and Septimius Severus. In imperial days it was one of the most luxurious palaces in Rome; the large atrium was surrounded by a two storied arcade supported by marble columns, between each of which were statues of the chief vestals in official dress, with laudatory inscriptions on the pedestals. In the centre of the court were fountains and probably the sacred grove; the ancient *lucus*. The Vestal virgins, the priestesses of the goddess Vesta, whose temple was opposite their house, were selected among the daughters of patrician families between six and ten years of age. They were exempt from the common law, had many privileges and great political importance, often interposing to save a life, or to restore harmony at times of crisis. They sat in seats of honour at public games and were almost the only citizens allowed to drive within the walls. Their duty was to watch by night and by day the sacred fire in the Temple, and to guard the *Palladium*. If the fire was allowed to go out, the Vestal in charge was scourged for her carelessness; if she violated her vow of chastity, she was condemned to be buried alive.

SANCTA MARIA ANTIQUA.   *Erected in the 6th cent.*

Photo ALINARI, ANDERSON, BROGI.

The *Temple of Antoninus and Faustina*, one of the most remarkable buildings in the Forum, was erected by the emperor Antoninus Pius himself, in honour of his deified wife Faustina, A. D. 141, whom he had proclaimed to the rank of the gods. On his death twenty years later the Senate added the name of Antoninus on the inscription and dedicated the temple to his worship also. The monolith columns (50 ft. high) of the portico are of the costly cipollino marble, the frieze on the entablature is elaborately sculptured with griffins in heraldic posture and separated by vases.

The interior of the temple was converted (12th cent.) into the church of San Lorenzo in Miranda, to which a baroque façade was added in 1602.

TEMPLE OF ANTONINUS AND FAUSTINA. A. D. 141.

RUINS OF THE REGIA. *In the rear is the basement of the temple of Antoninus and Faustina.*

The *Regia*, the traditional palace of Numa Pompilius was the house of the early kings. When monarchy was abolished it became the official residence of the Pontifex Maximus. Here were preserved the sacred spears of Mars, the important state archives, the ritual books and instruments, the tables of the calendar and the official records (*Fasti*), now in the Palazzo dei Conservatori.

THE BASILICA OF CONSTANTINE.

The *Arch of Titus*, erected to commemorate the victories of Titus and Vespasian in the Judæan war ending with the destruction of the city and temple of Jerusalem A. D. 70, was not completed until after the death of Titus and dedicated by Domitian A. D. 81. This splendid arch entirely faced with pentelic marble is one of the gems of the first century. The vaulting is decorated with rosettes in richly carved coffers and by splendid reliefs of the highest interest. On one side is represented a triumphal procession with captives and soldiers carrying the Jewish spoils including the table of the shew-bread and the seven-branched golden candlestick; opposite is seen the emperor Titus in a triumphal quadriga, driven by the goddess Roma while Victory holds a crown over his head. The relief in

The *Basilica of Constantine*, the largest building in the Forum, was begun by Maxentius A. D. 306, and completed with some alteration in its design by his conqueror Constantine. This great edifice which Michelangelo and Bramante studied for their plans of Saint Peter's, had a central nave with two aisles. The principal apse had a colossal statue of the emperor Constantine, fragments of which may be seen in the court of the Conservatori. Unlike other flat-roofed basilicas supported by ranges of columns, the concrete vault of this building was supported by a few huge piers. To these were attached immense monolith marble columns, one of which, removed by Paul V., is still standing in the piazza in front of Santa Maria Maggiore (p. 418).

ARCH OF TITUS A. D. 81.

the centre of the vault represents the Apotheosis of Titus, who is carried to heaven by an eagle.

In the Middle Ages the arch was used as a stronghold by the Frangipani family. In 1823 it was restored by Valadier by order of Pius VII., and the missing marble portions replaced by travertine.

Between the temple of Antoninus and Faustina and the Basilica of Constantine is the *Temple of Romulus*, a circular building erected by Maxentius A. D. 309 in memory of his son whom he deified and named after the founder of the city. Behind it stood the *Templum Sacræ Urbis*, erected A. D. 73, as a depository for the plans of the city, the cadastral registers and other documents relating to property.

Captives carrying the Jewish spoils.

Photo ALINARI, ANDERSON, BROGI.

ROME — MONUMENTS OF ANTIQUITY.

The first city of Rome, the Roma Quadrata, was built on the *Palatine*. Here, according to the legend, Romulus traced the boundaries of the future capital of the world. At first simple citizens lived on this hill: later at different times, amongst these dwellings, temples and palaces were built; the temples of *Cybele* and the *Lupercal*. During the Republic, the Palatine was inhabited by a large number of important men; the Gracchi, Fulvius Flaccus, Lucius Crassus, Scaurus, Hortensius, Cicero, Catiline, Mark Antony, Claudius, the father of Tiberius, and Octavius, the father of Augustus.

Augustus, who was born here, built his house which was destined in later years to become the palace of the Emperors. The part built by Augustus, which his successors added to, kept the name of *Domus Augustiana*. Tiberius enlarged the palace and these additions were called *Domus Tiberiana*; Caligula added still further to the buildings which reached down to the Forum. Before long the whole Palatine was not large enough for the depraved magnificence of Nero: he extended enormously the Imperial Palace (his Golden House) up to where later the Colosseum was built and as far as the Esquiline, where there were the gardens of Mæcenas.

The Emperors who succeeded him preferred larger sites, and chose abodes in the southern districts of the city. When Rome ceased to be the capital of the Empire, the buildings on the Palatine, were sacked and destroyed during the invasions of the barbarians, and in the Middle Ages fortresses were built over their ruins.

THE PALATINE SEEN FROM THE FORUM.

Of all the famous spots in Rome the *Colosseum* ranks foremost. The mighty edifice covers about six acres of ground, its external circumference is one third of a mile long, while the height of the external wall is more than a hundred and fifty feet. The emperor Vespasian commenced it and eight years later Titus after his return from the conquest of Jerusalem inaugurated it in A. D. 80. Its inauguration lasted 100 days, during which 5000 wild animals were killed and naval contests were exhibited. The Colosseum was also the scene of fearful barbarities during the persecutions of the Christians in the 2nd and 3rd centuries. During three hundred years it was used for gladiatorial combats: ten thousand men furnished with weapons and extremely skilled in the use of them, athletic and well fed, were always kept in readiness for the fatal service.

After a long abandonment the building was used as a fortress in the Middle Ages, and as an arena for bull fights. During the 15th, 16th and 17th centuries it was used as a sort of quarry and afforded building material for a number of churches and palaces, such as the Farnese, the Barberini, the Cancelleria and the Palazzo Venezia. Lastly, it was consecrated to the memory of the martyrs who perished in it during the Christian persecutions in the early days of the Church. The spot of their martyrdom was marked until 1872 by a tall cross, devoutly kissed by the faithful, and all around the arena stood the small chapels or "stations" used in the *Via Crucis* procession. "While stands the *Coliseum*, Rome shall stand..." *Byron*.

THE COLOSSEUM. (*Amphitheatrum Flavium*).

MAMERTINE PRISON or TULLIANUM.

ARCH OF JANUS QUADRIFONS. *Third century*.

The *Mamertine Prison*, one of the most ancient structures in Rome, is filled with mournful recollections. Ancus Martius hollowed it out of the rock on the declivity of the Capitoline hill making it a place of terror. Later, Servius Tullius enlarged it and added another dungeon more dreadful yet.

The prison consists of two chambers one below the other, the lower one illustrated here originally had no staircase and the prisoners were let down into it through a hole in the ceiling. In this dungeon perished Jugurtha, Vercingetorix, Sejanus and others; here too the accomplices of Catilina were strangled by order of Cicero. Conquered enemies generally were executed at the moment the conqueror ascended in triumph the steps of the Capitol. Beneath the floor is a fountain which, according to the legend, burst forth miraculously, to enable St. Peter to baptize his jailors Processus and Martinianus.

Supposed to have been erected at the intersection of two streets, it is one of the numerous edifices of the kind constructed as a shelter or as covered exchanges. It has four equal sides and 48 niches for statues.

Photo ALINARI, ANDERSON, BROGI.

ROME — *MONUMENTS OF ANTIQUITY.*

The *Arch of Constantine*, erected over the Via Triumphalis in celebration of Constantine's victory over Maxentius near the Milvian bridge in A. D. 312, is one of the best preserved of all ancient Roman edifices. As stated on the inscription, the Senate of Rome dedicated this arch to Constantine, because *by the will of God* and by his own virtues, he liberated the country from the tyrant Maxentius.

The arch is largely constructed of material and fragments taken from earlier buildings skilfully arranged in an architectural framework and producing an impression of considerable power by the harmony of its proportions. Its single defect perhaps is the abuse of richness.

TRIUMPHAL ARCH OF CONSTANTINE THE GREAT. A. D. 315.

The only sculptures upon it that belong to Constantine's period are the statues, victories and captives on the bases of the columns, and the long narrow reliefs placed beneath the medallions forming a frieze over the side arches. These reliefs represent the achievements of the emperor in war and peace and interesting views of the Forum and the Rostra.

Contrasting strongly with these 4th century rude examples of a decadent art are the other admirable reliefs taken from structures of the second century, in the use of which the portraits of Trajan and Marcus Aurelius were rechiselled to represent Constantine. Those from the period of Trajan are: the two large reliefs on the inner side of the central archway representing Trajan's triumphal entry into Rome, and Prætorian guards slaying the Dacians, and the two reliefs on top on either side of the arch; the eight medallions on the two façades depicting hunting and sacrificial scenes, and the statues of captive Dacians in *pavonazzetto* standing over the columns.

The eight reliefs on the attic on either side of the inscription belonged to a monument to Marcus Aurelius (like the three in the Pal. dei Conservatori, p. 504). Those on the north front represent (left to right): the emperor's triumphal entry into Rome, his arrival on the Capitol, the emperor distributing food to the people, and the submission of a German chief. Those on the south front: Captive Sarmatians brought before Marcus Aurelius. Discovery of the conspiracy of the Dacians, the emperor haranguing his soldiers, and the sacrifice of the *Suovetaurilia*. The arch was converted into a castle in 10th cent.

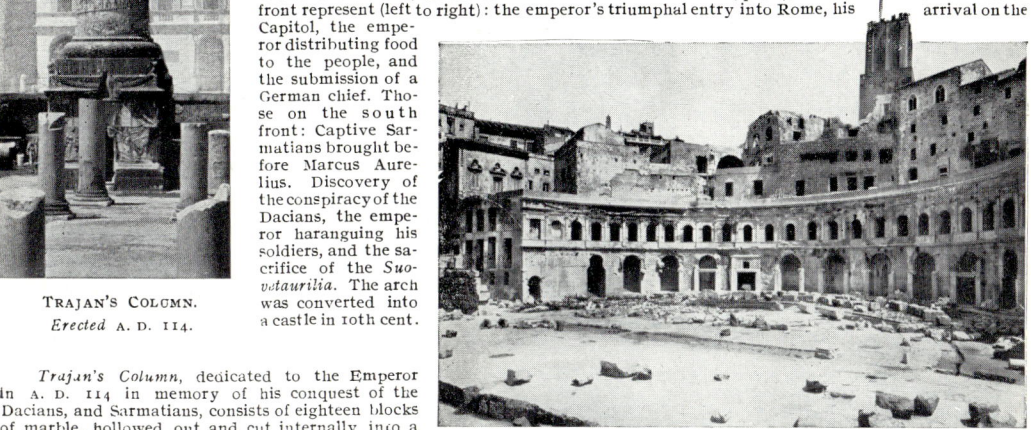

TRAJAN'S COLUMN.
Erected A. D. 114.

Trajan's Column, dedicated to the Emperor in A. D. 114 in memory of his conquest of the Dacians, and Sarmatians, consists of eighteen blocks of marble, hollowed out and cut internally into a winding staircase. Along the outside runs a spiral frieze 3-4 ft. wide and 650 ft. long, forming a series of scenes with about 2500 human figures representing the campaigns of Trajan against the Dacians.

HEMICYCLE OF TRAJAN'S FORUM (Mercati Traianei).

These admirable reliefs, more deeply worked in proportion as they gain height, celebrate the triumph of Roman discipline and determination over barbaric courage. They constitute a set of valuable pictures of military antiquities: costumes of warriors and their horses, engines of war, ships, canoes, quinqueremes, dwellings of the barbarians, priests of all theogonies, women of all ranks, marches, manœuvres, sieges, assaults, etc.

The column is about 12 ft. in diameter and 97 ft. high, the whole including the pedestal and the statue 108 ft. It was surmounted by a bronze statue of Trajan replaced in the 16th cent. by that of St. Peter. The base, decorated with trophies of war, formed the sepulchral chamber in which the ashes of Trajan, who died A. D. 117 in Cilicia, were deposited in a golden urn. In the interior of the column a staircase of one hundred and eighty-five steps ascends to the top.

The *Forum of Trajan*, planned by the architect Apollodorus, was begun after the emperor's return from the Dacian war and completed A. D. 114. It was a large complex of open areas and buildings, including a triumphal arch which gave entrance to a large square enclosed with a portico on three sides and the Basilica Ulpia on the fourth side. Beyond the basilica were two library buildings, the memorial column, given on this page, and a temple to the deified Trajan. The whole was considered not only the masterpiece of Roman architecture of the golden age, but one of the marvels of the world. On the east and west of the forum were two hemicycles designed to support the slopes of the Capitol and Quirinal hills, which were cut away to make room for this suite of buildings. The eastern hemicycle shown above had a double tier of shops and public offices.

— 401 —

Photo ALINARI, ANDERSON, BROGI.

ROME — THE RUINS OF ANTIQUITY.

BIRDS-EYE VIEW OF THE RUINS OF THE BATHS OF CARACALLA. A. D. 212.

The *Baths of Caracalla* or *Thermæ* Antoniniæ, begun by Caracalla in 212 and completed by Alexander Severus, were built in a style of luxury and magnificence almost incredible. The vast walls were covered with rare marbles, the floors with mosaics, arches supported by porphyry and granite columns, gilt bronze used freely for doors and capitals. There was accommodation for 1600 bathers at one time, but that was only the pretext for the great club house in which the indolent citizens were enabled to forget life and spend the day in « dolce far niente ».

The bath then was a highly luxurious and elaborate process: the visitor first entered the so-called *Apodyterium*, a room where he undressed and had the body gently massaged or anointed, he thence passed into the *Tepidarium*, a hall agreeably heated, in order to prepare the body for the great heat of the next room, the *Sudatorium* or perspiring hall, from which he passed into the *Calidarium*, or hot-water bath. From the *Calidarium* he returned to the *Tepidarium* and finally into the *Frigidarium* or cold bath. Various costly perfumes for anointing the body were used at the different stages. The bath over, the visitor would then prepare himself for the delights of the table.

In addition to the baths there were gymnasia for athletes, stadia for running and wrestling; libraries and reading rooms, halls and peristyles for conversation and walking in wet weather; galleries in which painters and sculptors exhibited their latest works; a stage for the reading of the latest poems; buffets for refreshments, stalls for articles of fashion; scent shops, etc. Service was furnished by means of underground passages, where an army of slaves could move swiftly without being seen. The baths opened at sunrise and closed at sunset, and remained in use until the 6th century, when the invading Goths damaged the aqueducts and rendered these and other thermæ useless.

Amongst the works of art found in the ruins are the Torso Belvedere (p. 451), the colossal group of the Farnese Bull, the Hercules of Glycon and the Flora in the Naples' Museum. The habits of luxury and idleness which were accentuated by the magnificent Baths of the emperors were among the causes of the decline of the Roman Empire.

The *Theatre of Marcellus*, begun by Julius Cæsar, finished by Augustus, who named it after his nephew, the son of Octavia, is said to have accommodated 12.000 spectators. Vitruvius praised the beauty and proportions of the structure, which has been a source of inspiration to artists.

The *Portico of Octavia*, adjoining the theatre of Marcellus, was erected by Augustus in honour of his sister, and as a place of shelter for the spectators in unfavourable weather.

It consisted of a double arcade with 270 columns enclosing an open space within which stood the temples of Jupiter and Juno.

THEATRE OF MARCELLUS. *Completed in* 13 B. C.

TEMPLE OF MARS ULTOR. *Forum of Augustus*.

The *Temple of Mars Ultor* in the Forum of Augustus was built by that emperor to the god *Mars the Avenger*, with whose assistance he had defeated Brutus and Cassius at Philippi 42 B. C., and thus avenged the murder of his ancestor Julius Cæsar. In this temple were preserved the Roman ensigns and the sword of Julius Cæsar.

The *Columbaria Codini*, containing cinerary urns chiefly of persons attached to the family of the Cæsars, is one of the numerous sepulchres of Imperial Rome (prior to Constantine the Great), which have been discovered since the Renaissance.

COLUMBARIA IN THE VIGNA CODINI. *First century*.

While the great families had their sumptuous tombs upon the Appian Way, and the poor were cast into the common ground, the columbaria were the burial places of the middle classes. They were deep excavations in the tufa rock with rows of niches resembling pigeon-holes, hence the name, which contained the urns in which the ashes of the dead were deposited. They were capable of containing the ashes of large numbers of persons, and were erected as family tombs or by societies, guilds and speculators who sold places for urns by subscription.

— 402 —

Photo ALINARI, ANDERSON, BROGI.

ROME — *THE RUINS OF ANTIQUITY.*

THE CAMPAGNA. RUINS OF THE CLAUDIAN AQUEDUCTS.
*Completed by Claudius in 52 A. D.
There were 14 aqueducts in Rome, with a total length of 360 miles.*

VIEW OF THE APPIAN WAY.
Begun in 312 B. C. A military road which formed the chief line of communication with Southern Italy.

THE CATACOMBS. (From a print.)

The *Catacombs* are a vast labyrinth of subterranean galleries where the early Christians buried their dead and held certain periodic services in their honour. In times of persecutions they were also used as places of hiding and worship.

They were begun in Apostolic times and continued to be used till the end of the 4th century, when there were in Rome at least 25 of the greater catacombs and 20 of the smaller, extending in all to about 500 kilometers of tunnelling. Like the Pagan sepulchres the catacombs were all situated from the first to the third milestone outside the city along the main highroads. The general plan was that of a *columbarium*, but since the Christian rite prescribed interment, recesses or *loculi* in the walls of the narrow galleries were substituted for the niches which held the cinerary urns. These *loculi* were deep enough to hold one, or two, or even three bodies which were wrapped in linen cloth; they were closed with hermetically sealed slabs, on which the relatives inscribed a name or prayer or words of faith and hope. Since much space was needed for burying so great a number of dead, large rooms were impossible except in rare cases, when a martyr or Pope had a chapel-tomb, or a rich family had a special vault (*cubiculum*), where sometimes sarcophagi were placed.

THE ARCH OF DRUSUS.

erected in the 2nd century, was probably used to carry the aqueduct for the Baths of Caracalla.

After the Peace of the Church in 313, burial in the catacombs was gradually given up, and it became the custom to bury the dead near the churches and to organize pilgrimages to the ancient Christian cemeteries of the catacombs which were made more accessible and adorned with new inscriptions and paintings. From the fourth to the seventh centuries pilgrims from all parts of Christendom continued to visit the graves of the martyrs in spite of barbarian invasions. Enormous quantities of corpses and bones were carried off by pilgrims and by invaders and exported to Germany, France or England, where the number of churches increased and the demand for bodies or relics of saints and martyrs became ever greater. The authorities consequently transferred innumerable bodies to the crypts of churches within the city, while twenty-eight cartloads of bones were deposited in the Pantheon. In course of time all the catacombs, except those under the church of St. Sebastian, became grown with vegetation and were entirely forgotten. It was not till the 16th century that the discovery of one of them led to the search for and retracing of the others.

The Catacombs were decorated with naïve paintings setting forth incidents in the Old and the New Testament, scenes of divine deliverance, miracles of mercy, of resurrection. There are also allegorical figures, like that of the Good Shepherd (Jesus), bringing back the lost sheep to the fold; the fish symbolized sometimes the Saviour, and sometimes the faithful; the anchor, hope in immortality; the dove, peace; the peacock, eternity; etc. The paintings are highly interesting as being the earliest examples of Christian art that have been preserved to us. The Catacombs of St. Calixtus and those of St. Sebastian on the Via Appia are the most interesting and most frequented.

It is believed that during the persecutions of the third century the bodies of the Apostles St. Peter and St. Paul, originally buried close to the spots where they suffered martyrdom, were exhumed and temporarily hidden in the Catacombs of St. Sebastian on the Appian Way.

THE PYRAMID OF CESTIUS.

The *Pyramid of Caius Cestius*, is about 117 ft. high. An inscription shows that Cestius, who died in 43 B. C. was a tribune of the people. At the foot of the pyramid is the *Old Protestant Cemetery*, which contains the graves of John Keats († 1821); Severn († 1879); Shelley († 1822); J. A. Symonds († 1893); A. Humboldt († 1859); and other illustrious men.

— 403 —

Photo ALINARI, ANDERSON, BROGI.

ROME — THE CHURCHES OF ROME.

According to an old tradition, Rome, at one time, possessed nearly one thousand places of Worship. A great many of them have now disappeared or are known only from their ruins, while others have been disfigured by alterations or are known only from the chronicles of the time. Yet, to day, every age, every style has its representatives in the churches of Rome, which are the oldest and the richest in the world.

And truly, it is impossible to conceive all the wealth that the liberality of princes, the love of art, the pomp relative to the Catholic worship and the devotion of the faithful have accumulated in these sacred edifices for a period of nearly two thousand years.

At every step the pilgrim meets with grand monuments and splendid tombs to the princes of the Church; priceless works of art in sculpture, painting and mosaic; everywhere a profusion of the rarest marbles, of bronzes of every description; altars loaded with silver, gold and precious stones which dazzle the eyes and excite admiration.

The plans of the churches of Rome are of various forms and may be classified and reduced to four: the *basilical*, the *circular*, the *Latin cross* and the *Greek cross*.

The " basilical form " consists of a rectangle and had its origin from the Roman basilicas which were used for the transaction of business and for administering justice. From these civil edifices the Christian basilica was gradually developed and acquired the grand proportions, the triple nave (St. Peter's and St. Paul's were exceptions) and the uniform symmetry of the columns; from the Roman houses, it obtained the *atrium*, a square court surrounded by a covered passage with a fountain in the centre The Christian basilicas of Rome which to day offer the best example of the classical form are S. Maria Maggiore (p. 419) and San Clemente (p. 423). The central nave much larger and higher than the side aisles from which it was separated by two rows of columns, was bounded at the end by a circular apse or *tribuna*. Towards the centre there was the *choir* surrounded by a marble screen or *chancel*. Between the apse and the choir a transversal nave or *transept* gave to the church the form of a cross. In the centre of the transept there was a canopy or *baldacchino supported by columns* enclosing the *altar*, below this there was a crypt or *confessio* which contained the tomb of a martyr or a highly revered relic of a saint. In the apse there was the *cathedra* where sat the bishop.

The "circular form" sprung in the IV. century and was inspired by ancient temples and mausoleums (Pantheon, Hadrian's tomb, etc.) and probably also by the round halls of Roman bathing establishments. This form was mostly used for *baptisteries* which primitively were separated from the church, but in the sixth century they were taken into the church-porch, and afterwards into the church itself.

The " Latin cross " has the form of a cross placed on the floor offering one arm longer than the three others—that which begins at the entrance of the church and runs up to the point of intersection.

The " Greek cross " has four arms equal in length and width.

The Basilica of St. Peter.   View showing the obelisk and Michelangelo's dome.

The Basilica of St. Peter is one of the wonders of the world, and perhaps the most stupendous of all. Nowhere else exists anything like it, and no one who has not seen it, can conceive its stateliness and its magnificence.

For nearly two hundred years, the greatest masters of the Renaissance exerted their genius and exhausted all the resources of their art while more than forty popes lavished their treasures in this unparalleled sanctuary, which stands on the site of the circus of Nero where thousands of the first Christians suffered martyrdom.

In the year 67 A. D. according to tradition, St. Peter was executed in the middle of the circus at the foot of the obelisk which now stands in front of his temple. Close by the circus existed a cemetery where the martyred Christians were buried; and in this cemetery the body of the Apostle was deposited. In the year 90 A. D. the bishop Anacletus, to mark *(Continued)*

Photo ALINARI, ANDERSON, BROGI.

ROME — BASILICA OF SAINT PETER.

The imposing façade is 124 yds. wide and 133 feet in height. It has eight columns of travertine 93 feet high and 8 feet in diameter. It is surmounted by a balustrade with statues of the Saviour and the Apostles 19 feet in height. The inscription on the frieze recalls that the pope Paul V. (Borghese), had the façade built in 1612.

The *Loggia della Benedizione* stands over the central entrance. In it the new pope used to be crowned, and from here he imparted his benediction to the people assembled below at Easter. The bas-relief beneath, by BUONVICINO, represents Christ handing the keys to St. Peter. The total height of the dome, including the cross, is 435 feet. The bronze ball on the top is 8 feet in diameter and can hold 16 persons.

The Piazza has the form of an ellipse and measures 215 yds. in its greatest breadth. The beautiful colonnade surrounding it erected by BERNINI in 1667 under Alexander VII., is 19 yds. wide and 25 yds. in height. It consists of four rows of columns leaving between them a central passage for carriages. There are 284 columns and 80 buttresses surmounted by 162 statues of saints each 12 ft. in height. The obelisk was brought from Egypt and formerly stood in Nero's circus (near the present sacristy). In 1586 Sixtus V., had it removed to its present site by D. FONTANA, who estimated its weight at about 320 tons. The height from the pavement to the cross is 133 feet. *(see p. 46)*.

PIAZZA AND BASILICA OF ST. PETER, and the Vatican.

« LA NAVICELLA ». St. Peter on the sea.
Mosaic by GIOTTO *and* CAVALLINI.

The ceiling of the portico is decorated with stucco and gold. Five entrances lead into the basilica. The first door on the right is the *Porta Santa*. The central entrance has bronze doors, belonging to the Constantinian basilica, executed by FILARETE in 1445 by order of Eugenius IV. The reliefs represent Christ and the Virgin, SS. Peter and Paul and their martyrdom, and events in the life of Pope Eugenius IV.; on the frame are mythological subjects, animals, fruits, and portraits of Emperors. At the two ends of the portico are equestrian statues: right, Constantine the Great; left, Charlemagne

PORTICO OF ST. PETER'S.

BRONZE DOORS. *By* A. FILARETE. A. D. 1445.

(Cont'd) the spot, erected a small oratory over the grave of St. Peter. Later, at the request of Sylvester I., Constantine the Great destroyed the old circus and over its northern foundations built the first great basilica to the Apostle.

The Constantinian basilica which was half as large as the present one, lasted for eleven hundred years, when in the middle of the 15th century ruin menacing it, the reigning pope Nicholas V., determined on its reconstruction on a more extensive scale. BERNARDO ROSSELLINO and LEON BATTISTA ALBERTI, the greatest architects of the day, were employed and work began in 1450. When Nicholas V., died in 1455 the walls of the new construction were only a few feet high and for nearly fifty years, under the succeeding popes, the work progressed very slowly until the election of the great Julius II. (1503), who had the talent for big undertakings. This pope, keen to detect genius, preferred BRAMANTE to all other architects and having formed the idea of erecting a monument to himself in his lifetime in the new basilica, gave fresh impulse to the enterprise. The old basilica *(Continued)*

Photo ALINARI, ANDERSON, BROGI.

ROME — *BASILICA OF SAINT PETER.*

INNER VIEW OF THE CUPOLA.

The inside diameter of the cupola is 139 feet, its height from the pavement to the lantern 438 feet. The dome has double walls and between them there is a staircase for ascending to the summit. The inscription on the frieze around the dome is in mosaic on a gold background, the letters are nearly five feet in height.

The *Cathedra of St. Peter* executed in 1667 is in gilt bronze and encloses the ancient episcopal wooden chair encrusted with ivory used by the Apostle. It is supported by four colossal figures of the Fathers of the Church.

The nave has a length of 630 ft. The immense roof is ornamented with sunken coffers richly gilded and stuccoed.

THE BRONZE BALDACCHINO (Canopy).

The concavity of the cupola is divided into sixteen compartments decorated with gilded stuccoes and mosaics representing the Saviour, the Virgin, the apostles and other saints.

The *Canopy*, erected by BERNINI in 1633 by order of Urban VIII., is entirely of bronze with gilt ornaments. It weighs over 700 tons and has a height of 95 feet. The gilding alone cost 40.000 scudi.

The pavement is inlaid with beautiful marbles after the designs of GIACOMO DELLA PORTA. The round slab of porphyry marked with † indicates the spot where Charlemagne and other medieval emperors were formerly crowned.

The interior is all enpanelled with beautiful marbles, the roof ornamented with sunken coffers richly gilded and stuccoed. In wandering about one is struck at first by the apparent want of magnitude. But, little by little, its enormous scale is appreciated. Gigantic statues, superb monuments, precious marbles, bronzes and gilded stuccoes are to be seen wherever the gaze turns. The chapels have cupolas all encrusted with dazzling mosaics. The altars are ornamented with a wealth of rare marbles. With a few exceptions all the pictures are in mosaic, executed with such accuracy of tints as to produce a genuine illusion. Everywhere there is magnificence and the brilliancy of precious stones.

VIEW OF THE CENTRAL NAVE.

(*Continued*) was gradually demolished and on April 18, 1506 the foundation stone of the new edifice was laid with great pomp by Julius II., in the presence of thirty-five cardinals. Bramante's plan was to erect a church in the form of a Greek cross, with rounded choir and transept and a gigantic cupola in the centre to be supported upon four colossal piers. He pursued the work with ardour, but when he died in 1514, only the four piers and the arches above them were completed.

Leo X., who had succeeded Julius II., in the previous year placed the work in the hands of GIULIANO DA SANGALLO, FRA GIOCONDO DA VERONA and RAPHAEL. The latter's plan was a church in the form of a Latin cross, but until his death neither he nor his colleagues who were divided between the Greek and the Latin form of cross achieved anything. The next architects were ANTONIO DA SANGALLO, BALDASSARE PERUZZI (1520) and MICHELANGELO (1546) then in his seventy second year. Paul III., the reigning pontiff, gave Michelangelo unlimited power to alter, pull down or remodel the building according to (*Continued*)

— 406 —

Photo ALINARI, ANDERSON

ROME — BASILICA OF SAINT PETER.

VIEW OF THE TRANSEPT.

STATUE OF ST. PETER. *Bronze of the 5th cent.*

The transept has a length of 449 ft. The dome is supported by four monster piers 234 ft. in circumference, each having two niches one above the other; the lower niches are occupied by four colossal statues 11 ft. in height, on the upper niches are four balconies designed by Bernini, here are recesses used as shrines for the greatest relics, which are exibited only in days of high festivals. Above are four enormous mosaic medallions of the Evangelists.

Including the sacristy and the crypt, the basilica contains 45 altars where 121 lamps are kept burning day and night; 390 statues in marble, bronze and stucco; 748 columns in stone, marble, alabaster and bronze.

The *Confessio* surrounded by a beautiful circular balustrade of marble, has 95 lamps which burn day and night. A double flight of marble steps leads down to the ancient chapel encrusted with precious marbles. Doors of gilded bronze belonging to the old basilica close the oratory which contains the bronze sarcophagus surmounted by a golden cross of St. Peter.

In front of the shrine is the kneeling statue of Pius VI., by CANOVA. The pope who died an exile in his last moments requested to be buried near the tomb of the Apostle.

The statue of St. Peter, a bronze of the 5th century, formerly stood in the old basilica, placed there by Saint Leo the Great in the year 445.

For ages this monument has been the object of such veneration that the kisses of the faithful have polished and worn its right foot.

On great occasions the statue is adorned with pontifical robes and jewels which are preserved in the sacristy.

The *High Altar* under the canopy stands over the primitive oratory erected by Anacletus in the year 90 A. D. over the grave of St. Peter.

Here only the pope or a specially authorized cardinal celebrates mass on high festivals.

THE CONFESSIO AND THE HIGH ALTAR.

STATUE OF PIUS VI. By CANOVA.

(*Continued*) the master's own ideas. Michelangelo, however, returned to Bramante's plan of a Greek cross, and began the dome on a different plan, declaring he would raise the Pantheon in the air. When he died in 1564, he had finished the drum of the dome and left designs and models for the completion of the work up to the lantern which his successor, GIACOMO DELLA PORTA, finished in 1590 under Sixtus V. After the death of Michelangelo, besides G. DELLA PORTA, the construction of the church was entrusted to VIGNOLA, PIRRO LIGORIO, and CARLO MADERNO. This last architect appointed by Paul V., returned to the plan of a Latin cross and completed the façade in 1614. The new Basilica was dedicated by Urban VIII., in 1626.

This great achievement of architecture in which all the artistic forces of the age contributed, occupied a period of 176 years in its construction. Its cost by the end of the seventeenth century, amounted to nearly ten million pounds sterling (Forty-five million dollars). The basilica may contain nearly seventy thousand persons.

— 407 —

Photo ALINARI, ANDERSON, BROGI.

ROME — BASILICA OF SAINT PETER.

Tomb of Pope Paul III. († 1549).
With statues of Justice *and of* Prudence.
Designed by G. della Porta.

Tomb of Pope Urban VIII. († 1644). *By* Bernini.

The tomb of Paul III., the finest monument in St. Peter's, is a masterpiece of Giacomo della Porta, pupil of Michelangelo. The statue of the pontiff in the act of giving the benediction is entirely of bronze. The beautiful reclining figures below, Prudence (right) and Justice (left) are in marble. The last one a supposed portrait of the Pope's sister-in-law was sculptured almost naked, but was draped by Lorenzo Bernini in a painted bronze tunic. The reclining figures recall those on the Medici Tombs in the church of San Lorenzo in Florence.

The tomb of Pope Urban VIII. (Maffeo Barberini), was designed by Bernini, who executed the bronze figure of the pontiff in the act of benediction, while the marble figures below representing Justice (right), and Charity (left), were done by his pupils. The gilded bronze skeleton on the sarcophagus symbolizes the genius of Death occupied in registering in his book the name of the deceased. The bees from the Barberini coat-of-arms may be seen flying over the monument, suggestive of the ended life of the occupant.

Urban VIII. was descended from a powerful Tuscan family, and was remarkable from his passion for building; the Barberini palace (p. 508) is a memorial of the magnificence and ambition of this pontiff. The ruthless way in which his family plundered ancient buildings to adorn their own palaces is the origin of the saying, « *Quod non fecerunt barbari, fecerunt Barberini* ». It was under the pontificate of Urban that Galileo, aged 70, was tried and condemned by the tribunal of the Inquisition in Rome.

Transversal View of the Interior, showing the Stuarts monument.
Everywhere precious marbles, gigantic statues in marble and in bronze, monuments.

Monument of the exiled Stuarts,
with busts of James (called the Third) and his sons Charles Edward, and Henry (Cardinal York).
Executed by Canova *in* 1819.
(George IV. contributed to its expense).

Photo Alinari, Anderson, Brogi.

CAPPELLA DELLA PIETÀ.

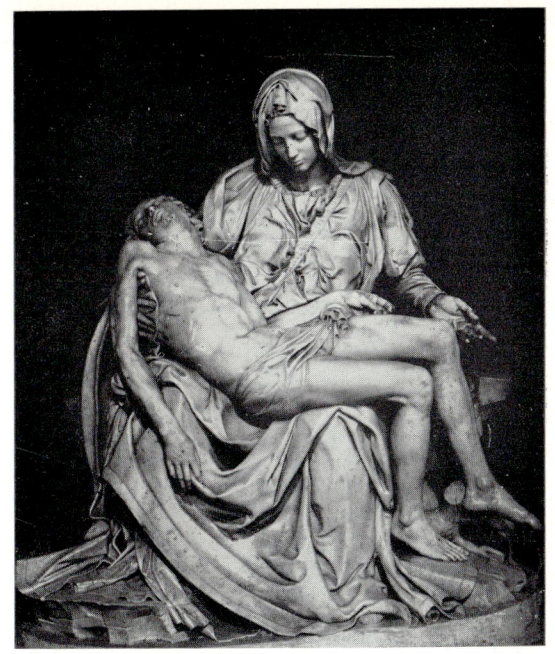

PIETÀ. By MICHELANGELO, 1499.

The aisles are rich in sepulchral monuments of popes and illustrious persons. The right aisle begins at the Porta Santa, the first chapel is named after MICHELANGELO's celebrated *Pietà*, executed in the artist's twenty-fifth year. This master-piece, modelled with the utmost delicacy, is the finest existing group of devotional sculpture; every line in the Virgin speaks of life, every line in the Christ of death.

To combine into a group two life-sized bodies in marble, was one of the most difficult tasks imaginable. Here Michelangelo accomplished what no other artist then living could have done. It is the only work ever signed by the master, whose name may be seen on the band crossing the breast of the Virgin. When critics observed to Michelangelo that the Madonna was too young, he answered that "Chastity enjoys eternal youth."

The chapel also contains the *Colonna Santa*, a spiral column which stood in the Confessio of the old basilica, said to have been brought from the Temple at Jerusalem, and to be the one against which Christ leaned when discoursing with the Doctors.

The marble-well which surrounds the base was added by Cardinal Orsini in 1438.

This splendid monument is the best work of the famous CANOVA who employed eight years in its completion. It was inaugurated on Holy Thursday in the year 1795 in the presence of great crowds of people among which, disguised as a priest, mingled the artist himself to hear the opinions on his work.

The statue of the pontiff in prayer is perfectly modelled. On the left stands Religion, on the right the genius of Death seems to give way to sorrow. Two lions symbolizing the strong character of the dead pope, seem to guard the entrance to the vault. One is wideawake and menacing, the other peacefully asleep and relaxed are the most beautiful production of modern sculpture.

Clement XIII., was a man of upright and pacific intentions, he refused to suppress the Jesuits, after they had been driven out from France and Spain.

TOMB OF POPE CLEMENT XIII.
(† 1709). By CANOVA.

MARTYRDOM OF ST. SEBASTIAN.
Mosaic after DOMENICHINO.

Photo ALINARI, ANDERSON, BROGI.

— 409 —

THE RETREAT OF ATTILA.
Marble relief by ALGARDI (1650).

ENTOMBMENT OF ST. PETRONILLA.
Mosaic after GUERCINO.

THE ARCHANGEL MICHAEL.
Mosaic after GUIDO RENI.

Algardi's relief was probably inspired by Raphael's famous fresco (p. 466). Attila, surnamed "the Scourge of God," from the terror he everywhere inspired, in the year 452 invaded Italy and devastated the northern provinces. His intention was of crossing the Apennines and assailing Rome. The powerless citizen in their despair sent an embassy of senators to deprecate the ravages of the Huns. The Bishop of Rome, Leo I. (the Great) was among the envoys. They found Attila and his vast army of 500.000 encamped near Mantua and, after the conference, to the astonishment of all Europe, Attila countermanded the march on Rome and withdrew his army. Tradition ascribes this marvel to the miraculous appearance in the sky of SS. Peter and Paul, and to the effect which Leo, as the head of the Church and vicegerent of the Deity, produced on the awe-struck mind of the pagan monarch.

St. Petronilla, the spiritual daughter of St. Peter, was asked in marriage by Flaccus, an influential heathen nobleman of Rome Fearing his power and not daring refuse him, she told him to return in 3 days and she would go home with him. Meanwhile she prayed earnestly to be delivered from the unholy union; and when Flaccus came to espouse her, he found her dead. In the lower part of Guercino's picture the saint is being let down into the grave, crowned with roses, while Flaccus stands by mourning; in the upper, Petronilla is already in paradise kneeling before Christ, having changed an earthly for a heavenly bridegroom.

TOMB OF GREGORY XIII. († 1585),
the rectifier of the calendar (ten days were dropped out of the year 1582), an event commemorated in a bas-relief upon the sarcophagus. By C. RUSCONI.

TOMB OF MATILDA († 1115).
The relief on the sarcophagus represents Gregory VII. granting absolution to Henry IV.
By BERNINI.

TOMB OF LEO XI. Medici († 1605),
with statues of Majesty and Liberality; on the sarcophagus: Abjuration of Henry IV. king of France.
Designed by ALGARDI.

Matilda (1046-1115), daughter of Boniface II. Marquis of Tuscany, stanch supporter for over thirty years of the Popes in the great quarrel with the Emperors concerning Investitures (see p. 474), was popularly known as "the great Countess." In 1077 she bequeated to the Holy See all her patrimonial estates which included Tuscany, Lucca, Modena, Mantua and Ferrara by an act of gift to Pope Gregory VII., a territory which constituted the greater part of the temporal dominion of the papacy, and a legacy that generated much evil in Italy. Upon her death she was buried in a Benedictine abbey near Mantua, whence her remains were brought here in 1635.

Photo ALINARI, ANDERSON, BROGI.

ROME — BASILICA OF SAINT PETER.

THE MASS OF ST. GREGORY THE GREAT.
Mosaic after A. SACCHI.

THE "TRANSFIGURATION"
Mosaic after RAPHAEL.

PUNISHMENT OF SIMON MAGUS.
Painting on slate by VANNI.

The basilica of St. place occupies the first place in the tradition of Christendom, both as an object of veneration and as an artistic monument. In addition to the usual religious services performed in the church, certain specially solemn ceremonies, which can only be carried out by the Pope, are held here. These are Beatifications, Canonizations and Holy Years.

The rite of beatification consists in the reading of a papal brief proclaiming the new Blessed, and the first act of "cultus" towards his image and relics, which is done during a solemn mass, celebrated in the great hall above the vestibule of the basilica. The rite of canonization is more solemn and complete. It is a declaration made by the Pope himself that a servant of God, renowned for his virtues and for miracles he has wrought, is to be publicly venerated by the whole Church, termed Saint, and honoured by a special festival. After the proclamation, the Pope celebrates the pontifical Mass in the Basilica.

The rite observed during Holy Years or Jubilees, is the passage of the faithful through the Holy Door (p. 405), which is always walled up but is opened with great ceremonies, at the beginning of the Holy Year and closed at the end of it by the Pope in person.

* * *

The doorway beneath the monument of Maria Clementina Sobiesky gives access to the Dome. The ascent may be made by lift or by the easy spiral stairway whose walls bear inscriptions recording the names of royalties who have ascended it. The roof of the church with its domes, work-shops and houses in which the workmen and custodians of St. Peter's live, presents the aspect of a village in miniature.

The summit of the façade affords a fine view of the city and the Campagna; from this point the visitor can best appreciate the stupendous size and proportions of the dome which rises 308 feet above the roof. A further flight of steps and staircase between the two shells of the cupola leads to the lantern.

From the circular inner galleries of the dome (175 and 240 ft. above ground) an impressive view of the interior of the dome and the church may be gained: the church seems like the bottom of an abyss, the faithful on the pavement below are like dots, the mosaics of the dome, which seen from below appear minute and delicate, are here found to be coarsely executed and deformed. The narrow loggia round the lantern, reached by an awkward staircase, commands a perspective that is almost unbounded. A perpendicular iron ladder ascends to the bronze ball, which seen from the ground has the effect of a melon, and which is capable of holding sixteen persons.

TOMB OF INNOCENT VIII. († 1492).
By the Brothers POLLAIUOLO.

BAPTISMAL FONT. *Designed by* C. FONTANA.

This font is said to be the upturned lid of the porphyry sarcophagus which contained the ashes of Hadrian in the Castle of Sant'Angelo, and in which Otho II. was subsequently buried.

The tomb of Innocent VIII., a bronze work of ANT. and PIERO POLLAIUOLO, is the oldest papal monument of the new basilica. The Pope is represented by two statues, the one stretched upon a sarcophagus, the other enthroned giving the papal benediction with the right hand, while in the left he holds a lance, representing the one (sent by the Sultan Bajazet) preserved in the basilica, said to be the same which pierced Our Saviour's side.

The four niches on either side of the Pope contain statuettes of the Cardinal Virtues, with their appropriate symbols; in the centre of the lunette above is a crowned woman, emblematic of Divine Providence or Charity, with figures of Faith, and Hope.

Photo ALINARI, ANDERSON, BROGI.

ROME — BASILICA OF SAINT PETER.

Silver gilt Candelabrum.
Designed by B. Cellini.

Dalmatic of Pope Leo III.,
worn at the coronation of Charlemagne. A. D. 800.

Silver Pyx
presented by the City of
Milan to Pope Leo XIII.

The treasury contains jewels, ornaments, church plate, copes and vestments of great value. The dalmatic of Leo III. said to have been embroidered at Constantinople, is worked in gold and silver. On the front the Saviour is represented in glory.

In the centre of a golden circle " Jesus Christ the Resurrection and the Life," holds an openbook, inscribed with the invitation, " Come, ye blessed of my Father." The Virgin Mary stands on the right of Our Saviour; the heavenly host and the company of the blessed form a circle of adoration around the central glory ; angels occupying the upper part, emperors, patriarchs, monks and nuns the lower. In the corners below appear (right) the Baptist, and (left) Abraham seated, a child in his lap and others standing at his side. On the back of the dalmatic is the Transfiguration.

It was in this dalmatic that in 1345 Cola di Rienzi robed himself for his election to the tribuneship.

Boniface VIII. († 1303).
By Arnolfo di Cambio.

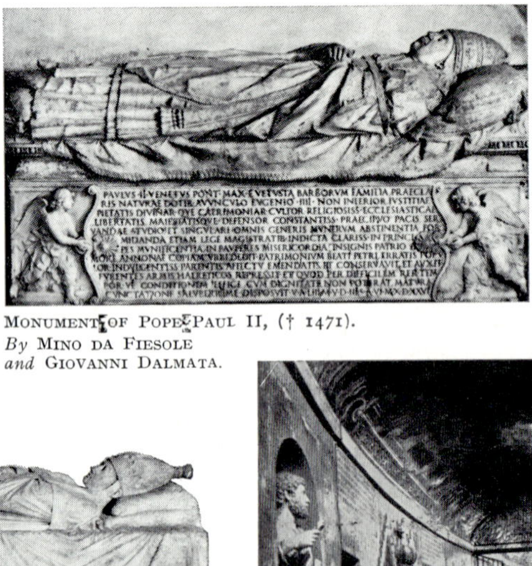

Monument of Pope Paul II, († 1471).
*By Mino da Fiesole
and Giovanni Dalmata.*

Sarcophagus of Boniface VIII. († 1303).
By Arnolfo. 14th cent.

The Pope's recumbent statue is interesting on account of the tiara with the double circlet first used by this pontiff. The triple circlet (now in use) dating from the time of Clement V. Boniface instituted the first Jubilee in 1300.

Sacre Grotte or Crypt. *Grotte Nuove.*

In the construction of the new basilica, to preserve it from dampness, a space of 13 ft. was left between the pavement of the old church and that of the new one. This space constitutes the " Vatican Grottos." In it were deposited the majority of the tombs and fragments of sculpture, frescoes and mosaics formerly located in the old basilica of St. Peter.

Besides the tombs illustrated here the *grottos* contain the sepulchral monuments of many popes and illustrious personages removed here from the old basilica, Nicolas I. († 867) ; Gregory V. (a German † 999) ; Nicholas III. (Orsini † 1280) ; Urban VI. († 1399) ; Marcellus II. († 1555) ; Calixtus III. and Alexander VI. Borgia.

— 412 —

APPENDIX

COATS OF ARMES
OF THE
Renaissance Popes

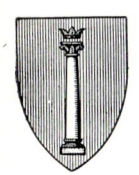

PAPAL INSIGNIA.

COLONNA	CONDULMER	PARENTUCELLI	BORGIA	PICCOLOMINI	BALBO
Martin V. 1417-1431	Eugenius IV. 1431-1447	Nicolas V. 1447-1455	Calixtus III. 1455-1458	Pius II. — Pius III. 1458-1464 1503	Paul II. 1464-1471

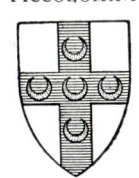

DELLA ROVERE	CIBO	BORGIA	MEDICI	DEDEL	FARNESE
Sixtus IV. — Julius II. 1471-1484 1503-1513	Innocent VIII. 1484-1492	Alexander VI. 1492-1503	Leo X. — Clement VII. 1513-1521 1523-1534 Pius IV. Leo XI. 1559-1565 1605	Hadrian VI. 1522-1523	Paul III 1534-1549

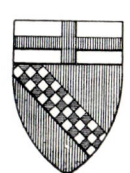

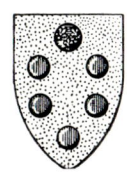

DEL MONTE	CERVINI	CARAFFA	GHISLIERI	BUONCOMPAGNI	PERETTI
Julius III. 1550-1555	Marcellus II. 1555	Paul IV. 1555-1559	Pius V. 1566-1572	Gregory XIII. 1572-1585	Sixtus V. 1585-1590

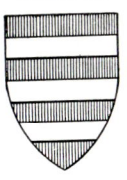

CASTAGNA	SFONDRATI	FACCHINETTI	ALDOBRANDINI	BORGHESE	LUDOVISI
Urban VII. 1590	Gregory XIV. 1590-1591	Innocent IX. 1591	Clement VIII. 1592-1605	Paul V. 1605-1621	Gregory XV. 1621-1623

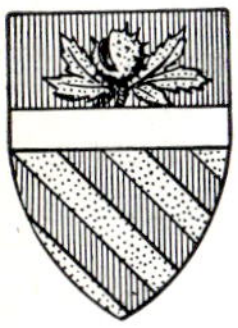

COATS OF ARMS OF THE POPES (Continued).

Family	Pope	Years
BARBERINI	Urban VIII.	1623-1644
PAMPHILI	Innocent X.	1644-1655
CHIGI	Alexander VII.	1655-1667
ROSPIGLIOSI	Clement IX.	1667-1669
ALTIERI	Clement X.	1670-1676
ODESCALCHI	Innocent XI.	1676-1689
OTTOBONI	Alexander VIII.	1689-1691
PIGNATELLI	Innocent XII.	1691-1700
ALBANI	Clement XI.	1700-1721
CONTI	Innocent XIII.	1721-1724
ORSINI	Benedit XIII.	1724-1730
CORSINI	Clement XII	1730-1740
LAMBERTINI	Benedit XIV.	1740-1758
REZZONICO	Clement XIII.	1758-1769
GANGANELLI	Clement XIV.	1769-1774
BRASCHI	Pius VI.	1775-1799
CHIARAMONTI	Pius VII.	1800-1823
DELLA GENGA	Leo XII.	1823-1829
CASTIGLIONI	Pius VIII.	1829-1830
CAPPELLARI	Gregory XVI.	1831-1846
MASTAI-FERRETTI	Pius IX.	1846-1878
PECCI	Leo XIII.	1878-1903
SARTO	Pius X.	1903-1914
DELLA CHIESA	Benedit XV.	1914-1922
RATTI	Pius XI.	1922-1939
PACELLI	Pius XII.	1939-1958
RONCALLI	John XXIII.	1958-1963
MONTINI	Paul VI.	Since 1963

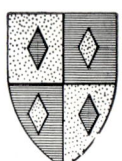

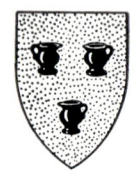

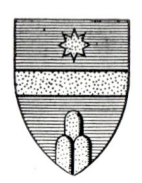

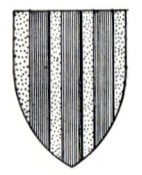

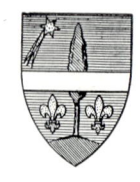

ROME — BARILICA OF SAINT PETER.

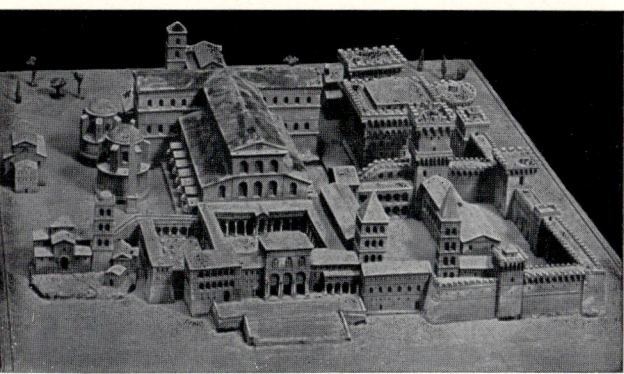

MODEL OF OLD ST. PETER'S, the Vatican and adjacent edifices.

Silver gilt Candelabrum.
Designed by A. POLLAIUOLO.

Old St. Peter's was approached by a flight of 35 steps which the pilgrims ascended on their knees. The atrium or quadriportico was entered by three gateways; it was paved with blocks of marble and surrounded by a colonnade. The fountain in the centre, a marsterpiece of the 6th cent. was composed of a tabernacle supported by eight porphyry columns with a dome of gilt bronze; the water flowing in innumerable jets from out of a bronze pine core (now in the Vatican). On festival days the atrium was used as a place in which to feed the poor; there were stalls also where pilgrims might buy food and objects of devotion. The walls of the portico were painted with frescoes, beneath which were ranged the tombs of the popes, kings and emperors. The façade of the church was adorned with mosaics, and the church itself was entered by five doors; funerals passed through the Porta *Iudicii*, "Judgment Door"; men entered by the Porta *Ravenniana*; the main entrance, opened only for Pope or Emperor, was called the Porta *Argentea*, from the silver ornaments affixed to it; the fourth door, *Romana*, was reserved for women; and the fifth, *Guidonea*, for tourists and pilgrims. Among the most notable of the early 'pilgrims' were Theodosius I.; Valentinian III., emperor of the East; with his wife Eudoxia; Totila; Luitprand, king of the Lombards; Carloman, king of France, Ethelwolf; king of the Anglo-Saxons.

Old St. Peter's was a church of pure basilical form with a wooden roof and five naves divided by four rows of antique columns. The interior was decorated with beautiful mosaics, gold and precious marbles taken from other ancient edifices. Beneath the high altar was the sarcophagus containing the remains of St. Peter. The basilica began to be the official mausoleum of the Popes in the fifth century. At first the place selected was not the interior of the church but the vestibule, and for over two centuries they were laid side by side under the floor, the graves being marked by a plain slab. When every inch of space had been occupied the aisles of the church were chosen, and the richness and magnificence of their tombs increased as time went on. In the course of time the basilica was surrounded by monasteries, chapels, churches, and buildings, that formed the beginnings of the Vatican palace.

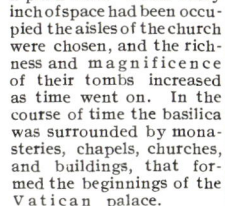

CHRIST between SS. Paul and Peter. *10th cent.*

In this mosaic, formerly placed in the atrium of the Old basilica, above the tomb of Otho II., St. Peter is seen holding three (instead of two) keys: they symbolize power, science and jurisdiction.

SARCOPHAGUS OF JUNIUS BASSUS. Prefect of Rome. († 359).

The reliefs represent scenes from the Old and New Testament: Sacrifice of Isaac, Adam and Eve, Seizure of St. Peter, etc. In the spandrels of the arches are smaller reliefs of lambs performing miracles; from right to left: Raising of Lazarus, Multiplication of the Loaves, Baptism of Christ, etc.

BRONZE MONUMENT OF SIXTUS IV. († 1484).
By ANTONIO POLLAIUOLO. A. D. 1493.

The monument of Sixtus IV. is one of the grandest works of the Renaissance. The fine figure of the Pope, dressed in robes of state, lies upon a bronze couch, the sides of which are panelled with sculptured figures of the seven Virtues and enriched with foliage, mouldings, tassels, etc., of the most admirable execution. On the concave sides are allegories of the ten Liberal Arts.

Photo ALINARI, ANDERSON, BROGI.

— 413 —

53. - *WONDERS OF ITALY*.

BASILICA OF SAINT JOHN in Lateran.

ST. JOHN IN LATERAN. *Designed by* A. GALILEI. 1734-36.

VIEW OF THE NAVE. *Designed by* BORROMINI.

CONSTANTINE the Great.
*Ancient statue in the atrium.
(From his Thermæ.)*

ST. JAMES the Greater. *By* RUSCONI.

Tabernacle and High Altar containing the heads of SS. Peter and Paul.

ST. MATTHEW. *By* RUSCONI.

The Basilica of *St. John in Lateran* is the "Mother and head of all churches"; founded by Constantine in or near the great Lateranus palace which he had presented to Pope Sylvester I., as his episcopal residence and which was occupied by all the popes until their secession to Avignon in 1307. The primitive church was dedicated to the *Holy Saviour* and became the cathedral of Rome and of the world, taking priority of all the churches in the city. Its canons to day still take precedence of the canons of St. Peter's. The Constantinian church was destroyed by earthquake in 898, but was re-erected and dedicated to John the Baptist. Nicholas IV. subsequently remodelled and beautified it. In 1308, a fire burnt it down and it was again rebuilt by Clement V., and repeatedly extended and modified by his successors, so that nothing of the original edifice is recognizable in the present church which dates mostly from the 17th century. St. John in Lateran is one of the four basilicas which have a *Porta Santa*, opened only during Holy Years.

The interior, remarkable for its austerity and grand proportions, is 426 feet in length and consists of a nave with double aisles, a transept and a choir. The columns of the primitive basilica, with the exception of two still visible at the end of the nave, were united in pairs and encased in twelve massive pilasters, in the niches of which are colossal statues of the Apostles, of the school of BERNINI; above these are reliefs of the Old (left) and New (right) Testament by ALGARDI; higher still are medallions of the prophets. The gorgeous ceiling sculptured with coats-of-arms of popes and emblems of the Passion, was designed by GIACOMO DELLA PORTA; the Cosmatesque pavement dates from 1420.

The High Altar, at which only the pope or a substitute appointed by him may celebrate mass, contains many relics, including the heads of SS. Peter and Paul, and a table from the catacombs used as an altar by St. Peter. The gothic tabernacle over the altar, decorated by a Sienese painter, dates from 1369. On the pavement in front of the Confession is the bronze Tomb of Pope Martin V. Colonna), by the Florentine sculptor SIMONE GHINI (*see opposite page*).

The transept may be entered from the portico on the north front of the church. The Altar of the Sacrament has four gilt bronze columns from the Constantinian basilica. Here is preserved the cedar table which, according to tradition, served for the Last Supper. The great ornament of the basilica is the Corsini chapel in the left aisle, built in honour of St. Andrea Corsini († 1302). It contains the tomb of Clement XII., and that of Cardinal Neri Corsini; in the vault of this chapel is a group of the *Pietà* by MONTAUTI.

CAPPELLA CORSINI. *Built by* A. GALILEI.

— 414 —

Photo ALINARI, ANDERSON, BROGI.

ROME — BASILICA OF SAINT JOHN in Lateran.

The Ancient Apse reconstructed under Leo XIII. contains precious mosaics executed in 1290 by *Jacobus Torriti*. The composition in the semidome represents the union of heaven and earth by baptism. Above the majestic head of Christ is represented the face of the Almighty enveloped in clouds. Beneath these two Persons of the Godhead, the Holy Ghost, descending like a dove, sheds the Trinal influence in the shape of rays upon the bejewelled Cross elevated on the summit of the mystic Calvary, the Mount of Paradise. In the centre of the cross is represented the Baptism of Christ and at its base is the « well of life », at which stags are drinking, symbolical of the faithful. From this well the four rivers of Paradise descend the mountain and gather into the mystical river « Jordanes » in which souls in the shape of children and all kinds of living things find the joy of existence. At the foot of the mountain appears the holy city, the New Jerusalem, a vast fortress in the midst of which rises the Tree of life, and the phoenix, the symbol of resurrection, reposing on its summit. The gate is guarded by an angel. Right and left is the Virgin, the Baptist, SS. Peter, Paul, John, Andrew, Francis of Assisi, Anthony of Padua and Pope Nicholas IV. The Apostles owbel are by *Camerino*.

MOSAICS IN THE APSE. By JACOBUS TORRITI (1290).

BONIFACE VIII., proclaiming the first Jubilee of 1300. *Fresco by* GIOTTO.

GRAVE OF MARTIN V. († 1431). *Bronze by* SIMONE GHINI.

PIETÀ OR DEPOSITION. *By* ANTONIO MONTAUTI.

GIOTTO's portrait of Boniface VIII. placed on the first pilaster of the right aisle, was originally painted for the portico of the adjacent Lateran palace, whence pontiffs used to give the papal benediction. In the picture the Pope is represented in the act of blessing from the loggia whilst a cleric reads the Bull of Indulgence. The plenary indulgence which Boniface published on the occasion of the Jubilee of 1300 to all who should make the pilgrimage, attracted over two million devotees to Rome, among these were Giotto and Dante.

During the many centuries in which the Lateran was the residence of the pontiffs, the basilica of St. John was not only the scene of the coronations, installations and entombments of the popes; being a papal cathedral it became also a much-favoured place of assembly for ecclesiastical councils. The most prominent of these was that of 1215 under Innocent III., at which, besides the Patriarchs of Jerusalem and of Constantinople, the envoys of England, France, Hungary, and Sicily, 412 bishops, with 800 priors and abbots from all parts of Christendom were present. At this council the errors of Joachim of Calabria, respecting the Trinity, were denounced as heresies; a series of resolutions provided for the institution of the episcopal inquisition, conventual discipline, marriage-law, and, on every Christian arrived at years of discretion, the duty was imposed of confessing and of receiving the Eucharist at least once annually.

Monument to Innocent III († 1215). *By* LUCHETTI.

Monument to Leon XIII († 1903). *By* TADOLINI.

Monument to Clement XII († 1740). *By* MONALDI.

— 415 —

Photo ALINARI, ANDERSON, BROGI.

ROME — THE LATERAN BAPTISTERY. San Giovanni in Fonte.

The *Lateran Baptistery*, an octagonal building, for a long time the only baptistery at Rome, was the model for all later buildings of the kind. In the centre is the porphyry bath in which, according to a Roman legend (p. 430) Constantine is said to have been baptized. (His baptism, however, did not take place until the approach of death in 337. In those days baptism was gladly put off as long as possible as it was the purification from all stains). The foundation of the baptistery is attributed to Constantine, but it was probably first built under Sixtus III. (ca. 432). The exterior, and the general arrangement of the interior, have been preserved without alterations; but the whole building has been repeatedly repaired and restored. The porphyry columns of the interior came from an imperial building.

ORATORY OF ST. VENANTIUS. *Mosaic of the 7th century.*

The paintings on the sides of the cupola, illustrating the Life of St. John the Baptist are by *Andrea Sacchi*; the frescoes on the walls representing the Vision of Constantine, his Victory over Maxentius, and his Triumphal entry into Rome are by *Carlo Maratta*.

On either side of the entrance are the oratories of the two Saint Johns, built by Pope Hilary in the 5th cent. The one on the right, dedicated to the Baptist, has bronze doors which sound a musical note in opening or shutting, said to have been brought from the Baths of Caracalla. The ceiling of the oratory of St. John the Evangelist is decorated with fine 5th cent. mosaics of birds and of flowers; in the centre is the Lamb with a nimbus, a symbol of the Creator.

The oratory of St. Venantius connected with the baptistery was erected in the 7th cent. by Pope John IV. and his successor Theodore I. In the semidome is Christ blessing and two angels, below stands the Virgin, in the attitude of prayer; on her right are SS. John the Evangelist, Paul, Venantius and Pope John IV. holding his oratory; on her left are SS. Peter, John the Baptist, Domnius and Pope Theodore; on the face of the arch above are the emblems of the Four Evangelists, and the cities of Jerusalem and Bethlehem, below are eight Slav saints, remarkable as showing the costumes of the period.

INTERIOR OF THE BAPTISTERY.
The Baptismal Font: an ancient bath in green basalt.

PROCESSION OF LEVITES.
Ancient relief in the Lateran cloisters.

PALAZZO DEL LATERANO. *Erected under Sixtus V., in* 1586.
Designed by DOMENICO FONTANA.

CLOISTERS OF ST. JOHN IN LATERAN.
By VASSALLETUS. 1300.

The "Lateran," was the residence of the Popes from the time of Constantine until the removal to Avignon (1307). The old palace, much larger than the present one, was burned down in 1308 and on its foundations *Domenico Fontana* erected the present building which has never used as a residence by the Popes.

The red granite obelisk beside the palace, originally erected by King Thotmes (15th century B. C.) in front of the Temple of the Sun at Heliopolis, and brought to Rome in A. D. 357 by Emperor Constantius, was set up on its present site by Pope Sixtus V. in 1588. It measures 105 ft. in height and is the largest obelisk in existence.

Photo ALINARI, ANDERSON, BROGI.

ROME — THE LATERAN. The Scala Santa, Triclinium or Tribune.

THE SCALA SANTA "Holy Stairs." (*Church of San Salvadore*).

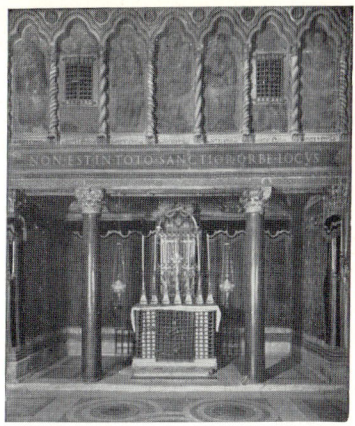

THE "SANCTA SANCTORUM" CHAPEL. *13th cent.*

The *Scala Santa*, a flight of 28 marble steps from the house of Pilate, and which our Saviour is said to have ascended, was brought to Rome by the Empress Helena the mother of Constantine the Great. It formed part of the old Lateran palace whence it was removed to its present site on the destruction of that building. The stairs may be ascended only on the knees (side stairs being provided for the descent); an indulgence for a thousand years — indulgence from penance — is granted for this act of devotion. There is no day on which worshippers may not be seen ascending these stairs; the multitude of the faithful who ascended them in the time of Clement XII. (1730-1740), was so great that he found it necessary to protect them by planks of walnut wood, which have been renewed three times.

The two groups in marble at the foot of the steps, "Christ before Pontius Pilate," and the "Betrayal of Judas," are by the sculptor JACOMETTI.

At the top of the stairs is the old private chapel of the popes, the 'Sancta Sanctorum,' a remnant of the famous Lateran palace. The chapel probably dates from the 6th cent. when it was erected to receive the relics brought by Gregory the Great from Constantinople; in 1278 it was completely rebuilt by a member of the Cosmas family for Pope Nicholas III.

Over the altar is a picture of our Saviour which, according to tradition, was begun by St. Luke and finished by « invisible hands ». This great relic was brought from Jerusalem to Rome in the 8th century to save it from the outrage of the Iconoclasts.

The pavement of the chapel is of beautiful cosmatesque work, the vault is decorated with 9th cent. mosaics representing the Redeemer sustained by six-winged seraphims; on the architrave supported by four gilded columns is the iscription, « Non est in toto sanctior orbe locus ». (There is not in the whole world a place more holy).

UPPER PART OF THE TRIBUNE erected by Pope Benedict XIV, A. D. 1743.

CHRIST giving the keys to Pope Sylvester and the labarum to Constantine.

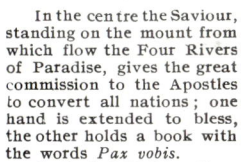

TRIBUNE of Benedict XIV.

ST. PETER giving the pallium to Leo III., and the banner to Charlemagne.

In the centre the Saviour, standing on the mount from which flow the Four Rivers of Paradise, gives the great commission to the Apostles to convert all nations; one hand is extended to bless, the other holds a book with the words *Pax vobis*.

On the left Christ enthroned, bestows the keys on Pope Sylvester and the labarum or

The *Tribune* erected by Benedict XIV. (adjoining the Scala Santa), is a reconstruction of a part of the state banqueting-hall built at the end of the 8th cent. by Leo III. in the old Lateran palace, in which the pope entertained Charlemagne after the coronation of 800 in St. Peter's, the memorable event which gave rise to the Holy Roman Empire.

standard of the Cross to the Emperor Constantine.

On the right St. Peter, with the keys in his lap, gives Leo III. the pallium (the emblem of spiritual supremacy vested in St. Peter and which he here confers on his earthly representative), and Charlemagne the banner (the emblem of temporal power). The figures of Pope Leo and Charlemagne are distinguished by the square nimbus or glory round their heads. Square shaped nimbuses were given to living persons only

— 417 —

Photo ALINARI, ANDERSON, BROGI.

ROME — *BASILICA OF SANTA MARIA MAGGIORE.*

BASILICA OF SANTA MARIA MAGGIORE.  **HIGH ALTAR AND CANOPY.**

Santa Maria Maggiore is one of the five patriarchal churches of Rome and, like St. Peter's, has a "jubilee door". Originally founded by Pope Liberius in 352, it was altered in the 12th cent. and again in the 16th cent. The façade by Fuga dates from 1743. The fine bell-tower, dating from the 13th century, is the loftiest and one of the best preserved in Rome. The column in front of the church has a bronze figure of the Virgin.

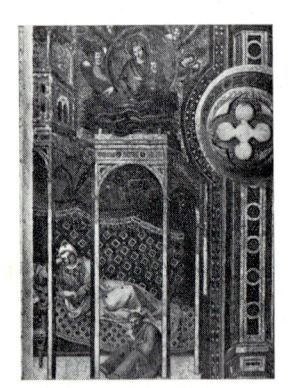

Vision of Pope Liberius. (*see p. 419*). Christ enthroned and Angels.  Johannes relates his dream to the Pope.

Mosaics by FILIPPO RUSUTI *and* GADDO GADDI *ca. 1300 (inner façade).*

The Borghese Chapel.  View of the decorations.  Altar with St. Luke's Madonna.

The Borghese chapel is encased with costly marbles. monumental statues, reliefs, paintings on gold backgrounds, gems, etc.

Photo ALINARI. ANDERSON, BROGI.

ROME — BASILICA OF SANTA MARIA MAGGIORE.

SANTA MARIA MAGGIORE OR BASILICA LIBERIANA. *Founded in the fourth century.*

Santa Maria Maggiore offers the best example of the classical basilical form. It is also named « S. Maria ad Nives », because a fall of snow determined the exact limits of its site. Tradition goes that in the year 352 the Virgin Mary appeared in a dream simultaneously to Johannes, a devout Roman patrician and to Pope Liberius, commanding them to build a church to her on the spot where they should find snow on the following morning (August 5th). The snow (a rare thing at that season) was found on the Esquiline hill and thither the Pope went in procession and marked out the foundations of the edifice which Johannes built at his own expense. The primitive church was completely rebuilt by Pope Sixtus III., who reigned from 432 to 440; and of this magnificent building, which since the 12th cent. has received frequent and extensive additions and alterations, there remain the nave with its Ionic marble columns and the interesting mosaics of the nave and of the great arch (p. 420). The High Altar rests on an ancient porphyry basin, said to have been the tomb of the patrician Johannes. In the Confessio are preserved relics of S. Matthias, and five boards of the Manger at Bethlehem. In the tribune are mosaics by Jacobus Torriti (p. 420). In the right transept is the sumptuous Sixtine Chapel — or Chapel of the Holy Sacrament — with tombs of Sixtus V. and Pius V. and a fine tabernacle in gilded bronze sustained by four angels. In the left transept is the Borghese Chapel containing tombs of Paul V. and Clement VIII. Nothing can exceed the costliness of the marbles with which this chapel is encased; monumental statues, bas-reliefs, gold paintings, gems, etc. Over the altar, between four fluted columns of jasper, is the miraculous painting of the Virgin and Child, painted by St. Luke, which St. Gregory the Great carried in procession to stay the plague that desolated Rome in A. D. 590. (*Continued*).

The magnificent ceiling by GIULIANO DA SANGALLO dating from 1498, was gilded with the first gold brought by Columbus from America, presented to Alexander VI. by Ferdinand and Isabella of Spain.

The pavement, of Cosmatesque design, dates from about 1150. Near the entrance is the tomb of Pope Nicholas IV. († 1292), and that of Pope Clement IX. († 1669).

A famous scene of violence occurred in this church in 1075, when Pope Gregory VII., was attacked while celebrating mass on Christmas eve, and carried off to a fortified tower by a supporter of the Emperor Henry IV. (see p. 474); on being rescued by the populace the next day, the pope, with characteristic fortitude, returned to the basilica offered thanksgivings to God, and finished the interrupted mass.

THE POPE TRACES THE PLAN OF THE BASILICA. *Relief by* MINO DEL REAME.

In the right transept is the chapel of the Holy Sacrament, or Sixtine Chapel, built by DOMENICO FONTANA for Cardinal Montalto before he became Sixtus V. The chapel, a veritable church in itself, is a work of extraordinary magnificence.

The fine tabernacle in gilded bronze in the centre covers the original altar consecrated for the primitive church of pope Liberius. In the *Confessio* is a statue of San Gaetano by BERNINI, and a group of the Holy Family by CECCHINO DA PIETRASANTA.

On the right wall of the chapel is the sumptuous monument of Pope Sixtus V. On the left wall, the monument of Pius V., with effigy in gilded bronze relief below; the reliefs represent the battle of Lepanto, which took place during the reign of the pontiff, and his sending assistance to Charles IX. of France for the persecution and utter destruction of the Huguenots.

CHAPEL of the Holy Sacrament, Sixtine Chapel. *Erected by* D. FONTANA.

Tabernacle in gilded bronze, with Angels bearing the chapel.

Photo ALINARI, ANDERSON, BROGI.

ROME — BASILICA OF

About eighty years after the foundation of the primitive basilica, Sixtus III. (432-440) re-erected the church and dedicated it to *Sancta Maria Mater Dei*. This pontiff had just resisted the heresy of Nestorius, Patriarch of Constantinople, who denied the divinity of Christ and would not allow to the Virgin Mary the title that had been given her as the « Mother of God ». Nestorius

MOSAICS ON THE ARCH OF TRIUMPH.

The mosaics on the face of the arch are divided into three courses. The subject matter is, apparently, the childhood of Christ :

1. The Annunciation to Mary and to Joseph who stands in front of the Temple. The Virgin is crowned and seated on a chair with angels right and left of her. The Holy Ghost descends from Heaven on one side, the angel Gabriel flies down on the other. The Virgin is represented in Roman attire; the Temple with closed doors behind her « symbolizes the abrogated Jewish Law », while the open sanctuary behind Joseph, and the burning lamp in its entrance « symbolizes the new universal Church ».

2. The Adoration of the Magi. The Child sits enthroned on an enormous Roman chair, a cross over his head proclaiming his divine origin; behind Him are four angels and between them is seen the star which guided the Magi. The figure to the left of Christ is intended for the Madonna; the one seated on a small throne to the right is an undefined personification; behind her two Magi standing and holding their offerings.

3. The Massacre of the Innocents. To the left is Herod enthroned, to the right a group of women, in an attitude of sorrow and resignation, carrying their little children.

4. The city of Jerusalem, a flock of sheep at the gate symbolizing the faithful.

Annunciation.   Nativity   Death of
CORONATION OF THE VIRGIN *By* JACOBUS.

The mosaic decoration of the apse was ordered by Pope Nicholas IV. and Cardinal Jacopo Colonna and was finished in 1296 by TORRITI. In a blue gold-starred circle representing heaven Christ and the Virgin are seated enthroned; on each side groups of angels gaze in adoration. To the left, behind the small kneeling figure of Nicholas IV. stand

Abraham and the 3 Angels.    Isac blesses Jacob.
Mosaics of the 5th cent. on the left wall of the nave.

The series of mosaics which adorn the Arch of Triumph and those on the architrave of the nave, are perhaps the finest examples of early Christian Art, and will stand as rare specimens of the form which the ideas of that time gave to the biblical characters. They have been considered to date from the pontificate of Sixtus III. (432-440), whose name is inscribed on the arch, and who dedicated the basilica to the Virgin. But Dr. Richter and Miss Taylor in an exhaustive work on the mosaics—*The Golden Age of Christian Art*— prove them to belong to an earlier date. Dr. Richter, a theologian and art critic,

SANTA MARIA MAGGIORE. The Mosaics.

had been deposed at the Council of Ephesus 431, where the dogma of Christ's divinity was confirmed, and in commemoration of this important event Sixtus enlarged the church and decorated the great arch and the nave with mosaics, the symbolism of which is interpreted (hypothetically) as an iconographic exemplification of the truths denied by the followers of Nestorius.

Phot. ANDERSON, Rome.

In a circle in the centre of the arch is represented the apocalyptic throne with the book of the seven seals, indicating the gospels. Upon the book is a 1 gemmed cross and behind it rises a larger veiled cross. On either side of the circle SS. Peter and Paul are seen standing, holding a book, and behind them are the symbols of the Four Evangelists.

Right of the throne:
2 1. The Presentation in the Temple. Nearer the centre of the arch stands the Virgin, crowned and holding the Infant Christ; near her stands Joseph who points to the prophetess Anna and three angels. To the right is Simeon who
3 bends forward reverently and stretches his hands to receive the Child. On the extreme right of the composition is the Temple.

2. This picture has been thought to represent the homage paid by the Egyptians to the Child Christ, when their idols fell at His coming. The composition consists
4 of two groups advancing processionally from right and left to meet each other. The group to the left is headed by a Prince and a Philosopher, the one to the right by the Child Christ who is followed by Joseph, Mary and three angels.

TORRITI (1296). *Mosaic decorations in the apse.*

SS. Peter, Paul and Francis of Assisi; to the right is the small kneeling figure of Cardinal Colonna and SS. John the Baptist, John the Evangelist and Antony of Padua. Below is the River Jordan with symbolical figures of men and animals. Lower still, are scenes from the life of the Virgin.

3. Visit of the Magi to Herod. To the left of the composition are the Magi to the right Herod and between them two priests.
4. The city of Bethlehem, with a group of five sheep at its gate symbolizing the mystic Flock of Christ.

Crossing of the Jordan.    The siege of Jericho.

Mosaics of the 5th cent. on the right wall of the nave.

finds that the subjects represented are closely connected with the religious thought of the 2nd century, with the writings of Justin Martyr, of Clement of Alexandria and Origen rather than to the doctors of the 5th century. The mosaics on the left wall of the nave represent scenes from the history of Abraham and Jacob; those on the right wall stories of Moses and Joshua. They are thirty-one in number (not including those which are lost); the style of these compositions is purely classic, and recalls the reliefs on the columns of Trajan and Marcus Aurelius rather than the mosaic pictures of the fourth and fifth century churches.

— 421 —   Photo ALINARI, ANDERSON, BROGI.

ROME — BASILICA OF SAINT PAUL Outside-the-Walls.

Founded in 386 by the Emperor Valentinian II., continued by Theodosius, and finished under Honorius on the site of a church built by Constantine over the tomb of St. Paul, this was the finest basilica at Rome until the great fire of 1823 which almost totally destroyed it. Immediately after the fire Leo XII. began the reconstruction, the whole world joining in the work, and the present church was consecrated by Pope Pius IX. in 1854. The plan and dimensions are the same as those of the original basilica.

The interior (394 ft. by 197 ft. and 75 ft. high) is most imposing. The 80 columns of grey granite were quarried near Baveno, on Lake Maggiore, and transported hither on rafts.

The main façade fronting the Tiber has modern mosaics and a quadriporticus borne by enormous monolithic columns of granite.

The High Altar is surmounted by a famous tabernacle the work of ARNOLFO DI CAMBIO (1285); the reliefs on its exterior represent scenes from the Old Testament, those on the inner surface symbolic animals.

All along the friezes of the nave and aisles, is a long series of mosaic portrait medallions of all the popes from St. Peter to Pope Benedict XV. († 1922).

The Triumphal Arch, spared by the conflagration, is adorned with 5th century mosaics ordered by Galla Placidia and representing Christ and the twenty-four Elders of the Apocalypse with crowns in their hands. Above, are the symbols of the Four Evangelists; below, the two princes

PASCHAL CANDLESTICK. By Vassalletus A. D. 1180.

THE TRIUMPHAL ARCH. *5th cent. mosaic.* THE TRIBUNE, *13th cent. mosaics.*

INTERIOR OF ST. PAUL'S OUTSIDE-THE-WALLS.

CLOISTERS OF ST. PAUL'S *by* VASSALLETUS (*13th cent.*).

of the apostles St. Paul and St. Peter pointing towards the Saviour.

The mosaics in the semidome of the apse, and those of the arch above it and opposite to it, are reconstructions of a work of the time of Pope Honorius III. (1225). In the centre is Christ enthroned, holding an open book, inscribed "VENITE BENEDICTI PATRIS MEI PERCIPITE REGNUM" (Matt. XXV, 34).

To the spectator's right stand SS. Peter and Andrew, to the left SS. Paul and Luke; at the feet of Christ kneels a diminutive figure of Honorius, by whom the mosaic was dedicated. Beneath are the apostles not included in the semidome, the palmtrees separating them are emblematic of their martyrdoms; in the centre is the "prepared throne" with the implements of the passion. All the apostles have scrolls bearing the articles of the Creed. The elaborate Paschal Candlestick near the high altar has scenes from the life of Christ and carvings of animals and foliage: soldiers taking Christ before Caiaphas, Pilate washing his hands, the Crucifixion with the Virgin and St. John, the Resurrection and the Ascension.

Photo ALINARI, ANDERSON, BROGI.

ROME — CHURCH OF SAN CLEMENTE.

SAN CLEMENTE, one of the best preserved of the medieval basilicas of Rome, consists of two churches, one above the other, standing on a foundation of the first century which is said to have been the house of the saint.

The lower church, discovered in 1857, dates from the 4th century for it is mentioned by St. Jerome in 392 and Gregory the Great delivered two homilies in it. During the Sack of Rome (1084) this early basilica was nearly destroyed and buried, as the level of the whole district had been greatly raised by the débris from the burnt edifices after the invasion of Robert Guiscard. The reconstruction of the new basilica was undertaken in 1108 by Pope Paschalis II. who, instead of building other foundations, completed the filling up of the half-hidden basilica and on its ruins erected the present upper church in which he placed several ornaments of the lower, such as the ciborium, the choir-screens, the ambones, the pillars and whatever else could contribute to the adornment of the new basilica while perpetrating the memory of the old.

San Clemente being a fairly exact copy of the lower church, offers a perfect example of the primitive church: everything is conventional and remains *in statu quo*—the atrium, the portico, the choir surrounded by a marble screen or cancellum, the ambones, the ciborium, the paschal candlestick and the cathedra.

SAN CLEMENTE. *Tribune mosaics of the 12th century.*

SAN CLEMENTE. *The upper church.*

The most remarkable thing of the interior is the mosaic decoration of the tribune (12th century). The centre of the composition is occupied by the Cross on which the Saviour is nailed, but very small in proportion; twelve doves, emblems of the Apostles (?), are on the arms of the cross; the Virgin and the Baptist beside it. Above, from a series of five concentric rainbow-like semicircles, signifying Heaven, issues the hand of God holding the crown of victory. To the right and left, within the circle, stands the paschal Lamb. Springing from the foot of the cross, a vine tree (allusive to His words who said « I am the True Vine »), spreads like a rolling frieze over the whole hollow of the tribune; the four Doctors of the Church, men and birds ensconced among its branches. From the base of the cross the four mystic rivers flow to the right and left, stags and peacocks drinking at their streams, while waterfowl and fish, the emblems of the faithful, swim in the river of life, and a whole array of the Christian symbols are ranged along the bank.

Below there is a procession of 13 sheep symbolizing our Saviour and the apostles. On the triumphal arch, is the Redeemer in the act of giving the benediction; on either side are the symbols of the Evangelists. Lower down to the left sit SS. Laurence—Paul, to the right SS. Peter—Clement; lower still are Isaiah, Jeremiah.

Finding of the widow's child.  St. Clement celebrating Mass.  The Translation of St. Cyril's remains.
Frescoes of the 11th century in the lower church of San Clemente.

— 423 —

Photo ALINARI, ANDERSON, BROGI.

ROME — BASILICA OF SAN LORENZO Outside-the-Walls.

FAÇADE AND CAMPANILE OF SAN LORENZO.

VIEW OF THE INTERIOR. *13th century.*

This is one of the seven pilgrimage churches of Rome. It occupies the site where Constantine erected a church in 330, over the graves of St. Lawrence and St. Cyriaca. Rebuilt and enlarged in the 6th cent., by Pope Pelagius II., the ancient edifice (which was entered from the rear of the present church) was again remodelled in the thirteenth century by Pope Honorius III., who reversed the plan of the building and added the present nave and portico.

The façade is adorned with modern paintings imitating mosaics and representing Christ, the Emperor Constantine, Pelagius II., Honorius III., Sixtus III., St. Lawrence and St. Stephen.

In the vestibule are early-Christian sarcophagi and 13th cent. frescoes with stories of SS. Lawrence, Stephen, Hippolytus and the legend of the Emperor Henry II. [†1024].

The interior of the basilica of St. Lawrence consists of two constructions: (*a*) the nave and aisles dating from the time of Pope Honorius III. (13th cent.); and (*b*) the sixth century church erected by Pope Pelagius which Honorius converted into a choir and crypt.

The nave has 22 antique granite columns and is paved with a 12th century Cosmatesque mosaic. On the walls above the entablature are modern paintings representing scenes in the life of St. Lawrence (left of the entrance), and St. Stephen (right). At the end of the nave are two Cosmatesque ambones, the one on the right for the gospel, that on the left for the epistle.

From here two flights of steps on each side of the Confessio ascend to the choir.

The vestibule of the original basilica was recently appropriated for the mausoleum of Pope Pius IX.

TRIUMPHAL ARCH of the Older Church. *Mosaics of the 6th cent.*

The Choir dates from the time of Honorius III. who erected a pavement half way up the columns of the older church and transformed it into a crypt and choir. Twelve magnificent fluted columns rise from the lower level of the Pelagian church, support the entablature which is made up of ancient friezes and cornices and bears a gallery formerly set apart for women. The high altar surmounted by a canopy dating from 1148, stands above the Confessio, where in a marble urn are deposited the remains of SS. Lawrence, Stephen and Justin. The mosaics on the triumphal arch represent Christ with (right) SS. Paul, Stephen and Hippolytus, (left) SS. Peter, Lawrence and Pope Pelagius offering his Church, and the holy cities of Bethlehem and Jerusalem. In the crypt are inscriptions referring to the notorious *Senatrices* Theodora and Marozia.

THE CHOIR AND THE HIGH ALTAR. *6th and 13th cent.*

MAUSOLEUM OF POPE PIUS IX. († 1878).

Photo ALINARI, ANDERSON, BROGI.

ROME — SANTA MARIA IN TRASTEVERE.

CHURCH OF S. MARIA IN TRASTEVERE.

THE INTERIOR. *The ceiling designed by* DOMENICHINO.

This was the first large church in Rome dedicated to the Virgin. Founded in the 2nd century by Calixtus I., on the site where a spring of oil miraculously welled up, on the night of the Nativity, the edifice was almost entirely rebuilt in 1140 by Innocent II., who is buried within it. The mosaics on the façade dating from this period represent the Madonna, at whose feet are small kneeling figures of Innocent II. and another pope, attended by ten virgins holding burning lamps (two of which are extinguished). In the porch there is the tomb of Card. Campeggio (the Campeius of Shakespeare), who was concerned in the negotiations for the divorce of Henry VIII. of England from Queen Catherine of Aragon. Under Nicholas V. (1450), the church was altered to its present form. The twenty-two massive columns of the nave were taken from pagan edifices; the ceiling, richly decorated with gildings and carved work, was designed by *Domenichino*, who also painted (on copper) the Assumption of the Virgin in the centre; the Cosmatesque pavement was laid in 1872 with old cubes of porphyry, and other marbles.

MADONNA WITH THE CHILD and Virgins.
Mosaics of the 12th cent. on the façade.

The mosaics in the semidome, like those on the arch, date from the time of Innocent II. In the centre is Christ and the Virgin, on her right St. Calixtus, St. Lawrence and Innocent II. holding a model of the church; on the left of Christ is St. Peter, St. Cornelius, Pope Julius and St. Calepodius. Beneath is the Lamb and the 12 sheep (the Apostles) issuing from Bethlehem and Jerusalem. Below are six scenes from the life of Mary, executed about 1300 by *Pietro Cavallini*. From left to right: the Birth, Annunciation, Nativity, Adoration of the Magi, Presentation in the Temple, and Death of the Virgin. The church contains a fine tabernacle for holy oil, by MINO DA FIESOLE (1471); and the tombs of Card. Philip d'Alençon, a member of the royal house of Valois [† 1397]; and Cardinal Pietro Stefaneschi [† 1417], by *Magister Paulus*.

MOSAICS IN THE TRIBUNE. *12th and 13th cent.*

The mosaics on the arch above the semidome date from 1140; in the centre, the cross with the Alpha and Omega flanked by the candlesticks and the emblems of the Evangelists; right and left standing figures of the prophets Isaiah and Jeremiah, above whom is the symbolic caged bird.

THE ANNUNCIATION. **THE ADORATION OF THE MAGI.**
Mosaics of the 13th century by PIETRO CAVALLINI.

Pietro Cavallini, a scion of the family of the Cosmati, was an artist of great talent and the founder of the Roman school of religious painting. The admirable mosaics on the lower portion of the apse representing scenes in the life of the Virgin Mary are well-composed and arranged in surroundings of Cosmatesque architecture.

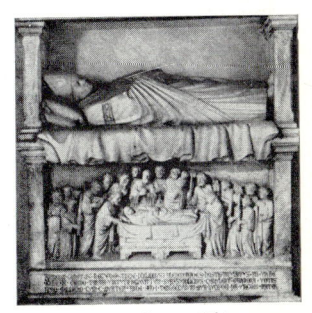

MONUMENT TO CARD. D'ALENÇON.
By Magister Paulus (15th cent.).

Photo ALINARI, ANDERSON, BROGI.

— 425 —

ROME — THE CHURCHES.

Church of Santa Maria in Cosmedin.
Founded in the 6th century.

The *Bocca della Verità*.
12th century.

Interior. (*Santa Maria in Cosmedin*).

The church of *Santa Mar.. in Cosmedin* founded in the 6th cent. upon the site of a very ancient Roman temple, has been many times rebuilt and altered. The present church and the fine campanile show the form given to them in the 12th cent. The interior, of basilical form, has delicate marble screens, beautiful ambones and a Gothic tabernacle.

In the portico is the 'Bocca della Verità, a marble disk representing a human face; in medieval times a suspected person was required, in taking an oath, to place his hand in the mouth of this mask, in the belief that it would close if he swore falsely. In the sacristy is an ancient mosaic representing the Adoration of the Magi.

St. Agnes between Honorius I. (left), and Symmachus.
Mosaics in the Apse. A. D. 625. (*Church of Sant'Agnese fuori le Mura*).

Temple of Vesta.

This charming little temple was probably erected in the first century. It is built entirely of marble, and now bears the name of *Santa Maria del Sole*. The ancient entablature and the roof have disappeared. The columns are 32 ft. high.

Sant'Agnese is one of the most interesting churches in Rome as it has preserved many characteristics of an early Christian basilica. Originally built by Constantine in 324 over the grave of the martyred St. Agnes, the church was restored under the papacy of Symmachus (498-514), and rebuilt by Honorius I. (625-40).

The nave has 16 antique columns taken from different pagan buildings; the gallery or matroneum above the aisles was reserved for women. The mosaic in the tribune dates from the time of Honorius, who is there represented holding the model of the church opposite to Symmachus. This work is specially interesting to art students for it marks the transition between the earlier and later styles; St. Agnes and the two pontiffs, the restorers of the church, take here the place usually occupied by Christ and the Apostles. The only indication of the Godhead is the Hand issuing from the clouds pointing to the saint, dressed in jewelled robes, in accordance with Byzantine ideas. These three solemn, hieratic figures are most impressive.

In the left aisle is the entrance to the Catacombs of St. Agnes, dating from the 1st to the 6th centuries and containing family vaults and private burial places. These are the best preserved in Rome.

On St. Agnes' Day (Jan. 21), a peculiar ceremony is celebrated in this church, when two lambs are placed on the altar and publicly blessed. They are afterwards tended by nuns until Easter, when their wool is employed in making *pallia*, which, after being worn by the pope, are sent to archbishops as a sign that they share in the plenitude of the episcopal office.

Sant'Agnese. *Early-Christian architecture.*

Photo Alinari, Anderson, Brogi.

ROME — THE CHURCHES.

CHURCH OF SANTA CECILIA.
(Founded in the year A. D. 230).

THE INTERIOR. ST. CECILIA, by STEFANO MADERNO.
(The statue of the Saint is under the high altar).

The church of *Santa Cecilia* is situated on the site of the house of the saint and its foundation dates from the 3rd cent. Primitively restored by Gregory the Great, and rebuilt in the 9th cent. by Paschalis I., it was remodelled in the 18th century by Cardinal Acquaviva, and again restored in 1900 at the expense of Cardinal Rampolla, who caused the sepulchral chapel of St. Cecilia and her co-martyrs to be gorgeously decorated in the Byzantine style with luminous mosaics.

The mosaics in the apse belong to the time of Pope Paschalis I. (817-24).

The ancient columns of the nave were encased in brick pilasters in 1822. The church contains several monuments. To the left of the entrance, that of the warlike Card. Fortiguerra, who played an important part in the contests of Pius II. and Paul II., with the Malatesta, Savelli and Anguillara families; to the right, that of Cardinal Adam of Hertford († 1398), an English prelate who was titular of this church.

Under the high altar is the pathetic statue of S. Cecilia by *Maderno*, who represented the body of the saint as it was found when her tomb was opened (in the presence of the artist), in 1599. In the *Confessio* beneath the high altar lies the body of S. Cecilia who, having converted her husband Valerianus, suffered martyrdom in the 2nd century. In the right aisle is the chapel of St. Cecilia, the ancient *calidarium* of the bath-room, in which, according to legend, the saint was trust into boiling water and afterwards beheaded. An old bronze caldron for heating water still exists there. The saint was originally buried in the catacombs of St. Calixtus on the Appian Way, but in 821 Pope Paschalis I. transferred her remains here.

THE REDEEMER. *Detail of the Last Judgment. Fresco by* P. CAVALLINI (1293).

This figure of Christ is a fragment of a fresco discovered in the year 1900.

The painting, a vast composition representing the Last Judgment, had been concealed since 1530 behind the stalls of the nuns' choir in Santa Cecilia, and its rediscovery caused a great sensation in the world of art as it recognized the existence at the end of the 13th century of a highly developed Roman school of painting of which Pietro Cavallini was its last and greatest exponent.

MOSAIC IN THE TRIBUNE. *9th cent.*

Christ with (left) St. Paul, St. Agata and Paschalis I. holding the church restored by him; on the right St. Peter, St. Valerian and St. Cecilia.

The church of *Santa Maria in Domnica*, occupies the site of the house of St. Cyriaca, where St. Lawrence (p. 471), distributed the treasures of the Church among the poor. The original church was rebuilt by Paschalis I. in 817, to which date the mosaics belong; and again entirely restored by Leo X., from the designs of *Raphael*.

On the arch, the Saviour with two angels, 12 Apostles and two large figures of prophets below. In the apse, instead of the usual figure of Christ, is the Virgin with the Child amid a host of angels; a diminutive figure of Paschalis, with a square nimbus, kneels at the Virgin's feet.

MOSAICS OF THE ARCH AND THE APSE. A. D. 817-824.
(Church of Santa Maria in Domnica).

— 427 —

Photo ALINARI, ANDERSON, BROGI.

ROME — THE CHURCHES.

When Christianity became the religion of the state in the fourth century, mosaic, which had hitherto been used more particularly for pavements, being more durable than painting, began to be preferred for the walls and arches of the churches. The early representations were purely emblematical, thus, the Apostles were figured as twelve sheeps with Christ in the centre as the Lamb of God standing on an eminence and crowned with a nimbus.

The earliest and only Christian mosaics of the 4th cent. known to us, are those on the ceiling of St. Costanza: they are of a purely decorative character. Those in the tribune of St. Pudenziana, of the end of the fourth century, have been several times restored. The mosaics in the tribune of Santi Cosma and Damiano which date from A. D. 525-30, are considered the most beautiful in Rome.

Santa Costanza, originally erected by Constantine as a mausoleum for his daughter Constantia, whose sarcophagus is now in the Vatican (p. 443), was converted into a church in 1256. The dome, 74 ft. in diameter, is supported by 24 granite columns. In the vaulting of the ambulatory are the earliest extant Christian mosaics, executed in blue on a white ground and depicting vintage scenes, birds, cupids and interlacing vine-traceries of exquisite workmanship. In some of the niches in the outer wall are other less artistic mosaics; in one is Christ standing on the mount whence flow the four rivers, on each side are SS. Peter and Paul; on another is seen Christ giving the keys to St. Peter.

CHURCH OF SANTA COSTANZA *built by Constantine as a mausoleum for his daughter.*

VINTAGE SCENE. *Early 4th cent. mosaic (Church of S. Costanza).*

SANTA PUDENZIANA. *Consecrated* A. D. 145.

MOSAICS OF THE TRIBUNE. A. D. 390. *(Church of Santa Pudenziana).*

The church of *Santa Pudenziana*, is traditionally the oldest church in Rome, supposed to occupy the site of the house of the senator Pudens, where St. Peter lodged from A. D. 41 to 50, converted the senator's daughters Praxedis and Pudentiana and baptized many thousands of converts. The church was several times restored and altered, especially in 1588. The façade with its mosaics is modern, the campanile dates from the 9th cent.

The 4th century mosaics of the tribune represent: in the centre, Christ enthroned: to His right and left are St. Peter and St Paul crowned by St. Pudentiana and her sister Praxedis; on either side Pudens and his family. The character and arrangement of the figures, the rich architectural background representing the heavenly Jerusalem, the emblems of the Evangelists on each side of the gemmed cross planted on the mystical mountain, are all alike remarkable.

PART OF THE CYPRESS-WOOD DOORS with sculptured scriptural scenes. *5th cent.* (Church of Santa Sabina.)

The church of *Santa Sabina*, supposed to occupy the site of an ancient temple, was presented (1222) by Honorius III., to St. Dominic, who made it the headquarters of his order. The most important monument in it are the wooden doors, unique in existing art, on which are 18 scenes from the Old and New Testaments: *A*) Miracles of Christ, *B*) Crucifixion, *C*) The Marys at the tomb, *D*) Miracles of Moses, and the prophet Elijah carried to heaven, etc.

Photo ALINARI, ANDERSON, BROGI.

THE PREDICTION OF ST. PETER'S TREASON. *Wooden door of Santa Sabina (5th century).*

THE ADORATION OF THE MAGI. *Wooden door of Santa Sabina (5th century).*

ROME — THE CHURCHES.

THE TRIUMPHAL ARCH. THE TRIBUNE ARCH. THE APSE.
Mosaics of the ninth century. (Santa Prassede).

CHURCH OF SANTA PRASSEDE. *Erected* A. D. 822.

The church of *Santa Prassede* stands over the house of Praxedis, sister of Pudentiana (p. 428), where an oratory was built (A. D. 150), as a place of security to which the primitive Christians might retire during the persecutions. The present building was erected in 822 by Pope Paschalis I. in whose time the mosaics were executed. The church was restored about 1450 by Nicholas V. and again in 1832 and 1869.

Santa Prassede contains more mosaics than any other church in Rome. Those on the arches are, as usual, taken from the Apocalypse.

On the arch of triumph is depicted the New Jerusalem, an enclosure studded with precious stones, with a gate at each end guarded by angels. Within, is the Saviour of the World attended by two angels, at whose feet are SS. Praxedis and Pudentiana (?). On each side of Christ are seated the 12 Apostles and the Baptist, offering Him their triumphal crowns. Outside the walls, groups of saints and martyrs are seen approaching, they are encouraged by angels to enter the City of God. Lower down, on each side, a host of the elect looking up to the holy city, await admission.

On the arch of the tribune is the Lamb on a throne with the sealed scroll below, at the side are the seven candlesticks with four angels and the emblems of the Evangelists; beneath are the twenty-four Elders bearing their crowns.

The Chapel of San Zeno, in the right aisle of the church is a veritable gem of mosaic decoration. Above the portal is a double row of busts; in the outer row

Christ blessing: on His right, SS. Paul, Praxedis and Pope Paschalis bearing the Church: on the left, SS. Peter, Pudentiana and Zeno. (Semidome).

CHAPEL OF SAN ZENO (or della Colonna).

Christ and the Apostles, with St. Pudens and St. Zeno below; in the inner the Virgin and Child, St. Praxedis, St. Pudentiana and other saints. The interior entirely lined with 9th cent. mosaics, was called, from its splendour, the "Garden of Paradise." On the vault is the Saviour's head supported by angels, on the walls St. Peter and St. Paul upholding the throne of God, the Virgin and the Baptist, St. John the Evangelist, St. Andrew and St. James, St. Agnes, St. Praxedis and St. Pudentiana. In a niche is a portion of the column at which our Lord is said to have been scourged.

The church of *SS. Cosma and Damian*, formed by the union of two ancient buildings, the *Ædes Sacræ Urbis* and the circular temple of young Romulus, was consecrated as a church by Felix IV. (526-30), in whose time the mosaics in the interior were executed.

The mosaics in the apse, though over restored are considered the most beautiful in Rome. In the centre stands Christ, sustained by clouds, bearing a roll in one hand, at his feet flows the river Jordan, the symbol of Baptism. On each side are SS. Peter and Paul presenting SS. Cosma and Damian to the Saviour, behind are St. Theodorus and Pope Felix presenting a model of the church. Underneath is the Lamb and the usual procession of sheep (the Apostles) issuing from the cities of Bethlehem and Jerusalem.

On the face of the arch is the Lamb on a gemmed throne, with the Book with seven seals (Revelation V.), flanked by the seven candlesticks, four angels and the symbols of the Evangelists.

SS. Felix, Cosma and Paul.
Tribune mosaics. (SS. Cosma and Damian).

SS. Peter, Damian and Theodorus.
Tribune mosaics. (SS. Cosma and Damian).

— 429 —

Photo ALINARI, ANDERSON, BROGI.

ROME — THE CHURCHES.

The medieval church of *Santi Quattro Coronati*, rebuilt by Pope Paschalis II. in 1112, and dedicated to four painters and five sculptors who suffered martyrdom under Diocletian for refusing to paint or carve images of pagan gods, is interesting particularly on account of the series of eight curious frescoes it contains, detailing the legendary history of the Conversion of Constantine the Great.

In the year 323, Constantine was attacked by an incurable leprosy as a punishment for persecuting the Christians. And on consulting his physicians, he was prescribed a bath of the warm blood of three thousand infants.

CONSTANTINE refusing the sacrifice of babes.   CONSTANTINE'S vision of SS. Peter and Paul.
Early 13th cent. paintings illustrating the legend of Constantine the Great.

But the piteous wailings and entreaties of the mothers who had been forced to bring their babes for the purpose so moved Constantine's pity that he renounced the prescribed remedy, and dismissed the mothers laden with gifts. On the following night SS. Peter and Paul appeared to him in a dream, and in guerdon of his having spared the innocent blood, prescribed the infallible cure for both physical and moral disease through the waters of baptism. Constantine, waking, sent soldiers to summon Sylvester, the Bishop of Rome, who diligently instructed the emperor in the Christian faith and admonished him to open the prisons. And on the evening of the Sabbath, bade make ready the bath of the palace (the Lateran), blessed the water, and baptized him. And Constantine being cleansed of his leprosy decreed that Christ alone should be adored in all the Empire and that the Bishop of Rome should be the chief over all the bishops of Christendom. He built basilicas and churches and gave up the palace of the Lateran to the Pope and bestowed on the Apostolic See many privileges and patrimonies. After this Pope Sylvester, crowned with the phrygium, entered Rome in triumph, Constantine himself leading his horse by the bridle. (Another scene of the "Donation" is in the Vatican p. 469).

CHURCH OF SANTO STEFANO ROTONDO. (5th cent.).

Santo Stefano Rotondo, the largest of the circular churches in Italy, was built on the foundations of a large market of imperial times during the pontificate of Simplicius (468-82). The original edifice consisted of three concentric rings, the largest being 213 ft. in diameter; in 1453 Pope Nicholas V., destroyed the outer intercolumniation and walled up the inner ring. In the interior are 32 frescoes by POMARANCIO representing scenes of martyrdom, interesting as legends.

San Gregorio Magno, originally built by Pope Gregory the Great (590-604), on the site of his father's house, dates in its present form mainly from the 17th cent. It was from this church that St. Augustine, who was a monk in the adjoining monastery, was sent by Gregory a missionary to England. Cardinal Manning was titular of this church from 1875-92, and Cardinal Vaughan after him.

In the atrium is the tomb of Sir Edw. Carne († 1561), ambassador of Henry VIII., to the Vatican, who was a member of the commission appointed to obtain the opinion of the foreign universities on the divorce of Catherine of Aragon, daughter of Ferdinand and Isabella of Spain. In the interior are 16 antique granite columns and a small chamber in which St. Gregory is said to have slept. Connected with the church are three chapels dedicated to St. Andrew, St. Silvia (mother of St. Gregory), and St. Barbara containing frescoes by *Domenichino* and *Guido Reni*, a statue of the Pope commenced by Michelangelo and completed by *Cordieri*, and a table at which St. Gregory, when abbott of the monastery, daily fed twelve poor men whom he served himself.

ST. GREGORY I. the Great. † 614.
By CORDIERI.

The pope has one hand raised in benediction, in the other he holds the book of his homilies. The Holy Ghost in the form of a dove (it prompted him when writing) is on his shoulder.

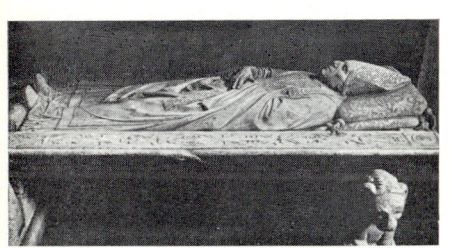

TOMB OF CARD. BAINBRIDGE. † 1514.
Archbishop of York.
(Church of S. Tommaso degl'Inglesi).

San Tommaso degl'Inglesi or *di Canterbury*, the church of the English College, was built in 1866-88, on the site of an earlier structure. It contains among others the beautiful tomb of Cardinal Bainbridge, Archbishop of York and British envoy to Pope Julius II. In the college are portraits of English cardinals, from Wolsey to Vaughan.

Tomb of Adrian VI.
By BALDASSARE PERUZZI.

SANTA MARIA DELL'ANIMA. *Erected in* 1500-14.

This is the national church of the Germans; Besides other monuments it contains the tomb of Adrian VI. [† 1523], the last non-Italian pope.

Photo ALINARI, ANDERSON, BROGI.

ROME — THE CHURCHES.

THE PANTHEON. *Erected in* 27 B. C.

THE PANTHEON. *Consecrated as a church* A. D. 609.

The *Pantheon*, is the only ancient edifice in Rome which has come to us in perfect preservation. Rescued from decay through its dedication to Christian worship, it may be considered a link between the life of the ancient and the modern city. Originally founded in the year 27 B. C. by Marcus Agrippa to commemorate the victory of Actium over Antony and Cleopatra, it was probably a rectangular building of ordinary temple type. After much damage caused by the great conflagration in the reign of the emperor Titus, A. D. 80, it was magnificently rebuilt by Hadrian, A. D. 110-125, on a larger scale and in a circular form, and dedicated to the gods of the seven planets: Jupiter, Mars, Apollo, Venus, etc. The columns and entablature of the portico, inscribed with Agrippa's name are perhaps those of the earlier building. A second inscription on the architrave records subsequent restorations under Septimius Severus and Caracalla. Closed and abandoned under the first Christian emperors, it was consecrated as a Christian church by Boniface IV, in 609, and dedicated to the Mother of God, under the name of *S. Maria ad Martyres*. On this occasion, a large quantity of the bones of martyrs were removed here from the catacombs. The portico is supported by 16 monolith granite columns, 46 ft. in height. The gilt bronze tiles that covered the dome, and the bronze trusses which carried the portico roof have disappeared; the ancient bronze doors remain.

The building within exists in its exquisite original form. The stupendous dome expanding in every sense like an interior firmament impresses the visitor with overwhelming effect. One looks around and finds nothing to arrest the eye; the groundplan is circular, the walls are circular, the ceiling is circular and the light descends from the single circular aperture in the top. The whole is on one plane of equality,—the diameter of the rotunda (143 ft.) is exactly equal to the height from floor to summit, the height from floor to cornice is equal to that from cornice to apex. All around are the chapels of the ancient gods, now occupied by saints. The architrave is borne by columns of giallo antico, pavonazzetto, porphyry and granite. The pavement, restored by Pius IX., is of costly marbles; below it runs a drain to carry off the rain which enters by the opening (28 ft. in diameter) in the dome. The Pantheon now contains the tombs of the Kings of Italy, Victor Emmanuel II. and Humbert I. It is also the burial place of Raphael, Giov. da Udine, Perin del Vaga, and other artists.

Santa Maria degli Angeli, is formed of one of the great halls of the Thermæ of Diocletian, the largest of all the ancient Roman baths. Pius IV., desiring to utilise the huge ruins commissioned Michelangelo to adapt the central hall (the *Tepidarium*) into a church and another portion into a monastery for the Carthusians (p. 500).

VIEW OF OLD ST. PETER'S. *15th cent. fresco in the Church of San Martino ai Monti.*

The church built by Michelangelo (1563) had the principal entrance to the south, in what is now the right transept. In 1749 in order to erect a chapel to the Beato Albergati, *Vannutelli* altered the orientation of the church. The main door was blocked up and the Albergati chapel erected on the site of the former porch, the side door on the west was converted into the principal entrance, the great nave became the transept, while the former transept was lengthened into a nave. In spite of this disfigurement the church remains one of the most imposing sacred edifices in Rome. The great transept (the former nave) is 300 ft. long, 89 ft. wide and 92 ft. high; the 16 granite columns are 45 ft. high. Most of the large paintings were once altarpieces in St. Peter's, where they have been replaced by copies in mosaic. Besides a colossal statue of St. Bruno, by *Houdon*, the church contains several monumental tombs, including those of the painters Carlo Maratta and Salvator Rosa, that of Pope Pius IV., designed by *Michelangelo*, and of Armando Diaz († 1928), the Italian *Generalissimo*.

CHURCH OF SANTA MARIA DEGLI ANGELI. *It is a part of* Diocletian's Baths *which* MICHELANGELO *converted into a church, in* 1563.

The church of S. Martino ai Monti originally erected in the 4th was modernised in the 17th cent. The interior contains 24 ancient columns and 15th cent. frescoes of the old basilicas of St. Peter's, St. John Lateran and the Council of 325, which was held here by St. Sylvester, when in the presence of Constantine the Great the heretical books of Arius, Sabellius and Victorinus were condemned and consigned to the flames.

— 431 —

Photo ALINARI, ANDERSON, BROGI.

ROME — THE CHURCHES.

CHURCH OF S. CROCE IN GERUSALEMME.

THE DISCOVERY OF THE HOLY CROSS. *By* PINTORICCHIO.

Santa Croce, one of the 'Seven Churches' of Rome, owes its origin to the Empress Helena, mother of Constantine, who in her zeal for Christianity made a pilgrimage to Jerusalem and brought back a collection of relics, including a portion of the Saviour's cross, for the purpose of forming a pilgrims' shrine for those who could not afford time and money for the journey to the Holy Land. The church she founded, was probably a hall of the Sessorian palace in which she resided; it was called *Basilica Heleniana*, or *Sessoriana*.

The primitive church was rebuilt by Pope Lucius II. in 1114, and modernized in 1743 by *Gregorini*, who added the baroque façade. The campanile dates from 1196. The sacred relics preserved in the church include a part of the Cross and of its inscription, one of the nails, thorns from the crown, and the finger with which St. Thomas convinced himself of the reality of the wound in the side of Christ. The tribune is covered with frescoes representing the Discovery of the Cross. The oldest part of the church is the chapel of St. Helena (ladies are not admitted except on March 20th), the floor of which is built upon a soil composed of earth brought from Jerusalem.

SANTA FRANCESCA ROMANA. *Façade by* C. LOMBARDI. 1608.

Santa Francesca Romana, built in the 9th cent., on the site of the Temple of Venus and Roma, was restored in 1216, when the campanile was erected, and again in 1612. Over the high altar is a miraculous Madonna, traditionally attributed to St. Luke; in the Confessio, a statue of S. Francesca, foundress of the Order of the Oblates, and below it a crypt containing her remains. In the tribune are interesting 12th cent. mosaics of the Madonna and four saints. In the right transept is the tomb of Gregory XI. († 1378), erected by the Senate in 1584, in gratitude for his having restored the papal court to Rome from Avignon. A relief by OLIVIERI represents the Pope's triumphal entry, with St. Catherine of Siena, who prevailed on him to return, walking beside his mule. The vacant papal throne is seen floating in the air. It is said that when Gregory returned there were only 17.000 inhabitants left in Rome. Near by, built into the wall, are two paving stones from the *Sacra Via* which, according to tradition, bear the imprint made by the knees of St. Peter, when he knelt to pray for the punishment of Simon Magus, who was displaying his magic by flying across the Forum.

GREGORY XI. entering Rome on his return from Avignon (1377). (S. *Francesca Romana*).

CHURCH OF SAN SEBASTIANO.

San Sebastiano is one of the seven basilicas visited by pilgrims, being erected over the catacombs where so many martyrs were buried. The present church dates from the 17th cent.; it contains the remains of the martyred saint, and the celebrated stone bearing the impression left by the Saviour's feet, when He met St. Peter fleeing from Rome, at the spot now marked by the chapel of 'DOMINE, QUO VADIS?'

The *Cemetery of the Capuchins* consists of four grim chambers containing holy earth from Jerusalem in which the monks are temporarily buried.

ST. SEBASTIAN. *Designed by* BERNINI.

CEMETERY OF THE CAPUCHINS, decorated with the bones of departed monks. (*Santa Maria della Concezione*).

Photo ALINARI, ANDERSON BROGI.

ROME — SANTA MARIA DEL POPOLO.

VIEW OF THE INTERIOR.
Renovated by Bernini in 1655.

VAULT FRESCOES IN THE CHOIR. By PINTURICCHIO.
A. D. 1508.

Santa Maria del Popolo, stands at the foot of the Pincian hill, near the site where Nero was buried. The primitive church, erected in 1099 by Paschalis II., was entirely rebuilt in 1480 by Sixtus IV. (Della Rovere), who added the adjoining Augustinian convent, in which Martin Luther resided while in Rome. Under the pontificate of Julius II. (1503-13 another of the Della Rovere popes), the church was completed and enriched with works of art by Raphael, Pintoricchio, Sansovino and other famous artists, many wealthy citizens connected with the papal court contributing to the expense. It then became the favourite burial place of cardinals and great personages whose sepulchral chapels and monuments, dating from the best period of the Renaissance, are the chief attraction of the church. On the high-altar is a miraculous image of the Virgin brought hither from the chapel 'Sancta Sanctorum' (see also p. 417). The vault of the choir was painted by *Pintoricchio*. In the centre is the Coronation of the Virgin, surrounded by Evangelists and sibyls; at the corners are the Fathers of the Church. Beneath are the splendid tombs of Card. Girolamo Basso Della Rovere, and Card. Ascanio Sforza, brother of Lodovico il Moro, Duke of Milan, erected by *Andrea Sansovino*, at the expense of Julius II. The two monuments are almost identical in design, in both the figure of the deceased is "no longer laid out in calm repose, but reclining in uneasy attitudes, which could not exist in life, or be maintained in death."

THE ALMIGHTY surrounded by symbols of the planets.
Mosaics in the dome of the Chigi chapel.

The Chigi chapel, founded in honour of Our Lady of Loreto, was constructed under the direction of *Raphael*. At the sides are the tombs of Agostino and Sigismondo Chigi, executed by *Bernini*; in the niches are four statues of prophets. Right of the entrance Habakkuk, by *Algardi*; left Daniel, by *Bernini*; right of the altar Elijah, by *Lorenzetti*; left Jonah, by *Raphael*. On the altar is the Nativity of the Virgin, by *Seb. del Piombo*, the bronze relief on the front, Christ and the Woman of Samaria, is by Lorenzetto; the wall paintings are by Salviati and Francesco Vanni.

TOMB OF CARDINAL GIROLAMO BASSO,
nephew of Sixtus IV.
By ANDREA SANSOVINO.

The dome of the chapel is adorned with mosaics executed by LUIGI DI PACE in 1516, from cartoons by RAPHAEL. The design represents the creation of the heavenly bodies. In the centre is God, the Prime Mover and Creator, whose will is executed by the angels around who move the planets, and in this way control the universe. In the panel above Him is the stellar sphere or firmament, in the other panels are the symbols of the seven lower heavens: Saturn, Jupiter, Mars, Apollo (the Sun), Venus, Mercury and Diana (the Moon). Each planet is portrayed by a pagan deity with appropriate action, enclosed within a segment of the zodiac, each is attended by a guardian angel. The scheme was probably suggested by Dante's lines in the *Paradiso*, II. 127-29.

THE CHIGI CHAPEL. *Designed by* RAPHAEL.

Photo ALINARI, ANDERSON, BROGI.

ROME — SANTA MARIA SOPRA MINERVA.

Church of Santa Maria sopra Minerva (Dominican).
The only Gothic church in Rome.

The Risen Christ.
By Michelangelo.

Grave of Fra Angelico
da Fiesole († 1455).

This church stands on the site of a temple of Minerva and (besides the 'Sancta Sanctorum,' p. 417), is the only ancient Gothic church in Rome. It was built about 1280 by two Dominican architects from Florence, *Fra Sisto* and *Fra Ristoro*; a century later (1370) the Dominicans moved their headquarters from Santa Sabina here and ever since the church has been in their charge. The imposing interior contains many remarkable monuments, tombs and paintings by eminent artists. Beneath the high-altar is preserved the body of St. Catherine of Siena; to the left of the high altar is Michelangelo's famous Christ with the Cross, a work of 1521, supposed to represent the Saviour as He appeared to St. Peter as the Apostle fled along the Appian Way.

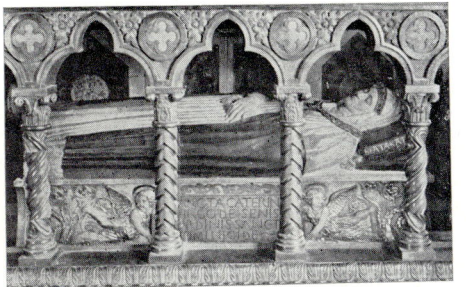

In the fourth chapel on the right is the "Annunciation," by *Antoniazzo Romano*, painted on a gold background, to commemorate the charitable Confraternity of the Santissima Annunziata, founded in 1640, for endowing poor girls. In the foreground is Cardinal Torquemada recommending three poor girls to the Virgin who gives them purses for their dowries. Above the Almighty appears in the clouds.

The monastery adjoining the church was the headquarters of the Inquisition. Giordano Bruno, the philosopher, received his death sentence here in 1600; and here in 1633, Galileo aged 70 was tried before its tribunal for the "heresy" of saying that the earth revolved round the sun, instead of the sun round the earth, as was then believed. Galileo was obliged to recant on his knees before receiving absolution; but as he rose he concluded his recantation with the exclamation, "Still, it moves." The monastery now contains the *Biblioteca Casanatense*. A Library of 200,000 volumes and manuscripts.

Tomb of St. Catherine of Siena († 1380).
Canonized by Pius II., her relics were deposited here (1461).

The Annunciation.
By Antoniazzo Romano.

Triumph of St. Thomas Aquinas.
Fresco by Filippino Lippi.

Triumph of St. Thomas. St. Thomas is enthroned amid allegorical figures defending the Catholic religion against heretics; Averrhoes lies prostrate under the feet of the saint, to the left stands the bearded figure of Arius with his demolished writings at his feet, opposite is Sabellius looking down on his book of heresies. On each side are groups of scholars listening to the teachings of the saint who displays an open book.

The tall personage seen on the right is symbolical of the Dominican Order and its mission of destroying heresy. The four maidens right and left of St. Thomas represent the Virtues: Theology holding a book, Astrology pointing to Heaven, Philosophy discussing with Grammar. Near the latter is a child reading.

View of the Transept (*see* p. 435).

Photo Alinari, Anderson, Brogi.

ROME — THE CHURCHES.

Sant'Andrea della Valle, begun in 1591 by OLIVIERI on the site of an earlier church, and completed by CARLO MADERNO, has an ornate façade and the largest dome in Rome, after that of St. Peter's. The immense and sumptuous interior with the large gold-framed frescoes by DOMENICHINO offers a fine example of the late Renaissance style. At the end of the nave are the sepulchral monuments of the two Piccolomini Popes: Pius II. († 1464), and Pius III. († 1503), which formerly stood in the old basilica of St. Peter. On the right is the Strozzi chapel in which are bronze copies of Michelangelo's group of the *Pietà* and his statues of Leah and Rachel. The paintings in the cupola executed by LANFRANCO, represent the Glory of Paradise. On the pendentives are the famous Evangelists by DOMENICHINO, which are considered one of the finest specimens of the master's work, wonderful compositions, in which the St. John, surrounded by angels, constitutes one of the finest efforts of the kind. DOMENICHINO also painted the frescoes on the vaulting of the apse which represent St. John the Baptist pointing to the Saviour, the Calling of SS. Peter and Andrew, the Flagellation of St. Andrew, St. Andrew revering the cross; and the six allegorical female figures of the Virtues beneath them.

TOMB OF PIUS II. (Piccolomini). († 1464). By PIETRO DA TODI.

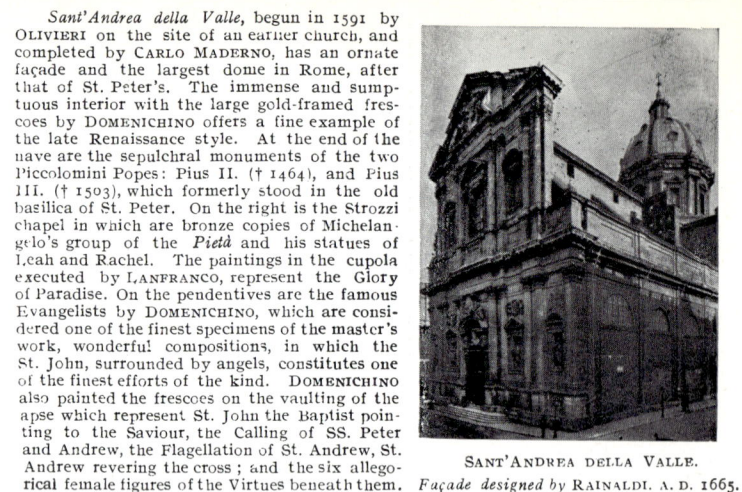

SANT'ANDREA DELLA VALLE. *Façade designed by* RAINALDI. A. D. 1665.

THE VOCATION of SS. Peter and Andrew. *Fresco by* DOMENICHINO.

ST. ANDREW beholds and reveres the cross on which he will be martyred. By DOMENICHINO. (*Church of Sant'Andrea della Valle*).

SAINT JOHN by DOMENICHINO.

TOMB OF BISHOP DURANDUS († 1296). By JOHANNES COSMAS.   TOMB OF POPE LEO X. († 1521 Medici). By ANTONIO DA SANGALLO, BACCIO BANDINELLI, RAFF. DA MONTELUPO.   TOMB OF CLEMENT VII. († 1534 Medici). (*Church of Santa Maria sopra Minerva*).

In the right transept is the fine Gothic tomb of Durandus, Bishop of Mendes; in the choir the tombs of Leo X. and Clement VII. and that of Cardinal Bembo. The most important events in the pontificate of these two popes were the daring protest of Martin Luther, the great Reformer, and the sack of Rome by the troops of the Emperor Charles V.

Photo ALINARI, ANDERSON, BROGI.

ROME — THE CHURCHES.

SAN GIORGIO IN VELABRO. *Founded in the 4th century.*
(On the left is the Arch of Janus).

SAN GIORGIO IN VELABRO. VIEW OF THE NAVE.

This church originally founded in the 4th cent. was rebuilt by Leo II. (682), and subsequently restored in the 13th cent., by Card. Stefaneschi, who added the portico. The twelfth century campanile stands close to the arches of the money-changers and of Janus. The interior has retained its basilica form, the 16 columns of the nave were taken from ancient edifices; beneath the high altar and the marble canopy is preserved the head of St. George, the young soldier, introduced by Richard Cœur-de-Lion to the English, who made him their patron saint.

The church of *Santi Giovanni e Paolo*, was founded in 398 and rebuilt by Pope Paschalis II. (1099-1118), after the terrible fire caused by Robert Guiscard's soldiery. The church occupies the site of the house of John and Paul, two court dignitaries under Constantine II., who were martyred by Julian the Apostate. Beneath the church are several rooms belonging to a Roman house with interesting pagan and Christian decorations.

The church of *Santi Apostoli*, founded in the 4th cent. in honour of the Apostles Philip and James the Less, was several times rebuilt. In the vestibule is the tomb of the engraver Volpato († 1802), with a figure of Friendship weeping before the bust of the deceased; in the interior many fine sepulchral monuments and paintings. In a corridor beside the church is a monument to Michelangelo, whose remains, now in Florence (p. 218), were originally interred here.

SS. GIOVANNI E PAOLO *(Apse)*.
Architecture of the 12th cent.

MONUMENT OF CLEMENT XIV. *By* CANOVA
On the pedestal Temperance *and* Charity.
(Church of Santi Apostoli).

SS. TRINITÀ DEI MONTI.

DESCENT FROM THE CROSS.
Altarpiece by DANIELE DA VOLTERRA.

SAN LUIGI DE' FRANCESI.
Façade by GIACOMO DELLA PORTA.

SS. Trinità dei Monti, erected in 1494 by Charles VIII., of France, and severely damaged during the French revolution, was restored in 1816, at the expense of Louis XVIII. It is now attached to the French Nunnery of the *Sacré-Cœur*, devoted to the education of girls. The interior contains many works of art and the famous 'Descent from the Cross,' the masterpiece of DANIELE DA VOLTERRA. (The Villa Medici near by, and the famous Spanish Steps are illustrated on page 510).

San Luigi de' Francesi, erected in 1589, is the national church of France. In the interior are paintings by *Domenichino*, and tombs of illustrious Frenchmen: the card. d'Ossat († 1604), etc.

Photo ALINARI, ANDERSON, BROGI.

— 436 —

56. - *WONDERS OF ITALY.*

ROME — CHURCH OF S. MARIA IN ARACOELI.

SANTA MARIA IN ARACŒLI. (*Church of the Altar of Heaven*).

VIEW OF THE NAVE.

This church occupies the site of the *Arx*, the citadel of ancient Rome. It was probably erected in the 6th cent. when it was called *Sancta Maria del Capitolio*.

Its present name is derived from an altar erected, according to tradition, by Augustus to commemorate the prophecy of the Tiburtine Sibyl respecting the birth of the Saviour. In the 13th cent. to mark the site, a copy of the Augustans altar, bearing the inscription *Ara Primogeniti Dei*, was placed within the chapel of St. Helena.

The imposing flight of 124 marble steps ascending to the principal entrance of the church, was built in 1348 as a votive offering for the delivery of the people of Rome from the black plague, which in medieval times, was regarded as a Divine punishment. The beautiful interior is full of interesting monuments sculptures and paintings.

The nave has 22 ancient columns of different sizes and styles, brought from the Forum and the Palatine. The rich ceiling was executed to commemorate the victory of the papal fleet over the Turks at Lepanto in 1571. Pope Innocent IV. conferred (1250) the church to the newly instituted Order of the Franciscans in whose charge it has been ever since. In the transept are the tombs of the Savelli, to which family Pope Honorius IV. (1285-87) belonged, and that of Card. Acquasparta, general of the Franciscans. This order was founded by St. Francis in 1209; it gave to the Church saints, popes, and Doctors such as Bonaventura, Roger Bacon, Alexander of Hales, Duns Scotus, Occam and others.

THE "SANTISSIMO BAMBINO."

THE TRANSEPT. At the end is the Chapel of St. Helena.

TOMB OF CARDINAL MATTEO OF ACQUASPARTA († 1302).

In the sacristy is the celebrated miracle working image of the *Santissimo Bambino*. It is a small figure carved out of olive wood from the Mount of Olives, swathed in gold and silver tissue. The Santissimo Bambino is, according to the popular belief, invested with extraordinary powers in curing the sick. Its aid is in constant requisition in severe cases, and its practice brings to it more fees than any physician in Rome. The Santissimo is always borne in a private coach under the care of two Franciscan monks; as it passes through the streets devout people kneel and cross themselves. Its gold crown adorned with pearls and precious stones and the countless sparkling diamonds, emeralds, and rubies by which it is covered, are votive offerings recording its miraculous powers.

DEATH OF SAN BERNARDINO OF SIENA.
Fresco by PINTORICCHIO (*Bufalini chapel, right aisle*).

TOMB OF LUCA SAVELLI (father of Honorius IV.) with an antique sarcophagus

Photo ALINARI, ANDERSON BROGI.

ST. TERESA, by BERNINI (*detail*). *Church of Santa Maria della Vittoria.*

This work, executed in 1647, is the masterpiece of Bernini; he himself considered it modestly as "the least bad thing he had done".

ROME — THE CHURCHES.

CHURCH OF THE GESÙ. A. D. 1570.
Rebuilt by VIGNOLA and DELLA PORTA.

INTERIOR OF THE GESÙ.

The *Gesù* is the principa church of the Society of Jesus in Rome. Erected at the expense of Card. Alessandro Farnese by GIAC. DELLA PORTA and VIGNOLA in 1575, it furnished the model for that sumptuous style called the architecture of the Jesuits. The interior is gorgeously decorated with coloured marbles, bronzes, sculptures, paintings and masses of gilding. On the vaulting is a remarkable fresco, the " Triumph of the Name of Jesus," by BACICCIO. In the right transept is the altar of St. Francis Xavier, with a painting (Death of St. Francis Xavier) by P. DA CORTONA.

In the left transept is the altar-tomb of St. Ignatius Loyola designed by Father ANDREA POZZI. It is here that the order have displayed their most dazzling magnificence. The columns are of lapis lazuli and gilded bronze, the silver plated colossal statue of the saint is a copy of the original by LEGROS in massive silver which Pius VI., caused to be melted to pay a war indemnity imposed by Napoleon. Above is a terrestrial globe, consisting of a single block of lapis lazuli. The urn, containing the remains of the saint, beneath the altar, is of gilded bronze ; right and left are marble groups of Religion and Faith.

The solemn *Te Deum* sung in this church on December 31st for the blessings received during the year, is one of the most famous traditional ceremonies.

Santa Maria della Vittoria, erected by order of Pope Paul V., in 1605, for the barefooted Carmelites, contains paintings by DOMENICHINO, GUERCINO, and the famous group of St. Theresa by BERNINI ; a work in the master's most affected manner. The figure of the saint, overmastered by emotion and in a state of collapse while the Angel of Death points an arrow at her heart, displays that ' passionate mysticism ' which characterized the Catholicism of Bernini's days. The execution of Bernini's work is masterly, whatever critics may think of the spirit.

ST. THERESA. *Group by* BERNINI.
(*Church of S. Maria della Vittoria*).

ALTAR OF ST. IGNATIUS OF LOYOLA.
(*Church of the Gesù*).

CRUCIFIXION. By GUIDO RENI.
(Church of S. Lorenzo in Lucina).
S. Lorenzo in Lucina, was founded by Pope Sixtus III., in 440.

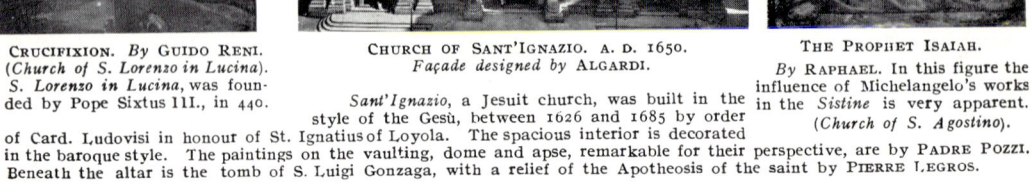

CHURCH OF SANT'IGNAZIO. A. D. 1650.
Façade designed by ALGARDI.

THE PROPHET ISAIAH.
By RAPHAEL. In this figure the influence of Michelangelo's works in the *Sistine* is very apparent.
(*Church of S. Agostino*).

Sant'Ignazio, a Jesuit church, was built in the style of the Gesù, between 1626 and 1685 by order of Card. Ludovisi in honour of St. Ignatius of Loyola. The spacious interior is decorated in the baroque style. The paintings on the vaulting, dome and apse, remarkable for their perspective, are by PADRE POZZI. Beneath the altar is the tomb of S. Luigi Gonzaga, with a relief of the Apotheosis of the saint by PIERRE LEGROS.

— 438 —

Photo ALINARI ANDERSON, BROGI.

THE FOUR SIBYLS.
Painted by RAPHAEL A. D. 1514

CUMAEAN SIBYL.

SIBYL OF TIBUR

Santa Maria della Pace, erected by Sistus IV., in 1484 to commemorate the peace made among the Italian powers, was restored under Alexander VII.

SANTA MARIA DELLA PACE.
Portico by PIETRO DA CORTONA.

Santa Maria della Pace, erected by Sistus IV., in 1484 to commemorate the peace made among the Italian powers, was restored under Alexander VII., by Pietro da Cortona, who added the Doric portico to the façade. The interior contains many paintings by eminent artists. The principal monument in the church is the celebrated fresco of the Four Sibyls, painted by Raphael above the first chapel (Chigi) on the right. Over the centre of the arch a little winged genius bearing a torch symbolical of the light of prophecy divides the groups, each consisting of two sibyls receiving their messages from angels. From left to right: the Sibyl of Cumæ, the Persian Sibyl, the Phrygian Sibyl and the aged Sibyl of Tibur. Great mastery is shown in the mode of filling and taking advantage of the apparently unfavourable space, a spirited diversity in the composition is created by the little angels holding the tablets. In another chapel is a fresco by *Baldassarre Peruzzi* representing the Cardinal Ponzetti (the donor) kneeling before the Virgin and Child with SS. Bridget and Catherine. The monastery court or cloisters dating from 1504, were designed by *Bramante*.

ALTARPIECE by B. PERUZZI. 1516.
(Santa Maria della Pace).

SAN PIETRO MONTORIO.
Erected A. D. 1480.

THE CLOISTERS. A. D. 1504. By BRAMANTE.
(Santa Maria della Pace).

San Pietro in Montorio, erected at the end of the 15th cent., at the expense of king Ferdinand and Isabella of Spain, owes its existence to the medieval tradition that here was the site of St. Peter's martyrdom.

Within the church are works by Perugino, Vasari and a 'Scourging of Christ' by SEBASTIANO DEL PIOMBO, from the designs of MICHELANGELO. Raphael's Transfiguration (page 487), was the high-altar-piece of this church for 300 years. In front of the high altar, without memorial, is the grave of the unhappy Beatrice Cenci (p. 494), who was beheaded as a parricide.

In the court of the adjoining monastery is the famous Tempietto of Bramante, erected in 1502, on the spot where St. Peter was then supposed to have suffered martyrdom. The terrace in front of the church affords a magnificent view of Rome.

SANTA MARIA DI LORETO.

Begun in 1507 by *Antonio da Sangallo the Younger*, this church has a remarkable octagonal interior and contains a beautiful statue of St. Susanna by *Duquesnoy*.

THE SCOURGING OF CHRIST.
By SEBASTIANO DEL PIOMBO.

THE "TEMPIETTO."
By BRAMANTE.
(Church of San Pietro in Montorio).

— 439 —

Photo ALINARI, ANDERSON, BROGI.

ROME — CHURCH OF SAN PIETRO IN VINCOLI.

San Pietro in Vincoli is also named *Basilica Eudoxiana*, after the Empress Eudoxia, who founded it in 442 as a shrine for the chains with which St. Peter was bound at Jerusalem and those used during the Apostle's captivity in Rome. The church was rebuilt in the 8th cent. and restored in 1475 and 1503 during the pontificates of the Della Rovere popes Sixtus IV. and Julius II., but the general form given to the building in the 5th cent. has been retained. The imposing nave is separated from the aisles by 20 marble columns from Hymettus, the vaulting is decorated with a painting by PARODI representing the Cure of a demoniac by the touch of the Holy Chains, which are now preserved in a bronze tabernacle under the high altar.

The church contains many works of art and tombs including that of the Florentine masters Pietro and Antonio Pollaiuolo, but the most important monument in it is the tomb of Julius II., the unfinished work of MICHELANGELO and "the tribulation of the sculptor's life."

In one of his most cherished projects, Julius II., had conceived the idea of erecting to his own memory a colossal mausoleum under the dome of the new basilica of St. Peter, the splendour of which was to surpass that of all past and present structures of the same kind. This vast undertaking was entrusted to Michelangelo, who received full powers and unlimited means. The four-fronted tomb which he designed (18 ft. high and 12 ft. wide), was to stand apart from wall or pillar, so as to allow free passage all round it; thirty-eight life-sized statues and about as

MONUMENT OF POPE JULIUS II. († 1513).
The *Moses* and the flanking figures of *Rachel* (left) and *Leah* (right) are by MICHELANGELO.
The figures above are by other sculptors.

many reliefs in bronze illustrating the feats of the great pontificate, were to adorn it. But the execution of this gigantic structure was subjected to so many vicissitudes and quarrels between the pope and the artist that the scheme was cut short by the death of pope Julius.

The side of the mausoleum (on a reduced scale and in a different style) which Michelangelo completed was set up in this church of which Julius had been titular cardinal, while his mortal remains were placed in the grave of Sixtus IV. in St. Peter's. Only the Moses, and the figures of Rachel and Leah, symbols of the contemplative and active life, are by the great master; the recumbent figure of the Pope is attributed to MASO DEL BOSCO, the sitting figures of the Prophet Elijah and that of the Sibyl at the side to RAFFAELLO DA MONTELUPO, the Madonna and Child above to the sculptor SCHERANO DA SETTIGNANO.

The Moses is one of Michelangelo's most celebrated sculptures and worthy of all admiration.

Moses, full of 'repressed movement,' and vibrating with wrath and passion, is represented as on the point of giving way to impulse, of starting up from his seat, in indignation at the idolatry of the Jews. The figure is colossal and animated by a superhuman power of execution. Thus, when brought face to face with it one's first impression is that of stupor. "The eye does not know where to rest" says Gregorovius, "in this the masterpiece of sculpture since the time of the Greeks. It seems to be as much an incarnation of the genius of Michelangelo as a suitable allegory of Pope Julius. Like Moses, he was at once lawgiver, priest, and warrior." In truth, when we recall the character of the mighty leader of the Hebrews, of the haughty Julius for whom the statue was made, and the proud nature of the master who modelled it, it is impossible to isolate from this creation the personalities of these three men which it epitomizes.

THE MOSES OF MICHELANGELO
Monument of Pope Julius II., Della Rovere
San Pietro in Vincoli.

Photo ALINARI, ANDERSON, BROGI.

ROME.   THE VATICAN.

VIEW OF THE BASILICA OF ST. PETER AND THE VATICAN.

In the foreground is seen one of the two beautiful fountains designed by *Maderna*, erected in the 17th century under the reigns of Sixtus V. and Innocent XI. The water forms a mass of spray, upon which the sun at times paints the most beautiful rainbows. It falls back into a basin of Oriental granite, and runs over the sides of this into an octagonal basin of travertine, about 28 ft. in diameter.

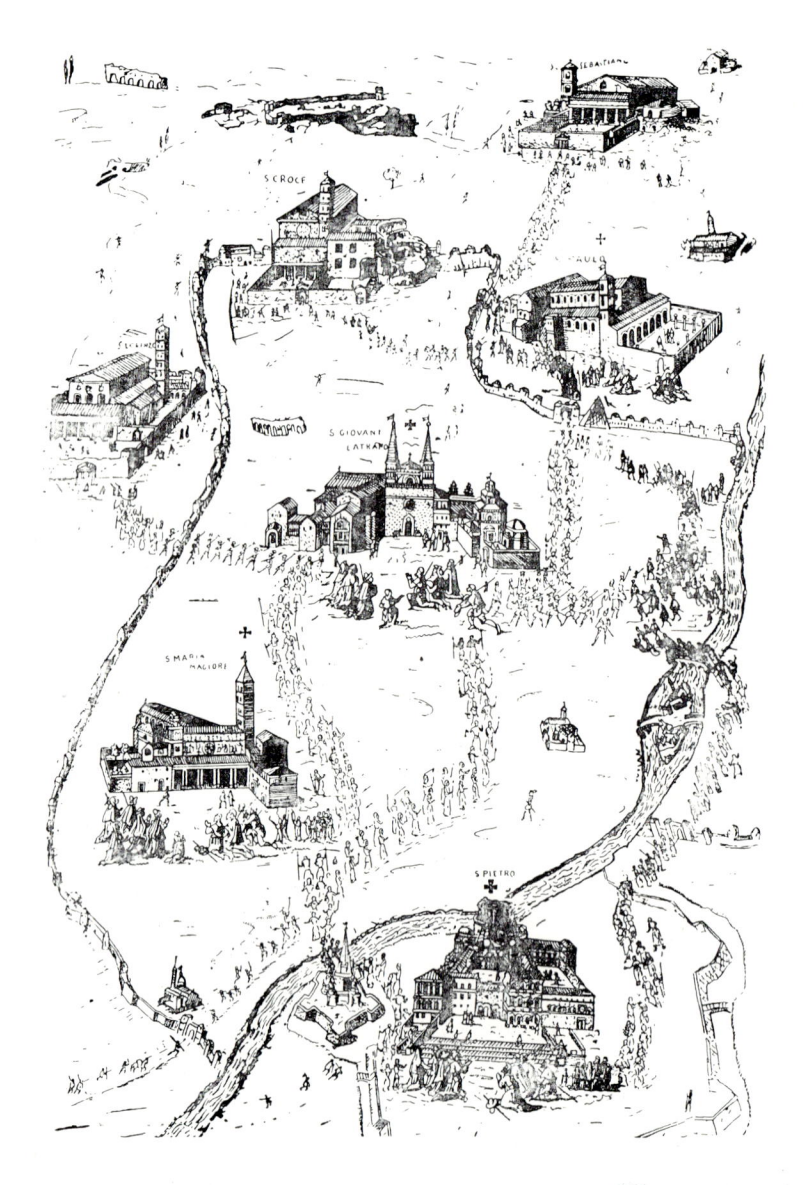

THE JUBILEE OF THE YEAR 1575. *After a printing of the epoch.*

THE PIAZZA OF ST. PETER AND THE VATICAN PALACE.

THE "COFFEE HOUSE" AND THE VATICAN GARDENS.
Above Fountain by *Maderno*, and the Pontifical Residence.

CORTILE DELLA PIGNA.

SCALA REGIA
Erected by BERNINI *in 1661.*

THE VATICAN PALACE.

THE VATICAN PALACE is an immense pile of buildings, irregular in plan and composed of parts constructed at different periods, without regard to general harmony. Originally a residence for the popes, erected by Symmachus A. D. 498 near the antecourt of the old church of St. Peter and afterwards gradually extended, here Charlemagne is said to have resided on the occasion of his coronation in St. Peter's in 800. This first building having fallen to decay Pope Eugene III., began a new building in 1150. Nicholas III., enlarged it in 1278; but the Lateran Palace continued to be the papal residence, the Vatican being used only for the reception of foreign sovereigns visiting Rome.

After the return of Gregory XI., from Avignon in 1377, the Vatican became the permanent residence of the popes. In 1450, Nicholas V., formed the idea of making it the most imposing palace in the world. But he died before accomplishing it. The building which he commenced was finished by Pope Alexander VI., and extended by subsequent popes. This part is now called "Appartamento Borgia." In 1473, Sixtus IV., added the Sistine Chapel and in 1490 Innocent VIII., erected the Belvedere in the garden. Julius II., added the Logge, and laid the foundations of the Vatican Museums.

Thenceforth the popes vied with each other in the extent and variety of their additions. The greatest architects and painters were employed: BRAMANTE, MICHELANGELO, RAPHAEL, POLLAIUOLO, SANGALLO, FONTANA, MADERNO, BERNINI and others. These additions have rendered it the largest palace in the world. It is said to possess 80 grand staircases, 200 smaller ones, 20 courts and about 11.000 halls, chapels, rooms and apartments. A comparatively small part of the building is used for the papal court, the greater part being occupied by the *Museums* which comprise the *Collections of Antiquities*, the *Library*, the *Borgia Apartment*, *Raphael's Stanze*, the *Sistine Chapel*, the *Picture Gallery*.

Photo ALINARI, ANDERSON, BROGI.

ROME — THE VATICAN. The Library. Museo Cristiano.

The *Vatican Library* was founded by Nicholas V. about 1450, and increased by Sixtus IV. who appointed Platina (p. 485) director. In 1588 Sixtus V. caused the present edifice to be erected by DOMENICO FONTANA. The great hall, decorated, gilded and furnished like a reliquary is 50 feet wide and 200 feet long. Seven large pillars, covered with frescoes divide it into two aisles. No books or MSS. are visible; they are all enclosed in illuminated cupboards, so that of a library there is no appearance whatever. Ranged along the bays and in the middle of the hall are all sorts of precious objects, porcelain vases, mosaic tables and other ornaments, gifts of foreign potentates. The whole establishment is of ideal magnificence, and arranged so as to give a festival to the eyes. The Library now contains about 260.000 printed volumes and 34.000 manuscripts, including illuminated manuscripts; a *Bible* of the 4th century in Greek; the *Codex Vaticanus*, that famous ancient manuscript of the Gospels; the *Menologium* or sacred calendar of the tenth century; the *Homilies* of Gregory the Great; the manuscripts of Virgil and of Terence; of the *Divina Commedia* of Dante; the *Affirmation of the Seven Sacraments* by Henry VIII. of England, which caused the Pope to confer on the King the title of "Defender of the Faith"; the correspondence of Henry VIII., and Anne Boleyn. All ages and all peoples have contributed their share to this treasure.

GREAT GALLERY OF THE VATICAN LIBRARY. *Biblioteca Apostolica Romana.*
In the gallery are seen gifts made to the Popes.

THE CROSS OF RAMBONA.
*Ivory diptych of the 9th cent.
Museum of Christian Antiquities.*

The Museum of *Christian Antiquities,* founded by Benedict XIV., contains (1) objects and curiosities from the catacombs dating from the first five centuries, — bronze and glass vessels used in funereal banquets, instruments of torture employed against the early sufferers of the faith terracotta lamps, seals, rings, personal ornaments, — all bearing emblems of the dove, the fish, the stag, the monogram, the anchor, the ship, the words 'salva' 'vivas' and other Christian symbols; (2) valuable ancient church-furniture, — reliquaries, gold and silver crosses, altarpieces, statuettes, pictures, gems, ivories, gospel book-covers, diptychs, etc. To these was lately added the famous "treasure" from the chapel of the "Sancta Sanctorum," which is exceedingly rich in enamels and Byzantine jewel-work, the most important of these is, perhaps, the beautiful cross illustrated here upon which are scenes from the life of the Virgin and the Saviour.

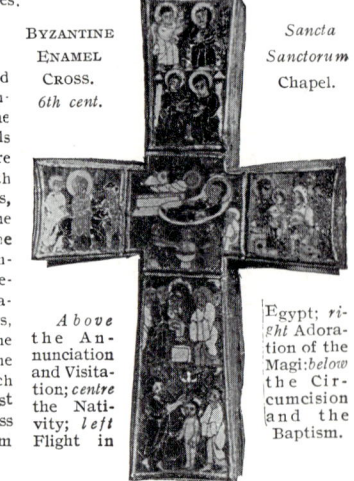

BYZANTINE ENAMEL CROSS. 6th cent.

Sancta Sanctorum Chapel.

Above the Annunciation and Visitation; *centre* the Nativity; *left* Flight in Egypt; *right* Adoration of the Magi: *below* the Circumcision and the Baptism.

— 442 —

Photo ALINARI, ANDERSON, BROGI.

ROME — THE VATICAN.   Museums of Antiquities.

GALLERIA DEI CANDELABRI.

MUSEO PIO-CLEMENTINO.

The *Vatican Museums* are the most ancient, the most splendid of the public museums of the world. A visit to these incomparable collections is an education, a life experience to be treasured in the memory for ever. For here only one may drink at the purest springs the teaching of divine and human letters,— architecture, sculpture, painting, —arts ancient as well as modern revealed by the most perfect models.

The museums of antiquities originated with the works collected by the Renaissance Popes Julius II., Leo X., and Paul III., in the Cortile del Belvedere. But the importance and arrangement of the present collections are due principally to the pontiffs of the 18th and 19th centuries, who enriched the museums with more than 2000 works of art, and built new galleries to contain them. Thus, the *Museo Pio-Clementino*, which includes the largest part of the sculptures, was built by Clement XIV., and Pius VI.; the *Museo Chiaramonti* and the *Braccio Nuovo* were added by Pius VII.; the Egyptian and Etruscan Museums were founded by Gregory XVI. The *Picture Gallery*, founded by Pius VII., and continually added to by his successors, was lately transferred into a new splendid building expressly designed by the architect Luca Beltrami, and erected by order of Pope Pius XI.

Even to-day in wandering through these galleries it is difficult to decide whether to admire most the magnificence of the collections or the beauty of the buildings in which they are housed.

SALA A CROCE GRECA.

Erectea under Pius VI., in the form of a Greek cross

The *Sala a Croce Greca*, so-called from its shape of a Greek cross, forms part of the beautiful constructions designed by SIMONETTI.

The entrance of this hall is guarded by two large sphinxes of red and grey Egyptian granite, found during the construction of Saint Peter's. On the pavement is a large mosaic with the bust of Minerva, sur-

HEAD OF MINERVA.
Ancient mosaic.

rounded by a band on which the phases of the moon and constellations are depicted. The ægis of the goddess is adorned with a head of Medusa. Ranged around the walls are important reliefs and statues. On the left wall is the gigantic sarcophagus in porphyry of the Empress Helena, the mother of Constantine the Great, adorned with reliefs representing Roman warriors hurling themselves on captive barbarians. On the right wall the porphyry sarcophagus of Constantia, daughter of Constantine, decorated with cupids and vintage scenes.

BACCHANALIAN SCENE.
Ancient relief.

AUGUSTUS as Pontifex
Ancient sculpture.

Photo ALINARI, ANDERSON, BROGI.

56*. - WONDERS OF ITALY.

ROME — THE VATICAN. Museums of Antiquities. Galleria dei Candelabri.

The *Galleria dei Candelabri*, an old loggia which was enclosed under Pius VI., owes its name to eight very tall Candelabra belonging to churches. These marble candelabras, are placed on triangular bases adorned with reliefs of Fauns, Dancing Bacchantes, and other mythological subjects such as Apollo and Marsyas, Jupiter and Minerva, Venus, etc. Besides numerous ancient sculptures this gallery contains a series of beautiful sculptured vases in different kinds of coloured marbles. The ceiling paintings, by Lodovico Seitz, represent partly incidents in the pontificate of Pope Leo XIII., partly allegorical scenes such as the Apotheosis of St. Thomas Aquinas, the Arts, and the Sciences under the Popes, etc. The pavement is formed with ancient marbles

GALLERIA DEI CANDELABRI. (300 ft. long).

VASE with reliefs representing Silenus with satyrs crushing grapes.

SARCOPHAGUS WITH THE MYTH OF PROTESILAUS AND LAODAMIA.

Protesilaus, a Greek warrior, was slain at the battle of Troy, hereupon his wife Laodamia begged the gods to be allowed to converse with him for only three hours. The request was granted : on the left is represented the death of the hero, and Mercury leading Protesilaus back to the upper world ; on the right Laodamia is on her bed weeping for the second death of her husband, and, Mercury again leading Protesilaus to Charon's boat which will carry him into Hades. The two figures standing in the centre are presumably portraits of the deceased who were buried in the sarcophagus. *Found on the Appian Way.*

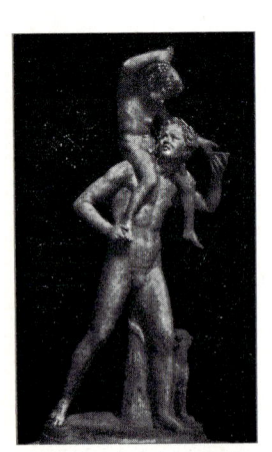

WELL HEAD with Bacchanalia scenes.

SATYR with the infant Bacchus. *Ancient sculpture.*

GANYMEDE carried off by the eagle. *After Leochares.*

GREEK GIRL RUNNING. *From a bronze of the 5th cent.* B. C.

— 444 —

Photo ALINARI, ANDERSON, BROGI.

ROME — THE VATICAN. *Museums of Antiquites. Galleria dei Candelabri, Sala della Biga.*

SARCOPHAGUS WITH THE RAPE OF THE LEUCIPPIDES. (*Galleria dei Candelabri*).

The *Sala della Biga*, a circular hall with a dome, was built by order of Pius VI., for the purpose of housing the famous Biga or chariot illustrated here. Besides this the hall contains several important pieces such as the Discobolus of Myron, an admirably posed figure of a young athlete hurling his discus; the Bearded Bacchus, at once majestic and benevolent in expression; the Discobolus of the Attic school; the draped figure of a Roman in the act of sacrificing; the huntress Diana, with a quiver on her shoulder and a dog by her side; the Charioteer, a curious figure of a victorious driver, with the straps twisted round the body, and finally, two sarcophagus-reliefs illustrating chariot racing in the circus.

BIGA or two-horse chariot.

The body of the chariot which for centuries served in the church of St. Mark as an episcopal chair, and the trunk of the right horse are alone ancient.

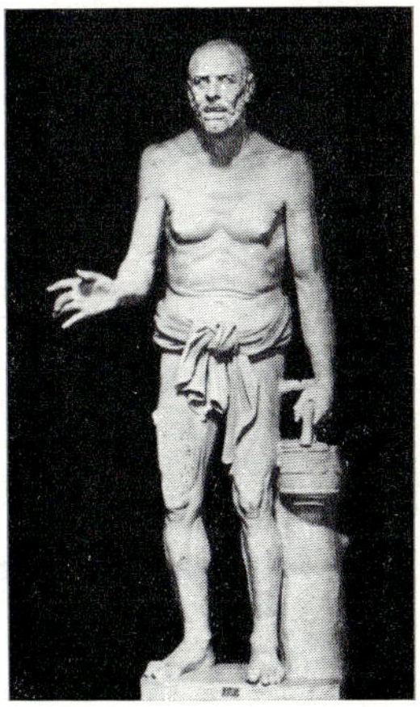

DIANA OF EPHESUS. *The symbol of fecundity.* (*Galleria dei Candelabri*).

SARCOPHAGUS WITH THE RACE OF PELOPS AND OENOMAUS. (*Sala della Biga*).

Pelops, son of Tantalus king of Phrygia, was betrothed to Hippodamia, daughter of Oenomaus, king of Pisa in Elis. An oracle having declared to Oenomaus that he should be killed by his son-in-law, he declared that he would bestow his daughter's hand upon the man who should conquer him in a chariot race, but that whoever was conquered should suffer death. This he did, because his horses were swifter than those of any other mortal. Pelops bribed Oenomaus' charioteer, who took out the linch-pins of the chariot which during the contest broke down and Oenomaus was killed. Thus Hippodamia (who with her mother is represented on the extreme left) became the wife of Pelops.

OLD FISHER. *School of Pergamum.* (*Galleria dei Candelabri*).

DISCOBOLUS OF MYRON. 5th cent. B. C.    BEARDED BACCHUS. 4th cent. B. C.    DISCOBOLUS. *Attic School.*
(*Sculptures in the Sala della Biga*).

Photo ALINARI, ANDERSON, BROGI.

ROME — THE VATICAN. Museums of Antiquities. Sala Rotonda.

THE BARBERINI JUNO.
School of Phidias.

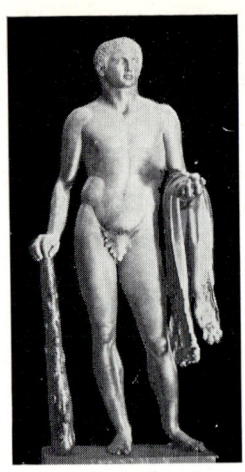

HERCULES.
Gilded bronze.

CLAUDIUS as Jupiter.
Found at Civita Lavinia.

ANTINOUS as Bacchus.
(The drapery is modern).

The *Sala Rotonda*, a large circular hall designed by SIMONETTI on the model of the Pantheon, was built for the purpose of housing the colossal statues and busts of ancient gods and emperors it contains. The floor space is occupied by an ancient mosaic found at Otricoli in 1780, representing the head of Medusa encircled by the Combat of Centaurs and Lapithæ. The rest of the mosaics which form the outer zone of the pavement represents Tritons, Nereids and other Marine deities swimming on the waves. In the centre is a magnificent basin of porphyry, probably the largest single piece known, sixteen yards in circumference, found in the baths of Titus. On either side of the entrance are two ancient hermæ representing Comedy and Tragedy, found in Hadrian's Villa.

SALA ROTONDA. *Erected under Pius VI. on the model of the Pantheon. Designed by* SIMONETTI.

BUST OF JUPITER (Otricoli).
4th century B. C.

The Jupiter bust given here, the finest and most celebrated of the numerous types extant, is remarkable for the unspeakable majesty which characterizes this prototype of the Olympian chief. The abundant hair falling on both sides in thick masses; the bold elevated eyebrows; the slightly parted lips superior to every motion; the pitiless impassibility of this ideal and manly beauty—all contribute to convey the idea of a superhuman being.

The *Sala Rotonda* contains in all eight colossal statues and ten busts which are considered among the most important in the Vatican. These are the *Head of Jupiter*, illustrated above; the so-called *Barberini Juno* whose noble female form is revealed with grace under the transparency of the peplum; the *Hercules* in gilded bronze, found near the Theatre of Pompey; the *Emperor Claudius*, represented as Zeus; the *Juno Sospita*, an archaic Latin image with curious attributes; the *Antinous*, the favourite of Hadrian, who deified him and consecrated a temple in his honour; the statue of *Hera* or Ceres, of the school of Phidias; the busts of *Julia Domna*, of *Faustina*, of *Plotina*, wife of *Hadrian*, of *Claudius* and of *Jupiter Serapis*, represented with the tresses of Pluto.

JULIA DOMNA, wife
of Septimius Severus.

BUST OF HADRIAN,
from his tomb.

FAUSTINA the Elder,
wife of Antoninus Pius.

Photo ALINARI, ANDERSON, BROGI.

ROME — THE VATICAN. Museums of Antiquities. Sala delle Muse.

URANIA.
Astronomy.

APOLLO MUSAGETES.
After SCOPAS?

MELPOMENE.
Muse of Tragedy.

BUST OF PERICLES.
Fifth cent. B. C.).

The *Sala delle Muse*, owes its name to the famous statues preserved here of Apollo and the nine Muses: Melpomene, Thalia (Muse of comedy), Calliope (epic poetry), Polyhymnia (lyric poetry), Erato (erotic poetry) Terpsichore (dancing), Clio (history), Euterpe (music), Urania. Among the muses are busts of Greek celebrities: Socrates, Plato, Sophocles, Pericles, Aspasia, Metrodorus, Æschines, Euripides, Epicurus and Alcibiades. On the walls reliefs of the Birth of Dionysius, and the Pyrrhic Dance, depicting the Greek love of rhythmic movement.

SALA DELLE MUSE. *Erected by order of Pius VI.*

SOCRATES.   SOPHOCLES.   PLATO (or ZENO?)
Ancient portrait-busts of Greek philosophers.

DANCING WARRIORS. PYRRHIC DANCE. *4th cent.* B. C.

The bust of Pericles is probably a copy of a famous work by *Cresilas*. Pericles (B. C. 495?-420), was a high-souled, nobly-bred man, great in all he thought and did. Born at Athens, he entered public life at thirty and soon became the head of the democratic party. He was distinguished as a general as well as a statesman, and frequently commanded the Athenian armies in their wars with Sparta and the neighbouring states. After having put down all rivalry in Athens, he established himself as absolute ruler with the consent of the citizens, reforming the laws, encouraging literature and the arts, and adorning the city with public buildings which made it the wonder and admiration of the world: hence the period of his rule is called the *Periclean Era*. The enemies of Pericles made many attempts to ruin his reputation, but failing in these, they attacked him through his friends (Phidias, Anaxagoras), and Aspasia. Aspasia, born at

BUST OF ASPASIA (?).

Miletus, was the most celebrated of the Greek Hetæræ; being attracted to Athens, came and settled in it, and became the consort of Pericles. She was remarkable for her wit, beauty and culture and her house was the centre of the best literary and philosophical society of Athens, and was frequented even by Socrates. Her character was often both justly and unjustly assailed.

— 447 —

Photo ALINARI, ANDERSON, BROGI.

ROME — THE VATICAN. Museums of Antiquities. Sala degli Animali.

The *Sala degli Animali*, contains a rich collection of representations of animals in white and coloured marble, which was begun by Pius VI., under the supervision of the sculptor Francesco Franzoni; nearly all are ornamental sculptures intended for the country houses of the wealthy Romans. A large part of the floor is paved with antique mosaics chiefly found at Palestrina.

Among the notable pieces here are the Attack on a young Stag; the Cow in grey marble, reminiscent of the famous cow of Myron; the Sow with her litter, of Virgil's Æneid; the Combat between a Bear and a Bull; the Whelp with a puppy; greyhounds running; a Panther in yellow alabaster inlaid with black marble spots, a Tiger in Egyptian granite; a Lion and the head of an Ass in grey marble, a Dolphin in serpentine, a Wild Boar, a Crocodile. Horses are rare, but an important place is taken by animals for food: ducks, cocks, hens, quails, a goose, a turkey, a lobster.... A truly unique collection; but this hall contains many other important works of art, such as the Meleager, given above, the group of the Sacrifice of Mithras, representing an Eastern form of sun worship introduced in Rome under the emperors; the Triton carrying off a Nymph; the Hercules dragging away the Nemean lion; the Hercules slaying Geryon; the bovine figure of the Minotaur; Commodus on horseback, which inspired Bernini with his equestrian statue of Constantine under the portico of St. Peter's.

Built into the walls are several reliefs and two exquisite mosaics from Hadrian's Villa at Tivoli, representing a Lion and Bull Fight, and a pastoral scene with the goddess Pales holding a sceptre. On the floor are mosaics of birds, fish and an eagle tearing a hare to pieces, mostly found at Palestrina.

SALA DEGLI ANIMALI. Hall of the animals.

MELEAGER. *Marble statue from a bronze original by* SCOPAS.

This celebrated figure, in which the mythological hero rests on his lance between his dog and the head of the Calydonian boar, was found about 1500 in a vineyard on the slopes Janiculum.

TRITON CARRYING OFF A NYMPH.

COW IN GREY MARBLE.

SOW WITH HER LITTER.

WHELP WITH A PUPPY.

STAG ATTACKED BY A HOUND.

MITHRAS SACRIFICING A BULL.

Photo ALINARI, ANDERSON, BROGI.

The *Galleria delle Statue.* This part of the Vatican, originally a summer-house of Innocent VIII., built by A. POLLAIUOLO, consisted of six rooms and a chapel dedicated to St. John the Baptist decorated with paintings by MANTEGNA and PINTORICCHIO. Clement XIV., converted it into a museum which was later extended by Pius VI., who connected it with the rest of the Vatican galleries. In the work of adaptation the frescoes by MANTEGNA were almost totally destroyed.

The Galleria delle Statue resembles a long avenue with a double procession of masterpieces and a perspective closing at one end with the sleeping Ariadne and at the other, with a majestic Jupiter seated sceptre in hand. On the floor of the gallery are fine examples of Oriental alabaster in the shape of a large bath and a vase. One of the best pieces here is the statue of Lucius Verus, whose cuirass is covered with small reliefs representing a Gorgon's head and a figure of Victory holding a cornucopia. The group of Æsculapius and Hygea is of Hellenistic origin, and the figure of the goddess of health leaning on the shoulder of her father most adorable. The Apollo Sauroctonos, trying his arrows upon lizards is a reproduction from the celebrated Praxiteles. The Wounded Amazon, in Parian marble, is of great antiquity for it was placed by Augustus in the portico of the physicians. The two seated personages at the end of the gallery are Menander and Posidippus, two famous Athenian comic poets, who flourished in the first half of the third century B. C. These fine statues which people used to take for Marius and Sulla, are important monuments of the gallery.

GALLERIA DELLE STATUE. *Museo Pio-Clementino.*

EROS OF CENTOCELLE
or "Genius of the Vatican."

APOLLO SAUROCTONOS.
After PRAXITELES.

WATER CARRIER.
Ancient sculpture.

LUCIUS VERUS.
A realistic portrait.

GALLERY LEADING TO THE ROOM OF THE BUSTS.
Near the arch seated statues of Menander (left), and Posidippus (right).

SLEEPING ARIADNE. *3rd century* B. C.

The figure of Ariadne is executed with masterly power. The gentle inclination of the head and the turn of the beautiful arms exhibit a charming picture of peaceful deep slumber. The pedestal of this noble piece is formed by a sarcophagus on which struggling giants are being turned into hydras. On either side are two superb candelabra found in Hadrian's Villa at Tivoli.

Photo ALINARI, ANDERSON, BROGI.

The *Sala dei Busti* or Hall of Busts, is rich in likenesses of the great or notorious people of the Roman Empire. There are Marcus Aurelius, Hadrian, Septimius Severus and his wife Julia Pia. the head of Caracalla—fine portrait of a restless tyrant, the helmeted head of Menelaus, part of a group with the dead Patroclos, the two half-figures of a Husband and Wife, on a cippus, an admirable work. The ceiling decorations date from the period of Innocent VIII.

CARACALLA.

MARCUS AURELIUS.

MENELAUS.

The *Cnidian Venus* is probably the best of the existing copies of the celebrated statue of Aphrodite made by PRAXITELES and long admired in the temple of the goddess at Cnidus. An adequate appreciation of its beauty is prevented by the modern metal drapery now hanging from below the hips.

PRAXITELES (born about 450 B. C.), was the first sculptor who gave prominence to corporeal attractions. Before his age a nude figure of the deity had scarcely been thought possible; in his unrobed Aphrodite the great master combined the utmost luxuriance of personal charms with a spiritual expression in which the queen of love herself appeared as a woman needful of love, and filled with inward longing, Phryne, the celebrated beauty, is supposed to have been Praxiteles' model for the statue.

APHRODITE (*Cnidian Venus*). After PRAXITELES.

VENUS in the bath. After Daedalus of Bithynia.

The *Gabinetto delle Maschere*, so named from the beautiful mosaic on the floor of masks from Hadrian's Villa, contains besides several fine statues of Venus, a Satyr in "rosso antico," an exquisite Dancing Girl, reliefs of the Labours of Hercules, a Bathing-chair, formed of a single piece of rosso antico, and other sculptures.

VASE with reliefs of Bacchanalian scenes.

CORTILE DEL BELVEDERE.

The *Cortile del Belvedere*, designed by Bramante, was originally a square court belonging to the summer-house of Innocent VIII. It was altered in 1775 under Clement XIV., when the present portico supported by 16 ancient pillars of Oriental granite was added. Eight large masks taken from the Pantheon occupy the pediments; eight reliefs occupy the intercolumnar spaces; statues, sarcophagi and other sculptures are arranged against the walls. Under the arches in separate cabinets are placed the most important pieces, which are given on the following page.

In the arcades adjoining the cabinets are many monuments worthy of note, such as the two Molossian hounds of the school of Pergamum; the sculptured frieze representing the combat of Artemis and Hecate with the Giants; the relief of Æneas and Dido in the harbour of Carthage; the relief from the *Ara Pacis* and several others.

ANCIENT SARCOPHAGUS with Bacchanalia scene.

Bacchanalia festivals were celebrated in honour of Bacchus. They arose in Egypt and were brought into Greece about 415 B. C. and called *Dionysia*. The Romans celebrated them every three years.

Photo ALINARI, ANDERSON, BROGI

ROME — THE VATICAN. Museums of Antiquities. Cortile del Belvedere.

The *Apollo Belvedere* was found near Rome at the end of the 15th century and was one of the first specimens of ancient sculpture placed in the Vatican. This most beautiful statue of the slayer of Laocoon, personifies the perfect ideal of youthful manliness, and is celebrated for its extra-ordinarily elegant attitude. The arms are restored and the god seems to have originally held the bow (or, most probably the *Ægis*) in his left hand.

The *Hermes*, one of the most beautiful statues in the world, is a work done in Greece and according to which Poussin fixed the proportions of the academic figure. It was found in the ruins of an edifice erected by Hadrian and was formerly called the Antinous of the Belvedere.

APOLLO BELVEDERE.
Ascribed to LEOCARES.

HERMES (*Mercurio*).
School of PRAXITELES.

APOXIOMENOS.
From a bronze by LYSIPPUS.

The famous group of the *Laocoon* discovered under Julius II. in 1506, among the ruins of the Palace of Titus, on the Esquiline, was termed by Michelangelo a "miracle of art." It is generally attributed to the Rhodian artists *Agesander, Athenodorus,* and *Polydorus*; but the date of the work is in dispute. The myth represented by the group is an episode of the Second Book of Virgil's "Æneid" and describes the destruction of the Priest Laocoon and of his sons by serpents sent by Apollo. This fate befell Laocoon in his effort to forestall the destruction of the city of Troy; he warned the Trojans against the trickery of the Greeks and adjured them not to admit the wooden horse into the city. The whole group is formed out of a single block of marble. Michelangelo modestly refused to restore it and the restoration of the missing arms was done by the sculptors *Montorsoli* and *Cornacchini*.

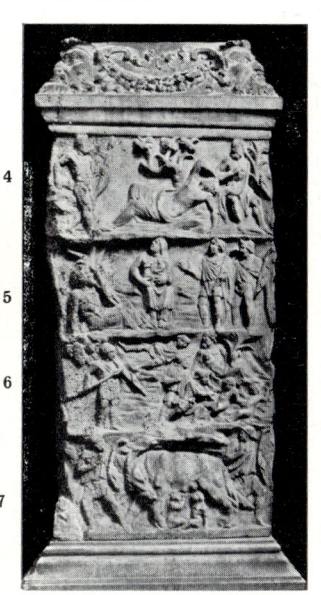

ARA CASAL.

LAOCOON. *School of Rhodes* (1st century B. C.)

Among the monuments of archæology in the Vatican is the so-called *Ara Casali*, a quadrangular pilaster intended to support some figure of a god or votive offerings. The reliefs on the sides represent: the corpse of Hector dragged by Achilles round the walls of Troy, and two scenes relating to the funeral of Hector; 4. Mars approaching Rhea Sylvia asleep, 5. Rhea Sylvia with Romulus and Remus, 6. exposure of the Twins on the bank of the Tiber, 7. the Twins suckled by the Wolf.

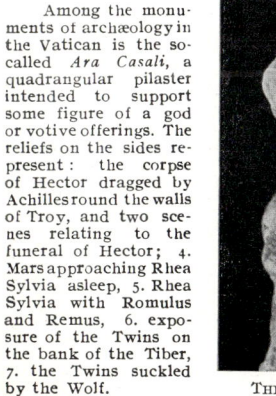

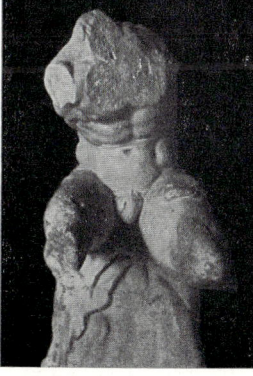

CANOVA'S *Perseus* and the two Pugilists were placed here in 1811 by Pius VII. to replace the Apollo Belvedere and Laocoon which Napoleon had taken to Paris.

The *Torso Belvedere*, is supposed to represent the trunk of a seated Hercules. The accuracy of its anatomy is so perfect, that its discovery caused a revolution in the field of art; Michelangelo studied it to such a degree that he was wont to call himself pupil of the Torso.

THE TORSO BELVEDERE.

PERSEUS. *By* CANOVA.

57. - WONDERS OF ITALY.

— 451 —

Photo ALINARI, ANDERSON, BROGI.

ROME — THE VATICAN. Museo Etrusco-Gregoriano. Museo Egiziano.

The *Etruscan Museum*, which was founded by Gregory XVI. in 1836, contains a magnificent collection, the result of excavations at Vulci, Toscanella, Tarquinii, and also antiquities collected in the Lateran under Pope Pius IX.

The exhibit comprises statues, bronzes, golden ornaments, vases, domestic utensils, paintings on canvas copied from the principal tombs in Southern Etruria representing games and dances in honour of the dead, and a vast collection of painted vases mostly the work of Greek potters, displaying the most exquisite skill of drawing and belonging to the finest period of Greek art (460-400 B. C.); all extremely interesting for the study of early-Italian art and fruitful in information as to the customs which the Romans borrowed from the Etruscan populations.

Hermes presenting the infant Bacchus to Silenus.

Amphora with various scenes.

Hector parting from Priam and Hecuba

THE ALDOBRANDINI NUPTIALS. MARRIAGE OF PELEUS AND THETIS. *Roman fresco of the first century found in* A. D. *1600.*

THE ALDOBRANDINI NUPTIALS.

The bridegroom is sitting at the foot of a couch, on which sits the bride, attired in white drapery, accompanied by a bridesmaid, who seems to be advising with her. Right and left of the picture groups of women making preparations for the wedding ceremony.

Until the discoveries at Herculaneum and Pompeii this fresco was considered the most precious specimen of ancient wall decoration.

QUEEN TUË mother of Rameses II.

ANTINOUS (*Hadrian's Villa*)

QUEEN ARSINOË wife of Ptolemy Philadelphus.

THE GODDESS SEKHMET *15th cent.* B. C.

The *Egyptian Museum*, founded by Pius VII. (1800-23), and Gregory XVI. (1831-46), commends itself for its diversity and allows us to penetrate more deeply into the life of this mysterious people. The collection comprises a number of valuable works including colossal statues of Egyptian divinities, statues of Ptolemy Philadelphus and his wife Arsinoë, two lions couchant inscribed with the name of Pharaoh Nektonebos (4th cent. B. C.), sarcophagi, mummy-cases, canopic jars, cast of the famous Rosetta trilingual inscription, which enabled Champollion to decipher the hieroglyphs on the obelisks, etc. There are besides several pieces of Græco-Roman sculptures imitating Egyptian works, the majority of which were found in Hadrian's Villa at Tivoli; among these is the colossal statue of Antinous illustrated above, in white marble, executed with a feminine exquisiteness of rounded and velvety outlines.

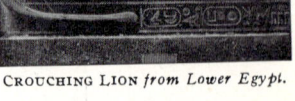

CROUCHING LION *from Lower Egypt.*

Photo ALINARI, ANDERSON, BROGI.

ROME — THE VATICAN. *Museums of Antiquities. Museo Chiaramonti.*

Hercules and Telephus.
After a Greek work 4th cent. B. C.

Hygeia.
Found at Ostia.

Ulysses handing the goblet to Polyphemus.

Female Divinity.
(Primigenia Fortune?).

Sarcophagus of Evhodus with the Myth of Alcestis. *Found at Ostia.*

Ulysses had been confined in the cave of the giant Polyphemus, whence he escaped after having intoxicated the monster. In this statue we see energy and patience put to the test rather than cunning.

The relief on the great sarcophagus of Junius Evhodus given here represents the myth of Alcestis. This romance of conjugal love carved on the marble is a homage of Evhodus 'to his very dear wife Metilia Acte,' as the inscription on the lid relates. These people, who had little dread of death, prepared tombs most tastefully adorned, and gallantly offered them like a madrigal to the loved object. The faces of Alcestis and her consort Admetus, are likenesses of Evhodus and his wife. In the centre Alcestis is seen on her deathbed bidding a last farewell to Admetus. On the left is Apollo leaving the house. On the right Hercules extending his hand to Admetus and leading back to him Alcestis, still wrapped in a shroud; whom he has rescued from Hades, represented by Cerberus. Behind are the Fates, on the extreme right sits Pluto and Proserpine.

Head of Vulcan. (Hephæstus).

Statue of Tiberius.
From Veii.

Museo Chiaramonti. *Founded by Pius VII.*

This valuable gallery, so called from its founder Pius VII. (Chiaramonti), was arranged by Canova. The corridor, divided into thirty compartments, is one hundred and fifty-five yards long and contains nearly eight hundred antique works of art: statues, bas-reliefs, busts, sarcophagi, etc.

Photo Alinari. Anderson, Brogi.

ROME — THE VATICAN. Museums of Antiquities. Braccio Nuovo.

MINERVA (Giustiniani). From a bronze, 5th c. B. C.

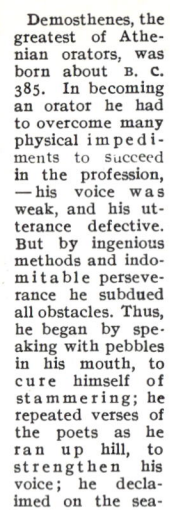

Demosthenes, the greatest of Athenian orators, was born about B. C. 385. In becoming an orator he had to overcome many physical impediments to succeed in the profession, — his voice was weak, and his utterance defective. But by ingenious methods and indomitable perseverance he subdued all obstacles. Thus, he began by speaking with pebbles in his mouth, to cure himself of stammering; he repeated verses of the poets as he ran up hill, to strengthen his voice; he declaimed on the sea-beach, amid the noise of the waves, to overcome a natural diffidence and accustom himself to the noise and confusion

DEMOSTHENES. From Polyeuctos' original.

of the popular assembly; he lived for months in a cave, engaged in constantly copying over again and again Thucydides' "History of the Peloponnesian War," in order to acquire a perfect mastery of the Greek language.

At 30 he began to obtain reputation as a public speaker, and his eloquence soon gained him the favour of the people. The influence he acquired he employed for the good of his country, and not for his own aggrandizement; he spent 15 years of his life in denunciation of Philip of Macedon, who had resolved to subjugate Greece, pronouncing against him his immortal "Philippics."

PUDICITIA. 2nd cent. B. C.

TYCHE. Fortuna.

THE BRACCIO NUOVO. *Side view.*
Designed by RAPHAEL STERN. A. D. 1817.

SILENUS and the infant Bacchus.

CARYATID. 5th cent. B. C.

This superb gallery expressly constructed to receive the marbles and works of art it contains, was added to the Museo Chiaramonti by Pius VII., in 1817-22 from designs by RAPHAEL STERN. The great hall, embellished with fourteen columns of Egyptian granite, alabaster, cipollino and giallo antico, is two hundred and thirty feet long by twenty-six feet broad, with a small exedra in the middle. The reliefs on the frieze are imitated from the columns of Trajan and Marcus Aurelius, and from various triumphal arches. Its magnificence, its sumptuousness may be likened to the famous buildings of ancient Rome.

The very mosaics of the pavement are important, especially that representing the Travels of Ulysses, whose vessel having doubled the rock of Scylla is passing near the islands of the Sirens. The hero, as recorded by Homer, is seen bound to the mast of the ship, which is steered by two of his companions.

NIOBE. *Attributed to* SCOPAS.

— 454 —

Photo ALINARI, ANDERSON, BROGI.

ROME — THE VATICAN. Museums of Antiquities. Braccio Nuovo.

SATYR REPOSING.
After PRAXITELES.

THE EMPEROR AUGUSTUS.
Found in the Villa of Livia.

WOUNDED AMAZON. From
an original by POLYCLETUS.

The cuirass worn by Augustus has elaborate reliefs. Central zone, Mars receiving the re-captured Roman ensign from a Parthian, on either side allegorical figures; below Earth with the children and the horn of Plenty; above *Cælus*, with the Sun in his chariot.

THE BRACCIO NUOVO. *Designed by* RAPHAEL STERN.

DORYPHORUS. (*lance-bearer*)
After the bronze by POLYCLETUS.

The *Braccio Nuovo* contains many gems of the sculptor's art, among which it is well to remark the *Apoxiomenos* (the scraper), one of the masterpieces of Lysippus; the *Wounded Amazon* and the *Doryphorus* of Polycletus, chief of the school of Argos, who devoted himself to the study of the human form and enjoined upon his pupils the results of his researches; the headless statue of Niobe, the Ganymede, the busts of Marc Antony, of Octavianus, of the emperors Hadrian, Claudius, Commodus, Probus; and of Julia, the daughter of Titus.

There are many copies of this statue; the best is the one found at Pompei, now in the National Museum in Naples.

The sixteen playing children clambering over the river god are symbolic figures and allude to the sixteen cubits' depth to which the Nile annually rises to irrigate the country around. The base, carved in imitation of the waves of the great river, represents hippopotami and plants.

THE EMPEROR DOMITIAN.

THE NILE. *Colossal group found near S. Maria sopra Minerva.*
This splendid piece was exhumed near a temple of Serapis.

— 455 —

Photo ALINARI, ANDERSON, BROGI.

ROME — THE VATICAN. Appartamento Borgia.

The *Appartamento Borgia* consists of six rooms which were occupied by Alexander VI. (Borgia), and his family. Here the pope lived in almost fabulous luxury for 11 years. Three of the rooms were decorated by PINTORICCHIO and his pupils with a series of frescoes of great magnificence. These pictures, a "wondrous conglomeration of elements sacred and profane," are full of interesting portraits of the notorious Pope Alexander, Lucrezia Borgia, and other such celebrities of that period. After the Pope's death, the place was vacated, the successive popes preferring the lighter rooms on the floor above. In 1889-97 Pope Leo XIII. caused the rooms to be restored.

SALA DEI PONTEFICI. Hall of the Pontiffs.
Decorated by GIOV. DA UDINE *and* PERIN DEL VAGA.

The *Hall of the Popes*—the antechamber of the Swiss guard—was decorated during the pontificate of Leo X., whose arms appear at each angle of the vaulting. The design represents allegories of the seven celestial bodies, surmounted by the signs of the Zodiac: Saturn drawn by dragons, Jupiter by eagles, Mars by wolves (?), Apollo by horses, Venus by doves, Mercury by cocks, Diana by nymphs. Between these are inscriptions recording the names and deeds of ten popes.

The *Sala del Credo* and the *Sala delle Sibille*, at the other end of the 'apartment,' were decorated by pupils of Pintoricchio. In the hall of the Creed are half-length figures of Apostles and Prophets, arranged in pairs, the apostles holding scrolls bearing a sentence or a passage of the Creed, the prophets' scrolls inscribed with prophetic sayings.

THE RESURRECTION OF CHRIST
by PINTORICCHIO (*Sala della Madonna*)

The *Sala della Madonna* or hall of the Mysteries, the most beautiful of the rooms, is adorned with frescoes representing events or mysteries in the life of Christ and the Virgin Mary. There are seven scenes: the Annunciation, the Nativity, the Adoration of the Magi, the Resurrection, the Ascension, the Descent of the Holy Spirit and the Assumption of the Virgin. This was the first room decorated by Pintoricchio. The compositions are of the simplest, there is no trace of violent emotions or dramatic power, the figures are all of that peaceful and primitive devotion suited to the demands of the early Church.

On the ceiling directly above each scene are medallions of prophets holding scrolls upon which is inscribed the prophecy referring to the scene represented on the wall beneath.

None of the painful scenes of the Passion of Christ are included in the series of paintings in the hall of the Mysteries. The Adoration of the Magi is followed by the *Resurrection*. Here the Risen Saviour is seen in a golden glory bordered with cherubs' heads, on the right are the guards in armour, on the left, most conspicuous of all, is the kneeling figure of the donor, Pope Alexander himself, clothed in a gorgeous mantle embossed with gold,—a splendidly realistic portrait of the pleasure-loving pontiff. The guard who kneels with a halberd in his hand is supposed to be a portrait of Cesare Borgia.

SALA DELLE ARTI LIBERALI. Hall of the Liberal Arts

This hall has seven frescoes representing symbolic impersonations of Grammar, Dialectics, Rhetoric (Trivium); and Geometry, Arithmetic, Music, Astrology (Quadrivium). Charming allegorical figures of queens surrounded by philosophers and disciples in each branch.

ARMS OF LEO X.
(Giovanni de' Medici)

THE BORGIA ARMS.

— 456 —

Photo ALINARI, ANDERSON BROGI.

ROME — THE VATICAN. Appartamento Borgia.

SALA DEI SANTI. Hall of the Saints.

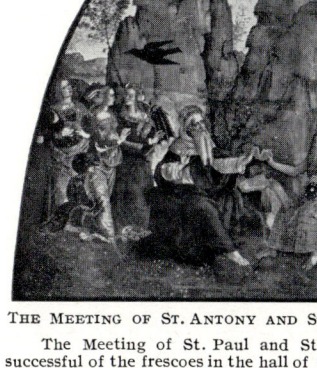

THE MEETING OF ST. ANTONY AND ST. PAUL THE HERMIT.

The *Sala dei Santi* or hall of the Saints is adorned with paintings representing episodes from the lives of various saints and one scene from the Old and one (the Visitation) from the New Testament. In these frescoes Pintoricchio has surpassed himself in fertility of invention and poetical feeling,—the grouping is varied, the action more lively.

The Meeting of St. Paul and St. Antony, is the most successful of the frescoes in the hall of the Saints. The scene represents the moment when the two aged hermits break the loaf of bread which the raven had brought them. Behind St. Paul are two disciples listening to the edifying conversation, while behind St. Antony stand three beautiful women with little horns, symbolizing the temptations of the world

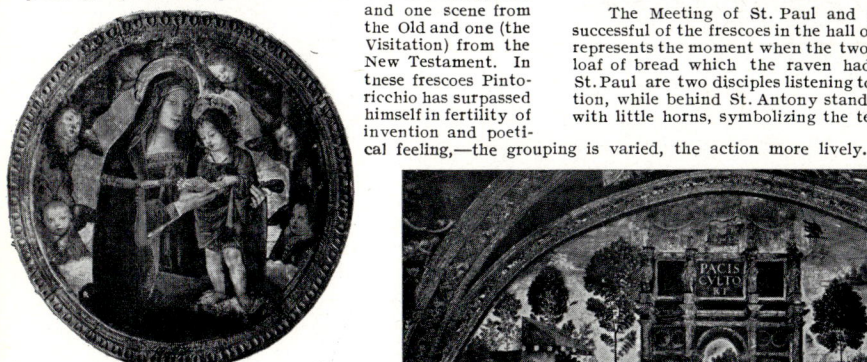

MADONNA AND CHILD.
The Virgin's face is supposed to be a portrait of Giulia Farnese.

The Dispute of St. Catherine is the most important of Pintoricchio's frescoes. Here the scene is laid in a charming landscape: on the left the emperor sits on a richly ornamented throne, and before him, standing, the youthful Catherine illustrates the points of her arguments upon her fingers.

St. Catherine was an Egyptian princess, famed for her learning. Her people, being Christians, were commanded by Maximianus, on pain of severest torments, to renounce their religion. The princess hearing the cries of her people sallied forth from her palace and confronted the tyrant, pleading for her fellow-Christians. And such was the power of her eloquence that the emperor being impressed by her wisdom and arguments, which left him without reply, decided to confront her with fifty of the most learned philosophers and rhetoricians of his empire. This is the moment represented by Pintoricchio. The learned old men stand in a group to the right, some discussing, some meditating doubtfully or watching the disputation, others searching their great books.

ST. CATHERINE OF ALEXANDRIA DISPUTING BEFORE THE EMPEROR MAXIMIANUS. By PINTORICCHIO.

Prince Djem.   St. Catherine.   Group of Philosophers.

Behind the throne is a crowd of courtiers, at the sides are two figures of striking aspect; the sad-eyed man in Greek dress in the foreground is said to be Andreas Paleologos, nephew and heir of Constantine III., who lost Constantinople to the Turks; the one in a white turban is supposed to be Prince Djem the son of the Sultan Mohamed II.

The Emperor is believed to be a portrait of Cesare Borgia, and St. Catherine his sister Lucrezia. In the background is the arch of Constantine bearing the inscription *Pacis Cultori* (to the Guardian of Peace).

— 457 —

ROME — THE VATICAN. Raphael's Stanze.

[Jurisprudence].
Justice.

The Fall.

[The Dispute of the Holy Sacrament].
Theology.

Punishment of Marsyas.

Judgement of Salomon.

Philosophy
[The School of Athens].

Astronomy.

Poetry.
[The Parnassus].

CEILING OF THE STANZA DELLA SEGNATURA.
Fresco by RAPHAEL. A. D. 1508.

Allegory of PHILOSOPHY.

ASTRONOMY or Study of the Globe.

STANZA DELLA SEGNATURA. *Showing* The School of Athens, and Parnassus.
Decorated by RAPHAEL *from 1508 to 1511.*

THE STANZE OF RAPHAEL, consist of a large saloon and four smaller halls corresponding to the four Borgia chambers which are immediately below them. In November of 1507 Pope Julius II. vexed at being constantly reminded of Alexander VI. gave up the Borgia Apartment and decided to inhabit the suite of rooms now known as Raphael's Stanze. These rooms had been already partly decorated by painters of distinction, one of whom, Sodoma, was then at work on the ceiling of the Stanza della Segnatura (so named from the signing of pardons—Segnature di Grazia—the granting of which was discussed here in the presence of the Pope). Sodoma was dismissed by Julius who handed over to Raphael the completion of the ceiling. The young artist (he was but 25 years old) achieved it with four medallions representing beautiful symbolical figures of the moral powers —*Theology, Philosophy, Poetry* and *Justice*. The Pope was so enchanted with the work that he assigned to Raphael the task of decorating the walls of the four rooms with frescoes. Raphael († 1520) did not, however, live to complete his task, and it was finished by his pupils. The frescoes which he executed are

— 458 —

Photo ALINARI, ANDERSON, BROGI.

ROME — THE VATICAN. Stanza della Segnatura. Ceiling.

Raphael commenced his work in the Vatican (see opposite), by completing the ceiling of the Stanza della Segnatura, upon which Sodoma had already painted the ornamental framework and the small panels with mythological figures imitated from antique reliefs.

The subjects painted by Raphael are the four medallions containing allegorical figures of the Virtues and the corner panels related with them: Theology and the Fall of Man, Poetry and the Punishment of Marsyas, Philosophy and the Study of the Globe, Justice and the Judgment of Solomon. It was upon these pictures that the whole scheme of decoration of the Stanza was based, the great frescoes on the four walls being illustrations of these subjects.

The most beautiful of the medallions is the Poetry, whose countenance expresses a sweet and serene inspiration; *Numine Afflatur*—inspired by the god, are the words inscribed on the tablets of the winged genii. Philosophy holds two volumes, one concerning morality, the other the study of external phenomena; the words *Causarum cognitio*—the knowledge of causes, are inscribed on the tablets. Theology, austere and chaste, points with her finger to the Trinity below; she holds the Gospels while two genii carry the tablets with the inscription *Divinarum rerum notitia*—the knowledge of things divine.

Justice, holds a sword of iron, the metal of force, in her right and the balance in her left hand. She is flanked by two angels and two genii each carrying a tablet inscribed with the words, *Jus suum* and *Unicuique tribuit*.

On the lower parts of the walls are small compositions in monochrome.

Allegory of POETRY.

ADAM AND EVE. THE FALL.

PUNISHMENT OF MARSYAS.

JUDGMENT OF SOLOMON.

large historical and symbolical compositions that embrace the whole of human knowledge,—they resume the different stages of development of the great artist's genius. In the *Stanza della Segnatura* (painted from 1508 to 1511), each of the four mural paintings is an illustration of the subject presented by the symbolical figure on the ceiling. In the *Stanza di Eliodoro* (painted from 1512 to 1514), the mural paintings refer to the Divine assistance granted to the Church against her foes, and to the miraculous corroboration of her doctrines. In the *Stanza dell'Incendio* (painted in 1517), the subjects of the walls tell the story of the acts of Leo X. who had succeeded Julius II. In the *Sala di Costantino* (painted after 1520), the scenes are from the life of the Emperor Constantine, in which he figures as the champion of the Church and the founder of her temporal Power. Here is depicted Constantine's Donation " of the city of Rome," to Pope Sylvester I.

Raphael was an artist of great genius in whom painting attained its culminating point of historic and dramatic development. His unparalleled popularity was due to his faculty for adaptation and intelligent imitation which made his art the synthesis and quintessence of all that was most fascinating in Italian art.

STANZA DELLA SEGNATURA. *Showing* The Disputa and Jurisprudence. *Decorated by* RAPHAEL *from 1508 to 1511.*

— 459 —

Photo ALINARI, ANDERSON, BROGI.

58. - WONDERS OF ITALY.

THE VATICAN.   Stanza della Segnatura.

"LA DISPUTA" (Theology or Religion). *Fresco by* RAPHAEL. A. D. 1509.

St. Pierre.

Adam.

St. John.

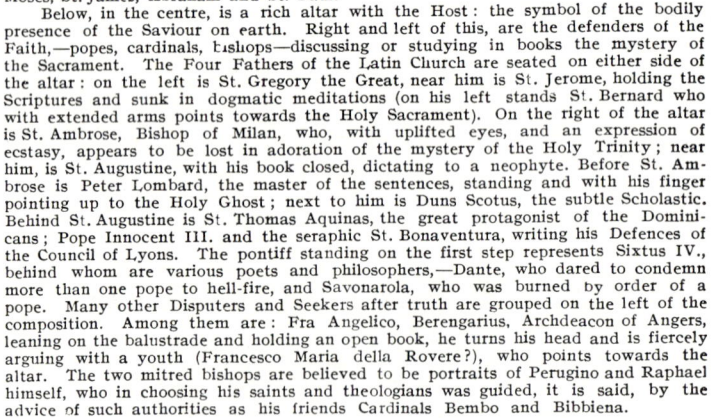

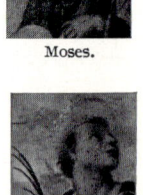

Moses.

St. Stephen.

St. George.

This great picture is divided into two principal parts: the upper part represents the glory of Heaven, the lower an ideal assembly of all the Church Dignitaries on earth who took part in the controversies on the Sacrament of the Eucharist.

Above, in the centre, is the Saviour enthroned and attended by the Virgin and the Baptist. Over the Saviour appears the half-figure of God the Father in the act of benediction, and below Him the symbol of the Holy Ghost in the midst of angels bearing the books of the Evangelists. On each side of Christ, in a semicircle, sit majestically Apostles, Patriarchs and Saints; from left to right: St. Peter, Adam, St. John Evangelist, David and St. Lawrence, then St. George, St. Stephen, Moses, St. James, Abraham and St. Paul.

Below, in the centre, is a rich altar with the Host: the symbol of the bodily presence of the Saviour on earth. Right and left of this, are the defenders of the Faith,—popes, cardinals, bishops—discussing or studying in books the mystery of the Sacrament. The Four Fathers of the Latin Church are seated on either side of the altar: on the left is St. Gregory the Great, near him is St. Jerome, holding the Scriptures and sunk in dogmatic meditations (on his left stands St. Bernard who with extended arms points towards the Holy Sacrament). On the right of the altar is St. Ambrose, Bishop of Milan, who, with uplifted eyes, and an expression of ecstasy, appears to be lost in adoration of the mystery of the Holy Trinity; near him, is St. Augustine, with his book closed, dictating to a neophyte. Before St. Ambrose is Peter Lombard, the master of the sentences, standing and with his finger pointing up to the Holy Ghost; next to him is Duns Scotus, the subtle Scholastic. Behind St. Augustine is St. Thomas Aquinas, the great protagonist of the Dominicans; Pope Innocent III. and the seraphic St. Bonaventura, writing his Defences of the Council of Lyons. The pontiff standing on the first step represents Sixtus IV., behind whom are various poets and philosophers,—Dante, who dared to condemn more than one pope to hell-fire, and Savonarola, who was burned by order of a pope. Many other Disputers and Seekers after truth are grouped on the left of the composition. Among them are: Fra Angelico, Berengarius, Archdeacon of Angers, leaning on the balustrade and holding an open book, he turns his head and is fiercely arguing with a youth (Francesco Maria della Rovere?), who points towards the altar. The two mitred bishops are believed to be portraits of Perugino and Raphael himself, who in choosing his saints and theologians was guided, it is said, by the advice of such authorities as his friends Cardinals Bembo and Bibbiena.

The monochrome pictures beneath represent: St. Augustine and the child on the seashore, Augustus and the Sibyl.

Fra Angelico.    Raphael.   St. Bernard.   St. Thomas.   Dante.   Savonarola.
                 Perugino.   St. Jerome.   Innocent III.
                                 St. Gregory.   St. Bonaventura.

— 460 —

THE VATICAN.   *Stanza della Segnatura.*

THE SCHOOL OF ATHENS (Philosophy or Knowledge).   *Fresco by* RAPHAEL. A. D. 1510.

This composition, forming a pendant to the « Disputa » opposite, represents an imaginary assembly of all the philosophers of Asia and Greece and their scholars. Here Raphael has done away with the intervals of time and space which separated so many illustrious men, and presents them as contemporaries.

In a wide spacious hall conceived in the noble style of Bramante, with colossal statues of Apollo and Minerva on either side, the greatest minds af all ages and climes are brought together. A flight of four steps raises the more distant figures above the nearer groups. Among the former Plato and Aristotle, the princes in the realm of thought, stand together in the centre, as if disputing on their doctrines. Plato holds the « Timaeus » in one hand and with the other points to heaven,—an attitude significative of his system of speculative philosophy; while Aristotle, holding the « Ethics » with a calm gesture is pointing to the earth, —thereby implying that all true philosophy must be derived from investigation and experience. On each side of these masters is a row of attentive auditors. To the left is seen Socrates in argument with a group of five persons, to whom he explains in order (counting on his fingers) his principles and their conclusions. On the opposite side, others are engaged in conversation or in study. Lying upon the steps in front is Diogenes the Cynic, apparently unaware of the crowds around him. In the foreground to the left is the bald-headed Pythagoras, busily writing upon his knee, and behind him Empedocles; the youth in a white mantle is a portrait of Francesco Maria, Duke of Urbino, a nephew of Julius II.; the figure resting his foot on a marble block is said to be Anaxagoras, lastly, the man supporting his head with his left hand Heraclitus. In the group to the right is seen Archimedes (a portrait of Bramante) stooping and drawing a diagram with a compass; several pupils watch him, the different degrees of their intelligence being most strikingly represented. Behind them are Zoroaster (a portrait of Castiglione the author of the *Cortegiano*) and Ptolemy holding celestial and terrestrial globes; they turn towards two figures close to the edge of the picture which are portraits of Raphael and Sodoma. Earlier Art can show nothing in the leat comparable to the varied arrangement of these figures.

The monochrome pictures beneath represent: Astrologers in conference, the Siege of Syracuse, and Death of Archimedes.

Alcibiades.   Socrates.   Plato.   Aristotle.
Duke of Urbino.   Anaxagoras.

Photo ALINARI, ANDERSON, BROGI.

"JURISPRUDENCE" *or* The Three Cardinal Virtues: Fortitude, Prudence, Temperance. *Fresco by* RAPHAEL.

CIVIL LAW: Justinian entrusts the Roman Code to Tribonian. *By* RAPHAEL.

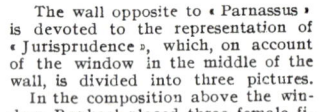

The wall opposite to « Parnassus » is devoted to the representation of « Jurisprudence », which, on account of the window in the middle of the wall, is divided into three pictures.

In the composition above the window Raphael placed three female figures, personifications of Prudence, Fortitude and Temperance, the virtues without whose aid the science of law cannot be applied to daily life. Prudence sits in the centre and has a double visage, in front her countenance is beautiful and young, at the back aged and bearded—in allusion to her knowledge of the past and her power of looking into the future. She is attended by two cherubs, one offers her the mirror of Truth, the other the Torch of Penetration. On the left is Fortitude caressing a lion and armed with an oak branch (Julius II.'s badge). On the right is the figure of Temperance holding a bridle denoting self-control.

The Pandects or Digest (fifty books) of the decisions, writings and opinions of the old Roman jurists, executed in A. D. 528-533 by direction of the Emperor Justinian, formed the leading compilation of the Roman civil law (*corpus juris civilis*). The original copy of the Pandects, discovered by the Pisans when they captured Amalfi in 1137, is now preserved in the Laurentian Library at Florence, the oldest Public Library to exist in Europe (see p. 238).

CANON LAW: Gregory IX. presenting the Decretals to a Jurist. *By* RAPHAEL.

This picture is in allusion to the claim of the Church to legislative authority. The Pope's face is a portrait of the reigning pontiff Julius II.; the cardinal to the left in front is Giovanni de' Medici (afterwards Leo X.), behind him, full face, is Alessandro Farnese (afterwards Paul III.). The decretals formed the second part of the canon law; being edicts and judicial replies of the Popes to cases submitted to them from time to time for adjudication.

Moses giving the Law to the Israelites.

Alexander placing Homer's poems in the tomb of Achilles.

Augustus preventing Virgil's friends from burning the Æneid.

Photo ALINARI, ANDERSON, BROGI.

THE VATICAN.   Stanza della Segnatura.

PARNASSUS.
(Apollo and the Muses. - Poetry or Imagination).
Fresco by RAPHAEL.

This fresco is the glorification of poetical life and exalted sentiment.

On the heights of Mount Parnassus Apollo sits under laurel trees playing the violin,—a fine figure of an inspired performer. Around him are grouped the nine Muses. Two of them are seated on either side of Apollo, the others stand about in the background.

Right and left of this central group are the poets of antiquity and of modern Italy, who have been fostered by the Muses. In the group to the left is the imposing figure of the blind Homer with upturned face, reciting verses, which a seated youth eagerly listens to and transcribes; behind him are Dante (in profile) and Virgil. Below are the Lyric poets: Alcæus, Corinne of Thebes, Petrarch and Anacreon, engaged in conversation, with the voluptuous figure of Sappho seated and holding a scroll on which her name is inscribed. The face of the latter is said to be a profile of the famous courtesan Imperia, who was loved by all the wealthiest and greatest men. Foremost in the group to the right of the window is Pindar, seated, speaking with an air of enthusiasm, while Horace and Ovid (?) listen to him with reverence; behind them is Sannazzaro, who wrote the *Arcadia* and sang the Virgin, and, higher up, Boccaccio and Terence, conversing, and Ariosto and Aristophanes halting.

Apollo is playing the violin, and this instrument is said to have been chosen out of compliment to Giacomo Sansecondo, a famous violinist and a friend of Raphael. The Muse sitting on the right of Apollo is identified as Calliope, holding on her knee the trumpet of Fame; this, again, is a profile of the celebrated Vittoria Colonna, Michelangelo's « holy flame »—the consolation and last joy of the noble old man. Behind Calliope are Melpomene with the mask of tragedy, Terpsichore and Polyhymnia embracing each other. The Muse Erato sits on the left of Apollo, and behind her are Clio, Thalia, Euterpe and Urania.

Consecrated to the revival of ancient literature, this picture breathes all the enthusiasm of the sublime years which characterized the golden age of the Renaissance in Rome. The composition is symmetrically arranged notwithstanding the unfavourable character of the space to be covered: the figures are treated with great freedom, and the impression conveyed is most pleasing.

Calliope.   Apollo.   Erato.

The decoration of the Stanza della Segnatura was executed by Raphael in about three years, and that of the Stanza di Eliodoro in about two years. "The knowledge expressed in these frescoes is so thorough," writes Symonds, "that we wonder whether in his body lived again the soul of some accomplished sage."... "If, after estimating the range of thought revealed in these works, we next consider the labour of the mind involved in the distribution of so many multitudes of beautiful and august human figures, in the modelling of their drapery, the study of their expression, and their grouping into balanced compositions, we may form some notion of the magnitude of Raphael's performance."

— 463 —   Photo ALINARI, ANDERSON, BROGI.

ROME — THE VATICAN. *Stanza di Eliodoro.*

THE SACRIFICE OF ISAAC.

The *Sacrifice of Isaac* painted above the "Mass of Bolsena," stands as a lesson to those whose faith wavers. Abraham's faith in God was tried when the injunction came 'Offer up thy son.' Yet he did not attempt to object or intercede; he still retained his confidence that 'the everlasting covenant' could not fail... 'and Abraham stretched forth his hand, and took the knife to slay his son.' It was enough; God required no more. His faith and duty had not been found wanting. Scenes *from the Old Testament painted by* BALDASSARE PERUZZI *on the ceiling of the* Stanza di Eliodoro. (See also p. 465).

THE COVENANT OF ABRAHAM.

The paintings in the *Stanza di Eliodoro* illustrate the triumphs of the Church over her enemies, and the miracles by which her power has been attained. The Miracle of Bolsena, officially recognized at the time by Pope Urban IV., vindicates the dogma of "transubstantiation:"—that the bread and wine of the Eucharist is, after consecration by a priest, converted mystically into the body and blood of Christ. This dogma was confirmed by the Council of Trent, in 1562, and is known (by Roman Catholics) as the doctrine of the Real Presence, the actual presence of Christ in the Eucharist.

THE MASS OF BOLSENA.
Fresco by RAPHAEL.

This picture represents a famous miracle which occurred in 1263. A young Bohemian priest who doubted the dogma of transubstantiation, was celebrating Mass in a church at Bolsena, when, in elevating the host, blood issued from five gashes in the wafer, resembling the five wounds of our Saviour. Thereupon the priest seeing this was immediately convinced of the truth.

In this fresco, the scene is laid in the choir of a church. The priest is gazing on the bleeding wafer with an expression of embarrassement, astonishment and shame. Opposite kneels Julius II. watching the priest, with an expression of reproof, and attended by two cardinals, one of whom is Raffaello Riario cousin of Julius II. (p. 211, 484). The miracle was officially recognized and the Feast of Corpus Domini was instituted, for which St. Thomas Aquinas composed the office. This picture illustrates the infallibility of the Church and the suppression of the schism by Julius II. (1512).

GROUP OF WOMEN AND CHILDREN.  POPE JULIUS II.  SWISS PAPAL GUARDS.

Among the spectators of the miracle are some admirable portraits. "This picture," writes Layard, "is remarkable not only for its well-connected composition, but for its highly characteristic forms; the courtly humility of the priests, the rude hardy forms of the Swiss, the various ways in which the people manifest their sympathy, and above all the *naïveté* of the choristerboys and of the youths who look over the inclosure of the choir; all this is connected satisfactorily and naturally with the two principal personages."

— 464 —

Photo ALINARI ANDERSON, BROGI.

ROME — THE VATICAN. *Stanza di Eliodoro.*

Jacob's Vision represents a flattering allusion to the promises of the reign of Leo X. and to the destinies of the Medicean House. "And Jacob, while he slept, had a vision... a ladder set upon the earth and the top of it reached to heaven: and the angels of God ascending and descending on it... and the Lord stood at the top, and said I am the Lord God... the land whereon thou liest, to thee will I give it and to thy seed, which should be numerous as 'the dust of the earth'."

JACOB'S VISION.

MOSES AT THE BURNING BUSH.

MIRACULOUS EXPULSION OF HELIODORUS FROM THE TEMPLE. *Fresco by* RAPHAEL.

The story which forms the basis of this picture is told in the Apocrypha (Maccab. ii. 3). Money belonging to widows and orphans, was stored in the Temple of Jerusalem; on this treasure Seleucus, King of Asia, designed to lay hands and despatched Heliodorus, his treasurer, to Jerusalem to accomplish this profanation. But while Heliodorus and his men were in the temple and about to carry off their plunder "there appeared unto them a heavenly horseman in golden armour, and he run fiercely and smote at Heliodorus who fell suddenly to the ground, and was compassed with great darkness."

In this composition Raphael has represented the successive incidents of the story in one picture; the scene being laid in the vestibule of the temple, which is seen at the back. On the right, beneath the fiery horse whose terrible rider is followed by two celestial emissaries rushing impetuously through the air and armed with scourges, the sacrilegious Heliodorus lies prostrate on the ground, while his companions attempt to carry off the booty. In the background, Onias, the high priest, is seen praying at the altar for the divine interposition. To the left are amazed spectators and, huddled together, the widows and orphans who were to have received the money; here, in the foreground, appears the figure of Julius II. carried on his *sedia gestatoria*, beholding the miracle. The foremost of the two chair-bearers is thought to be a portrait of the celebrated engraver Marcantonio Raimondi.

The picture, remarkable for its vigour of expression, is an allusion to Julius II.'s success in liberating the States of the Church from foreign enemies, and his efforts to protect Italy from the invasions of the French.

HELIODORUS.

— 465 —

ROME — THE VATICAN. *Stanza di Eliodoro.*

ATTILA REPULSED FROM ROME BY POPE LEO I. *Fresco by* RAPHAEL.

The invasion of Italy in the year 452 by Attila, King of the Huns, forms the subject of this picture.

The barbarian King in the midst of his cavalry shrinks back in horror at the miraculous apparition in the heavens of St. Peter and St. Paul, each sword in hand, who warn back the invaders. The Apostles are enveloped in a brilliant light, visible only to Attila and his Huns; the latter struck with terror and thrown into confusion are already retreating. In the distance are seen the flying standards of the barbarian host, trumpeters and burning villages. On the left of the picture the Pope advances on a white mule followed by his court. The Pope's features are those of Leo X. (he is represented twice and may also be recognized as one of the attendant cardinals), the priest bearing the cross is said to be a portrait of Raphael himself, while his old master Perugino, riding a white horse accompanies him as mace-bearer.

In this composition Raphael has transferred the scene where the event actually took place (see p. 410) to the vicinity of Rome. The contrast between the papal group and the disorderly army of the Huns is emphasized by the calm confidence of the Pope. « The great processional cross », writes Cruickshank, « is opposed to the spears and banners of the Huns. It is the victory of the spiritual over the temporal power, and the ruins of ancient Rome in the background suggest the triumph of Christianity over Paganism ».

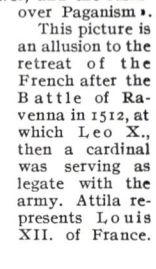

This picture is an allusion to the retreat of the French after the Battle of Ravenna in 1512, at which Leo X., then a cardinal was serving as legate with the army. Attila represents Louis XII. of France.

ATTILA, the "Scourge of God," the murderer of men, the devastator

ATTILA, KING OF THE HUNS.

whose very war-horse left a trail where no grass ever grew again, ravaged Europe and inspired terror everywhere. In the year 452 he collected a vast army and swept down like a typhoon upon Italy. His intention was of assailing Rome, but first he began by devastating and pillaging the northern provinces, extorting heavy tribute to reward his Huns. Aquileia Padua, Vicenza, Verona, Bergamo were either burnt to the ground or sacked; the citizens were powerless and panic prevailed everywhere, when suddenly, to the astonishment of all Europe, Attila retreated with his army over the Alps and marched into Pannonia. He died shortly after his arrival there of an uncommon effusion of blood on the day of his nuptials with a maiden named Ildico, the last of his numerous wives. His body was enclosed within three coffins, of gold, of silver and of iron, and immense treasures,—the spoils of nations— were thrown into his grave, which was dug by captives who, it is said, were afterwards inhumanly killed, lest they should reveal the spot.

MURAL DECORATION.

— 466 —

Photo ALINARI, ANDERSON, BROGI.

ROME — THE VATICAN. *Stanza di Eliodoro.*

DELIVERANCE OF ST. PETER FROM PRISON. *Fresco by* RAPHAEL.

This fresco, remarkable for its contrasting effects of light, is divided in three parts, and, according to the story, represents how Peter lay in prison and was called by an angel at night; how, still dreaming, he went out accompanied by the angel, and how the watch was roused when his flight was discovered.

In the centre is the dungeon where the angel is seen awakening the Apostle who, with hands folded as in prayer, sits asleep between two slumbering watchmen. The angel, in a glory, bends down to him, lays a hand on his shoulder and points with the other towards the door. *On the right* the angel is leading Peter away, while the guards sleep on the steps. Here again the light proceeds from the angel,—' an incomparable type of a swiftly-moving guiding force '—while the Apostle with widely opened eyes walks away like a dreamer. *On the left* a soldier with a lighted torch rouses his comrades to help search for their prisoner.

This picture, one of Raphael's most admirable compositions, is in allusion to the captivity of Cardinal Giovanni de' Medici (before he was elected Pope Leo X.) after the Battle of Ravenna (1512), where he was taken prisoner by the French. However, while the French retreated towards Milan he managed to escape, while the army was crossing the Po, and with his brother Giuliano returned to Florence.

CARVED DOOR.

The carved interlaced diamond rings on the door represent the private crest of Lorenzo de' Medici, father of Leo X.

STANZA DI ELIODORO. *Showing* " The Liberation of Peter."

The mural paintings in this room were almost entirely executed by *Raphael* in 1512-14. The decoration of the ceiling is the work of *Baldassare Peruzzi*.

— 467 —

Photo ALINARI, ANDERSON, BROGI.

59. - *WONDERS OF ITALY.*

ROME — THE VATICAN. Stanza dell'Incendio.

The paintings in the Stanza dell'Incendio were executed in 1517 from Raphael's designs; they represent scenes from the reigns of Leo III. and Leo IV. The scenes, however, were designed in allusion to episodes in the history of the then reigning pontiff Leo X. The ceiling was decorated by Perugino, master of Raphael.

The principal fresco here, the *Conflagration of the Borgo* (which gave the name to this room), represents a fire which occurred in the Leonine City in the year 847, miraculously extinguished by Pope Leo IV. with the sign of the Cross. The traditional incident is represented in the background where the flames are seen threatening the old church of St. Peter (cfr. p. 413). On the loggia is Leo IV. surrounded by church dignitaries; on the steps below is seen a crowd of excited people, some kneeling in prayer, others gesticulating violently. In the foreground are groups exhibiting the terrors of a conflagration: distracted mothers and their children imploring succour, women carrying water to assist men who endeavour to extinguish the flames, a youth is letting himself down from a wall, while a woman prepares to drop her baby to a man below. On the left is seen Æneas carrying off his father Anchises, followed by his wife Creusa and their child Ascanius. This fresco is intended to refer to the success of the conference at Bologna in 1515 (see below). The Pope thought that he had by a diplomatic miracle extinguished the conflagration that was then threatening Europe.

THE CONFLAGRATION OF THE BORGO.

THE BATTLE OF OSTIA.

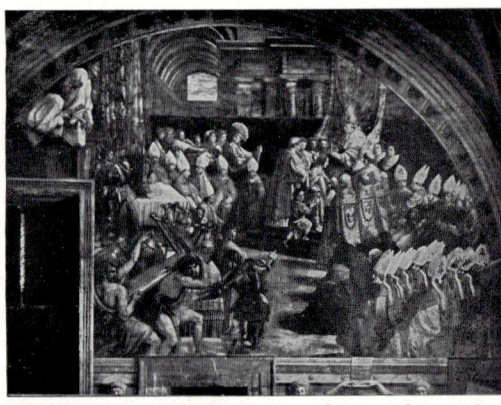

THE CORONATION OF CHARLEMAGNE IN ST. PETER'S. A. D. 800.

The historical event which forms the basis of this picture is the naval victory at Ostia, obtained by the allied fleets of Pope Leo IV. and the towns of Naples and Amalfi, over the Saracens in the year 846. A storm brought in answer to the prayers of the Pope, destroyed the Saracen fleet. The Pope is represented as Leo X., the cardinals behind him are portraits of Giulio de' Medici (afterwards Clement VII.) and Bibbiena (an admirer of Raphael). The fresco is in allusion to the crusade against the Turks proclaimed by Pope Leo X.

On Christmas day at the celebration of Mass in Old St. Peter's Pope Leo III. placed a golden crown on Charlemagne's head. (Charles had already visited Rome in 774. On this occasion the momentous ceremony of the Donation likewise took place in St. Peter's, where Charles confirmed and extended the older Donation made to the Holy See by his father King Pipin). In the picture the Pope has the features of Leo X., and the emperor those of Francis I. The picture is intended to refer to the meeting of Leo X. and Francis I. at Bologna in 1515.

OATH OF LEO III.

This event took place two days before the coronation of Charlemagne. The Pope stands at the altar, and with his hands on the gospels is clearing himself on oath of the calumnies of his enemies. On the left of the picture is Charlemagne (standing, his back turned to the spectator) who, not being yet crowned emperor, is dressed as a Roman Patrician, with a gold chain on his shoulders.

Photo ALINARI, ANDERSON, BROGI.

ROME — THE VATICAN. Sala di Costantino.

SALA DI COSTANTINO.

CLEMENCY. *Attributed to Raphael.*

The paintings in this room were executed under Clement VII. (Giulio de' Medici), after the death of Raphael who had made preliminary sketches for some of the representations. They are illustrative of the victory of Christianity through the instrumentality of Constantine, and the establishment of the Church.

Victory of Constantine over Maxentius. The scene is laid on the left bank of the Tiber, with Ponte Molle on the right. In the centre the emperor Constantine is advancing victoriously, with a spear levelled at Maxentius who is sinking in the Tiber; in the sky appear triumphant angels. This grand composition 18 feet long full of movement, was designed by RAPHAEL and executed after his death.

VICTORY OF CONSTANTINE OVER MAXENTIUS AT PONTE MOLLE. *By* GIULIO ROMANO.

VISION OF CONSTANTINE.
Fresco by GIULIO ROMANO.

CONSTANTINE'S DONATION of Rome to Pope Sylvester.
Fresco by RAFFAELLO DAL COLLE.

This fresco represents Constantine addressing his soldiers regarding the apparition of the Holy Cross, which he beheld when marching from the Rhineland to Rome in order to attack Maxentius, and which he adopted as his ensign or *labarum* of war. While the emperor addresses his army there is a renewal of the supernatural apparition in the sky.

The scene is represented in Old St. Peter's. The Emperor kneels at the feet of the pope and offers him as a symbol of the Donation, a golden statuette of an armed soldier. On this Donation was based the power of the Pope to bestow the crown of the empire, Charlemagne and all succeeding emperors received their crowns by virtue of this gift.

Another large wall fresco here depicts the *Baptism of Constantine* (see pp. 416, 430). In addition there are paintings of eight popes flanked by allegorical figures.

— 469 —

Photo ALINARI, ANDERSON, BROGI.

ROME — THE VATICAN. *Raphael's Logge.*

Separation of light from darkness.

The Temptation (The Fall).

Expulsion from Paradise.

Abraham and the three angels.

Destruction of Pharaoh in the Red Sea.

Moses strikes the rock for water.

Moses at the burning bush.

Finding of Moses.
Specimen of vault decorations designed by Raphael.

RAPHAEL'S LOGGE decorated in 1517-19 by pupils of Raphael from his designs. The vaulting of each of the 13 bays contains four Biblical scenes, which are popularly known as *Raphael's Bible.*

Painted decoration and stucco mouldings.

Jacob and Rachel at the well.

Finding of Moses.

Solomon's Judgment.

— 470 —

Photo ALINARI, ANDERSON, BROGI.

ROME — THE VATICAN. Chapel of Niccolò V.

ST. STEPHEN PREACHING TO THE PEOPLE.   ST. STEPHEN BEFORE THE COUNCIL.

Fresco by FRA ANGELICO DA FIESOLE. A. D. 1450.

One of the gems of the Vatican is the chapel of Pope Nicholas V., decorated by Fra Angelico about 1450. The frescoes arranged in two series on the three walls of the chapel illustrate the life and martyrdom of SS. Lawrence and Stephen. On the upper part of the walls are represented the following scenes: 1. Stephen ordained deacon by St. Peter; 2. Stephen distributes the alms of the Church to the widows and the orphans; 3. He preaches to the people; 4. He is brought before the council at Jerusalem; 5. He is dragged away to his martyrdom; 6. He is stoned to death.

On the lower part of the walls: 1. St. Lawrence ordained deacon by Sixtus II.; 2. The same pope about to be led away to prison for refusing to give up the treasures of the Church to the prefect Decius, delivers them to S. Lawrence, commanding him to distribute them among the poor; 3. Distribution of the treasures; 4. The saint is arraigned before the prefect and is condemned to be broiled alive; 5. He converts his gaoler; 6. Martyrdom of St. Lawrence.

In these remarkable frescoes Fra Angelico, then in his 61st year, not only displayed a vigour equal, but superior, to that of his youth. The composition is for the most part admirable throughout the series; the draperies are noble and dignified; the architecture in the backgrounds is in the richest Cinquecento style. Although in immediate proximity to the famous Stanzas painted by Raphael, nevertheless these frescoes, in virtue of their air of perfect devotion and calm contemplative worship, excite the enthusiasm of all true admirers of Christian art.

ST. LAWRENCE receives the Church's treasures.    ST. LAWRENCE distributing the Church's treasures.

Photo ALINARI, ANDERSON, BROGI

ROME — THE VATICAN. Chapel of Niccolò V.

ST. LAWRENCE DISTRIBUTES THE CHURCH'S TREASURES.
By FRA ANGELICO.

PROCLAMATION OF THE DOGMA (8 DEC. 1854) OF THE IMMACULATE
CONCEPTION OF THE VIRGIN. By FRANCESCO PODESTI.
Sala dell' Immacolata

SALA DELL'IMMACOLATA
Decorated by PODESTI.

The wall paintings in the *Sala dell'Immacolata Concezione*, executed by PODESTI, by order of Pius IX., commemorate the celebration of the Dogma of the Immaculate Conception. These frescoes are especially interesting for their portraits of contemporary prelates who took part in the ceremony.

The large composition opposite the window is divided in two sections; in the lower part is the scene of the Promulgation of the Dogma, December 8, 1854: here the Pope is seen surrounded by numerous cardinals and by his Court; in the upper part of the fresco is the Virgin Mary between the Almighty and the Saviour, with St. Peter on one side and St. Paul on the other. Right and left of this central group are the other apostles, the saints, patriarchs, and angels.

On the left wall are represented the Theologians and the Prelates who gathered in the Vatican at the last discussion of the Dogma. On the right wall, Pius IX., and his Court are seen venerating the image of the Blessed Virgin.

The *Galleria Geografica*, is so named from the enormous maps of the Italian provinces painted on the walls. There are in all forty maps designed by the Dominican IGNAZIO DANTI and executed by his brother Antonio about 1585 under the pontificate of Gregory XIII., the reformer of the calendar, by whose order the gallery was furnished with marble benches and a double row of Hermes, ancient busts of: Homer, Socrates, Hesiod, Antisthenes, Athene, Aphrodite, etc. The ceiling is gorgeously decorated with gilding, cofferwork or stucco framing medallions and historical and religious paintings by *Tempesta* and other artists.

GALLERIA GEOGRAFICA. Gallery of Maps. (164 yds. long).

— 473 —

Photo ALINARI, ANDERSON, BROGI.

ROME — THE VATICAN. SALA REGIA. Cappella Paolina.

The sumptuous *Sala Regia*, or Royal Hall, begun under Paul III., by Antonio da Sangallo the Young, originally served as a vestibule to the Sistine and Pauline chapels and for the reception of foreign ambassadors to the Holy See. The rich stucco decorations of the ceiling are by *Perin del Vaga*; those on the walls above the seven doorways by *Daniele da Volterra*.

The large mural frescoes by *Vasari, Salviati, Federico Zuccari, Sermoneta* and others, represent glorious events in the history of the papacy, and illustrate the temporal power of the Church. The most important paintings are: the Donation to the Holy See by King Pepin (A. D. 754); its Confirmation by Charlemagne (A. D. 800); Gregory VII., absolving the Emperor Henry IV., at Canossa (1077); the Reconciliation of Alexander III., and Frederick Barbarossa in St. Mark's at Venice (1177); the Excommunication of Frederick II., by Gregory IX. (1239); the League against the Turks and the Battle of Lepanto (1571); the Return from Avignon of Gregory XI. (1377); the Massacre of St. Bartholomew and death of Coligny (1572).

SALA REGIA, erected by A. DA SANGALLO. Completed in 1573.

The painting by *Zuccari* reproduced on this page represents the celebrated penance of the Emperor Henry IV., before the Pope Gregory VII., at Canossa, which marked the final act of that terrible dispute between the popes and the emperors, which distracted Italy for generations.

Hildebrand, the son of a Tuscan carpenter, rose to eminence as a monk of the Benedictine Monastery of Cluny, where he won a reputation for his learning and the extreme austerity of his life in an age of undisguised immorality. He became sensible of the formidable evils tending to the corruption of the clergy, due to their dependence on the Emperor for investiture into their benefices, and set himself with all his might to effect a total purging of the Church from its foulness, and especially from the guilt of simony. For some years before his actual election to the Papal throne he had begun to exercise an immense control over the councils of the

GREGORY VII. (Hildebrand), absolving Henry IV., at Canossa (1077). Fresco by ZUCCARI.

THE RETURN OF GREGORY XI., FROM AVIGNON. Fresco by VASARI.

Church, and he was personally responsible for the epoch-making resolution (1060), which declared that the choice of a new Pontiff was vested in the College of Cardinals alone. As soon as he assumed the Tiara in 1073, he began to dispute with the Emperor Henry IV. about the question of « investiture ». And in the council of 1075 he caused to be passed a decree vehemently condemning as simony investiture by layman, declaring null the bestowal by King or Emperor of the Episcopal ring and staff to a bishop, deposing certain bishops whom Henry had instituted and excommunicating several of Henry's officials to whom these prelates had, he alleged, paid money for favouring their appointment. In great indignation, the Emperor protested against so decided an infringement of a custom which had been followed since the time of Charlemagne. He assembled a council of his ecclesiastics at Worms, and there a decree was passed declaring that Gregory was deposed. The Pope retaliated by a solemn sentence of excommunication on the Emperor. The issues were now clear: the Emperor strove to make the Church a feudal dependency, the Pope to render the Church, with all its temporalities, independent of the State. The struggle between Church and State or the « War of the Investitures » had begun. The Pope's sentence made the German nobles turn against the Emperor, and they informed Henry that unless he obtained remission of the ban within the year they would renounce their fealty and he would lose his throne. The final act of that terrible duel is well known. Accompanied by his wife and by the excommunicated bishops and officials, Henry crossed the Alps in the depth of winter in order to ask absolution of the Pope who was then staying at the Castle of Canossa, the Countess Matilda's stronghold (*see* p. 410) in the Apennine Mountains. For three weary days the Emperor was kept waiting amidst the snow before the castle-gate, clad only in a coarse woollen shirt as a penitent, and there, fasting, he awaited in humble patience the pleasure of the stern Pontiff. At last he was admitted, threw himself on his knees and received absolution, but on very hard terms. (*See also* p. 557).

THE CRUCIFIXION OF ST. PETER. By MICHELANGELO (Cappella Paolina).

Photo ALINARI, ANDERSON, BROGI.

ROME — THE VATICAN. *Sistine Chapel.*

VIEW OF THE SISTINE CHAPEL.
Erected in 1473 by order of Pope Sixtus IV., from the designs of the architect Giovanni de' Dolci

This magnificent chapel, in itself as large as a church, was erected by GIOVANNI DE' DOLCI, under Sixtus IV., in 1473, whence its name of *Sistine*. BOTTICELLI, PERUGINO, SIGNORELLI, ROSSELLI, PINTORICCHIO, GHIRLANDAIO and other famous Florentine masters in 1482 executed a series of beautiful frescoes on the upper part of the long walls. In 1508, Julius II., nephew of Sixtus IV., entreated MICHELANGELO to decorate the ceiling, which was completed in the fall of 1512. Nearly twenty years later, Clement VII. again requested Michelangelo, then in his sixtieth year, to paint on the altar wall the celebrated « Last Judgment ». This occupied the great master for eight years, and was finished in 1541 under Paul III. The sculptured white marble screens and the handsome singing gallery are the work of MINO DA FIESOLE. The pavement is of Cosmatesque mosaic. The altar, where only the pope officiates, is beautifully inlaid with mother-of-pearl.

Photo ALINARI, ANDERSON, BROGI.

ROME — THE VATICAN. Sistine Chapel.

THE LAST JUDGMENT. THE RESURRECTION OF THE DEAD.
Painted by MICHELANGELO. A. D. 1534-41.

This vast painting measuring about 66 ft. in height and 33 ft. in width is the largest and most comprehensive in the world. At first sight it appears confused and intricate, but careful study will enable the spectator to appreciate the mathematical severity of the composition which is divided horizontally into four bands or planes of grouping.

1) On the top, in the semicircular compartments, are groups of angels bearing the instruments of the Passion.

2) Immediately below, in the centre, Christ as Judge with the Virgin on his right while on his left the saints and martyrs hold up the symbols and instruments of their martyrdom: St. Peter showing the keys, St. Lawrence with the gridiron, St. Bartholomew with his skin and the knife with which he was flayed, St. Catherine with the wheel, St. Sebastian with the arrows, saints showing the crosses upon which they suffered martyrdom. On the opposite side (to the right of Christ) Adam and Abel, groups of women witnessing the resurrection and symbolising the final scope of the human race.

3) In the centre, the seven angels of the Apocalypse sounding the trumpets to awaken the dead, while other angels show to the damned the books of Judgment; on the right the condemned ones are delivered to the fury of the demons, each figure typifying one of the seven capital sins, Envy (the malignant) hopeful of rising to the group of the happy ones, has been grabbed and drawn downwards by the devils, Avarice holding the keys of her treasure, Luxury punished in the most cruel manner. To the left group of figures ascending more or less rapidly (according to the weight of their sins) to present themselves to the High Judge, three figures whose faces appear to be reflections of the same self ascending together, they are supposed to typify brotherly love: purity, charity, piety.

4) In the lowest division, on the left the dead emerging from their graves shake off their shrouds and resume their human form, Michelangelo himself in the garb of a monk touching the head of a resuscitated old man points to the Almighty above; a grotto here is supposed to represent Purgatory; on the right Charon with his boat having reached Hell is striking down the rebellious with his oar. The latter are awaited by the judge Minos, whose face is a portrait of Biagio da Cesena, master of the ceremonies to Paul III. He had censured the picture on account of the nudity of the figures, and Michelangelo revenged himself by painting him with an ass's ears and a serpent round his body amongst the condemned.

Photo ALINARI, ANDERSON, BROGI.

ROME — THE VATICAN.   Sistine Chapel.

ZACHERIAS.

The ceiling of the Sistine Chapel is considered Michelangelo's masterpiece and the most powerful piece of painting in existence. When the despotic Pope Julius II. ordered the master to paint the Sistine Chapel, Michelangelo at first rebelled, saying he was a sculptor not a painter, but once inspired with the idea he entered into it with enthusiasm. Unversed as he was in fresco painting and being diffident of his powers in this new department of art, he summoned some of the best painters from Florence to execute the frescoes from his cartoons ; Michelangelo, however, was not satisfied with their performances, and having mastered their secret, dismissed them, obliterated what they had done and shut himself all alone in the chapel to begin work.

He commenced the frescoes on May 10th 1508 and worked on them earnestly for four years. His scheme was to give an epitome of the events recorded in the book of Genesis regarding the expectance and the preparation for Christ's coming.

The ceiling of the chapel forms in its section a flattened arch ; the central, narrow, oblong portion, a flat surface. In order to avoid confusion and subject to a certain order the different scenes and the multitude of figures (over two hundred) which he intended to create, Michelangelo invented an imaginative structure with cornices in bronze and marble, vertical pilasters adorned with bas-reliefs, and an entablature on which appears to rest the vaulting which forms nine sections devoted to the Biblical scenes. On the lower part of this vaulting runs the great series of seated Prophets and Sibyls, colossal figures of wonderful beauty, dignified and full of individual character. In the pointed arches and lunettes he painted the ancestors of the Virgin in calm expectation ; in the four corners of the ceiling, scenes in the history of the people of Israel. Lastly, he placed a great number of nude decorative figures, in grey, bronze or bright colour, in the empty spaces of the framework to support the architectural forms and connect the whole. These figures of youths, symbols of human force and vitality, are among the most striking examples of Michelangelo's art.

In viewing this stupendous undertaking the spectator will readily observe that the combined genius of an architect, sculptor and painter was required to produce a result so admirable.

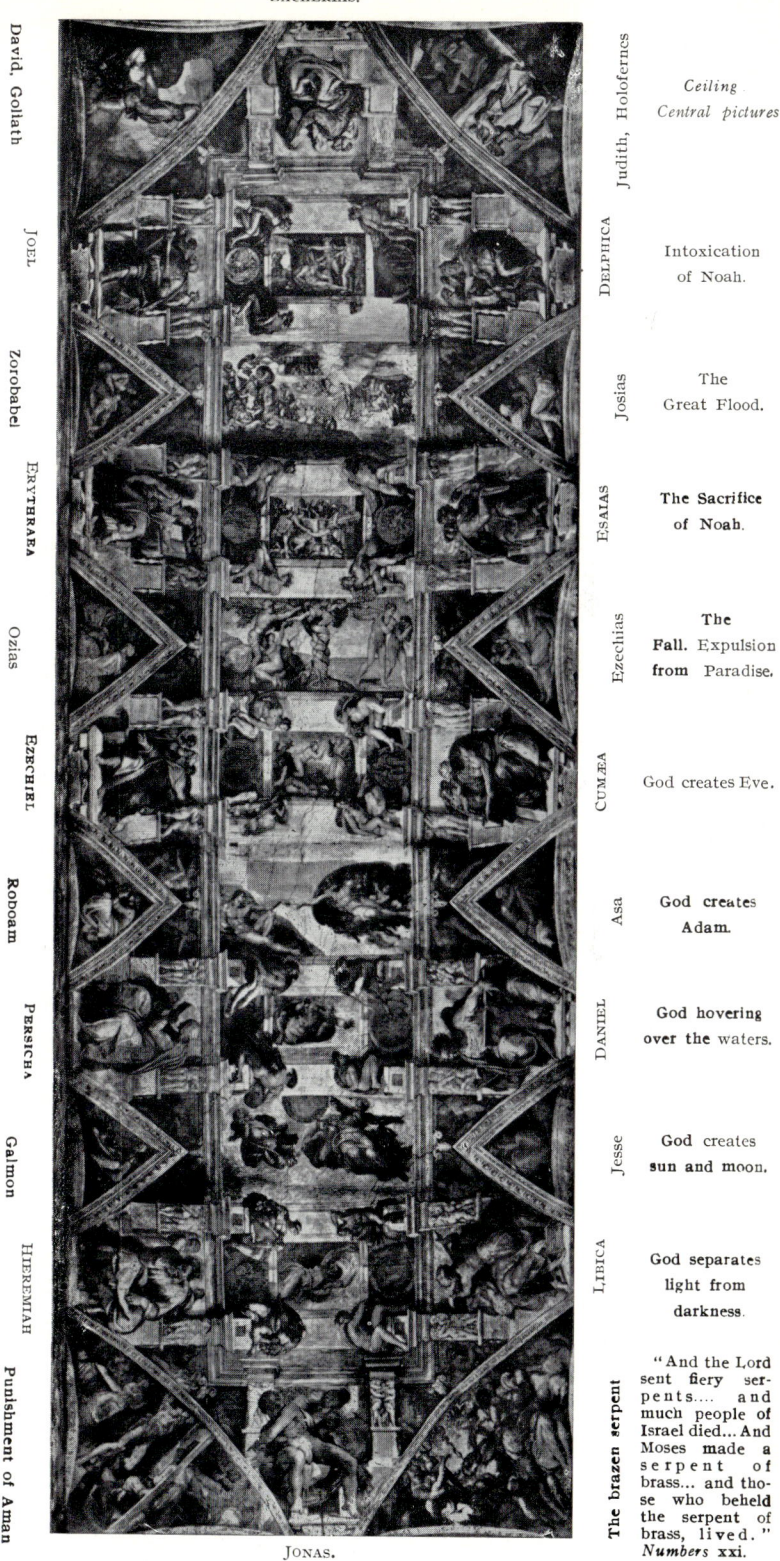

David, Goliath — JOEL — Zorobabel — ERYTHRAEA — Ozias — EZECHIEL — Roboam — PERSICHA — Galmon — HIEREMIAH — Punishment of Aman

Judith, Holofernes — DELPHICA — Josias — ESAIAS — Ezechias — CUMÆA — Asa — DANIEL — Jesse — LIBICA — The brazen serpent

Ceiling Central pictures

Intoxication of Noah.

The Great Flood.

The Sacrifice of Noah.

The **Fall.** Expulsion from Paradise.

God creates Eve.

God creates Adam.

God hovering over the waters.

God creates sun and moon.

God separates light from darkness.

"And the Lord sent fiery serpents.... and much people of Israel died... And Moses made a serpent of brass... and those who beheld the serpent of brass, lived." *Numbers* xxi.

JONAS.

THE CEILING. By MICHELANGELO. A. D. 1508-12.

— 477 —

ROME — *THE VATICAN. Sistine Chapel. Michelangelo's Frescoes.*

The Erythræan Sibyl.  | The Prophet Jeremiah.  | The Prophet Isaiah.

Drunkenness of Noah.

Sacrifice of Noah.

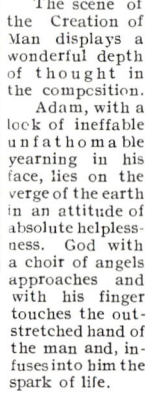

Below: The Creation of Man. *Centre:* God creates Eve. *Above:* The Temptation. The Expulsion. In the centre: is the Tree of Knowledge of Good and Evil, round which is coiled the tempting serpent; on the left our first parents are plucking " the fruit of that forbidden tree, whose mortal taste brought death into the world, and all our woes, with loss of Eden."

The scene of the Creation of Man displays a wonderful depth of thought in the composition. Adam, with a look of ineffable unfathomable yearning in his face, lies on the verge of the earth in an attitude of absolute helplessness. God with a choir of angels approaches and with his finger touches the outstretched hand of the man and, infuses into him the spark of life.

— 1478 —

ROME — THE VATICAN.   Sistine Chapel. Michelangelo's Frescoes.

THE PROPHET DANIEL.   THE LIBYAN SIBYL.   THE DELPHIC SIBYL.

THE GREAT FLOOD.   Detail of the ceiling.

On the left, the unfortunates take refuge on a cliff emerging above the waters in an effort to save themselves together with their children; other fugitives burdened with chattels are labouring to ascend this last vantage ground: mothers shelter their infants, a husband carries a wife on his shoulder, a man has climbed a tree. On the right, some of the unlucky ones have improvised a tent, here one man bears in his arms a lifeless form which he has rescued from the water, the father and mother stretch their hands towards it. In the centre, others are piling up into a boat which soon will be swallowed up by the waves. In the distance is the Ark triumphant, on which people are eagerly rescued from destruction.

FIGURE OF A SLAVE.    JUDITH AND HOLOFERNES.   FIGURE OF A SLAVE.
Detail of the ceiling.

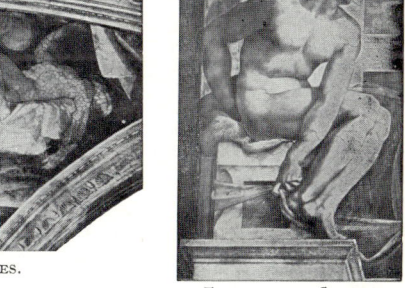

The youths beneath the central panels of the ceiling are perhaps the most beautiful creations of the great master.

Photo ALINARI, ANDERSON, BROGI.

ROME — THE VATICAN. Sistine Chapel. (Left wall).

The frescoes on the long walls of the Sistine (six on each side of the chapel), were executed about 1483 under the direction of Botticelli. The subjects which illustrate episodes from the lives of Christ and Moses were probably decided by Sixtus IV. The acts of Moses, the forerunner of Christianity, are represented as symbolically parallel to those of Christ, its founder and head. Thus, the Old Testament scenes of promise on the left wall are in every instance faced by corresponding scenes of fulfilment from the New Testament which embody the same idea.

Events in the Life of Moses. (The old dispensation).

Journey of Moses. The Circumcision. In the background, at the foot of the hill, Moses and his family take leave of Jethro; on the left the leader of Israel sets out for Egypt in a long procession, Zipporah with her children, attended by women with burdens on their heads

The Circumcision. Group of spectators.

follows; in the centre the Angel of God with drawn sword and outstretched arm bars the way to Moses, who had neglected the command to circumcise his son; on the right Zipporah is seen circumcising her child, while Moses watches the ceremony surrounded by a crowd of men. In the background groups of people dancing.

Journey of Moses. The Circumcision. By Perugino and Pintoricchio.
Typifying the institution of the monotheistic Church.

The Leading into the Wilderness. In the centre Moses draws water from a well for the flocks of the daughters of Jethro (a scene full of idyllic charm); right Moses slays the Egyptian and beyond he escapes to the land of Midian; left background he removes the sandals from his feet and kneels before the burning bush; left foreground Moses leads the Israelites into the wilderness.

The Leading into the Wilderness. By Botticelli.
Typifying the ministry of Moses as leader of the people.

Departure of the Israelites for the Promised Land. Death of Pharaoh in the Red Sea. On the left the Israelites, headed by Moses who stands between Aaron and Miriam, watch God's vengeance on the Egyptians. On the right Pharaoh and his host are submerged in the surging waters from which rises the pillar of fire which guided the Israelites. In the background across the water to the right Pharaoh is seen enthroned in front of his palace. This fresco is said to commemorate the victory (1482) of the Pope's troops over Alphonso of Naples, who had conspired against the papal throne.

Departure of the Israelites for the Promised Land.
Death of Pharaoh in the Red Sea. By Piero di Cosimo.

— 480 —

Photo Alinari, Anderson, Brogi.

ROME — *THE VATICAN. Sistine Chapel. (Right wall).*

The two series begin at the altar and end on the entrance wall with scenes of the Resurrection of Christ, and Contest for the body of Moses. The greatest interest of these pictures centres in the fine contemporary portraits introduced in the compositions. The three frescoes which had been painted on the altar wall — the Assumption of the Virgin, the Nativity and the Finding of Moses — were destroyed to make room for Michelangelo's "Last Judgment" (p. 476).

EVENTS IN THE LIFE OF CHRIST. (The new dispensation).

The Baptism of Christ in the Jordan. In the centre is the baptism, St. John pours water over the head of Christ, above whom hovers the Holy Ghost; higher up is the Eternal

Father blessing. Behind are three youths waiting their turn to receive the rite; in the background on the left St. John preaches to the people; on the right Christ on a cliff exhorts his listeners to repentance.

THE BAPTISM OF CHRIST IN THE JORDAN. *By* PINTORICCHIO.
Typifying the office of entrance into the Christian Church.

Cleansing of the Leper. Temptation of Christ. In front of a noble building stands a Jewish altar with the burning cedar-wood, on the right the leper supported by two friends is led to the altar, while his wife advances from the opposite side carrying a basket with the doves on her head. In the foreground the high-priest receives the sacrificial blood from an assistant. The scenes of the temptation of Christ are introduced in the background: on the left Satan disguised as a friar, proposes that Christ should turn the stones into bread; lower down Jesus descends a stairway closely followed by three angels; in the centre on the top of the building Satan invites the Saviour to cast himself down; on the right Christ commands the devil begone, while three angels place some food on a table.

The youth in white presenting the bowl is believed to represent the Church, and the High Priest the Synagogue. The building in the centre represents the Hospital of Santo Spirito finished under the pontificate of Sixtus IV. Among the spectators to the right are several portraits of members of the Confraternity of the Holy Ghost, instituted for the purpose of tending the sick.

CLEANSING OF THE LEPER. TEMPTATION OF CHRIST. *By* BOTTICELLI.
Typifying the ministry of Christ.

The Calling of the First Disciples. In the background to the left, Christ calls Peter and Andrew, who are drawing their nets; in the foreground they kneel before their Master. In the middle distance to the right Christ, attended by Peter and Andrew, summons James and John who sit in a boat which their father Zebedee backs

in from the lake. The Saviour and the four disciples are distinguished by haloes, all the other personages, about fifty, are supposed to be portraits of members of the Florentine colony then living in Rome; the fifth person in the front row to the right is Giovanni Tornabuoni, treasurer of the pope. In the distance is the Lake Tiberias between two ridges.

THE CALLING OF THE FIRST DISCIPLES.
Fresco by DOMENICO GHIRLANDAIO.

Photo ALINARI, ANDERSON, BROGI.

ROME — *THE VATICAN. Sistine Chapel. (Left wall.)*

Events in the Life of Moses. (The old dispensation).

The Giving of the Law. The Worship of the Golden Calf. Moses kneeling on Mount Sinai receives from God, who appears in a glory of an-

THE GIVING OF THE LAW. THE WORSHIP OF THE GOLDEN CALF.
Fresco by COSIMO ROSSELLI.

gels, the tables of the Law. In the centre Moses followed by Joshua is seen casting the tables to the ground at the sight of his people worshipping the golden calf. On the left of the picture Moses, with rays issuing from his head, once more attended by Joshua, presents the second tables to the people, who receive them with humility. In the background on the right is the scene of the punishment commanded by Moses.

Punishment of Korah, Dathan and Abiram. In the centre, Moses lifts his rod in indignation calling vengeance upon the rebellious Levites, who have come with censers, to dispute his authority, while Aaron with the triple tiara on his head, calmly swings his own censer and celebrates the appointed sacrifice. On the right, one of the blasphemers is going to be stoned; on the left, is the open abyss where the schismatics are swallowed up by the earth, while Eldad and Medad hover above and prophesy in the name of the Lord. In the rear is the Arch of Constantine.

PUNISHMENT OF KORAH, DATHAN AND ABIRAM. *By* BOTTICELLI.

Promulgation of the Law. Death of Moses. On the right raised upon a high seat Moses for the last time reads the Law to the Israelites. In the background an angel shows to Moses the distant Promised Land which he will not enter; he is seen descending the hill leaning upon his staff. On the left Joshua sorrowfully kneels before the aged Moses and receives from him the staff of office and the assurance that the Israelites shall enter the Promised Land. In the distance (left) the dead body of Moses, stretched on the ground, is bewailed by mourners. Moses, prophet and mediator, stands out as one of the greatest figures in history.

PROMULGATION OF THE LAW. DEATH OF MOSES. *By* SIGNORELLI.

Photo ALINARI, ANDERSON, BROGI.

ROME — THE VATICAN. *Sistine Chapel. (Right wall).*

EVENTS IN THE LIFE OF CHRIST. (The new dispensation).

Sermon on the Mount. Healing of the Leper. In the background on the hillside Christ followed by his disciples approaches; on the left standing on a hillock He preaches to the crowd of people gathered around; on the right the Saviour cleanses the leper who kneels and worships Him. The scene is peopled with graceful groups of attentive women and faces of lifelike serenity.

SERMON ON THE MOUNT. HEALING OF THE LEPER.
Fresco by COSIMO ROSSELLI.

Christ giving the keys to St. Peter. In the foreground Peter kneels reverently before Christ, who gives him the golden keys, the rest of the Apostles stand on either side; in the middle distance to the left of the spacious piazza is represented the payment of the tribute money (Matt. XVII. 24-27); on the opposite side are two episodes in which the Jews attempt to stone Christ. In the background is the Temple of Jerusalem and two triumphal arches.

CHRIST GIVING THE KEYS TO ST. PETER. *By* PERUGINO.
Typifying the divine institution of the priesthood.

The Last Supper. The scene is composed in the traditional form, Christ has gathered about Him for the last time, the twelve apostles. Judas sits in front of the curving table by himself, a little devil perched on his shoulders urges him to treason. On either side of the picture two personages have been introduced, on the floor are pots and pans and two cats playing. Beyond the open loggia are three scenes from the Passion: the Agony in the Garden of Olives, the Kiss of Judas and the Crucifixion.

THE LAST SUPPER. *Fresco by* COSIMO ROSSELLI.

— 483 —

Photo ALINARI, ANDERSON, BROGI.

ROME — THE VATICAN. Picture Gallery.

Phot. Faccioli, Rome]. With permission of the Vatican Museums].
SALA DI GIOTTO. Early Florentine School.

ST. NICOLAS DA BARI GIVES THREE BALLS OF GOLD TO THREE POOR GIRLS.
By GENTILE DA FABRIANO.

The *Pinacoteca* or Gallery of Pictures, recently transferred into a splendid new building expressly designed by the architect LUCA BELTRAMI for Pius XI., passes for a wonder, because it is composed of pictures amongst which are some of the world's masterpieces. Pius VII., who instituted it, placed there the pictures given back by the French (1815), most of which had been taken from churches during the invasion of the Papal States, and since that time the gallery was enriched by the addition of works from other papal collections and from suppressed convents.

The collection completely re-organized by its eminent Director, is of great interest to students of art, the pictures being wisely arranged according to school and order of time in the fifteen halls, the first two of which are set apart to works and altarpieces by the early Florentine and Sienese masters.

MADONNA AND CHILD.
By VITALE DA BOLOGNA.

GREAT ALTARPIECE from Old St. Peter's. *By* GIOTTO A. D. 1300.

ANGELS PLAYING. *Detail of a fresco by* MELOZZO DA FORLÌ.

Giotto's "Altarpiece," recently restored, was executed for the high altar of the old basilica of St. Peter's. On the front in the central panel, our Saviour enthroned in the act of benediction surrounded by adoring angels. At the feet of Christ, the kneeling figure of Cardinal Stefaneschi, nephew of Boniface VIII., for whom the work was executed in 1300. In the left panel, Crucifixion of St. Peter; in the right panel 'Decapitation of St. Paul.' On the predella is the Madonna enthroned between two angels holding censers, saints and apostles.

On the reverse side in the central panel, St. Peter attended by two angels sits in pontificals, holding the keys and giving his blessing; in the foreground to the left, St. George recommends the Cardinal Stefaneschi, who holds a model of the altarpiece itself, opposite two patron saints of the donor. In the side panels figures of SS. Andrew and John, James the Elder and Paul.

"This altarpiece alone would justify the assertion that Giotto was the founder of a school of colour, and that, in this respect, he was as great in pictures on wood as in fresco." Crowe and Cavalcaselle.

Photo ALINARI, ANDERSON, BROGI.

ST. FRANCIS *By* MARGHERITONE D'AREZZO. (XII sec.).

MADONNA ENTHRONED AND SAINTS. *By* GIOVANNI BONSI.

PERUGINO (1446-1524), owed much of the excellence of his works to the Florentine painters. He had an instinct for airy compositions, and golden, transparent colours, an exquisite sense of reverie and ecstasy. His figures show a graceful delicacy of attitude and a simplicity of expression.

MADONNA ENTHRONED AND SAINTS. Painted by PERUGINO. A. D. 1495.

This altarpiece painted for the church of San Pietro at Perugia, is one of the most valuable pictures in the gallery, alike for its own beauty and for its interest in the history of art.

SIXTUS IV. RECEIVING PLATINA. *Fresco by* MELOZZO DA FORLÌ.

Melozzo's fresco representing Sixtus IV. receiving Platina is one of the most interesting pieces of portraiture for it gives the likenesses of an important historical family. Near the Pope stand two of his nephews—Pietro Riario on the right of the papal chair, and facing him is Giuliano Della Rovere (afterwards Pope Julius II.). In the centre is the kneeling figure of Platina, Librarian of the Vatican, and the historian of the Popes. His face is that of a scholar; the finely-cut mouth, and abnormally square jaw denote the power of his will. Behind the librarian stand two other nephews of the Pope—Cardinal Giovanni Della Rovere and Girolamo Riario, who became celebrated in connection with the conspiracy of the Pazzi. These personages are treated with a master hand and the beauty of the picture is enhanced by the architectural background.

— 485 —

Photo ALINARI, ANDERSON, BROGI.

ROME — THE VATICAN. Picture Gallery.

The "Coronation of the Virgin," one of RAPHAEL's early works, was painted for the church of San Francesco at Perugia, and for many years it passed as a work by Perugino. In the lower part are the twelve Apostles gathered round the Virgin's tomb, and having found only lilies and roses they are gazing heavenwards. In the centre, between SS. Paul and Peter, the Apostle Thomas is seen holding the sacred girdle which the Virgin dropped him while ascending to heaven. In the upper part the Virgin, surrounded by lovely angels, her hands joined in adoration, is receiving the crown from the hands of her Son.

In the *predella*: Annunciation, Adoration of the Magi, Purification.

RAPHAEL'S "Madonna di Foligno," was originally placed over the high altar in the church of Ara Cœli. It was painted for Sigismondo Conti, secretary of Julius II., as a votive offering in gratitude of his escape during a bombardment of Foligno. In the distance is a view of Foligno, into which a bomb falls; to the right St. Jerome presents Sigismondo Conti to the Madonna, to the left St. Francis of Assisi and St. John the Baptist.

CORONATION OF THE VIRGIN.
Altarpiece by RAPHAEL.

MADONNA DI FOLIGNO. *By* RAPHAEL. A. D. 1512.

PIETÀ.
By GIOVANNI BELLINI.

CRUCIFIXION OF ST. PETER.
By GUIDO RENI.

THE VISION OF ST. ROMUALDO.
By ANDREA SACCHI.

MADONNA.
By SASSOFERRATO.

ANDREA SACCHI'S picture of the "Vision of St. Romualdo," is a far famed work. The Saint seated under a large tree is in the act of relating a vision (represented in the background) to a group of five brother monks: "in a dream he saw a ladder resting on the earth, and the top of it reaching to heaven; and the brethren of his Order ascending by twos and by threes."

MARRIAGE OF ST. CATHERINE. *By* MURILLO.

ADORATIONS OF THE SHEPHERDS. *By* MURILLO.

Photo ALINARI, ANDERSON, BROGI.

— 486 —

ROME — THE VATICAN. Picture Gallery.

The "Transfiguration," is Raphael's last great work. It was left unfinished at the time of his death and completed about 1522. The composition and the upper part of the picture are by Raphael's own hand; the lower part was executed by Francesco Penni and Giulio Romano. Above is Christ hovering between Moses (left) and Elias; Peter, James and John prostrate on the summit of Mount Thabor, hide their eyes from the dazzling heavenly light. Below are the other apostles who are being requested to heal a boy possessed of a devil. For 300 years this picture was on the high-altar of the church of San Pietro in Montorio (p. 439).

The ‹Entombment› is one of CARAVAGGIO's best works, powerfully painted, but devoid in religious expression. The contrast of vivid light and deep shadow is very striking. The sorrowful figure of Mary, exausted with weeping, has seldom been surpassed.

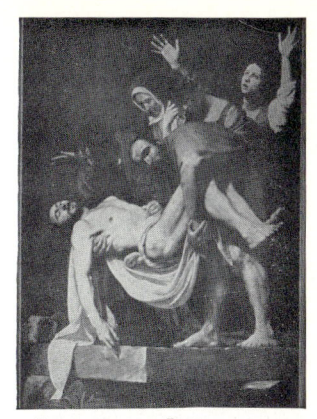

THE TRANSFIGURATION. By RAPHAEL and GIULIO ROMANO.

ENTOMBMENT. By CARAVAGGIO.

ANNUNCIATION. By BAROCCI.

BAROCCI's works have considerable resemblance to those of Correggio in delicacy of light and shade. 'His pencil may be said to have been dedicated to religion: so devout, are the sentiments expressed in his pictures.'

MADONNA OF S. NICCOLÒ DE' FRARI.
By TITIAN. A. D. 1523.

COMMUNION OF ST. JEROME.
By DOMENICHINO.

The picture of St. Jerome, one of the three works by LEONARDO that remain in Italy, has been long admired as a study of movement. 'Alone in the desert, the Saint has literally lost himself in God.... his body has become, as it were, a mere shadow.'

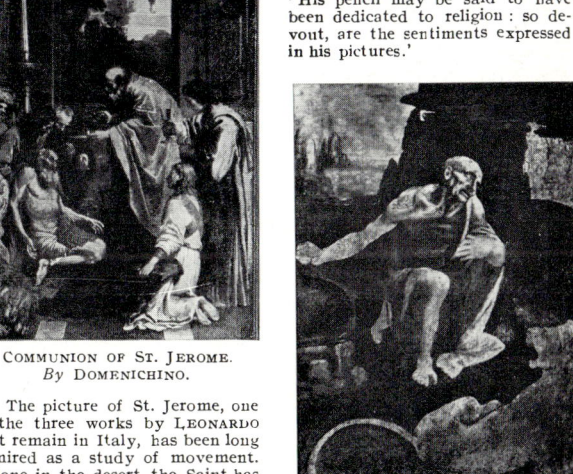

ST. JEROME with the Lion.
By LEONARDO DA VINCI.

— 487 —

Photo ALINARI, ANDERSON, BROGI.

Among the treasures of the Vatican, Raphael's Tapestries are not the least important. They are nine in number and are displayed (together with another series) in the *Galleria degli Arazzi*, Pinac. Vaticana (1933).

In the years 1515-16, Raphael made ten designs or cartoons for tapestries which Leo X. intended to hang on the lower, unpainted part of the walls in the Sistine Chapel. The tapestries from these cartoons were executed at Brussels, under the direction of Bernard van Orley, a pupil of Raphael, who had returned to his native country, and they were used for the first time in the Sistine Chapel on December 26th 1519, when they excited widespread enthusiasm. After that, the tapestries suffered many vicissitudes. During the Sack of Rome (1527), they were carried off and seriously injured, but some twenty years later found

THE MIRACULOUS DRAUGHT OF FISHES.

their way back to the Vatican. In 1798, they were again carried off by the French and were sold to a Genoese Jew who burned one of them for the purpose of extracting the gold and silver threads used in the weaving. The experiment, fortunately, was not successful and in 1808 the remainder were repurchased by Pius VII. They are now sadly dilapidated, but the beauty of their execution and the compositions are among the marvels of our art. The subjects of the principal scenes were chosen from the lives of the Apostles Peter and Paul, the joint founders of the Roman Church. The decorations on the side borders represent allegories of the Virtues, the Seasons, the Fates, the Constellations, etc. The bronze colour borders below the tapestries that deal with St. Peter illustrate events in the life of Leo X. until his election to the

THE DEATH OF ANANIAS.

pontificate; those below the St. Paul tapestries represent further incidents in the life of that apostle. All these decorations were designed by Giovanni da Udine, Raphael's pupil.

The principal scenes are: Christ giving the keys to St. Peter—« Feed my Lambs ». The Healing of the Lame Man. Sacrifice at Lystra. St. Paul preaching at Athens. The Death of Ananias. Conversion of St. Paul. The Miraculous draught of Fishes. St. Paul in prison at Philippi. The Blinding of Elymas.

The original cartoons themselves remained at Brussels, serving as models for several series. Seven of these were seen in the manufactory in 1630 by Rubens, who recognized their worth, and effected their purchase for King Charles I. of England; they are now exhibited in the South Kensington Museum, the others have disappeared.

ST. PAUL PREACHING AT ATHENS.

— 487A —

THE MIRACOLOUS DRAJGHT OF FISHES. (Detail).

ROME — GALLERIA BORGHESE.

VIEW OF THE CASINO OF THE VILLA BORGHESE.

The *Villa Borghese*, now officially styled "Villa Umberto Primo," is a magnificent park laid out in the 17th cent. by Cardinal Scipio Borghese and placed at the disposal of the people of Rome. In 1902 it was purchased by the state and handed over to the City of Rome. The Villa which is now connected with the Pincian gardens forms one great public park.

THE GREAT HALL or SALONE (*Ground Floor*).

The floor of the great hall is inlaid with ancient mosaics of gladiators in action, interesting for the equipment and weapons of the combatants. The large fresco on the ceiling, executed by MARIANO ROSSI, represents the Dictator M. Furius Camillus at the Capitol interrupting the peaceparley with the Gallic chief Brennus (389 B. C.).

The *Casino*, formerly used as a summer residence by Cardinal Scipio Borghese, consists of two floors; the lower one containing ancient and modern sculptures, the upper the important picture gallery removed from the Palazzo Borghese.

The present collection of antiques, assembled here by Prince Camillo Borghese in 1820, after his marriage with Pauline Bonaparte, to replace an earlier and more valuable collection purchased by Napoleon and sent to the Louvre, consists largely of sculptures found in exploring the vast Borghese estates.

HALL OF PAULINE BORGHESE.
(*Ground Floor*).

PRINCESS PAULINE BORGHESE *sister of Napoleon I. as Venus Victrix.* By CANOVA (1757-1822).

Among the modern statuary are several works by BERNINI, and the reclining statue of Pauline, who as queen of Beauty, holds the golden apple triumphantly. It is one of CANOVA's best works thanks to the beauty of his most celebrated model.

RAPE OF PROSERPINE.   APOLLO AND DAPHNE.   DAVID. (The sculptor's portrait).    ÆNEAS AND ANCHISES.
Marble sculptures by GIAN LORENZO BERNINI (1598-1680).

— 488 —

Photo ALINARI, ANDERSON, BROGI.

ROME. GALLERIA BORGHESE

Holy Family. *By* Andrea del Sarto.

ROME. — GALLERIA BORGHESE. First Floor.

MADONNA AND CHILD AND ST. JOHN.
By LORENZO DI CREDI.

PORTRAIT OF CARDINAL CERVINI.
By PONTORMO.

MADONNA AND CHILD AND ANGELS
By SANDRO BOTTICELLI.

The Infant Jesus is holding a pomegranate in his left hand. " All Sandro's poetic sentiment," writes Signor Venturi, " inspires this painting, all the tenderness of his soul is expressed in the attitudes of the charming youthful figures which surround the noble group. The hands of these angels do not touch but they seem to caress the things they touch. The background is a piece of garden trellis.

This is one of the most beautiful works of the *gentilissimo* Florentine master."

THE GREAT HALL (*First floor*).
Ceiling: Council of the gods.
By LANFRANCO.

The *Borghese Gallery*, located on the first floor, contains one of the finest collections of paintings in Rome. In spite of the removal of several of its treasures, one of the principal merits of the collection is that it includes examples of almost every school and particularly works by Ferrarese masters of the sixteenth century.

But the gem of the gallery is Titians' so-called « Sacred and Profane Love », the masterpiece of the painter's youthful period and one of those poetic creations that produce an indelible impression upon the beholder.

CHRIST BLESSING.
By MARCO DA OGGIONE.

THE ENTOMBMENT. *By* RAPHAEL.

Painted at Perugia in A. D. 1507 when Raphael was only twenty-four years of age; it is the last picture he painted before coming to Rome. The execution is extremely beautiful, the action powerful, the expression of the heads and the modelling of Christ's body are perfect. The predella is in the Vatican.

The work has a touching story; it was painted for Atalanta Baglioni, to be set over the tomb of her murdered son, the tyrant Astorre.

PORTRAIT
By RAPHAEL.

HOLY FAMILY.
By ANDREA DEL SARTO.

THE SORCERESS CIRCE.
By DOSSO DOSSI.

VENUS.
By A. DEL BRESCIANINO.

Photo ALINARI, ANDERSON, BROGI.

62. - *WONDERS OF ITALY.*

ROME — GALLERIA BORGHESE.

ST. JEROME. *By* BAROCCI.

SIBYL. *By* DOMENICHINO.

MADONNA AND CHILD. *By* C. DOLCI.

MADONNA. *By* CARAVAGGIO.

MADONNA. *By* FRANCIA.

THE CHASE OF DIANA. *By* DOMENICHINO.

The Chase of Diana, or Nymphus Bathing and Shooting. This is one of the famous works of the master; full of charm and with plenty of animation everywhere. It represents Diana and her Nymphs enjoying themselves — some of the maidens are shooting at a mark, while others are bathing. The goddess herself with her arms raised is in the act of applauding. Safe a few ingenious variations all the nymphs appear to have been portrayed from the same model.

"The picture shows indeed neither quite pure forms nor Venetian fullness of life", writes Burckhardt, "but splendid motives, and a truly idyllic character".

PORTRAIT. *By* ANT. DA MESSINA.

ST. DOMINIC. *By* TITIAN.

ST. STEPHEN. *By* FRANCIA.

Photo ALINARI, ANDERSON, BROGI.

ROME — GALLERIA BORGHESE.

SACRED AND PROFANE LOVE. (*Amor Sacro e Profano or Earthly and Heavenly Love*). By TITIAN (ca. 1515).

This exquisite allegorical picture in which the influence of Giorgione may be traced, is one of the most fascinating of Titian's early productions. The name by which it is now known does not explain its symbolism very clearly; possibly it represents Venus persuading Helen to listen to Paris, or, Helen inducing Medea to follow Jason... "The charm of such works," writes Vernon Lee, "is that they are never explicit; they tell us, like music, deep secrets, which we feel but cannot translate into words." The superb nude figure holding aloft a burning lamp is meant for Heavenly Love.

"The meaning of the picture," writes Burckhardt, "is exemplified in all possible ways: the complete covering of the one figure, even with gloves; the plucked rose; on the sarcophagus of the stream, the bas-relief of a Cupid wakened out of sleep by Genii with blows from their whips; the rabbits; the pair of lovers in the distance. It is perhaps only an allegory, but of a rare kind, in which the allegorical sense which can be expressed is lost in comparison with an inexpressible poetry".

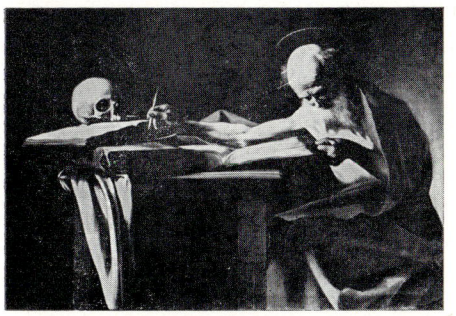

ST. JEROME. *By* CARAVAGGIO.

The Three Graces. A work of great originality and rich colouring. Venus is in the act of bandaging the eyes of her son, while attendant nymphs hold his bow and arrow.

ST. ANTHONY PREACHING TO THE FISHES. *By* P. VERONESE.

THE THREE GRACES, *by* TITIAN (1565).

DANAË WITH CUPIDS, *by* CORREGGIO.

The "Danae" remains the most *correggiesque* of Correggio's pictures. The aërial perspective and the chiaroscuro of this panel are admirable. The head of the daughter of the king of Argos is imitated from that of the Medici Venus, but the painter has given her a more youthful figure, and an expression of ingenue pleasure.

— 491 —

Photo ALINARI, ANDERSON, BROGI.

ROME — *THE FARNESINA. Myth of Psyche.*

1. **Venus pointing out Psyche to Cupid** with contempt directing him to plunge her into an unworthy passion.

10. **The Banquet** by which the gods celebrate the marriage of Psyche.

2. **Cupid showing Psyche to the Graces.**    3. **Venus, Ceres and Juno.**    4. **Venus ascending to Olympus.**

The *Galatea* (in a saloon adjoining the entrance hall), was executed by RAPHAEL himself in 1514. The « goddess of the sea » is borne over the waves in a shell; tritons and sea-nymphs sport joyously around her while Cupid discharge their arrows from above. ' The utmost sweetness, the most ardent sense of pleasure, breathe from the work; everything lives, feels, vibrates with enjoyment.'

While working at this picture Raphael is reported as saying: that he could do nothing with models, but relied on the idea of beauty which occurred to him spontaneously.

The Galatea. *By* **Raphael.**

The « FARNESINA », built in 1508-1511, was the gay summer residence of the Papal banker Agostino Chigi, an enthusiastic admirer of art and patron of Raphael. On the ceiling of a large hall which serves for vestibule there are twelve fascinating frescoes displaying the famous fable of Cupid and Psyche in a light and airy series, most graceful in conception and treatment. The whole composition was designed and begun by RAPHAEL in 1517, and then executed by his pupils *Giulio Romano, Francesco Penni* and *Giovanni da Udine*. On the flat part of the ceiling two large pictures represent the Council of the Gods, who decide the dispute between Venus and Cupid, and the Marriage of Psyche; the accessory subjects, illustrative of the incidents in the fable, are distributed in the pendentives. Raphael was indebted for his version of the myth to the famous work of Apuleius, much read during the Renaissance period, and which may be briefly recounted as follows : A certain king has three daughters, of whom, Psyche, the youngest, excited by her beauty the jealousy and envy of Venus. In order to avenge herself, the goddess bids her son Cupid to inspire Psyche with a love for the most contemptible of all men : but Cupid is so stricken with her beauty that he becomes enamoured of her and shows her to the Graces. He visits her by night only, warning her to repress her curiosity as to his appearance. But instigated by her envious sisters, Psyche disobeys the injunction. While Cupid sleeps she lights a lamp and looks upon him, and, to her amazament, beholds the most handsome and lovely of the gods. In the excitement of joy and fear, a drop of heated oil falls from her lamp on his shoulder and awakens her lover who upbraids her for her mistrust and quits her in anger.

— 492 —

ROME — THE FARNESINA. *Myth of Psyche.*

8. Mercury carrying Psyche to Olympus where she will become immortal and be reunited with Cupid for ever.

9. COUNCIL OF THE GODS before whom Venus and Cupid plead their causes.

5. Venus complaining to Jupiter.  6. Mercury flying in search of Psyche.  7. Psyche presenting Venus with the box of Proserpine.

Psyche left alone wanders about filled with despair. Venus in the meantime informed of her son's attachement, imprisons him, and seeks assistance from Ceres and Juno to find Psyche, but they refuse to aid her. She then goes to complain to Jupiter, imploring him to send Mercury to her assistance. Jupiter listens to her prayer and sends forth Mercury to seek for Psyche, whom Venus now ill-treats in every conceivable manner, imposing upon her the hardest and most humiliating labours. Finally she is ordered to bring Proserpina's casket from the infernal regions, and even this, with the invisible assistance of Cupid, she succeeds in accomplishing. Cupid, escaped from captivity, begs Jupiter to grant him Psyche. Jupiter embraces the irresistible infant and commands Mercury summon the gods to deliberate and to conduct Psyche to Olympus, where she will become immortal and be united to her lover for ever.

In this pleasing story Psyche is the symbol of the human soul, which is purified by passions and misfortunes, and thus prepared for the enjoyment of true and pure happiness.

In spite of restorations the frescoes produce a charming and brilliant effect owing to the indestructible beauty of the designs, which are among the most charming creations of the master. Though Pagan in sentiment, and naturally in accordance with the tastes of the age, the scenes are neither coarse nor sensual; a nobility of proportion, never overstepping the bounds of refinement, being preserved throughout the series.

THE MARRIAGE OF ALEXANDER AND ROXANA. *By* SODOMA (1512).
Alexander conducted by Cupids to the nuptial couch of Roxana offers her a crown.

— 493 —

Photo ALINARI, ANDERSON.

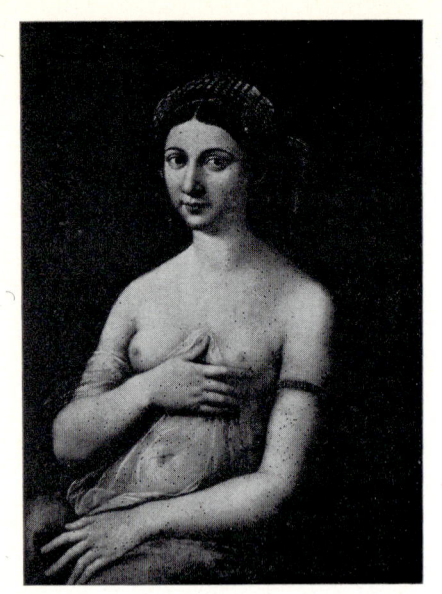

ROME — GALLERIA NAZIONALE D'ARTE ANTICA. (Barberini).

«LA FORNARINA».
By RAPHAEL.

TRIPTYCH. By FRA ANGELICO.

The triptych by Fra Angelico shows *in the central panel* the Last Judgment: above, the Saviour makes the sublime gesture that decrees the end of the world; below, the open empty tombs, to the right the Condemned, most of them monks, are hurried to hell by a devil, to the left the Blessed look up to the Saviour. *In the left panel* is the Ascension of Christ; *in the right panel* the Descent of the Holy Ghost.

THE WOMAN TAKEN IN ADULTERY. *By* TINTORETTO.

The Barberini Palace houses part of the collection of the National Gallery of Ancient Art, which was founded in 1895 uniting the Corsini and Torlonia collections, and was later considerably increased. Here are exhibited works from the 13th up to the 16th centuries and, in the last two rooms, some important paintings from the following centuries.

MARY MAGDALENE.
By PIERO DI COSIMO.

ERASM OF ROTTERDAM. *By* METSYS.

HENRY VIII. OF ENGLAND. *By* HOLBEIN.

PHILIP II. OF SPAIN.
By TITIAN.

Photo ALINARI, ANDERSON, BROGI.

ROMA — GALLERIA NAZIONALE D'ARTE ANTICA (Corsini), CASINO ROSPIGLIOSI.

The *Palazzo Corsini* was built in the 15th century for the Riario family from whom it was acquired by Clement XII, in 1739, for his nephew Card. Neri Corsini whose name it has always retained. The palace was purchased by the State in 1884 and became the seat of the *Accademia Nazionale dei Lincei*, of the *Biblioteca Corsiniana* and of the *Galleria Nazionale d'Arte Antica*. This one fills twelve rooms and saloons with a collection of Italian paintings of the 17th and 18th centuries and with an important group of foreign works.

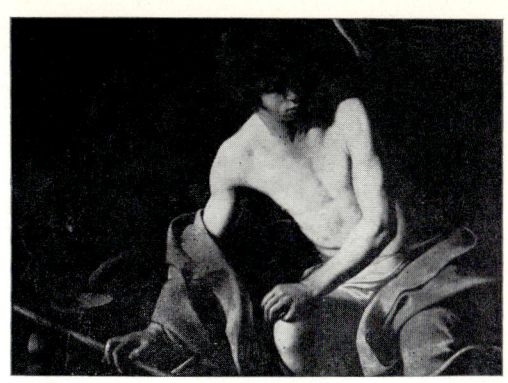

BEATRICE CENCI. *Attribuited* to G. RENI.

ST. JOHN THE BAPTIST. *By* CARAVAGGIO.

The portrait of Beatrice Cenci, whose lovely face and large brown eyes meet those of the spectator, is thus in part described by Shelley: "There is a fixed and pale composure upon the features; she seems sad and stricken down in spirit, yet the despair thus expressed is lightened by the patience of gentleness. Her head is bound with folds of white drapery from which the yellow strings of her golden hair escape, and fall about her neck. The moulding of her face is exquisitely delicate; the eyebrows are distinct and arched; the lips have that permanent meaning of imagination and sensibility which suffering has not repressed, and which it seems as if death scarcely could extinguish.... In the whole mien there is a simplicity and dignity which, united with her exquisite loveliness and deep sorrow, is inexpressibly pathetic."

« ECCE HOMO ». *By* GUERCINO.

SAINT AGNES. *By* CARLO DOLCI. (*Painting in the Corsini Gallery*).

MADONNA AND CHILD. *By* CARLO DOLCI.

PORTRAIT OF BERNINI. *By* BACICCIA.

AURORA. *Fresco by* GUIDO RENI. *Ceiling of the hall of the Casino Rospigliosi.*

The "Aurora," is one of the most beautiful works of the master. Apollo, the god of the sun, is seated on his chariot drawn by four fiery steeds; to the right Aurora (Dawn) is arising into the air and is throwing flowers before the chariot of Apollo. Seven female figures are dancing gracefully around the chariot; they are the Hours that pass. Above the horses a little cupid with a flaming torch represents Lucifer, or the morning star. "There is nothing gracefully or more delicately painted, than this fresco in which nature and the love of the antique combine with poetry to ennoble the subject...."
The *Rospigliosi-Pallavicini Palace*, was built in 1603 by Cardinal Scipione Borghese on the site of the Baths of Constantine. Later it belonged to the Bentivoglio family and to Cardinal Mazarin. The French Embassy was here until 1704.

Photo ALINARI, ANDERSON, BROGI.

ROME — GALLERIA DORIA.

THE DAUGHTER OF HERODIAS with the head of John the Baptist. *By* TITIAN.

HALL OF THE MIRRORS in the Doria Gallery.

The *Doria Gallery*, is situated in the Palazzo Doria-Pamphili, the most magnificent perhaps of the Roman palaces, erected at the end of the 15th and reconstructed in the 17th century.

The gallery contains numerous fine pictures of the different schools of painting, partly collected by Donna Olympia Maldachini, sister-in-law of Pope Innocent X., partly acquired in the time of the great admiral Andrea Doria of Genoa (p. 32).

DOUBLE PORTRAIT (*Detail*). *By* RAPHAEL.

THE ANNUNCIATION. *By* FRA FILIPPO LIPPI.
[A distinguished scholar of Lippi was Botticelli].

POPE INNOCENT X. *By* VELASQUEZ.

This world-renowned picture, painted in 1650, surpasses all other portraits produced in the same century.

The Pope was high in complexion: his ruddy skin, seeming to shine with moisture, stands forth as in a blaze from a hood of red satin with a purple-coloured background. The skilful manner in which the various reds are blended, the *life* which circulates under the features.... give to this portrait a superior rank.

PORTRAIT OF ANDREA DORIA. *By* SEBASTIANO DEL PIOMBO.

It is the masterwork of Sebastiano's portraits. Its largeness worthy of Michelangelo is joined to a deep expression of the admiral's personality.... a remarkable work and one of the most lifelike portraits.

THE REST ON THE FLIGHT TO EGYPT. *By* CARAVAGGIO.

LANDSCAPE. *By* CLAUDE LORRAIN.

JOANNA OF ARAGON. *By* LEONARDO.

THE "MILL." *By* CLAUDE LORRAIN.

— 496 —

ROME — GALLERIA COLONNA.

VENUS. (IL "GIORNO"). By VASARI.

GREAT HALL OF THE COLONNA GALLERY.

The *Colonna Gallery* was founded in 1572, to consecrate the glory of Marc'Antonio Colonna, who commanded the papal fleet against the Turks at the Battle of Lepanto (1571). The collection comprises many important paintings and numerous family portraits of the highest value. The Palazzo Colonna, one of the oldest and finest in Rome, was begun by Pope Martin V. (Colonna), in 1430, and completed in the 17th and 18th cent. The great hall, 150 ft. long, hung with mirrors upon which are painted children and flowers, is gorgeously decorated with bas-reliefs, statues and frescoes illustrating the battle of Lepanto.

The princely Colonna family is famous as one of the most powerful of the great Roman families; some of its members rose in eminence as generals, prelates and statesmen in the service of the Church or other powers. The popes Marcellinus, Sixtus III., and Adrian III., are said to have belonged to this family; a detailed record of which would be a history of Rome.

PORTRAIT OF VITTORIA COLONNA, poetess and friend of Michelangelo. By G. MUZIANO.

PORTRAIT OF MARIA MANCINI. By NETSCHER.

GUIDOBALDO of URBINO. By GIOVANNI SANTI.

(*Portraits in the Colonna Gallery*).

JAMES, DUKE OF YORK. (Called "The Baby Stuart").

CALYPSO. (*School of Titian*).

THE VIOLINIST. By RAPHAEL (1518).

VANITY. (*School of Titian*).

(*Accademia di San Luca, founded in 1577 by F. Zuccari*).

— 497 —

Photo ALINARI, ANDERSON, BROGI.

63. - *WONDERS OF ITALY*.

ROME — THE MUSEUMS. Villa Giulia. Villa Albani.

CISTA FICORONI.

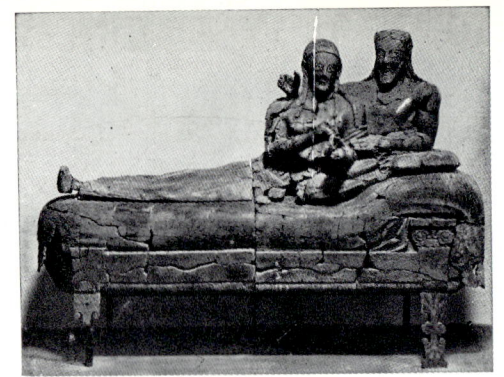

ETRUSCAN SARCOPHAGUS of Cerveteri.

APOLLO OF VEII.

THE VILLA GIULIA.

Built by *Vignola* from 1550 to 1555 as a pleasure house of Pope Julius III., the *Villa Giulia* contains since 1889 a museum of pre-Roman antiquities brought from the Necropolis of Veius, of Falerius, of Praeneste etc. There are to be found sarcophagi of terra-cotta, Greek and Italic vases, vessels, caskets, statuettes, busts and other objects discovered in the Etruscan tombs; including the famous Cista Ficoroni found at Praeneste.

THE VILLA GIULIA. Built in 1555, for Pope Julius III.

MODEL OF ETRUSCAN TEMPLE.

MINERVA.    ORPHEUS AND EURYDICE.    ANTINOUS.
Ancient sculptures in the Villa Albani.

The *Villa Albani*, was built about the year 1759 for Cardinal Albani, a great lover and connoisseur of antiquities, who gathered together here under the direction of his friend Winckelmann an important collection of statues, busts, bas-reliefs and other ancient monuments. A large number of the statues were taken to Paris by order of Napoleon I., and instead of being returned to Rome they were sold to the "glyptotheca" of Munich; nevertheless this villa may be regarded as a rich museum of antiquities. The ceiling of the Great Hall has an admirable fresco representing the *Parnassus: Apollo and the Muses*, by Raphael Mengs.

VESTIBULE OF THE VILLA ALBANI.

APOLLO AND THE MUSES. By RAPHAEL MENGS. *Ceiling of the Great Hall.*

Photo ALINARI, ANDERSON, BROGI.

APOLLO OF VEII, (*Detail*). About 500 B. C.

ROME — CASTEL SANT'ANGELO. *Papal Apartments.*

HALL OF THE COUNCIL.

CHEMICAL LABORATORY AND PHARMACY. 17th cent.

Story of Cupid and Psyche.

Story of Cupid and Psyche.

BEDROOM OF POPE PAUL III. (Farnese).

The *Castel Sant'Angelo* is connected with the Vatican by a corridor built by Alexander VI., intended for the escape of the Popes to the castle, *e. g.* in 1494 on the occasion of the invasion of Charles VIII.; in 1527 during the sack of Rome; etc.

The Papal apartments commenced by Alexander VI. and completed by Paul III. consist of a series of beautifully decorated rooms which no visitor to Rome should fail to see. The Library or Reception Room is embellished with frescoes by various pupils of the school of Raphael; the ceiling is moulded in gilt and painted stucco. Another room has a frieze representing the story of Perseus by Perin del Vaga. The Council Room, decorated by the same artist, illustrates the life of Alexander the Great. The bedroom of Paul III. has a gorgeous carved and gilded ceiling and a frieze painted by Perin del Vaga representing scenes from the story of Cupid and Psyche. Beneath the Papal apartments are the dungeons in which Beatrice Cenci and many others were incarcerated. In 1538, Benvenuto Cellini was thrown in one of these dungeons as a prisoner of state. He was accused of having stolen jewels belonging to the Apostolic treasury.

Fragment of the frieze and gilded stucco mouldings, in the Library or Reception Room.

Photo ALINARI, ANDERSON, BROGI.

ROME — NATIONAL MUSEUM. Museo delle Terme.

MERCURIUS FACUNDUS.
School of Myron.

ANCIENT SARCOPHAGUS WITH RELIEFS OF THE MYTH OF JASON AND MEDEA.

The *National Museum* or *Museo delle Terme*, situated in a part of the Baths of Diocletian was founded (1899) to house the ancient remains unearthed in Rome since 1870. The magnificent collection, enlarged by the antiquities from the Boncompagni-Ludovisi Collection, is rich in matchless masterpieces and rivals the largest museums in the world.

A BRIDE burning incense.

SLEEPING ERINYS. Medusa

THE BIRTH OF VENUS. *Fifth century* B. C.
Ancient marble known as the Ludovisi throne.

The *Ludovisi Throne*, as it is called, appears to be composed of the sides and the back of a great marble throne or altar. It is one of the most interesting Greek works of the last century of the Archaic Period. On the back can be seen Aphrodite who is arising out of the foam of the sea and is supported by two nymphs; desire and joy are expressed on the face of the goddess. On one side of the throne is a naked young girl who plays on her flute the praises of love; on the other side a young bride closely draped drops some incense in a brazier in honour of Venus.

HEAD OF A GODDESS.
Marble of the 5th cent. B. C.

ROMAN GIRL.
3rd cent. B. C.

GAUL AND HIS WIFE.
3rd cent. B. C.

MARS RESTING.
After LYSIPPUS.

JUNO LUDOVISI.
Greek, 4th cent. B. C.

APOLLO WITH THE LYRE.
Colossal statue.

BACCHUS AND SATYR.
(*Praxiteles*).

— 501 —

ROME — NATIONAL MUSEUM. Museo delle Terme.

DAUGHTER OF NIOBE.
School of Cresilas, 5th cent. B.

VENUS GENETRIX.
Found on the Palatine.

APHRODITE OF CNIDOS.
School of Praxiteles.

SATYR POURING WINE.
After Praxiteles.

The statue of a *Daughter of Niobe* (Niob de) found in the "Orti Sallustiani" is remarkable for its touching expression of anguish seen on her face. She has just been pierced in her back by an arrow shot by Apollo and she is seen sinking to the ground; she is making with her arms a desperate effort to draw the arrow out of her body. In that position her cloak falls down and leaves nearly all her beautiful body uncovered.

The *Venus of Cyrene*, represents the goddess who has just emerged from the sea and is arranging her hair. There is so much warmth in that exquisite marble flesh, so much grace that whil contemplating it, the lovely figure seems to come to life.

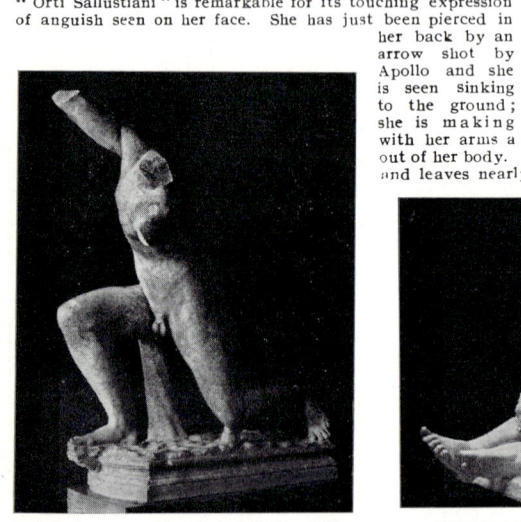

EPHEBUS OF SUBIACO. *From the Villa of Nero.*

STATUE OF A YOUTH RESTING. (ADONIS).

VENUS OF CYRENE.
School of Praxiteles.
4th cent. B. C.

ORESTE and ELECTRA.
School of Pasiteles.

THE GREAT CARTHUSIAN CLOISTERS.
Constructed in 1565 from designs by Michelangelo.

The *Cloisters*, are supported by 100 Doric columns. Under the arcades are many sculptures. A cypress tree said to have been planted by Michelangelo died in 1909.

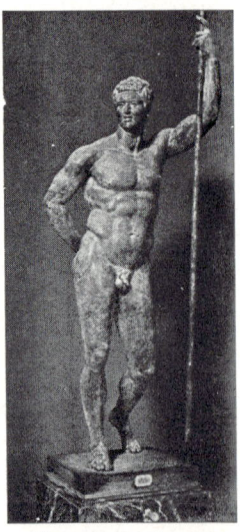

HELLENISTIC PRINCE
Greek bronze.

— 502 —

Photo ALINARI, ANDERSON, BROGI.

ROME — NATIONAL MUSEUM. Museo delle Terme.

The *Pugilist Resting* is a very beautiful specimen of the Hellenistic period, found during the construction of the Teatro Nazionale. The man of strong physique has just finished his fight; exhausted, he has sunk down heavily; he looks at the crowd around him or talks to a friend. His face is bruised and wounded by the blows of his opponent, his nose is swollen and blood flows from his open wounds. His hands are bound with long strips of leather, tied by metal fasteners. All the marks of his rough trade are chiselled with intense realism. It is a magnificent bronze work of the third century B. C. signed by Apollonius who is also the author of the Torso of the Belvedere.

THE PUGILIST.
Bronze 1st cent. A. D.

DANCING GIRL.
5th cent. B. C.

STATUE OF APOLLO.
Found in the Tiber.

THE DISCOBOLUS OF MYRON.
(*Plaster cast reconstruction*).

MUSE or NYMPH. *Hellenic art of the 3rd cent.* B. C.
These marbles were found on the Palatino.

THE MAIDEN OF ANTIUM.
Greek. 4th cent. B. C.

The *Maiden of Antium*, found in 1878 at Porto d'Anzio, is a masterpiece of Greek Art; the sculptor seems to have belonged to the school of Lysippus and to have left the influence of Praxiteles. She carries on a tray offerings for an act of adoration; her attitude is full of reverence for the ceremony she is performing.

« VESTALIS MAXIMA »
From the House of the Vestals.

ALTAR FROM OSTIA.
Marble of the Flavian period.

BACCHUS. *Bronze of 2nd cent.* B. C. *found in the Tiber.*

ROME — THE CAPITOL.

APPROACH TO THE CAPITOLINE HILL AND THE SENATOR'S PALACE.

THE EMPEROR MARCUS AURELIUS.

The *Capitoline* is the smallest but the most famous of Rome's Seven Hills. It was the stronghold and the religious centre of the ancient city. It consisted of a rocky platform, rising above the Forum valley, accessible only from it and having precipitous cliffs on every other side. There was a depression in the middle (the present piazza), while the extremities rose into two elevations upon which stood the *Arx* or citadel and the *Temple of Juno Moneta* (the site is now occupied by the church of Aracœli) and the great *Temple of Jupiter Capitolinus* (the site on which the Pal. Caffarelli now stands). On the slope towards the Forum was the *Tabularium* or record-office. This edifice, still standing, was used in the 13th cent. for the erection of the *Senator's Palace* which originally overlooked the Forum and, then as now, was used by the municipal administration. In 1536 on the occasion of the entry of Charles V. in Rome, Michelangelo was charged with the embellishment of the Capitol. He began by opening the grand staircase shown in our illustration, which gives access to the piazza above from the side opposite that of the Forum ; altered the Senator's palace by making a new façade towards the piazza, in the centre of which he placed the *Equestrian Statue of emp. Marcus Aurelius* (formerly near the Lateran), and designed the two side palaces (the *Capitoline* and the *Conservatori*) erected after his death. Thus, it may be said that Michelangelo reversed the Capitol and it now presents a magnificent aspect. Half-way up the staircase on the left is a bronze statue of Cola di Rienzi, who was killed by the mob near this spot ; and cages with eagles and a she-wolf to commemorate the legendary origin of Rome. On the summit right and left by the balustrade are colossal statues of Castor and Pollux standing beside their horses, found in the Ghetto, near the theatre of Balbus ; adjoining them are the so-called "Trophies of Marius" ; statues of Constantine and his son Constans ; and two milestones. The staircase on the left of our illustration leads up to the Church of Aracœli (p. 437). An inscription there states that the expenses for the construction of the steps, in 1348, were defrayed by charitable contributions. The Pope's absence from Rome (the Holy See had been removed to Avignon, where it remained till 1377), explains the necessity of private enterprise.

THE WOLF of the Capitol (5th cent. B. C.). The twins, Romulus and Remus are by A. POLLAIUOLO. (15th cent.).

THE SENATOR'S PALACE. Designed by Michelangelo.

1. Triumphal entry into Rome.   2. Sacrifice to Jupiter.   3. Conquered enemies pardoned.
Ancient reliefs representing events in the life of the emperor Marcus Aurelius.

THORN EXTRACTOR. Græco-Roman bronze.

The three reliefs reproduced above, now in the *Palazzo dei Conservatori*, belonged to a monument erected in honour o Marcus Aurelius on the occasion of the victories he gained on the Germanic barbarians near the Danube in 167-175. The events they represent are analogous to those sculptured on the Aurelian column (p. 395), and belong to the same series as the eight panels on the attic of the Arch of Constantine (p. 401). 1. Marcus Aurelius accompanied by Victory rides in a chariot adorned with splendid reliefs ; the figure behind the horses is an impersonation of the *Populus Romanus*. 2. Marcus with head veiled, stands in front of a tripod throwing incense in the flames ; to the right the sacrificial attendant with his axe, leading the bull. 3. The Emperor, riding with the prefect Bassæus at his side, receives the submission of two conquered chieftains.

Photo ALINARI, ANDERSON, BROGI.

ROME — *PALAZZO DEI CONSERVATORI*

HALL OF THE PUNIC WARS or SALA DI ANNIBALE.

GREAT HALL OF THE HORATII AND CURIATII.

The *Palazzo dei Conservatori* (of the town-councillors), contains a fine collection of ancient sculptures, bronzes and other works of art together with various important objects found in recent times in street making in the city and its neighbourhood.

On the first floor are the *Halls of the Conservators* (Town-Councillors) and the *New Capitoline Museum*. On the second is the *Picture Gallery* founded by pope Benedict XIV., and containing a number of valuable works of art.

The *Halls of the Conservators*, consist of eight rooms most of which adorned with historical frescoes and other objects of art. In one of the halls are fragments of the *Fasti Consularis*, or lists of Roman consuls and generals who had celebrated a triumph, found near the Regia (p. 399); another hall (Sala di Annibale) illustrated here, is painted with scenes from the Punic Wars: the great hall, given above, has a coffered ceiling and frescoes representing the Combat of the Horatii and Curiatii, the Finding of Romulus and Remus, the Foundation of Rome, the Rape of the Sabines, and other episodes from the history of Rome under the early kings.

ROMULUS AND REMUS. *By* RUBENS.

ST. SEBASTIAN. *By* GUIDO RENI.

The RAPE OF EUROPA. *By* PAOLO VERONESE.

PRESENTATION AT THE TEMPLE. *Attributed to* F. FRANCIA *and formerly to* FRA BARTOLOMEO.

MARSYAS ready to be flayed.

CHARLES I. OF ANJOU King of Naples and Sicily.

VENUS known as the Esquiline Venus

The statue of Charles of Anjou, the Nero of the Middle Ages, is the only medieval portrait statue in Rome, and of high historical value. It is roughly sculptured, the expression of the face stolid and coarse, but its lineaments are individual.

Charles, who was the brother of St. Louis, King of France, came to Rome in 1265 to be invested with the Senatorial office, and the following year, after defeating king Manfred the bastard of Frederick II. at Benevento, he was crowned King of Sicily. Then at the battle of Tagliacozzo, in 1268, he defeated the youthful Conradin, Frederick's grandson, put him to death and became king of Naples; but owing to his cruelties he lost his kingdom after the terrible tragedy of the Sicilian Vespers, in 1280.

Photo ALINARI, ANDERSON, BROGI.

— 505 —

ROME — CAPITOLINE MUSEUM.

LAUGHING SILENUS in red marble. *From a Greek bronze.*

THE CAPITOLINE MUSEUM.
Built under Innocent X., from Michelangelo's designs.

The *Capitoline Museum*, was founded by Clement XII., and augmented by Benedict XIV., Clement XIII., Pius VI. and other popes. Besides many admirable ancient masterpieces the museum contains a unique collection of portrait busts of members of the various imperial families and other celebrities.

MINERVA (Cfr. with the Minerva on p. 454).

ANTINOUS. *Ancient sculpture.*

HALL OF THE DYING GAUL.
(Sala del Gladiatore).

SATYR OR FAUN.
By PRAXITELES.

This is the *Marble Faun* of Hawthorne's beautiful romance.
" The whole statue " he writes, " unlike anything else that ever wa wrought in the severe material of marble, conveys the idea of an amiable and sensual creature, easy, mirthful, apt for jollity, yet not incapable of being touched by pathos."

THE DYING GAUL (2nd or 1st cent. B. C.).

This is probably an original work by an artist of Pergamus and likely belonged to a group which was placed on the *Acropolis* at Athens by Attalus I. of Pergamus to commemorate certain victories upon the Gallic hordes which had invaded Asia Minor. It represents a warrior, mortally wounded, sitting on his shield ; the blood pours from his wounded breast, his head sinks forward, his eyes are dim with pain, the lips half parted by a sigh : his whole expression and pose is of an absolutely tragic realism. It is a work at once realistic and pathetic.

PERSEUS delivering Andromeda.
*Marble relief
from a Greek original*

— 506 —

Photo ALINARI, ANDERSON, BROGI.

ROME — CAPITOLINE MUSEUM.

EROS WITH THE BOW.

CUPID AND PSYCHE.

GREEK PHILOSOPHER.

VENUS OF THE CAPITOL.

The celebrated *Venus of the Capitol,* regarded as the perfect type of feminine grace, is reminiscent of the Medici Venus and derives from the Cnidian Aphrodite of PRAXITELES. She is represented in the act of stepping into the bath after having laid aside her last garment. By an involuntary impulse of womanly modesty she covers her lap and bosom with her hands, while her head turns shyly to one side.

'HALL OF THE EMPERORS'.
(Sala Imperatori).

The valuable Collection of busts which forms one of the attractions of the museum has been arranged, according to etiquette, in two distinct salons.
In one of them are 84 busts of Roman emperors, empresses and their near relatives; the most remarkable are—besides the Cæsars—those of Agrippina, wife of Germanicus; Messalina, third wife of Claudius; Poppæa, Nero's second wife; Julia, daughter of Titus; Plotina, wife of Trajan; Julia Sabina, wife of Hadrian; Lucilla, wife of Lucius Verus; Faustina the Elder, and many others.

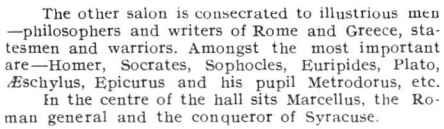

The other salon is consecrated to illustrious men —philosophers and writers of Rome and Greece, statesmen and warriors. Amongst the most important are—Homer, Socrates, Sophocles, Euripides, Plato, Æschylus, Epicurus and his pupil Metrodorus, etc.
In the centre of the hall sits Marcellus, the Roman general and the conqueror of Syracuse.

DRUNKEN OLD WOMAN.
The expression of rapture on the face of the *old woman,* who is clasping with arms and legs her friend, a corpulent amphora, has been wonderfully rendered,

MARCELLUS of Syracuse. Roman general.

PORTRAIT OF A ROMAN LADY.

DOVES. *Mosaic.*
The celebrated mosaic of the *Four doves on a basin of water,* imitated from that of Pergamus which Pliny so much admired, was found in Hadrian's Villa in the year 1737.

BUSTS OF ROMAN EMPERORS. *Capitoline Museum.*

This magnificent statue of a seated matron, with head-dress set with pearls, called *Agrippina,* is but the portrait of an unknown Roman lady. It is a work from an original of the 5th century, particularly interesting for the pose and for the skilful arrangement of the drapery.

— 507 —

Photo ALINARI, ANDERSON, BROGI.

ROME — THE PALACES.

The massive and imposing *Palazzo Venezia*, was built, with stones taken from the Colosseum, about the year 1445, probably on the plans of Leon Battista Alberti, for Cardinal Pietro Barbo who became Pope in 1464 under the name of Paul II. Here he placed his collections of works of art and made it his principal residence. Many Popes took up their abode here, and Charles VIII., King of France, lived here in 1494. Pope Pius IV., gave it to the Republic of Venice to be the residence of the Ambassador to the Holy See; in 1797 it became the Austrian Embassy, and since 1916 it has belonged to the State.

THE PALAZZO VENEZIA. *Begun in 1445.*

POMPEY THE GREAT.
Ancient statue. Palazzo Spada.

The *Palazzo Spada* was built under the papacy of Paul III., according to the plans of MAZZONI. The façade, by BORROMINI, is decorated with statues and ornaments intermingled with bas-reliefs in plaster: the other walls are decorated in the same way. The building was bought by the State in 1926, it is now the meeting-place of the Italian Council of State. The most interesting feature in this palace is the famous statue (11 ft. high) of Pompey holding the globe, found in 1552; it is supposed to be the same one that was in the Curia, at the foot of which the great Julius Cæsar was assassinated.

THE PALAZZO SPADA. *Begun. in 1550.*

BUST and relief representing the *fasces* in the courtyard of the Massimi alle Colonne Palace.

The *Palazzo Massimi alle Colonne*, is a masterpiece of the Renaissance of Rome. It was built according to the plans of BALDASSARE PERUZZI about the year 1534, who, in order to follow the curve in the road, built a circular façade, reinforced by six gilt columns. The very picturesque courtyard is decorated with bas-reliefs in plaster and old statues. The *fasces* or tied rods seen in the relief reproduced above were the emblem of supreme power in ancient Rome.

The Court.   THE PALAZZO DELLA CANCELLERIA. *15th century.*   The Façade.

COURT OF PALAZZO MASSIMI ALLE COLONNE.
Begun in 1532 by BALDASSARE PERUZZI.

The *Palazzo della Cancelleria*, is the noblest example of early Renaissance architecture. The façade is built with blocks of travertine taken from the Colosseum. The beautiful two-storied arcade of the court is a distinctive feature of Italian fifteenth century palaces. This palace, according to the Lateran Treaty of 1929, is the property of the Holy See.

The *Palazzo Barberini*, one of the most imposing, contains the Barberini Gallery (p. 494).

PALAZZO BARBERINI.
Begun in 1624. Baroque façade by MADERNO.

Photo ALINARI, ANDERSON, BROGI.

— 508 —

ROME — THE PALACES.

CHRIST IN A GLORY. By MELOZZO.

THE PALAZZO DEL QUIRINALE. *Begun in 1574.*

PRINCIPAL PORTAL. By BERNINI.

The *Quirinal Palace*, the residence of the Kings of Italy since 1870, was begun towards 1574 by Pope Gregory XIII., on the ruins of Constantine's Baths, from designs by FLAMINIO PONZIO. It was continued and enlarged by DOMENICO FONTANA, CARLO MADERNO, BERNINI, etc. In summer it was the residence of the Popes. On the Grand Staircase there is a magnificent fresco by MELOZZO, representing "Christ in a cloud of Angels," once in the church of Santi Apostoli. The *Sala Regia* is decorated by a frieze painted by Lanfranco and Saraceni; at the side is the *Pauline Chapel* built in the same shape and dimensions as the Sistine Chapel. In front of the palace there are two colossal statues: the Horse Tamers, belonging to the Thermæ of Constantine, attributed to Phidias and Praxiteles, and an obelisk erected by Pius VI. in 1787.

THE SALA REGIA. (State Apartments).

THE THRONE ROOM.

TRIUMPH OF BACCHUS AND ARIADNE. By A. CARRACCI. (Farnese Palace).

THE FARNESE PALACE. *Begun in 1512.*

PALAZZO TORLONIA. *Attributed to* BRAMANTE. 1496.

The *Farnese Palace*, the residence of the French Embassy, is one of the most beautiful in Rome. Begun in 1512 by Cardinal Farnese who became Pope Paul III., according to the plans of ANTONIO DA SANGALLO, it was continued under the direction of MICHELANGELO and completed by GIACOMO DELLA PORTA. Stones from the Colosseum and the Theatre of Marcellus were used in its construction. The magnificent Banqueting Hall is decorated with mythological scenes the work of ANNIBALE CARRACCI and his pupils. The large painting in the centre is given above.

COURT of the Farnese Palace.

— 509 —

Photo ALINARI, ANDERSON, BROGI.

ROME — THE PALACES, THE MONUMENTS.

Monument to Cola di Rienzi. By Masini.

Monument to Garibaldi. Erected in 1895. By Gallori.

Monument to Goethe. By Eberlein. Figures from Goethe's poems.

Fountain of the Acqua Paola. Erected by Fontana in A. D. 1611 by order of Paul V., with pillars from Old St. Peter's.

The Scala di Spagna (Spanish Steps).

The Academy of France. Villa Medici.

The *Piazza di Spagna (Spanish Square)* takes its name from the Palazzo di Spagna which is situated here; it is the residence of the Spanish embassy to the Holy See since the 17th cent. The Grand Staircase (137 steps), illustrated here, leads to the terrace of the church of *Santa Trinità dei Monti* (page 436). It was built 1725 at the expense of M. Gouffier, the French Ambassador in Rome. At the foot of the steps, there is a quaint fountain shaped like a boat, called the *Barcaccia*. To the south, stands the column of the *Immacolata*, erected by Pope Pius IX, in the year 1854, to commemorate the proclamation of the Dogma of the Immaculate Conception.

This palace, situated in a charming position on the Pincian hill, was built in the 16th century for cardinal Ricci da Montepulciano. Later, it became the property of the Grand Dukes of Tuscany, it was called the "Villa Medici."
In 1803 Napoleon bought it and transferred here the Academy of Fine Arts, founded by Colbert in 1665 during the reign of Louis XIV. The young French artists came here after winning in Paris the "grand prix" of painting, sculpture, architecture, engraving, and musical composition, to acquire greater proficiency in three years. The perimeter of the garden is two kilometres. Messalina took refuge and was killed in the woods beyond.

Court of the Mattei palace. 17th cent.

Palazzo Chigi. Begun in 1562, by Giacomo della Porta and completed by Carlo Maderno
(now the seat of the Ministry of Foreign Affairs). The beautiful marble fountain in the foreground is the work of Giacomo della Porta.

Palazzo Montecitorio. Begun in 1650 by Bernini.

— 510 —

Photo Alinari, Anderson, Brogi.

ROME — THE FOUNTAINS.

FONTANA DEL TRITONE. *By* BERNINI.

The *Fontana del Tritone*, is the most original of the fountains of Rome: four dolphins solidly bound together form a base for the basin, a large granite shell on which sits a vigorous Triton who blows from his conch into the sky a stream of water falling round like a shower of pearls.

FONTANA DELLE TARTARUGHE.
By GIACOMO DELLA PORTA (1585).

It is the most beautiful of the fountains. Leaning against the small original basin, are four charming bronze figures of youths, holding with hand and foot a dolphin, while with the other hand they push the tortoises to drink in the upper basin. The movement is at first almost invisible; but it is creates with such art as to impart life to the whole. The four bronze figures of the youths are the work of the Florentine *Taddeo Landini*.

FONTANA DI TREVI (Centra :part). *Erected in 1735.*

Rome is the city of fountains. The *Fontana di Trevi*, erected by order of Pope Clement XII. in 1735, is the largest and most celebrated of the public fountains in Rome. Tradition goes that if on the eve of departure from Rome you throw a coin into the water, you cannot remain absent from Rome for ever; destiny will bring you back. Fountains are to be seen everywhere in Rome; wherever one goes he hears the pleasant sound of babbling waters. On every piazza, fountains, embellished with sculptures, elaborate marble basins, o belisks, etc., spirt and splash streams of pure waters.

FONTANA DI PIAZZA NAVONA. *Designed by* BERNINI.

ACQUA FELICE. *By* DOMENICO FONTANA.

— 511 —

ROME — THE ENVIRONS. Frascati. Tivoli.

Only fifteen miles from Rome is FRASCATI, charmingly situated on a slope of the Tusculan hills It is a favourite resort of the Roman nobility and is famous for its beautiful, shady 16th century villas commanding glorious views of the vast Roman Campagna. Nothing can describe the charm of these villas: Aldobrandini, Falconieri, Mondragone, Torlonia, Ruffinella....

TUSCULUM, the birthplace of Cato, and which Cicero made so famous by his *Tusculan Disputations* and other works; is within a short distance of Frascati.

TIVOLI: TEMPLE OF THE SIBYL.

FRASCATI: VILLA ALDOBRANDINI. A. D. 1603.

THE WATERFALLS OF TIVOLI.

TIVOLI, the ancient *Tibur*, according to tradition was built by the Sicules over 400 years before the foundation of Rome. When Camillus conquered it in 380 B. C. he had some famous temples built: the temples of the Sibyl, Vesta, and Hercules.

Under Augustus it became the pleasure resort of the Romans. Many famous people had villas here, amongst whom Mæcenas, Sallust, Cassius, Catullus, Propertius, Horace.... Zenobia, the famous queen of Palmyra, was imprisoned here. Under Hadrian the city enjoyed its greatest prosperity, but later it was sacked by the barbarians.

RUINS OF HADRIANS' VILLA AT TIVOLI.

The *Villa "Adriana,"* was the favourite residence of the Emperor Hadrian. The emperor, on his return from his travels in the Empire, so as to remember those places that had impressed him most in Greece and Egypt, had exact reproductions in miniature made of the monuments he had so much admired, and filled them with statues which he had brought back from these different countries for instance: the Lyceum, and the Pecile of Athens, the Valley of Tempe, and even Hades, according to the imagination of the poets. There were Theatres, Baths, Temples, a road and a magnificent Imperial Palace.

Photo ALINARI, ANDERSON, BROGI.

TIVOLI. THE VILLA D'ESTE.

    This is one o fthe finest villas of the Renaissance period, and was built in 1549 from design by PIRRO LIGORIO for Cardinal d'Este. The unfinished Casino is decorated with frescoes by the ZUCCARO Brothers; the park laid out in terraces on the hillside, though neglected, is magnificent in its beauty and affords many picturesque points of view. Its grottoes of mosaic where water drips in drops, its ruined ornamental fountains, its pieces of green water filled with lotus, the lofty cypresses all around, the ilexes... lend a strange charm to the villa and produces the impression o fa palace of romance and adventure.

ROME — THE ENVIRONS

FRASCATI: VILLA ALDOBRANDINI.
Built in 1603 by order of Cardinal Aldobrandini from designs by GIACOMO DELLA PORTA.

FRASCATI: VILLA MONDRAGONE.

Frascati is charmingly situated on a slope of the Tusculan hills. It is a favourite resort of the Roman nobility and is famous for its beautiful, shady and well-watered sixteenth century Villas, commanding glorious views of the vast Roman Campagna. Nothing can describe the charm of these villas, Villa Aldobrandini, Villa Falconieri, Villa Mondragone, Villa Torlonia, Villa Ruffinella.... Tusculum. birthplace of Cato and which Cicero made so famous, is within a short distance of Frascati.

FRASCATI: VILLA ALDOBRANDINI.

FRASCATI: VILLA TORLONIA.

CAPRAROLA: VILLA FARNESE.

TARQUINIA: PALAZZO VITELLESCHI. *Gothic style.*

The Palazzo Farnese at Caprarola, and the Villa Lante near Viterbo, are two of the most magnificent chateaux of the Renaissance period built by VIGNOLA.

Photo ALINARI, ANDERSON, BROGI.

CIVITA CASTELLANA: THE CATHEDRAL. *Portico by L. Cosmato (1210).*

The *Cathedral* of CIVITA CASTELLANA, wose origin is very ancient, was probably rebuilt in the 11th century; the façade, with a great portico, divided into two parts by a central archway, is the work of Jacopo di Lorenzo and his sons (1210). The central archway, shaped like a triumphal arch, is a brilliant forerunner of the Renaissance in its classical form.

TUSCANIA, which is given a definitely Medieval character by the towers and ruins of the old Castle, has ancient churches: the *Church of San Pietro* and the one of *Santa Maria Maggiore* already existing in the 8th century, but rebuilt after the year 1000 according to the architectural ideas of the Lombard master. The two churches were in the first place part of two monasteries then became bishop's sees; they are also like each other in structure, although Santa Maria Maggiore, flanked by a powerful bell-tower, is more balanced and harmonious in its lines.

TUSCANIA. Church of San Pietro.
Erected in the 8th cent. and restored in 1040.

The upper part of the façade is covered with figures of men, devils and beasts in high relief; within, the church is a veritable museum of Pagan fragments.

TUSCANIA. Santa Maria Maggiore.
Erected in 8th cent. and rebuilt in the 12th cent.

The columns separating the nave from the aisles have capitals carved in the rude style of the 9th century; the pulpit has reliefs of the same period.

Photo ALINARI, ANDERSON, BROGI.

VITERBO — THE PALACE OF THE POPES (1266) AND THE LOGGIA (1267).

VITERBO. This little town in Latium hardly existed before the Middle Ages, but from the 11th century onwards its importance increased and in the following century the Popes took to living there. Of several conclaves held in this town the most famous still remains the one preceding the election of Gregory X which lasted two years and ten months. On that occasions, the Captain of the People, following the advice of St. Bonaventura, locked up all the cardinals in the palace, had the roof of their meeting room removed and at the same time cut short their food supplies. The marks of the roof having been taken off, the holes made in the floor for the cardinals' tent-pegs are still visible. Ten years later, on account of the imprisonment of two cardinals by the daring citizens, the Papal Court, that had brought prosperity to the town, removed itself from Viterbo.

In the grand Romanesque churches, built between the 11th and 12th centuries, the architects expressed their preference for the ancient basilica form of church. The *Cathedral*, built round about 1192, is a splendid example of this return to classical forms. But the buildings that have survived best are the Medieval Gothic ones, which reveal a new conception of the Gothic style that produces spectacular contrasts of light and shade. The most wonderful works of these Gothic architects are the *Palace of the Popes* (1266), which is largely occupied by an immense hall, and its ancient *Loggia* (1267) where the multi-coloured marbles add to the picturesqueness of its appearance. The Alessandri Palace, the Marzatosti and the Farnese ones, the numerous houses with an outside staircase shaped like a balcony, stand as witnesses of a school of architects full of original ideas that flourished until the 15th century.

In the year 1271, during the celebration of Mass the cathedral of Viterbo was the scene of an awful deed. Here Guy de Montfort, son of Earl Simon of Leicester, and viceroy in Tuscany for Charles of Anjou, assassinated Henry of Cornwall, nephew of Henry III. to avenge the death of his father at the battle of Evesham in 1265, where his body had been despitefully treated. The heart of the murdered prince Henry was put in a golden cup and brought to Westminster Abbey, where it was placed near the shrine of Edward the Confessor, † 1066.

THE CATHEDRAL, *built in 1192*.

LATIUM: SUBIACO, ANAGNI, FOSSANOVA, OSTIA.

SUBIACO. VIEW OF THE MONASTERY.

Upper church of "Il Sacro Speco".

Subiaco, about 45 miles from Rome, was the cradle of Western monasticism. Around the end of the 5th century St. Benedict retired to live in a cava near Subiaco, now one of the chapels of the *Sacro Speco*, and here, a few years later, founded the Orders of the Benedictines. The present buildings are of the 12th and 13th centuries.

EPISCOPAL THRONE. *By* VASSALLECTUS. 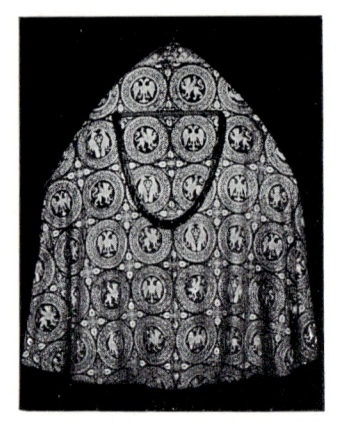 DALMATIC (COPE) OF BONIFACE VIII.
(*Cathedral of Anagni*).

Anagni, only a few miles from Rome, in the middle ages was frequently a papal residence. The cathedral founded in 1074 has a beautiful mosaic pavement, one of the first examples of Cosmatesque work. In the choir is a bishop's throne and a fine candelabrum dating from 1263. The church contains also ancient papal vestments and a statue of Pope Boniface VIII., born at Anagni.

In the year 1303 the quarrel between the Pope and King Philip le Bel of France came to a head. Boniface had come to Anagni intending to excommunicate the king from the cathedral, but on the night of Sept. 7th 1303 the partisan of Philip le Bel entered Anagni, attacked the Papal palace, and forced their way into the presence of Boniface, whom they found seated on his throne wearing the tiara and the papal robes. The angry men dragged him off his throne and attempted to strike him. After being kept prisoner for three days, Boniface was liberated by the people and taken back to Rome where he died a month later.

CHURCH OF FOSSANOVA.
Erected A. D. 1187-1208.

OSTIA. PIAZZALE DELLE CORPORAZIONI.
MOSAIC BEFORE THE « CELLA » OF MERCHANTS OF CORN.

The Church (and Abbey) of Fossanova, is situated along the Appian Way, between Rome and Terracina. It was built on the plans of the early Cistercian abbeys of France by monks from Clairvaux. In the Middle Ages it was a much frequented halting place for travellers who were hospitably received by the monks. St. Thomas Aquinas died here in 1274.

According to tradition *Ostia Antica*, the most important harbour of ancient Rome, was founded in the 7th century B. C. Together with the principals monuments of the town, like the Theatre, the Thermae and the Forum, also the *piazzale delle Corporazioni* is very interesting; it was surrounded by arcades divided in *cellae* which formed the offices of the roman commercial representations or guilds.

— 516 —

Photo ALINARI, ANDERSON, BROGI.

BAY OF NAPLES: NISIDA.

CAMPANIA

NAPLES
POMPEII SORRENTO CAPRI AMALFI RAVELLO PAESTUM

CLOISTER OF THE CARTHUSIANS.
Monastery of San Martino.

Photo ALINARI, FOTOCELERE.

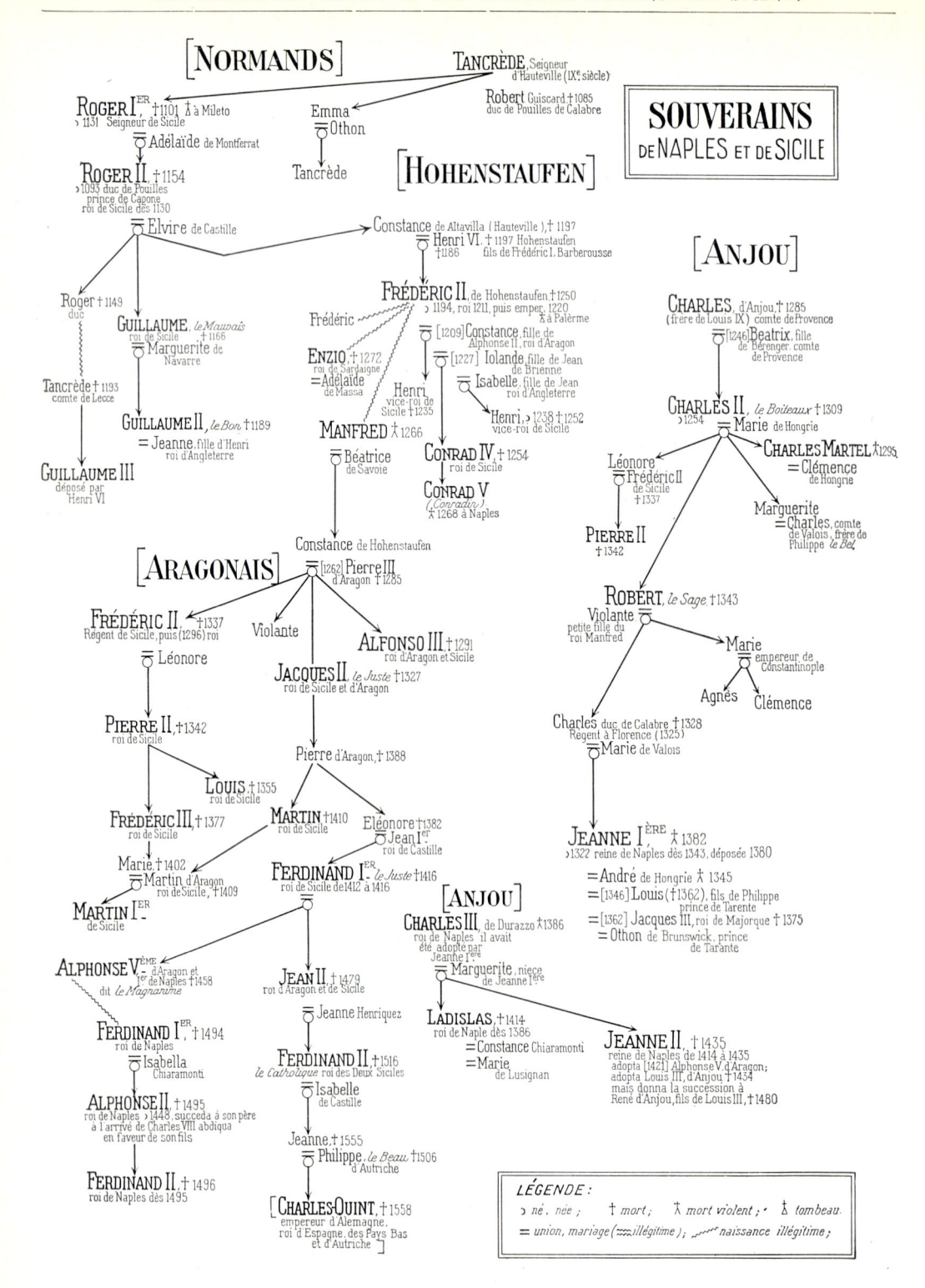

GENEALOGICAL CHART OF THE KINGS OF NAPLES AND SICILY.

SOUVERAINS DE NAPLES ET DE SICILE

[NORMANDS]

TANCRÈDE, Seigneur d'Hauteville (IXe siècle)
- Robert Guiscard †1085, duc de Pouilles de Calabre
- ROGER Ier †1101 ☩ à Mileto, ›1131 Seigneur de Sicile
  = Adélaïde de Montferrat
- Emma = Othon
  - Tancrède

ROGER II †1154, ›1095 duc de Pouilles, prince de Capone, roi de Sicile dès 1130
= Elvire de Castille

- Roger †1149, duc
- GUILLAUME, le Mauvais, roi de Sicile †1166
  = Marguerite de Navarre
- Tancrède †1193, comte de Lecce
- GUILLAUME II, le Bon †1189
  = Jeanne, fille d'Henri, roi d'Angleterre
- GUILLAUME III, déposé par Henri VI

[HOHENSTAUFEN]

Constance de Altavilla (Hauteville), †1197
= Henri VI †1197 Hohenstaufen †1186 fils de Frédéric I. Barberousse

FRÉDÉRIC II, de Hohenstaufen †1250, ›1194, roi 1211, puis emper. 1220, ☩ 1250 à Palerme
- Frédéric
- ENZIO, †1272, roi de Sardaigne = Adélaïde de Massa
- [1209] Constance, fille de Alphonse II, roi d'Aragon
- [1227] Iolande, fille de Jean de Brienne
  - Henri, vice-roi de Sicile †1253
- Isabelle, fille de Jean roi d'Angleterre
  - Henri, ›1238 †1252, vice-roi de Sicile

MANFRED ☩ 1266
= Béatrice de Savoie
- Constance de Hohenstaufen

CONRAD IV †1254, roi de Sicile
- CONRAD V (Conradin) ☩ 1268 à Naples

[ARAGONAIS]

[1262] Pierre III d'Aragon †1285
- FRÉDÉRIC II †1337, Régent de Sicile, puis (1296) roi
  = Léonore
  - PIERRE II †1342, roi de Sicile
    - FRÉDÉRIC III †1377, roi de Sicile
      - Marie †1402
        = Martin d'Aragon roi de Sicile, †1409
        - MARTIN Ier de Sicile
- Violante
- ALFONSO III †1291, roi d'Aragon et de Sicile
- JACQUES II, le Juste †1327, roi de Sicile et d'Aragon
  - Pierre d'Aragon, †1388
    - LOUIS †1355, roi de Sicile
    - MARTIN †1410, roi de Sicile
      = Eléonore †1382
      = Jean Ier de Castille
    - FERDINAND Ier, le Juste †1416, roi de Sicile de 1412 à 1416

ALPHONSE Vème d'Aragon et Ier de Naples †1458, dit le Magnanime

FERDINAND Ier †1494, roi de Naples
= Isabella Chiaramonti
- ALPHONSE II †1495, roi de Naples, ›1448, succéda à son père, à l'arrivée de Charles VIII abdiqua en faveur de son fils
  - FERDINAND II †1496, roi de Naples dès 1495

JEAN II †1479, roi d'Aragon et de Sicile
= Jeanne Henriquez
- FERDINAND II †1516, le Catholique roi des Deux Siciles
  = Isabelle de Castille
  - Jeanne, †1555
    = Philippe, le Beau †1506 d'Autriche
    - CHARLES-QUINT, †1558, empereur d'Alemagne, roi d'Espagne, des Pays Bas et d'Autriche

[ANJOU]

CHARLES, d'Anjou, †1285, (frère de Louis IX) comte de Provence
= [1246] Beatrix, fille de Bérenger, comte de Provence

CHARLES II, le Boiteaux †1309, ›1254
= Marie de Hongrie
- CHARLES MARTEL ☩ 1295
  = Clémence de Hongrie
- Marguerite
  = Charles, comte de Valois, frère de Philippe le Bel
- Léonore
  = Frédéric II de Sicile †1337
  - PIERRE II †1342

ROBERT, le Sage †1343
= Violante, petite fille du roi Manfred
- Marie
  = empereur de Constantinople
  - Agnès
  - Clémence
- Charles duc de Calabre †1328, Régent à Florence (1325)
  = Marie de Valois
  - JEANNE Ière ☩ 1382, ›1322 reine de Naples dès 1343, déposée 1380
    = André de Hongrie ☩ 1345
    = [1346] Louis (†1362), fils de Philippe prince de Tarente
    = [1362] Jacques III, roi de Majorque †1375
    = Othon de Brunswick, prince de Tarente

[ANJOU]

CHARLES III, de Durazzo ☩ 1386, roi de Naples "il avait été adopté par Jeanne Ière"
= Marguerite, nièce de Jeanne Ière
- LADISLAS, †1414, roi de Naple dès 1386
  = Constance Chiaramonti
  = Marie de Lusignan
- JEANNE II, †1435, reine de Naples de 1414 à 1435, adopta [1421] Alphonse V d'Aragon; adopta Louis III, d'Anjou †1434 mais donna la succession à René d'Anjou, fils de Louis III, †1480

LÉGENDE:
› né, née ; † mort ; ☩ mort violent ;· ⚰ tombeau.
= union, mariage (≈≈ illégitime); ⌐ naissance illégitime ;

— 518 —

NAPLES: VIA CARACCIOLO AND VIEW OF MERGELLINA.

NAPLES

HISTORICAL SKETCH

FOUNTAIN FIGURE.
Bronze from Herculaneum.

THE origin of this celebrated city is ascribed to a Greek colony from Cumæ, a town of great antiquity founded in 1056 B. C. by Æolians from Chalcis in Eubœa. In 326 B. C. the city was conquered by the Romans and rose rapidly into importance, but the Greek language and customs prevailed till the end of the imperial age. During this last period the favorite winter residences of the Roman nobility were in her neighbourhood, and the names of the most celebrated poets are connected with her history. Virgil composed some of his most beautiful poetry here; Augustus often sojourned here while the emperors Tiberius, Claudius, Nero, Titus and Hadrian were among the chief benefactors of Naples.

In 536 A. D. the town was captured by Belisarius and again by the Goths a few years later. But the citizens soon threw off their yoke and contrived to maintain their independence till 1130, when, after a long siege, the city succumbed to the Normans. From that time the history of Naples, like that of most of the Italian states, is replete with incidents of long and fearful contention. Discord and revolution followed in turn; no dynasty being sufficiently long established on the throne to settle the affections of the people in its favor. Frederick II. (1212-50) of Hohenstaufen was followed by the Angevin dynasty (1268-1442); and again by the Spanish House of Aragon (1442-1503), and the Spanish viceroys (1504-1707). After the Spanish war of succession Naples fell under the domination of Austria (1713), and at the close of the Austrian war of succession, to the Bourbons (1743). For another century Naples was the scene of incessant revolts and disturbances, but with Garibaldi's triumphal entry at the head of the valorous Piedmontese troops in 1860 Naples was finally annexed to the Kingdom of Italy.

— 519 —

Photo ALINARI, FOTOCELERE.

NAPLES — *THE CITY*.

View of Naples, the Bay and Mount Vesuvius.

The Castel dell'Ovo seen from Via Caracciolo.

The wonderful Mediterranean coast offers no lovelier feature than the Bay of Naples — one of the maritime gateways to Italy — and the approach to it by sea, has a fascination all its own.

Naples itself occupies one of the finest situations in the world, at the base and on the slopes of a range of hills which rise in an amphitheatre on the north shore of the magnificent Bay. The beauty of the city as seen from the sea is incomparable and today it possesses the same fascination that she had when Cicero and Lucullus built their villas here, and when the potentates of Greece and Rome left their capitals to pass their days in indolence and luxury upon her shores.

The Stock Exchange. Corso Umberto I.
The beautiful fountain in the centre dates from 1595.

Piazza Trieste e Trento.
From this square to the Museum runs Via Roma (Toledo), the principal street of Naples opened in 1570 by the Viceroy Don Pedro de Toledo.

— 520 —

Photo ANDERSON, FOTOCELERE.

NAPLES — *THE CITY*.

THE MONASTERY OF SAN MARTINO (ON THE HILL) SEEN FROM THE HARBOUR.

Naples offers attractions as a permanent residence at all times of the year; its delightful climate, its azure skies, its warm and bright sunshine in winter and refreshing sea-breezes of summer have long been sung. There are very instructive hours to be spent in visiting the old churches replete with Gothic monuments; long mornings and afternoons amidst the endless galleries of the National Museum filled with the antiquities of Pompeii and Herculaneum; beautiful drives along the sea-front and over the hills affording the most glorious views over bay and mountains. Finally, what could be more attractive than the numerous excursions to the Environs of Naples? Sorrento, Amalfi, Ravello: those dazzling cities basking in sunshine; the islands of Capri and Ischia rising from waters of sapphire and presenting a truly magic aspect.

MONUMENT TO VICTOR EMMANUEL II. († 1878).
Executed by FRANCESCHI *and* LEONE.

GALLERIA UMBERTO I. (The " Arcade ").
Built in 1887-90 from designs by E. ROCCO.

— 521 —   Photo ALINARI, ANDERSON, BROGI, FOTOCELERE.

66. - WONDERS OF ITALY

NAPLES — *CASTEL NUOVO.*

The CASTEL NUOVO, begun by Charles I. of Anjou in 1283, was erected in a style like the French fortresses of the period. In 1443-70 Alphonso I. added the grand triumphal arch, which is considered one of the finest works in Naples.

For over three hundred years the Castel Nuovo was the home of the kings of Naples, the royal palace of Anjou and Aragon and the residence of the Spanish viceroys.

During the rule of the tyrants, its walls and chambers were the scene of unnumbered tragedies and barbarities.

VIEW OF THE CASTEL NUOVO. *Designed by* GIOVANNI PISANO (*13th cent.*).

The triumphal arch over the entrance to Castel Nuovo was begun A. D. 1443 by order of Alphonso I. to commemorate his conquest of the city and the downfall of the old House of Anjou.

This lofty monument of white marble framed between two gloomy towers, is very striking. Every inch of space is covered with beautiful sculptures worked with the utmost care. On the top are the four cardinal virtues in niches; in the centre a large relief represents the king in a triumphal car, surrounded by a crowd of people. The figures are sculptured in bold alto-relief. Among the sculptors upon the reliefs were Isaia da Pisa, Silvestro d'Aquila, Pietro di Martino and probably Giuliano da Maiano.

TRIUMPHAL ENTRY INTO NAPLES OF ALPHONSO I. OF ARAGON (June 2. 1442).

THE TRIUMPHAL ARCH. *Des. by* LUCIANO LAURANA.

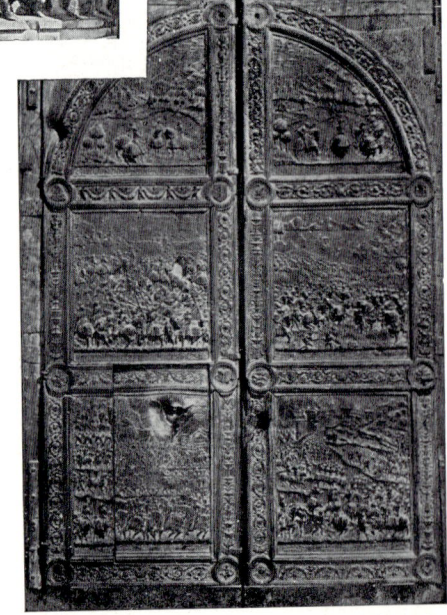

THE BRONZE DOORS. *By* G. MONACO (*15th cent.*). *The reliefs represent the victories of Ferdinand I.*

— 522 —

Photo ALINARI, ANDERSON, FOTOCELERE.

NAPLES — CHURCH OF SANTA CHIARA.

Santa Chiara is one of the principal and most interesting of the churches in Naples. It was originally erected by Robert the Wise in A. D. 1310 and decorated with frescoes by *Giotto*. In the eighteenth century the interior was re-decorated in the rococo style and Giotto's paintings were whitewashed. The exterior still retains its severe Gothic aspect of the fourteenth century but the interior has lost its charm and resembles rather a large magnificent hall. Besides many interesting early sculptures, the church contains such wonderful Gothic monuments of the Anjou dynasty that it is called the Westminster Abbey of Naples. At the back of the high altar is the

Church of Santa Chiara.
[This church and the adjoining monastery was greatly damaged in the last war].

magnificent tomb (42 ft. in height) of king Robert the Wise († 1343) embellished with numerous statues and reliefs of saints. In the lower part, the figure of the king with the crown and barefooted, attired in the garb of a Franciscan, lies recumbent upon his sarcophagus, while on a higher story of the monument he is dressed in royal robes and enthroned in all his earthly splendour. In the upper part, statues of St. Francis and St. Clare present the kneeling king and his wife to the Virgin. On the top, in a mandorla, is the figure of the Saviour in glory.

Monument to King Robert of Anjou († 1343).
By the Florentine brothers Giovanni *and* Pacio.

Scenes from the life of St. Catherine.
Reliefs of the fourteenth century.

Lower part of the Monument to King Robert.

In the niches in front of the sarcophagus are figures of the king with his two wives, Violante and Sancia, and of his son Duke Charles of Calabria with his wife Mary of Valois, and their daughter the famous Queen Joanna I.

Choir of the Clarisses.

The nuns' choir is situated behind the tribune. Originally decorated by Giotto, this choir, like the church, was entirely repainted in the 18th cent. The frescoes represent scenes from the life of Christ and the Virgin.

Photo Alinari, Anderson, Brogi.

NAPLES — *THE CHURCHES.*

CHURCH OF SAN FRANCESCO DI PAOLA.

The church is an imitation of the Pantheon at Rome; it was built by Ferdinand I. from designs of P. Bianchi (1817). In the interior, the dome is supported by thirty-two columns: those at the sides of the high-altar are of Egyptian breccia; the altar is inlaid with lapis-lazuli and jasper. There is a gallery above for the use of the king and its family. These works of art are by Italian artists of the 19th century.

CHURCH OF S. M. DEL CARMINE and Piazza del Mercato Nuovo.

Statue of Conradin. By THORWALDSEN.

CHURCH OF SAN GIOVANNI A CARBONARA. *Erected in 1344 from designs by* MASUCCIO.

The Church of S. Maria del Carmine now contains the remains of the unfortunate prince Conradin of Hohenstaufen.

The cruel tyrannical rule of Charles of Anjou who was abetted by the Pope, had become intolerable in Southern Italy, and the oppressed people looked towards Germany for help. Conradin, a handsome youth, the grandson of Frederick II. decided to try his fortunes against the French usurper. In the year 1267 he crossed the Alps and made his way direct to Rome. The enthusiastic people came out to meet him, and with much pomp the young king was led to the Capitol and acclaimed Emperor. But his hour of triumph was short-lived. Impatient to meet his foe, he soon, perhaps too soon, led forth his troops, and at the battle of Tagliacozzo, near Rome, lost all he had striven for. With a few of his faithful companions Conradin escaped and embarked on a fishing vessel in the hope of reaching Pisa, but was captured and delivered into the hands of Charles, who had cruelly slaughtered most of his important prisoners. Conradin was imprisoned in the Castel dell' Uovo and after a mock trial, Charles pronounced the sentence of death on the young king and twelve of his companions. On October 29th 1268 the pitiable execution took place at Naples in the Piazza del Mercato, beneath a window from which Charles could look down upon the bloody spectacle. Conradin, the « bright and brave lad », only 16, is said to have shown no terror, but to have embraced his companions and, throwing out his glove (in symbolic protest) amid the mute multitude that looked on, laid his head on the block exclaiming: « Ah, my mother, what sorrow I have caused thee ! »

In 1847 a statue, designed by Thorwaldsen, was erected over the tomb of Conradin, the last of the Hohenstaufen.

THE BAPTISM. *Fresco by* ODERISIO. (*Church of the Incoronata*).

SCOURGING OF CHRIST. *By* CAVALLINI. (*Church of S. Maria Donna Regina*).

Photo ALINARI, ANDERSON, BROGI.

NAPLES — THE CHURCHES.

The Cathedral of San Gennaro (St. Januarius).
Begun in 1272.   Rebuilt in the 15th cent. Façade of 1788.

Church of Sant'Eligio.
Gothic portal of the 14th cent.

The interior contains the monuments of Charles I. of Anjou († 1285) brother of St. Louis; Charles Martel († 1301) King of Hungary, and his wife Clementia, daughter of Rudolf of Hapsburg. In the right aisle is the celebrated *Cappella del Tesoro* built in 1608 at a cost of five million francs, and dedicated to St. Januarius (San Gennaro), patron of Naples. The liquefaction of the blood of the saint preserved here takes place thrice a year. The rapidity of the miracle is considered essential for the prosperity of Naples.

Dead Christ.   *By* G. Sammartino.   *18th century sculptures in the Cappella Sanseverino*   **Modesty.**   *By* A. Conradini.

Monument to Sigismond.
Church of SS. Severino e Sosio.
In the sacristy of San Domenico are coffins of ten princes of Aragon.

San Domenico Maggiore.
Erected in 1289, Gothic style.

Monument of King Ladislaus.
Executed by A. Ciccione (15th cent.).
(Church of S. Giovanni a Carbonara).

— 525 —

Photo Alinari, Anderson, Brogi.

NAPLES — THE PALACES.

The *Palazzo Reale* was begun in 1600 by the Viceroy Count de Lemos, from designs by Domenico Fontana, a Roman architect. The building was restored in 1840, after a fire. The façade consists of three stories in the Doric, Ionic and Corinthian styles. The marble statues in the niches represent the Neapolitan dynasties of the last eight centuries; Roger of Normandy, Frederick II. of Hohenstaufen, Charles I. of Anjou, Alphonso I. of Aragona, Charles V., Charles III. of Bourbon, etc.

THE ROYAL PALACE.
By D. FONTANA (1600).

THEATRE OF SAN CARLO.
Founded in 1737. One of the largest opera-houses in Italy.

THE PALAZZO CUOMO-FILANGIERI (1464-90).
It contains a museum of weapons and majolica.

The *Teatro San Carlo* was founded in 1737 by Charles III of Bourbon, and built by Angelo Carasale, a Neapolitan architect, from a design of the Sicilian Giovanni Medrano. Within it has been entirely rebuilt after a fire in 1816, in harmony with the original plan. It is one of the largest opera-houses in the world.

The *Royal Palace of Capodimonte* is situated above the town, on the hill which bears that name. It was begun in 1738 by Charles III. and completed in 1839 under Ferdinand II. The building was designed by Medrano, the architect of the Teatro San Carlo. In the interior, at the second floor, is the *National Gallery of pictures*; at the first floor is a Museum containing a collection of majolicas and porcelains from Sèvres, Vienna, Meissen, Venice and from the former manufactory of Capodimonte.

THE ROYAL PALACE
OF CAPODIMONTE (1738).

Photo ALINARI, ANDERSON, BROGI.

NAPLES — *NATIONAL MUSEUM.*

GREEK TOMBSTONE.
Archaic sculpture 5th cent. B. C.

THE BATTLE OF ALEXANDER. *Mosaic found in the House of the Faun at Pompeii in 1831.*

THE NATIONAL MUSEUM is one of the most important of the public museums of Europe. Besides the collections of the kings of Naples and the numerous works of Greek art brought from Rome, formerly the property of the Farnese family, the museum contains an unrivalled collection of antiquities excavated at Pompeii and Herculaneum, which consists of a great many marble and bronze statues, statuettes, candelabra, lamps, tripods, braziers, jugs, house and kitchen-utensils of every description, weapons of gladiators and warriors, trade and surgical instruments, bracelets, toilet-articles, money-chests coins, mosaics and several hundreds of wall-paintings executed some nineteen centuries ago.

PALLAS (*Herculaneum*).
Archaic style.

THE PRIESTESS EUMACHIA.
Pompeii.

M. NONIUS BALBUS. Senior.
Honorary statue from Herculaneum.

ARTEMIS. *Archaic work with traces of painting. End of the 6th cent. B. C.*

THE CREATION OF MAN. Prometheus and, lying on the ground, the man as yet uninspired with life, surrounded by beneficent gods: Mars, Juno, Mercury, Neptune. (*Found at Pozzuoli*).

— 527 —

Photo ALINARI, ANDERSON, BROGI.

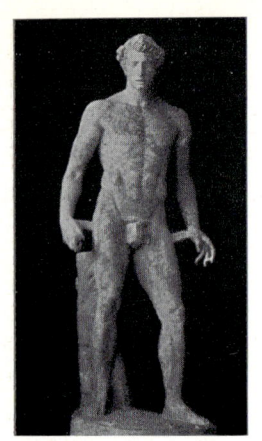

NAPLES — NATIONAL MUSEUM. Marble Sculptures.

WOUNDED GLADIATOR in a fainting condition.

ORPHEUS AND EURYDICE (ca. 360 B. C.).

After his return from the Argonautic expedition Orpheus married the nymph Eurydice. His wife having died, he followed her into the abode of Hades. Through the charms of his lyre Orpheus was permitted to bring his consort out of Hades on condition that he should not look back upon his restored wife till they had arrived in the upper world. The anxiety of love, however, overcame the poet, and just as they were about to pass the fatal bounds, he looked round to see that Eurydice was following him. The scene, full of pathos illustrated here, represents Hermes, the conductor of departed souls, with gentle gesture holding back Eurydice to consign her again to the invisible world, while she bids a last affectionate farewell to her husband.

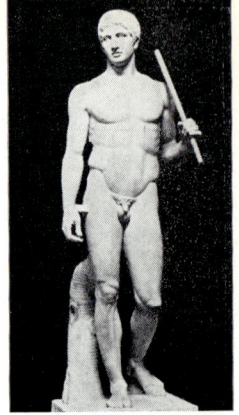

DORYPHORUS. *After the bronze original by* **POLYCLETUS**.

PUGILIST (Sorrento). *Ancient sculpture.*

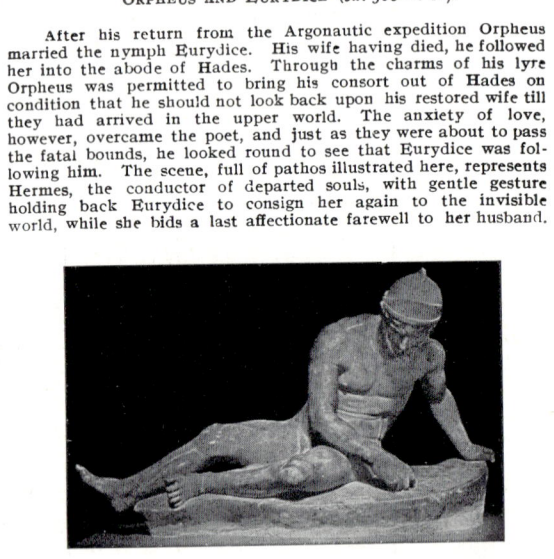

WOUNDED GAUL. The attitude and expression of this warrior, with blood pouring from his wounded breast, is tragic and painful.

GLADIATOR. *Ancient sculpture.*

Aristogeiton was strongly attached to the young Harmodius who returned his affection. Hipparchus endeavoured to withdraw the youth's love to himself, and, failing in this, resolved to avenge the slight by causing Harmodius' sister to be publicly insulted. This outrage determined the two friends to slay both Hipparchus and his brother Hippias. In the group illustrated here the two Athenians are represented in the act of rushing to the attack, the sword of the younger being raised to strike, while Aristogeiton is at hand to protect his brave friend, as soon as the time comes for him to interfere. After the deed was done (514 B. C.), Harmodius and Aristogeiton obtained among the Athenians of all succeeding generations the character of patriots, deliverers and martyrs.

ORESTES AND ELECTRA. *Eclectic School of* **PASITELES** *(Found at Pozzuoli).*

ARISTOGEITON AND HARMODIUS. *After a bronze original by* **ANTENOR** *(4th cent. B. C.).*

Photo ALINARI, ANDERSON, BROGI.

MOSAIC OF THE BATTLE OF ALEXANDER (*detail*), *found at Pompeii* (see p. 527).

THE FARNESE BULL (TORO FARNESE), *found in 1540 in the Thermæ of Caracalla at Rome.*

    The famous group of the *Farnese Bull,* hewn out of a single block of marble, was executed by the Rhodian sculptors APOLLONIUS and TAURISCUS. Its restoration was superintended by Michelangelo. The group represents the punishment which Zethus and Amphion, the two sons of Antiope (standing in the rear), devised to inflict upon Dirce to avenge the wrongs of their mother who for many years had been treated with the greatest cruelty by Dirce. They put her to death by tying her to a bull, who dragged her about till she perished.

NAPLES — NATIONAL MUSEUM. Marble Sculptures.

"APHRODITE."
A replica of the Medici Venus.

MINERVA (Athena).
(Farnese Collection).

FLYING VICTORY (Nike).
A replica of the Greek original.

Venus, the goddess of love and beauty, called *Aphrodite* by the Greeks, was the daughter of Jupiter and Dione, or, according to some poets, she was sprung from the foam of the sea, near the island of Cyprus or Cythera. She married Vulcan and was the mother of Cupid. She surpassed all the other goddesses in beauty, and hence received the prize of beauty from Paris. She likewise had the power of granting beauty and invincible charms to others.

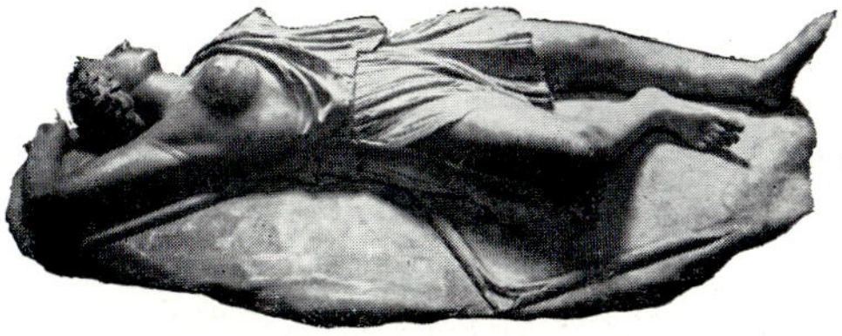

DEAD AMAZON. *Ancient Sculpture.*

The *Amazons* were a nation of famous warlike women from Caucasus, who lived in the neighborhood of the modern Trebizond. All their life was employed in wars and manly exercises. Their right breast was burnt off that they might hurl a javelin with more force and make a better use of the bow. They constantly occur in Greek mythology.

THE FARNESE FLORA. *4th cent. B. C.*

SATYR AND BACCHUS.

In Greek mythology the « satyri » are connected with the worship of Bacchus, and symbolize the luxuriant, vital powers of nature. They are described as fond of wine and were often represented either with a cup or a thyrsus in their hands.

HERA (Farnese Juno) *5th cent. B. C.*

This colossal statue, probably a copy of a smaller Greek original, was found in the Baths of Caracalla at Rome. In spite of its huge proportions the figure is graceful, particularly in the charming arrangement of the tunic. The head, arms, feet and accessories are modern.

Juno, the sister and consort of Jupiter, is here majestically represented, with a beautiful forehead, and with a grave expression commanding reverence. The light tunic clinging to the body like a wet drapery enhances the classic beauty of the forms. The head is modern.

Photo ALINARI, ANDERSON, BROGI.

NAPLES — NATIONAL MUSEUM. *Marble Sculptures.*

VENUS (Victrix) OF CAPUA.

BUST OF HOMER. († ca. 850 B. C.).
A fine portrait of the blind poet.

BUST OF EURIPIDES. († 406 B. C.).
The Greek tragedian.

This beautiful statue of the goddess of love resembles greatly the Venus of Milo in the Museum of the Louvre. The arms and the nose are modern. It was found at Capua in the 18th century, and probably is a Roman work from a Greek original.

PSYCHE OF CAPUA.
(School of PRAXITELES).

GANYMEDE WITH THE EAGLE.

Psyche, "the soul," occurs in the later times of antiquity, as a personification of the human soul. This sadly mutilated torso; one of the most charming sculptures in the museum, was found in the amphitheatre of Capua.

FRAGMENT OF A BACCHIC CORTEGE.
This exquisite relief still bearing traces of painting was discovered at Herculaneum.

The *Farnese Hercules* is the work of the Athenian GLYCON, and is a copy of an original by LYSIPPUS. Hercules is represented as resting from his successful accomplishment of the eleventh labour imposed on him. In the right hand, which is resting against the back, he holds the golden apples of the Hesperides. This statue was found in 1540 (together with the group of the Farnese Bull) in the Baths of Caracalla at Rome.

THE FARNESE HERCULES.

Photo ALINARI, ANDERSON, BROGI.

— 530 —

NAPLES — NATIONAL MUSEUM. Marble Sculptures.

BUST OF DEMOSTHENES.
(† 322 B. C.).
The great Athenian orator.

BUST OF JULIUS CAESAR. († 44 B. C.).
Considered to be a good likeness of the greatest man of antiquity.

VENUS CALLIPYGUS (Aphrodite).
This exquisite figure of the goddess of love is of a remarkable perfection and refined charm. The drapery is skillfully disposed.

CROUCHING VENUS.
Ancient Sculpture.

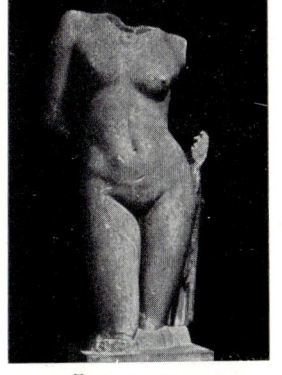

TORSO OF VENUS.
Attributed to PRAXITELES.

THE NUPTIALS OF HELEN AND PARIS.
Venus trying to induce Helen to follow Paris who stands talking with Heros. Seated above is Peitho the goddess of persuasion.

DIANA OF EPHESUS.
The symbol of fecundity.

ISIS.
Egiptian divinity.

THE INFANT BACCHUS HANDED OVER TO A NYMPH. (*Gaeta Vase*).

Photo ALINARI, ANDERSON, BROGI.

NAPLES — NATIONAL MUSEUM. Bronze Sculptures.

The Naples' Museum contains an unrivalled collection of ancient bronzes discovered at Herculaneum and Pompeii. Their respective origins is distinguished by their *patina* or incrustation. The bronzes from Herculaneum are of a dark, black-green colour, whil those from Pompeii, which were much exposed to moisture, are oxydised, and of a light, bluish green colour.

This figure of a drunken faun (or satyr) reclining on a half-empty skin of wine is modelled with great life-like truth.

DRUNKEN FAUN. *(Found at Herculaneum)*.

MERCURY RESTING. *(Found at Herculaneum, 1758)*.

« We here see the messenger of Jupiter resting for a moment, his right hand supported on a rock, and his left, which holds the rod, carelessly hanging over his knee; one leg is stretched out, the other drawn back, and the head is slightly bent forward with an intelligent expression of countenance. It is a fresh picture of elastic youth, resigning itself to a moment's easy repose after preceding effort; one of the numerous ideas which the palaestra afforded to Greek sculptors. It is evidently an original, probably of the time and school of Lysippus ». — *Lübke*.

BOAR ATTACKED BY HOUNDS. *(Group found at Pompeii)*.

AUGUSTUS. *(Herculaneum)*.

EQUESTRIAN STATUE OF NERO (or Caligula ?). *(Found at Pompeii)*.

AUGUSTUS. *(Herculaneum)*.

Photo ALINARI, ANDERSON, BROGI.

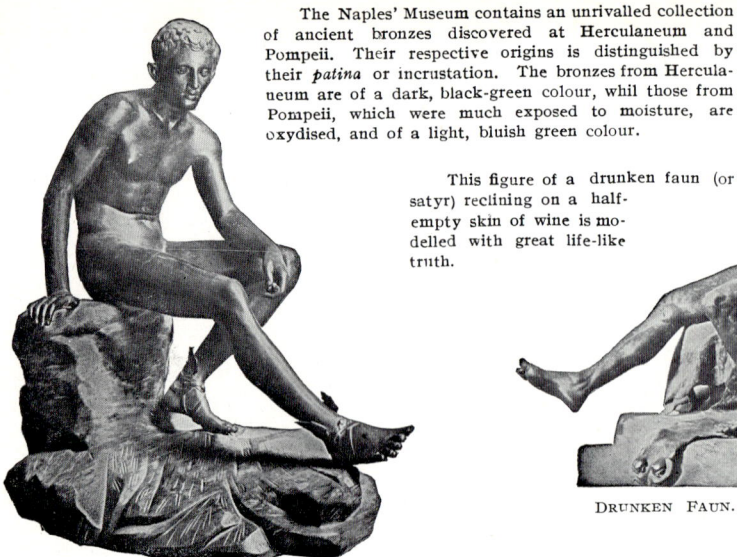

NAPLES — NATIONAL MUSEUM. Bronze Sculptures.

APOLLO SHOOTING (*Pompeii*).    PERSEUS (*Pompeii*).    SATYR WITH A WINE-SKIN.

The profusion of bronze sculptures found at Pompeii and Herculaneum, the masterly casting and chiselling of these works testify to the high degree of development of this branch of art in those ancient times.

DANCING FAUN marking the time by snapping his fingers. (Found at Pompeii in 1830).

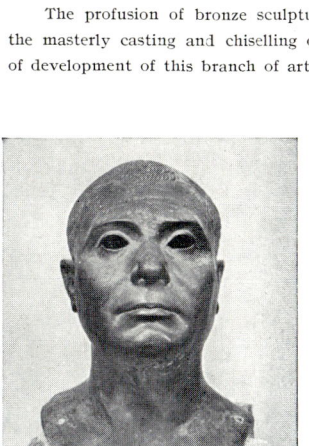

NORBANO SORICE. (Found at Pompeii).    DANCING WOMAN. (Herculaneum). 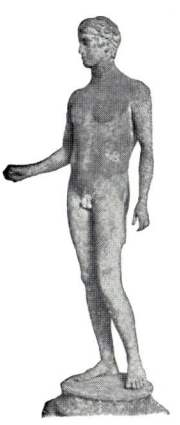   BACCHUS. (Pompeii).    DYONISUS or PLATO. (Herculaneum, 1750).

BERENICE. (Found at Herculaneum).    PORTRAIT OF L. CÆCILIUS JUCUNDUS. Banker (Found at Pompeii).    PTOLEMY APION (?). (Found at Herculaneum).

Photo ALINARI, ANDERSON, BROGI.

NAPLES — NATIONAL MUSEUM. *Bronze Sculptures.*

VENUS.
arranging her hair.

FLYING VICTORY.
(*Pompeii*).

LISTENING NARCISSUS.
(*Found at Pompeii in 1862*).

SILENUS. (*Pompeii*).
used as the bearer of a vase.

ANGLING FISHERMAN.

POMPEIAN BRONZE COOKING STOVE.

SLEEPING SATYR.
(*Found at Herculaneum, 1756*).

AMAZON.
(*Found at Herculaneum*).

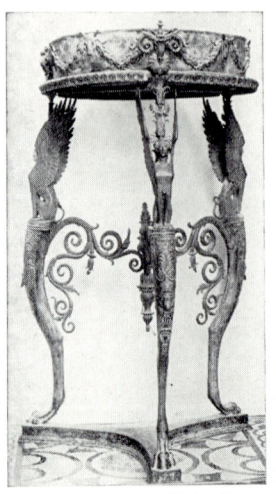

BRONZE STAND (*Tripod*).
From Herculaneum (?)

RUNNER *or* WRESTLER.
(*Found at Herculaneum in 1754*).

— 534 —

Photo ALINARI, ANDERSON, BROGI.

NAPLES — NATIONAL MUSEUM. *Cameos, vases.*

TAZZA FARNESE.

This celebrated ornamental vessel of grey-brown onyx, with admirable reliefs inside and out, is the largest cameo of its kind The subject of the inner relief has been differently interpreted by art critics. Some refer it to the occasion of an inundation of the Nile, which is impersonated by the old man sitting on the left; others, to a spring festival instituted at the foundation of Alexandria (Egypt), where this marvellous cameo was executed. The relief on the outside represents the Head of Medusa.

NUPTIALS OF BACCHUS.
(*Southern Italy*).

ORPHEUS
in the infernal region.

BLUE GLASS VASE.

CAMEO.

CAMEO.

This beautiful vase, rivalling with the famous Portland vase, was used as a cinerary urn. It is decorated with exquisite reliefs appropriately cut in a layer of pure white glass on a blackground of dark blue glass, representing two vintage scenes: Cupids making wine, singing and playing. On the band at the bottom are goats and sheep in pasture. The vase is made up of two layers of glass, one blown subsequently into the other, and was found in a house in the street of the Tombs at Pompeii.

— 535 —

Photo ALINARI, ANDERSON, BROGI.

NAPLES — NATIONAL MUSEUM. *Pompeian Paintings.*

Bacchante.  — Punishment of Cupid.  — « Flora ». Girl plucking flowers.

Wall paintings from Pompeian houses

Wounded Eneas being medicated. *On the left Venus brings healing herbs.* — Theseus after the slaughter of the Minotaur. *Right and left are thankful figures.* — Hercules' son suckled by the hind. *The father's amazement is well expressed.*

COMEDY SCENE. This mosaic picture, discovered at Pompeii, is one of the most beautiful examples which the museum possesses. It represents three actors disguised under feminine vestments and a child. The first, dressed as an old woman, beats expressively on a pair of castanets. The other, similarly disguised, standing in a suitable attitude, plays on a big tambourine. Their heads are covered with a white cloth, and they seem to dance to the accompaniment of their instruments. Behind, another actor plays on a double tibia, while the child holds a bag-pipe. The composition and the drawing are admirable, the drapery well treated and the work executed minutely and with great skill.

COMEDY SCENE. *A work by* Dioscurides of Samos. — PEACOCKS DRINKING. (*From Pompeii*).

— 536 —

Photo ALINARI, ANDERSON, BROGI.

NAPLES — NATIONAL MUSEUM. Pompeian Paintings.

THE SACRIFICE OF IPHIGENIA.

While carried to the altar by Ulysses and Diomede, Iphigenia appeals to her father (left) who hides his face in grief. The augur Calchas (right) is doubtful whether to strike the fatal blow.

WOMEN PLAYING WITH ASTRAGALI.

This picture is a very precious cinnabar painting on marble: a rare example of its kind.

PAQUIUS PROCULUS AND HIS WIFE.   SAPPHO.
These realistic genre portraits are of special interest.

SCENE IN A FULLERY.
Inspection of cloth; carding; bleaching frame.

THE THREE GRACES.
An often repeated grouping.

MARS AND VENUS.
On the left Cupid stands watching.

PERSEUS AND ANDROMEDA.
On the left the sea-monster.

Photo ALINARI, ANDERSON, BROGI.

NAPLES — *NATIONAL GALLERY.*

HOLY FAMILY, *by* RAPHAEL.

FRANCESCO GONZAGA, *by* MANTEGNA.

The National Gallery, in the Royal Palace of Capodimonte, though it does not rival in wealth of masterpieces the galleries of Florence, Rome, Venice or Siena, is nevertheless an important gallery of painting only second to these in Italy. The Neapolitan school of painting never came to have much importance; but the gallery can boast of fine works of every other school in Italy.

PARABLE OF THE SEVEN BLIND MEN, *by* P. BRUEGHEL THE ELDER (1568).

Photo ALINARI, ANDERSON, BROGI.

HOLY FAMILY. *By* RAPHAEL.    MADONNA AND CHILD. *By* B. LUINI.    ST. JOHN BAPTIST. *By* B. LUINI.

DANAË. *By* TITIAN (1545).

THE RACE OF ATALANTA AND HIPPOMENES. *By* GUIDO RENI.

Danaë, the beautiful daughter of Acrisius, king of Argos, was confined in a brass tower by her father to prevent the fulfilment of an oracle declaring that his daughter's son would kill him. Jupiter, who was enamoured of her, found access to her in the form of a shower of gold, and she became the mother of Perseus. Mother and son were both enclosed in a chest and cast in the sea by Acrisius. But Jupiter saved them and in time Acrisius, in a public game, accidentally met his fate by the hand of his grand-son who in throwing a discus had crushed his foot.

Atalanta's beauty gained her many admirers. To free herself from their importunities she proposed to run a race with them (the suitors starting first). Any one who could outstrip her would be made her husband; failure to do so being death. Many of the suitors perished in the attempt: at last Hippomenes whom Venus had provided with three golden apples from the Hesperides, accepted the risk, and during the course artfully dropped them one after the other. Atalanta stopped to gather the apples and lost the race, whereupon Hippomenes claimed the prize.

PENITENT MAGDALENE. *By* TITIAN (1567).

HOLY FAMILY. *By* SEBASTIANO DEL PIOMBO.

MADONNA (*La Zingarella*). *By* CORREGGIO.

Photo ALINARI, ANDERSON, BROGI.

MOUNT VESUVIUS, HERCULANEUM.

Vesuvius, for the last three hundred years the only active volcano near Naples, rises in solitary majesty from a base nearly thirty miles in circumference. Its height varies according to the different effects of the eruptions, — from about 4000 to 4300 feet. The upper part of the *mountain* is divided into two peaks; the northeast one is called Monte Somma, the southern is Vesuvius proper.

The first record of its activity (after centuries of quiet), dates from A. D. 63 when a fearful earthquake did immense damage at Herculaneum and Pompeii. A few years later, on August 24th, 79, just as the previous damage was nearly repaired, a terrific eruption took place with appalling fury devastating the country around and blotting out from the world the flourishing cities of Pompeii and Herculaneum.

Since that terrible day a great number of eruptions, of various intensity are recorded; the most recent being that of 1906. On April 4th, 5th and 6th the lava began to overflow in streams down the upper part; during the night of the 7th enormous masses of broken stones were thrown from the summit-crater while the lava-torrent descended through the village of Boscotrecase, which it completely destroyed, down to Torre Annunziata. On the next day the crater continued to pour forth huge volumes of ashes which covered the villages around to the depth of five or six feet, while black dust and smoke reached even as far as Naples.

VIEW TAKEN FROM THE BRINK OF THE CRATER.

According to tradition HERCULANEUM was founded, by Hercules. The place was inhabited by the Oscans, an aboriginal race, by the Etruscans and the Samnites, then it was occupied by the Romans. Many villas were built here, owing to its fine situation on a hill near the sea. The town was entirely destroyed by the eruption of Vesuvius in A. D. 79, buried under 50-100 ft. of ashes and lava. Herculaneum was discovered accidentally in 1719, when the sinking of a well revealed the ancient theatre at a depth of 90 ft. The excavations progressed during the 18th and 19th centuries and many fine bronzes, now in the National Museum of Naples, were discovered here.

HERCULANEUM: THE HOUSE OF THE STAGS (*Casa dei Cervi*).

Photo ALINARI, ANDERSON, BROGI.

RUINS OF THE TEMPLE OF APOLLO.    THE TEMPLE OF APOLLO (as it was).

POMPEII

HISTORICAL SKETCH

BOY WITH A DOLPHIN.

Pompeii, is unique, the most precious storehouse of ancient knowledge the world possesses. Founded by the Oscans about the fifth century B. C., at an early period it became influenced by Greek civilization. This is proved by the remains of architecture which may be seen to-day. After the Samnites wars (343-290 B. C.) Pompeii fell under the domination of the Romans and, owing to its excellent situation at the mouth of the river which made Pompeii a convenient port, it became a flourishing town with some thirty thousand inhabitants, and in course of time was completely Romanized. In the last days of the Republic it was a favourite retreat of wealthy Romans and, later, also favoured by the emperors.

Previous to its final destruction a fearful earthquake occurred in 63 A. D. and a large part of the buildings of the city were thrown down. This calamity gave the prosperous and enterprising inhabitants an opportunity of re-building their town in a style more in harmony with the architecture of imperial Rome. The new houses and temples had not long been rebuilt or restored when the final catastrophe came on the 24th of August, 79 A. D.

Early in the morning of the fateful day there was a severe shock of earthquake, then a dense shower of ashes came down to the depth of about three feet; and those who appreciated the greatness of the danger had time to escape. But many of them probably returned to save their valuables, while others, striken with terror, went back into their houses to find shelter. Unfortunately the ashes were soon followed by fragments of red-hot pumice stones, which rained down to the depth of eight or ten feet, and succeeded by a fresh shower of volcanic ashes lasting all day. Pompeii and Stabiae on the south side of Vesuvius were completely buried, while Herculaneum on the west side, was covered to the depth of 60 ft. with the same materials, but here the ashes being mingled with torrents of rain, hardened into a kind of tufa stone, and the modern town of Resina was built over its site.

From the number of skeletons discovered, it has been estimated that about two thousand persons perished at Pompeii. After its catastrophe the very name of Pompeii was forgotten and her place was known no more, until in the 18th century excavations were commenced and most of the ruins have been extricated of the ashes and rubbish accumulated during seventeen centuries. To-day a whole antique city, which represents almost our only source of acquaintance with ancient domestic life, lies before our astonished eyes, and in wandering through her streets, we find it difficult not to give reins to imagination and sentiment.

POMPEII — *THE DEAD CITY.*

VIEW OF THE BASILICA.

This was the most magnificent and architecturally the most interesting building at Pompeii. It is oblong in shape and measures 220 ft. by 80 ft. It was chiefly devoted to business transactions and to the administration of justice.

PART OF THE COLONNADE OF THE FORUM.

The colonnade surrounding the Forum on three sides was, in greater part, built in two stories, the lower of the Doric the upper of the Ionic order. The upper gallery was approached by stairways some of which are still preserved.

THE WATER GATE (*Porta Marina*).
The Arch on the left has a path for foot passengers.

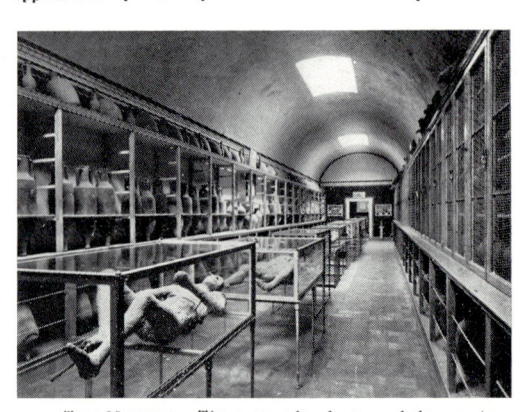

THE MUSEUM. These records of agony help us to realize the unspeakable horrors of the great eruption.

The Museum contains several casts of human corpses and one of a dog. The bodies of those who perished in the storm of ashes which covered Pompeii left perfect moulds in the ashes which afterwards hardened. In 1863, Signor Fiorelli, the Director of the excavations, filled these moulds with soft plaster of Paris and succeeded in preserving the figures and the pathetic attitudes of the deceased.

VIEW OF THE STABIAN GATE.

VIEW OF THE SMALL THEATRE.

Besides an amphitheatre Pompeii possessed a large uncovered theatre and a smaller covered one. The latter illustrated here had a seating capacity of 1500; the seats were of masonry, cut in such a way that the person sitting in front was not disturbed from the feet of one sitting on the upper seat behind.

Photo ALINARI, ANDERSON, BROGI.

POMPEII — *THE DEAD CITY.*

The Forum was the central point of the town and here the most important religious festivals were celebrated. It served also as the favorite promenade and lounging place, where people met to discuss affairs of mutual interest or indulge in conversation. Six streets converge to the Forum, but only pedestrians could enter it. Including the colonnade the Forum measures approximately 497 ft. in length by 156 ft. in breadth; the open space in the center was paved with large slabs of travertine. Here were erected statues of emperors, illustrious men and citizens who had rendered distinguished services to the community. On the north side, the Forum was dominated by the *Temple of Jupiter*, flanked on both sides by triumphal arches. On the west by market buildings and the *Temple of Apollo*. On the northeast (near the temple of Jupiter) is the *Macellum*, a provision market, and south of it the *Sanctuary to the City Lares*; adjoining it is the *Temple of Vespasian* and next the *Building of Eumachia*, probably used as a bazaar for the sale of clothing. The southeast corner of the Forum is occupied by the *Comitium*, voting place; the southern side by *Municipal Buildings* and the southwest corner by the *Basilica*. No private houses opened on the Forum.

VIEW OF THE FORUM LOOKING NORTH TOWARDS VESUVIUS.

COLONNADE OF THE PALAESTRA.
(*Barracks of the Gladiators*).

SCHEME OF WALL DECORATION.

VIEW OF THE TEMPLE OF ISIS.

THE TEMPLE OF ISIS.

The temple of Isis was probably built in the first century B. C. An inscription over the entrance indicates that, after the earthquake of 63 A. D., it was restored by N. Popidius Celsinus, a boy six years of age, and that in recognition of his generosity, he was admitted into the rank of the decurions.

— 543 —

Photo ALINARI, ANDERSON, BROGI.

POMPEII — *THE DEAD CITY.* House of the Vettii.

CUPIDS AS GOLDSMITHS. *Wall painting in the House of the Vettii.*

SPECIMEN OF WALL DECORATION.

PERISTYLE IN THE HOUSE OF THE VETTII. *Partly rebuilt and replanted.*

The House of the Vettii is a museum in itself. In no other house in Pompeii will the visitor obtain an impression of the aspect presented by a peristyle in ancient times; nowhere else are the wall decorations so effective, the excellently preserved compositions so remarkable both for the drawing and exquisite finish.

VIEW OF A (DINING?) ROOM. *House of the Vettii.*

THE INFANT HERCULES *strangling the serpents.*

Most of the better class Pompeian houses were built in one story and consisted of a single series of apartments. They were entered from the street by a narrow passage (*vestibulum*) leading to a court (*atrium*). This atrium, the chief feature of Pompeian houses, was surrounded by a covered passage and in the center had an *impluvium*, or reservoir for rain water connected with the cistern. The roof of the atrium sloped inwards from all sides and had a rectangular opening in the middle (*compluvium*), which gave light and air to the atrium and the sleeping rooms opening into it. (*Continued*).

— 544 —

Photo ALINARI, ANDERSON, BROGI.

POMPEI — *THE DEAD CITY*.

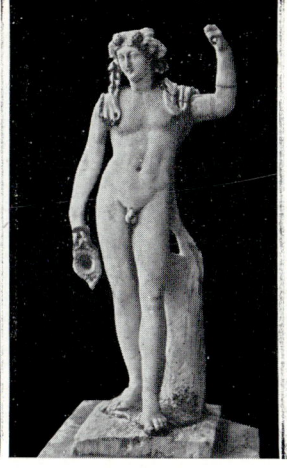

A CORNER OF THE PERISTYLE.   YOUNG BACCHUS.   KITCHEN *with cooking-apparatus*.
(*House of the Vettii*).

The House of the Vettii, unlike other Pompeian buildings from which every object of value and every painting of importance have been removed to the Museum of Naples, has been allowed to remain in the same condition in which it was unearthed in 1894. It therefore affords the best insight into the domestic details of a wealthy man's Roman household.

HOUSE OF THE GILDED CUPIDS (*Casa degli Amorini Dorati*). PERISTYLE.

(*Continuation*). At the rear of the atrium was a large chamber (*tablinum*), probably used as a reception room, on the right or left of which was the *andron*, a sort of hall or passage connecting the atrium with the *peristyle* beyond. The peristyle (connected with a side street by a separate entrance) consisted of an open court with dining rooms (*triclinium*) and business rooms opening into it. It was enclosed by a colonnade and had a garden in the middle. The kitchen had no particular location. Few houses had private baths, the public baths being preferred and patronized. Second story rooms destined principally for the slaves are rarely found.

Photo ALINARI, ANDERSON, BROGI.

POMPEII — *THE DEAD CITY.*

COMMEMORATIVE ARCH.
The bronze statue of Caligula which once surmounted this arch is now in the Museum at Naples.

THE THERMÆ (*Tepidarium*).
This chamber was heated by means of a large bronze brazier. The niches around were used for depositing clothes.

THE STABIAN BATHS (*The largest and oldest establishment at Pompeii*).

The Apodyterium (Dressing room for women).   *Dressing room for men.*

The Stabian Baths are the largest in Pompeii and were designed for both men and women. Though less extensive than the baths of Rome the arrangement of their essential parts was the same. First there was a court, *palaestra*, surrounded by a colonnade: it was used for gymnastic exercises and had a shallow open-air swimming tank. From the palaestra a passage or anteroom led to the dressing room, *apodyterium*; next to which was the *tepidarium*, a moderately heated room, and the *calidarium*, a room in which hot baths were given.

VIEW OF THE HOUSE OF THE TRAGIC POET.
In the foreground the *impluvium* and a cistern curb. At the right, the andron. In the centre, the *tablinum*; beyond, the *peristyle* and the shrine.

MOSAIC IN THE HOUSE OF THE TRAGIC POET.
BULWER in his « Last Days of Pompeii » represents the house of the Tragic Poet as the dwelling of Glaucus.

Photo ALINARI, ANDERSON, BROGI.

POMPEII — *THE DEAD CITY.*

RUINS OF A BAKERY WITH MILL-STONES.
The mills were probably turned by slaves or asses.

STREET OF THE TOMBS. The burying-places of the Greeks and Romans were at a distance from their towns.

THE VILLA OF DIOMEDES.

SEMICIRCULAR NICHE (Street of the Tombs).

In a subterranean vault of the Villa of Diomedes a number of skeletons were discovered in one spot near the door. There were jewels and coins and several wine amphoras. It seems that the inmates, who had sought protection here, had rushed to the door and in their attempt to open it had been suffocated with the sulphureous vapours in the air.

TEMPLE OF FORTUNA AUGUSTA (*Strada del Foro*).

VIEW OF THE AMPHITHEATRE.

At intervals in the streets are placed big stepping-stones for the convenience of foot-passengers in wet weather, which owing to the lack of drains turned these streets into regular watercourses.

Photo ALINARI, ANDERSON, BROGI.

SORRENTO — La "Gentile."

VIEW OF CASTELLAMMARE.

THE COAST OF SORRENTO AS SEEN FROM THE SEA.

SORRENTO. CAMPANILE OF THE CATHEDRAL.

SORRENTO. VIEW OF THE HARBOUR.

THE «TARANTELLA». *The famous popular dance.*

The Tarantella, usually performed with the assistance of exhilarating music in the Sorrentine hotels, is a most graceful dance expressive of old-fashioned courtship and full of rhythmical movement and display of peasant-finery.

« The Tarantella is a choreographic love-story, the two dancers representing an enamoured swain and his mistress. It is the old theme — ' the quarrels of lovers is the renewal of love. ' Enraptured gaze, coy side-look; gallant advance, timid retrocession; impassioned declaration, supercilious rejection; piteous supplication, softening hesitation; worldly goods' oblation, gracious acceptation; frantic jubilation, maidenly resignation. Petting, wooing, billing, cooing. Jealous accusation sharp recrimination; manly expostulation, shrewish aggravation; angry threat, summary dismissal. Fuming on one side; pouting on the other. Reaction, approximation, explanation, exoneration, reconciliation, osculation, winding up with a grand *pas de circonstance*, expressive of confidence re-established and joy unbounded. »*

* W. A. J. STAMER, *Dolce Napoli*

— 548 —

Photo ALINARI, ANDERSON, BROGI, FOTOCELERE.

SORRENTO — La "Gentile."

View of Sorrento and the Castellammare Road.

SORRENTO, the ancient *Surrentum*, already in the days of imperial Rome was a place of no small importance and was frequented by the proud inhabitants of the capital who came here to enjoy sunny leisure. The numerous remains of Roman villas and medieval walls and towers easily testify to its former importance and prosperity. And truly, the lovely shores of Sorrento, its enchanted gardens, its blossom-filled groves upon steep cliffs, the intoxicating perfume of orange flowers, combine to make it a place of delight and an ideal resort at all times of the year. The hotels are charmingly situated amid flowering gardens or on a terrace overlooking the sea, whence a series of magnificent views over the bay and surrounding country may be enjoyed. In spring and autumn Sorrento is frequented almost exclusively by Americans and English; its situation however, admirably adapts it for a summer residence when the delight of bathing in the limpid waters of the Bay is added to the other attractions of society gatherings and gaieties.

Sorrento is the birthplace of Torquato Tasso, poet and author of the famous epic poem, *Jerusalem Delivered*. Many notable personages sojourned here, among whom: Shelley, Byron, Stendhal, Musset, Lamartine, Renan, Bourget, Longfellow, Nietzsche, Grieg, Ibsen.

Owing to its topographical position, Sorrento is a convenient centre and starting point for many attractive excursions on foot, or carriage or motor, about this beautiful region.

Neighbourhood of Sorrento. View of Capri.

Photo FOTOCELERE.

CAPRI — The "Pearl of the Mediterranean."

CAPRI. VIEW OF THE MARINA GRANDE.

THE island of Capri lies in the Bay of Naples, and its picturesque outline forms one of the most charming features in the view of the bay itself. It is noted in history as the place where the emperor Tiberius († 37 A. D.) spent the last ten years of his life, and remains of several villas built by him are still to be seen. Famed for its bold, picturesque scenery, the island long has been a favorite resort of artists and tourists. It would be impossible to paint a word picture of this fairy-like island, with its bold cliffs rising precipitously from the sea, its terraced hills with blooming groves of oranges and vines, the white sunny houses, all with flat roofs, the villas with their gay approaches, the magnificent road to Anacapri affording a panorama which is wonderful in its display of colour, a point of observation from which one of the loveliest pictures in the world may be enjoyed, and, last but not least, the marvellous Blue Grotto and the enchanting sea that lies along the shore and encircles the island.

CAPRI. THE PIAZZA AND CAMPANILE.

ARCO NATURALE (Natural Archway).

Photo ANDERSON, FOTOCELERE.

CAPRI — The "Pearl of the Mediterranean."

THE ROAD LEADING TO THE MARINA PICCOLA.

MONTE SOLARO AND THE ROAD TO ANACAPRI.

VIEW OF THE BLUE GROTTO.

VILLA S. MICHELE AND THE OLD ROAD TO ANACAPRI.

The Blue Grotto is the most famous of the caves in the rocky shores of Capri. It can only be entered from the sea and the entrance being scarcely 3 ft. high access is possible only by small boats when the sea is quiet. Visitors must lie flat down in the boat which is carried in by the wave, and they suddenly find themselves in a marvellous place. The water is liquid sapphire, the rocky vaulting glistens with a beautiful pale blue light, the drops of spray tossed up by the movement of the oars fall like phosphorescent silver: the whole effect presents a scene of truly magic beauty and fascination.

SOUTHERN COAST AND THE FARAGLIONI.

VIEW OF THE ISLAND OF CAPRI.

Photo ALINARI, ANDERSON, BROGI, FOTOCELERE.

AMALFI — *An Artist's Idyll.*

VIEW OF AMALFI FROM THE TERRACE OF THE CAPUCHIN MONASTERY.

AMALFI once made laws governing Mediterranean waters and possessed colonies in the distant soil of Africa and Asia. It is first mentioned in the 6th century; in the 9th century it shared with Venice and Gaeta the Italian trade with the East, and in the year 848 its fleet sent to the assistance of pope Leo IV., against the Saracens. An evidence of its sea-power are the *Tavole Amalfitane*, a maritime code which was recognized through the Mediterranean until 1570. Amalfi took a conspicuous part in transporting the early Crusaders to Palestine, where the Amalfitani built many churches and founded a hospital in Jerusalem, whence the most renowned Order of St. John of Jerusalem, or Knights hospitallers, took their name. In the 12th cent. it was a prosperous republic with a powerful fleet and a population of 50.000, until the Normans subdued it and its importance declined. The town is most singularly situated,—surrounded on one side by overhanging mountains and rocks, while on the other spreads the illimitable blue of the Mediterranean, veiled with the softest haze. The hills rise terrace-wise above the town, gaily coloured houses, villas surrounded with orange groves and medieval towers are mingled in picturesque variety half buried in the foliage of the vine. The Old Capuchin monastery, the well known hotel perched up on the hill, is the realization of a pleasant dream, for here one may pass his hours in perfection of leisurely comfort. To **Amalfi** is commonly attributed the honour of having given birth to Flavio Gioia, the inventor of the mariner's compass.

Photo ALINARI, ANDERSON, BROGI.

AMALFI — *An Artist's Idyll.*

AN OLD WATCH-TOWER.

OLD MONASTERY NOW A HOTEL.

VALLEY OF THE MILLS.

CLOISTERS OF THE CAPUCHIN MONASTERY.

The Cathedral is in Lombard-Norman style; has bronze doors made at Constantinople before 1066; Campanile from 1276.

CATHEDRAL OF ST. ANDREA (11th cent.).

GENERAL VIEW OF AMALFI AND (right) THE VILLAGE OF ATRANI.
The Amalfi coast viewed from the sea, is the most enchanting of all the Italian shores.

— 553 —

Photo ALINARI, ANDERSON, BROGI.

70. - WONDERS OF ITALY.

THE AMALFI ROAD — *Positano*.

POSITANO from the hill-side.
Gulf of Salerno.

RIVIERA DI AMALFI.

The Amalfi or *Corniche* Road, which stretches from Castellammare, for forty miles, along the shores of the blue Mediterranean, to Salerno, is considered to be without rival for beauty and scenic views. The road is almost the whole way hewn in the cliffs of the coast and frequently supported by viaducts nearly five hundred feet above the sea-level. Smiling villages, each with its note of individual charm, are scattered all along the coast.

It is difficult to furnish an efficient description of the attractions of this district without seeming to indulge in exaggeration. Here is the realm of the olive-tree, which clothes the foot of the hills; greyish yellow rocks, silver-gray foliage of the olive; dark green groups and groves of orange and lemon trees; gaily coloured villages, a graceful campanile here, a picturesque tower, standing solitary there; a blue sky above, a blue sea below; a series of never ending enchantments, — such is the character of this exquisite coast scenery.

VIEW OF THE HIGH ROAD FROM POSITANO TO AMALFI.

Photo ALINARI, ANDERSON, BROGI, FOTOCELERE.

THE AMALFI ROAD — *Atrani, Maiori, Vietri.*

CETARA. (Villages between Amalfi and Salerno). VIETRI SUL MARE.

WATCH-TOWER *near* CETARA. VIEW OF ATRANI.

The picturesque village of Atrani, a suburb of Amalfi, boasts of an interesting little church, *S. Salvatore a Bireta,* wherein the doges of Amalfi were elected and buried; its beautiful Byzantine bronze doors date from 1087.

MAIORI. OLD FOUNTAIN AT MINORI. (*XIIIth century*).

Watch-Towers are found all along the shores of the Gulf of Salerno for the purpose of keeping guard against the incursions of the Saracens. In the ninth century, the Mohammedons or "Saracens" of Arabia and North Africa constantly infested the coasts of Southern Italy, committing the most audacious acts of piracy and devastation.

Photo ALINARI, ANDERSON, BROGI.

RAVELLO. CAMPANILE OF THE CATHEDRAL.

VIEW OF RAVELLO.

The celebrated old town of Ravello was probably founded by patrician families of Amalfi; it is beautifully situated on a high plateau four miles to the northeast of the latter town and commands a most fascinating view of the coast and the bay of Salerno. The curious penetrating charm of this place, the marvel of its view across the fabled sea, appealed so strongly to the most romantic spirit of our generation that Richard Wagner, signing his name in the visitor's book of the local hotel, added the words, " Klingsor's Zaubergarten ist gefunden."

In the eleventh century, when in the zenith of its fame and prosperity, the town was entirely girdled by walls and towers and possessed four monasteries, thirteen churches and a great many private places. The Cathedral with its bronze doors, its mosaics and Norman sculptures; the Palazzo Rufolo, a perfect Alhambra, are now left to recall the memory of its period of greatness.

RAVELLO. MARBLE PULPIT IN THE CATHEDRAL (*13th cent.*).

SALERNO. MARBLE PULPIT IN THE CATHEDRAL (*12th cent.*).

GENERAL VIEW SALERNO.

The town of Salerno, which gives the name to its gulf, is the terminal point of the famous « Corniche Road ». In the Middle Ages, under the successive rules of the Lombards, the Normans and the houses of Hohendtaufen and Anjou, the town attained a high degree of prosperity and possessed a most excellent school of medicine. The Cathedral, erected in 1084 by Robert Guiscard, is now the most interesting place in town. Besides the beautiful pulpit, it contains, among others, the tomb of Pope Gregory VII. and of Hildebrand, one of the greatest men, a reformer, almost a martyr, dead in exile, as he said, because he loved justice.

Hildebrand, the son of a Tuscan carpenter, rose to eminence as a monk of the Benedictine Monastery of Cluny, where he won a reputation for his learning and the extreme austerity of his life in an age of undisguised immorality. He became sensible of the formidable evils tending to the corruption of the clergy, due to their dependence on the Emperor for investiture into their benefices, and set himself with all his might to effect a total purging of the Church from its foulness, and especially from the guilt of simony. For some years before his actual election to the Papal throne he had begun to exercise an immense control over the councils of the Church, and he was personally responsible for the epoch-making resolution (1060), which declared that the choice of a new Pontiff was vested in the College of Cardinals alone. As soon as he assumed the Tiara in 1073, he began to dispute with Emperor Henry IV. about the question of « investiture ». And in the council of 1075 he caused to be passed a decree vehemently condemning as simony investiture by layman, declaring null the bestowal by King or Emperor of the Episcopal ring and staff to a bishop, deposing certain bishops whom Henry had instituted and excommunicating several of Henry's officials to whom these prelates had, he alleged, paid money for favouring their appointment. In great indignation, the Emperor protested against so decided an infringement of a custom which had been followed since the time of Charlemagne. He assembled a council of his ecclesiastics at Worms, and there a decree was passed declaring that Gregory was deposed. The Pope retaliated by a solemn sentence of excommunication on the Emperor. The issues were now clear: the Emperor strove to make the Church a feudal dependency, the Pope to render the Church, with all its temporalities, independent of the State. The struggle between Church and State or the « War of the Investitures « had begun. The Pope's sentence made the German nobles turn against the Emperor, and they informed Henry that unless he obtained remission of the ban within the year they would renounce their fealty and he would lose his throne. The final act of that terrible duel which was destined to distract Italy for generations to come is well known. Accompanied by his wife and by the excommunicated bishops and officials, Henry crossed the Alps in the depth of winter in order to ask absolution of the Pope who was then staying at the Castle of Canossa, the Countess Matilda's stronghold in the Apennine Mountains. For three weary days the Emperor was kept waiting admist the snow before the castle-gate, clad only in a coarse woollen shirt as a penitent, and there, fasting, he awaited in humble patience the pleasure of the stern Pontiff. At last he was admitted, threw himself on his knees and received absolution, but on very hard terms. The terms imposed were intolerable and Henry broke them, elected a Pope (Clement III.) of his own, and accompanied by him entered Rome at the head of an army. Gregory VII. took refuge in the castle of Sant'Angelo, and sent an appeal to Robert Guiscard, Duke of Apulia and Calabria. The latter accompanied by 40.000 warriors forced his way into Rome, put Henry to flight and delivered the Pope. But the city was given over to pillage, and innumerable churches and monuments were reduced to ruins. Gregory himself was shocked at the state in which the city was restored to him, and found it advisable to leave it with his rescuers and retire to Salerno where he died the following year (1085).

FRAGMENT OF THE BRONZE DOORD OF THE CATHEDRAL.
These doors presented by Landolfo Butromile in 1099 were executed at Constantinople.

Photo ALINARI, ANDERSON, BROGI.

PÆSTUM — And its Wonderful Temples.

VIEW OF THE TEMPLE OF NEPTUNE.

PÆSTUM, the *Poseidonia* of the Greeks, was founded five hundred years before Christ, by a Sybarite colony, afterwards a Roman city under the name of Pæstum. It was surprised and destroyed by the Saracens at the beginning of the 10th century. The city today has disappeared from the earth, only the magnificent lines of columns in the three Doric temples remaining to testify to the greatness of its past.

TEMPLE OF CERES.   **TEMPLE OF NEPTUNE.**

It is impossible to imagine a higher effort of man's creative genius than in these temples, which seem to be built for eternity.

VIEW OF THE BASILICA.

This temple less imposing and inferior in beauty of proportion to the temple of Neptune, is divided into two halves and was probably intended for the worship of dual divinities.

Photo ALINARI, ANDERSON, BROGI.

POZZUOLI. BAJA. ISCHIA.

The district between Naples and Cumæ — Pozzuoli, Baja, Misenum — comprised in ancient times under the title of the *Phlegræan Fields*, is exceedingly rich in classical associations. It was here that Greek civilization, attracted by the beauty of the seaboard, first gained a footing in Italy. Subsequently, the Romans, appreciating the glorious climate and delightful surroundings, erected there innumerable palatial villas and temples on which was lavished all that wealth and splendour could furnish. Of all this magnificence to day there remains nothing: the volcanic nature of the region and the convulsions of the soil have left only a few ruined buildings to recall the glamour of the past. But the natural beauties still possess the same old charms they had when emperors, philosophers and statesmen came here to enjoy their leisure.

POZZUOLI. TEMPLE OF SERAPIS OR « SERAPEUM ».

POZZUOLI. THE SOLFATARA.

Pozzuoli, the *Puteoli* of the Romans, was in ancient times the principal port in Italy, for the traffic with the East and Egypt. The Apostle Paul landed here in A. D. 62 and spent seven days at Pozzuoli (Acts, XXVIII), before proceeding to Rome. The decline of the Roman empire, the barbarian devastations of the middle ages and the convulsions of the volcanic soil reduced the once prosperous town to a fishing village; only its ruins remain to day to testify of its past.

The *Solfatara*, is the crater of a half extinct volcano which has not been in full activity since A. D. 1198. The ground around is hot and sounds hollow when stamped on; steam jets charged with sulphureous gases (which attain a temperature of 220° Fahrenheit) emerge continously from numerous fissures in the ground.

The city's principal sights are given here.

POZZUOLI. THE ROMAN AMPHITHEATRE.

VIEW OF BAJA AND ITS MEDIEVAL CASTLE.

The *Amphitheatre* finished under Vespasian, is a large and well preserved monument with interesting substructures. Here, during the reign of Diocletian, St. Januarius, the patron of Naples, and his companions were imprisoned and vainly exposed to the fury of the wild beasts, before they were put to death near the Solfatara.

Baja, was the most fashionable watering-place of antiquity. Augustus, Nero and other Roman emperors rivalled each other in embellishing it and erecting magnificent villas for their sojourn. But the fall of the Empire was also the ruin of Baja. Later the Saracens plundered it and gradually the town was almost abandoned.

THE LAKE LUCRINUS.

The *Lake Lucrinus*, famous in antiquity for its oysters, is only half a mile distant from the celebrated *Lacus Avernus*, which, owing to its gloomy surroundings was regarded by the ancients as the entrance to the infernal regions.

ISCHIA. THE CASTLE OF ALPHONSO I. OF ARAGON.
Built about 1450.

Photo ALINARI, ANDERSON, BROGI.

CAMPANIA.

VIEW OF THE MONASTERY OF MONTECASSINO. *Founded by St. Benedict in 529.*

This is the principal and most ancient of the Benedictine monasteries. Erected on the site of a temple of Apollo, the abbey has been repeatedly destroyed by the Lombards, the Saracens, and other invaders, the edifice now standing being of the 17th century. Of the original monastery only a few architectural fragments now remain; the bronze doors of the church, executed at Constantinople in the middle of the 11th century, are inscribed with a list, inlaid in silver, of all the possessions of the abbey in 1060, which at that time was esteemed the richest in the world. Its abbot was the administrator of a diocese composed of 37 parishes, and the revenues at the end of the 16th century were valued at 500.000 ducats. It was from here that monastic life spread over barbarous Europe in the darkest period of the Middle Ages; here Paulus Diaconus wrote his history of the Lombards; here the arts and sciences, found an asylum with the brethren who faithfully guarded them for posterity, and the world's debt to the early Benedictines for their safe preservation of whatever remained of ancient civilization is very great. The Library of the monastery, once of world-wide fame, still possesses a collection of about 10.000 volumes and many valuable manuscripts executed by the monks. In medieval times students of literature and other arts were received into the monasteries so that they became the centres of actual schools of Art. The Monastery, completely destroyed in the last war, has now been reconstructed.

BENEVENTO. ARCH OF TRAJAN. A. D. 114.

CAPUA. RUINS OF ROMAN AMPHITHEATRE. *Constructed of travertine, it dates from Imperial times.*

In 1266 Benevento was the scene of the conflict between Charles I. of Anjou and the chivalrous and accomplished young king Manfred, in which the latter lost his throne and his life, through the treachery of his allies.

CASERTA. THE ROYAL PALACE. *Erected in 1752 by* VANVITELLI *for Charles III.*
The façade is 800 ft. long and 135 ft. high. In its vastness this palace recalls the Escurial.

Photo ALINARI, ANDERSON, BROGI.

SULMONA. PALAZZO COMUNALE. *Early 16th cent.*

THE ABRUZZI - APULIA

AQUILA TROIA TRANI BRINDISI BARI LECCE BITONTO

Traceried window at Sulmona.

THE ABRUZZI.

AQUILA. SANTA MARIA DI COLLEMAGGIO. A.D. 1287.   CHIEF PORTAL. S. Maria di Collemaggio.

The marble façade inlaid with red, has splendidly-wrought portals. The interior contains the tomb of Pope Celestine V.

SULMONA. PORTAL OF S. MARIA.    SULMONA. PORTAL OF THE CATHEDRAL.    SULMONA. PALAZZO TABASSI.

TORRE DEI PASSERI. SAN CLEMENTE IN CASAURIA.   PULPIT of San Clemente in Casauria.

Founded in the 9th cent. on the site of an old Benedictine abbey and rebuilt by the Cistercians in 1176.

Photo ALINARI, ANDERSON.

APULIA — THE CATHEDRALS

FRAGMENT OF BRONZE DOOR *executed by* ODERISIO *in 1119-27. Byzantine style. (Cathedral of Troia).*

TROIA. THE CATHEDRAL. A. D. 1093-1125.
The upper part of the façade in Apulian style, 13th cent.

APULIA and most of Southern Italy, once belonged to the beautiful and much praised *Magna Grecia*, of which there remains scarce the shadow of a shade. From the beginning of the eleventh century,—when the Normans* made their first appearance in Italy— till the middle of the twelfth century Apulia enjoyed ever increasing prosperity. During this period the cities enriched by commerce and agriculture, acquired a spirit of emulation, independence, and enterprise. Art flourished and developed under the Norman rulers and it was during this romantic period of her history that the noble churches were built whose façades and portals with their gates of bronze furnish us with the most important examples of sculpture.

* Among whom was the notorious Robert Guiscard and his ten brothers, the progeny of Tancred of Hauteville.

FRAGMENT OF BRONZE DOOR *executed by* BARISANUS *in 1175. Byzantine style (Cathedral of Trani).*

TROIA. PULPIT OF THE CATHEDRAL.

TRANI. PORTAL OF THE CATHEDRAL.

TRANI. THE CATHEDRAL. *Erected* A. D. 1100.
Photo ALINARI.

— 563 —

71*. - WONDERS OF ITALY.

APULIA.

General view of Brindisi

Brindisi, an important station for the trade between Europe and the East, is famous in history; it formed the termination of the Appian Way and was the chief port of the Romans. In the Middle Ages it was the embarkation place of the Crusaders.

Canosa. Episcopal Throne (1089).

Bari. Chair of S. Elia (1098).

Greek Marble Column *indicating the termination of the Appian Way* (Brindisi).

Bitetto. The Cathedral. *Façade of the 13th cent.*

Portal of Bitetto Cathedral. *Gothic style.* A. D. 1435.

Altamura. The Cathedral. *Restored* A. D. 1316.

Photo Alinari, Fotocelere.

APULIA — THE CATHEDRALS.

BARI. CHURCH OF SAN NICOLA.
Begun A. D. 1087. It contains the relics of the saint.

LECCE. CHURCH OF SS. NICOLA AND CATALDO.
Built by Count Tancred A. D. 1180. *Dome in Byzantine style.*
Lecce, an archiepiscopal see of Apulia, was an independent countship when the Counts of Norman blood (Bohemund *et al.*) took it (11th cent.).

BITONTO. PORTAL OF THE CATHEDRAL.

BITONTO. THE CATHEDRAL. A. D. 1175-1200.

ALTAMURA.
PORTAL OF THE CATHEDRAL. 1330.

BITONTO.
LOGGIA OF THE CATHEDRAL. 1200.

RUVO.
PORTAL OF THE CATHEDRAL. *13th cent.*
Photo ALINARI.

ANDRIA (Bari). CASTEL DEL MONTE. *Erected in 1240 by the Emperor Frederick II. of Hohenstaufen.*

This castle, about ten miles south of the city, was the favourite residence of Frederick, whose second and third wives, Violanthe and Isabella of England, were buried in the cathedral. The Castle which still defies the hand of time, is perhaps the most wonderful and original structure of the kind in the world. The edifice, built in 1240 by the Emperor Frederick II. as a fortress and a palace is as beautiful as its general plan is ingenious and its workmanship admirable. Its plan is octangular, with eight powerful octagonal turrets at the angles ; it measures one hundred sixty-seven feet at its extreme breadth and about nine hundred feet in circumference ; the walls are all one hundred feet high and about eight feet thick. The vaulted ceilings and the marble doorway are reminiscent of classic art ; whilst the sculptured ornaments recall the origin of the founder of the Great School of Pisan sculpture.

ALBEROBELLO. THE TRULLI.

Photo ALINARI.

TORRALBA. NURAGO.

The *nuraghi* were the fortified dwellings of the earliest inhabitants, built of large blocks of stone shaped externally like a circular tower or truncated cone, containing rooms inside. Some are more complicated in construction. They were both a house and a fortress, the permanent residence of the chief and a fortified tower where, in case of attack, all the tribesmen living in huts around it found shelter and protection.

SARDINIA

CAGLIARI SASSARI
SACCARGIA UTA ORISTANO

CAGLIARI. TORRE DELL'ELEFANTE.
By GIOVANNI CAPULA, 1305.

Photo ALINARI.

SARDINIA.

SARDINIA, called by the ancients *Sandaliota*, on account of its shape resembling to a sandal, is for its extent the second island od the Mediterranean Sea.

The preistoric era has left many traces in the island whose civilisation dates back to the neolitic period. This period is plentifully afforced by the small hewn-cut grottoes where the dead were buried, but the greatest and most characteristic historical period is that represented by the *nuraghi see pag.* 566 A) built during the Bronze Age and the early Iron Age. Over 6.000 nuraghi are scattered over the island, spread or grouped, according to the nature of the ground, but more numerous along coasts and valleys to defend them against the invaders. There are other megalithic buildings known as the Giants' Tombs consisting of a long low corridor covered with a mound of earth.

The story of Sardinia dates back approximately to the apogee of the Carthaginians's power that, in the 7th century, invaded a great part of the Sardinian coasts. The Roman rule sprung up in 238 B. C. After the Roman civilisation the island knew the barbaric invasions of the Vandals; in 534 it passed under the Byzantium rule and from the 8th century to the year 1000 many Arabian raids took place in the island. Beginning from the year 1004 its coasts were a theatre of war between Genoa and Pisa; in 1200, however, Pisa succeeded in establishing its might over the island. In 1323 Sardinia became a Spanish feud, under the Aragonese kings, and finally in 1718 was ceded, in exchange for Sicily, to the Duke Amedeo II of Savoy who assumed the title of Kings of Sardinia.

Cagliari, the Caralis of the Roman, lies on an extensive bay bounding the flat district at the south of the island; an avenue ascends to the Castle with is ancient gates, towers and walls. The Cathedral, originally of Pisan origin, has been altered and modernized. There is an University, founded in 1596 by Philip III of Spain; an interesting Museum of antiquities with a picture gallery; the remains of a Roman amphiteatre.

Sassari is the second town of Sardinia. The Cathedral is a baroque building while the church of Santa Maria di Betlem maintains its severe Gothic façade of Pisan period. In the Sanna Museum there is a collection of antiquities and a Gallery conteining paintings mostly of the 17th an 18th century; the most important work is the Madonna with Child by Bartolomeo Vivarini dated 1473.

CAGLIARI. THE NATIONAL MUSEUM FIGURINES FOUND AT UTA.

CAGLIARI. THE ROMAN AMPHITEATRE.

Photo ALINARI

THE CATHEDRAL.
Portal of the right transept.

PULPIT OF THE CATHEDRAL (*detail*).
Executed by GUGLIELMO D'INNSBRUCK.

The Cathedral, built in the 14th cent., was altered in the 17th cent. The side portals and the wings of the gothic chapels of the transept are the only parts keeping the medieval structure of the building.

The reliefs of the pulpit's panel reproduced here represent " The symbol of the Evangelist and story of Christ " and are carved not on a smooth surface but on a inlaid one, in the manner of the Byzantine. The pulpit was sculptured for the Cathedral of Pisa from 1159 to 1162 and given in 1312 to that of Cagliari. At first it was a single *ambo*, laid on the lions that to day are situates on the sides of the high altar ; in 1600 it was divided in two pulpits.

MADONNA AND CHILD, WITH ST. ANNE.   MADONNA AND CHRIST.
Triptych by GERARD DAVID *in the Cathedral.*   ST. MARGARET.

This tryptich is named of Clemente VII for it was stolen in Rome, during the town's pillage, under his pontificate (May 1527.) It was afterwards left in Cagliari by the Spanish soldier who had stolen it and had repented of his theft.

Photo ALINARI.

SARDINIA.

MADONNA AND CHILD,
by BARTOLOMEO VIVARINI, 1473.

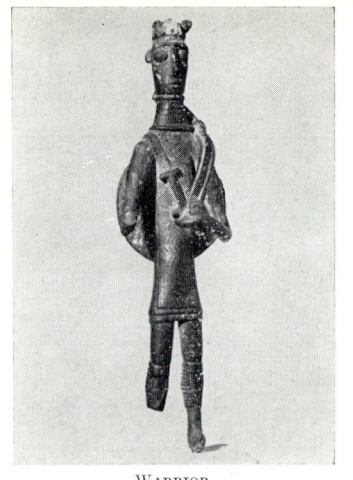

WARRIOR,
a little nuraghe's bronze.
SASSARI. MUSEO SANNA.

VASE WITH RELIEFS,
found at Oristano.

UTA. THE CATHEDRAL.
Romanesque style. 12th cent.

SACCARGIA. BADIA DELLA TRINITÀ.
Pisan style. 12th cent.

CHURCH OF ST. GIUSTA.

Built on a high hillock near Oristano, it has a façade of Lombard-Pisan style of the first half of the 12th century.

The interior, with its three aisles, has marble and granite columns some of which come from Roman buildings.

Photo ALINARI.

PALERMO. MONTE PELLEGRINO.

SICILY

PALERMO
TAORMINA SYRACUSE AGRIGENTO
MESSINA SEGESTA CEFALÙ

THE ETNA AS SEEN FROM TAORMINA.

Photo FOTOCELERE.

TEMPLE AT SEGESTA (5th cent. B. C.). *One of the best preserved Doric temples in Sicily* (See p. 581).

SICILY

" Italy without Sicily leaves no image in the soul
" Sicily is the key to all."
— GOETHE.

SICILY possesses an abundance of spendid ruins and presents to historians and archæologists a field the more tempting since it has been so little tilled, and a new world to travellers who delight in the romantic and picturesque. Nowhere else in Europe (within the limits of so small a territory) are there to be seen so many well preserved specimens of the work of the master builder of ancient and medieval times.

It has been well said that " Sicily is the Archæological Museum of Europe, " for in Sicily are to be seen the fragments of cyclopean structures reared by prehistoric builders; foundations of walls laid by Phoenicians and Carthaginians; temples, theatres, and fortresses of Greek construction; bridges, acqueducts and amphitheatres erected by Roman engineers; remains of edifices built by Byzantine architects; mosques and towers of Saracenic origin; while of Norman churches, castles, palaces, — who can tell the mumber or describe the magnificence?

TEMPLE OF CASTOR AND POLLUX AT GIRGENTI. (5th cent. B. C.).

— 568 —

Photo ALINARI, ANDERSON, BROGI.

GENERAL VIEW OF PALERMO.

PALERMO

PALERMO, is the capital of Sicily, and its largest city. It lies fronting a beautiful bay and encircled by mountains; the plain, enclosed by a semicircle of hills, is named from its singular form and luxuriant fertility, the " Conca d' Oro," the Golden Shell; and within this shell lies Palermo like a splendid pearl.

The city was founded by the Phoenicians, from whom it passed into the hands of the Carthaginians. Later it was conquered by the Romans and subsequently by the Goths. From the sixth to the eleventh century the city was in turn ruled by the Byzantine emperors and by the Arabs, but in 1072 the Normans, led by the progeny of Tancred of Hauteville, obtained possession of the town and it then became the centre of a brilliant architectural activity; palaces and villas, churches and monasteries were erected with such splendour and magnificence as to make of Palermo one of the most glorious cities of Southern Italy.

CHRONOLOGICAL SKETCH OF THE HISTORY OF PALERMO.

B. C.
700. Foundation of *Panormus* (Palermo), by the Phœnicians.
350. Panormus becomes an important stronghold of the Carthaginians.
276. It is conquered by Pyrrhus, King of Epirus, only for a short time.
274. The Romans capture the town.
246. Hamilcar Barca, the Carthaginian general makes an unsuccessful attempt to recover the city.
20. Under Augustus Palermo becomes a Roman municipium.

A. D.
440. Invasion of the Goths.
535. Palermo is reconquered by Belisarius, general of the Byzantine emperor Justinian.

A. D.
831. The Saracens take possession of the city. Under their rule it is made the capital of an emirate and rapidly attains great prosperity, rivalling with Cordova and Cairo in oriental splendour.
1072. The Normans conquer the city and make it the centre of trade between Europe and Asia.
1194. The emperor Henry VI. of Swabia is crowned at Palermo. The German rule lasts for 60 years.
1198-1250. Frederick II. of Hohenstaufen. Under his rule a new era begins, the city becomes the seat of Italian poetry and the centre of scientific learning in Europe.

A. D.
1266. Charles I. of Anjou obtains possession of the city.
1282. The rebellion of the " Sicilian Vespers " puts an end to the misrule of Charles. The House of Anjou is expelled.
1300. The Spanish Aragonese domination begins.
1320. The Chiaramonte in power.
1647. Revolt against the tyrannical rule of the Spaniards.
1713. Sicily is allotted to Victor Amadeus of Savoy, until
1718. when it comes under the rule of the Neapolitan Bourbons.
1860. Victorious entry of Garibaldi Sicily is annexed to the Kingdom of Italy.

— 569 —   Photo ALINARI, ANDERSON, BROGI, FOTOCELERE.

72. - WONDERS OF ITALY.

PALERMO — THE ROYAL PALACE.

COURT OF THE ROYAL PALACE.

THE ROYAL PALACE AND TOWER OF SANTA NINFA.

The Royal Palace occupies the site of an ancient Saracenic edifice to which additions were made by Roger II. and his successors William I., the Bad, William II., the Good, Frederick II., and King Manfred. The palace was afterwards further altered and to day the central part or *Torre di Santa Ninfa*, is the only original relic of Norman times.

On the second floor are the former state apartments, the most important of which is the *Sala di Re Ruggiero* with fine ancient mosaics, and a hall containing portraits of the viceroys.

The palaces of "La Zisa" and "La Cuba" belong to a group of pleasure-residences built by the Norman kings on the outskirts of Palermo. La Zisa (Arab. *El' Aziz*: magnificent), is the best preserved civil edifice of the 12th century. La Cuba (Arab. *kubbeh*: a dome), was built in imitation of La Zisa. The greater part of the splendid park with which it was once surrounded has disappeared, and only one of the numerous pavilions erected by William II. in his gardens now remains standing (see p. 584).

LA ZISA. Arabo-Norman Palace.
Begun in 1160 by William I.

LA CUBA. Arabo-Norman Palace.
Erected by William II. in 1182.

THE GRAND THEATRE. One of the largest theatres in the world.

THE CATACOMBS OF THE CAPUCHINS.

Photo ALINARI, ANDERSON, BROGI.

CAPPELLA PALATINA. Royal Chapel.
Built in 1130 by King Roger II. Norman Saracenic style.

Among all the many places of interest, which attract the stranger to Palermo, there is not one, perhaps, which produces a more powerful impression on the visitor than the Cappella Palatina. Built in the Norman style about 1130 by King Roger II. and dedicated to St. Peter, this chapel is the most splendid of any ecclesiastical interior in Christendom. The floor is covered with inlaid marbles and coloured mosaics; the nave is separated from the aisles by columns of Egyptian granite and cipollino; the walls are richly adorned with rare marbles and glittering mosaics representing scenes from the Old Testament, the lives of Christ, St. Peter, and St. Paul; the beautiful roof, curiously carved, and decorated with an Arabian inscription, is reminiscent of the Alhambra. To the right is a gorgeous pulpit and a carved marble candelabrum exquisitely mellowed by age. The royal throne, facing the altar, bears the arms of Aragon and those (added subsequently) of Savoy.

Photo ALINARI, ANDERSON, BROGI.

PALERMO — THE CATHEDRAL.

THE CATHEDRAL. *Erected* A. D. *1169-85.*

The Cathedral or church of the *Assunta*, erected by the archbishop Walter of the Mill (Gualterius Offamilius), an Englishman sent by Henry II. of England as tutor to William II. of Sicily, is one of those striking structures which abound in Italy. Built in 1169-85 on the site of an earlier church which had been used as a mosque, the edifice has been many times rebuilt and altered. The southwestern front with its fine portico and two towers dates from the second half of the 15th century; the old Campanile (left), connected with the church by two arches spanning the street, dates from the 12th century.

The façade with the great triple-arched porch seen in our illustration is practically original 12th century work and shows best the character of the ancient building. The inharmonious dome was added in 1781-1801 by the architect Ferdinand Fuga, who likewise modernised the interior.

A host of statues of holy or distinguished natives — bishops, popes, and saints — surrounds the enclosure in front of the edifice, which is beautiful in the golden colour of its stone, and splendid in the richness of its Saracenic-Norman decoration.

TOMB OF FREDERICK II. Hohenstaufen († 1250).　　　INTERIOR OF THE CATHEDRAL.

The interior contains porphyry sarcophagi which shrine the bones of the Hautevilles and their representatives: King Roger, "mighty duke and first King of Sicily" († 1154); his daughter Constance, wife of Henry VI.; Emperor Henry VI. († 1197); his son the great Emperor Frederick II. († 1250); Constance of Aragon, wife of Frederick II.; William, Duke of Apulia, son of Frederick III. of Aragon, king of Trinacria. These magnificent tombs constitute one of the most interesting groups of royal sepulchres in the world.

Photo ALINARI, ANDERSON, BROGI.

THE CHURCHES.

CROWN OF CONSTANCE OF ARAGON (*Cathedral*).

The Norman church of *Santo Spirito* (see below), founded in 1173, is especially interesting for its historical associations. For it was here that as the church bell was ringing for vespers on Easter Tuesday 1282, an insult offered to a Sicilian bride on her very way to church by a French soldier who insisted upon searching her for concealed weapons, led to the memorable rebellion against the hateful rule of Charles of Anjou, and the massacre of the French in Sicily, known as the *Sicilian Vespers*. The rising spread to the city, where a republic was proclaimed. In a few weeks the whole of Sicily was in the hands of the rebels.

CHURCH OF SAN GIOVANNI DEGLI EREMITI.

CLOISTERS OF SAN GIOVANNI DEGLI EREMITI. *Arabo-Byzantine architecture.*

San Giovanni degli Eremiti is one of the most picturesque and characteristic relics of Norman times in Sicily. The church was founded in 1132 by King Roger on the site of an older monastery. The five red domes, rising directly from the plain, perpendicular walls, present quite an Oriental appearance, and show that Moslem architects have been given a free hand in its building. In a diploma bearing the date of 1148, Roger grants the buildings to the monastery (Sancti Johannis) "for the love of God, and the salvation of our mother; and our father, the great Count Roger I. of the most serene

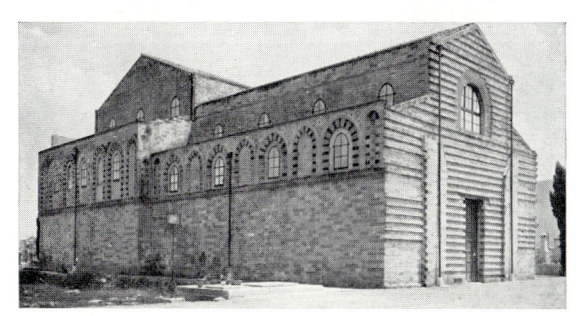

CHURCH OF SANTO SPIRITO or DEI VESPRI. *12th cent.*

Duke Robert Guiscard, our uncle, of most blessed memory and also for the welfare of the soul of our consort, Queen Elvira." Under the Normans the church was the favourite burial place of great personages.

The Cloister, with its luxuriant vegetation presents quite a charming picture.

— 573 —

PALERMO — THE CHURCHES.

CAMPANILE OF "LA MARTORANA" OR SANTA MARIA DELL'AMMIRAGLIO.

La Martorana originally built in 1143 in the Norman style by Georgios Antiochenos, the grand-admiral of King Roger I., was subsequently altered and presented in 1433 to a convent of nuns by Eloisa Martorana. The church was richly decorated by Greek artists with mosaics, among which are the portraits of King Roger in the act of being crowned by Christ, and that of Georgios kneeling at the feet of the Virgin Mary.

The Campanile which dates from the 12th century is a jewel of Norman architecture.

CHURCH OF "LA MARTORANA". *12th cent.*

ROGER I. CROWNED BY CHRIST. *Mosaic, church of La Martorana.*

STUCCO RELIEFS. *By* SERPOTTA. *Oratorio di San Lorenzo.*

CHURCH OF S. MARIA DELLA CATENA. *15th cent*

Santa Maria della Catena, owes its name to the chain (catena) with which the mouth of the neighbouring harbour used to be closed. The church was erected about the end of the 15th century, on the site of an earlier edifice. Its triple-arched porch with the two corner-pilasters exhibits a remarkable combination of Gothic and Renaissance styles.

The church of *San Cataldo*, hard by that of La Martorana and built about the same time, in the Norman-Arabic style, has a battlemented frieze, with al-Koran texts.

CHURCH OF SAN CATALDO. *Begun in 1161.*

Photo ALINARI, ANDERSON, BROGI.

— 574 —

PALERMO — MONREALE.

APSES OF THE CATHEDRAL.    **WEST FRONT OF THE CATHEDRAL.**

Erected in 1174-89 by order of William II., this is the most conspicuous monument of Byzantine-Norman Art in Sicily.

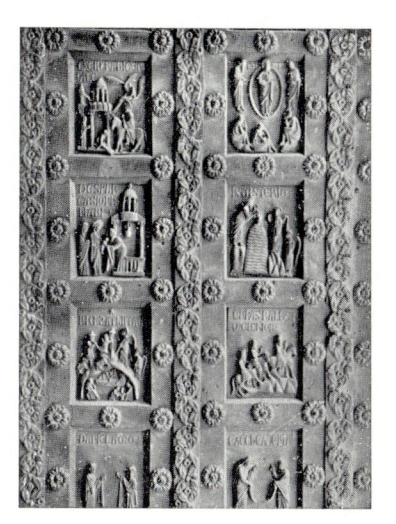

The *Cathedral of Monreale* and the adjoining Benedictine monastery were erected in 1174-89 by order of King William II. called the Good. All that man's genius could devise, has been realized to create this triumph of ecclesiastical architecture.

The church originally dedicated to the Assumption of the Virgin Mary, is in the form of a Latin cross 333 ft. long and 131 ft. wide. The magnificent portal approached by an 18th century porch, has bronze doors executed in 1186 by *Bonanno da Pisa*, adorned with reliefs from the Scriptures; the bronze doors on the right side of the church are the work of *Barisano da Trani*, who executed them about 1190. The wonderful interior has granite pillars with sculptured capitals of great beauty and delicate workmanship; the floor is of variegated and inlaid marbles; the walls are richly adorned with dazzling mosaics which portray scenes from the Old Testament downward.

BRONZE DOORS.
By BONANNO DA PISA (1186).

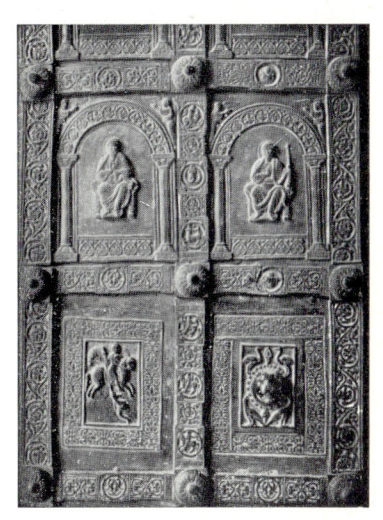

BRONZE DOORS.
By BARISANO DA TRANI (1190).

DOORWAY OF THE CATHEDRAL.
Arabo-Norman style.

CLOISTERS OF THE BENEDICTINE MONASTERY.
Early 13th cent.

— 575 —

Photo ALINARI, ANDERSON, BROGI.

PALERMO — MONREALE.

INTERIOR OF THE CATHEDRAL OF MONREALE.

SCULPTURED CAPITAL.

CHRIST, THE APOSTLES AND SAINTS.
Mosaic in the tribune of the Cathedral.

WILLIAM II. presents the church to the Virgin.

The walls of the cathedral are entirely encrusted with the most splendid specimens of Norman-Byzantine mosaics which cover an area of about seventy thousand square feet. The mosaics in the nave illustrate scenes from the Old Testament; those in the aisles and in the transepts subjects from the history of Christ; on the arches of the transepts are scenes from the life of the Apostles St. Peter and St. Paul. In the right transept are the tombs of William I. and William II. who married Joan of England, daughter of Henry II. (Thomas à Becket was his Chancellor).

In the tribune is a colossal half-length figure of the Saviour, holding an open book, on which " I am the Light of the World " is written in Greek and Latin; in the space below is the Virgin Mary holding the Child, saints, prophets and patriarchs. The royal throne seen on the left is surmounted by a mosaic portrait of King William II. receiving the crown direct from Christ (not from the pope!). The marble throne on the right designed for the archbishop is surmounted by a mosaic picture in which King William is represented in the act of offering a model of the cathedral to the Madonna.

Photo ALINARI, ANDERSON, BROGI.

PALERMO — MONREALE.

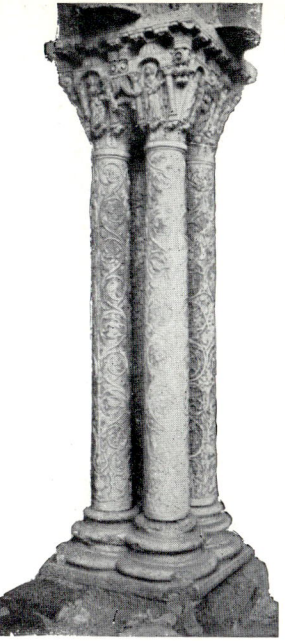

GROUP OF FOUR COLUMNS.
Cloisters of the Monastery.

SCENES FROM THE OLD TESTAMENT.
Mosaics on the walls of the Cathedral.

CLOISTERS OF THE BENEDICTINE MONASTERY. *Early 13th century.*

The magnificent cloisters are the most superb examples of 12th century architecture in existence. The court, which is 169 feet square, is surrounded by pointed arches resting on coupled columns of marble, with a group of four columnes at each angle. There are altogether 216 columns in pairs, encrusted with mosaics in varying patterns, with ever-varied classical capitals of marvellous beauty " all the religion, all the poetry of their age, sculptured in stone ". At the southern angle of the cloisters is a little square court with a fountain in the centre thoroughly Saracenic in character, reminiscent of the Alhambra.

— 577 —

73. • WONDERS OF ITALY.

PALERMO — *MUSEO NAZIONALE.*

COURT OF THE MUSEUM.  HALL OF SELINUNTE. *Showing the metopes.*

The *Museo Nazionale*, situated in the suppressed monastery of the Philipines, contains very remarkable collections of Sicilian-Greek terracottas and sculptures and other antiquities, besides a picture gallery and specimens of Sicilian needle work and embroideries. The Sala di Selinunte, contains the famous *Metopes of Selinus*, very important in the evolutionary development of Hellenic sculpture, from the beginning of the archaic period, to that shortly before its perfection.

The three metopes illustrated here, belong to a 6th century temple; they represent (1) A Quadriga, with the horses in bold relief, beside the charioteer; (2) Perseus, protected by Athena, beheading the Medusa, from whom Pegasus rises; (3) Hercules carrying off the Cercopes, the pigmy robber brothers. The Medusa is almost distorted, the exaggerated thickness of the limbs, the fixed expression of the face, with large staring eyes is almost horrible. The other figures are formless and heavy. Old traces of red pigment increase the primitive character of the work.

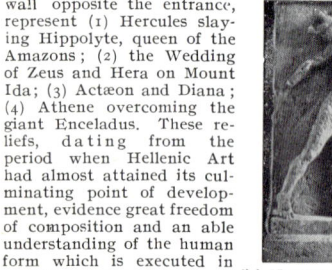

QUADRIGA.   PERSEUS KILLING MEDUSA.   HERCULES WITH CERCOPES.
Sixth century B. C. *metopes from a Doric temple at Selinunte.*

The four metopes on the wall opposite the entrance, represent (1) Hercules slaying Hippolyte, queen of the Amazons; (2) the Wedding of Zeus and Hera on Mount Ida; (3) Actæon and Diana; (4) Athene overcoming the giant Enceladus. These reliefs, dating from the period when Hellenic Art had almost attained its culminating point of development, evidence great freedom of composition and an able understanding of the human form which is executed in an extremely life-like manner.

HERCULES AND HIPPOLYTE.   PUNISHMENT OF ACTÆON.   ATHENE AND ENCELADUS.
Fifth century B. C. *metopes from a Doric temple at Selinunte.*

ORPHEUS PLAYING THE LYRE. *1st cent.* A. D.
Mosaic Pavement (20ft by 16).

ETRUSCAN SARCOPHAGUS.
This is a noble example of ancient art.

— 578 —

Photo ALINARI, ANDERSON, BROGI.

TAORMINA.

The Græco-Roman Theatre. *In the distance is the volcano Etna.*

The Badia Vecchia.

Palazzo Santo Stefano.

TAORMINA, the ancient *Tauromenium*, is a spot of infinite loveliness, the land of *Dolce Far Niente*.

The town lies in an elevated position of wonderful, almost unique beauty: affording magnificent views combining sea and sky of a marvellous blue, miles of curving coast line and picturesque mountain scenery, while the majestic pyramid of Mt. Etna on one side constitutes a scene of indescribable charm and beauty.

The Græco-Roman Theatre has the finest site of any theatre in the ancient world. Situated four hundred feet above the level of the sea, this theatre is one of the most striking monuments of antiquity.

The theatre itself is semicircular and is 377 feet diameter on the outside. Its perfection of structure was celebrated, as a voice upon the stage could penetrate to every part of the building when it was occupied by an audience of 40,000. Taormina was the landing place of Timoleon and of Pyrrhus. The Badia Vecchia and the palaces Santo Stefano and Corvaia are considered among the most interesting Gothic buildings sextant.

The Cathedral. *Gothic portal.*

Palazzo Corvaia. *Gothic architecture.*

— 579 —

Photo ALINARI, ANDERSON, BROGI.

SYRACUSE.

GENERAL VIEW OF SYRACUSE.

The famous VENUS ANADYOMENE.
A Greek work of the 3rd cent. B. C.

THE GREEK THEATRE (5th cent. B. C.).

SYRACUSE, is one of the great cities of antiquity, and the most interesting place in Sicily. Without visiting it, it is impossible to understand its geographical and historic significance.

In 734 B. C. a colony of Corinthians led by Archias, drove out the Phoenician settlers and established themselves on the isle of *Ortygia*, lying close to the mainland, and afterwards united to it by a bridge. Owing to the fertility of the soil, the colony increased so rapidly, that within a century of its foundation it was in a position to found new colonies in other parts of Sicily. In her palmiest days Syracuse had a circuit of 14 miles, enclosing five separate quarters, and is said to have contained over half a million inhabitants. She had two ports, the smaller port was capacious enough to receive a large fleet of ships of war; there were several quarries of limestone (*Latomiæ*), of which the city was built, and in which unfortunate prisoners of war were confined.

The most important event in the history of Syracuse was the long siege of the city by the Athenians which ended in the total destruction of the great Athenian land and sea armaments in 413 B. C.

After a prosperous period, owing to internal dissensions, the city fell under the rule of tyrants, the last of whom, Hieronymus, allied himself with the Carthaginians against Rome, during the Punic Wars. A Roman army, therefore, under Marcellus was sent against Syracuse, and after a siege of two years, during which the celebrated Archimedes assisted his fellow-citizens by the construction of various engines of war, the city was taken and plundered (Archimedes was slain by a soldier who did not know him). From this time Syracuse sank to the condition of a Roman provincial town and finally was sacked and nearly destroyed by the Saracens in A. D. 878.

With the aid of the Normans (1085), the portion of Ortygia was rebuilt, and this constitutes the modern city, which has interesting relics of its former greatness.

SARCOPHAGUS OF ADELFIA.

Photo ALINARI, ANDERSON, BROGI, FOTOCELERE.

SYRACUSE, SEGESTA.

SEGESTA   The Greek Theatre.   5th cent. B. C.
This theatre resembles in its position that of Taormina, it is hewn in the rock and has a diameter of 165 yds.

SEGESTA.   The Doric Temple.
This is a Roman structure of the period of Augustus. It has a length of 77 yds. and is 44 yds. in width.

SEGESTA, originally *Egesta*, one of the most ancient cities of Sicily, claimed to have been founded by Trojan fugitives in the 12th century B. C. The ancient town was in continual warfare with Selinous, and after the destruction of the latter (B. C. 409), it became a subject-ally of Carthage. But during the First Punic War (B. C. 264), the inhabitants allied themselves with the Romans and changed the name of their town from Egesta to Segesta. The city, however, was finally abandoned in consequence of the ravages of the Saracens in A. D. 900. Its existing ruins comprise a temple and a theatre.

The Temple, which stands upon a lonely hill (900 ft.), is one of the grandest and best preserved monuments of Doric architecture in Sicily. Its length is 200 ft.; width 86 ft.; the 36 unfluted columns surrounding it are 30 ft. in height and 6 ft. in thickness. The edifice was probably never completed (*see also* p. 568).

The Theatre, is hewn in the rock and has a diameter of 205 ft. It commands fine views of the surrounding country.

SYRACUSE.   THE AMPHITHEATRE. (1st cent. B. C.).

AURIGA.   *Bronze found at Delphi.*

SYRACUSE.   LATOMIA DEL PARADISO.

SYRACUSE.   LATOMIA AND CONVENT OF THE CAPUCHINS.

The "Latomie," which form one of the characteristics of Syracuse, are places of which no photographs give any notion. They are vast excavations hewn in the rock to a depth of about 100 feet below the level of the soil. The Latomie were used as burial-places and sometimes as prisons for captive enemies. The Latomia del Paradiso possesses extraordinary acoustic properties.

Photo ALINARI, ANDERSON, BROGI.

MESSINA. View of the Town with the Cathedral.

CATANIA, an ancient city at the foot of Etna, is the most important town in Sicily after Palermo. It has been several times devastated by earthquakes and the eruptions of Etna, particulary that of 1693. The present town with its imposing buildings, dates from the reconstructions of the eighteenth century. Vincenzo Bellini (1801-35), the composer, was a native of Catania.

The Cathedral, begun under Roger I. in 1092 and rebuilt after the earthquakes of 1169 and 1693, contains among other things a chapel dedicated to St. Agatha († 253), the patroness of the city; the monument of the composer Vincenzo Bellini; sarcophagi of the Aragonese sovereigns Frederick II. († 1337), King Louis († 1355), Frederick III. († 1377), Queen Constance († 1363), and others

CATANIA. The Cathedral. Begun in 1092.

MESSINA, the ancient *Zankle*, is situated on the Straits of Messina, which separates Sicily from the mainland; here are the famous Scylla and Charybdis of the ancients. It was first colonised in the 5th cent. B. C.; in 264 B. C. it was involved in war with Carthage, and later it became a Roman town of great importance. Messina was a well planned, flourishing and beautiful city, but its monuments have been greatly damaged by the last earthquake of 1908. The cathedral, now restored, dates from 1092 and contains works of art of the 16th century. The Museo Nazionale, is formed of works of art saved from the earthquake.

The environs present excellent points of view towards Calabria; the *Fata Morgana* (a mirage), is frequently noticed at the Straits.

CEFALÙ. The Cathedral (*12th cent.*).

MOSAICS in the tribune. Cefalù Cathedral.

The *Cathedral of Cefalù*, founded by Roger II. in 1131, is a noble monument of Norman architecture. The façade dates from 1240: the impressive interior built in the form of a Latin cross (length 243, width 92 ft.) has 16 columns with Byzantine and Romanesque capitals. The tribune is decorated with mosaics dating from 1148, considered to be the oldest and best preserved in Sicily (cfr. with p. 576). The beautiful cloisters adjoining the church, are reminiscent of those at Monreale.

Photo ALINARI, ANDERSON, BROGI, FOTOCELERE.

AGRIGENTO (GIRGENTI).

VIEW OF AGRIGENTO (GIRGENTI).

AGRIGENTO (Girgenti), the ancient *Acragas*, was the second city of Sicily in point of population, but first in point of wealth during the Greek period. Its site (about 1000 ft. above the sea) was one of the stateliest on which any city was ever planted. To-day only the ruins of the temples remain to testify to the greatness of its past.

The Greek temples at Girgenti are the most majestic in the ancient Hellenic world. The glorious Temple of Concord given here is the best preserved and is probably the best specimen of Doric architecture in existence.

The Cathedral, occupies the site of the ancient Acropolis, the highest part of the modern town; in the Chapter House is a magnificent Roman sarcophagus, with reliefs of great delicacy and purity of style, representing four episodes in the story of Hippolytus and Phædra.

TEMPLE OF CONCORD. *Doric style.*

PHAEDRA PINING FOR LOVE.
Relief on a marble sarcophagus in the Cathedral.

TEMPLE OF JUNO LACINIA.
(5th cent. B. C.).

Photo ALINARI, ANDERSON, BROGI, FOTOCELERE.

PALERMO. "La Cubola."
Remains of a pavilion once belonging to the Saracenic palace of La Cuba, erected by the Norman King William II. in 1182. Boccaccio chose this place for the scene of one of his novels.

"Farewell, land of love, Italy,
"Sister-land of Paradise:
"With my own feet I have trodden thee,
"Have seen with mine own eyes:
"I remember, thou forgettest me,
"I remember thee."

C. G. ROSSETTI

ARMORIAL BEARINGS AND PORTRAITS OF THE GONZAGAS OF MANTUA.
Fifteenth century relief in the *Accademia Virgiliana, Mantua*.

INDEX

WITH HISTORICAL SKETCH

The letters *a b c* after the page number signify that the reference will be found:
a in the upper part of the page; *b* in the middle: *c* in the lower part of the page.

AARON

AARON, elder brother of Moses, leads the Israelites out of Egypt, in their march to the Promised Land of Canaan, 480, 482. [He is the traditional founder and head of the Jewish priesthood].
Abbey of Monte Cassino, founded by St. Benedict, 560. [Now completely destroyed in the World War].
Abelard, Peter [† 1142], noted French phylosopher and theologian, 77. [He was a great teacher in his day, renowned for his dialectic ability and his learning, his passion for Heloïse (whom he secretly married) and consequent misfortunes].
Abijah, King of Judah, 380.
Abiram, a levite who conspired against Moses, 482.
Abraham, Hebrew patriarch, ancestor of the Jews, 98, 380, 420; offers up Isaac, 205, 229, 315, 462.
Abruzzi, a highland district, in the Apennines, in Central Italy, 561 sq.
Absalom, a son of David, 340. [He rebelled against his father, defeated in " the wood of Ephraim, " was killed by Joab David's captain].
Accademia (Academy) di Belle Arti, at Venice, 138; at Florence, 289; at Siena, 346; *dei Lincei*, at Rome, 496. The Platonic academy founded by the Medici 312; Academy of France, 510.
Acciaiuoli, Niccolò, of an illustrious Florentine family, grand seneschal of Queen Giovanna of Naples, 312.
Achab, seventh king of Israel, 340 *b*.
Achilles, the great hero of the Iliad, 387. [He was invulnerable except in the heel, at the point where his mother held him as she dipt his body in the Styx to render him invulnerable].

Acquasparta Matteo d' [† 1302] General of the Franciscans, orders monum't to Benedict XI., 360; his tomb, 437. [In 1300, he was sent by Boniface VIII. to Florence to pacify the Bianchi and the Neri, but was unsuccessful).
Acre, St. Jean d', pillars of, 112. [The ancient Ptolemaïs, during the crusades Acre was a strong place and seaport in Syria, taken at an enormous sacrifice of life, by Richard Coeur de Lion in 1191; in 1517 it became part of the Turkish empire. General Allenby captured it (1918) from the Turks].
Acropolis at Athens, sculptures from, 506. [The fortified nucleus of the citadel commanding the city of ancient Greece].
Actæon, mythical huntsman, Greek relief at Palermo, 578. [He was changed into a stag for surprising Diana when bathing, and afterwards devoured by his own dogs].
Actium, 431. [A town at the entrance of a gulf in Greece, where in 31 B.C. Augustus gained his naval victory over Antony and Cleopatra].
Acts of the Apostles, 101, 228, 240.
Adam and Eve, fresco by Masolino, 241; by Michelangelo, 478; by Raphael, 470; symbolism of, 114.
Adeodatus (12th cent.), sculptor, 326.
Admetus, King of Pherae, 453 *b*, 495.
Adonis, the favourite of Aphrodite, 501. [He was of remarkable beauty; being mortally wounded by a boar was changed by Venus into a flower, the anemone, the colour of his blood, by sprinkling nectar on his body; he was permitted to return each year from the underworld to his mistress for six months].

ÆSCULAPIUS

Adoration of the Kings (Magi, 262), painting by Botticelli, 261; Gentile da Fabriano, 257; Ghirlandaio, 246, Mantegna, 271; Bonifazio Veronese, 34; Albert Durer, 273; Ben. Bonfigli, 364*. Early Christian mosaic, 420; relief, 188.
Adoration of the Shepherds, The, painting by Ghirlandaio, 244; Hugo van der Goes, 272; Fiorenzo di Lorenzo, 364.
Adorno, illustrious family in Genova, of the Ghibelline party, several of whom were doges of the Republic, 34.
Adrian, Roman emperor. See Hadrian.
Adrian IV. (Nicholas Breakspeare) [† 1159], Benedictine Abbot (the only English pope), 333.
Adrian VI. [† 1523], of Utrecht, Pope, minister of Charles V., 42, 430.
Adriatic, The « Queen » of the, 82; annual symbolic ceremony connected with, 151. [The Adriatic Sea, 450 m. long, separates Italy from Dalmatia and Albania].
Æneas Piccolomini. See *Piccolomini*.
Æneas, the Trojan hero, carrying off his father Anchises, 468 *a*, is wounded and medicated, 536 *b*.
Æneid, episodes from Virgil's, 448 *a*; Augustus appreciation of, 462 *c*. [Æneid, an epic poem by Virgil, of which Æneas is the hero].
Æschines [† 314 B.C.], celebrated Athenian orator, 447.
Æschylus [† 456 B. C.], the father of the Greek tragedy, 447.
Æsculapius, god of medicine, and the healing art, 398 *b*; 449 *a*. [He is commonly represented in a long cloak, with bare breast, his usual attribute is a club-like staff with a serpent coiled round it, and often accompanied by his daughter Hygieia, the goddess of health].

— 585 —

74. - WONDERS OF ITALY.

Ærarium publicum (the state treasury), in ancient Rome, 397.
Aërial perspective, beauty of, in Masaccio' paintings, 240 b.
Agatha St. [† 253], 582 b. [A Sicilian virgin, she suffered martyrdom under Decius in 251; is represented in art bearing a pair of shears: the instruments with which her breasts were cut off].
Agilulf [† 616], Lombard King, 77.
Agliè, castle at, 14.
Agnes St. [† 303], a virgin who suffered martyrdom under Diocletian, 426 b; peculiar ceremony on her festival, in St. Agnes' church in Rome, ib.
Agnus Dei, Lamb of God,—applied by John the Baptist to Christ, relief on Giotto's campanile, in Florence, 217.
Agostino di Duccio [† 1482], Florentine sculptor, 300, 360.
Agrate Marco, sculptor, his statue of St. Bartholomew, 52.
Agrippina, wife of Germanicus, 507.
Ahasuerus, King of Persia, 202, 271, 286.
Aix, the ancient *Aquae Sextae*, 272. [It was the scene of the defeat of the Teutones by the Romans; successively occupied by Visigoths; several times plundered by Franks and Lombards; taken by Saracens in 731; during the middle ages it became the capital of the County of Provence, and reached its zenith after the 12th century, when the houses of Aragon and Anjou made it a centre of art and learning].
Alahambra, The, 556, 571, 575.
Alaric [† 410], King of the Goths, 48, 392.
Alassio, Riviera di Ponente, 45.
Albano, The Lake of, near Rome, 513.
Alberico da Barbiano, famous condottiere, of the 14th century, 74.
Alberti Leon Battista [† 1472], Florentine architect, erects the Rucellai palace, 305; and the façade of S. Maria Novella at Florence, 223; becomes architect of St. Peter's, Rome, 405; designs the Duomo at Rimini, 188.
Albertinelli Mariotto [† 1515], Florentine painter, his famous "Visitation of the Virgin," in the Uffizi, 263.
Albigenses, the, 223 b. [It is the usual designation of a sect of heretics, especially the Catharist heretics which sprung in the south of France in the 12th and 13th centuries against which pope Innocent III. proclaimed a crusade, afterwards carried on by the Inquisition till their annihilation].
Albizi, Giovanna degli, Florentine beauty, 225. [The Albizi, a powerful Florentine family, were the rivals of the Medici and the Alberti].
Alboin, King of the Lombards, 166 b.
Alborghetti, Venetian sculptor, 128.
Albornoz [† 1367], Spanish cardinal and statesman, 188.
Alcæus, of Mytilene (B. C. 611), poet, 463.
Alcestis, her romance of conjugal love, carved on marble, 453 b.
Alcibiades [† 404 B. C.], Athenian general and politician, 447, 461.
Aldo Manuzio, famous Venetian printer, his valuable books, 78.
Aldobrandeschi, old nobles of Siena, 329*.

Aldobrandini, illustrious family of Tuscany, 452; A. Nuptials, *ib.*; Villa A. at Frascati, 512, 513.
Alemagna, Giov. d' (15th cent.), Venetian painter, 134, 138, 142.
Alençon, the Cardinal D', 425.
Alessi Galeazzo [† 1572], architect, follower of Michelangelo, 28, 31, 38, 63.
Alexander Severus [† 235], Roman emperor, 402. [He was a wise, virtuous and pious prince; in an expedition against the Germans, who were causing trouble on the frontiers of the empire, fell a victim to an insurrection among his troops not far from Mainz].
Alexander the Great [† 323 B. C.], King of Macedonia, mosaic of the defeat he inflicted on Darius at Issus, 527; his appreciation and safeguard of Homer's poem, 462 c; painting representing his nuptials with Roxana, 493; paintings representing episodes of his life, 499 b; bronze statue from Herculaneum, 535; allegory of his triumphs, 287 a; of his ascension to heaven, 94. [He had Aristotle for tutor, and on the death of his father ascended the throne at the age of 20. After subduing Greece had himself proclaimed generalissimo of the Greeks against the Persians; conquered the army of Darius, subdued the principal cities of Syria, overran Egypt, and crossing the Euphrates and Tigris routed the Persians; hurrying further south he swept everything before him, till his soldiers refusing to advance, he returned to Babylon, where he suddenly fell ill of fever and in a few days died at the age of 32. He is said to have slept every night with his Homer and his sword under his pillow, and the inspiring idea of his life is defined to have been the right of Greek intelligence to override and rule the merely glittering barbarity of the East].
Alexander III. (Orlando Bandinelli)[†1181] Pope, and Frederick Barbarossa, German Emperor, gives a nuptial ring to the Republic of Venice, 151 b; excommunicates the emperor Frederick Barbarossa, 474 a, 516 c; is reconciliated with Barbarossa, 95 b; paintings in allusion to this event, 125 a; his triumphal entry into Rome, 333. [He was a Sienese and teacher of canon law at Bologna; in 1153 he became papal chancellor, and was the leader of the cardinals opposed to Frederick Barbarossa. In 1159 he was chosen to succeed Adrian IV., a minority of the cardinals, however, electing the cardinal priest Octavian, who assumed the name of Victor IV. This antipope, and his successors Paschal III. and Calixtus III., had the imperial support. But after his defeat at Legnano (1176) the emperor finally recognized him as Pope. He took the part of Thomas à Becket against Henry II. of England; excommunicated William the Lion of Scotland, and put the Kingdom under the interdict. He held the third Lateran council in Rome 1179].

Alexander V. (Filargo) [† 1410], Pope, 176. [Franciscum monk, originating from Candia, was elected in Pisa in 1409].
Alexander VI. (Roderigo Borgia) [† 1503], Pope, quoted, 131; his enmity for Savonarola, 252; architectural work in Sant'Angelo, 395, 499; receives first gold brought from America, 419; adds to the Vatican, 441; his portrait by Pintoricchio, 456.
Alexander VII. (Chigi) [† 1667], Pope, erects the colonnade of St. Peter's, 405; restores the church of S. Maria della Pace, in Rome, 439.
Alexandria (Egypt), 60, 110.
Alfieri Vittorio [† 1803], famous tragic dramatist, 219 c. [Born at Asti, of rich and noble parents until the age of 16 remained at the Academy of Turin, though he learned very little there. The successive seven years he spent travelling about Europe visiting most of the capitals, indulging in a series of amorous adventures and wasting much time in dissipation. He studied Voltaire, Rousseau, Montesquieu and after his return to Italy Plutarch's *Lives*, wherein he found a stimulus to literary composition. On the success of his first drama "Cleopatra," he determined to devote himself to the composition of tragedies (his literary reputation rests chiefly on 19 of his tragedies, all strictly classical in form). In 1777 he met the Countess of Albany, a new love, and on the death of her husband Charles Edward Stuart, they settled in Florence, where they lived for the rest of his life. On his death he was buried in Santa Croce, and there the Countess of Albany caused a monument by Canova to be dedicated to the memory seven years later].
Alfred the Great [† 901], King, 69. [The most celebrated and greatest of the Saxon kings].
Algardi Alessandro [† 1654], sculptor and architect, his relief of Attila, 410; reliefs at St. John in Lateran, 414; at S. Maria del Popolo, 433; façade of Sant' Ignazio, 438.
Alighieri. *See* Dante.
Allegorical paintings, remarkable: Veronese's "Apotheosis of Venice," in the Doges' palace, 126; "The Triumph of Death," in the Pisan Camposanto, 320; "Good and Bad Government," in Palazzo Pubblico, at Siena, 332; "Pictorial Chronicles of Peace and War," in the Sienese Archivio, 349; the "Infallibility of the Church," famous fresco in the Vatican, 464.
Allegories of St. Francis of Assisi, famous paintings by Giotto illustrative of the vows of the franciscan order, in *San Francesco*, at Assisi, 369 sqq.
Allegory of the Church, by Bellini, 270; of Love, 36, 297; of Michelangelo's sculptures in the Medici chapel, 236 sq.
Allori Cristofano [† 1621], Florentine painter, 273 c; the "Judith and Holofernes," 285 a.
Alphonso of Este. *See* Este.
Alphonso I., King of Naples, 330 his triumphal arch, 522; his castle of Ischia, 559.

Alps, The, 11, 12, 13. [The vastest mountain system in Europe, occupying an area of 90.000 sq. miles. Their peaks mostly covered with perpetual snow].

Altamura (Apulia), Duomo of, 564, 565.

Altichiero da Zevio [† ca. 1390], Veronese and Paduan painter, his frescoes in the chapel of San Giorgio, at Padua, 158; in Sant'Anastasia, Verona, 162.

Altinum, ancient Town of the *Veneti*, 91.

Amadeo Giov. Ant. [† 1522], Milanese architect, his work on the Duomo at Milan, 51; façade of Certosa at Pavia, 70; Colleoni chapel, Bergamo, 75.

Amadeus VI. [† 1383], of Savoy, 16.

Amadeus VIII. [† 1451], first duke of Savoy, 18. [He retired into a monastery on the death of his wife; was elected pope as Felix V., but was not acknowledged by the Church].

Amalasuntha [† 535], daughter of Theodoric, erects a mausoleum in which the bones of her father were laid, 181.

Amalfi, 552; its capture and discovery of the Pandects, 238, 462; its fleet goes to the assistance of pope Leo IV., against the Saracens, 468; her *Tavole Amalfitane*, 552; invention of the mariner's compass there, 552; its famous Road, 554 *sq*.

Aman, minister of Ahasuerus, 477.

Amati, The (16th-17th cent.), violin-makers of Cremona, 77.

Amazones, a fabulous race of female warriors, 529.

Ambrose, St. [† 397], one of the 4 Latin doctors, 54; becomes Bishop of Milan, 48; life and miracles, 54; consecrates church in Florence, 233; converts St. Augustine, 354.

America, symbolically represented, 27.

Amidei, a wealthy 13th cent. Florentine family (the kinsmen of the proud Uberti and Fifanti), whose feud with the Buondelmonti was supposed to have originated the Guelph and Ghibelline factions in Florence, 192.

Ammannati Bartolommeo [† 1592], Florentine architect and sculptor, his works at Florence: rebuilds Santa Trinita Bridge, 194; erects Fountain of Neptune, 196.

Amorites, a pre-Israelite people, 335.

Amphitheatre, Roman, at Verona, 166; at Pola, 170; at Rome, 400; at Pozzuoli, 559; at Capua, 560.

Anacapri (Island of Capri), 550.

Anacletus [† 91], Bishop of Rome, 404.

Anacreon [† 478 B. C.], famous lyric poet of Athens, 463.

Anagni, scene of Papal tragedy, 516.

Ananias, a follower of the Apostles, striken to death when reproved by Peter for lying, 472.

Anatomy, first lessons of, 173.

Anaxagoras [† 428 B. C.], celebrated Greek philosopher, 461; cited, 447.

Anchises, Trojan prince, father of Æneas, in Raphael's painting, in Vatican, 468 *a*.

Ancona, important sea-port, 189.

Andrea da Firenze [† 1377], Florentine painter, decorator of the Spanish Chapel, at Florence, 228.

Andrea del Castagno [† 1457], Florentine painter, his frescoes in Sant'Apollonia, Florence, 253.

Andria (Apulia), Castel del Monte, 566.

Andromeda and Perseus, sculpture by Cellini, 198; Pompeian fresco, 537.

Angelico, Fra (Giov. da Fiesole) [† 1455], Florentine painter, character of his art, 250; frescoes in San Marco, Florence, 248 *sq*.; and easel paintings, 250 *sq*.; picture at Perugia, 364; frescoes in the Vatican, 471; frescoes at Orvieto, 384; presumed portraits, 460; burial place, 434.

Angilbertus (9th century), Archbishop, 55.

Anjou, dynasty in Naples, 519; their abominable rule, 524; their stronghold, 522; burial place of some of them, 523, 525. [Anjou, the name of a French territory annexed (1203) to the crown of France. In 1246 King Louis IX. gave it as an appanage to his son Charles, count of Provence, whose descendants became (1268-1442) Kings of Naples]. See also *Charles, René*.

Anne of Brittany [† 1514], duchess of Brittany and queen consort of France, 313. [She was scarcely 12 years old when she succeeded to her father Francis II., duke of Brittany. By her marriage, first to Charles VIII. then to Louis XII., the duchy was added to the crown of France].

Ansaldo, architect at Genoa, 38.

Ansano, St., evangelizes the people of Siena, 329. [Martyrised in 303].

Anselm, St. [† 1109], archbishop of Canterbury, 12. [He was an able, high principled, God-fearing man, and a calmly resolute upholder of the teaching and authority of the Church].

Antelami [† 1196], Parmesan sculptor, 180.

Antichrist (Simon Magus), The, 323, 382.

Antinous, Hadrian's favourite, 446, 452.

Antioch, 39; the King of, 240.

Antisthenes [† 365 B. C.], Greek philosopher, 473.

Antonello da Messina, Sicilian and Venetian painter, his work in Venice, 140; remarkable portrait in the Borghese Gallery, 489.

Antoninus Pius [† 161], Rom. emp., 399.

Antony Mark (Marcus Antonius) [† 30 B.C.], the Triumvir, pronounces oration at Julius Caesar's funeral, 398 *a*; resides on the Palatine, 400 *a*; his defeat at Actium, 431 *a*; his liaison with Cleopatra, 149 *c*.

Antony of Padua, St. [† 1231], Franciscan friar born at Lisbon, histor. sketch, 155 *b*; portrait, in Rome, 421 *b*.

Antony the Great, St. [† 356], an Egyptian hermit, known as the founder of ascetism, 255 *b*, 457.

Aosta (the ancient *Augusta Praetoria*), 12. [A town in a fertile Alpine valley, the birth place of St. Anselm].

Apelles (4th cent. B. C.), celebrated painter of antiquity, 261.

Aphrodite, celebrated statue in the Vatican, 444. See also *Venus*.

Apocalypse (*The Revelation*), the, 421, 429.

Apocrypha, story from the, 465.

Apollinaris St., 187.

Apollo and the Muses, celebrated fresco by Raphael, in the Vatican, 463.

Apollo Belvedere, famous Greek statue by Leocares, in the Vatican, 451.

Apollodorus of Damascus [† ca. 185 A. D.], famous Greek architect, 401.

Apollonius of Tralles (2nd cent. B. C.), Greek sculptor, 451, 491.

Apostles, The, symbolised as sheep, 94, 187, 429; places where they preached, 108, as represented by Leonardo, 57.

Apothecaries, The Patron saint of, 231.

Apoxiomenos, celebrated marble statue, in the Vatican, 455.

Apparition of the Virgin to St. Bernard: painting by Orcagna, 289; Fra Bartolommeo, 289; Filippino Lippi, 245.

Appian Way, The, 403, 564; its termination, 564.

Appius Claudius, censor, 513.

Apuleius, a student of Plato, author of the « *Golden Ass* », 79, 492.

Apulia (ancient territory of *Magna Grecia*), period of its prosperity, architecture, sculpture, 563 *sqq*.

Aqueducts in Rome, the, 391, 403.

Aquila (Abruzzi), churches of, 562.

Aquileia (Venetia), 91, 110, 169.

Aquinas, St. Thomas [† 1274], Allegory of his Glorification, great fresco in S. Maria Novella, 228; famous painting, at Pisa, 317 *; his death-place, 516; his portrait in the Vatican, 460; composes office for the feast of Corpus Domini, 464. [An Italian of noble birth, studied at Naples, became a Dominican monk, sat at the feet of Albertus Magnus and went to Paris].

Ara Pacis, Rome, relief from the, 255.

Arabo-Norman architecture in Sicily, 574.

Arabs, their capture of Palermo, 569.

Aragon, Tullia of, famous courtesan, 76.

Aragonese Kings of Naples, *s*. Chart VII., p. 586; their rule of Naples, 519.

Arazzi, Raphael's cartoons for the, 472.

Arbia, scene of Montaperti battle, 329.

Arc, Joan of. See Joan of Arc.

Arca di Sant'Agostino, at Pavia, 69; di San Domenico, at Bologna, 176.

Arcadia (land of simplicity and bliss), 463.

Arch, Memorial: of Augustus, 12, 171; of Septimius Severus, 396; of Ianus, 400; of Drusus, 403; of Constantine, 401; of Titus, 399; of Trajan, 560.

Archeological Museum of Europe, 568.

Archimedes of Syracuse [† 212 B. C.], 461, 580. [The greatest mathematician of antiquity, a man of superlatively power, well skilled in all the mechanical arts and sciences of the day. When Syracuse was taken by the Romans, he was unconscious of the fact, and slain, while busy on some problem, by a Roman soldier, notwithstanding the order of the Roman general that his life should be spared. He discovered how to determine the specific weight of bodies while he was taking a bath, and was so excited over the discovery that, it is said, he darted off stark naked on the instant through the streets, shouting " *Eureka! Eureka!* I have found it! I have found it!"].

Archives, at Siena, 330. [In 1859, the stately palazzo Piccolomini became the repository of the State Archives, one of the important collections in Italy].

Arena, Chapel, at Padua, famous for its frescoes by Giotto, 157.

Aretino Pietro [† 1556], celebrated pamphleteer, portraits of, 284. [A licentious, satirical writer, was called the "Scourge of Princes;" he died after an uncontrollable fit of laughter which seized him at the story of the adventure of a sister].

Arezzo, 356. [An ancient Tuscan city, birth place of Mæcenas, Petrarch, Guido Monaco, Fra Guittone, Giorgio Vasari, Pietro Aretino].

Ariadne, daughter of Minos, King of Crete, famous painting by Tintoretto, 120; the Sleeping A., in the Vatican, 449; the Triumph of A., 509.

Arians, baptistery of the, at Ravenna, 185. [Of or pertaining to Arius. See below].

Aribert, Archbishop of Milan, inventor of the *Carroccio*, 49.

Ariosto † 1533], illustrious Italian poet, visits the court of the Gonzagas (Mantua), 78 b; and that of the Estes, at Ferrara, 178 c; his portrait in the Palazzo Vecchio, 201 a; and in Raphael's fresco of "Parnassus," Rome, 463 b. [He spent his life mostly in poverty; his fame rests on his great work "Orlando Furioso," a poem in 46 cantos depicting the madness of Roland induced by the loss of his ladylove through her marriage to another].

Aristophanes (5th cent. B. C.), great comic dramatist of Athens, 463.

Aristotle [† 322 B. c.], Greek philosopher, portrait in Florence, 287; in Rome, 461; in Venice, 114. [At Athens he taught in the Lyceum, where it was his habit to walk up and down while teaching, from which circumstance his school got the name of Peripatetic. He was the oracle of the scholastic philosophers and theologians in the Middle Ages, is the author of a great number of writings which covered a vast field of speculation, of which the progress of modern sciences goes to establish the value. His philosophy has influenced the world for 2000 years].

Arius [† 336], founder of Arianism, 228, 323, 434. [A presbiter of the church of Alexandria, he held that Christ was the first and noblest of all created beings, but that, as there was a time when he was not, he was not the Eternal Son of God, and that there was no Trinity, as the Son was not of the same substance as the Father. He was condemned first by a local synod which met at Alexandria, and then by a General Council held at Nicea in 325].

Ark of Noah, 98, 453. [Constructed by the Patriarch by God's command for the preservation of the human race and the dry-land animals, during the prevalence of the deluge].

Ark of the Covenant, 205 b. [It was a chest of acacia wood overlaid with gold; contained the two tables of stone inscribed with the Ten Commandments, the gold pot with the manna, and Aaron's rod].

Arkesilaos, sculptor of ancient Greece, his "Venus Genetrix," in Rome, 502 b.

Armorial bearings of the House of Medici, 1; of the Florentine republic, 197; of Florentine podestas, 292.

Armoury, collections of, in Turin, 22; in the Bargello, 293, and in the Stibbert museum of Florence, 308.

Arms of Florence, 197, 235; of Siena, 329.

Arno, The river, 194, 195, 313. [It rises in mount Falterona, in the Apennines, about 25 m. from Florence; runs through the beautiful Casentino valley, Florence and Pisa and falls into the sea 7 m. west of Pisa, after a course of 155 miles].

Arnold of Brescia [† 1155], political and religious, Italian reformer, his birth place, 77 a; attempts an insurrection in Rome, 392. [He studied theology in Paris and upon his return to Italy he became a canon regular; his life was rigidly austere; he declaimed against the corruption of the clergy and the temporal ambitions of the high dignitaries of the Church. At last, after his failure of an insurrection in Rome, he was burned alive and his ashes thrown into the Tiber].

Arnolfo di Cambio [† 1301] (pupil of Niccolò Pisano), Florentine architect and sculptor, his works in Florence: builds the Palazzo Vecchio, 197 a; begins the construction of the Cathedral, 209; and the church of Santa Croce, 218; contributes work to the pulpit of the Siena cathedral, 336; designs the Fontana Maggiore, in Perugia, 358; initiates the construction of the Orvieto cathedral, 379; builds the Castle of Poppi, in the Casentino, 389; executes the marble tomb of pope Boniface VIII., in Rome, 412; and the fine tabernacle over the highaltar, at St. Paul's outside-the-walls, in Rome, 422. [He was faithful to his master's teachings; in his creations, however, he resisted the lure of the Gothic, tempering it with Tuscan grace; had an instinct for proportion preserving a geometric regularity of form].

Arpie, Madonna delle, by del Sarto, 263.

Arquà, death city of Petrarch, 170.

Arringhieri, portrait by Pintoricchio, 337.

Arti or Trade Guilds, of Venice, 92, 93; their importance in Florence, 231.

Artists' jokes, 222.

Arts and Sciences, medieval centres, 560.

Arx, The, of Rome, site of, 437, 504.

Asa, King of Judah, 380, 477.

Ascension of Christ, mosaic at Venice, 101.

Aspasia of Miletus (5th cent. B. C.), consort of Pericles, her bust in the Vatican, 447.

Assisi, the Land of Mysticism and birth place of St. Francis and of St. Clare, 365.

Assumption of the Virgin, The, painting by Perugino in the Uffizi, 265; Rosso Fiorentino in the Annunziata, 243; Andrea del Sarto in the Pitti, 277; Titian in Venice, 131; relief by Orcagna in Or San Michele, 232; legend of the Assumption, 277.

Asti, birthplace of Alfieri, 14.

Astragals (dice), 537.

Atalanta and Hippomenes, myth of, 539.

Athaulfus, King of the Visigoths, marries Galla Placidia, 171 C.

Athena, Olympian deity. See Minerva.

Athenodorus of Rhodes, pupil of Polycletus, sculptor, 541.

Athens, compared with Florence, 193.

Atrani, view of, 555.

Atrium, the St. Mark's', 95 *sqq.*, 99; of Old St. Peter's, 413.

Attalus I., King of Pergamus, 506.

Attila [† 453], the « scourge of God », his invasions of Italy, sacks Milan, 48 a; destroyes Aquilea, Padua, Altinum, 81*; relief in St. Peters' representing his repulse, 410 a; the same scene as represented by Raphael, in the Vatican Stanzas, 466 a; is placed in Hell by Orcagna, 323; his burial amidst immense treasures, the spoils of nations, 466.

Augustine, St. [† 430], Bishop of Hippo; Theologian, Father of the Latin Church, and Founder of the Order of Augustinians; stories from his life in Gozzoli's frescoes, at San Gimignano, 354; painting of him by Botticelli, 239; by Simone Martini, 345 c; his baptism, 54 a; his grand Tomb, at Pavia, 69 c. [He was born in Numidia, Africa, the son of a pagan father and a Christian mother, St. Monica, he studied rethoric in Carthage; after a youth of dissipation in 383 went to Rome hoping to find employment there as a teacher of rethoric, failing in this the following year went to Milan and there he came under the influence of Ambrose, bishop of the city; imbued with the theology of St. Paul he was converted to Christ; became bishop in 396; took up an active part in the Church controversies of his age, opposing especially the Pelagians. His most famous works are his "Confessions," his spiritual autobiography and the *De Civita Dei*, the "City of God." The Order he founded had 200 Houses in England at the time of the Reformation].

Augustine, St. [† 613], founder of the Christian Church in England, and first archbishop of Canterbury, 430.

Augustus [† 14 A. D.], first of the Roman emperors, 171, 392, 462; erects a temple to Julius Cæsar, 398; the Theatre of Marcellus, 402; restores the House of the Vestal Virgins, 398; places an altar on the Capitoline hill, 437; rebuilds the basilica Julia, 397; his residence, 400; his Forum, 402; his Temple, 398; his statue, 455.

Aurelianus [† 275], Roman emperor, 391.

Aurora, famous fresco by Guido Reni, Casino Rospigliosi, Rome, 494.

Austria, her rule in Italy, annexes Milan 48; takes Venice 81*; annexes Trento 168; and Trieste, 169.

Avanzo Jacopo, Bolognese painter, 158.

Avaricious, Dante's verdict on the, 227.

Alvernia or Verna, mount, 366.

Avernus, lake, near Naples, 559 c.

Averrhoes [† 1198], Arabian heretic, philosopher Commentator, 228, 317*, 323.

Avignon (France), made the seat of the « Apostolic See », 192, 228; return of the Popes from, 345, 392, 394, 416, 432, 474. [For seventy years, the years of the so-called 'Babilonian captivity,' the popes continued to reside at Avignon where they raised enormous masses of the *Palais des Papes*, that still overhang the city and the Rhone river].

BABEL, Tower of (Gen. XI.), 98, 322.
Baby Stuart, by van Dyck, 21 a.
Bacchanalia games, 445b, 450c. [A festival originally of a loose and riotous character, in honour of Bacchus; celebrated by the Romans every three years with an orgiastic procession at night. The licentiousness to which it gave rise caused its prohibition in A. D. 186].
Bacchantes Pompeian fresco of a, 536.
Baccio d'Agnolo [† 1543], Florentine architect and sculptor, 305.
Baciccio of Genoa [† 1709], painter, 438.
Baciocchi Elisa, sister of Napoleon, 325.
Baglioni, The, despots of Perugia, 382.
Bagnaia, the Villa Lante at, 513.
Baiæ, resort of old Roman nobility, 559.
Balaam, prophet, 380.
Baldovinetti Alessio [† 1499], Florentine painter, 255 c.
Baldwin of Flanders, 273 b.
Bale (Basle), Council of, 338.
Balia, the, at Siena, 333. [In the early days of communal freedom, there were few available administrative precedents, and each separate transaction was wont to be carried through by a *Balìa*, or commission of *boni homines*, expressly chosen for the purpose. All the great offices of the State, all councils had their origin in *balìe*, or temporary committees, which, in the course of time, became permanent. The first of the *balìe* to become permanent was that which had charge of the financial affairs of Siena, the *Biccherna*].
Balilla, Genoese boy-hero, 26.
Bambaia (Agostino Busti) [† 1548], Milanese sculptor, 62.
Bamberg (Bavaria), 273 b.
Bambino, in S. Maria Aracoeli, Il Santissimo, his miraculous powers, 437.
Bambinos, della Robbia's tondos of, 246.
Banco di San Giorgio, the, at Genoa, 26.
Banco, Nanni di. [† ca. 1420], Flor. sculptor, 209, 230.
Bande Nere, Giov. delle. See Medici.
Bandello Matteo [† 1562], Italian novelist, 79. [He received a very careful education and entered the church. In 1550 he was raised to the bishopric of Agen, in France where he resided for many years. He wrote a number of poems, some of which furnished themes and incidents for Shakespeare and other dramatists of his time, but his fame rests entirely upon his collection of *Novelles* or tales, of which Boccaccio's *Decameron* is the best known example].
Bandinelli Baccio [† 1560], Florentine sculptor, his group of Hercules and Cacus, 197; statue of Giovanni delle Bande Nere, 233; contributes work on the Medici tombs in S. Maria sopra Minerva, in Rome, 435.
Banks, the, in medieval times, 231.
Baptism, Rite of, by the Apostles, 108.
Baptistery, The: of Ravenna, 185; of Venice, 108; of Florence, 204 sqq.; competition for the latter's bronze doors, 205; Michelangelo's appreciation for Ghiberti's doors, ib.; mosaics in the dome, 208; the Lateran B., 416.
Barabino Carlo, Genoese architect, 31.
Barbarossa. See *Frederick I*.

Barberini, a powerful family from Tuscany, 408; Barberini palace, in Rome, 494.
Bardi, the, Florentine bankers, 221; their loan to Edward III. of England, 231.
Bari (Apulia), churches of, 524 sq.
Barocci Federico [† 1612], Roman painter, his St. Jerome, in the Borghese, 490; the Annunciation, in the Vatican, 487; the Madonna del Popolo, in the Uffizi, 268.
Bartholomew, St., Apostle, statue at Milan, 52; Michelangelo's, 476.
Bartolo di Fredi, Sienese painter, 346.
Bartolommeo, Fra (Baccio della Porta) [† 1517], Florentine painter, 486; his portrait of Savonarola, 252; work in San Marco, 248; his Deposition, 280; and Risen Christ, 279; his Apparition of the Virgin, 289; altarpiece, 325.
Basaiti Marco, Venetian painter, 144.
Baseggio, Venetian architect, 115.
Basilica, example of early Christian, 419.
Bassano Francesco, painter, 124, 125, 127.
Battisti Cesare, Italian patriot, 168.
Battle, The: of Campaldino, 192, 389; of Constantine, 496; of Legnano, 48; of Lepanto, 81*, 121, 474; of Marignano, 48; of Ostia, 468; of Pavia, 48, 69; of Ravenna, 48, 61, 181, 466; of Tagliacozzo, 313, 505, 524.
Baveno, summer resort, 68*.
Bayard (Pierre Terrail), Chevalier de [† 1524], French Knight, 77.
Beatifications at St. Peter's, Rome, 411.
Beatrice Cenci [† 1599], her exquisite beauty, 494; her portrait by Guido Reni, ib.; her imprisonment, 499; her burial place, 439.
Beatrice (Portinari), Dante's, 168, 304.
Beatrice d'Este, her marriage with Lodovico Sforza, 72; her portraits in Milan, 61; her tomb at Pavia, 72.
Beatrice of Lorraine [† 1076], Countess of Tuscany, 318.
Beccafumi Domenico [† 1551], 335, 340.
Beccaruzzi, painter, 74.
Becket, Thomas [† 1170], archbishop of Canterbury, 576.
Belisarius [† 565], famous general under Justinian, 393; his capture of Naples, 519.
Bellagio, famous summer resort, 66.
Bellincion Berti, his offer to a German emperor, 389.
Bellini Gentile [† 1507], painter, 61, 140.
Bellini Giovanni [† 1516], brother of the above, Venetian painter, work at Genoa, 35; at Milan, 60; his altarpieces in the Frari, 131; S. Zaccaria, 134, and in the Academy Venice, 139, 140*; his allegory of the Church, 270.
Bellini Vincenzo [† 1835], operatic composer: *Norma, Sonnambula*, etc. 582.
Beltraffio [† 1516], Milanese painter, 62.
Bembo Bernardo, erects tomb of Dante, 181; Bembo Pietro [† 1547], Cardinal and writer, 78b, 201, 435, 460.
Benassai, patrician Sienese family, 330.
Benedetto da Rovezzano [† 1556], Florentine sculptor, 303.
Benedict St. (480-543), founder of Western Monachism, life and works, histor. sketch, 515 b; scenes from his life, 257 b; founds Montecassino, 560.
Benedict XI. (Boccasini) [† 1304], Pope, presumed portrait, in the Spanish chapel, 229; his tomb at Perugia, 360.

Benedict XIV. (Lambertini) [† 1758], Pope, erects a Tribune adjoining the Scala Santa, 417 c; founds a museum of Christian Antiquities, in the Vatican, 442 c; a Picture Gallery, in the Palazzo dei Conservatori, 505 a.
Benedictines, Order of, worlds' debt to, 560
Benefactors of Genoa, their beneficent scheme and reward, 26.
Benevento, 329; arch of Trajan at, 560.
Benevolent Societies, at Florence, 247.
Benozzo Gozzoli. See Gozzoli.
Bentivoglio, lords of Bologna, 172, 175, 382.
Benvenuti Pietro [† 1844], painter, 235.
Benvenuto di Giovanni, Sienese painter, his work in the church of San Giovanni, at Siena, 342 a; his altarpiece in the Accademia, 347 a; the Tavolette di Biccherna, 349 a.
Berengar I. the Marquess of Friuli [† 924], King of Italy, 70.
Berengar II. [† 966], King of Italy, 69.
Berengarius [† 1088], theologian, archdeacon of Angers, 460.
Berenson, Mr. B. (Art Critic), 241, 258.
Bergamo, 74; tombs of the Colleoni at, 75.
Bergamo, Stefano da, sculpt. 361.
Bernard of Clairvaux, St. [† 1153], Doctor of the Church, founder and first abbot of the Cistercians, his devotion for the Blessed Virgin, 245, (56), 460.
Bernard of Menthon, St. [† 1008], founds hospice on the Alps, 13.
Bernardino da Siena, St. [† 1444], founder of the *Osservanti*: Franciscan preacher, singular success of his preachings, 337; founds a convent, 351; Oratorio at Perugia, 360; see also, 437.
Bernardino di Mariotto, painter, 364*.
Bernini Giovanni Lorenzo [† 1680], Roman architect and sculptor, his works in Rome: erects colonnade of St. Peter's, 395, 405; and the bronze canopy, 406; drapes nude figures, 408; his tomb of Countess Matilda, 410; his St. Teresa, 438; builds Scala Regia in the Vatican, 441; sculptural works in the Borghese Gallery, 488; his fountains, 511; other works, designs balconies overlooking transept of St. Peter's, 407 a; drapes nude marble figure there, 408 b; renovates church of S. Maria del Popolo, 433.
Bertoldo di Giovanni [† 1491], Florentine sculptor, teacher of Michelangelo, contributes work on bronze pulpits, in S. Lorenzo, 233; his Crucifixion, in the Bargello, 294 c; designs bronze medals of the Pazzi conspiracy, 303.
Bessarion, Cardinal, his gift to Venice, 87.
Biagio da Cesena, his criticism of Michelangelo and ensuing punishment, 476.
Bianca Cappello, celebrated beauty, 312.
Bianchi, The, Italian faction, 326.
Bibbiena, Cardinal, friend of Raphael, his portrait in the Pitti, 279; in the Dispute, 460; in the Battle of Ostia, 468 c.
Bible, The, 97; of Raphael, 470.
Biblical scenes, at Orvieto, 380 sqq.; in S. Maria Maggiore, 420; in Sistine 477.
Biblioteca Apostolica Vaticana, 442.
Biblioteca Laurenziana, Florence, 238.
Biblioteca San Marco, Venice, 87.
Biccherna, Tavolette di, Siena, 347.
Bigarelli Guido [† ca. 1250], Lombard architect and sculptor, 314.

Biliverti, Florentine painter, 277.
Birth of the Virgin, The, painting by Ghirlandaio, 224; by del Sarto, 243.
Birth of Venus, The, by Botticelli, in the Uffizi, Florence, 260; ancient relief, in the Therme, Rome, 500.
Bishops, their rule, 48, 49, 168, 329; their election in medieval times, 474, 557.
Bissone, Giovanni da, sculptor, 38.
Bitetto (Apulia), churches of, 564.
Bitonto (Apulia), churches of, 565.
Black Plague, 192, 329, 437.
Blessed Virgin, enthusiasm for, 242, 245.
Blue Grotto, at Capri, description, 551.
Boar at Florence, the bronze, 309.
Boboli (Garden of), 275.
Boccadi Leone, The, at Venice, 127.
Boccaccio Giovanni [† 1375], humanist and poet, sketch of his career, 253; presumed portraits in the Cappella degli Spagnuoli, 229 c; in the Orvieto cathedral, 382 a; in the Parnassus, 463 b; a painted page of his *Decameron*, 179 b; his statue in the Portico of the Uffizi, 254*; traditional meeting place of his friends, 310; extols forest of Ravenna, 171; supposed scene of his *Decameron*, 584.
Boccanegra Simon, doge of Genoa, 26.
Boccatis Giovanni [†,1480], painter, 364*.
Boccherini Luigi [† 1805], composer, 325.
Boëthius [† 525], statesman, philosopher, his portrait, in S. Maria Novella, 228 c; his burial place, in S. Pietro in Ciel d'Oro, 69 b. [He was a profoundly learned man, held the highest offices in Rome under Theodoric: but his integrity and opposition to injustice roused the ill-will of his enemies, who accused him of treason. It was during his confinement in Pavia, that he wrote various famous works, among which the *De Consolatione philosophiae*, which King Alfred translated into Anglo-Saxon. He was canonised as a martyr, and his influence was great during the Middle Ages].
Bohemond [† 1108], Guiscard's son, 565.
Boiardo Matteo Maria [† 1494], poet, author of "Orlando Innamorato," 178.
Boleyn Anna [† 1536], wife of Henry VIII. of England, records of her correspondence, 442 a; is portrayed in a Venetian painting, 143 c.
Bologna, 173 sqq.; leaning towers, 172; churches, 174-176; picture gallery, 176*; palaces, 177*; Fount. of Neptune, 173.
Bolsena, the Miracle of, 379, 386; Raphael's fresco of the Mass of, 464.
Bonanno [† ca. 1183], Pisan architect and sculptor, his famous leaning tower, 312* sq.; his bronze doors at Pisa, 313*; at Monreale, 576.
Bonaparte, a name made famous by Napoleon I. See *Napoleon*.
Bonaventura St. [† 1274], great Theologian, and Franciscan friar, known as the « Seraphic Doctor », 460.
Bonfigli Benedetto, Umbrian painter, 364.
Brindisi, the ancient *Brundusium*, 564.
Brescia, birth place of Arnold of B., 76 sq.
Brienne, 192 c. [Brienne-le-Château, the capital town of a French countship, was captured in the 10th cent. by an adventurer named Engelbert and from him sprang the noble house of Brienne].

Boniface VIII. (Benedetto dei Caetani) [† 1303], Pope, Dante's verdict on, 227; his bust, 407; his portrait by Giotto, 415; place of birth, 516; his Dalmatic, outrage and death, *ib.*; his tomb, 412. [He was born of noble family at Anagni; studied canon and civil law in Italy and possibly at Paris, and after being appointed to canonicates in these two countries, in 1265 was sent to England, to assist in the reconciliation of Henry III. and the baronial party. In 1291, he became cardinal-priest; and after the abdication of pope Celestine V., he was crowned pope (1295) at Rome. By his attempt to exercise his authority in temporal as well as in spiritual affairs, he involved the papacy in many controversies with European kings and princes. The attempt to build up great estates for his family made most members of the noble Colonna family his enemies; the policy of supporting the interests of the house of Anjou in Sicily, proved a failure. In 1300, he instituted the *First Jubilee*, and received Dante as the ambassador of Florence; he humbled Eric of Denmark; but the most noted conflict, was that with Philip IV. (the Fair), of France. He died in 1303, and with him the medieval Papacy came to an end; was buried with the utmost magnificence in a splendid chapel, which he had built and adorned with mosaics, and where a grand tomb was erected to him; nothing remains now but the fine sarcophagus, which bears the majestic figure of the pope by Arnolfo del Cambio].
Book of Psalms, poem from, 213.
Book of Wisdom, quotation from, 228.
Bordone Paris [† 1571], Venetian painter, his famous painting at Venice, 144.
Borghese Gallery, at Rome, 488; B. chapel, in S. Maria Maggiore, 418. [A noble 13th cent. family of Sienese origin, a wealthy member of which, Marcantonio Borghese settled in Rome and was the father of Camillo, who, under the title of Paul V. became pope in 1605; a Prince Borghese married Pauline Bonaparte, sister of Napoleon; the B. palace at Rome, is one of the most magnificent in the city].
Borgia Apartments, in the Vatican, 456 sqq. [A suite of five rooms occupied by Alexander VI. Borgia or *Borja*, a Spanish family which in the 15th c. settled in Italy; Alfonso B., in 1455 became pope Calixtus III; Roderigo, his nephew (1431-1503), became pope in 1499 under the name of Alexander VI].
Borgia Cesare [† 1507], Cardinal and military leader, attacks Forlì, 190 b; enters Urbino and expels its duke, 190: presumed portraits of him in various picture galleries, 382, 456.
Borgia Lucrezia. See Lucrezia.
Borgia Roderigo. See Alexander VI.
Borgo San Sepolcro, frescoes at, 356.
Borgognone Ambrogio [† ca. 1523], Milanese painter, his painting in the Brera, 59; in the Ambrosiana, 61; prepares designs for Certosa di Pavia, 70 a.
Borromean Islands, The, 68.

Borromeo Carlo, St. [† 1584], Cardinal Archbishop, 52. [He was the son of count Borromeo of Arona and Margarita de' Medici; his uncle pope Pius V. created him cardinal and Archbishop of Milan, when he was charged with the supervision of the Franciscans, the Carmelites and the knights of Malta. In 1576, when Milan was visited by the plague he went about giving directions for accomodating the sick and burying the dead, avoiding no danger and sparing no expense. He was canonized in 1610. Contrary to his wishes a memorial was erected to him in the Duomo of Milan, and a statue 70 ft. high above Arona, by his admirers who regarded him as the leader of a Counter-Reformation].
Botticelli (Alessandro Filipepi) [† 1510], Florentine painter, his works in Florence, 260 sqq.; in Turin, 20; in Milan, 61; in Sistine, 480 sq.; Borghese, 489. [He was a profound student of Dante, whose Divine Comedy he illustrated. His range of subjects was immense. It extended from great scriptural compositions to events in classic history, including allegorical and classic subjects. All these he treated in a form which was the natural outcome of the *Renaissance*, but with a *verve*, naïveté, and pathos peculiar to himself].
Bourbon, Charles Duke of [† 1527], Constable of France, is appointed governor of Milan, 48 b; sacks Rome and is wounded by Benvenuto Cellini, in an affray, 392 b.
Bourbons, of Parma, 325; Naples, 519.
Braccio da Montone, condottiere, 74.
Bramante Donato [† 1514], Umbrian, Lombard and Roman architect and painter, 73, 190; his style of architecture, 390 b; is appointed architect of St. Peter's, 405 c; and of the Vatican, 441; designs the Cortile Belvedere, 450. [He was born in Urbino, in 1444, studied painting under Mantegna and Piero della Francesca, and architecture under Luciano Laurana. Went to Rome about 1500 and began to be consulted on nearly all great architectural works].
Bregna Andrea [† 1470], sculptor, 335.
Brennus, Gallic chief, sacks and burns Rome, 392 a; parleying with the Romans on the Capitol, 488. [He was a leader of the Gauls who invaded Italy in 390 B. C., after taking and pillaging Rome, invested the Capitol for six months, accepted the offer of the Romans to ransom themselves with a thousand pounds' weight of gold; but as the gold was being weighed out he threw his sword and helmet into the opposite scale, adding, *Vae Victis*, "Woe to the conquered"].
Bronze casting in ancient times, works in Nation. Museum, Naples, 533.
Bronze horses of San Marco, Venice, 91.
Bronzino Angelo [† 1572], Florentine painter, 201; paints a remarkable picture, in San Lorenzo, 234.
Browning Robert [† 1889], English poet, 150; his 'Guardian Angel,' 189; 284

Brunelleschi Filippo [† 1446], Florentine architect and sculptor, designs Pitti Palace, 275; enters competition for the baptistery doors, 205; his trial plate compared with that of Ghiberti, 205; erects dome of the cathedral, 209; the Pazzi chapel, 218; his friendship for Donatello, 222; his Crucifix, 223; designs San Lorenzo, 233, 234; Santo Spirito, 239; the Foundling Hospital, 246. [He was born at Florence in 1379; entered the gild of goldsmiths, then went to Rome, studied hard and quickly perfected himself in the knowledge of sculpture, perspective and geometry; in 1407 he returned to Florence just at the time when it was resolved to complete the cathedral with a dome. The task was finally entrusted to him, but he did not live to see the completion of his great work, considered one of the triumphs of architecture. He died and was buried in the cathedral of Florence, his native city].

Bruni Leonardo [† 1414], historian, 219.
Bruno Giordano [† 1600], philos., 434.
Bruno St. [† 1101], austerities of the Order founded by him, 312, 431.
Brutus Marcus Junius, one of Julius Cæsar's murderers, 402, 291.
Bucentaur, famous Venetian galley, 151; solemnly burned down by Napoleon, *ib*.
Buon, Bartolommeo and Giovanni, Venetian architects, works: 113, 115, 147, 153.
Buonaccorsi, Florentine bankers, 182 *c*.
Buonarroti. *See* Michelangelo.
Buonconte Guido, famous Ghibelline captain, 190*.
Buondelmonti-Amidei, tragedy of, 192 b. [The Buondelmonti, a medieval family leaders of the Guelph party. One of them, Buondelmonte de' Buondelmonti was murdered by the Amidei in 1215, in revenge for an insult to their family. Buondelmonte, a handsome knight, having pledged himself for political reasons to marry a maiden of the Amidei, and having capriciously thrown her over for one of the Donati. In consequence of this murder a bitter feud arose between the partisans of the Buondelmonti and those of the Uberti (a member of whose family had been implicated in the deed) which resulted in the introduction into Florence of the Guelph and Ghibelline factions; an event forming a turning point in the history of the city].
Buonsignori, Sienese patricians, 329*.
Buontalenti Bernard [† 1608], Florentine architect, 475.
Buonvicino Ambr. [† 1622], sculptor. 405.
Burckhardt Jacob [† 1897], Swiss historian and Art critic, 490, 491 [He is the author of "The Civilization of the Renaissance in Italy" which remains a standard work].
Burdens, the, of medieval Christians, 227.
Burial place of: Fra Angelico, 421; Botticelli, 239; the Medici, 234, 235, 236; Petrarch, 170; Ghiberti, 219; Andrea del Sarto, 243; Amerigo Vespucci, 239; of early Christians, 433.
Burning of Vanities, at Florence, 197.

Busketus, Pisan architect, 313, 315.
Byron (George Gordon, lord of) [† 1824], ode on Italy, 9; helps in burying corpses of Shelley and Williams on the Viareggio beach, 43 *c*; celebrates Bridge of Sighs, 75 *c*; visits Petrarch's house, at Arquà, 170 *c*; extols the Pine forest of Ravenna, 171; his poem on *Parisina*, 178 *b*; sojourns at Sorrento, 549; his retreat Ravenna, 181 *b*.
Byzantine Art, 99 *sqq.*; 571 *sqq.*
Byzantium (modern Constantinople), 91.

Cà d'Oro (Golden House), 151, 153.
Cadore, Titian's birthplace, 143.
Cæcilia Metella, tomb of, 392.
Cæsar Julius [† 44 B. C.], greatest man of antiquity, plans the building of the Basilica Julia, 397 *b*; begins the Theatre of Marcellus, 402 *b*; his Temple in the Forum, 348 *a*; his assassination, 392 *b*; his murder avenged, 402 *c*. [His family was of patrician rank and traced a legendary descent from Iulus, the founder of Alba Longa, son of Æneas and grandson of Venus. Eloquent, energetic with a wonderful political ability, he took up the cause of the people against Pompey; was created consul. His conquest of Gaul (50-51) gave him the military glory and also a devoted army; having freed himself of his adversaries he became absolute ruler of Rome].
Cagliostro (Giuseppe Balsamo) [† 1795], Sicilian impostor, 191*.
Cagnacci Guido [† 1681], painter, 490.
Caiaphas, the High Priest of the Jews who condemned Christ to death, 422.
Calcio, il, the Florentine football, 192 *b*. [In the 15th cent. the Piazza in front of the Church of Santa Croce, which in early days was given over to the solemn chants of the Franciscan monks and the harmless plays of children, became the scene of the city's welcome to, and entertainment of, her distinguished visitors. Together with Tournaments, Parades and Exhibitions, a game of *Calcio* was introduced. Twenty or more noble youths formed equal sides, clad in blue and red respectively; the rules, the players and the ball were as today, only the artistic tendencies of the Florentines surrounded them with splendid pageantry].
Calendar, correction of the, 392, 410, 473.
Caliari Gabriele, Venetian painter, 119.
Caligula [† 41], Roman Emperor, famous for his barbarous cruelties, 400.
Calixtus I. [† 223], Pope, 425.
Calixtus III. (Alfonso Borgia) [† 1458], Pope, 338, 412. [He was responsible for introducing his nephew, the notorious Rodrigo (afterwards pope Alexander VI.) to Rome].
Calvin John [† 1564], Reformer, 178.
Cambrai, League of, 81*, 123.
Camillus Marcus Furius [† 365 B. C.], Roman hero, 202, 488.
Campaldino, the battle of, 190*, 192, 389.
Campania, 517 *sqq*.
Campione, Bonino da [† 1374], Lombard sculptor, 62; 69; 159.

Campione, Marco da, Lomb. sculptor, 51.
Campione, Matteo da [† 1396], Lombard architect, 48 *a*; 64 *a*; 69 *b*.
Camposanto (burying ground), of Genoa, 39; of Pisa, 322.
Canaletto, Antonio Canale [† 1768], Venetian painter, 271.
Candelabrum, the, in the Duomo, Milan, 52; in St. Paul's, Rome, 422.
Candlestick, the seven-branched, 399.
Canon Law, fresco by Raphael, 462.
Canonizations at St. Peter's, Rome, 411.
Canosa (Apulia), churches of, 564.
Canossa, castle of, 178*, 474, 557. [It was the countess Matilda's stronghold, in the Apennines, where the emperor Henry IV. humbled himself and begged absolution from pope Gregory VII].
Canova Antonio [† 1822], Venetian and Roman sculptor, his statue of Pius VI., 407; tomb of the Stuarts, 408; of Clement XIII., 409; of Clement XIV., 436; his Perseus in the Vatican, 451; arranges the Museo Chiaramonti, *ib.*; his figure of Pauline Borghese, 286 and 488; his own tomb at Venice, 130.
Canterbury, 430.
Cantorie or Singing Galleries, in Florence, 212, 213.
Caparra, Il (Niccolò Grosso) [† 1509], famous Florentine blacksmith, his work way of doing business, 304.
Capitol, The, of Rome, 504.
Capponi Piero, Florentine patriot, 301.
Caprarola, the Palazzo Farnese at, 513.
Capri, and its attraction to artists, 550.
Caprina, Meo del, Florentine architect, 18.
Capua, Roman amphitheatre at, 560.
Capuchins, Order of the, 366; cemeteries of the, 432, 553.
Capulets, the, of Shakespeare's play, 165.
Caracalla [† 217], Roman emperor, 396, 431, 450; the baths of, 402; sculptures found there, 530 *sq*. [He was the son of Septimius Severus, his reign, which began with the murder of his brother Geta, was a series of crimes, follies and extravagances; he put to death twenty-thousand persons, among other the jurist Papinianus. Finally, he was himself assassinated at Edessa by one of his guards].
Caracci Annibale, Bolognese painter, his Triumph of Bacchus, in the Farnese palace, 509; the Bacchante, 268 *c*.
Caravaggio [† 1609], Lombard, Roman and Neapolitan painter, his work at Florence, 268; his Entombment, 487; other works at Rome, 490, 495; work at Perugia, 361.
Carbone, architect, 34.
Carducci Giosuè, Italian poet, 173.
Careggi, the Medici Villa at, 312.
Carmagnola, famous condottiere, 74.
Carmelites, The Order of the, 249.
Carne, Sir Edward, ambassador of King Henry VIII. of England, 430.
Caroline (Amelia of Brunswick) [† 1821], queen of George IV., of England, 68.
Carolingians, 329. [The 2nd Frankish dynasty of kings and emperors who ruled France in the 8th-9th cent.].
Carpaccio Vittore [† ca. 1523], Venetian painter, his paintings of Sant'Ursula's Legend, 141; and of Saint George's, 146.
Carrara, The della, seigneurs of Padua, 82.

— 591 —

Carrara, its marble-quarries, 43.
Carriera Rosalba [† 1757], 144, 270.
Carroccio, The, 329; its invention, 48, 49.
Carthage, at war with Rome, 392 a.
Carthaginians, architectural ruins of, 568.
Carthusians Order, a branch of the Benedictines, 71, 312, 517.
Cartoons, fate of Michelangelo's and Leonardo's, 200 (of Raphael's, 472.
Casanova de Seingault [†1798], notorious adventurer, 84.
Casauria, San Clemente in, 562.
Caserta, the palace at, 560.
Cassino. See *Montecassino*.
Cassius Longinus, one of the murderers of Julius Cæsars, 402.
Cassius Titus, Roman orator, 512.
Cassoni, their use in medieval times, 298.
Castel del Monte, at Andria, 566.
Castel Durante, 190 a.
Castellammare, view of, 548.
Castiglione Baldassar [† 1529], statesman and author, his birth-place, 79 c; his description of court life at Urbino, 190 c; his portrait, 461 b.
Castiglione d'Olona, Masolino da Panicale's frescoes at, 63.
Castruccio Castracane [† 1328], is lord of Pisa, 313 c; and of Lucca, 325 b; his portrait in the Palazzo Medici, 307c.
Catacombs, at Rome, 403, 426.
Catasto, 192, 349. [Register of Income Tax, containing names of Taxpayers].
Cathedra, Episcopal, 406, 516, 504, *ib.*
Catherine de' Medici, *See* Medici.
Catherine of Alexandria, St. [† 307], 59, 457.
Catherine of Aragon [† 1536], queen of Henry VIII. of England, 425.
Catherine of Siena, St. [† 1380], histor. sketch, 345; her house now converted into a chapel, 350 c; her portrait by Andrea Vanni (a contemporary painter), 344 a; portrait by Vecchietta, 433 a; Sodoma's famous altarpiece of the *Svenimento*, 344; prevails upon pope Gregory XI. to remove Holy See from Avignon, 345, 432 b; her tomb, 434 b; canonization, by Pius II., 339 c.
Catherine Sforza, Lady of Forlì, 190 b, 496.
Catiline [† 61 B. C.], Roman conspirator, is defeated at Pistoia, 326 a; his accomplices' fate, in the Mamertine prison, 400 c. [An able Roman patrician, but unscrupulously ambitious; frustrated in his designs, he formed a conspiracy against the State. This was discovered and exposed by Cicero in an oration which he delivered in the Forum, in consequence of which Catiline was declared public enemy and killed in a battle near Pistoia].
Catino Sacro (cup of Last Supper), 28, 39.
Cato [† 149 B. C.], the Censor, 512.
Cats, in Florence, 238; symbolism of, 252.
Catullus Caius Valerius [† 54 B. C.], great Latin lyric poet, 159, 512.
Cavallini [† 1300], Roman painter, and mosaicist, his mosaic work in S. Maria in Trastevere, 425; paintings in the church of S. Cecilia, 427; and in S. Maria Donnaregina, Naples, 424 c.
Cavour, Camillo Benso, Count of [† 1861], great Italian statesman, 16.
Cefalù (Sicily), cathedral of, 582.
Celestine II. (Guido di Castello) [† 1144], Pope, 389.

Celestine V. (Pietro di Morone, St.) [† 1296], Pope, his burial place, 562.
Cellini Benvenuto [† 1571], Florentine sculptor and goldsmith, 254*; bronze Perseus, 198; bust of Cosimo I., 294; portrait of Francis I., 298; other works in the Pitti, 287-288; in the Bargello, 303; candelabrum in St. Peter's, 412; cause of his imprisonment, 499; his autobiography, 238.
Cemetery, The, of the Capuchins, 432, 573; of Staglieno, at Genoa, 40.
Cennini's printing-press, 192 a. [He was Ghiberti's partner, in designing and casting the famous Baptistery Gates, and the first Florentine printer from type].
Centaurs, their mission in hell, 227.
Cerberus, three-headed dog that guarded the entrance to Hades, 453.
Cernobbio, summer resort, 66.
Cesarea (Palestine), 28, 39.
Cetara, on the Amalfi coast, view of, 555.
Champollion Jean François [† 1832], French Egyptologist, 452.
Charlemagne (Charles the Great) [† 814], place of his coronation, 69, 402; forms a Frankish kingdom in Italy, 48; his coronation as emperor of the West, 406, 468; Dalmatic of, 412; his residence in the Vatican, 441; plunders Theodoric's palace, at Ravenna, 181. [He was the son of Pepin le Bref; he became sole ruler on the death of his brother Carloman, in 771; he subjugated by his arms the southern Gauls, the Lombards, the Saxons and the Moors of Spain, with the result that his kingdom extended from the Ebro river to the Elbe. He devoted himself to the welfare of his subjects, enacted laws, patronised letters, established schools; when he died was buried at Aix-la-Chapelle].
Charles Albert [† 1849], King of Sardinia, 22.
Charles Edward (the Young Pretender), his sepulchral monument, 408.
Charles of Bourbon (the Constable), is appointed Governor of Milan, 48; his sack of Rome and death, 392.
Charles of Anjou, Duke of Calabria, 523.
Charles I. of Anjou [† 1285], the Nero of medieval times, 329, 515; begins the Castel Nuovo, at Naples, 522; his tyranny and cruelty, 524; puts Conradin to death, *ib.*; his statue in the Capitoline museum, 505; his burial place, 525.
Charles I. of England [† 1649], of his children, 21; purchases cartoons, 472.
Charles II. of England, 21.
Charles IV. [† 1378], H. Rom. Emp., 325.
Charles V. [† 1558], Holy Roman Emperor, 80b; appoints Andrea Doria admiral of his fleet, 32c; defeats the French at Milan, 48 b, 69 a; confines Francis I. of France, in a cell at Portofino, 43 c; his conquest of Florence, 192 b, of Siena, 329; Rome sacked and burned by his troops, 435 c; is crowned with the Iron Cross, 65 b; by pope Clement VII. at Bologna, 174; the gorgeous armour he wore, 293 a; Michelangelo's preparations and alterations on the Capitol for his triumphal entry into Rome, 504 a.
Charles Martel (Angevine line) [† 1296] claimant to throne of Hungary, 525.

Charles VIII. [† 1498], King of France, his invasion of Italy, 80 b, 301, and his pretensions on Florence, *ib.*; his alliance with Lodovico il Moro, 48 b; who urges him to attack Naples, 72 c; defeats Piero de' Medici, 192 a; breaks his promise to the Pisans, 313 c; erects the church of S. Trinita dei Monti, in Rome, 436 c; intimidates the popes in Rome, 499 a; establishes his residence in the Palazzo Venezia, 508 a.
Charon, and his warning, 227.
Charybdis, a dangerous whirlpool, 582.
Chastity, Giotto's allegory of, 370.
Chaucer Geoffrey [† 1400], poet, 69.
Chianti champaign, wine region, 328*.
Chigi Agostino, Papal banker, at Rome, his gay summer house, 492; his stately palace, in Rome, 510.
Childe Harold, Byron's, 85.
Children, abandoned, how cared for, 246.
Chioggia, Battle of, 26.
Chosroës, King of Persia, 220.
Christ, symbolised as Shepherd, 185, 503; as a Lamb, 429; symbol of His body and blood, 464; earliest representation of, on the cross, 324; proclaimed King of Florence, 192, 197.
Christendom, in the Middle Ages, 229.
Christian Art, early, 182|*sqq.*, 420, 428, 503.
Christian basilica, type of the, 423.
Christianity, is recognized as State religion, by Constantine, 48.
Christians persecutions of, 191*, 392, 403.
Christina [† 1689], queen of Sweden, 496.
Christmas Feast, institution of the, 372.
Church Militant, fresco of the, 229.
Church, allegories of her triumph, 464.
Ciccione, A., Neapolitan sculptor, 525.
Cicero [† 43 B. C.], Roman orator and statesman, impersonates *Rethoric*, 228c extols Tusculum, 512 a; orders execution of Catiline's accomplices, 400 c.
Cigoli (Lod. Cardi da), painter, 282.
Cima da Conegliano, Venetian painter, his Baptism of Christ, 136 b; altarpiece in the Academy, 142 c.
Cimabue [† 1302], Florentine painter, his Rucellai Madonna, 223; altarpiece in the Uffizi, 256; mosaic at Pisa, 315; his presumed portrait, 229; his contribution to art, 256; work at Assisi, 373.
Cincinnatus Lucius Quintus (5th century B. C.), Roman dictator, 363.
Cione, Benci di, Florentine architect, 198.
Circe, mythical sorceress, redoutable for her beauty and incantations, 387.
Circles of Hell, the, 227.
Circumcision, institution of, 98; 480.
Cistercians, The, their church at Chiaravalle, 56; abbey at San Galgano, 351; at Fossanova, 516; in the Abruzzi, 562; order of the Cistercians, 245, 249.
Città di Castello (Umbria), 389.
City of God, the, 429 a. [St. Augustine's name for the Church, as distinct from the cities of the world, and the title of a book of his defining it].
Ciuffagni Ber., Florentine sculptor, 231.
Civil Law, fresco by Raphael, 462.
Civita Castellana, 514.
Civitali Matteo, of Lucca [† 1501], sculptor, 28, 325.
Clara of Assisi, St. [† 1263], portraits 373, 374; life and works, *ibid*.
Classis, ancient naval port, 182.

— 592 —

75. - WONDE

Claude Lorrain [†1682], painter, works, 495.
Claudius Appius, censor in 312-307 B. C. ; began the construction of the Aqueducts and the Appian Way, 391, 403.
Claudius Tiberius Drusus [† 54], Roman Emperor, 446, 532.
Clemency, figure of, by Raphael, 469.
Clement of Alexandria [† 220], Greek Father of the Church, 421.
Clement of Rome, St. [† 100], Pope, 423
Clement III., Antipope, accompanies the emperor Henry IV. to Rome, 557 c.
Clement V. (Bertrand de Got) [† 1314], Pope, 227, removes Apostolic See to Avignon, 228, 392, 414.
Clement VII. (Giulio de' Medici) [† 1534], Pope, his portraits by Raphael, 267, 468 ; orders decorations for the Vatican, 469 ; plans the Laurentian Library, 238 ; completes the Medici Chapel, 236 ; asks Michelangelo to paint the Last Judgment, 475 ; crowns Charles V., emperor of the Holy Roman Empire, 174 ; his mitre in the Pitti, 288 ; his tomb, 435.
Clement VIII. (Aldobrandini) [† 1605], Pope, 419.
Clement IX. (Rospigliosi) [† 1669], Pope, 419.
Clement XII. (Corsini) [† 1741], Pope, restores the Scala Santa, 417 ; founds the Capitoline museum, 506 ; erects the Fountain of Trevi, 511 ; purchases the Corsini palace, 496 ; his tomb, 415.
Clement XIII. (Rezzonico) [† 1769], Pope, 65, 506 ; his monument by Canova, 409.
Clement XIV. (Ganganelli) [† 1774], Pope, adds to the Vatican Museums, 449, 450 ; his tomb, 436.
Clementia of Hapsburg, 525.
Cleomene, Greek sculptor, 255.
Cleopatra [† 60 B. C.], Queen of Egypt, Guercino's picture of her, 34 c ; Tiepolo's painting in Venice, 149 c ; the Pantheon in Rome founded to commemorate her defeat, 431 a. [A woman of great beauty and charms ; at the age of 17 she became queen of Egypt, and distinguished herself for her amours ; first fascinated Julius Cæsar, whom she accompanied to Rome and there openly lived as his mistress, until his assassination, when she returned to Egypt. Subsequently she became the ally and mistress of Mark Antony ; their connection being highly unpopular at Rome, Octavian declared war upon them and defeated them at Actium (31 B. C.). Cleopatra escaped to Alexandria, where Antony joined her. Having no prospect of ultimate success, she accepted Octavian's proposal that she should assassinate Antony, and enticed him to join her in a mausoleum which she had built in order that " they might die together. " Antony committed suicide, in the mistaken belief that she had already done so. Octavian refused to yield to the charms of Cleopatra who, according to tradition, put an end to her life by applying an asp to her bosom, to escape the shame of being taken to Rome to grace the triumph of the victor].
-gy, in medieval times, 474, 557.

Clermont (France), Council of, 39.
Clitumnus, source of the, 390.
Clouet François, French painter, 21. 269.
Coducci Moro, Venetian architect, 88.
Cola di Rienzi. See Rienzi.
Colbert Jean-Baptiste, minister of king Louis XIV., of France, 510.
Coligny, Gaspard de [† 1572], French admiral, a leader of the Huguenots, 474.
Colleoni Bartolommeo, famous condottiere, his chapel and monument at Bergamo, 75 ; his reputation, 132 ; his equestrian statue at Venice, 83, 132.
Colombina, the, 309.
Colonna, great Roman family who played a considerable part in the history of the Church, 497, 516. Vittoria Colonna. See *Vittoria*.
Colosseum, The, at Rome, 394, 400.
Colours, mystical value of, 244.
Columbarium, 402.
Columbus Christopher [† 1506], Navigator, stately monument in his honour, at Genoa, 27 ; his portrait by Signorelli, 382 b ; his discovery of a new continent undermines Venice's commercial supremacy, 81* ; brings gold from America for Roman basilica, 419 b.
Combs, ancient ivory, 296.
Como, the cathedral, 65.
Compagnie di Ventura, 74.
Compass, the discovery of, 552.
Competition, for the Florentine baptistery gates, 205 ; for the cathedral, 209.
Condottieri (soldiers of fortune), 74.
Conegliano, Cima da [† circa 1518], Venetian painter, 136.
Conradin of Hohenstaufen, 190*, 329 ; attempts to regain his inheritance, 524 ; is defeated by Charles of Anjou, 505 ; and put to death, 524.
Conspiracy, of the Pazzi, 211, and of Luca Pitti, 261 ; to murder the Medici.
Constable of Bourbon (Charles of Bourbon), the, 48, 392.
Constance, a descendant of the Hautevilles, mother of Frederick II., of Hohenstaufen, 572.
Constantia, daughter of Constantine the Great, 443 b ; her mausoleum, 428.
Constantine the Great [† 337], Roman Emperor, his Edict of Milan, 48 ; removes bronze horses from Nero's arch, 91 ; founds basilica of St. Peter, 405 ; of St. John in Lateran, 414 ; the Baptistery, 416 ; other churches erected by him, S. Costanza, 428 ; S. Clemente, 423 ; chapel over the grave of St. Paul, 422 a ; and of St. Agnes, 426 b ; his baptism, 416 ; his conversion, 430 ; gives privileges to Bishop of Rome, 430 ; presents relics of Magi to Milan, 57 ; frescoes in the Vatican representing his « Donation », and his battle against Maxentius, 468, 469 ; his Triumphal Arch in Rome, 401 ; the so-called basilica of Constantine, 399.
Constantine III., Eastern Emperor, 457.
Constantinople (Istambul), 61, 81*, 91.
Conti Niccolò, Venetian sculptor, 128.
Contino Antonio, Venetian architect, 86.
Convent life in Venice, peculiar, 149.
Coppo di Marcovaldo, Sienese painter, 343.
Cordieri Nicolas, sculptor, 430.
Corinne of Thebes, Greek poetess, 463.
Cornacchini Agostino, sculptor, 451.

Cornaro, Caterina [† 1510], queen of Cyprus, portrait, 269.
Corniche Road, The Italian, 554 sq.
Coronation of the Virgin, 420 ; painting by Botticelli, 260 ; Fra Angelico, 249 ; relief by Luca della Robbia, 239.
Coronation place, of Lombard Kings and German Emperors, the portico of Sant'Ambrogio, Milan, 54 ; in the cathedral of Monza, 64 ; in San Michele, Pavia, 70 ; in St. Peter's, 406.
Corporale, Santo, 386.
Corpus Christi procession, at Venice, 140 ; origin of Feast, 464, 386.
Correggio (Antonio Allegri da) [† 1534], Parmesan painter, his works at Parma, 180 ; in the Uffizi, 269 ; in the Borghese Gallery, 491 ; his style, 269.
Corsini, a Florentine princely family, 496.
Cortegiano, Il, a manual for courtiers, 190.
Cortigiane honeste, the so-called, 76.
Cortona, 356 ; Pietro da C. [† 1669], painter, his paintings in the Pitti, 276, 280.
Cosimo dei Medici. See *Medici*.
Cosimo Rosselli. See *Rosselli*.
Cosini Silvio, of Pisa, sculptor, 32.
Cosmati, The, work in S. Maria in Trastevere, 425 ; tomb of bishop Durandus, 435 ; cathedral of Civita Castellana, 514.
Cossa Francesco, Ferrarese painter, 178.
Costa Pietro, sculptor, 16.
Costumes, Florentine, 225, 240, 293.
Cottonian Collection (British Museum), 96.
Council, The, of Bale, 338 ; of Constance, 192, 208 ; of Ephesus, 420 ; Episcopal, at Florence, 306 ; of Lyons, 460 ; of Trent, 168, 177*, 464 ; of Worms, 557 ; of the Ten, at Venice, 127.
Courtesans, treated with respect, 76.
Crassus Lucius, Roman orator, 391, 400.
Creation of Man, The, mosaics in Venice, 96 ; marble reliefs, at Orvieto, 380 ; Michelangelo's frescoes, in the Sistine, 477, sqq. ; ancient relief in Naples, 527.
Creation mosaics at Venice, 96, 97.
Credence tables, origin of, 296.
Credi, Lorenzo di [† 1537], Florentine painter, his altarpiece in the Turin Gallery, 20 ; the Adoration of the shepherds, in the Uffizi, 262.
Crema, view of the cathedral, 77.
Cremona, the home of violin-makers, 77.
Cresilas, Greek sculptor, 447, 501.
Cressy (Crécy), Battle (1346) of, 231.
Crivelli Carlo, Venetian painter, 61, 163.
Cromwell Oliver [† 1658], 14.
Cronaca (Simone Pollaiuolo) [† 1508], Florentine architect, 200, 305.
Cross, The True, Legend of, 220 ; its appearance to Constantine the Great, 469 ; miracles of, 140.
Crucifix, The, earliest appearance and evolution of, 324.
Crucifixion of Christ, great fresco in the Cappella Spagnuoli, 229 ; in S. Maria Maddalena de' Pazzi, 247 ; in San Marco, Florence, 249 ; Tintoretto's in Venice, 147. (Limoges enamel, 288).
Crusades, 39, 309, 313, 329, 564.
Cumæ, 559.
Cupid and Psyche, myth of, 79, 492, 499.
Curiatii, the Three, 505.
Cyprus, sovereigns of, 55, 140, 269.
Cyril St. [† 869], apostle of the Slav, 423.

— 593 —

OF ITALY.

DALMATIC, the, of Boniface VIII., 516; of Leo III., worn at the coronation of Charlemagne, 412.
Danaë, myth of, 539 (see also 491).
Dandolo, Andrea, 107, 109. Enrico, 91, 125.
Daniel, hero and author of the book bearing his name, 380, 477.
Dante Alighieri [† 1321], the great Poet of Italy, his sojourn at Verona, 164; his monument at Trento, 168; his Divina Commedia, 210, 219; his conception of hell, 227, 323; his verdicts on offenders, 227; his letter to the Florentine Republic, 238; delivers speech at San Gimignano, 352; place of birth, 304; of baptism, 204; of death, 181; memorial in Santa Croce Florence, 219; portrait by Giotto, 298; presumed portraits by Orcagna, 226, 227; by Raphael, 460, 463; by Signorelli, 383; picture in the Duomo, Florence, I, 210; quoted, 70, 155, 157, 190*, 245, 254*, 370, 313, 329, 389, 219, 442, 515. [One of the world's universal poets: he was born at Florence in May 1265; in his youth learned all that the schools and universities of the time could teach him; fought as a soldier; did service as a citizen; at 35 filled the office of chief magistrate of Florence. While but a boy of ten, he first met Beatrice Portinari, a very beautiful girl of his own age and rank, the love for whom was to be the guiding-star and inspiration of his life. In some civic Guelf-Ghibelline strife he was banished from Florence and his property confiscated (1302). Henceforth he wandered all over Italy; he was without home in this world; and "the great soul of Dante... homeless on earth... made its home more and more in that awful other world... over which, this timeworld, with its Florences and banishments, flutters as an unreal shadow, " a world of souls: his Divine Comedy, the most remarkable of all modern Books, is the result of his exile. He died after finishing it, at the age of 56; left many other Works and a considerable number of canzoni, ballads and sonnets.
Danti Ignazio, Dominican painter, 202, 473.
Danti Vincenzo, of Perugia, 204.
Daphne, a nymph beloved by Apollo, transformed into a laurel as he attempts to seize her, famous group by Bernini, in the Borghese gallery, 488 c.
David Gerard, Dutch painter, 36, 566 c.
David, King of Israel, statue of, by Donatello, 295; by Michelangelo, 291; by Verrocchio, 295; by Bernini, 458; D. King of Israel, 213, 228, 380.
Dawn, Michelangelo's figure of, 236.
Day, Michelangelo's figure of, 236.
Death, medieval conception of, 321.
Decameron, The, by Boccaccio, 253; scene of the D., 310, 584; first printed edition of the *Decameron*, 78. [Florentine edition issued, 1950, by the Publishers of " Wonders of Italy "].
Decretals, The, papal documents, 462.
Dedication of Siena to the Virgin, 329.
Deliverance of St. Peter, The, fresco by Masaccio, 241; by Raphael, 467.

Demosthenes [† 322 B. C.], Athenian orator, 422; his bust in Naples, 531.
Denis St. (3rd century), first bishop of Paris, patron saint of France, 436.
Denmark, a prince of, 277.
Deposition, The, painting by Fra Bartolommeo, 280; Francia, 20; Giottino, 256*; Perugino, 279; Titian, 143; marble group by Michelangelo, in the Duomo, at Florence, 211.
Desdemona, House of, at Venice, 152. [She was the wife of Othello the Moor, who, in Shakespeare's play of that name, kills her on a groundless insinuation of infidelity, to his bitter remorse].
Desiderio da Settignano [† 1464], Florentine sculptor, his tomb of Marsuppini, 218; works in the Bargello, 298, 300.
Devotion of the Dominicans, symbol of; represented in Fra Angelico's painting in San Marco, Florence, 248.
Diacre Paul [† 801], historian, 560.
Diana, the Chase of, famous painting by Domenichino, 490 b.
Diaz [† 1500], Portuguese Navigator, 81*.
Diaz Armando [† 1928], Italian marshal and Duca della Vittoria, 431.
Dido, the founder of Carthage, 450.
'Dieu me l'a donnée', Napoleon's motto, when he placed the Iron Crown on his own head, 64.
Diocletian [† 313], Roman Emperor, 116, 191*, 329, 430, 431, 500.
Diogenes the Cynic [† 323 B. C.], 461.
Dionysus Areopagita, theologian, 228.
Diotisalvi, Pisan architect, 314.
Dispersion, The, 98.
Disputa, The, famous fresco by Raphael, in the Vatican, 460.
Divina Commedia, The, 210 c. [The great poem of Dante consists of three *Cantiche*, each containing 33 Cantos of about 145 lines, and the Inferno has an extra, introductory Canto].
Djem, Turkish prince, who was interned in the Vatican, 457 c.
Dogma of the Immaculate Conception of the Virgin, 473.
Dogs, of Saint Bernard, 12.
Dohrn Anton [† 1909], naturalist, 526.
Dolceacqua (Liguria), 45.
Dolci Carlo [† 1686], Florentine painter, his Magdalene, in the Pitti, 285 c; the Madonna and Child, in the Borghese gallery, 490 a; and in the Corsini, 496 b.
Dolci Giovanni de' [† 1486], architect, 475.
Domenichino (Domenico Zampieri) [†1641], Bolognese painter, works at Rome, the Chase of Diana, 490; the Communion of St. Jerome, 487; the Martyrdom of St. Sebastian, 409 and the Sibyl, 490; frescoes at S. Andrea della Valle, 435; at S. Gregorio Magno, 430; other works, designs ceiling of S. Maria in Trastevere, 425 a; his paintings in S. Luigi dei Francesi, 436 c; and in S. Maria della Vittoria, in Rome, 438 b.
Domenico di Bartolo, Sien. painter, 345.
Dominic, St. [† 1221], Founder of the Order of Dominicans, life, 223; his sojourn at Rome, 428; his magnificent tomb, in San Domenico, Bologna, 176.
Dominicans, a religious order of preaching friars, founded by St. Dominic, 223, 229, 434.

Donatello (Donato dei Bardi) [† 1466], Florentine sculptor, his rare faculties and new departure in art, 299; works: Marzocco, 196, 294; relief in Milan, 63; equestrian statue of Gattamelata, 155; Judith and Holofernes, 196; Tomb of John XXIII., 208; statue of Poggio Bracciolini, 211; singing gallery, 212; statues on Giotto's Tower, 215; Annunciation, 219; wooden Crucifix, 222; statues on Or San Michele, 230; pulpits in San Lorenzo, 233; and bronze doors, 234; terracotta bust of San Lorenzo, 234; tomb of Giovanni de' Medici, 234; bronze David, 295; St. George, 295; St. Johns, 295; terracotta bust of Uzzano, 295; stone relief of little St. John, 295; relief of St. Cecilia, 299; fountain in the Pitti, 275; Cantoria at Prato, 328; works at Siena, 337, 342; *see also* 254*.
Donation of Rome to Pope Sylvester, 430, 469; its confirmation by Charlemagne, 468; value of donations, 226.
Donatish, a sect of heretics founded by Donatus, 354 c.
Donizetti Gaetano [† 1848], Italian musical composer, 74 a. [He studied at Bologna, and devoted himself to dramatic music; produced over sixty operas, among which *Lucia di Lamermoor*, the *Daughter of the Regiment*, *Lucrezia Borgia*, *Linda di Chamounix*, *La Favorita*, *Don Pasquale*, *L'Elisir d'amore*, etc. He won the popular ear by his flow of melody and by his rare skill in writing for the voice].
Doria Andrea, the great admiral of Genoa, 32; castle, 45; portrait, 495.
Dosso Dossi [† 1542], Ferrarese painter, his work at Rome, 489.
Dove, Celestial, symbolism of, 228, 256.
Drunkenness of Noah, 452.
Dryden John [† 1700], English poet, 171.
Duccio Agostino [† 1482], sculpt., 360.
Duccio di Buoninsegna [† 1320], Sien. painter, 256, 341, 346.
Duns Scotus [† 1308], the « Doctor Subtilis », 460 b; quoted, 437 b. [The greatest British medieval philosopher; he became a Franciscan; studied at Oxford where he lectured to crowds of auditors on the *Sentences*].
Dupré G. [† 1882], sculptor, 16, 285.
Duquesnoy François, Belgian sculptor, 439.
Dürer Albrecht [† 1528], German painter, his Adoration of the Kings, in the Uffizi, 273 b; picture of Cardinal Albert, in the Corsini, Rome, 496 c.
Dust of the earth, the, 465.
Dyck, Anton van [† 1641], Dutch, painter, 20*, 33, 34, 35, 273, 282, 283, 496.

EARTHQUAKES, consequences of, 540 *sq.*
Easter Eve, ceremony, at Florence, 309.
Eberlein Gustav, sculptor, 510.
Edict of Milan (A. D. 313), issued by Constantine granting toleration, 48.
Edward the Confessor [† 1066], King of England, 515. [The last of the royal Saxon line; a feeble monarch of ascetic proclivities, was buried in Westminster Abbey which he had rebuilt, and canonised for his pie†

Edward III. [† 1377], of England, borrows money from Florentine bankers, 231 b. [He began the One Hundred Years' War with France, memorable for the heroic achievements of Edward the Black Prince, the king's eldest son; associated with his reign are the glorious victories of Cressy (Crécy). He founded the "noble order" of the Garter].

Edward IV. [† 1483], of England, bestows the Order of the Garter on Federigo di Montefeltro, 190.

Egyptians, homage paid by them to the Child Christ, 421.

Elections, ceremony of, papal, 338; unprincipled, 252; long protracted, 515.

Eleonora of Portugal, her meeting before the wedding, with the Emperor Elect Frederick III., outside the Porta Camoglia, Siena, 339.

Eleonora of Toledo, consort of the Grand-Duke Cosimo I., de' Medici, 202; her magnificent apartment, *ib.*

Elias of Cortona [† 1253], Franciscan friar, disciple of St. Francis, 369 c.

Elijah, a Jewish prophet, 428 c.

Elizabeth and the Virgin Mary, 263.

Elymas, Jewish magician, 472.

Embriaco G., Genoese military leader, 39.

Emilia, 171 *sqq.* Emilian way, the, 180.

Empedocles (5th cent. B. C.), philosopher, statesman and orator, 461.

End of the World, the, 383.

Engraving, origin of the art of, 212.

Enzo, King, son of Frederick II., 172.

Ephesus, Council of, 421.

Epicur [† 270 B. C.], Greek phil., 447, 507.

Epitome of human progression, 217.

Erasmus Desiderius [† 1536], the greatest humanist of the Renaissance, 496 b.

Este, one of the oldest of the former reigning houses of Italy, which played a great part in the history of medieval and Renaissance Italy: Chart III., p. 587; gayety and splendour of their court, at Ferrara, 178; their castle, 190*.
  Alphonso I., husband of Lucrezia Borgia, third Duke of Ferrara, 179*.
  Beatrice, 73.
  Borso, first Duke of Ferrara, 179*.
  Ercole I., 2nd Duke of Ferrara, 179*.
  Ercole II., 4th Duke of Ferrara, 179*.
  Isabella, 179*.
  Lionello d'Este, Marquis, 179*.
  Niccolò III., husband of the unfortunate Parisina, 179*.

Esther, consort of King Ahasuerus, 286.

Etna, Mount, 567, 579 [On the East coast of Sicily, 10,700 ft. in height, the highest European volcano].

Etruria, ancient region of Italy, 254, 377.

Etruscan antiquities: 173, 355, 388, 578 c.

Euclid [† 283 B. C.], geometrician, 228 c.

Eugenius III. (Paganelli) [† 1153], Pope, commences the Vatican palace, 441.

Eugenius IV. (Condulmer) [† 1447], Pope, 338; bronze doors to St. Peter's, 405. [His pontificate was marked by a schism, the issue of which was that the Council of Bale deposed him, and elected the duke of Savoy (Amadeus) in his place, in 1439; afterwards he was enabled to return from his exile to Rome, and restored the papacy to its former position].

Euripides [† 406 B. C.], Greek tragedian.

Eurydice, wife of Orpheus, 498, 528.

Evesham, Battle of, 515.

Exarchs of the Byzantine emperors, 181.

Excommunications: of the German emperor Henry IV., and of his officials, 474, 557; of Frederick Barbarossa and Frederick II. 516 c. [An ecclesiastical punishment formulated in the 3rd cent., inflicted upon heretics and offenders against the Church laws and violators of the moral code. It varied in severity according to the degree of offence; in its severest application it involved permanent exclusion from the sacraments of the Eucharist, from the rites of Christian burial, and the rights and privileges of a religious community. In medieval times such a sentence proved most terrifying, even to the boldest!]

Executions in Florence, place of, 292.

Ezechiel, great prophet, 477; the Vision of, picture by Raphael in the Pitti, 278.

Ezzelino da Romano, Vicar of Frederick II. of Hohenstaufen, 167, 178*.

FABIUS, Rom. general, the "Delayer," 363.

Fabriano, Gentile da. See *Gentile*.

Fabris, Emilio de [† 1883], Florentine architect and painter, 209.

Falcone, architect, 33.

Faliero, the name of one of the oldest and most illustrious Venetian families, 81*; Doge Marino Faliero [† 1355], 117 b; absence of his portrait in the Hall of the Great Council, 124 c.

Fall, The, of Man, 97, 380, 470, 478.

Fano, ruled (14th c.) by the Malatesta, 189.

Farinata degli Uberti. See *Uberti*.

Farnese, Italian princely family which ruled the duchies of Parma and Piacenza for two centuries, 177; Alessandro Farnese, cardinal (afterwards pope Paul III.), 426 b; erects the palazzo Farnese, at Rome, 409; famous works of Greek art formerly the property of the family, now exhibited in the Naples' Museum, 527 *sqq.*

Farnesina, the Villa, at Rome, 492.

Fasces, the emblem of official authority in ancient Rome, 502, 508.

Fata Morgana the, 582.

Fates, The Three, goddesses who presided over the destinies of individuals, 276 c, 280. See also, 227, 453.

Fathers of the Church, Latin, 406; 108.

Faun, Michelangelo's mask of a, 291.

Faustina Annia Galeria, wife of the emperor Antoninus Pius, 399, 446.

Federighi A., Sienese architect and sculptor, his Loggia della Mercanzia, 331; the Holy water basins, 337.

Federigo d'Urbino. See *Montefeltro*.

Felix IV. (Saint) [† 530], Pope, 429.

Felix V. (Amadeus VIII.) [† 1451], Antipope, 338. See *Eugenius IV.*

Feltre, Vittorino da. See *Vittorino*.

Ferdinand I. [† 1494], King of Naples, 522.

Ferdinand of Aragon (the Catholic) [† 1516], his gift of gold, 419.

Ferrante (Ferdinand I.), of Naples, 73.

Ferrara, court life at, 178.

Ferrari Gaudenzio [† 1546], painter, 20.

Ferri Ciro, Roman painter, 283.

Fiammetta, Boccaccio's sweetheart, 253; reputed portrait of, 229.

Ficino Marsilio*[† 1499], eminent Italian philosopher and writer, 225, 312. [He was recognized as the earliest Platonist of the Renaissance; in 1463 became president of a Platonic school, founded by Cosimo de' Medici, where he spent many years spreading and instilling the doctrines of Plato. His religious beliefs were a strange blend of Platonism and Christianity, but were the foundation of a pure life, while his interest in classic studies helped to further the Renaissance].

Fiesole, 310; Fra Angelico da. See *Angelico*; Mino da F. See *Mino*.

Filarete (Antonio di Pietro), Florentine sculptor, architect, 405.

Filippino Lippi, Fra Filippo. See *Lippi*.

Filippo Benizzi, St., his miracles, 242.

Finiguerra Maso [† 1464], Florentine engraver, 212.

Fiorenzo di Lorenzo [† 1525], Umbrian painter, 364, 365*.

Fish, miraculous draught of, 472.

Fisherman presenting St. Mark's ring to the doge, Bordone's painting of, 144.

Flabellum, the, use of, 297.

Flaccus Fulvius, Roman general, 400.

Flagellants, medieval fanatics, 376.

Flatterers, Dante's verdict on, 227.

Flavians, illustrious family of Rome, which gave the emperors Vespasian, Titus, and Domitian, 400.

Flavio Gioia, inventor of the mariners' compass, 552.

Flood, the Great, as represented by Michelangelo, 479; mosaic in Venice, 98.

Florence, 192 *sqq.*; History, 192; her part in the development of Art, 193; Yriarte's appreciation of F., 194. *Palaces*: Davanzati, 304; Guadagni, 305; Medici (Riccardi), 306; Pitti, 275; Podestà, 291, 304; Rucellai, 305; Strozzi, 305; Vecchio, 8, 197, 200. *Churches*: Santissima Annunziata, 242; Badia (the Abbey, A. D. 1285), 245; Baptistery (S. Giovanni, A. D. 1200), 204; Cathedral (S. Maria del Fiore), 209; Santa Croce (begun 1294), 218; San Lorenzo (begun 1419), 233; Santa Maria del Carmine, 240; Santa Maria Novella (begun 1278), 223; Or San Michele (erected 1337), 230; San Miniato al Monte (11th cent.), 311; Ognissanti (S. Salvadore), 239; Santo Spirito (begun 1436), 239; Santa Trinita (A. D. 1250), 244. Foundling Hospital, 246; Monastery of San Marco, 248, *sqq.*; Sant'Apollonia, 253. *Galleries*: Uffizi, 255 *sqq.*; Pitti, 276 *sqq.*; Academy, 289 *sq.*; Corsini, 308. *Museums*: of S. Maria del Fiore, 212; of Michelangelo, 308; of the Bargello, 291 *sqq.*; Etruscan, 254; Stibbert, 308; *Environs*, 310 *sq.*

Florentines, enterprise of the, 231.

Florin, the gold, 192, 231 c. [It was stamped with the image of St. John the Baptist, the city's patron saint had 24 carats of pure gold; was first used at Florence in 1252, an era of great prosperity in the annals of the Republic; before which time their most valuable coinage was of silver].

Fogazzaro Antonio [† 1911], Italian poet and novelist, 167.

Foix, Gaston de [† 1512], French military leader, his tomb at Milan, 62; 181.

Foligno, 357. [In 1434 was ruled by the famous Trinci family].

Fontana Domenico [† 1607], Roman architect, erects obelisk in the Piazza of St. Peter's, 405 (46); rebuilds Lateran palace, 416; his work in S. Maria Maggiore, 419; is appointed architect of the Vatican and builds the Library, 441, 442; his fountains, 510, 511.

Fontebranda, oldest of the Sienese fountains, was recorded by Dante, 342.

Foppa Vincenzo, Lombard painter, 59.

Forks and Knives, 296.

Forlì, birthplace of Melozzo, 188.

Fornarina, La, Raphael's sweet heart, 494.

Fornovo, Battle of, 80 b.

Fortune, vicissitudes of, 335.

Forum, at Rome, 396; at Pompeii, 543.

Foscari, Doge Francesco [† 1457], histor. sketch, 152 c; his palace on the Grand Canal, ib.; builds a chapel in St. Mark's, 103 b; his marble effigy, on the Porta della Carta, 113; his tomb 131 a.

Foscolo Ugo [† 1827], poet, 219.

Fossanova, Abbey of, 476.

Foundling Hospital, the, at Florence, 246.

Francesca da Rimini, scene of her tragedy, 190*(quoted 181). [She was the daughter of Guido da Polenta, lord of Ravenna; was given by her father in marriage to Lanciotto, son of Malatesta, lord of Rimini, a man of extraordinary courage, but deformed in his person. His brother Paolo, who unhappily possessed those graces which the husband of Francesca wanted, engaged her affections; and being taken in adultery, they were both put to death by the enraged Lanciotto. This pathetic love story has been immortalized in Dante's *Inferno*, V., 116].

Francesca (Frances), St. [† 1440], founder of a monastery of nuns called the Congregation of Oblates of Mary, now known as the Collatines, 432.

Francesca, Piero della. See *Piero*.

Francesco di Giorgio [† 1502], Sienese architect and painter, his great altarpiece of the Coronation of the Virgin in the Academy, 348 a; contributes work on the Siena cathedral, 335; on the Milan cathedral, 51.

Francia (Francesco Raibolini) [† 1517] Bolognese painter, his realistic St. Peter Martyr, in the Borghese gallery, 490 a; his Entombment, in Turin, 20

Franciabigio (Francesco di Cristofano) [† 1525], Florentine painter, 243, 459.

Francis I. [† 1547], King of France, 32. painting in the Vatican in allusion to his meeting (1515) with pope Leo X., at Bologna, 468 c; at the head of a large army enters Milan and drives out Duke Francesco Sforza, 48 b (1522); orders a magnificent tomb for Gaston de Foix, 63 c; breaks faith with his admiral Andrea Doria, 32; is defeated and taken prisoner (1525), at Pavia, by the troops of Charles V., 70 a; and detained at Portofino, 42 c; his gorgeous bronze helmet and shield, in the Bargello, 296 a; casket, 288.

Francis of Assisi, St. [† 1226], founder of the Franciscans, historical sketch, 366 a; life and miracles: as depicted by Giotto, at Assisi, 369, 370, 371, 372, 373; and at S. Croce, in Florence, 221; by Benedetto da Maiano, in the same church, 219; by Domenico Ghirlandaio, in Santa Trinità, 244.

Francis Xavier, St. [† 1552], a Spaniard of noble parentage and one of the first members of the Society of Jesus, 438.

Franciscans (**Minorites**), Order of, 366.

Franco Matteo, Florentine poet, 244.

Franks, The, in Italy, 48. [Germanic tribes, who overran and made the conquest of Central Gaul, in the 5th century; originally dwelling between the Rhine, the North Sea and the Elbe. They were redoubtable warriors and were generally of great stature].

Frascati, and its villas, 512, 513.

Frederick I. [† 1190], Holy Roman Emperor, called "Barbarossa" or "Redbeard," by the Italians; receives the Lombard crown at Pavia, 69; painting representing his investiture as emperor (1155), at Rome, 333 b; undertakes (1158) an expedition into Italy, and is excommunicated by the pope Alexander III., 516 c; invades Lombardy (1162) and nearly destroys Milan, 48; new expedition against Italy (1176), his defeat by the Milanese, 48; his humiliation (1177) at Venice, and Reconciliation with Alexander III., 95; painting in the Vatican, 474 a.

Frederick II. [† 1250], of Hohenstaufen (son of Emperor Henry IV., grandson of Barbarossa), Holy Roman Emperor, King of Sicily and Jerusalem, defeats (1237) the Milanese, 48 c; his son king Enzo († 1272), is kept a prisoner for 25 years by the Bolognese, 172 b; he is excommunicated (1239) by pope Gregory IX., 474 a, 516 c; his rule of Naples, 519 c; his natural son Manfred is killed (1266), at the battle of Benevento, 505; his grandson Conradin is barbarously beheaded (1267), in the market-place at Naples, 524 c; he erects a fortress-palace in Apulia, 566 a; his residence in Palermo, 570 a.

Frederick III. [† 1493], Emperor Elect, 179*; and Eleonora of Portugal, 338.

French Academy, at Rome, 510.

French invasion, of Italy, 48, 301, 465.

Friars, mendicant, 366; preaching, 223.

Froment Nicholas, French painter, 272.

Fungai Bernardino, Sienese painter, 349

Furius Camillus, dictator, 363 b; 488 a.

Gaddi Agnolo [† 1396], Florentine painter frescoes, Legend of Holy Cross, 220.

Gaddi Gaddo [† 1327], Florentine painter, and mosaicist, his work at Rome, 410.

Gaddi Taddeo [† 1366], Florentine painter and architect, erects the Ponte Vecchio, 195; converts a corn market into a church, 230; frescoes in Santa Croce, 222; work at Perugia, 364; other frescoes attributed to him, 228.

Gaggini Domenico [† 1492], sculptor, 28.

Gai Antonio, Venetian sculptor, 87.

Galatea, The, of Raphael, 492. [A nymph whom Polyphemus made love to, but who preferred the shepherd Acis to him, whom therefore he made away with by crushing him under a rock, in consequence of which the nymph threw herself into the sea].

Galilei Alessandro, Flor. architect, 414.

Galileo Galilei [† 1642], physicist, astronomer, and mathematician, histor. sketch, 219 c. his "Tower," in Florence, from which he made his astronomical observations, 311 c; his experiments at Pisa, 312*, 315; his condemnation and acquittal, 219, 434; his famous motto, *ib.*; his tomb in Santa Croce, Florence, 219; 254*

Galla Placidia, Empress, 171; her portrait, 76; decorates church in Rome, 422; her mausoleum at Ravenna, 185.

Galliera, the Duchess of, 34, 36.

Gallori Emilio [† 1924], Flor. sculptor, 510.

Galvani Luigi [† 1798], Italian discoverer of galvanism, 173.

Ganymede, Trojan prince, 445.

Garda, the Lake of, 67.

Garibaldi Giuseppe [† 1882], Italian hero, his monument in Rome, 510; death of his wife, 171. [He began life as a sailor, associated himself enthusiastically with Mazzini for the liberation of his country; took part in the defence of Rome against the French; joined the Piedmontese against Austria, and in 1860 assisted in the overthrow of the Kingdom of Naples and the union of Italy under Victor Emmanuel II.].

Garofalo (Benvenuto Tisi) [† 1559], Ferrarese painter, 490.

Garter, Order of the, conferred on Federigo of Urbino, 190 b. [The "most noble" Order of the Garter was instituted about 1348. It probably owes its origin to the following incident: the Countess of Salisbury while dancing with Edward III. having let fall her left leg blue garter, the king hastening to pick it up to render it to the Countess, perceived a sort of jeering smile on his courtiers' faces, whereupon: *Honni soit qui mal y pense*, "Evil be to him that evil thinks," he said. And there and then he instituted the Order of the Garter, which was placed under the protection of St. George. It is the highest order of knighthood and is designed K. G.; the knights are distinguished by a garter of blue velvet bearing the inscription in gold letters *Honni soit qui mal y pense*, worn on the left leg below the knee, and the queen on the arm; election to the order lies with the sovereign].

Gattamelata, famous commander, 155; his equestrian statue at Padua, inspires the Colleoni monument, 132.

Gelasius II. [† 1119], Pope, 315.

Genealogies: of former reigning Houses of Italy. Visconti, 73; Sforza, 73*; Gonzaga, 80*; Este, 178* *sq.*; Montefeltro, 190*; Della Rovere, 190 b; Medici, 287*; Kings of Naples and of Sicily, 518.

Genesis, scenes from, 96, 215, 380, 477.

Genga Girolamo, of Urbino, painter, 265.

Genoa, 26 *sqq*. History, 26; description, 27; churches, 28 31; palaces, 32 39, Camposanto, 40.

Gentile da Fabriano [† 1427], Umbrian painter, his magnificent altarpiece: Adoration of the Kings, in the Uffizi, 257 b; in the Vannucci gallery, 364;

George, St. [† 303], martyr and patron saint of England, his chivalrous legend, 146; Carpaccio's paintings ibid.

George IV. [† 1830], King of Great Britain, contributes to the expense in the Stuarts' Memorial, 408 c.

Georgics, Virgil's celebrated Poem, 78.

Geryon, mythical monster, 448.

Geta Publius Septimius [† 212], 396.

Gherardesca (Della), great bankers in the 14th century, 231 b; Ugolino della Gherardesca, lord of Pisa, 313 c. [An illustrious family of Tuscany, lords of Gherardesca, near Piombino, among their members was the famous Ugolino, who was defeated by the Genoese in 1288, when Ruggieri, Archbishop of Pisa, caused him to be imprisoned in a tower, with two of his sons, and his two grandsons also; the key of the prison was thrown into the Arno, and all food being withheld from them, in a few days hey died of hunger. See Dante's *Inferno*, xxxiv.].

Ghetto, the, in Florence, 192 a.

Ghibellines, histor. sketch, 309 c; quoted, 192 a, 313 b.

Ghiberti Lorenzo [† 1455], Florentine sculptor, his contest for the baptistery gates at Florence, 205; works: the bronze doors, of the baptistery, 206 sq.; the bronze sarcophagus of St. Zenobius, 210 a; statue of John the Baptist, at Or San Michele, 231 a; designs a screen for the Duomo, 303 b; executes two reliefs for the marble font in San Giovanni, at Siena, 242 b; his burial place, 219 c.

Ghirlandaio (Domenico Bigordi) [† 1494], Florentine painter, and master of Michelangelo, his character and innovations in sacred art, 224; works at Florence: his frescoes in S. Maria Novella, 224, 225; in Santa Trinita, 244; in Ognissanti, 239; picture in the Innocenti, 246; in the Uffizi, 262; at San Gimignano, 352; in the Vatican, 481.

Ghirlandaio Ridolfo [† 1561], son of Domenico, Florentine painter, decorates the cappella dei Priori, in the Palazzo Vecchio, 202 b; his mosaic of the Annunciation, on north side of the Duomo, 209 c; in the Pitti, 276 c.

Giambologna [† 1608], Florentine sculptor, works at Florence: group in the Loggia de' Lanzi, 199; equestrian statue of Cosimo I., 196; statue in Or San Michele, 231; the flying bronze Mercury, 294; his fountain at Bologna, 173; bronze doors, at Pisa, 315.

Giambono Michele, painter, 103.

Giocondo da Verona, Fra [† 1515], architect, designs the Palazzo del Consiglio, at Verona, 164 b; his collaboration in the building of St. Peter's, 406 c.

Giordano Luca [† 1705], Neap. painter, 306

Giorgione (Giorgio Barbarelli) [† 1510], Venetian painter, his altarpiece at Castelfranco, 145; his 'Concert' in the Pitti Gallery at Florence, 284.

Giottino [† 1380], Florentine painter, pupil of Giotto, his Deposition, 256*.

Giotto di Bondone [† 1337], Florentine painter, architect and sculptor, his influence on the development of Art, 221; works in Florence: the Campanile, 214 sqq.; his part on the Duomo, 209; on the Campanile, 215; altarpiece in the Uffizi, 256; portrait of Dante, 298; presumed portraits of G., 229, 254*, 369; his meeting with Dante, 155; his frescoes at Padua, 156 sq.; at Assisi, 369 sqq.; his works at Rome, mosaic of the "Navicella," in St. Peter's, 405 b; his fresco of Boniface VIII. proclaiming the first Jubilee of 1300, 415 b; his great Altarpiece, for the Old basilica of St. Peter's, now in the Vatican gallery, 484; decorates the nuns' choir in Santa Chiara, at Naples, 523 c; and the residence of the Scaligers, lords of Verona, 164 c.

Giovanni da Milano [† 1369], Florentine painter, pupil of Giotto, decorates the Cappella Rinuccini, in Santa Croce, 222 a.

Giovanni da Vicenza (Fra) [† 1281], Dominican preacher, his strange power of persuasion and extraordinary eloquence, 166 c.

Giovanni delle Bande Nere [† 1526], father of the Grand-Duke Cosimo I. de' Medici, famous condottiere and greatest commander of the 16th century, 233 a; his career, 74 b; his marble bust, in the Bargello, 301 c.

Giovanni di Paolo, Sienese painter, 347.

Giovanni di Stefano, Sienese painter, 335.

Girdle, Our Lady of the, relief by Nanni, 209; by Orcagna, 232; story of the G., 277; depository of the G., 328.

Girgenti (Agrigento), temples at, 543, 568.

Girolamo da Cremona, miniaturist, 338.

Girolamo dai Libri [† 1556], Veronese painter, 163.

Giunta di Pisa (ca. 1255), painter, 324.

Glycon, Greek sculptor who worked in Rome, his famous Hercules, found in the Baths of Caracalla, now exhibited in the National Museum, in Naples, 530 c.

Gobelin tapestries, in the Pitti palace, at Florence, 286. [The famous Gobelin manufacture in Paris, was originally founded as a dyehouse by the Gobelin family of France; it was early established as a tapestry Works; was made a royal manufactory under Louis XIV., in 1662, and has since been owned by the French government].

Godfrey de Bouillon [† 1100], « Defender Baron of the Holy Sepulchre », 39, 309.

Goes, Hugo van der [† 1482], Flemish painter, his magnificent Tryptich, painted at Bruges, in Uffizi 272 a.

Goethe (Johann Wolfgang) von [† 1832], greatest of German poets, 510, 568.

Gold, brought by Columbus, 419.

Golden Ass, the, of Apuleius, 79; also, 492.

Golden altarpiece, in Venice, 107.

Golden Book, of the Venetian Republic, 83 b, 117 a, 124 c, 150 b. [The official register of Venetian nobility in which were inscribed in golden letters the names of Patrician families whose members were garanteed admission to the Great Council, which possessed supreme authority in the State. This record of peerage was destroyed in 1797, during the Napoleonic wars].

Golden Fleece, the, 303 c. [An Order of knighthood founded in 1429, by Philip III. (the Good), duke of Burgundy, on the day of his marriage with Isabella of Portugal at Bruges, and instituted for the protection of the Church].

Golden Legend, of Jacopo da Varagine [† ca. 1298], illustrating episodes in the life of: St. Ursula, 141: St. Mark, 142.

Golden Rose, given to the city of Florence by the Pope, 192a. [A wrought gold ornament set with gems, generally sapphires, which is blessed by the pope on the fourth Sunday of Lent, which was therefore called " Rose Sunday "; and afterwards perfumed and sent as a mark of special favour to some civil community or distinguished individual, who has during the year shown most zeal for the Church. The ceremony originated with Gregory the Great, and its use introduced by pope Leo IX].

Goldfinch, Raphael's Madonna of the, 267; symbolism of the, 244.

Gonzaga, House of, princely family who ruled Mantua, Chart IV, p. 587; brilliancy of their court, at Mantua, 78.
    Elisabetta, Duchess of Urbino, 190; her virtues and accomplishment, ib.
    Federigo II., (1519-40), 79.
    Gian-Francesco II. (1484-1519), husband of Isabella d'Este, 78.
    Lodovico (1444-78), husband of Barbara Hohenzollern, 78.

Good Government, allegory of, 331.

Good Shepherd (the Saviour), 503 a.

Gospel narratives, of St. Luke, 262 a, 277.

Goths, seat of government, in Italy, 181 a; their invasion of Italy; Milan, 48 a; Venetia, 82*; Rome, 410 c; Naples, 519 b. [A Teutonic people who, about the 2nd century settled on the shores of the Black Sea; one branch, the Ostrogoths, was conquered by the Huns, while another, the Visigoths (West Goths) crossed the Danube and invaded the Roman Empire thrice besieging Rome and, in 410 sacked the city; in 466 they set up a kingdom at Toulouse, and later in Spain until 711. The Ostrogoths having regained their independence, with Theodoric conquered Italy in 488; but after Justinian reconquered Italy, in 535, they disappeared as a nation].

Gozzoli Benozzo [† 1497], Florentine painter, favourite pupil of Fra Angelico; his frescoes: at Florence, 306; at Pisa, 322; at San Gimignano, 354.

Graces, The Three, group of, at Siena, 338; in Botticelli's " Primavera, " 261 a; in Raphael's myth of Psyche, 492 b; in a Pompeian painting, 537 c.

Gradara, Castle of, 190 B.

Graffiti, in the Sienese cathedral, 340.

Grail, The Holy, the famous talisman of Arthurian romance, 28.

Granacci Francesco [† 1543], painter, 267.

Gratz, the Bishop of, 40.

Greccio, a burgh in Umbria, 372.

Gregorian Calendar, introduced by pope Gregory XIII., in 1582 to substitute the ancient calendar which allowed the year 11 minutes too much, 410 c. [Britain adopted it in 1751].

— 597 —

Gregorini Domenico, Roman arch., 432 *a*.
Gregorovius F. [† 1891] (Historian), 440.
Gregory the Great, St. [† 604], Pope, stops plague in Rome, 395, 419; delivers homilies in San Clemente, 423, 442; sends St. Augustine to convert the Anglo-Saxons, 427; brings holy relics from Constantinoples, 417; restores church of S. Cecilia, 427; portrait in Vatican, 460; statue, 430; the Mass of St. Gregory, 411.
Gregory VII. (Hildebrand) [† 1085], Pope, reforms of, 474, 557; his quarrel with Henry IV., *ibid.*, 410, and 392; is attacked while celebrating Mass, 419; is besieged in the Castel Sant'Angelo, 395; receives the patrimonial estates from Mathilda of Tuscany, 410.
Gregory IX. (Ugolini) [† 1241], Pope, 462; excommunicates Frederick II., 474, 516; his vision of St. Francis, 372.
Gregory X. (Visconti) [† 1276], Pope, curious election of, 515.
Gregory XI. (Pierre Roger de Beaufort) [† 1378], Pope, restores seat of papacy to Rome, painting in Siena of his journey, 345 *a*; marble relief on same subject, 432 *b*; fresco in Vatican, 474 *a*; stops at Portofino, 42 *c*.
Gregory XIII. (Buoncompagni) [† 1585], Pope, rectifies the calendar, 410; orders the building of Map Gallery in the Vatican, 473; begins Quirinal palace, 509.
Gregory XVI. (Cappellari) [† 1846], Pope, creates the Etruscan and Egyptian museums in the Vatican, 452; and the Lateran museum, 503.
Grieg Edoard [† 1907], Norwegian composer of Scottish origin, 549 *b*. [Born in 1843 in Bergen; he entered (1858) the Leipzig Conservatorium, where he came under the influence of the Mendelssohn and Schumann romantic school; thence he went to Copenhagen founding there the Concert Society Euterpe; in 1870, he was in Rome where he met Liszt, who gave him his approbation; in 1866 he settled in Christiania (Oslo); during the years 1888-1896 he made several visits to London. His works inspired by the folk tunes of his country include the famous music to Ibsen's *Peer Gynt*, the *Solvejg's Lied, Ich liebe dich, et al*].
Grimaldi, patrician family of Genoa, 44. [An ancient Guelph family whose members, soldiers, generals, admirals played an important part in the history of Genoa. One of the Grimaldis having expelled the Saracens from Monaco, in the 10th century, received from the emperor Otto I. the lordship of that city; its territory (area 8 sq. m.) in course of time divided into the 3 communes of Monaco, Montecarlo and La Condamine, became a principality, under French protection. In 1731, the last descendant was succeeded by his daughter, wife of Jacques Goyon count of Matignon and Thorigny, who succeeded his wife and took the name of Grimaldi].
Grimani, noble Venetian family, Cardinal Domenico, 128, 143, 149; Doge Antonio, father of the above, 119, 149.
Gritti, Doge Andrea, of Venice, 121.

Grosso Niccolò. *See* Caparra.
Grotius Hugo [† 1645], Dutch jurist, 282.
Grottanelli, noble family of Siena, 330*.
Gruamons (Gruamonte), of Pisa, sculptor, 326, 327.
Gualdrada, the beautiful daughter of Bellincion Berti (Dante's *Paradise*, XV), her story and resolute modesty, 389; her refusal to kiss the German emperor Otho IV., 202 *a*.
Guardi Francesco [† 1793], painter, 149, 271.
Guarini Giov. Battista [† 1612], Italian Poet, author of *Pastor Fido*, 178.
Guarini Guarino, Modenese architect, his works in Turin: erects the Palazzo Carignano, 16 *b*; the Chapel of the Holy Shroud, 18; San Lorenzo, 19.
Guarnieri, the duke of, 74.
Guastalla (Emilia), 80 *b*.
Gubbio, the Palazzo dei Consoli at, 390. [In the history of artistic handicrafts the city was famous for its *Majolicas*].
Guelphs, the pernicious influence of their rule in Florence, 309; strife of Guelphs and Ghibellines, in Milan, for predominance between the *Della Torre* and the *Visconti*, 48; in Verona, between the *Capulets* and the *Montagues*, 165 *c*; in Florence, between the *Bianchi* and the *Neri*, 192 *a*, 196 *b*; in Pistoia, the Blacks and the Whites, 326 *a*; in Siena 329; in San Gimignano, the *Salvucci* and the *Ardinghelli*, 352; in Orvieto, 377 *c*.
Guercino, il (Giov. Francesco Barbieri) [† 1666], Bolognese and Roman painter, his Sibyl, 33; Cleopatra, 34; his famous Angel, at Fano, 189.
Guglielmo, Fra, Pisan sculptor, assistant of Nicolò Pisano, his work on the Arca of St. Dominic, at Bologna, 176; completes the façade of San Michele, at Pisa, 317; pulpit, at Pistoia, 327.
Guidarello Guidarelli, his monument, 181.
Guidetto, Pisan architect, 325.
Guido d'Arezzo known as Guido Monaco (11th cent.), inventor of the musical scale, 171 *c*.
Guido da Polenta. *See* Polenta.
Guido da Ravenna, abbot of Pomposa, 161 *C*.
Guido da Siena, painter, 333.
Guidoriccio da Fogliano, general, 333.
Guilds, of Florence, 231; of Venice, 93. [In the 13th cent. the *Arti* or Guilds acquired a great importance in Florence].
Guiscard Robert [† 1085], famous Norman adventurer, 563; one of the founders of the kingdom of Naples, obeying pope Gregory VII. appeal enters Rome at the head of forty thousand warriors, puts the Germanic emperor to flight, pillages the city, 557 *c*; and nearly destroys the basilica of San Clemente, 423 *a*; King Roger's love for him, 573 *c*.
Guy de Montfort. *See* Montfort.

Hadrian Publius Ælius [† 138], Roman Emperor, 446; rebuilds the Pantheon, 431; restores the temple of Castor and Pollux, 398; consecrates the temple of Venus and Roma, 502; his tomb at Rome, 395; Villa at Tivoli, 512.
Hagar, mother of Ishmael, 98.
Haggai, Hebrew prophet, 106.

Hannibal [† 183 B. C.], Carthaginian general, his expedition from Africa to Italy, 392 *b*; crosses (216 B. C.) the Alps with a large army, 21 *a*; Hall of Hannibal, on the Capitol, 505 *a*.
Hapsburg or Habsburg, 525. [The name of the royal house which has played a leading part in the history of Europe from the 12th century until the conclusion of the first Great War, in 1918].
Harpies, abode of, 227; Madonna, 263.
Hauteville, Normandy castle, 563, 569, 572.
Hawkwood, Sir John [† 1393], famous English commander, 74.
Hebrews, scenes from history, 480 sqq.
Hector, Trojan prince and warrior, 451.
Helen of Troy, the most beautiful woman of ancient Greece, 491.
Helena, St. [† 327], the mother of Constantine the Great, builds church at Nazareth, 189; story of her discovery of the True Cross, 220; brings fragment of it to Rome, 432; and a nail of the same, 65; the Scala Santa, 417; sarcophagus of H. in the Vatican, 443.
Heliodorus, treasurer of Seleucus Philopator, driven from the Temple, 465.
Hell, picture by Angelico, 251; fresco by Orcagna, 227, 323; by Signorelli, 384, 385.
Henrietta-Maria Queen of England, 283 *c*.
Henry II., of Saxony [† 1024], surnamed the "Saint," Roman Emperor, 70; legend of his death, 226; *see also*, 424.
Henry II. [† 1189], King of England, 572.
Henry II. [† 1559], King of France, 273 *b*. [He was the second son of Francis I.; was married to Catherine de' Medici, by whom he had seven children, six of them came to the throne. He died from a wound received when tilting with the count of Montgomery].
Henry III. [† 1056], son of Conrad I., Holy Roman Emperor, 329.
Henry III. [† 1272], King of England, 515
Henry III. [† 1589], of Valois, King of France, his entry into Venice, 118; his residence, 152; Lineage of, 273 *b*.
Henry IV. [† 1106], Emperor, his quarrel with Pope Gregory VII., 395, 474, 575; his excommunication and humiliation *ib.*, 410, 474, 575.
Henry VI., of Hohenstaufen [† 1197], father of Frederick II., 572.
Henry VII., of Luxembourg [† 1313], Emperor of Germany, confirms the power of the Visconti at Milan, 48, 73; is crowned with the Iron Crown, 65; ravages Cremona, 77; presumed portrait of him, 229; his tomb, 319.
Henry VIII. [† 1547], King of England, 143; his divorce from Catherine of Aragon, 425; receives the title of "Defender of the Faith," 442; his correspondence with Anne Boleyn, *ib.*; his portrait by Holbein, 496.
Heraclitus [† 475 B. C.], Greek phil., 461.
Heraclius, Emperor of the East, 220.
Herculaneum, 527, 532 sq., 540 sq.
Hercules, famous Greek statue, at Naples, 530; H. and Cacus, by Bandinelli, 197.
Heretics, symbolically represented, 229.
Hermits, Life led by the first, curious painting, in the Uffizi gallery, 255 *b*.
Herod the Great [† 4 B. C.], King of Judæa, 421.

Herod Antipas [† 39 A. D.], son of Herod the G., King of Judæa, 108.
Hesiod (8th cent. B. C.), Greek poet, 473.
Hetæræ, the, a class of women who flourished in the 15th - 16th centuries in Italy, 76 b; their predecessor in Classical Athens, 447 c.
Heywood, Mr. W. (Art Critic), 349.
Hilairy or Hilarius St., Pope, 416.
Hippolyte, queen of the Amazons, 578.
Hippolytus, son of Theseus, 318, 503.
Hohenstaufen, German family whose members occupied the imperial throne (from 1138 to 1250), 313. See under *Conradin, Frederick, Henry.*
Holbein Hans, the Younger [† 1543], German painter, his portrait of Richard Southwell, in the Uffizi, 273 c; that of Henry VIII. of England, 496 c.
Holofernes, Assyrian general of Nebuchadnezzar, Donatello's group, 196 c; Botticelli's Judith and H., in Uffizi, 261c; Michelangelo's, in Sistine, 477 c, 479 c.
Holy Cross, The, Legend of, 220.
Holy Grail. See *Grail.*
Holy House of Nazareth, the, 189.
Holy Roman Empire, 48, 392.
Holy Sepulchre, the, Godfrey de Bouillon insulted on its threshold, 39 c; pieces of flint from the H. Sepulchre, 309 a.
Holy Shroud, the, 18.
Holy Spirit, Descent of the, 100, 228.
Homer (ca. 900 B. C.), great epic poet of Greece, his marble bust, in the National museum, at Naples, 530 a; his likeness in Raphael's "Parnassus," in the Vatican, 463 b; his poems stored in Achille's tomb, 462 c.
Homeric Legend, scene from the, 387.
Honoria, daughter of Galla Placidia, 76.
Honorius [† 423], son of Theodosius, Emperor of the West, 48, 76.
Honorius I. [† 638], Pope, 426.
Honorius III. (Cencio Savelli) [† 1227], Pope, confirms the Orders of the Dominicans, 176, and Franciscans, 244.
Honorius IV. (Giacomo Savelli) [† 1287], Pope, his memorial in Ara Cœli, 437.
Honthorst (Gherardo delle Notti) [† 1656], Dutch painter, 266.
Horace Quintus Flaccus [† 8 B. C.], famous Latin poet, 439.
Horatii, the Three, 505.
Horatius Cocles, Roman hero, 363.
Horses in Venice, lack of, 84.
Hospice of St. Bernard, 12.
Hospitallers Knights 552.
Houdon J.-A. [† 1828], French sculp., 431.
Howells William [† 1920], Am. novelist, 85c.
Hugo, Count of Tuscany, 245.
Humbert I. (Biancamano) [† 1056], founder of the Savoy dynasty, 13.
Humbert I. [† 1900], King of Italy, 431.
Huns, The, their invasion of Italy, 81; invade *Venetia*, 81 a; their intention of assailing Rome miraculously frustrated, 410 a, 416 a. [A horde of barbarian Mongol peoples, who invaded Europe, first in the 4th century settling in Hungary and imposing their supremacy on the Ostrogoths and other Germanic peoples; and second under Attila in the 5th century, when they invaded Gaul and threatened Rome].
Hygieia, mith. goddess of health, 449.
Hypocrites, Dante's verdict on, 227.

Iconoclasts, the, breakers of images, in the 8th century, 417.
Ignatius of Loyola, St. [† 1556], founder of the Society of Jesus, 30, 438.
Ilaria del Carretto, tomb of, 316.
Imperia, famous courtesan, to a dazzling beauty she joined a refined and cultured mind, 463.
Impostors, Dante's verdict on, 227.
Indulgences for a thousand granted by the Church, 417.
Industry, Veronese's allegory of, 121.
Inferno (Hell), Dante's idea of, 227, 323.
Influence, of the Franciscans, and the Dominicans, on Art, 221.
Inghirami, Cardinal, 279.
Innocent II. (Papareschi) [† 1143], Pope, rebuilds S. Maria in Trastevere, 425 a.
Innocent III. (Conti) [† 1216], one of the greatest popes in history, holds (1215) a Council in the Lateran, 415 c; his portrait in the Stanza della Segnatura, 460 b; his dream regarding the collapse of St. John in Lateran, 372 a. [He was born about 1160, studied at Paris and at Bologna; in 1198, on the death of Celestine III., he was unanimously elected pope. He was successful in asserting the power of the Church, and made nearly all Christendom subject to its sway; of all the triumphs the greatest was his victory over King John of England; promoted the 4th Crusade and crusades against the Livonians and Albigenses; confirmed the Rule of St. Francis and did much to reform the morals of the clergy; personally he was a man of blameless life].
Innocent IV. (Fieschi) [† 1254], Pope, 437; canonizes Peter of Verona, 55.
Innocent VIII. (Cibo) [† 1492], Pope, erects the Vatican Belvedere, 441; his tomb by the brothers Pollaiuolo, 411.
Innocent X. (Panfili) [† 1655], Pope, 495.
Innocent XI. (Odescalchi) [† 1689], Pope 65. [He opposed Louis XIV., of France].
Inquisition, the Spanish, its headquarters in Rome, 408, 434; practice of, 223.
Inquisitors, symbolically represented, 229.
Institutes of Gaius, the, 163.
Investitures, War of the, 410, 474, 557.
Iphigenia, the sacrifice of, 537.
Iron Crown, The, of Lombardy, 64.
Isaac, sacrifice of, competition bronze plates in the Bargello, 205; fresco in the Vatican, 464; painting at Pisa, 315.
Isabella d'Este, her accomplishments and patronage of the arts and letters, 78; her home, at Mantua, ib.
Isabella of Aragon, wife of Sforza, 73.
Isabella of Spain [† 1504], 419, 439.
Isaia da Pisa, sculptor, 522.
Ischia, view of the Castle at, 559.
Isis, Egyptian divinity, 543.
Isola Bella, views of, 9, 69*.
Isotta da Rimini (Isotta degli Atti), celebrated beauty, the mistress of Sigismondo Malatesta, tyrant of Rimini, 188 a; her effigy on a bronze medal, in the Bargello, 303 a.
Israel, Kingdom of, 480 sqq.
Italian beauties, famous, 303.
Italian Lakes, The. See Lakes.
Italian Schools of Painting, chart of, 590.
Ivory works, in the bishop's palace, at Ravenna, 186 a; in the Bargello, 297.

Jacob, Hebrew patriarch, his Vision of a ladder which reached to Heaven, in the Stanza di Eliodoro, in the Vatican, 465 a; his effigy on the Orvieto cathedral, 381 b; scene of his meeting with Isaac, bronze panel from Ghiberti's famous baptistery gates, 206.
Jacobello del Fiore, Venetian painter, 138.
Jacopo di Piero, sculptor, 386.
Jacopo da Varagine [† ca. 1298], Archbishop of Genoa, 141. [He was born near Genoa; joined the Dominicans in 1244; early in 1292 was consecrated archbishop of Genoa, where he distinguished himself by his efforts to appease the civil discords of the city. He is the author of the *Golden Legend*, a popular religious work, dealing with the legendary lives of the great saints].
James, Duke of York (the Baby Stuart), his portrait by van Dyck, 20*, 494.
James I. [† 1437], King of Scotland, 338.
Janus, the Roman god of doorways, 436.
Jason, chief of the Argonauts, 491.
Jehoshaphat, King of Judah, 380.
Jenner Edward (1749-1822), discoverer of inoculation, 36.
Jeremiah, one of the four great prophets, his image in Raphael's Disputa, 460 b; in Domenichino's picture, in the Vatican gallery, 487 c; in Ribera's work in the Borghese gallery, 490 c.
Jericho, 205; fall of, 421.
Jerome St. [† 420], Father of the Church 362, 460, 487, 490.
Jerusalem, portion of Holy Shroud brought away from, 18 c; expedition to drive the infidels therefrom, 39 c; the Holy Cross carried to and from the city, 220; scenes of the Crucifixion of Jesus therein, 229 a, 147 b; a Florentine plants the first banner on its city walls, 309 a.
Jerusalem Delivered, by Tasso, 549 b. [A great heroic poem whose subject is the First Crusade, the capture of Jerusalem and the establishment of Godfrey de Bouillon as its first Christian king. The action of this long poem in twenty cantos is enriched by episodes of great beauty, battles, religious ceremonies, stratagems... and many characters forming a gallery of portraits. The fiery Rinaldo; impulsive Tancred, a mirror of gallantry; the indomitable Soliman, the chivalrous Saracens Emireno, Argante. The passion of love in the three principal pagan female characters too is exquisitely painted. The beautiful witch Armida, sent forth by the infernal senate to sow discord in the Christian camp, there converted to the true faith by her adoration for a crusading knight; brave Clorinda, donning armour and fighting in due with her devoted lover, and receiving baptism from his hands in her pathetic death; Erminia seeking refuge in the shepherd's hut, calls up the sweetest image conceivable of womanly tenderness and devotion].
Jesse, father of King David, 477.
Jesuits (the Society of Jesus), 409, 438
Jethro, the priest of Midian, 480.
Joachim of Calabria (Joachim of Floris) [† 1202], mystic theologian, 415.

— 599 —

Joan of Arc, St. (the *Maid of Orleans*), 339 a. [A French heroine born 1412 of poor parents, but nursed in an atmosphere of religious enthusiasm, was subject to visions and ecstasy. She seemed to hear voices from heaven calling her to devote herself to the deliverance of her country which, at the time, was occupied by an English army of invasion. Went to Chinon, persuaded Charles VII. she had received a divine mission to help expel the English ; raised the siege of Orleans and took part in other conflicts ; but was captured by the Burgundians and handed over to the English. Charged with witchcraft and heresy ; tried and condemned ; was burned alive at Rouen (1431); her ashes being thrown into the Seine. An official inquiry in 1456 annulled the sentence, her innocence proclaimed, and in 1920 she was canonized].

Joanna of Aragon, wife of Ascanio Colonna, her portrait by Leonardo, 495.

Joanna I. [† 1382], Queen of Naples, 523.

John the Baptist St. [† 30], the Precursor, repository of his ashes, 29 ; his life, mosaics at Venice showing scenes from his life, 108 ; paintings by Giotto, in Santa Croce, 221 a ; reliefs by Ghiberti, on baptistery, 205 ; the Lateran basilica, dedicated to, 414 b.

John, Knights of St., 552. [A religious order instituted 1110, for defending pilgrims to Jerusalem; on the fall of the city went to Cyprus and were named *Knights of Rhodes ;* thence settling in Malta took the name of *Knights of Malta*].

John XXIII. (Cossa) [† 1419], pope, 208.

Joseph, son of Jacob, History of, 23 ; paintings by Andrea del Sarto, 286.

Joshua, Moses' minister, 205b; 421c; 482c.

Jovius Paulus (Giovio Paolo), histor., 64.

Jubilee, its institution, 415.

Judas Iscariot, one of the twelve Apostles, who betrays Christ and, for money, delivers Him to His enemies, 54, 483.

Judgment, The Last, fresco by Giotto, at Padua, 157; mosaic in the Florentine baptistery, 208 ; in St. Mark's, Venice, 102 ; fresco by Orcagna, 226, 322; by Signorelli, at Orvieto, 384 ; fresco by Michelangelo, 476 ; fourteenth century fresco, at Toscanella, 514 ; fourteenth century fresco in the Camposanto, at Pisa, 322 ; painting by fra Angelico, 251 ; relief at Orvieto, 381.

Judgment of Solomon, 114 ; J. of Adam and Eve, Byzantine mosaic, 97.

Judith, Jewish heroine, 196 ; 261 ; 477.

Jugurtha, King of Numidia, 400.

Julian the Apostate [† 363], Roman emperor, orders martyrdom of John and Paul, two court dignitaries, 436 a ; his interview with St. Martin bishop of Tours, 368b ; is placed in Hell, 323b.

Juliet, house and tomb of, at Verona, 164 ; Romeo and J., 165.

Julius II. (Giuliano della Rovere) [† 1513], Pope, restores the Sforza to the duchy of Milan, 48 ; his part in the League of Cambray, 123 ; lays foundation stone of new St. Peter's, 406 ; adds Logge and founds Vatican museums, 441 ; orders Michelangelo to paint ceiling in the Sistine chapel, 475, 477 ; and Raphael to decorate the *Stanze* in the Vatican, 458 sqq. ; restores the churches of S. Maria del Popolo, 433, and S. Pietro in Vincoli, 440 ; his portraits by Raphael, 267, 462, 464, 465 ; part of his monument, 440.

Julius III. (Del Monte) [† 1555], Pope, his pleasure house turned into a museum of antiquities, 498 a.

Junius Bassus, sarcophagus of, 413.

Juno, chief Roman and Latin goddess, especially worshipped by women at all critical moments of life, 446.

Jupiter, principal deity of the Romans, his marble bust, in the Vatican. 446 b ; his role in the myth of Psyche, 492.

Jurisprudence, fresco by Raphael, 462.

Justin Martyr, St. [† 165], early Christian apologist, and philosopher, 421.

Justinian I. [† 527], surnamed the Great, East Roman emperor and jurist, 184, his mosaic effigy, in San Vitale, Ravenna, 184 a ; impersonates Civil Law, 228 c ; entrusts Roman code to Tribonian, Raphael's fresco, in the Vatican, 462 ; original of his Pandects, 238 c.

Justus van Ghent, Flemish painter, 190.

Juvara Filippo, Sicilian architect, 17, 19.

Juvenal [† ca. 122], poet satirist, 238.

Keats John [† 1821], poet, 403 c.

Kings of Italy, 15|a, 17 a, 18 c, 431 b, 521 c.

Kulmbach (John Snes) [† 1522], german painter, 273.

La Bella Simonetta, her portrait, at Ognissanti, 239 b ; in Botticelli's Birth of Venus and Primavera, 260, 261.

Ladislaus [† 1414], King of Naples, 525.

Lakes, the Italian, Como, 67 sq. ; Maggiore, 68* sqq. ; Garda, 68*.

Lamartine Alphonse [† 1869], poet, 549.

Landi, Neroccio di Bartolomeo, pain.. 345.

Landino Cristoforo[†1504],humanist,225.

Lanfranc [† 1089], of Canterbury, 70.

Languages, confusion of, at Babylon, 98 ; method for the mastery of, 454.

Laocoon, Trojan hero, priest of Apollo, 451 b.

Last days of Pompei, the, 541.

Lateran, the basilica, 414; the Museum 503.

Latium, 391 sqq.

Laura, Petrarch's, 229, 238.

Laurana Francesco [† 1502], of Dalmatia, sculptor, bust of B. Sforza, 300 a.

Laurana Luciano, architect, 190.

Laurentian Library, at Florence, 238.

Law, regarding street shrines, 245.

Laws, regarding extravagance in private life. See *Sumptuary laws.*

Lawrence, St. [† 258], martyr, deacon of St. Sixtus II., life and works 424 ; Angelico's frescoes in the Vatican, 471 ; Bronzino's fresco of his martyrdom, 234 ; Titian's painting, 134.

Leaning Tower, of Pisa, 312*, 313 ; of Bologna, 172.

Le Brun, Elizabeth [† 1842], painter, her self portrait, in the Uffizi, 274 b.

League of Cambrai, 78, 81*, 123.

League of Lombard Cities, against Frederick Barbarossa, 48 c., 329. [After his lawyers had assembled at Roncaglia, and Frederick I. attempted to re-establish his rights in Italy regarding the popes and the republics, a coalition or league was formed (1167), between the cities of Cremona, Mantua, Bergamo, Brescia... This league was soon joined by other cities : Milan, Parma, Padua, Verona, Piacenza, Bologna and others. In the years 1168-1174, during the absence of the Emperor from Italy even in Rome the imperial cause was waning, and the relations between the pope and the league became closer, and Alexander III. (in whose honour the fortress-city of Alessandria had just been rapidly built), became the leader of the alliance. Frederick entered Italy at the head of a large army and attacked Alessandria, but he was compelled to withdraw his troops after five months of ineffectual siege ; and shortly afterwards he was totally defeated (1176) by the allies at Legnano, 10 miles north-west of Milan. The meeting of pope Alexander III. and Frederick Barbarossa, at Venice, in 1177 (see p. 95 b), resulted in a truce of six years with the Lombard Republics; while the Peace of Constance (1183) which ended the struggle, left only a shadowy authority to the emperor in Italy. The League was successfully revived, in 1226, against Frederick II.].

Lecce (Apulia), church of S. Niccolò, 565.

Lecceto, convent of, 351.

Legend, The, of the Holy Cross, 220 ; of St. Lawrence and Henry II., 226 ; of the Sacred Girdle, 277 ; of St. Francis, 372, 373 ; of St. Martin, 368 ; of St. Lawrence, 471 ; of St. George, 146 ; of St. Ursula, 141 ; Homeric L., 387.

Legros Pierre [† 1719], French sculptor, his Apotheosis of S. Luigi Gonzaga, in the Jesuit church, at Rome, 438 c.

Leicester, one of the oldest towns in England, 515 c. [The earldom of Leicester originally belonged to the Beaufort family ; in 1207, Simon, count of Montfort, nephew and heir of Robert de Beaumont was confirmed in the possession of the earldom by King John, but it was forfeited when his son, Simon de M., was attainted in 1265]. See *Montfort.*

Leo I. the Great, St. [† 461], Pope, 407, orders the ancient bronze statue of St. Peter, to be placed in the Old Constantinian basilica of the Apostle, 407 a ; he confers with Attila, 410 a; and prevents the Huns from attacking Rome, 466. [He held the See from 440 to 461 ; he took stern measures (443) against the Manichæans, who had become very numerous in Rome ; on the irruption of the Huns into Italy (452); hearing of Attila's intention of assailing Rome, he rushed north and meeting the Barbarian near Mantua persuaded him to turn back. He, however, was less successful with Genseric, when the Vandal chief arrived under the walls of Rome].

Leo II. St. [† 683], Pope, 436.
Leo III. St. [† 816], Pope, receives the Pallium from St. Peter, 417; takes an oath of compurgation (B. C.), 468 c crowns Charlemagne (A. D. 800) in Old St. Peter's, 468 b; the dalmatic he wore at the said coronation, now preserved in St. Peter's treasury, 412 a. [On April 25th 799, Leo was attacked while riding in procession through the city; the object of his assailants was, by depriving him of his eyes and tongue, to disqualify him for the papal office; but this barbarous deed was not executed].
Leo X. (Giovanni de' Medici) [† 1521], Pope, his entry into Florence, 201; creates cardinals, ib.; allusion to his reign, 465; allusion to his captivity by the French, 467; his defeat of the French, 48, 466; his meeting with Francis I., of France at Bologna, 468; period and feature of his reign, 392; plans the Medici chapel, 236, and the decorations in the atrium of the Annunziata, at Florence, 242; appoints new architects for St. Peter's, 406; commissions Michelangelo to build façade of San Lorenzo, 233; orders Raphael to prepare designs for tapestries, 472; portraits of him by Raphael: in the Uffizi, 267; in the Vatican, 462 and 466; his tomb in Rome, 435; hall of Leo X., in Florence, 201.
Leo XII. (Della Genga) [† 1829], Pope, rebuilds the basilica of Saint Paul's, 422.
Leo XIII. (Pecci) [† 1903], Pope, undertakes reconstructions at St. John in Lateran, 415, and restorations in the Borgia Apartments, 456; paintings in reference to his pontificate, 445; his gift from Milan, 412; his tomb, 415.
Leonardo da Vinci [† 1519], Florentine painter, 487; many sided genius, 57; his Annunciation in the Uffizi, 264; his picture of Beatrice d'Este, 61; of Joanna of Aragon, 495; his head of Christ, in the Brera, 59; his lost cartoon, 200; his celebrated « Last Supper », 57; his own portrait in the Uffizi, 274; in the Palazzo Vecchio, 201; quoted: his famous Last Supper compared to Tintoretto's, 129; the work of his master, at Venice, 132 b; his statue placed in the Portico of the Uffizi, at Florence, 254.
Leonidas, King of Sparta, 363.
Leonora (Eleonora) of Aragon, consort of Duke Ercole I., of Ferrara, 178, 586. [She was the daughter of Ferrante I., king of Naples; when the Duke had reconciled himself with Ferrante and obtained the hand of the King's daughter in marriage, he despatched (June 1473) a noble company, among whom was the poet Boiardo, to fetch the bride. As they returned with her, they passed through Rome, where the princess was entertained with extravagant splendour by Card. Pietro Riario, the Pope's nephew. The entertainment lasted four days during which she witnessed a series of pantomimes profane and sacred. She was a highly cultured lady of many accomplishments and the mother of Isabella and Beatrice d'Este].

Leopardi Alessandro [† 1522], Venetian sculptor, his bronze pedestals, in St. Mark's square, 88 c, 89 c. the monument of cardinal Zeno, 109 c; tomb of Doge Vendramin, 133; collaborates with Verrocchio in Venice, 132.
Letters of Credit, origin of, 231.
Levi, Feast of, 135; by Veronese, 139.
Liberal Arts, 214, 336 c.
Liberale da Verona, painter, his illuminated missals at Siena, 338 c.
Liberius [† 366], Pope, 418, 419.
Library, The, Laurentian, at Florence, 238; of San Marco, at Venice, 87; 149; of the Siena cathedral, 338; of the Vatican, 442.
Lictors a class of attendants who escorted magistrates in ancient Rome, 502.
Ligorio Pirro, is appointed architect of St. Peter's, 407 c; prepares designs for the Villa d'Este, at Tivoli, 512 c.
Liguria, 25 sqq.
Lily of Florence, origin of the, 209.
Lion of St. Mark, the, represented as holding a book, on St. Mark's façade, 91 a; doge Foscari kneels before it, 113; risks to have his claws cut by pope Julius II., 123 b.
Lions, medieval symbolism of, 177.
Lippi Filippino [† 1504], Florentine painter, works in Florence: frescoes in S. Maria Novella, 225; in the Brancacci chapel, 240; picture in the Badia, 245; in the Uffizi, 260*, 262; fresco at Prato, 328; at Rome, 434.
Lippi, Fra Filippo [† 1469] (father of the above), Florentine painter, his style, 259; pictures in the Uffizi, 259; in the Pitti, 285; fresco at Prato, 328; carries off Lucrezia Buti, 285; works in the Doria gallery, Rome, 495.
Lipsius Justus [† 1606], philosopher, 282.
Literature, Petrarch's influence on, 253.
Liutprand [† 744], King of the Lombards, his grave, at Pavia, 69.
Logge of Raphael, the, in the Vatican, 470. [They form a triple open portico, of which the two lower stories are supported by pilasters, and the third by columns. The part painted by Raphael is that on the middle tier. The Loggia of the lower story is covered with stuccos and arabesques executed by Giovanni da Udine from the designs of Raphael].
Lombard Peter [† 1160], bishop of Paris and famous theologian, his figure introduced in the Triumph of St. Thomas, 228; and in Raphael's Disputa, 460.
Lombardo Antonio [† 1516], son of Pietro, Venetian sculptor, 109.
Lombardo Pietro [† 1515], Venetian architect, his work on the Doges' façade, 115; and in the court of the palace, 116; his relief of Doge Loredan before the Virgin, 128 a; the Tomb of Doge Mocenigo, 133 b; he designs the church of S. Maria de' Miracoli, in Venice, 135; the Tomb of Dante, in Ravenna, 181.
Lombardo Tullio [† 1532], son of the last, Venetian sculptor, works on the façade of the Scuola di San Marco, 133; executes a marble statue of St. Francis, 134 b; and the monument of Guidarello Guidarelli, at Ravenna, 181 c.

Lombards, The, found *Lombardy*, their dominion of Milan, 48 b; choose Pavia as the seat of their government, 69 a. [The Lombards or Langobards (long-beards), a Germanic people who in the sixth century invaded Northern Italy and occupied Lombardy, which is named after them. They had adopted Christianity in its Arian form, but later, abandoning their Arian faith they gradually became Italianised and after the overthrow of the dynasty, by Charlemagne, in 774, they became merged in the Italians].
Lombardy, 47 sqq.
Longfellow, H. W. [† 1882], American poet, 393; visits Sorrento, 549.
Longhena, Ven. arch., 129 a; 136 c; 152 b.
Lorenzetti, The (brothers), Ambrogio and Piero, Sienese painters, 320 sqq.
Lorenzetti Ambrogio [† 1350], Sienese painter, his frescoes in the Palazzo Pubblico, at Siena, 331, 333; other works attributed to him, 256, 343, 346.
Lorenzetti Pietro, Sienese painter, 256*.
Lorenzo Monaco, Don [† 1424], Florentine painter, adds figures on his pupil's altarpiece, 251 c; his great retable, in the Uffizi gallery, 257 a; the Madonna and Child, at Pisa, 317 b; the Tabernacle, the Siena 347 b.
Loreto, and its Sanctuary, 189.
Lorrain Claude [† 1682], French painter, his Landscape and the Mill, in the Doria gallery, at Rome, 495 c.
Lotto Lorenzo [† 1556], Venetian painter, his painting in the Accademia Carrara, at Bergamo, 74 c; the altarpiece of St. Antoninus, in SS. Giovanni e Paolo, Venice, 132 the Annunciation, at Recanati, 189 c; the Three Ages of Man, in the Pitti gallery, 280 c.
Louis IV. of Bavaria [† 1347], 80 b.
Louis, St. (Louis IX. King of France) [† 1270], he belonged to the Third Order of St. Francis, his figure in Lorenzo Monaco's Coronation of the Virgin, 257 b; his brother, Charles of Anjou, comes to Rome to take up Senatorial office, 505 c.
Louis XI. of France, 273 b.
Louis, St. [† 1297], bishop of Toulouse, his effigy, in the Uffizi, 257 b; scene of his Burial, painting by Bonfigli, 364 a.
Louis Gonzaga, St. [† 1591], Jesuit, 438.
Louis XII. [† 1515], King of France, invades Italy, 48; the Battle of Ravenna and L., 62; his designs on Milan, 73; his part in the League of Cambray, 123; impersonates Attila, in a Vatican painting, 466 b.
Louis XIV. [† 1715], King of France, founder of the Acad. of Fine Arts, 510.
Louis XV. [† 1774], King of France, portrait of his daughters, in the Uffizi, 273 a. [He was indolent and frivolous; fell under the domination of Madame Pompadour and Madame du Barry].
Louis XVIII. [† 1824], King of France, erects the church of SS. Trinita de' Monti, in Rome, 436 c.
Louvre, Art gallery, in Paris, 289, 161, 488.
Lucca, and it medieval churches, 325.
Lucius Verus, Roman emperor, 449.
Lucius II. (Caccianemici)[† 1145], Pope, rebuilds Santa Croce Gerusalemme, 432 a.

— 601 —

Lucrezia Borgia, becomes Duchess of Ferrara, 178; her portrait in the Vatican, 457 c. [She was the sister of Cesare Borgia; her father gave her in marriage to a nephew of the king of Naples, who was murdered by her brother's assassins; when she married the Duke of Ferrara. She died in 1519; was celebrated for her beauty and her patronage of letters, though she has been accused of enormities].
Lucrezia Buti, mother of Filippino Lippi, impersonates the Virgin Mary, 285 b.
Lucrezia del Fede, wife of Andrea del Sarto, her portrait introduced by her husband in the frescoes he painted, in the atrium of the SS. Annunziata, 243 a; and in the Madonna delle Arpie, in the Uffizi, 263; and in the Assumption, in the Pitti, 277 a; her's and her husbands portraits, 280 c.
Lucullus, celebrated epicurean, 520.
Luini Bernardino [† 1533], Milanese painter, works attributed to him, 59, 61, his works in the Brera gallery, 59; in the Ambrosiana, 61 a; and in the Poldi Pezzoli, at Milan, 61 c; his Salome, in Uffizi, 268 b; other works, 559 a.
Luke, St., the patron saint of artists, statue of him, in the Florence cathedral, 211 c; at Or San Michele, 231 a; episode from his Gospel, painted by Albertinelli, in the Uffizi, 263 a; picture of the Saviour, begun by him and finished by "invisible hands," 417 c; his picture of the Madonna, in S. Maria Maggiore, in Rome, 418 c; another picture traditionally attributed to him, in S. Francesca Romana, 432 b.
Luther Martin [† 1546], the great German religious Reformer, his protest against the system of indulgences and the corruptions of the hierarchy 435 c; he visits Rome, 392 b; and takes up his residence in the convent adjoining S. Maria del Popolo, 433.
Lysippus (4th cent. B. C.) Greek sculptor, one of his masterpieces, in the Vatican, 455 b; his statue of Mars resting, in the Terme Museum, 500 c; copy of his Hercules, 530; and the bronze Mercury, in the Naples' Museum, 532 a

MACHIAVELLI NICCOLÒ [† 1527], statesman and historian, his literary labours, 219; his opinion on the *Parte Guelfa*, 309; his tomb, 219; *see also* 254*.
Macrino d'Alba, Piedmontese painter, 20.
Maderna Stefano, Lombard sculptor, 427.
Maderno Carlo [† 1629], Roman architect, 360; is appointed architect of St. Peter's, 407, and of the Vatican, 441; completes the church of S. Andrea della Valle, 435; works on the Barberini, 508; Quirinal, 509; and Chigi palaces, 510; the tomb of Benedict XI. at Perugia, 360.
Mæcenas Gaius [† 8 B. C.], a wealthy Roman, his patronage of letters, 400, 512.
Magellan (Fernand de) [† 1521], 167.
Magi (wise men), of ancient Persia, 262.
Magna Grecia, 563.
Magnificat, The, 260.
Mahomet II. [† 1481], Turkish Sultan 61.

Maiano, Benedetto da [† 1497], Florentine sculptor and architect, his works at Florence: the Strozzi palace, 305; the pulpit in Santa Croce, 218; a doorway in the Palazzo Vecchio, 202; a bust of Mellini, 301; at Siena: 344, 329; altar at San Gimignano, 353.
Maiano, Giuliano da [† 1490], Florentine architect, works on the building of the *Santuario Santa Casa*, at Loreto, 189 b; sculptures attributed to him, 522 c.
Maiori, on the Amalfi road, 555.
Maitani Lorenzo, reliefs at Orvieto 379 b.
Malatesta, a family of Condottieri, lords of Rimini, remove precious marbles from Sant'Apollinare, in Ravenna, 187 a; employ Leon Battista Alberti to remodel the Rimini cathedral, 188 a; build the Gradara castle, scene of Francesca da Rimini's tragedy, 190*; bronze medals, in the Bargello to commemorate their effigies, 303 a; their portraits, in the Orvieto cathedral, 382 b.
Malavolti, Sienese family, 329, 347.
Malebolge or evil pits, Dante's, 227.
Mancini Maria, famous beauty, 497.
Manfred [† 1266], King of Sicily, 313, 329, 360, 505, 518. [He was the natural son of the emperor Frederick II. of Hohenstaufen; contemporaries praise his noble and magnanimous character; he was renowned for his physical beauty and great intellectual attainments. In conjunction with the Ghibellines of Tuscany his forces defeated the Guelphs at Montaperti (1260); later, in a battle with Charles of Anjou, he was defeated and slain near Benevento, and as he had been excommunicated by pope Urban IV., his body was not laid in consecrated ground but cast unburied upon the banks of the river Verde].
Manichæans, 354. [Believers in the doctrine of Mani or Manichæus, a Persian of the 3rd century, who taught a dualism derived from Zoroaster, e. g., that man's body is the product of the Kingdom of Darkness (Evil), but that his soul springs from the Kingdom of Light (Good)].
Manna, The, Gathering of, 129.
Manners, in Renaissance Italy, 78, 79, 190.
Mantegazza Antonio and Cristoforo, Lombard architects, 70.
Mantegna Andrea [† 1506], Paduan painter, pupil of Squarcione, work in Milan, 59, 60; at Mantua, 78, 79, 80; at Venice, 138; at Padua, 158; at Verona, 161; at Florence, 271; at Naples, 538.
Mantua, 78; court life at, *ib.*; Congress of Mantua, 339. See also *Gonzaga*.
Manzoni Alessandro [† 1873], Italian poet and novelist, author of the historical love-story *I Promessi Sposi*, 48.
Maratta Carlo [† 1713], Roman painter, his altarpiece, in the Pitti, 277 c; decorates the Lateran baptistery, 416 a; the Madonna, in the Corsini gallery, 496 c; his tomb, 431 c.
Marcellus Marcus Claudius [† 23 B. C.], 402.
Marches, The, 189 sq.
Marconi Rocco [† 1529], painter, 148.
Marcus Aurelius Antoninus [† 180], Roman emperor and Stoic philosopher, column of, 395; equestrian statue on the Capitol, 504; in the Vatican, 450.

Marescotti, Sienese family, 330.
Margaret of Cortona, St. [† 1297], 486.
Marguerite of Valois, portrait, 21.
Mariano, Lorenzo di (Marrina), Sienese sculptor, works in Siena, 337, 345 c.
Mariners' compass, the, 552.
Marius Caius, Roman general, 449, 504.
Mark Antony. See Antony.
Mark, St. [† 67], one of the Four Evangelists, stories from the life of, 90, 91, 102, 110, 111; Miracle of, by Tintoretto, 142; Discovery of his body, 61, and its Translation, 148.
Marot Clement, French poet, 178.
Marriage of the Virgin, The: painting by Raphael, 59; fresco by Luini, 64; panel by Fra Angelico, 250; fresco by Franciabigio, 243; relief by Orcagna, in Or San Michele, 232.
Mars, a Roman deity especially connected with warfare, 500; his spears preserved in the Forum, 399 b; Temple in his honour, built by Augustus, 402 c.
Marsyas, a legendary flute-player of Phrygia, his Punishment, painting in the Vatican, 459 b; statue 505 c.
Martin of Tours, St. (4th century), legend of, scenes from his life, painted by Simone Martini, in a chapel, at Assisi, 368.
Martin V. (Otto Colonna) [† 1431], Pope, begins the building of Palazzo Colonna, 497 a; his bronze grave, in St. John in Lateran, 415 b.
Martinengo, noble italian family, 77.
Martini Simone [† 1344], Sienese painter, works at Siena, 333, 345; at Assisi, 366, 368; portrait of Petrarch, 238; the Annunciation at the Uffizi, 256*.
Mary of Valois, tomb of, 523.
Masaccio (Tommaso Guidi) [† 1428], Florentine painter, his contribution to the development of art, 222, 240, 255*; his frescoes in the Brancacci chapel, 240; Holy Trinity in S. Maria Novella, 223.
Masolino da Panicale [† 1440], Florentine painter, fresco at Castiglione d'Olona, 64, and at Saronno, *ib.*, at Florence, 241; Perugia, 361.
Massegne, Jacobello and Pier Paolo delle, Venetian sculptors, 105, 176.
Master of Ceremonies, his traditional warning at Papal elections, 338.
Matilda of Tuscany [† 1115], known as the Great Countess, 474, 557; her gift to the Holy See, 410; her tomb in St. Peter's, by Bernini, 410; her hospitality to Gregory VII., 557.
Matteo di Giovanni (di Bartolo) [† 1495], Sienese painter, 340, 345.
Mausoleum of the Medici Grand-Dukes, at Florence, 235; of Theodoric, 181.
Maxentius M. Aurelius Valerius [† 312], Roman emperor, his defeat, 469.
Maximilian Ferdinand-Joseph [† 1867], emperor of Mexico, archduke, 169.
Maximilian I. [† 1519], Emperor Germany his stay at Portofino, 43 a; his part in the League of Cambrai, 123 b.
Maximin, Archbishop, 186.
Maximinus Galerius Valerius [† 314], 457.
Mazzini Giuseppe [† 1872], patriot, 40.
Mazzoni Guido [† 1518], Modenese sculptor, character of his work, 177.
Medallions of infants, terracotta, 246.
Medals, in the Bargello, 303.
Medea, legendary sorceress, 491, 500, 503.

Medici, the name of a famous ancient Guelph family of Tuscany, their first appearance at Florence, 192; their banking activity, 231; their original home, 306; residence in the Palazzo Vecchio, 202, 203; in the Pitti palace, 275; in the Villas outside Florence, 312; their rule of Florence, 194; expelled and recalled, 192; victims of the Pazzi conspiracy, 211; escape assassination, 261; their palace plundered, 301; memorable scene within its walls. *ibid.*; their work for the world, 194; erect church of San Lorenzo, 233, and found the Laurentian Library, 238; endow the Uffizi Gallery, 254*; the Pitti Gallery, 276; rebuild the monastery of San Marco, and commission Fra Angelico to decorate its walls, 248; paintings in allusion to their deeds, the Primavera, by Botticelli, in the Uffizi, 261 *a*; the Journey of the Magi, by Gozzoli, in the Medici palace, 306 *b*; their tombs at Florence, 234, 235, 236, 237; at Rome, 435; portraits of some of them, the equestrian statue of Cosimo I., in the Piazza della Signoria, 196 *a*; in Vasari's fresco, Palazzo Vecchio, 201 *a*; in Ghirlandaio's frescoes, 244; in Santa Trinita; in Botticelli's Adoration of the Magi, 261 *c*; in Bronzino's pictures, in the Uffizi, 266 *b*; and Raphael's, Ghirlandaio's frescoes, in Santa Trinita, 244; in Botticelli's Adoration of the Magi, 261 *c*; in Bronzino's pictures, in the Uffizi, 266 *a*; and Raphael's, in the Uffizi, 267; in a Florentine mosaic, Duke Cosimo II., Museo degli Argenti, at the Pitti, 288 *b*; in Cellini's wax medallion of Duke Francis I., in the Bargello, 298 *a*; marble busts, in the Bargello, 301; in Gozzoli's frescoes, in the Medici palace, 306; in Raphael's frescoes, in the Vatican, 462 *b*, 466 *a*, 468 *b*. Armorial bearings of the M., 1; genealogical charts of the Medici families, 287 *A*, 287 *B*.
    Alessandro de', 192.
    Catherine de', 192, 306.
    Cosimo the Elder, takes (1429) government of Florence, 192 *c*; is overthrown (1433) by the Albizi, *ib.*; returns (1434) from exile, and resumes government until his death (1464), *ib.*; builds the Old Sacristy, in San Lorenzo, 234; founds the Laurentian Library, 238; finances the rebuilding of the Monastery of San Marco, 248; orders Donatello to execute the bronze David for the courtyard of the Medici palace, 295 *b*; builds the Villa of Careggi, which became the favorite residence of Lorenzo the Magnificent, 312 *c*.
    Cosimo I. Grand Duke of Tuscany, 192, 196, 203, 294, 329.
    Cosimo II., Grand Duke, 288.
    Ferdinand I., Grand Duke, 235.
    Ferdinand II., Grand Duke, 287.
    Ferdinand III., Grand Duke, 278*.
    Francis I., Grand Duke, 294, 298, 312.
    Gian Gastone, last Grand Duke, 287.
    Giovanni de', father of Cosimo the Elder, 192, 234, 246.

Medici (continued):
    Giovanni de', Cardinal (afterwards Leo X.), 192, 236, 244, 462, 466, 467.
    Giovanni de', son of Cosimo the Elder, 234.
    Giovanni natural son of Cosimo I., 235.
    Giovanni de', (delle Bande Nere), famous military leader, 233, 301.
    Giuliano de', 192, 211, 236, 260, 261, 303, 381.
    Giuliano de' (afterwards Duke of Nemours), 192, 236, 244.
    Giulio de' (afterwards Clement VII.), 192, 288. See Clement VII.
    Ippolito de', Cardinal, 285.
    Lorenzo de', the Magnificent, 192, 211, 233, 234, 236, 238, 252, 261, 266, 287, 301, 303, 306, 312.
    Lorenzo de' (afterwards Duke of Urbino), 192, 236.
    Maria de', 266.
    Piero de' (the Gouty), 192, 234, 238, 261, 275, 301, 306.
    Piero de' (the Unfortunate), 244, 301.
Medieval legend, a suggestive, 226.
Medusa, one of the three Gorgons, in Cellini's bronze Perseus, 198 *a*; in the Etruscan Tomb of the Volumni, at Perugia, 390 *c*; in ancient mosaic, in the Vatican, 443 *b*; in the Tazza Farnese, National Museum, Naples, 538 *a*; in ancient Metopes from Selinunte, in the Palermo museum, 578 *b*.
Melchizedek, King and Priest, 98, 380, 420.
Meleager, the hero of Calydon, 448.
Meloria, Naval Battle (1284) of, 126, 313.
Melozzo da Forli [† 1494], Umbrian painter, decorates the *Santa Casa*, at Loreto, 189 *b*; figure of the Archangel, in the Uffizi, 265 *c*; the Christ in Glory, in the Quirinal palace, Rome, 509 *a*.
Memling Hans [† ca. 1494], painter, his great altarpiece of The Passion of Our Lord, at Turin, 21 *c*; illuminated work in the Breviarium Grimani, 149 *b*; his panel of St. Benedict, in the Uffizi, 272 *c*.
Memmi (Lippo), Sienese painter, 256*.
Menaggio, famous summer resort on Lake Como, 68.
Menander [† ca. 290 B. C.], a Greek comic poet, 449.
Mendicant Friars, origin of, 366.
Menelaus, king of Sparta, and husband of the beautiful Helen, 450.
Mengs Raphael [† 1779], painter, 494, 498.
Mercenaries, soldiers serving for pay, 74.
Merchants, Patron Saint of, 231.
Mercury, god of merchants, Giambologna's bronze statue, in the Bargello, 294 *a*; ancient bronze, in the Naples' museum, 532; M.'s role, in the Myth of Psyche, in the Farnesina, 493.
Messalina [† 48], notorious Roman woman, wife of Claudius, bust of her, in the Capitoline museum, 507 *b*; takes refuge in Pincian gardens and is killed, 510 *b*. [She was only 26 years old].
Messiah, *i. e.* the "anointed,", 382.
Messina, 582. Antonello da Messina. See *Antonello.*
Metal works on Florentine palaces, a distinguishing mark nobility, 304.
Methuselah, Hebrew patriarch, 229.
Metrodorus, a Greek philosopher, 447, 507.
Michael, the Archangel, 395, 410; his mission on earth, 226.

Michelangelo Buonarroti [† 1564], Florentine sculptor, architect, painter and poet, his art and personality, 236, 237, 267, 440; his themes in sculpture, 289; his appreciation of Ghiberti's gates, 205; of the cathedral's dome, 209; of the Laocoon group, and the Belvedere Torso, 451; his sense of humour, 290; Torregiano's brutality to him, 240; assists Ghirlandaio in S. Maria Novella, 224; his sculptural works: the tombs in San Lorenzo, 236, 237; meaning of his allegorical figures, *ibid.*; statues of David, 290, 291; of Christ with the Cross, 434; of Bacchus, 291; of Moses, 440; of Captives, 289; bust of Brutus, 291; group of the Pietà, 409; statue of St. Gregory the Great, 430; of the Deposition, 211; group in the Palazzo Vecchio, 200; relief of the Madonna with the Book, 291; of the Madonna on the Steps, 308; of the Battle of the Centaurs, 308; his mask of a Faun, 291; other sculptures attributed to him, 176, 335; his pictorial works: the Ceiling, 477 *sqq.*, and the Last Judgment, 476, in the Sistine Chapel; the Crucifixion of St. Peter, 474; cartoon, 255*B*; for the Scourging of Christ, 439, and the Deposition, 436; tondo of the Holy Family in the Uffizi, 267; cartoon for the Palazzo Vecchio, 200; his architectural works: the Medici chapel in San Lorenzo, 236; the Laurentian Library, 238; architect of the Vatican, 441, and of St. Peter's, 404 *sq.*; converts Roman baths into a church, 431; study of Constantine's basilica, 504; reverses and arranges the Capitol, 504; directs building operations of Palazzo Farnese, 509; prepares designs for the façade of San Lorenzo, at Florence, 233; restores the colossal group of the Farnese Bull, 531; his defence of Florence, 311; his friendship for Vittoria Colonna, 463, 497; his death and funerals, 218; tomb of M., *ib.*; memorials of M., 308; portraits of M., in Vasari's fresco, Palazzo Vecchio, 201 *a*; his bust in Santa Croce, 218 *c*; his statue, in Portico of the Uffizi, 254*; his likeness in the Uffizi, 274; marble statue of his Boyhood, in the Pitti, 285; M. quoted, 28, 147, 174, 180, 255*, 385.
Michelino (Domenico di), painter, 210.
Michelozzo (Michelozzi) [† 1472], Florentine architect and sculptor, builds the Medici palace, 306; designs the monastery of San Marco, 248; the courtyard of the Palazzo Vecchio, 200; restores the church of the Annunziata, 243; contributes work on the tomb of John XXIII., 208; on statue of St. Matthew, 230; on Cantoria, at Prato, 328; his relief in the Bargello, 295; in S. Croce, 191; his portal 63.
Middle Ages, elementary instruction in the, 214; Mysticism of the, 226.
Mieris Frans, van, Dutch painter.
Milan: history, 48; description, 49; the Duomo, 51 *sqq.*; Sant'Ambrogio, 54; Sant'Eustorgio, 55, 57; S. Maria delle Grazie, 56; Brera Gallery, 58 *sqq.*; Ambrosian Library, 61; Archeological Museum 62; Palaces, 63.

Milton John [† 1674], author, 14, 385.
Minerva called Athena by the Greeks, the goddess of wisdom and all the liberal arts, 434, 454, 529, 578.
Mino da Fiesole [† 1484], Florentine sculptor, his monument to Count Hugo, 245; reliefs in the Bargello, 299; bust of Bishop Salutati, 310; work at Rome, the sepulchral monument of pope Paul II., 412 b; the marble reliefs, in S. Maria Maggiore, 419 b; the Tabernacle for Holy oil, in S. Maria in Trastevere, 425 b; the marble screens and the singing gallery, in the Sistine chapel, 475; the pulpit, at Prato, 328.
Mino del Pellicciaio, Sien. painter, 342, 343.
Minori, on the Amalfi coast, 555.
Minorites (Franciscans), Order of, 366.
Minotaur, a fabulous Cretan monster having the body of a man and the head of a bull, 448, 536.
Miracles: of Bolsena, 386, 464; of St. Francis, 369, 372, 373; of St. Gennaro, 525; of SS. Peter and John, 240, 241; of SS. Peter and Paul, 242, 466; of the True Cross, 140, 220; of St. Mark, 142, 144: of Filippo Benizzi, 242.
Mirandola Pico della [† 1494], great humanist, 312. [Renaissance scholar].
Misericordia at Florence, origin of, 147.
Mission of 14th century painters, 226.
Mithras, a Persian or Assyrian deity, 448 c.
Modena, its Romanesque cathedral, 177.
Molmenti Pompeo [† 1928], writer, 149.
Monaco, Principality of, 44.
Monastic Orders, 249.
Monks of St. Bernard, labours of the, 12.
Monogram of Christ, The, in mosaic, in St. Mark's, Venice, 100 a; on Doorway of the Palazzo Vecchio, at Florence, 197 b; designed for tablets, by St. Bernardino da Siena, 333 a, 337 b; on Roman sarcophagus, in Lateran 503 b.
Monreale, monastery of, 575 sqq.
Montagues, the, of Shakespeare, 165.
Montaperti, Battle of, 192, 329.
Montauti Antonio, Roman sculptor, 415.
Monte Bianco, 13. Monte Rosa, 11, 12.
Montecarlo, famous gambling place, 44.
Montecassino, Benedictine abbey, 560.
Montefalco, 357. [Early Umbr. art].
Montefeltro, The, Lords of Urbino, 190; Genealogy of, 190*.
Federigo I. Duke of Urbino, 190; his rule and patronage of the arts and letters, ib.; is invested with the Order of the Garter, ib.; his portrait by Piero della Francesca, 258 b; and at Urbino, 190.
Guidobaldo, Duke of Urbino, 190.
Montelupo (Raffaello da) [† 1567], Florentine sculptor, his statue of St. John the Ev., at Or San Michele, 231 b; works on the Tombs of the Medici Popes, at Santa Maria sopra Minerva, 435 c; executes statue of the Prophet Elijah and that of a Sibyl, for the monument to pope Julius II., 440 b.
Monte Oliveto Mag., Sodomas' frescoes, 354.
Monteverde Giulio [† 1917], sculptor, 36.
Montferrat, 26. [The Marquisate of Montferrat, a territory south of the Po and east of Turin, was held by a family who were in the 12th century one of the most considerable in Lombardy].
Montfort, Guy de, his sacrilege, 515 c.

Monfort Simon de, Earl of Leicester [† 1265], father of the preceding, 515 c.
Months, allegories of the, medieval reliefs on St. Mark's façade, 92, sculptures 114.
Montorsoli, fra Giovanni [† 1563], Florentine sculptor, 30, 32.
Monza, 64 (and 48).
Moral precepts, pictures conveying, great frescoes, in S. Maria Novella, 226 a; and in the Cappella degli Spagnuoli, in Florence, 226, 229; mural paintings, in the Palazzo Pubblico, at Siena, 332.
Moretto da Brescia (Alessandro Buonvicino) [† 1555], painter, 35, 76, 135.
Moriale, Fra, famous condottiere, 74.
Moroni Giovanni Battista [† 1578], 270.
Morosini, Doge of Venice, 111, 127, 132.
Mosaics, early Christian, 182 sqq., 418; Byzantine, 90, 96 sqq., 571, 574, 577.
Mosca Simone [† 1553], sculptor, 386, 388.
Moses (ca. 1500 B. C.), Hebrew law-giver, reliefs on the Doges' palace, 114 b; in Tintoretto's Gathering of the Manna, church of St. George, at Venice, 129 b; in the Triumph of St. Thomas, 228 b; in the Christ in Limbo, 229 b; in Giorgione's Ordeal of Fire, in the Uffizi, 270 c; in Perugino's frescoes, in the Collegio del Cambio, at Perugia, 362 b; his Stoning, ancient mosaic, in S. Maria Maggiore, Rome; in Peruzzi's Burning Bush, Vatican Stanzas, 465 a; events from his Life, frescoes on left wall of the Sistine chapel, 480; statue of Moses by Michelangelo, 440.
Mozart Wolfgang [† 1791], composer, author of Marriage of Figaro. Don Giovanni, Magic Flute, 170.
Murat Joachim [† 1815], K. of Naples, 190*. [He was the son of an innkeeper, received Napoleon's sister to wife and was loaded with honours and rewarded with the crown of Naples].
Murillo Bartolomé Esteban [† 1682], Spanish painter, picture of St. Francis in prayer, Palazzo Bianco, Genoa, 36 b; his Madonna and Child, in the Pitti, 282 a; the Marriage of St. Catherine, in the Vatican Gallery, 486 c; the Madonna and Child, in Corsini Gallery, 496 c.
Muses, goddesses presiding over the liberal arts, allegories, in the Palazzo Schifanoia, Ferrara, 179 c; Statues of Muses, in the Vatican, 447 a.
Musset, Alfred de [† 1857], French romantic poet, play-writer and novelist, 549. [He took up law and medicine but could endure no profession; his Contes d'Espagne et d'Italie, had an immediate success; in 1833 began his liaison with George Sand, invoiving him in the ill-fated expedition to Venice, whence he returned the following year shattered in health].
Muziano [† 1592], Roman painter, 497.
Myron, Greek sculptor, his Discobolus, in the Vatican, 444; the Marsyas, 503.
Mysticism in medieval times, 226.
Myth, The, of Psyche, in Giulio Romano's paintings, at Mantua, 79; in Raphael's great series, in the Farnesina, Rome, 492, 493; myth of Protesilaus, 444; myth of Alcestis, 453; of Peleus, 503; of Atalanta and Hippomenes, 539; of Danaë, ib.; of Orpheus and Eurydice, 528.

NAPOLEON I. (Bonaparte) [† 1821], Emperor of the French, establishes the Ligurian Republic, 26; coronation, 48, his motto, 64; his sword at Turin, 23; orders completion of the Duomo, at Milan, 51; takes possession of Venice, 81*, and completes the Piazza San Marco, 88; his opinion of the same, 89; carries off St. Mark's bronze horses, 91; orders the burning of the Bucentaur, 151; gives Lucca to his sister, 325; adds Tuscany to his dominions, 192, 329; purchases art collection for the Louvre, 488; removes Apollo Belvedere and Laocoon group to Paris, 451; purchases the Villa Medici at Rome, 510. [Born at Ajaccio in 1769, he was trained at the military schools of Brienne and Paris, where he received a solid grounding in the work of an artilleryman and an officer; at 20 he came into the upheaval of the Revolution, which favoured the ambitious. He first distinguished himself at the siege of Toulon (1793), and was promoted general of brigade; the following year he received the command of the Italian campaign; in 1795, during an insurrection in Paris he had a chance to do a great, vital service to the Republic; and was rewarded first with the hand of Josephine de Beauharnais, and then nominated Commander in Chief of the Army of Italy; after the defeat of Austria and his famous victories at Lodi, Arcola, Rivoli..., "miracles of genius and courage," he was received in Paris with an enthusiasm which excited his ambition; his plan to strike a blow at England was accepted by the Directoire, and he set out (1798) to conquer Egypt, which he overran, but his fleet was destroyed by Nelson (the whole story of Napoleon up to Waterloo turns on this, henceforth he was to struggle against England, and in that struggle he was in the end to be vanquished). In 1799 he returned to France, overthrew the government of the Directory and established his own dictatorship; four years later he was invested with the imperial dignity. Henceforth began that long array of wars against Europe, which contributed to inspire all the nations around with a sense of terror of his name; but with his unfortunate expedition into Russia (1812), his glory began to wane and the tide to turn; he was finally defeated at Lützen by the Allies, who invaded France and entered Paris in 1814, upon which he was compelled to abdicate at Fontainebleau and retire to the island of Elba (April 1814); the following year (March 1815) he returned to France and resumed power: but in vain. The Powers with England at their head leagued against him and crushed him (June 1815) at Waterloo. By this defeat he had forfeited the throne, and was again compelled to abdicate. Having surrendered to the British he was shipped off to the island of St. Helena, in the south Atlantic, where after six years of misery, he died in May 1821].

Naples, history, 519, 522, 523, 524 sqq.; 526; Museum, 527sqq.; environs, 540 sqq.
Narni, its Bridge of Augustus, 390.
Nattier Jean-Marc [† 1766], French painter, his lovely portraits of Louis XV' daughters Marie Adelaide and Anna Henriette, in the Uffizi, 273 a.
Navicella, La, mosaic by Giotto, in the Portico of St. Peter's, 405 b. [The famous "Navicella," or Christ saving St. Peter from the waves, executed by order of Cardinal Stefaneschi, symbolizes the Ship of the Church Militant ploughing her way through the sea of this World. The vessel manned by eleven of the Apostles, all betraying embarassment and consternation, struggles with the winds, allegorically represented by two demons above blowing through long horns. The four Evangelists in the sky, with actions of sympathy for those in the ship, represent the supernatural aid of heaven which neutralizes evil spirits and maliciousness. In the left corner of the composition is an angler with his line, figurative of the Church's vocation to fish for souls. On the right is seen the Saviour supporting St. Peter when about to sink in the water on which he had attempted to walk, signifying that, without faith in Christ and the strength of His sustaining arm, neither Church nor Churchman is sufficient to stand on the yielding water of human infirmity].
Nazareth, House of, now at Loreto, 189.
Negroponte, Fra Antonio, painter, 135.
Nemours, the duke of, 236.
Neoptolemus, son of Achilles, 387.
Neri (Blacks), the, Italian faction, 314.
Nero Claudius Cæsar [† 68], Roman Emperor, his burning of Rome, 392; his equestrian statue, 532; site of his circus, 404; arch's bronze horses, 91.
Neroccio, Sienese painter, 258. 345.
Nervi (Liguria), seaside resort, 43.
Nestorius [† 451], Patriarch of Constantinople, celebrated heresiarch, 420.
Netscher Gaspard, Dutch painter, 497.
Nevers-Rethel, dukedom of, 80 b.
Niccolò da Bari, St., miracles, 256.
Niccolò da Foligno, painter, 484.
Niccolò da Uzzano, his bust by Donatello, in the Bargello, 295.
Niccolò Pisano. See Pisano.
Nicholas III. (Gaetano Orsini) [† 1280], Pope, his part in the building of the Vatican, 441; orders the reconstruction of the Sancta Sanctorum chapel, 417; his grave, 412; Dante's verdict on him, 227.
Nicholas IV. (Girolamo Masci) [† 1292], Pope, restores St. John in Lateran, 414; disposes for the decoration of apse of S. Maria Maggiore, 420; his tomb, 419.
Nicholas V. (Parentucelli) [† 1455], Pope, begins a new St. Peter's, 405; orders the restoration of several churches at Rome, 425, 429, 430; his grand idea of rebuilding the Vatican, 441; founds the Vatican Library, 442; orders Fra Angelico to decorate his chapel, 471; appoints Æneas Sylvius Piccolomini bishop of Trieste and Siena, 338.
Nicolaus, sculptor (ca. 1100), 160, 177.

Nietzsche Friedrich Wilhelm [† 1900], German philosopher, 549.
Nigetti, Florentine architect, builds the Medici mausoleum, at Florence, 235.
Night, Michelangelo's figure of, 236 sq.
Nile, marble group, in the Vatican, 455 c.
Niobe, the legendary queen of Phrygia, 501; famous group in the Uffizi gallery, Florence, 255.
Noah, patriarch, 114, 229; 98, 478.
Normans (Northmen), the, in Italy, 519; Genealogy of, 518; their Conquest of Naples, 519 b; subjugate Amalfi, 552c; monuments erected by them, at Ravello, 556 b; their patronage of Art, in Apulia, 563 b, 569. [Normans is the name of those colonists from Scandinavia who in the 9th century settled in Gaul and founded Normandy; adopted the French language and manners and from there set forth, in small organized groups, on new errands of conquest (11th-12th cent.), chiefly in the British Isles and in Southern Italy, where they obtained (1030) first the County of Aversa, and later (1053) they seized Apulia from Byzantine emperors, and Salerno from the Lombards, founding the Duchy of Apulia and Calabria. After the 13th century they ceased to exist as a distinct people].
Notaries, Patron Saint of, 231.
Novara, its remarkable church, 14.
Numa Pompilius, King of ancient Rome, his sculptured figure on columns supporting the Doges' palace, in Venice, 519 b; in Perugino's paintings, at Perugia, 363 b; his traditional palace in the Forum, in Rome, 399 b.
Numbers, quotation from the Book of, the Serpent of brass, 477 c.
Nuncio, the Papal, 151.
Nuns, their life in religious houses, 149 b.
Nuptials, The, of Beatrice d'Este, 72; of Isabella of Aragona, ib.; of Helen and Paris, 531; of Cupid and Psyche, 492; of the Adriatic Sea, 151; the so-called Aldobrandine nuptials, 452; of Alexander the Great, 493.

OAK, the, device of Julius II. (Della Rovere), 462.
Obedience, Giotto's allegory of, 370; group in admonition to, 114.
Obelisk of St. Peter's, in the Vatican, 400; story of its erection, 45.
Observantes, Order of the, 366.
Occam, William of [† 1347] English scholastic philosopher, surnamed the « Doctor Invincibilis », and Singularis, a monk of the Order of St. Francis of Assisi, 437 b.
Octavius Caius, Roman general, father of the emperor Augustus, 400.
Oderisio of Benevento, his gates on the cathedral, at Troia, 563.
Oderisio of Gubbio, painter, 390, 524.
Oliver, Paladin of Charlemagne, 163.
Olympus, the fabled residence of the gods, in Sabatelli's ceiling painting, in the Pitti, 276 b; in Raphael's frescoes, in the Farnesina, Rome, 493 a.
Onias, High Priest of the Jews, 465.
Opera House, the, at Milan, 49 c; at Naples, 526.

Orcagna Andrea [† 1368], Florentine architect, sculptor and painter, designs the Loggia de' Lanzi, 198; decorates the Strozzi chapel, 226; executes tabernacle of Or San Michele, 232; altarpiece in the Academy, 289, 320 sqq.
Ordeal of fire, Moses,' 270 c; St. Francis, 219 b. [In medieval times trial by fire was considered an efficacious means of proving one's innocence].
Ordelaffi, The, seigneurs of Forlì, 171.
Ordinances of Justice, 192.
Origen of Alexandria [† 254], a distinguished and influential theologian, 421.
Orley, Bernard van [† 1540], Flemish painter, the Vatican tapestries, 472.
Orpheus and Eurydice, myth of, 528 a; relief in the Villa Albani, Rome, 498 b.
Orsini, a powerful Roman princely family of the middle ages, 409.
Orsini Clarice, wife of Lorenzo, 233.
Orta, Lake of, 24.
Orvieto, 377; cathedral of, 378 sqq.; Museo dell'Opera, 387; palaces, 388.
Oscans, primitive inhabitants of Italy, the Founders of Pompeii, 541 a.
Ostia, Battle of, 468, 516.
Otho I. [† 973], Emp., 44, 178*.
Otho II. [† 983], Emperor of the Holy Roman Empire, appoints Count Ugo as his Viceroy in Tuscany, 245 b; part of his sarcophagus now used as a baptismal font, 411 b.
Otho III. [† 1002], German Emperor, releases Pomposa from the authority of Ravenna, 171; his legacy to Ravenna, 186.
Otho IV. [† 1218], of Brunswick, German Emp., his reward to the estimable Gualdrada, 389 (and 202).
Ovid Publius Naso [† 17 A. D.], great Latin poet, 463.

PACIFICUS, [† 846] deacon of Verona, 163.
Padua, Sant'Antonio, 155; Arena chapel, 156; Eremitani chapel, 158.
Paganini Nicolò [† 1840], Italian violinist, his instruments in Genoa, 37 b.
Pagan sculptures on church fronts, 514 a.
Paganism in Italian art, its character illustred by Giulio Romano's mural paintings, in the Palazzo del Tè, at Mantua, 79; and by those in the Farnesina, at Rome, 493.
Pageants, record of Florentine, 306.
Painting, Italian Schools of, 255 c, 590.
Palaces: Florentine, 304 sqq.; Roman, 508 sq.; Sienese, 330; Venetian, 148 sqq.
Palatine Hill, the, at Rome, 400.
Palatium, the, of Theodoric, 183.
Paleologus John VII. [† 1448], Emperor of the East, 307 c. [Paleologus, the name of an illustrious Byzantine family which first appears in history in the 11th century, whose descendants for two centuries became emperors of the Orient; the last of them, the younger brother of John VII., died in 1453. The conquest of Constantinople (Istanbul), in 1452, by the Turks dispersed the Paleologi. A younger branch held the marquisate of Monferrat from the year 1305 to 1533].

— 605 —

Paleologes (Andreas), the heir of Constantine III, 457.
Palermo, history, 569; palaces, 570; Cappella Palatina, 571; Cathedral, 572; churches, 573 sqq.; Museum, 578.
Palimpsest, discovered by Niebhur, 163.
Palio, the, at Siena, 350.
Paliotto, the, of Sant'Ambrogio, 54; of St. Mark, 107; of Città di Castello, 389.
Palladio Andrea [† 1580], Vicentine and Venetian architect, 167; work at Brescia, 77; at Venice, 119, 129.
Palladium (image of Pallas, *Minerva*), 426.
Pallas and the Centaur, Botticelli's, 260.
Palma il Giovane [† 1628], Venetian painter, decorates the Hall of the Senate, 122 *c*; and the Hall of the Great Council, in the Doges' palace, 124 *c*; his picture of the Allegory of Cahbrai, 123 *a*; and Venice crowned by Victory, 125 *a*; painting of the Last Judgment, 127 *b*; completes the painting of the Pietà, which Titian had left unfinished when he died, 143 *b*.
Palma il Vecchio [† 1528], Venetian painter, his altarpiece of Santa Barbara, in S. Maria Formosa, 136 *a*.
Pandects of Justinian, discovery of the, 462 *b*; their originals now in the Laurentian Library, 238 *c*.
Pannonia, 466.
Pantheon, the, at Rome, 430; of Florence, so-called, 218; of Venice 130.
Paolo Uccello. See Uccello.
Papacy, the: first germ of its power, 430; prerogatives of the emperors, 474, 557; election of the popes transferred to the cardinals, *ib.*; curious elections at Viterbo, 515; war between the P. and the Empire, 333, 474, 557; the P. and king Philip of France, 516; noted Papal excommunications, 252, 515, 557; transference of Papal Court to Avignon, 392; its return to Rome, 345, 432; pictorial career of a Renaissance Pope, 338, and worldliness of another, 499.
Paradise, Ghiberti's so-called gates of, 205; Signorelli's fresco of, 385; Orcagna's fresco at, 227; Tintoretto's painting of, 103, 124; Rivers of Paradise, ancient mosaics, 101, 415.
Parenzo, the cathedral, 170.
Paris Bordone. See Bordone.
Parisina, Byron's heroine, 178.
Parma, the Cathedral, 180; Correggio's paintings at, 180.
Parmigianino (Francesco Mazzola) [†1540], Parmesan painter, 268.
Parnassus symbolic residence of poets, famous fresco by Raphael, in the Vatican, 463; painting by Mengs, in the Villa Albani, 498 *c*.
Parodi Giovanni Battista, Genoese architect and sculptor, 34, 38.
Parte Guelfa, La, at Florence, 309.
Partecipazio, Doge Giovanni, 90.
Paschal I. [† 824], Pope, rebuilds the church of Santa Cecilia, 427 *a*; and that of Santa Prassede, at Rome, 429 *a*.
Paschal II. (Rainerio) [† 1118], Pope, orders the reconstruction of the church of San Clemente destroyed during the sack of Rome, by Robert Guiscard, 423 *b*; erects the church of Santa Maria del Popolo, 433 *a*; rebuilds the church of Santi Giovanni e Paolo, 436 *b*.

Passavanti, Fra Jacopo [† 1357], Dominican author, 228.
Patareni. See *Manicheans*.
Patriarchal life, reliefs of, 216.
Patrizio (Patrick), Well of San, 388.
Paul, St., "the Apostle of the Gentiles," the first Christian missionary and theologian, 422; *see also* 414.
Paul, St. (4th century), a hermit in the Thebaid, 255 B, 457.
Paul II. (Pietro Barbo) [† 1471], Pope, 179*; his monument in St. Peter's, 412; his favourite residence, 508.
Paul III. (Alessandro Farnese) [† 1549], Pope; gives Michelangelo unlimited powers for the construction of St. Peter's, 406; his portrait as Cardinal, 462; his apartment in Sant'Angelo 499; begins the Palazzo Farnese, 509; his connection with Michelangelo's 'Last Judgment.' 476; his tomb, 408.
Paul V. (Camillo Borghese) [† 1621], Pope, builds façade of St. Peter's, 405; the church of S. Maria della Vittoria, 438; Janiculum fountain, 510; tomb, 419.
Pauline Borghese, sister of Napoleon, remarkable portrait of the beautiful, 488.
Pavement, in Florence, used as pattern for fabrics, 208.
Pavia, 69; the Certosa of, 70 sqq.
Pawnshops in Florence, 192.
Pazzi, powerful Ghibelline family, chapel of the, 218; memorials of, 309; conspiracy of, 211; historical account of it, *ibid.*; medals commemorating same, 303; portraits of conspirators, 485.
Peace, allegorical figure of, 332.
Pebbles, used for improving the voice, 454 *a*.
Pegasus, 179, 578.
Peitho, goddess of persuasion, 531.
Pelagius II. [† 590], Pope, orders the reconstruction of the basilica of San Lorenzo, at Rome, 424.
Peleus. a King of Thessaly, 503.
Pelican, the, symbolism of, 249.
Pellico Silvio [† 1854], Italian patriot, 84.
Peloponnesian War (B. C. 431), the, 454.
Pendulum, invention of the, 315.
Penelope, faithful wife of Ulysses, 202.
Penni Francesco [† 1528], Roman painter, collaborates in the decoration of the Farnesina, 492 *b*.
Pensieroso, il, by Michelangelo, 237.
Pentecost, The, mosaic in St. Mark's Venice, 100; fresco in the cloisters of S. Maria Novella, Florence, 228.
Pepin (or Pipin) [† 768], a member of the Carolingian family, King of the Franks, his attack on the Lombards, 48, and the Byzantines, 392; his Donation, to the Holy See, 468.
Pericles [† 429 B. C.], Athenian statesman and orator, 447 (and 76, 363).
Persecutions of the Church, 191*; 392; 400. [The persecutions of the early Christians at the hands of Imperial Rome, are usually reckoned ten in number. viz., those under Nero A. D. 64, Domitian 95, Trajan 107, Hadrian 125, Marcus Aurelius 165, Severus 202, Maximinus 235, Decius 249, Valerianus 257, and Diocletian 303].
Perseus, a Greek hero, 506, 578; the, of Benvenuto Cellini, 198, 294; account of its casting, *ibid.*; P. of Canova, 451; P. and Andromeda, 537.

Persia, envoys of, at Venice, 119.
Persius Flaccus [† 62 A. D.], satirist, 355.
Perspective, Paolo Uccello's attempts, 258.
Perugia, views of the city, 358; churches, 360 sq.; Pinacoteca Vannucci, 264 sq.; Collegio del Cambio, 362 sq.; tomb of the Volumni, 390.
Perugino (Pietro Vannucci) [† 1524], Umbrian painter, characteristics of his work, 265; his Assumption in the Uffizi, 265; his Deposition in the Pitti, 279; his great Crucifixion, at Florence, 247; at Siena, 345; works in the Perugian gallery, 364; and the church of S. Pietro, 361; frescoes in the Collegio del Cambio, 362, 363; frescoes in the Sistine Chapel, 480 sq.; altarpiece in the Vatican, 485; portraits of him, 460, 466.
Peruzzi Baldassarre [† 1537], Sienese architect and painter, 329; begins the Belcaro castle, 351; is appointed architect of St. Peter's, 406; decorates ceilings in the Vatican, 464, 465; executes the Romb of pope Hadrian VI., 430 *c*; the Altarpiece in S. Maria della Pace, 439 *b*; prepares designs for the Palazzo Massimi, in Rome, 508 *b*.
Peruzzi, the, Florentine bankers, 221; their loan to Edward III. of England, 231 *b*. [The Peruzzi Bank consisted of three brothers, who lived with their wives and children in the Via de' Peruzzi, near Santa Croce; the combined families numbered thirty-one persons, who were served by upwards of twenty domestics of all grades. In 1345 the two banking-houses Bardi and Peruzzi, which were considered 'The Pillars that sustained a great part of the Commerce of Christendom,' became bankrupt; king Edward III., of England owing them some nine thousand gold florins Their failure involved, of course, a multitude of Florentine citizens, and was a heavy misfortune to the Republic. The Florentine bankers and merchants made their cash-reckonings in *lire*, *soldi*, and *denari*—the origin of the English £. s. d. Twenty *soldi* went to the pound and twelve *denari* to the *soldi*. The spot values of these coins were constantly varying, hence the standard coin for all important transactions was the florin in gold, first coined in 1252].
Pesaro family, the, 131.
Pestum, the Greek temples at, 558.
Peter Lombard [† 1160], bishop of Paris, his figure in Raphael's Disputa, in the Vatican, 460 *b*.
Peter, St., the Chief of the 12 Apostles, his landing in Italy, 321; his approval of St. Mark's gospel, 110; baptizes his jailors, 400; his deliverance, 467; converts the daughters of the senator Pudens, 428; his flight along the Appian Way, 432, 434; sites of his martyrdom, 404, 429; his relics, 407, 414; the Crucifixion of St. Peter, painting by Michelangelo, 474.
Peter the Hermit [† 1115], preacher of the First Crusade, 39.
Peter of Verona, St. [† 1252], Dominican preacher, 248; his death and tomb at Milan, 55.

Petrarch Francesco [† 1374], famous Italian lyric poet, sketch of his career and his contribution to literature, 253; his gift to Venice, 87; his friendship for Simone Martini, 368; his portrait by the same, 238; his residence, 70; death at Arquà, 170; other portraits of him, 226 b, 229 c, 253, 254* c, 463 b.

Petronilla, St. adopted daughter of the apostle Peter, 410.

Petrucci, seigneur of Siena, 351, 382.

Phaedra, her story sculptured on ancient sarcophagus, in the Pisan Camposanto, 318 c; and in the Lateran museum, 503 c; the famous sarcophagus at Girgenti, 533 c. [She was carried off by Theseus to Athens and became his wife; there she became enamoured of Hippolytus, son of Theseus, but finding her advances rejected, she hanged herself, leaving a letter in which she accused her stepson of an attempt upon her virtue. Theseus placed a curse on his son, and by the agency of the god Poseidon he was killed while riding in his chariot near the sea].

Pharaoh, king of ancient Egypt, 480; the Dream of, mosaic, 99; ivory, 186.

Phidias (5th century B. C.), Greek sculptor, his statue of Juno, in the Vatican, 446 a; the Horse Tamers, in front of the Quirinal palace, 509 b.

Philip le Bel [† 1314], King of France, his partisans strike pope Boniface VIII. in his palace at Anagni, 516 c; his figure in the Church Militant, in S. Maria Novella, Florence, 229 c.

Philip II. [† 336 B. C.], King of Macedon, father of Alex. the Great, 454.

Philip II. [† 1598] (son of Charles V.), King of Spain, 329; Van Dyck's portrait of him, 35 c; Titian's portraits, in the Pitti, 276 c; in the Corsini gallery, Rome, 496 a; he bears cost of coffin which contains the rest of San Carlo Borromeo, in the Milan cathedral, 52 c.

Philip IV. [† 1665], King of Spain, portrait in the Pitti, by Velasquez, 277.

Philosophy, Raphael's fresco of, 460.

Phocas [† 610], East Roman emperor, 397.

Phoenicians, The, in Sicily, 568, *sqq.*

Phryne (4th century B. C.), celebrated Greek courtesan, 444 b. [Her real name was Mnesarete, she lived at Athens and acquired so much wealth that she offered to rebuild the walls of Thebes. On the occasion of a festival of Poseidon at Eleusis she laid aside her garments, let down her hair, and stepped into the sea in the sight of the people, thus suggesting to the painter Apelles his great picture of Aphrodite Anadyomene, for which Phyrne sat as a model. She was also the model for the statue of the *Cnidian Venus*, by Praxiteles. When accused of profaning the Eleusinian mysteries, she was brought before the judges; and when it seemed that the verdict would be unfavourable, her advocate rent her robe and exposed her bosom, which so moved the judges that they acquitted her, to preserve to the artists the image of divine beauty thus recognized in her].

Physicians, Patron Saint of, 231.

Pia de' Tolomei, lady of Siena, 329.

Piacenza, and its Municipal palace, 177.

Piccadilly Circus, the, of Palermo, 570.

Piccinino Niccolò, famous condottiere, 74; his medal portrait by Pisanello, 303.

Piccolomini, illustrious family of Siena. 329, 330. See also *Pius II., Pius III.*

Pico della Mirandola. See *Mirandola.*

Piedmont, 11 *sqq.*

Piero della Francesca [† 1492], Umbrian painter, his portrait of a Lady, in the Poldi-Pezzoli, Milan, 63 a; the Sigismondo Malatesta, at Rimini, 188 b; the Portrait of Federico di Montefeltro and Battista Sforza, his wife, in the Uffizi, 258 b; his famous frescoes at Borgo San Sepolcro, 356; and those of The Legend of the Holy Cross, in the San Francesco, at Arezzo, *ib.*

Piero di Cosimo [† 1521], Florentine painter panel of Perseus liberating Andromeda, in the Uffizi, 263 c; the Mary Magdalene, in the Corsini gallery, Rome, 496 b; his famous frescoes in the Sistine Chapel, 480 c.

Piero di Giovanni, sculptor, 386.

Pietà (Deposition), The: by Fra Bartolommeo, mosaic, 280; by Bellini, 61; by Francia, 20; by Perugino, 279; by Raphael, 489; by Michelangelo, 211, 409; by Montauti, 415; by Titian, 143; by Roger van der Weyden, 272.

Pietro del Minella, Sienese painter, 340.

Pigafetta Antonio [† 1525], navigator, and companion of Magellan, 167 a.

Pigeons of San Marco, Venice, 89.

Pilate Pontius, Roman governor of Judæa, basin in which he washed his hands after surrendering Christ to the Jews, 175 a; marble steps from his palace brought to Rome by the Empress Helena, 417 a; relief of him on Roman sarcophagus, in the Lateran 503 b.

Pillage of Rome, under Gregory VII., 474.

Pindar [† 443 B. C.], greatest lyric poet of Greece, 463.

Pinerolo, the 'Nice of Piedmont,' 14.

Pintoricchio (Bernardino Betti) [† 1513], Umbrian painter, his great altarpiece at Perugia, 365*; designs graffiti for the Sienese Duomo, 335, 340; his portrait of Arringhieri, 337; decorates the Piccolomini Library, 338 *sq.*; the Borgia Apartment, 456; his part in the Sistine decoration, 454; frescoes in Ara Coeli, 437; in S. Maria del Popolo, 433; in Santa Croce, Rome, 432; portraits of him, in Signorelli's Antichrist, Orvieto cathedral, 382 a in his mural paintings, in the Siena cathedral, 338 c.

Piola, Genoese painter, 34, 39.

Piombo Seb. del. See *Sebastiano.*

Pisa, history, 313; palaces, *ib.*; cathedral and baptistery, 314 *sq.*; churches, 317 *sq.*; Camposanto, 318 *sqq.*; museum, 324; Leaning Tower, 312*.

Pisanello (Vittore Pisano) [† 1455], Veronese painter and medallist, 162, 303.

Pisano Andrea [† 1348], Pisan and Florentine sculptor and architect, works at Florence: the baptistery gates, 204; is appointed architect of the Duomo, 209; executes reliefs on Giotto's campanile, 215 *sqq.*; and the bust of Boniface VIII., at Rome, 412.

Pisano Giovanni [† 1331], Pisan architect and sculptor, his influence on Art, 316*; his famous pulpit at Pisa, 316*; and at Pistoia, 326; contributes work on the Sienese pulpit, 336, and on the Fontana Maggiore, at Perugia, 358; designs façade of cathedral, at Siena, 334; the Castel Nuovo, at Naples, 522; other works attributed to him, the Tomb of Benedict XI., in the church of San Domenico, Perugia, 360 c; Prato cathedral, 313 a.

Pisano Niccolò [† 1280], father of Giovanni, architect, sculptor, 254*; draws inspiration from Roman sarcophagus, 318; his pulpit, at Pisa, 316; contributes work on the Sienese pulpit, 335, and on the Perugian fountain, 358; his reliefs on the Arca di San Domenico, at Bologna, 176.

Pisano Nino [† 1368], sculptor, 317, 324.

Pistoia, the ancient *Pistoria*, 326 *sq.*

Pittacus, one of the seven sages of ancient Greece, 363.

Pitti Luca, Florentine banker, 231, 275.

Pius II. (Æneas Sylvius Piccolomini) [† 1464], Pope, his career and end, 330, 338, 339; his tomb, 435.

Pius III. (Piccolomini) [† 1503], Pope, orders the construction of the Libreria, in the Siena cathedral, 338 b; his Sepulchral monument, in Sant'Andrea della Valle, Rome, 435 a.

Pius IV. (Giovanni Medici or Medighino) [† 1565], Pope, 431, 508.

Pius V. St. (Ghislieri) [† 1572], Pope, 329, 419.

Pius VI. (Giovanni Angelo Braschi) [† 1799], Pope, his contribution to the Vatican, 443, 444, 445, 446, 447, 448, 449; adds to the Capitoline museum, 506; erects the Quirinal obelisk, 509; pays war indemnity to Napoleon, 438; his kneeling statue by Canova, 407.

Pius VII. (Luigi Chiaramonti) [† 1823], Pope, his contribution to the Vatican museums, 453, 454; creates the picture gallery, 484; makes arrangements for Raphael's tapestries, 472; instructs Canova to execute statues to replace those taken by Napoleon, 451; restores the arch of Titus, 399, and that of Constantine, 401.

Pius IX. (Mastai-Ferretti) [† 1878], Pope, his political designs and subsequent consequences, 392; consecrates the basilica of St. Paul's, 422; creates the Christian museum at the Lateran, 503; orders the decoration of the Sala dell'Immacolata Concezione, at the Vatican, 473; and erects a memorial column, 510; his contribution to the Pantheon, 431; his mausoleum at San Lorenzo, 424; his portrait in the basilica of St. Peter's, 407.

Pius XI. (Ratti) [† 1939], Pope builds new picture gallery, in Vatican 484. [The Lateran Treaty with Italy was signed in 1929 under his pontificate, in his encyclicals he condemned Nazism and antisemitism].

Pius XII. (Eugenio Pacelli) [born 1876], Pope since 1939, 413*. [During the World War he issued many appeals for peace, and exercised his influence to protect the Jews in Italy].

— 607 —

Placidia (Galla Placidia Augusta) [† 450], empress, daughter of Theodosius the Great, 185; orders mosaics for St. Paul's, in Rome, 422.

Plague, memorial of the, at Venice, 83, 129; at Rome, 437; at Siena, 331; ravages of the P., at Florence, 230.

Platina, Director of the Vatican Library, in presence of Sixtus IV., 485.

Plato [† 347 B. C.], great philosopher of Athens, his figure in Raphael's School of Athens, in the Vatican, 461; bronze bust, in the Naples' museum, 533 b.

Platonic academy, in Florence, 312.

Pliny the Elder [† 79 A. D.], Roman naturalist, 65.

Pliny the Younger [† 125], Author and orator, governor of Bithynia, 66, 159.

Pluto, god of Hades, 453.

Po, largest river in Italy, 467.

Poccetti (Bernardo) [† 1612], Florentine painter, 273 c.

Podesti Giulio, painter, 473.

Poggio a Caiano, Medici villa at, 312.

Poggio Bracciolini [† 1459], humanist, 211.

Pogliaghi Lodovico, Milanese sculptor, 51.

Pola, the Roman amphitheatre at, 170.

Polenta, Guido da, Lord of Ravenna, 181, 190*; Francesca da, 181, 190*.

Political doctrine, expressed in painting, at Siena, 332.

Poliziano Angelo [† 1494], poet, his portrait in Ghirlandaio' frescoes, in S. Maria Novella, 225 c; and in Santa Trinita, Florence, 244 b; visits the court of the Gonzagas, at Mantua, and in a few days composes his famous drama Orfeo, 78 b.

Pollaiuolo Antonio [† 1498], Florentine architect, sculptor and painter, his monument of Sixtus IV. in St. Peter's, 413; his candelabrum, 412; his bust in the Bargello, 301, and group of Hercules and Antæus, 294; contributes work on the monument of Innocent VIII., 411; on the Capitoline Wolf, 504; on the Dossale of the Florentine baptistery, 212; on the sacristy of S. Spirito, 239; is appointed architect of the Vatican, 426; his St. Jerome, in the Pitti gallery, 281.

Pollaiuolo Piero [† 1495], Florentine sculptor and painter, his picture at Turin, 20; his part on the tomb of Pope Innocent VIII., 411.

Polo Marco [† 1323], celebrated traveller, 135; his portrait, 495.

Polycletus [† 460 B. C.], Greek sculptor, his Doryphorus in the Vatican, 455, and at Naples, 528; his Amazon, 455.

Polydorus (ca. 100 B. C.), sculptor, 451.

Polyphemus, the most famous of the Cyclops, 453.

Polyxena, sacrifice of, on the tomb of Achilles, 378 a; the Rape of P., marble group, in the Loggia de' Lanzi, Florence, 199.

Pomarancio (Circignani), painter, 430.

Pompeian mosaics, 536; frescoes, 537.

Pompeii, historical account of its destruction, 541; plan of its houses, 544; of its baths, 546; views: of the Forum, 543; of House of Vettii, 544 sq.; of baths, 546; of amphitheatre, 547; treasures yielded from P., 527.

Pompey the Great [† 48 B. C.], triumvir, famous statue, in the Palazzo Spada, Rome, 508 a.

Pomposa, abbey of, 172.

Ponte, Antonio da [† 1597], architect, 82, 85

Pontormo (Jacopo Carrucci) [† 1557], Florentine painter, 489; his Visitation in the Annunziata, Florence, 243; his portrait of Cosimo de' Medici, 266.

Popes, The: 412*; their burial place in early times, 412, 413; decadence of Rome by their residence at Avignon, 392; fresco of their return to Rome, 345; bas-relief of the same subject, 432; their residence before removal to Avignon, 416; present residence, 441; other residences, in Rome, Castel Sant'Angelo, 499 b; at Anagni, Papal palace, 516 c; in Viterbo, The Gothic palace, 515 c; in Florence, the Monastery of S. Maria Novella, 223 a.

Poppæa Augusta, a woman of surpassing beauty, but licentious morals, wife of the emperor Nero, 507.

Poppi, view of the Castle at, 389.

Pordenone [† 1539], Venetian painter, 122.

Porta, Giacomo della [† 1604], Lombard architect and sculptor, is appointed architect of St. Peter's, 407, and designs its pavement, 406; his masterpiece the tomb of Paul III., 408; other works attributed to him: at St. John in Lateran, 414; at San Luigi dei Francesi, 436; at the Gesù, 438; at the Farnese palace, 509; Chigi, 510; the fountain of the Tartarughe, 511.

Porta, Guglielmo della [† 1577], Lombard and Roman sculptor, decorates a Chapel, in the Genoa cathedral, 28 c; erects SS. Annunziata, Genoa, 31 a.

Porta Santa (Jubilee Door) in St. Peter's, 405 b; in St. John in Lateran, 414 b. [It is opened by the Pope in person on the Christmas-eve of the Jubilee, which ordinarily takes place every 25 years. The pope begins the demolition of the door by striking it three times with a silver hammer].

Portinari. See Beatrice.

Portland vase, the, 538.

Portofino, on the Italian Riviera, 9, 43.

Portrait of a duchess, a striking, 269.

Portraits, of the Popes, 422; of distinguished artists, in the Uffizi, 274.

Porziuncola, the Cradle of the Franciscan movement, at Assisi, 375 b. See also p. 189 b.

Positano, the scenic beauties of, 554.

Poverty, Giotto's allegory of, 370.

Pozzuoli, 559.

Prato, 328.

Praxiteles (4th century B. C.), Greek sculptor, works attributed to him or to his School, the celebrated Statue of Aphrodite, in the Vatican, 450 a, the Apollo Sauroctonos 449 b, the Hermes, 451 a, the Satyr reposing, 455 a: all in the Vatican museums; the Bacchus and Satyr, in the Terme museum, 500 c, the Satyr pouring wine, 501 a, the famous Venus of Cyrene, and the Aphrodite, 501, in the Terme, Rome. the Psyche of Capua, 530 b, and the Torso of Venus both in the Naples' Museum, 531 b.

Preaching Friars, Order of, 223.

Predis, Ambrogio de [† ca. 1520], pupi of Leonardo, Lombard court painter to Lodovico Sforza, 268.

Presentation in the Temple, painting by Titian, in the Academy, Venice, 143; frescoes by Taddeo Gaddi and G. da Milano revealing character of Giottesque art, 222; Fra Bartolommeo's, 505.

Priam, the last King of Troy, 452.

Primavera, Botticelli's allegory of, 261.

Printing (invented about 1450), office established at Mantua, 78; Florence, 192

Priscian (6th c.), Latin grammarian, 228.

Privileges, to the Church of Ravenna, 187.

Prometheus, Greek hero, 527 c.

Propertius Sextus Aurelius [† 15 B. C.], greatest of elegiac poets of Rome, 512.

Proserpine, goddess of agriculture and queen of Hades, Bernini's marble group, of The Rape of P., in the Borghese gallery, 488 c; relief in the Myth of Alcestis, in the Vatican, 453 b; frescoes in the Myth of Psyche, 493.

Protesilaus, a hero of Thessaly who took part in the Trojan war, 445.

Provenzano Salvani, Sienese patriot, 329.

Psalms, Book of, 213.

Psyche, in Greek mythology the personification of the human soul, torso at Naples, 530; myth of, in the Villa Farnesina Rome, 492; in the Castel Sant'Angelo, 499; in the Palazzo del Tè, at Mantua, 79; marble group, 507.

Ptolemy Claudius (2nd century A. D.), Egyptian astronomer, 228, 461.

Ptolemy Philadelphus [† 246 B. C.], the son of Antony and Cleopatra, 452.

Public Libraries, Petrarch's patronage of, 253; oldest Public Library, 238.

Puccini Giacomo [† 1924], Italian operatic composer, author of Manon Lescaut, La Boheme, Madame Butterfly, Tosca, the unfinished Turandot, 325.

Punic Wars (struggle between Rome and Carthage), 505 a, 580.

Purgatory, Dante's, 210, 227.

Purification, the painting by Tintoretto, 144; relief by Orcagna, 232.

Purim, Jewish festival, 286.

Purity, emblems of, 256.

Pyrrhic dance, ancient relief, 447.

Pyrrhus, [† 272 B. C.], King of Epirus, 579.

Pythagoras [† 510 B. C.], celebrated Greek philosopher and mathematician, his figure in the Triumph of St. Thomas Aquinas, 228 c; in Raphael's School of Athens, 461 b; on reliefs of Giotto's Campanile, 217 b.

QUADRIVIUM, meaning of, 214, 456.

Quarrels, between Pope and Emperor, 474. 333, 557; between Pope and King, 516.

Queen of Sheba, the, 205, 220.

Quercia, Jacopo della, Sienese sculptor, joins competition for the baptistery gates, at Florence, 205; his tomb of Ilaria del Carretto, at Lucca, 325; his work on the Sienese baptismal font, 342; his reliefs on the portal of San Petronio, Bologna, 174; the tomb of Bentivoglio, 175.

Quirinal palace, ancient residence of the popes, afterwards of kings of Italy, 509.

Rabbinic legend, 270.
Rabbits, symbolism of, 179, 491.
Raffaello dal Colle, Roman painter, 469.
Raimondi, Marc'Antonio [† 1527], Bolognese and Roman engraver, 465.
Rainaldi Carlo, Roman architect, 435.
Rainaldus, Bishop of Ravenna, 186.
Rainaldus, Pisan architect, 313.
Rampolla del Tindaro (Mariano) [† 1913], cardinal, 427.
Rapallo, on the Italian Riviera, 42.
Rape of Europa, painting by Veronese, at Venice, 120.
Rape of Sabines, 396.
Raphael Santi of Urbino [† 1520], Umbrian Florentine and Roman painter, his three periods or manners, 267; his originality and fertility of invention, 459, 463. Works at Florence: the Goldfinch Madonna, 267; Young St. John, ib. the "Donna Gravida," of the Pitti, 276; portrait of Angelo Doni, 278 and Maddalena Doni, ib.; Madonna del Granduca, 278*; Madonna della Sedia, 278; La Donna Velata, 281; Frescoes in the Vatican: Disputa, 460; School of Athens, 461; Parnassus, 463; Jurisprudence, 462; ceiling Stanza della Segnatura, 459; Mass of Bolsena, 464; Expulsion of Heliodorus, 465; of Attila, 466; Liberation of St. Peter, 467; his part in the decoration of the Stanza dell'Incendio, 468; prepares designs for the Battle of Constantine, 469; designs decoration of the Logge, 470; the tapestries, 472; the Galatea, 492; the Transfiguration, 487; Madonna di Foligno, 486; Deposition, 489; Sibyls in S. Maria della Pace, 439; the prophet at Sant'Agostino, 438; myth of Psyche, in the Villa Farnesina, 492; is appointed architect of St. Peter's, 406; and the Vatican, 411; the Chigi Chapel, 433; other works attributed to him, the Violinist, and the Fornarina, in the Barberini, 494; the Fontana delle Tartarughe, 511. Works in various cities: the Sposalizio, at Milan, 58; the S. Cecilia, at Bologna, 176*; Madonna della Tenda, at Turin, 20; Holy Family, at Naples, 539; fresco at Perugia, 363. His own portrait, in the Uffizi, 274; other presumed portraits of him, 339, 382, 460, 461, 466. His last resting place, 431; Symond's opinion of his works, 463; R. quoted, 174, 180.
Ravello, its Norman architecture, 556.
Ravenna, palace and mausoleum of Theodoric, 181; tomb of Dante, ib.; memorial chapel of Galla Placidia, 185; the baptistery, 185; Sant'Apollinare in Classe, 187; Sant'Apollinare Nuovo, 182, 183; San Vitale, 184; Byzantine Art at R., 186; the Pineta of R., 171 the Battle of R., 181, 466, 467.
Real Presence, the, 460, 464.
Recanati, 189.
Redemption, Promise of, 380, 381.
Reformation, the, 76, 435.
Regula Monachorum, 515.
Rehoboam, King of Israel, 380.
Rembrandt, H. van Ryn [† 1669], Dutch painter, 274.
Renan Ernest [† 1892], French philosopher and Orientalist, 549.

Renée of France, daughter of Louis XII., Duchess of Ferrara, 178.
Reni Guido [† 1692], Bolognese painter, his Assumption, 30, and St. Sebastian, at Genoa, 35; the Apostle Peter weeping, at the Pitti, 282; the Archangel Michael, 410; St. Sebastian, 505; the Aurora, at Rome, 494; the portrait of Beatrice Cenci, ib.; the Christ on the Cross, 438; frescoes at San Gregorio, 430; Atalanta and Hippomenes, at Naples, 539.
Republic of San Marino, the, its foundation and peculiarities, 191*.
Resurrection of the Dead, the, as represented in the paintings by Signorelli, in the Orvieto cathedral, 382 c; by Michelangelo, in the Sistine Chapel, 476; in the Reliefs on front of the Orvieto cathedral, 381 c; in Mosaics, baptistery, Florence, 208 b.
Rhea Sylvia, mother of Romulus and Remus, 451, 502.
Rialto Bridge, at Venice, 82.
Riario Girolamo, his part in the Pazzi, conspiracy, 211, 485; Pietro R., 485; Raffaello R., 464.
Riccio (Andr. Briosco), Paduan sculptor and architect, 161.
Richard I. [† 1199] (surnamed Cœur de Lion), King of England, embarks for Palestine, 43; is confined upon his return, 169; introduces St. George to the English, 436.
Rienzi, Cola di [† 1354], Roman tribune, his statue on the Capitoline Hill, 510 a; spot where he was killed, 504 b.
Rimini, 188; Castles of the Lords of R., 190*; medals commemorating their effigies, 303 a.
Ring of St. Mark, story of the, famous painting by Bordone, 144.
Rivers of Paradise, the, 101, 415.
Riviera, The Italian, 41 sqq.
Rivo Alto. See Rialto.
Rizzo Antonio, Venetian architect, his bronze Giants, 88 a; and statue of Eve, in Venice, 177 c; begins building of eastern wing of Doges' palace, 115 c, 116 a.
Robbia, Andrea della [† 1525], nephew of Luca, Florentine sculptor, works: 302; executes Medallions of Swaddled Infants, on Foundling Hospital, in Florence, 246 c; his works in the Bargello, 302 b; his great Coronation of the Virgin, in Siena, 351.
Robbia, Giovanni della [† 1529], son of Andrea, Florentine sculptor, works: Andrea, Florentine, sculptor, 302; his works in the Bargello, 302 c; in the sacristy of S. Maria Novella, 223 b; his famous reliefs of the Seven Works of Mercy, on the Portico of the Ospedale del Ceppo, at Pistoia, 327.
Robbia, Luca della [† 1482], Florentine sculptor, his invention or discovery, 302; his bronze doors in the Duomo, 210; and in San Lorenzo, 234; his Cantoria, 213; his group of the Visitation, at Pistoia, 327; terracotta reliefs: over the Doors of the Sacristies, in the Duomo, 211 a; at Or San Michele, 231 b; at Ognissanti, 239 a; at the Badia, 245 a; in the Bargello, National Museum, Florence, 302 ab.

Robert Guiscard. See Guiscard.
Robert of Anjou [† 1343], King of Naples, 329.
Rodari, Tommaso and Jacopo, Lombard sculptors, 65.
Roger the Norman, King of Sicily, 531.
Rogers Samuel [† 1855], English poet, his ode on Venice, 81; on Florence, 193; on Bay of Naples, 518.
Roland, legendary French hero, Paladin of Charlemagne, 163.
Roman Empire, extent of the, 392; Forum, 396, 397; monuments, their influence on art, 305.
Romanino Girolamo, Brescian painter, his Altarpieces, in Brescia, 76 c, 77 b.
Romano Antoniazzo, painter, 434.
Romano Cristoforo, Lombard sculptor, his works at Pavia, 72.
Romano Giulio [† 1546], Roman and Mantuan painter and architect, decorates the Palazzo del Tè, at Mantua, 79; the Sala di Costantino, in the Vatican, 469; completes Raphael's "Transfiguration," 487; work at Farnesina, 492.
Rome, history and description, 392; burning of Rome, by Nero, ib.; pillage of Rome, by the Gauls, ib.; by the Vandals, ib.; by Robert Guiscard, 423; by the troops of Charles of Bourbon, 392. **Roman antiquities**: Colosseum, 400; Castel Sant'Angelo, 395, 499; Pantheon, 431; Forum, 396; Palatine, 400; Triumphal arches, 396, 399; Aqueducts, 391, 403. **Churches**: Sant'Agnese, 426; Sant'Agostino, 438; Sant'Andrea della Valle, 435; Santi Apostoli, 436; Capuchins, 432; Santa Cecilia, 427; San Clemente, 423; San Cosimo e Damiano, 429; Santa Costanza, 428; Santa Croce, 432; Santa Francesca, 432; Gesù, 438; San Giorgio in Velabro, 436; San Gregorio Magno, 430; Sant'Ignazio, 438; Santi Giovanni e Paolo, 436; S. John Lateran, 414; San Lorenzo fuori, 424; San Lorenzo in Lucina, 438; San Lorenzo in Miranda, 399; San Luigi de' Francesi, 436; Santa Maria degli Angeli, 431; Santa Maria Aracoeli, 437; Santa Maria in Cosmedin, 426; Santa Maria di Loreto, 439; Santa Maria Maggiore, 418 sqq.; Santa Maria sopra Minerva, 434; Santa Maria della Pace, 439; Santa Maria del Popolo, 433; Santa Maria ad Martyres (Pantheon), 431; Santa Maria del Sole, 426; Santa Maria in Trastevere, 425; Santa Maria della Vittoria, 438; San Paolo fuori, 422; San Pietro in Montorio, 439; San Pietro in Vaticano, 404 sqq.; San Pietro in Vincoli, 440; Santa Prassede, 429; Santa Pudenziana, 428; Santi Quattro Coronati, 430; Santa Sabina, 428; San Stefano Rotondo, 430. **Museums**: Capitoline, 506; Lateran, 503; Terme, 500; Vatican, 443 sqq. (see below). **Palaces and Galleries**: Barberini, 494, 508; Borghese, 488 sq.; Cancelleria, 508; Colonna, 497; Corsini, 496; Doria, 495; Farnese, 509; Farnesina, 492 sq.; Medici, 510; Rospigliosi, 494; Spada, 508; Vatican, 441 sqq. (See under Vatican); Venezia, 508. **Fountains** 511; **Environs** of Rome, 512* sqq.

Romeo and Juliet, scene of their affection, 164, 165.
Romulus, Legendary Founder of Rome, 400 a, 504 b.
Romuald, St. [† 1027], founder of the Camaldolese (reformed Benedictines), 486.
Rosa Salvatore [† 1673], Neapolitan painter, his sepulchral monument, 431 c.
Rosalba Carriera. See *Carriera*.
Rosamund, Alboin's bride, 166.
Rosary, Institution of the, 136.
Roses, thornless, at Assisi, 375.
Rosselli Cosimo [† 1507], Florentine painter, his paintings in the SS. Annunziata, Florence, 242 a; in the Sistine Chapel, 482 a, 483 a.
Rosselli Matteo [† 1650], painter, 284.
Rossellino (Antonio Gamberelli) [† ca. 1478], Florentine sculptor, his works in Santa Croce, 218 b; in the Bargello, 299 b, 300 c; Sepulchral monument to Cardinal Jacopo of Portugal, 311 b.
Rossellino Bernardo [† 1464], Florentine architect, designs the Palazzo Rucellai, Florence, 305 c; the Piccolomini, Siena, 330 c; is appointed architect of St. Peter's, Rome, 405.
Rossetti Christina Georgina [† 1894], sister of Dante G. R., English poetess, 584.
Rossi Mariano, painter at Rome, 488.
Rosso Fiorentino [† 1541], Florentine painter, his paintings in the SS. Annunziata, 243 c; in the Uffizi, 266 c; in the Pitti, 280 c.
Rostra, the, a platform for speakers in the Forum, 397, 401.
Rothschilds, prototypes of the, 231 b. [The name of a Jewish family, famed for its activity and magnitude in financial transactions; they began as money-lenders in Frankfort].
Rovere, family of Della: Francesco Maria, Duke of Urbino, his portraits by Raphael, 460, 461; remarkable portrait of his wife, 269; Giovanni, Cardinal, 485; Giuliano, Cardinal (afterwards Julius II.), escorts Charles VIII. into Florence, 301; his portrait by Melozzo, 485; Vittoria, Grand-Duchess of Tuscany, her portrait in the Pitti, 283. Genealogy of the, 190 A.
Rovezzano, Benedetto da. See *Benedetto*.
Roxana, wife of Alexander the Great, 493.
Royal Palace, at Rome, 509; Caserta, 560; Florence, 275, 286; at Genoa, 33; at Naples, 526; at Palermo, 570; at Turin, 22, 23; at Venice, 148.
Rubens Peter Paul [† 1640], Flemish painter, master of Van Dyck, 21; his works in Genoa, 30, 36; in the Pitti, 281, 282; portrait of his first wife, 273; his own portrait, 274; his discovery of Raphael's cartoons, 472; his work in the Conservatori, 505.
Rucellai, illustrious Florentine family 305; the Madonna R., 223.
Ruskin John [† 1900], Author and Art Critic, his opinion on St. Mark's mosaic, Venice, 105 a; his admiration for Cimabue's Madonna, at Assisi, 373 c; description of Giotto's Campanile, 217 a.
Rustici Giovanni Francesco [† 1652], Florentine sculptor, 204.
Rusuti Filippo, mosaicist, 418.
Rutelli Mario of Palermo, sculptor, 394.
Ruvo (Apulia), Cathedral of, 565.

SABELLIUS, schismatic, in the third century, who denied the dogma of the Holy Trinity, 228, 431, 434.
Sabines, The Rape of the, 396; Giambologna's group of, 199: Stradano's, 202.
Sacchi Andrea [† 1661], Roman painter, his Mass of St. Gregory the Great, 411 a.
Sacconi Giuseppe [† 1905], architect, 615.
Sacraments, The Seven, in art, 214.
Sacred and Profane Love, by Titian, 491.
Sacrifice of Isaac, 206, 315, 464.
St. John of Jerusalem, 552.
Saint Peter's, Basilica of, at Rome. Space occupied by the edifice, 240,000 square feet; styled one of the wonders of the world; its construction lasting nearly two hundred years, while forty popes lavished their treasures in this great Sanctuary of the Christian world, 404 b; historical sketch and number of architects employed, ib. Size of its imposing Façade, 405 a; form and measurements of the Piazza, number of Columns and colossal Statues of the Colonnade, 405 b; Portico and bronze Doors of main entrance, ib. Length of the Nave, diameter of the Cupola, weight of the bronze Baldacchino, over the Tomb of the Apostle, 406 a. Spot where Emperors used formerly to be crowned, and respective lengths of principal churches of Christendom, as inscribed in bronze figures on the pavement: St. Peter's, 205 yds; St. Paul's, *London*, 170 yds; Cathedral, *Florence*, 149 yds; Cathedral, *Milan*, 148 yds; San Petronio, *Bologna*, 132 yds; St. Paul's, *Rome*, 139 yds; St. John in Lateran, 122 yds; Cathedral, Antwerp, 119 yds; St. Sophia, Istanbul, 118 yds, 406. Size of Transept and of the monster Piers supporting the Dome, 407 a; number of Altars, of Statues, of Columns contained in the church, 406 b. Sepulchral Monuments of the Popes, Pictures in mosaic, et al., 408, 409, 410. Ceremonial rites of Beatifications, and of Canonizations, 411 a; Ordinances observed by the faithful during Jubilee Years, ib. Ascent to the Inner Galleries, and to the Dome, their colossal proportions, 411 b. The Treasury, jewels, churchplate, copes and vestments of great value; the Crypt or *Vatican Grottoes*, 412. Model and historical sketch of the Old Constantinian Basilica, 413.
Salerno, 557. [Landing stage of the Allies in Sept. 1943].
Salimbeni, wealthy family of Siena, 329.
Sallust [† 34 B. C.], Roman historian, 512.
Salomé the Dancer, daughter of Herodias, the 'damsel' connected with the death of John the Baptist, represented in mosaics in St. Mark's baptistery, 109 a; in Luini's panel, in the Uffizi, 268 b; in Titian's picture, Doria gallery, Rome, 495 a; in Giotto's frescoes, in Santa Croce, 221 b.
Salutation, The, of Elizabeth, 263.
Saluzzo, birthplace of Silvio Pellico, 447.
Salviati, Francesco de' [† 1563], Florentine painter, 202.
Sammartino G., Neapolitan sculptor, 525.
Samuel, prophet, and last judge of the Hebrews, 380.

San Carlo, theatre in Naples, 526.
San Clemente a Casauria, church of, 562.
San Fruttuoso, the Abbey of, 43.
San Gimignano, 352 sqq.
San Giorgio, the Banco di, at Genoa, 26.
San Giovanni, Giov. (Manozzi) da [†1636], Florentine painter, 287.
San Leo, castle of, 191*.
San Marco, basilica of, at Venice, 90 sqq.; monastery of, at Florence, 248 sqq.
San Marino, the Republic of, 191*.
San Remo, on the Italian Riviera, 44, 45.
Sancta Sanctorum, Chapel of (church of San Salvadore), a remnant of the Old Lateran Palace, 417 a; its Treasure in enamels and Byzantine jewel-works now in the Vatican, 442 c.
Sangallo, Antonio da, Florentine architect, is appointed architect of St. Peter's, 406; contributes work on tombs of the Medici Popes, 435; builds the Sala Regia, in the Vatican, 411, 474; designs the Palazzo Farnese, 509; begins church of S. Maria di Loreto, 439; his work at Orvieto, 388.
Sangallo, Francesco da [† 1576], Florentine architect, 301.
Sangallo, Giuliano da [† 1516], Florentine architect and sculptor, 189; work in Florence, 239; Siena, 330; Rome, 406.
Sanmicheli (or Sammicheli) [† 1559], Venetian and Veronese architect, builds the Palazzo Grimani, in Venice, 150 a; the Marble rood-screen, in the Verona cathedral, 163 b; the Palazzo Bevilacqua, Verona, 166 c; his Marble Altarpiece, Orvieto cathedral, 386 c.
Sannazzaro Jacopo [† 1530], Italian poet, Ode to Sorrento, 518 c; his Portraits, in Florence, 201 a, and in the Vatican, 463 b. [He wrote *Arcadia*, a pastoral medley: verse and prose].
Sano di Matteo, Sienese painter, 331.
Sano di Pietro [† 1481], Sienese painter his works at Siena, pictures of San Bernardino, in the Palazzo Pubblico, 333 a; in the Cathedral, 337 a; illuminates choir Books, in the Piccolomini Library, 338 c; his great Altarpiece, in the Accademia, 347 a; in the Oratorio di San Bernardino, 343 c; paints Tavolette of Tax Registers, 349 a.
Sansedoni, Sienese family, 329.
Sanseverino, the Count of, 349.
Sansovino Andrea (Andrea Contucci) [† 1529], Florentine sculptor, 433.
Sansovino, Jac. (Jacopo Tatti) [† 1570], Florentine and Venetian architect and sculptor, designs the Library of San Marco, 87; the staircase of the Doge's palace, 117; executes bronze doors in Saint Mark's, 108; his group on the Baptistery at Florence, 204; his Bacchus in the Bargello, 303; his work in the cathedral, at Genoa, 29.
Sant'Angelo, the castle of, at Rome, 395. the Papal apartments within, 499.
Santa Casa, the, at Loreto, 189.
Santa Fiora, 329. [A county in the Maremma, belonged to the Ghibelline family of Aldobrandeschi].
Santa Margherita (Liguria), 42.
Santa Sabina, Rome, 428; miracle in the monastery of, 248.
Santi Giovanni [† 1494], father of Raphael, Umbrian painter, 487.

Sappho (6th cent. B. C.), lyric poetess of Greece, her Portrait, in Raphael's Parnassus, 463 *b*; supposed P., in the Naples' Museum, 537 *b*. [In spite of her renown little is known of her history; she was contemporary with Pittacus and with the poet Alcæus, with whom she may have exchanged verses; she was the centre of a feminine literary coterie at Mytilene; is said to have been a woman of strong passions and questionable morality, but her lyrics are among the masterpieces of antiquity, though only two of her poems survive fragmentarily].
Saracens, the, invade and pillage the Ligurian coast, 26 *a*; threaten to desecrate the House of Nazareth, in which the Holy Virgin was born, 189 *a*; are deprived of Sardinia by the Pisans, 313 *b*; destroy the Abbey of Montecassino, 560 *a*; their conquest of Palermo, 569 *c*; they sack and nearly destroy Syracuse, 580 *c*; and Segesta, 581 *a*; specimens of Saracenic architecture, at Palermo. 570 *a*, 571, 573 *a*, 574 *c*. [Saracens was the current designation among the Christians in medieval times for the Arabs and Mohammedans. extended to all the non-Christian races with whom the Crusaders came in conflict].
Saracini, illustrious family of Siena, 330.
Sardinia, Mediterranean island, 566 *A* sgg.
Sarto, Andrea del [† 1531], Florentine painter, character of his art, 263; frescoes in the Annunziata, 242, 243; in the Cloisters of Lo Scalzo, 247 *b*; his famous Last Supper, in the Convent of San Salvi, 253 *a*; his masterpiece the Madonna delle Arpie, in the Uffizi, 263. The Assumption, in the Pitti, 277 *a*; the Disputa, 279 *a*; the St. John, 280 *b*; Annunciations, 279 *b* and 281 *a*; Holy Family, 283 *b*; Panels with the Story of Joseph, 286 *a*, all in the Pitti gallery. The picture of St. Agnes, Pisa cathedral, 315 *c*; The Holy Family, Borghese gallery, Rome, 489 *c*. affection for his wife, 277 *a*; portrait of her, 280 *c*; own portraits, 243 *a*, 263 *c*, 274 *b*, 280 *c*; grave, 243 *b*.
Sassetta (Stef. di Giovanni), Sienese painter, his great Altarpiece, in Siena, 351 *a*.
Sassoferrato (Giov. Battista Salvi) [†1685], Roman painter, the ' Blue Madonna, ' 486 *b*; The Three Ages of Man, 491 *b*.
Satan, symbolical representation of, 371.
Saturnalia, 397 *a*. [A festival in ancient Rome in honour of Saturn, in which poor and rich, young and old, enjoyed and indulged in merriment without restraint]
Savonarola Girolamo [† 1498], Dominican Friar and moral reformer: organizes the « burning of the vanities », 197; advises on politics, 200; style of his oratory in the Duomo, 210; his prophecies and denunciations of ecclesiastical corruption, 252; enmity of Alexander VI. for S., *ib.*; place of execution, 197; his portrait by Fra Bartolommeo, in San Marco, 252 *c*; another portrait of him appears in Raphael's Disputa, in Vatican, 460 *c*.
Savoy, House of, 13, 17*.
Savoy (Genealogical Table of), 16*.

Scala, opera theatre, in Milan, 49 *c*.
Scala Santa, « Holy Stairs », indulgences attached to, 417.
Scala, The Della, or Scaligers, Lords of Verona, 49*c*; their splendid dwellings, 164*b*; their hospitality to exiled Dante, 181 *b*.
Scalza Ippolito, of Orvieto, sculptor, 388.
Scamozzi Vincenzo [† 1616], Venetian architect, 120.
Scapulary, the Holy, 145.
Scarpagnino (Antonio Abbondi) [† 1549], Venetian architect, 115, 116.
Scaurus M. Æmilius [† 88 B. C.], Roman consul, 400.
Scherano da Settignano, sculptor, 440.
Scipio, celebrated Roman general, 363.
Scopas [† 350 B. C.], Greek architect and sculptor, his statue of Meleager, in the Vatican, 448 *a* (see also the Niobe, in the Uffizi, 255 *c*).
Scoppio del Carro, the, at Florence, 309.
Scotus Duns. See *Duns Scotus*.
Scuola, the, meaning of name, 147.
Sebastian, St. [† 288], story of his martyrdom, 265; painting of, by Genga in the Uffizi, *ib.*; by Guido Reni, 35, 505; by Domenichino, 409; by Sodoma, 285; by Veronese, 137.
Sebastiano del Piombo (Luciani) [† 1547], Venetian and Roman painter, Altarpiece, in San Giovanni Grisostomo, 135 *a*; the Portrait of a Lady, in the Uffizi, 270 *c*; Altarpiece, in S. Maria del Popolo, Rome, 433 *c*; the Scourging of Christ, S. Pietro in Montorio, 439 *c*; Holy Family, Naples Museum, 539 *c*.
Sedia gestatoria (portable state chair of the Pope), 465.
Segala Francesco, Paduan sculptor, 109.
Segesta, Greek temples at, 568, 582.
Seitz Ludovico [† 1908], painter, 445.
Sejanus Lucius Ælius [† 31 A. D.], favourite of the emperor Tiberius, 400.
Selinunte, metopes from, 578.
Seraphs, Byzantine representation of, 97.
Servites, Order of the, 242.
Servius Tullius [† 534 B. C.], sixth king of Rome, 400.
Settignano, Desiderio da. See *Desiderio*.
Seven-branched candlestick, the, 399.
Seven Deadly Sins, the, 146 *b*.
Seven Works of Mercy, the, 327 *b*.
Severn Joseph [† 1879], English portrait painter, 403.
Severus Lucius Septimius [† 211], Roman emperor, memorial arch in Rome, 396; restores the Pantheon, 431.
Sforza, the name of a famous Italian family of condottieri who became Dukes of Milan, 48 *sq.*, 70 *sqq.*; Lineage of the, 73*.
    Catherine (illegitimate), the Lady of Forli, 190 *b*.
    Francesco, founder of the dynasty, Duke of Milan, 48, 63, 73.
    Francesco, son of Lodovico, 73.
    Galeazzo Maria, assassinated, 73.
    Gian Galeazzo, 73.
    Lodovico (il Moro), his court and patronage of the arts and letters, 48 *sq.*; charges Leonardo to paint the ' Last Supper,' 57; portraits of him and his family, in the Brera, 62; sketch of his career and end, 72; his monument, *ib.*
    Maximilian, 73.

Shakespeare William [† 16:6], great English poet and dramatist, origin of his *Romeo and Juliet*, 165 *c*; subject of his *Campeius*, 425 *a*.
Sheba (ancient kingdom of southern Arabia), the Queen of, Veronese's Painting, in the Picture Gallery, Turin, 21 *b*; her Reception in the Temple 205 *b*.
Shelley, Percy Bysshe [† 1822], English Author and Poet, 403; his description of Beatrice Cenci's portrait, 494; sojourns at Sorrento, 549.
Shrines and Tabernacles, at Florence, 245.
Sibyls, Raphael's, 439; Michelangelo's, 477. [Fabled women of antiquity endowed with visionary prophetic power or "second sight."].
Sicilian Vespers (massacre of the French, in Sicily, A. D. 1280), 505.
Sicily, the largest island in the Mediterranean, 567 *sqq*.
Siege of Florence, 311; of Jericho, 421.
Siena, description, 328; palaces, 329; Palazzo Pubblico, 331 *sqq.*; cathedral, 334 *sqq.*; museum, 340; churches, 341 *sqq.*; picture gallery, 344 *sqq.*; Archivio di Stato, 347; environs, 351.
Sigismondo Malatesta. See *Malatesta*.
Sigismund [†1437],Holy Rom. emp.: King of Hungary and Bohemia,13,78,80*B*,340.
Signorelli Luca [† 1523], Umbrian painter, 386*; his celebrated Frescoes, in the Cathedral, at Orvieto: History of Antichrist, and Resurrection of the Dead, 382; the End of the World, 383; the Last Judgment: the Blessed ascending to Heaven, the Condemned descending into Hell, 384; the Punishment of the Wicked, Paradise, 385.
Signoria, *or Priors*, at Florence, 196.
Simon Magus (the Antichrist), heretic and sorcerer, 323, 382, 411, 432.
Simone Ghini [† 1491], sculptor, 414.
Simone Martini. See *Martini*.
Simonetta (Vespucci), La Bella, reputed portraits of her, 239, 260, 261.
Simonetti Michelangelo, architect, 443,446.
Simonists (the sin of Simon, Acts viii. 18-24), Dante's verdict on, 227.
Simplicius, St. [† 483], pope, 430.
Sins, the Seven capital, 476.
Sirens, 454 *c*. [In Greek mythology a class of nymphs who were fabled to lure the passing sailor on to the rocks ruining him by their melodious singing].
Sistine chapel, The, 475 *sqq.* (quoted 147).
Sivori Camillo (1815-1894), violinist, 37.
Sixtine Madonna, Raphael's model, 281 *c*.
Sixtus II., St. [† 258], Pope, ordains St. Lawrence, 471.
Sixtus III., St. [† 440], pope, founds the Lateran baptistery, 416; rebuilds Santa Maria Maggiore, 419; and decorates with mosaics its triumphal arch, 420; founds San Lorenzo in Lucina, 438.
Sixtus IV. (Della Rovere) [† 1484], Pope, adds Sistine chapel to Vatican, 441, 475; rebuilds Santa Maria del Popolo, 433; Santa Maria della Pace, 439; restores San Pietro in Vincoli, 440; appoints Platina as Librarian, 485; creates duchy of Urbino, 190, 190 *A*; his part in the Pazzi conspiracy, 211; his sepulchral monument in St. Peter's, 413; his portrait by Melozzo, 485; and by Raphael, in the Vatican, 460.

Sixtus V. (Felice Peretti) [† 1590], Pope, builds the new Lateran palace, 416; and the Vatican Library, 442; erects obelisk in the piazza S. Pietro, 45, 405; orders the completion of St. Peter's dome, 407; accords privileges to Loreto, 189; his grave, 419.
Slanderers, Dante's verdict on, 227.
Socrates [† 399 B. C.], Athenian philosopher, 447, 461.
Sodom, of Israel, 98.
Sodoma (Antonio Bazzi) [† 1549], Lombard and Sienese painter, his style, 348; works attributed to him, Altarpiece, Turin gallery, 20 c; St. Sebastian, Pitti, 284 b; Abraham's Sacrifice, Pisa cathedral, 315 c; SS. Vittore and Ansano, Palazzo Pubblico, Siena, 333 c; Christ bound to the column, Descent from the Cross, Christ in Limbo, and three pictures in the Siena Academy, 450; his Painting of the Marriage of Alexander and Roxana, in the Farnesina, 493 c; his portrait in the Vatican *Stanze*, 461 c.
Sogliani Giov. Ant. [† 1544], painter, 248
Solari Cristoforo [† 1525], Milanese architect and sculptor, 51, 73.
Solari Giovanni (15 th cent.), architect, 51.
Solfatara, sulphureous exctinct volcano, 559.
Solomon [† ca. 937 B. C.], King of Israel, his figure, on Ghiberti's bronze gates, 205 b; in The Triumph of St. Thomas Aquinas, 228 b; in the Legend of the Holy Cross, in Santa Croce, 220 b; in Perugino's paintings, at Perugia, 362b; the Judgment of S., famous relief, on Doges' palace, Venice, 114 a; same subject painted by Raphael, in the Stanza della Segnatura, Vatican, 459 b.
Sophocles [† 405 B. C.] tragic poet, 167, 447.
Sordello [† ca. 1267], a Provençal poet, 79.
Sorrento, famous summer residence: enchanted gardens with orange 518, 548 sq.
Sorte Cristoforo, of Verona, 123.
Spagna, Lo (Giov. di Pietro) [† 1530], Umbrian painter, his work in Perugia, 361 a; in the Vatican gallery, 485 a; decorates the cell in which St. Francis lived and died, 375 c.
Spanish Chapel, at Florence, 228.
Spannocchi, Sien. bankers to the Pope, 330.
Speakers, suggestions for public, 432.
Spinazzi Innocenzo, Florentine sculptor, his monument of Machiavelli, 219 c.
Spinello Aretino [† 1410], Florentine painter, decorates the sacristy of San Miniato, with stories of St. Benedict, 311 c; his mural paintings, in the Palazzo Pubblico, Siena, with stories from the life of pope Innocent III. and the Struggle between the Papacy and the Empire, 333 b.
Spoleto, 389 sq.
Sposalizio, The, by Raphael, 58; S. or wedding of the Adriatic Sea, 151.
Spring, Botticelli's allegory of, 261.
Squarcione, Francesco [† 1474], Paduan painter, 158.
Stags, symbol of, 185.
Stamer, W. A. J. (Author), 548.
Stammering, how to cure, 432.
Steen Jan [† 1679], Flemish painter, 272.
Stephen, St. [† 33 A. D.], protomartyr of the Christian Church, 230; 471.

Stern Raphael, architect, 454.
Stigmata, St. Francis receiving the, 366 a; Maiano's marble relief on pulpit of Santa Croce, Florence, 219 b. [Stigmata designate the Holy wounds or marks received by Christ at His crucifixion on Calvary; and which He, as a token of His Passion, imprinted on St. Francis' hands and feet, as well as on his side].
Stradano (Jan van der Straet), 202.
Stradivari, family of violin-makers, 77.
Street lighting, old practice of, 245.
Stresa, its gardens, villas, 68.
Strozzi, the name of an ancient and noble Florentine family, wich was already famous in the 14th century, 225, 226, 305.
Strozzi Bernardo (il Cappuccino or il Prete Genovese), painter, 35, 36, 37.
Stuart, portraits of princes of the House of, 20*, 21; monument of the Stuarts in St. Peter's, Rome, 408. [Stuart or Stewart, a family which inherited the Scottish throne in 1371 and later, upon the death (1603) of Queen Elizabeth, the English. It commenced with Robert II. and ended with James II. king of Great Britain and Ireland, who was deposed. Henry, titular Duke of York and known as the Cardinal of York, was the last of the royal family of Stuart; he died at Frascati and was buried in the *Grotte Vaticane* or crypt of St. Peter's].
Stupinigi, castle of, 24.
Styx, the, or Stygian lake, 227, 384.
Subiaco, its far-famed monasteries, 515.
Sulmona, churches, palace, 561 sq.
Summa Theologia, The, 320.
Sumptuary laws, 298. [Laws or regulations to prevent extravagance in private life by limiting expenditure for clothing, furniture, food, etc. They were common in ancient Greece and Rome, and during the 13th-15th centuries].
Superga, memorial church at, 15.
Supper, The Last, fresco by Andrea del Castagno, 253; by Ghirlandaio, 252; by Cosimo Rosselli, 483; by Andrea del Sarto, 253; by Leonardo da Vinci, 57; by Tintoretto, 129; by Bonifazio Veronese, 270; relief by Gruamons, 327.
Surgery, in Roman times, 536.
Susa, 11 sq.
Sustermans Justus [† 1680], Flaming painter, 277, 283.
Swabia, 569. [One of the duchies of medieval Germany, cradle of the Hohenstaufen emperors].
Sybaris, on the Gulf of Taranto, 558.
Sylvester I. St., Bishop of Rome, baptizes the Emperor Constantine, 430; requests him to build a basilica to the Apostle Peter, 405; receives the Keys of the Church, 417; and the « Donation », of Rome, 469.
Sylvia, St. [† 604], mother of St. Gregory the Great, 430.
Symbolical represent. of Saviour 185, 503 and the Apostles, 94, 186, 423, 429.
Symonds John Addington [† 1893], English Author and Art Critic, 66, 180, 210, 226, 227, 236 sq., 253, 284, 321, 382 sqq., 403, 463.
Syracuse, its great antiquity, 580.

TABULARIUM, public archives, 396, 398, 504.
Tacitus [† 120 A. D.] Roman hist., 238.
Taddeo di Bartolo, painter, 333, 346, 364.
Tadolini Giulio, sculptor, 415.
Tafi Andrea, Florentine mosaicist, 208.
Tagliacozzo, Battle of, 505 c, 524 b.
Taine, Hippolyte Adolphe [† 1893], eminent French critic and historian, 173.
Talenti Francesco [† ca. 1380], Florentine architect, 209, 217.
Tancred of Hauteville, Norman seigneur father of Robert Guiscard, 563, 569.
Taormina, its celebrated theatre, 579.
Tapestries, origin of, 273B; Raphael's, 472 Gobelin's, 286; in the Uffizi gallery, 273 B.
Tarantella, at Sorrento, 548.
Tarquins, the kings of ancient Rome, 398.
Tasso Torquato [† 1595], Italian poet, 178, 549. See under *Jerusalem Delivered*
Tassoni Alessandro [† 1635], poet, 177.
Tauriscus, Greek sculptor, 491.
Tavolette di Biccherna, at Siena, 349.
Telescope, constructed at Florence, 219.
Temperance, symbol of, 462.
Temptation of Christ, fresco 481.
Temptations of the world, symbols of typified by beautiful women with horns, in Pinturicchio's frescoes, Borgia apartments, Vatican, 457 a; Temptations of St. Anthony, remarkable painting, in the Uffizi, Florence, 255 B.
Terence Publius [† ca. 159 B. C.], Roman comic poet, his image in Raphael's Parnassus, 463 b; fragments of his manuscripts, in the Vatican Library, 442 a; and in the Laurentian, 238 b.
Terni, its Waterfalls, 390.
Theodolinda (6th c.), Lombard Queen, 64. [She played an important part as the mediator between the Lombards and the Catholic Church].
Theodora [† 548], notorious consort of Justinian, 184.
Theodora, (10th c.) Roman *Senatrix* 395.
Theodore, St., patron of Venice, 184.
Theodore I. [† 649], Pope, 416.
Theodoric the Great [† 526], king of the Ostrogoths, 166 sq.
Theodosius the Great [† 395], Emp., 48.
Theresa, St. [† 1582], a Spanish nun, the founder of reformed Carmelites, 438.
Thinker, The, statue by Michelangelo, 237.
Thomas Aquinas, St. [† 1274], the Angelic Doctor, his Apotheosis, in Traini's uncommon painting, at Pisa, 317 b; his Glorification, in the great fresco in the Spanish chapel, S. Maria Novella, Florence, 228 c; a Chapel dedicated to him, in the same church, 226 a; his death in the Abbey of Fossanova, on the Appian Way, 516 a.
Thomas, St., Apostle, incredulity of, 277, 432; group by Verrocchio, 231.
Thorwaldsen [† 1844], Dan. sculptor, 524.
Thucydides, Athenian historian, 454.
Tiara, the, symbol of sovereignty, 412, 557 [worn by the Pope only when he appears as sovereign—using the mitre when celebrating].
Tiberius Claudius Nero [† 37], second Roman Emperor, marble statue of him, in the Vatican, 453 c; enlarges the Imperial palace, on the Palatine, 400 a; builds several villas on the

island of Capri, where he spends the last ten years of his life, 550 b.
Tiepolo, Giov. Batt. [† 1770], Venetian painter, 136 c; decorates the Colleoni chapel, at Bergamo, 75 b; works in Venice: decorates the Hall of the Four Doors, 119 a; the Hall of the Senate, in the Doges' palace, 122 a; paints ceiling in church of I Gesuati 136 c; the remarkable Invention of the Holy Cross, now in the Academy, 145 b; the Institution of the Rosary, 136 c; frescoes, in the Labia palace,149 c.
Timoleon. celebrated general, 579.
Tino da Camaino, sculptor, 323, 337.
Tintoretto (Jacopo Robusti) [† 1594], called il Furioso, Venetian painter, his way of drawing, 147. Paintings in Venice: the great Paradise, 124; Ariadne and Bacchus, 120; the Dead Christ, 122; the Nuptials of St. Catherine, 121; other works in the Doges' palace, 118 sq.; in S. Rocco, 147; the Academy, 142, 148; in St. Mark's, 102 sq.; in San Giorgio Maggiore, 129; in S. Maria dell'Orto, 137; in S. Maria della Salute, 129; the Finding of the body of St. Mark, 61. Pictures in Uffizi, 269; in Pitti, 283; at Rome, 497.
Titian Vecelli [† 1576], Venetian painter character of his work, 269; his Presentation in the Temple, St. John, and Pietà, 143; the Assumption, and the Pesaro altarpiece, 131; picture in the Doges' palace, 119; in the Library of St. Mark, 148; in the church of I Gesuiti, 134; in S. Salvatore, 136; in S. Maria della Salute, Venice, 129; other works attributed to him, 95, 122; his Reclining Venus, Flora, and portrait of Catherine Cornaro, in the Uffizi, 269; his 'La Bella,' 284; the Mary Magdalen, 283; portrait of Philip of Spain, 276; other portraits in the Pitti, 284, 285; the Frari altarpiece, in the Vatican, 487; Sacred and Profane Love, 491; Education of Cupid, 491; Danaë, 539; other works attributed to him, 77, 495, 496, 539.
Titus Flavius Vespasianus [† 81], Roman emperor, completes the Colosseum, 400; restores Pantheon, 431; his Arch, 399.
Tivoli, the Villa Adriana; Este, 512 sq.
Tobias and the Angel, story of, 20, 277.
Todi, birth place of Jacopone da T., 390.
Tolentino, 190*.
Tolomei, illustrious family of Siena, 330.
Tombs, evolution of, at Venice, 130; pagan T., 402; early Christian T., 403; tombs of illustrious Englishmen, 403.
Tommè Luca, Sienese painter, 324, 347.
Tornabuoni, Florentine family, 224, 481.
Torregiano, Florentine sculpture, his brutality to Michelangelo, 240.
Torriti Jacobus (end of 13th cent.), mosaicist, 208, 415, 420.
Torso Belvedere, the, 451.
Toscanella, its medieval churches, 514.
Totila [† 552], King of Ostrogoths, 395.
Tournaments in Florence, 218.
Tower, of Babel, 98, 322; of Galileo, 311.
Towers, Leaning, at Bologna, 172; at Pisa, 312*; medieval towers, in Florence, 304 a; in San Gimignano, 352 a.
Trade Guilds. See Arti.
Traini Francesco [† ca. 1347], Pisan painter, his remarkable picture of St. Thomas Aquinas, in Pisa, 317*.
Trajan (Marcus Ulpius Trajanus) [† 117], Roman emperor, 114, 329, 363; creates a marvellous forum, 393, 401; restores the temple of Castor and Pollux, 398; memorial column of T., 401; its reliefs, 503; his triumphal arch, 560.
Trani, the cathedral of, 563.
Transfiguration, The, early mosaic, at Ravenna, 187; Perugino's, 363; Raphael's painting, in the Vatican, 487 a.
Transubstantiation, Dogma of, 386, 464.
Trasimene, 356. [A historic lake, associated with Hannibal's memorable victory over the Romans, 217 B. C.
Travels, of Marco Polo, 135.
Treaty of Versailles, 168; of Vienna, 26.
Tree of Knowledge, the, 478.
Trelawny Edward John [† 1881], friend of Shelley, author, 43.
Tremezzina, view of, 38.
Trento, 168. Council of, see Council.
Trevi Fountain, at Rome, tradition attached to it, 511.
Tribonian [† 545], the famous jurist and minister of Justinian, 462.
Tribute Money, fresco by Masaccio, in the Brancacci chapel, at Florence, 240.
Trinacria, 572. [Name used by Virgil for Sicily].
Trieste, chief seaport of Adriatic, 169.
Trissino Giorgio [† 1550], author, 167.
Triumph of Death, great medieval fresco in the Camposanto, Pisa, 320, 321.
Triumphal Arches, at Rome, 398; at Benevento, 560; at Rimini, 171.
Triumphs, of Apollo, Venus, etc. allegorical frescoes, at Ferrara, 179.
Trivium, meaning of, 214, 456.
Troia (Apulia), cathedral of, 563.
Troy, Jean-François de [† 1752], French painter, 286.
True Cross, Legend of the, 220.
Tura Cosimo [† 1495], Ferrarese painter, decorates residence of Borso, 178 a.
Turin, 15. Monuments and palaces, 16, 17; churches, 18, 19; picture gallery, 20, 21; Royal palace, 22, 23.
Turks, The, crusades against, 338, 468.
Tuscany, 191 sqq.
Tusculum, birth place of Cato, 512.
Tyrants, group in public square symbolical of liberty, as a warning to, 196.
Twilight, Michelangelo's figure of, 236.

UBERTI, an old aristocratic family in Florence, among its members Farinata, a leader of Ghibelline faction, 329, who in the 13th century courageously opposed the demolition of Florence, 197 c. 329.
Uccello Paolo [† 1475], Florentine painter, and investigator of perspective, his famous Calvary Battle, 258 a.
Udine, Giovanni da [† 1564], Roman painter, 431; prepares designs for Laurentian coloured glass windows, 238 a; decorates the Borgia Apartments, 456 b; works on Raphael's Tapestries, in the Vatican, 472 b; assists Raphael on the Farnesina paintings, 492 b.
Uffizi Gallery, The, at Florence, 255 sqq.
Ugolino da Siena, painter, 256.
Ugolino tyrant of Pisa. See Gherardesca.

Ugolino di Vieri, of Siena, 386.
Uguccione della Faggiuola, 313, 325.
Ulysses, Greek hero, kills the sorceress Circe, 387 b; his escape from the giant Polyphemus, 453 a; carries Iphigenia to the altar of sacrifice, 537 a; his passage near the islands of Sirens, 454c
Umberto I., King of Italy, 170, 431.
Umbria, its valleys, mountains, 357 sqq.
Umiliati, The, leading wool manufacturers in Florence, 239.
Unicorn, the, 179. [A fabolous animal like a horse but with one straight horn on its forehead; it is an emblem of female chastity].
Uovo, Castello del, at Naples, 517.
Urban II. (de Lagny) [† 1099], Pope, organizes the first crusade, 39.
Urban IV. (Pantaleone) [† 1264], Pope, his connection with the Miracle of Bolsena, 386, 464.
Urban V. (de Grimoard) [† 1370], Pope, his quarrel with Bernabò Visconti, 62.
Urban VI. (Prignano) [† 1389], Pope, 41.
Urban VIII. (Barberini) [† 1644], Pope, dedicates basilica of St. Peter, at Rome, 407; and orders bronze canopy for the same, 406; his part in the condemnation of Galileo, 408; his tomb by Bernini, in St. Peter's, 408 a.
Urbino, a celebrated centre during the Renaissance of refined society, and the resort of literary celebrities, 190. See also under Montefeltro and Rover.
Ursula, St., Dream of, by Carpaccio, 141; Legend of St. Ursula, ib.
Uta (Sardinia), its Roman. cathedral, 566 d
Uzzano (Niccolò da), Donatello's bust, 295.

VAGA, Perin del [† 1547], Roman painter, 32; works in the Vatican, 456, 462, 474; in the Castel Sant'Angelo, 499; his grave, 81.
Valadier Giuseppe [† 1839], Roman architect, 399.
Valentinian II. (Flavius) [† 315], Roman emperor, 422.
Valentinian III. (Flavius Placidus) [† 455], emperor of the West, 185.
Valle, Andrea della, architect, 158.
Valois, House of, 273 B.
Vandals, the, 392 c. [A fierce nation of Teutonic race akin to the Goths, who early in the 5th c. invaded the Roman provinces in Gaul and Spain and Rome destroying monuments and works of art in the city].
Van Dyck. See Dyck.
Vanities, the burning of, 197.
Vanni Andrea, Sienese painter, 344.
Vanni Francesco [†1609], painter,411,433.
Vannucci Pietro. See Perugino.
Varagine, Jacopo da, Archbishop of Genoa and author of the 'Golden Legend,' 141.
Vasari Giorgio [† 1574], Florentine painter and architect, and writer on art, 147; decorates the Palazzo Vecchio, 200, 201, 203; completes the Laurentian Library, 238; builds the Uffizi palace, 255; designs Michelangelo's tomb, 218; his portrait of Lorenzo de' Medici, 266; his work at Pisa 313; at Rome, in San Pietro in Montorio, 439 b; in the Vatican palace, 474a

Vassalletus Jacobus, architect, sculptor and mosaicist, 416, 422, 516.
Vatican, The, at Rome, views of, 411; extent of, *ib.*; the Scala Regia, 441; and Sala Regia, 474; the Apostolic Library, 442; Galleria de' Candelabri, 445; Sala a Croce Greca, 443; the Sala della Biga, 444; Sala Rotonda, 446; Sala delle Muse, 447; Sala degli Animali, 448; Galleria delle Statue, 449; Cortile Belvedere, 450; Museo Etrusco, 452; Museo Egiziano, *ib.*; Museo Chiaramonti, 453; Braccio Nuovo, 454, 455; the Appartamento Borgia, 456; the Stanze of Raphael, 458 sqq.; the Logge, 470; chapel of Niccolò V., 471; Raphael's Tapestries, 472; Sala dell'Immacolata Concezione, 473; Galleria Geografica, *ib.*; Sistine Chapel, 475 sqq.; Picture Gallery, 484 sq.
Vaughan Herbert [† 1903], cardinal and archbishop of Westminster, 430.
Vecchietta [† 1480], Sienese architect, sculptor and painter, executes the statues for the Loggia della Mercanzia, at Siena, 331 c; a picture of St. Catherine of Siena, in the Palazzo Pubblico, 333 a; the magnificent bronze Tabernacle in the Duomo, 335 a; collaborates in the decoration of the baptistery, 342 a.
Vela Vincenzo, Lombard sculptor, 19.
Velasquez (Diego Rodriguez de Silva y) [† 1660], Spanish painter, his portrait of Philip IV. of Spain, 277; and of Pope Innocent X., 495.
Velata, La Donna, Raphael's portrait of a lady, in the Uffizi, 281 c. [It is supposed to be the portrait of the woman Raphael loved, whom he used as a model for the Sistine Madonna].
Venetia, 81 sqq.
Veneziano Domenico [† 1461], pain., 258.
Venice, history, 81*; origin of site of the city, 81; description, 81; the Bridge of Sighs, 85; Library of San Marco, 87; Piazza of San Marco, 88 sqq. *Saint Mark's Church*: façades, 90-94 and 112; atrium, 95-99; interior, 100-111. The *Doges' Palace*: Porta della Carta, 113; façades, 114-115; courtyard, 116; staircases, 117; vestibule, 118; Sala delle Quattro Porte, 119; Sala del l'Anticollegio, 120; Sala del Collegio, 121; Sala del Senato, 122-123; Sala del Maggior Consiglio, 124-126; Sala della Bussola, Scrutinio, etc., 127; Museo Archeologico, 128. *Churches*: S. Caterina, 135; S. Francesco, *ib.*; I Frari, 130 sq.; I Gesuati, 135; I Gesuiti, 134; S. Giorgio Mag., 129; S. Giovanni Crisost., 135; SS. Giovanni e Paolo, 132 sq.; S. Giovanni in Bragora, 136; Madonna dell'Orto, 137; S. Maria dei Miracoli, 135; S. Maria Formosa, 136; S. Maria della Salute, 129; S. Moisè, 137; Pietà, 135; Redentore, 134; S. Salvatore, 136; S. Sebastiano, 137; I Scalzi, 136; S. Zaccaria, 134. *Academy*, 138-144. *Scuole*: I Carmini, 145; San Giorgio, 146; San Rocco, 147. *Palaces*, 148-152. *Canals*, 85, 153. *Environs*, 154. Marriage of V. with the Adriatic, 151; V. personified, 121, 125, 126, 133.
Ventimiglia, 44.
Venturi Adolfo, Italian art critic, 489, 495.

Venus, the Roman goddess of beauty and of love, she was regarded as the tutelary goddess of Rome and had a temple in her honour in the Forum (its site now occupied by a church), 432 b. Marble statues, *in Rome*: the V. of Cnidus, 444 a; the V. drying her hair, 450; the V. of Cyrene, 561 a; Birth of V., 500 b; the V. Genetrix, 502 b; the V. of the Esquiline, 503 c; the V. Victrix, by Canova, 488 b; *in Florence*: the Medici V., 255 c; the V. coming from the bath, by Canova, 286 a; *in Naples*: the V. of Capua, 530 a; the V. Callipygus, 531 a; the Crouching V., 531 b; replica of the Medici V., 529 a; *in Syracuse*: the V. Anadyomene, at Syracuse, 580 b.
Vercelli, 24.
Vercingetorix [† 46 B. C.], Gallic leader, place of death, 400 [In 53 B. C., when Cæsar conquered Gaul Vercingetorix chivalrously gave himself up on behalf of his beaten countrymen: five years later Cæsar led him in his triumph to Rome and had him executed, according to the old brutal custom, at the foot of the Capitol].
Verde, the Conte (Amadeus VI.), 16.
Verona, history, 159; San Zeno, 160 sq.; churches, 161-163; palaces, 164-166 Roman amphitheatre, 166.
Verona, Fra Pietro da. See *Peter Martyr*.
Verona Giambattista da (16th century), sculptor, and wood-worker, 163.
Veronese (Bonifazio dei Pitati) [† 1553], Veronese and Venetian painter, the Adoration of the Magi, in Genoa, 34 c; the Lazarus and Dives, Academy, Venice, 143 c; the Last Supper, in the Uffizi 270 a.
Veronese Paolo (Paolo Caliari) [† 1588], Veronese and Venetian painter, his works in Venice, the greatpainting representing the Feast in the House of Levi, 139 a; and his Madonna and Saints, in the Academy, 142 a; the Allegory of Mars and Neptune, and Venice honoured by Peace and Justice, in the Sala del Collegio, Doges' palace, 119 c, 121 a; the Rape of Europa, Sala dell'Anticollegio, 120 b; Venice crowned by Glory, great ceiling painting Hall of the Great Council, 126; Youth and Old Age, Sala dei Dieci, 127 b; the Nuptials of St. Catherine, church of S. Caterina 135 b; Martyrdom of SS. Marcus and Marcellinus, and Apotheosis of St. Sebastian, in the church of S. Sebastiano, 137; decorates the ceiling of the Library of San Marco, 148 a. Works *in Florence*, Esther in presence of Ahasuerus, and Martyrdom of St. Justina, Uffizi gallery, 271 a. *In Rome*, St. Antony of Padua preaching to the fishes, and Venus, Cupid and Satyr, Borghese gallery, 490 c, 491 c; replica of the Rape of Europa, Palazzo de' Conservatori, 505 b. *In Turin*, the Queen of Sheba before Solomon, Picture gallery, 21. [Veronese's inventive power and his fertility of imagination conduced to extraordinary productiveness, thus, all the galleries of Europe contain examples of his art.].

Verrocchio (Andrea dei Cioni called *del*) [† 1488], Florentine sculptor and painter, his reputation as a teacher, 299; his Baptism of Christ in the Uffizi, 264; sculptural works in the Bargello, 295, 299, 300, 301 sqq.; his bronze group of the incredulity of St. Thomas, 231; the Medici tomb in San Lorenzo, 234; his fountain piece in the Palazzo Vecchio, 200; his part on the baptistery *dossale*, 212; his equestrian statue of Colleoni, at Venice, 132.
Versailles Treaty (of 1919), 81*, 168.
Vespasian Titus Flavius [† 79], Roman Emperor, begins the Colosseum, 400; temple in the Forum in his honour, 397; arch in commemoration of his victories, in the Judæan Wars, 399 b. [He was of humble parentage; during his reign the temple of Janus was shut at Rome].
Vespucci Amerigo [† 1512], navigator, 239; portraits of him and of his family, in Ghirlandaio's painting, church of Ognissanti, Florence, 239 a. [He was born at Florence in 1451; his uncle Antonio to whom he owed his education, was a Dominican and friend of Savonarola; he was placed as a clerk in the commercial house of the Medici at Seville and Cadiz; thence he made several voyages for the New World and, according to the accounts he left which made it appear that he had preceded John Cabot, from him the two continents derived their name].
Vespucci family, The, gortraits of, 239.
Vesta, Temple of, at Rome, 393*, 417.
Vestals, duties and privileges of, 398.
Vesuvius, Mount, 540. [For the last 300 years the only active volcano near Naples; its terrific eruptions of A. D. 63 and 79 devastated the country around blotting out the flourishing Roman cities of Pompeii and Herculaneum].
Vezzolano, the Abbey of, 24.
Vicentino Andrea [† 1614], painter, 118.
Vicenza, the city of Palladio's creations, 167.
Victor Emmanuel II. [† 1878], first King of united Italy, called 'father of his country,'; monumentse rected in his honour: n Turin, 16 a; in Naples, 521 c; in Rome, 393 a. [The great memorial in Rome designed by Sacconi, is the most colossal white marble structure in the world; some 500 ft. in length and over 200 in height; situated on the slope of the Capitoline hill facing the Corso, it is adorned with numerous statues and sculptural works, fountains, a series of grand staircases and a gigantic equestrian statue in gilded bronze of the king. The base on which it stands is called the *Altar of the Fatherland*; here rests the nameless 'unknown warrior' who fought in the Great Wars].
Victorinus C. Marius [† 370], philosopher and grammarian, 431.
Victory, bronze statue, at Brescia, 177; marble in the Pitti, 5.
Vienna, Treaty of, 26.
Vietri sul Mare, 555.
Vieusseux library, at Florence, 309.

— 614 —

Vignola (Giacomo Barozzi) [† 1573], Roman architect, one of his great works, the church of Santa Maria degli Angeli, erected on the site of the first oratory of St. Francis, Assisi, 375; is appointed architect of St. Peter's Rome, 407 c; rebuilds the church of the Gesù, 438 a; builds the Villa Albani, for pope Julius III., 498 a.
Villa d'Este, Cernobbio, 66; Tivoli, 512*
Vinci, Leonardo da. *See* Leonardo.
Violante, Queen of Naples, 523.
Violins, the, of Paganini and Sivori preserved in the Town Hall, in Genoa, 37 b; original home of the famous 17th cent. manufacturers of V., Stradivari, Amati, Guarnerio, 77 b.
Virgil [† 19 B. C.], great Latin poet, 78. portraits of him, at Orvieto, 386 c, in the Vatican, 463 c; episode of his Æneid, 451 b; his residence in Naples, 519 b; some of his manuscripts preserved, in the Laurentian, 238 b, and the Vatican Libraries, 442 a.
Virgin Mary, honours paid to the, 242, 329.
Visconti, celebrated Italian family, Lords of Milan, 48 *sq.*, 72, 73.
    Azzo, the murderer of his uncle, 73.
    Bernabò, 49 c; his monument in Milan, 62; his barbarous cruelties, *ib.*; quarrels with the Pope and compels the Papal envoys to eat the bull of excommunication with which they served him, *ib.*
    Filippo Maria, Count of Pavia, 48, last of the Visconti, 73.
    Galeazzo II., "viper" of Milan, 73.
    Gian Galeazzo, his treachery to his uncle, 23; his love of the arts, *ib.*; founds the Duomo, at Milan, 50, 53; the Certosa, at Pavia, 70; his ambition, 330*; career, and end, 72; his monument at Pavia, *ib.*
    Giovanni, Archbishop of Milan, 72.
    Giovanni Maria (assassinated), 72.
    Matteo 1l. [† 1355], poisoned by his brothers, 72 a.
Visitation, The, story of, 262; picture by Albertinelli, *ib.*; by Pontormo, 243; group by Luca della Robbia, 327.

Vitale da Bologna, painter, 484.
Vitelli, The, Lords of Sinigaglia, 382.
Viterbo, scene of the murder of prince Henry of Cornwall, 515.
Vitruvius Pollio [† ca. 26 B. C.], Roman architect, 159, 167.
Vittoria Alessandro [† 1608], Venetian sculptor, 130.
Vittoria Colonna., poetess and friend of Michelangelo, 497 b.
Vittorino da Feltre [† 1446], humanist, his teachings at the court of Mantua, 78 b; his effigy on bronze medals, 303 c.
Vivarini Alvise [† ca. 1504], Venetian painter, 132, 134, 138.
Vivarini Bartolommeo [† ca. 1499], Venetian painter, 130, 142.
Voice, how to strengthen the, 432.
Volta Alessandro [† 1827], physicist, 66.
Volterra, ancient Etruscan city, 355.
Volterra, Daniele da (D. Ricciarelli) [† 1566], Roman painter, 436, 474.
Volumni, Tomb of the, near Perugia, 390.

Wagner Richard [† 1883], composer, 150, his appreciation of Ravello, 556.
Waldenses, the, 14 b. [A Christian community founded about 1170, in the south of France, by a rich citizen of Lyons; they lived in voluntary poverty, refused to take part in wars, rejected the Dogma of Transubstantiation; driven by persecutions from country to country, they finally settled in Savoy and Piedmont, where they still dwell].
Walter of Brienne, Duke of Athens, Seigneur of Florence, 192.
Wax portrait of Francis de' Medici, 298.
War, Rubens' allegory of its consequences, 282; W. of the Investitures, 474, 557.
William, Duke of Apulia, 572.
Wenceslaus, Emperor of Germany, 72.
Westminster Abbey, 218, 515, 523.
Weyden, Roger van der [† 1464], Flemish painter, work in Turin, 21 b; his Deposition, in the Uffizi, 272 c.
Wiligelmus (Guglielmo), sculptor, 160, 177.

William the Conqueror [† 1087], King of England, 69.
William II. (the Norman), King of Sicily, orders the building of the Monreale cathedral, Palermo, 570.
Wolf of the Capitol, The, 505.
Wölfflin Heinrich, Art Critic, 267.
Wolsey Thomas [† 1530], English cardinal and statesman, 430.
Wolvinus, goldsmith, his work, 54.
Women, their position in Italy during the Renaissance, 76.
Woolen manufactory in Florence, 239.
Works of Mercy, the Seven, 327.
World, the End of the, by Signorelli, 383.
Worms, the Council of, 474, 557.
Worship of the Virgin Mary, 242, 245.
Wrestlers, group of the, at Florence, 255.

York, Henry [† 1807], Cardinal of, 408 c. [The last of the Stuart royal family. See under *Stuart*].
Yriarte Charles [† 1898], French author, his admiration for Florence, 194.

Zacharias, father of John the Baptist, 224.
Zandomeneghi, Venetian sculptor, 130.
Zara, the Duomo of, 170.
Zebedee, father of the Apostles James the Major and John Evangelist, 144, 481.
Zeno San [† 380], Bishop of Verona, 160.
Zevio, Altichiero da, Paduan painter his work in Verona, 162 b.
Ziani (Sebastiano) [† ca. 1179], Doge of Venice, 115, 125, 333.
Zocchi Cesare [† 1922], sculptor, 168.
Zodiac, the Signs of, in the Florentine Baptistery 208 c.
Zoroaster, founder of the ancient Persian religion, 461.
Zuccaro Federico, Roman painter, the Founder of the *Accademia di San Luca*, Rome, 494 c; decorates the Sala Regia, in the Vatican, 474 a; his picture of Frederick Barbarossa at the Pope's feet, in the Doges' palace, 125 b.

Ensign of the Silk - Weaver's Guild.
Terracotta by The della Robbia.
(*Church Or San Michele, Florence*).

— 615 —

The attractions of Italy have not been exhausted in this comparatively modest volume, and many interesting cities have not been mentioned.

There is no other country in the world which possesses an equal number of cities remarkable for their architecture, their statuary, their paintings and their decorations. Only the principal places, unrivalled in their treasures of art, have been included, but " in almost every alley of almost every country town, the past lives in some lovely statuette, some exquisite wreath of sculptured foliage, or some slight but delicate fresco, a variety of beauty undreamed of."

OLD PRINTING SHOP IN FLORENCE.

READERS desirous of purchasing the original photographs reproduced in this volume may apply to

FRATELLI ALINARI
I.D.E.A.
8, Via Nazionale, Florence.

D. ANDERSON
7,ᴀ Via Salaria, Rome (34).

GIACOMO BROGI
13, Corso dei Tintori, Florence.

FOTOCELERE
19, Via Marochetti, Torino.

PRINTED AT THE " IMPRONTA PRESS " FLORENCE.